THE
CAPITAL
COMPANION

THE
CAPITAL
COMPANION

A STREET-BY-STREET GUIDE
TO LONDON AND ITS INHABITANTS

PETER GIBSON

With colour photographs by Simon McBride

MICHAEL JOSEPH

TO THE FIVE PEOPLE I LOVE
MOST IN THE WORLD

First published in Great Britain 1985 by
Webb & Bower (Publishers) Limited
9 Colleton Crescent, Exeter, Devon EX2 4BY
This paperback edition published 1988

Designed by Malcolm Couch

Production by Nick Facer

Copyright © Peter Gibson 1985

Colour photographs Copyright © Webb & Bower
Simon McBride 1988

British Library Cataloguing in Publication Data

Gibson, Peter
The Capital companion.
1. London (England)–Description–1981-
–Guide-books
I. Title
914.21'04858   DA679

ISBN 0-86350-073-0

Typeset in Great Britain by P&M Typesetting Ltd.,
Exeter, Devon

Printed in Great Britain by
Butler & Tanner Ltd, Frome and London

Introduction

Capital Companion contains the biographies of over 780 people who have lived in London since the time of Elizabeth I and historical explanations of the names of nearly 400 streets where they lived. Under the streets are listed 1500 or so addresses, many made famous by their occupants.

All the entries are alphabetical, whether street or person. So, in a typical example, we have: CHESTERTON, followed by CHEYNE ROW, CHEYNE WALK, CHOPIN and Agatha CHRISTIE. Anyone who appears in capital letters under a street reference or in a biography, also has a personal biography under his or her name.

Each biography has a two-column introduction. On the left-hand side is the person's surname, underneath his christian names and title, if any, followed in italics by his occupation. On the right-hand side is (when known) his place and date of birth, place and date of death and, finally, place of burial. Under these two columns appears a list of streets, with dates, where the person lived. These are cross-referenced to street entries for further information.

The street entries are self-explanatory. The nearest underground station is noted, followed by an historical introduction and an entry for each relevant street number.

Abbreviations have been reduced to a minimum and only two require explanation. The first (LCP and a date) means that a plaque (usually round, blue and ceramic) has been placed on the house by the Greater London Council or its predecessor, the London County Council, during that year. The second (P and a date) or merely (P) means a plaque has been affixed by some other authority, society or individual. (P) on its own records the existence of the plaque, but the date affixed has been lost.

London has been a large city, a 'crossroads of the world' almost, for hundreds of years and provided a wealth of famous and infamous people from which to choose. So, bringing *Capital Companion* to this stage has been an editorial problem of *exclusion* rather than *inclusion*. The biographical details cover some of the people who have lived in London since Elizabeth I came to the throne in 1558. Inevitably a number of 'favourites' had to be left out.

The area covered by the *Companion* is roughly a rectangle, four and a half miles long by three miles wide (7.25 × 4.8 kilometres) centred on Leicester Square: some 640 acres (260 hectares). Thus, it spans from Notting Hill and Kensington in the west to Hackney in the east, from Camden Town in the north to Pimlico in the south. Of course, many 'celebrities' who are not mentioned have lived (or live) outside this arbitrary area and many more inside it. But a start has been made.

A Select Dictionary
of the
People and Streets of London
from
Elizabeth 1
to the Present Day

ACACIA ROAD, NW8   *Jubilee line to St John's Wood*

It was mostly built in 1830 on the border of St John's Wood Farm. Elm Tree
and Oak Tree Roads had already been built, and it is thought that there
really *was* an acacia tree (or 'locust-tree') at the corner with Finchley Road.

37, Violet Cameron was installed here by her lover, the 5th Lord
LONSDALE. Here she gave birth to a daughter, whose father most
certainly was not Violet's husband, a M. Bensaude.

43A, Bernard MILES, 1946. On September 9, 1951, MILES produced *Dido
and Aeneas* (in a hall at the back of the house) with Kirsten Flagstad
singing Dido. From this small beginning grew the 'Mermaid Theatre',
which first opened – as the only playhouse in the City of London – by
Puddle Dock, Blackfriars Bridge on May 28, 1959.

ADAM   Kirkaldy, August 2, 1728
Robert   London, February 17, 1792
Architect   Westminster Abbey, South Transept

1-3, Adelphi Terrace, WC1 (P 1950) 1778-1785

Robert and his brother James (1730-1794) were sons of William Adam of
Maryburgh and both studied in Italy. Robert became joint architect of the
King's Works with Sir William CHAMBERS; a post to which his brother
succeeded in 1769. Both Adams were proponents of the *Palladian* style.
Their greatest project in London was the *Adelphi* (Greek for 'brothers')
which, shamefully, was almost entirely demolished in 1936.

The venture reduced the brothers to near bankruptcy and eventually they
were forced to organise a lottery to sell off the entire scheme.

ADAM STREET, WC2   *Circle and District lines to Embankment*

Named after the ADAM brothers whose *Adelphi* project was nearby.

2, Samuel WYATT (one of the numerous brothers Wyatt who were
considered second only to the architectural Adams) lengthened the first
floor windows of this house in 1790, for his client, a Mr Thomas
Williams.

4, William BUTTERFIELD, 1850s. By this time a well-established
architect, soon to start work on the buildings for Keble College,
Oxford.

ADAMS   Boston, Mass., February 16, 1838
Henry   Washington D.C., March 27, 1918
Historian

22, Queen Anne's Gate, SW1, 1880s

Henry was grandson of John Quincey Adams, 6th President of the United
States, 1767-1848, who had been married to Louise Johnson in the Church of
All Hallows, London EC4, in July 1796. He graduated from Harvard in 1758
and at one time acted as Secretary to his father, Charles, when he was
American Minister to *England*.

In 1870 Henry was appointed Professor of History at Harvard and remained
so until 1877. For much of these seven years he was editor of the *North
American Review*. His finest work was the nine-volume edition of the *History
of the United States,* which was published between 1889 and 1891. French
history also appealed to him and his book *Mont Saint-Michel and Chartres* was

a sensitive and intelligent study of French Medievalism – perhaps the best by any non-French writer. It was published only five years before his death in 1918.

ADDISON	Milston, Wilts., May 1, 1672
Joseph	London, June 17, 1719
Essayist	Westminster Abbey
	(Henry VII's Chapel)

Holland House, W8, 1716–1719 (destroyed by bombing, Second World War)

Addison was educated at Charterhouse School and Queen's College, Oxford, where he took his MA in 1693. Only four years later he published his poem, *The Peace of Ryswick* which, incredible to think of today, secured for him a pension of £300 per annum.

His marriage to the Dowager Countess of Warwick (by which time he had already moved into Holland House) was not happy. The 'jocose tradition' had it that, '…he kept a bottle of wine at each end of the room, so that in his walks backwards and forwards he might take a glass at each'.

He had established a journal called *The Spectator*, which was intended to '…bring philosophy out of the closets…', the first number appearing on March 1, 1711. It appeared daily until December 6 the following year. At its peak it enjoyed a circulation of 10,000 copies, which was an astounding total for its day.

Addison was an ardent Hanoverian and King George I made him Chief Secretary for Ireland – a thankless task even then. However, Addison was a better essayist than politician and he resigned in March 1718 on the grounds of 'ill health'. Probably he *was* ill. He died a little over a year later of *dropsy*.

ADDISON ROAD, W14   *Metropolitan line to Shepherd's Bush*

Named after the essayist Joseph ADDISON, who married the Dowager Countess of Warwick in 1716. As a 'Holland', she and her family owned most of the property here about, hence Holland Park and other related names. All the other 'Addisons' in the area have the same root.

2,   David LLOYD-GEORGE, for ten years after 1928. The Liberal Party were out of office, though he was still an MP for Carnarvon Boroughs.

14,   John GALSWORTHY, from the time when he (at last!) married Ada in September 1905. They lived here for seven years and, for the time, it had the very advanced feature of a 'fitted bathroom'.

31,   Arthur ROPES ('Adrian Ross') 1910.

67,   Chaim WEIZMANN (LCP 1980) 1917–1920. He moved here in the year that the 'Balfour Declaration' was made.

70,   Sir Edward POYNTER, from 1905 until his death here in 1919.

Between numbers 21 and 24 stands Oakwood Court. On this site, on March 10, 1804, the 2nd Lord Camelford killed his opponent in a duel.

ADELPHI TERRACE, WC2   *Jubilee, Northern or Bakerloo lines to Charing Cross*

Named after the ADAM brothers; they began to develop the area in 1768. Sadly, it has been completely 're-developed'; mostly by 1938.

1,   Robert ADAM (P 1950) 1778–1785.

1A,   John GALSWORTHY had a top floor flat here in 1912–1918.

1A,   J.M. BARRIE, 1919. His books were kept in a large room in the flat which had a huge fireplace at one end and often a dining table was laid out at the other. On June 19, 1922, Siegfried Sassoon went to a dinner party at Barrie's. Sassoon wrote in his diary of that evening; 'I found J.M.B. stumping about the room with his hands in his pockets. I'd forgotten his dwarfish exterior and facial shabbiness. … He has the melancholy face of a sexually frustrated man.' Amongst other guests that evening were: Herbert Asquith, son of the Prime Minister and novelist: 1881-1947, and Asquith's wife; 'Lady Cynthia, in old gold or something like that'. She was the daughter of the 11th Earl of Wemyss. Later she became Barrie's secretary and he left all his copyrights to her. This house was turned into the Caledonian Hotel and the King of the Sandwich Islands died here of smallpox.

4,   Richard d'Oyle CARTE, 1888-1901.

5,   David GARRICK, from 1772 until his death in 1779. He died in a little room at the back and his widow died in the same room 43 years later. The ceiling of the Garrick's front drawing room was painted by Antonio Zucchi, ARA (husband of Angelica KAUFMANN, 1726-1795).

8,   Thomas HARDY, 1862-1867, when he was an architectural assistant to Sir Arthur BLOMFIELD. He used to pencil 'caricatures' on the white marble of the ADAM fireplaces.

10,   G.B. SHAW, 1899-1927. It was here on March 22, 1922 that the Shaws met T.E. LAWRENCE, 'Lawrence of Arabia'. The friendship, begun at this meeting, lasted until Lawrence's death (by accident) in 1935. When Shaw moved from here in October 1927, an American 'fan' of Shaw's tried to buy the fireplace in the flat. The landlords forbade the sale.

AGATE   Manchester, September 9, 1877
James Evershed   June 6, 1947
Theatre Critic

14, Doughty Street, WC1, 1935

In his capacity as drama critic for the *Sunday Times* from 1923, film critic for the *Tatler* and literary critic for the *Daily Express,* Agate managed to make a large number of enemies, but not one of them could accuse him of not being a very hard worker.

He published a series of autobiographies – nine in all, the last being posthumous – which were fairly titled *Ego One, Ego Two* and so on. In one of these he put down an estimate of the number of words he had written – all of them sold. In 1938 he reckoned he had written (and mostly typed himself) 448,000 words in one year which had only earned him between £5,000 and £6,000.

Arnold BENNETT described Agate as, '... rather coarse-looking and therefore rather coarse in some things. Fattish. Has a reputation for sexual perversity.' So he had. Agate was a homosexual and went in for the 'rough trade'. But BENNETT's moral standing was not much better! The difference was that BENNETT was heterosexually inclined.

AIRLIE GARDENS, W8   *Central line to Holland Park*

Named after the 5th Earl of Airlie (1826-1881) who lived nearby at Holly Lodge.

10,   Ford Madox FORD, c.1903. Not long after moving here, he founded the *English Review.*

13,   William ROTHENSTEIN 1929-1935, during which time he was knighted.

AKENSIDE   Newcastle, November 9, 1721
Mark   London, June 23, 1770
Physician   St James's, Piccadilly

33, Craven Street, WC2, 1759-1761
12, Old Burlington Street, W1, from 1762 until he died here.

Son of a Newcastle butcher, Akenside originally studied theology as a student in Leyden. Here he met a Mr. Joseph Dyson. They formed a firm friendship and Dyson gave him an annual allowance of £300. At the age of eighteen he began what was to be his one published work, *The Pleasures of Imagination*. When he eventually became a doctor he was appointed as one of the physicians to King George III. Possibly conscious of his humble origin, he adopted a haughty and pedantic manner which did not add to his already small popularity.

A Dr. Lettsom, pupil of Akenside, wrote; '...one leg...was considerably shorter than the other, which obliged him to wear a false heel. He had a pale, *strumous* countenance, but was always very neat and elegant in his dress. He wore a large white wig and carried a long sword.'

Akenside's poetry was published in a collected volume in 1772. Sir Edmund GOSSE described Akenside as, '... a sort of frozen Keats.'

ALBANY, Piccadilly, W1   *Piccadilly and Bakerloo lines to Piccadilly Circus*

Albany is a courtyard leading off Piccadilly itself, near its eastern end on the north side. It is easy to miss and is in any case, a 'private' courtyard. Off it was the one-time home of HRH the Duke of York (the favourite son of King George III). The original building was begun in 1802, but even before he moved in, the Duke was plunged in debt and he was obliged to sell it. The house was then gradually converted into 'bachelor apartments' and really became the first block of flats in London.

A 1, Herbert Beerbohm TREE, in the early years of the 20th century.

A14, Sir Robert SMIRKE, 1811-1832 at a rent of £126 per annum. Later on, in this apartment, lived a Mr. O'Hagan. In 1887 he was the first to ask permission of Albany Management Committee (granted) to instal electric light.

B 3 and **B 4,** J.B. PRIESTLY.

B 5, Lord CLARKE, 1975. He had been made a Life Peer in 1969.

C 1, Sir Harold NICOLSON, 1952-1968. Sir Harold shared this apartment with Colin Fenton.

E 1, Sir Compton MACKENZIE. He was originally offered this apartment in 1912 at a rent of £180 per annum, but he felt he could not afford the price just then.

E 6. In 1889, the occupant, an innovative man called Posen, installed one of those new-fangled telephones.

F 3, Lord MACAULAY, 1846. Previously, he had been in E 1, which was smaller and where he had had, '...an entrance hall, two sitting rooms, a bedroom and a kitchen, cellars and two rooms for servants – all for 90 guineas [£94.50 per annum]'. In 1850 his library in F 3 amounted to 6,100 books – he counted them himself, together with, '...several hundreds more, mostly novels, behind them.'

G 1, John LANE, 1890s. This apartment has a door leading onto Vigo Street at the back of Albany. A drawing of the doorway was used on the front cover for Lane's book catalogues. (The Spanish naval port of Vigo was captured by the British Navy in 1719 and the street was patriotically named thus soon after.) Before Lane had this apartment, it was occupied by Douglas Cook, the editor of the *Saturday Review* He used G 1 as an office as well as his home.

G 2, Edward KNOBLOCK, 1914-1935. He moved here at the time when his first play, *My Lady's Dress* was winning him fame and some fortune.

ALBANY STREET, NW1   *Metropolitan and Circle lines to Great Portland Street*

The Duke of York, usually the second son of the monarch, carries the titles of York and Albany. New York is called after the Duke of York who became King James II, and the capital of the State is Albany. *This* Albany is after Frederick, Duke of York and Albany, who was the second – and favourite – son of King George III. Most of the names around Regent's Park are names directly connected with that fertile monarch's 15 children.

55, Henry MAYHEW (P 1953) 1840-1851. The first occupier of this house was John Nosworthy, a plasterer who worked for John NASH, the architect responsible for most of the building around the Park.

166, The ROSSETTI family, 1858.

197, Edward LEAR, c.1830.

197, Constant LAMBERT. He took this house after his second marriage in 1947 and it was still his address when he died in 1951.

ALBERMARLE STREET, W1   *Piccadilly, Victoria and Jubilee lines to Green Park*

General Monk (1608-1670) who was largely responsible for the Restoration of the Monarchy in 1660, was rewarded by King Charles II with the Dukedom of Albermarle. It was the second Duke, however, the spendthrift Christopher, whose name lives on here. He sold his house – for demolition – in an attempt to clear his debts. Sir Thomas Bond began building the street around 1684 and it first appeared in the rate books in 1685.

13, Charles James FOX. It was while he lived here that Samuel ROGERS first knew him.

36, Emma HAMILTON stayed here in 1810. Her husband, Sir William and her lover, Lord NELSON, were both dead and she was desperately short of money.

50, John Murray (1778-1843). He was BYRON'S publisher and it was in the dining-room here that Byron met Sir Walter Scott, for three consecutive weeks, at Murray's 'get-togethers' (hence Byron's allusions to 'Mr Murray's four o'clock visitors'). In 1898 Lady Monkswell dined with Murray's successors, '...at their nice old-world house ... up whose stairs – nice wide stairs with a pretty, twisted balustrade – so many poets and writers have walked...'.

ALDFORD STREET, W1   *Piccadilly line to Hyde Park Corner*

When Mary Davies (aged 12!) married Sir Thomas Grosvenor in 1677, she became the wife of a man who owned the villages of Belgrave, Eccleston, Kinnerton, Minera, Waverton, Claverton, Balderton, *Aldford,* Churton and Beeston (to name a few!). These village names are perpetuated in the street names of 'Belgravia' and much of the area around Grosvenor Square (the family name of the Dukes of Westminster is Grosvenor). Until 1886 Aldford Street was actually known as Chapel Street.

7, John G. WINANT (LCP 1981) 1942-1946. The house had been lent to him through the kindness of Winston CHURCHILL. .

13, 'Beau' BRUMMEL, in 1816. (His house has been demolished.)

18, Moreton FREWEN, 1886-1892, brother-in-law of Winston CHURCHILL. Frewen's son, Hugh and his sister Claire were born in this house. The house was a gift from Frewen's father-in-law, Leonard Jerome of New York.

ALDINGTON   Hampshire, July 8, 1892
Edward Godfrey (Richard)   United States, July 27, 1962
Author

4, Kensington Church Walk, W8, 1913

Aldington was educated at Dover College and afterwards at London University. He started 'writing' practically as soon as he could write at all and was literary editor of the *Egoist* before he was 21. The magazine was the periodical of a group of *literati* who called themselves 'The Imagists'. Amongst them was Hilda Doolittle who lived with Aldington for a few months before he married her in 1913. They were eventually divorced in 1937.

He served in the Armed Forces in World War One and on his return to 'civvy-street' worked as a translator and reviewer on a freelance basis. All the time he worked at his poetry and his first collection entitled *War and Love* was published in 1919.

From poetry he turned to novels. His *Death of a Hero* in 1929 collected good reviews. From fiction, biography was the next step. Soon after the outbreak of the 1939-45 war he moved to America and published *Wellington*, which won the Tait Black Prize in 1946. Two more biographies were on 'the Lawrences'; D.H. in 1950 and T.E. in 1955. He had already dealt with himself, in literary terms, when he published his autobiography, *Life for Life's Sake* in 1941.

ALDWYCH, WC2
Piccadilly line to Aldwych (Mondays to Fridays only)
otherwise District or Circle lines to Temple

It *could* be derived from the Saxon *eald wic* meaning 'Old Settlement'. Today's Aldwych, however, is really rather new (1905). Legend says that Alfred the Great (849-899) having kicked the Danes out of London, allowed them to make a settlement here. In 1398 the name 'Aldwich' makes its first documentary appearance. Drury Lane nearby, was once known as 'Via de Aldewyche'.

11, Ivor NOVELLO (LCP 1973) 1914-1951. Ivor moved in here with his mother and died in the top floor flat.

At the east end of the Aldwych is a statue of W.E. GLADSTONE, a bronze by Sir William Hamo THORNYCROFT, erected here in 1905.

ALEXANDER
(Sir) George
Actor, Manager

Reading, June 19, 1858
Chorley Wood, March 16, 1918

57, Pont Street, SW1 (LCP 1951) 1896-1918

He was born George Alexander Gibbs Samson, but adapted it better to suit the needs of an actor. He began to act with Sir Henry IRVING in 1881, though he had made his début in Nottingham two years earlier. He stayed with Irving for eight years, until he began in stage management and, in 1891, took over the St. James's Theatre. (Which, alas, became the victim of London's property developers after the Second World War, despite a vigorous opposition mounted by the theatrical world.) He was to manage this theatre until his death.

Oscar WILDE entered into contract with Alexander, who produced three Wilde plays and had two of them, *Lady Windermere's Fan* and *The Importance of Being Earnest* running in the West End in 1895 when Wilde was sent to prison for homosexual behaviour. The plays were taken off, but at Wilde's bankruptcy sale Alexander bought the acting rights of both of them. He made a few – voluntary – payments to Wilde after he was released from prison in 1897 and bequeathed the rights to Vyvyan HOLLAND, Wilde's younger and surviving son.

ALEXANDER PLACE, SW7
Piccadilly, District and Circle
lines to South Kensington

Much of the land around here belonged to the Thurloe estate (hence Thurloe Square etc). John Alexander was one of the estate's heirs.

11, Ruth DRAPER, 1939. She wrote, '...the room is filled with flowers, the quietness is audible, a Sir Joshua' [REYNOLDS] 'hangs above the mantelpiece – of a lovely young man in grey satin and fur - the house is charmingly furnished in the best possible taste – and I love it.'

17, James LEES-MILNE until 1946.

ALLENBY	April 23, 1861
(Viscount) Henry Edmund Hynam	London, May 14, 1936
Field Marshall	St George's Chapel,
	Westminster Abbey

24, Wetherby Gardens, SW5 (LCP 1960) 1928-1936

He was educated at Hailebury College. Then on to Sandhurst, after which he joined the Inniskilling Dragoons, seeing service in South Africa for three periods between 1884 and 1902.

In 1914, he was in command of the First Cavalry Division of the British Expeditionary Force. In 1917 he captured the important Vimy Ridge but was unable to press on further east against the German Army. He was posted to Palestine where, by clever manoeuvre, he outwitted the Turkish Army and, on December 9, 'redeemed his promise to give the British people Jerusalem as a "Christmas present"'. Damascus fell to him in October 1918, bringing the whole Middle Eastern campaign to a close.

He was appointed High Commissioner for Egypt and, by his vigilance and stern discipline, foiled subversive risings in that country.

His peerage was given to him in 1919. Not only was Allenby a soldier through and through, he was a classicist who could (and *did*) quote Greek in the original, much to the confusion of his fellow soldiers! He was also a keen ornithologist and built an aviary in the back garden of Wetherby Gardens.

ALMA-TADEMA	Dronsyp, Holland, January 8, 1836
(Sir) Laurence	London, June 25, 1912
Artist	St Paul's Cathedral

44, Grove End Road, NW8 (LCP 1975) 1886-1912

Originally intended for medecine, Alma-Tadema studied at the Antwerp Academy of Art, eventually settling in England in 1873. He became a Royal Academician six years later. He had become a British citizen almost as soon as he came to live in London and was knighted in 1899. Most of his paintings portrayed Greek or Roman 'domestic' scenes and were once described as, '...vapid in content but with skilful imitation of statuesque women and marble baths.'

ANDERSON	London, June 9, 1836
Elizabeth Garrett	December 17, 1917
Physician	Aldeburgh, Suffolk

20, Upper Berkeley Street, W1 (LCP 1962) 1860-1874

In 1865 Elizabeth Garrett became the first Englishwoman to qualify and practise as a doctor in Britain, by passing the Apothecaries' Hall Examination, despite strong opposition from practically all sides. Five years later she became Visiting Physician at the London Hospital in the East End. The University of Paris gave her a degree the same year.

She married J.G. Anderson in 1871 and their daughter, Louisa, born in 1872, wrote a biography of her mother in 1939. Louisa became a doctor too and organised the first hospital to be managed entirely by women in the First World War, later becoming Head of the Military Hospital in Endell Street in Holborn.

ANSTEY, F. See GUTHRIE, T.A.

ARBUTHNOT	Arbuthnot, Scotland, 1675
John	London, February 27, 1735
Physician	St James's, Piccadilly

11, Cork Street, W1, from 1729 until he died here

Having obtained his medical degree at Aberdeen University, Arbuthnot eventually became Chief Physician at the Royal Hospital, Chelsea where he remained many years.

He was a friend of Dean Swift and Alexander POPE. Swift said that the Doctor was a man who, '...could do everything but walk'. This strange opinion was prompted by the fact that Arbuthnot had a strange, uncoordinated and slouching gait.

Arbuthnot happened to be at the Epsom Races, where the Derby is now run, when Prince George of Denmark, the drunken husband of Queen Anne, was taken ill. The Doctor's services were called upon, with apparent success, as he was appointed Physician in Ordinary to the Queen.

It was Arbuthnot who created 'John Bull' as the prickly, archetypal Englishman, when he published *The History of John Bull* in a series of pamphlets in 1712. Arbuthnot described 'John Bull' as, '...an honest, plain-dealing fellow, choleric, bold and of a very inconstant temper...a boon companion, loving his bottle and his diversion.' Originally 'John Bull' appeared in Arbuthnot's satire, *Law is a Bottomless Pit,* in 1712 and critics feel that Arbuthnot did not 'invent' John Bull, but merely 'established' him.

ARCHER	Perth, Scotland, September 23, 1856
William	London, December 27, 1924
Dramatic Critic	

34, Great Ormond Street, WC1, 1890s
27, Fitzroy Square, W1, 1923-1924

To Archer falls much of the credit in bringing Henrik Ibsen's plays to London. He came south to London when he was 22 and in 1913 he was made the first President of the newly formed 'Critics' Circle'.

The *World* magazine (whose offices were at 1, York Street, Covent Garden) used Archer as their dramatic critic for many years after his first 'crit.' appeared in the *World* in 1884. When Cosmo Hamilton, a playwright, took the *World's* editorial chair, Archer, '...in his dry Scotch way, said that he would be perfectly prepared to step aside when anything of mine' [Hamilton's] 'was produced in London if I thought it desirable and thus would be spared the unhappy necessity of jumping on his editor.'

Archer turned playwright once or twice and Hamilton genuinely admired Winthrop Ames's production of Archer's play, *The Green Goddess,* which he had seen in New York with George Arliss in the leading role. Archer always *claimed* that he had dreamed the whole plot of *Green Goddess.*

ARGYLL STREET, W1 *Central, Bakerloo and Victoria lines to Oxford Circus*

The London home of the Dukes of Argyll was near here (on the east side of the street). They sold the house in 1830 to the Earl of Aberdeen.

10, Major-General William ROY 1779-1790. Despite its present exterior, this is basically one of the only two surviving buildings on the Argyll's original estate.

29 (formerly 30) Madame de STAEL 1813-1814. Her second husband, 20 years younger than she, had died of tuberculosis.

31, George LYTTLETON, 1743-1749. He had married Lucy Fortescue the previous year.

39, James NORTHCOTE, 1804-1806. Benjamin HAYDON, then only

18, came to see Northcote here and thought him 'wizened' (Northcote was then not yet 60 and had another 20 years to live).

ARLINGTON STREET, W1   *Piccadilly and Victoria lines to Green Park*

This street was developed about 1689 by Henry Bennet, Earl of Arlington. He was one of the clique of five men whose initials made up the word 'Cabal'. They were the most influential men in the Court of King Charles II between 1667 and 1674. The others were: Clifford; Buckingham; Ashley and Lauderdale. The land had been granted to him by the King and sold by Arlington to a man called Pym for £10,000.

3,   Sir Osbert SITWELL was born here in December 1892. So, too, was his sister, Edith, before him. Their father, Sir George, had taken the house on a short lease to enable him to attend more easily to his Parliamentary duties. It was, '...a nice house with electric light' (still very unusual for the London of 1890).

5,   Sir Robert WALPOLE (LCP 1976) from 1742 until he died here in 1745. He left it to his son, Horace, who lived here until 1779, when he moved to Berkeley Square.

9,   Charles James FOX.

17,   Horace WALPOLE was born here in 1717. The house was built by William Kent, 1685-1748.

17,   John Lothrop MOTLEY, 1869-1870, when he was United States Minister to Britain. In a letter to the Duchess of Argyll he wrote, '...yellow fog enwraps London and at my library table, being close to a large window looking out on the Green Park, I am just able to write with candles, while the depth of the room is as dark as night. Piccadilly is entirely invisible...'

20,   Lord SALISBURY, from 1878 until his death in 1903.

22,   called successively Beaufort House, Hamilton House, Walsingham House then Wimborne House, when it was redecorated and lived in by Lord HOUGHTON. The interiors were used by HOGARTH, between 1742 and 1744, as 'models' for his series of paintings, *Marriage à la Mode*. The paintings are now in the National Gallery.

ARMSTRONG-JONES   London, March 7, 1930
Anthony Charles Robert
(Lord Snowdon)
Photographer

25, Eaton Terrace, SW1, here born

Son of Ronald Armstrong-Jones and Anne Messell (who, after a divorce in April 1959, became the Countess of Rosse). 'Tony A-J' surprised the world (*including* Fleet Street!) by becoming the fiancé of HRH Princess Margaret, younger – and only – sister of HM Queen Elizabeth II. He had made his way in the cut-throat world of professional photography, developing great skill. After his marriage to Princess Margaret in 1960, he continued working and probably his Royal connections brought him commissions.
They had two children, Viscount Linley (b.1961) and Lady Sarah (b.1964) but, as all too many forecast, the marriage of the Princess and the Photographer came apart. Lord Snowdon married again, to Lucy Lindsay-Hogg (née Davis) – in 1978 – and they had one daughter. The Princess (born on August 21, 1930) found remarriage a difficult problem because her sister, Queen Elizabeth, would (apart from what is believed to be a hostility to divorce) be unlikely to adopt a compromising attitude to her sister's affairs when she, the Monarch, is *Defender of the Faith*. However, the Queen went out of her way to show that her ex-brother-in-law was not a *pariah* and has encouraged him in his profession as a very good photographer.

In 1963 he was made Constable of Caernarvon Castle, in Wales, and in that capacity, was largely responsible for the imposing and moving ceremony in the castle attendant upon HRH Prince Charles (as the Sovereign's eldest son) being formally 'crowned' as Prince of Wales.

Lord Snowdon was at school at Eton and in his time, none of the boys was allowed a radio in their studies. They were, however, permitted anything they made themselves. So Armstrong-Jones built himself a radio! The powers-that-be, therefore *had* to allow him to use it. His ingenuity and skill can be seen in the aviary he designed for the London Zoo, which is on the north side of that establishment. His son would have appeared to have inherited his father's practical gifts and has set out to be a designer of furniture.

ARNE Covent Garden, March 12, 1710
Thomas London, March 5, 1778
Composer St Paul's Church, Covent Garden

32, King Street, WC2, here born
215, Kings Road, SW1, 1770's

Arne's father (also Thomas) had a prosperous upholstery business and was sometimes referred to as 'Crown and Cushion' (or even 'Two Crowns and a Cushion as he had worked for Queen Anne and, after her death in 1714, for George I.) There was enough money in it to be able to send young Thomas to Eton. He was always set on music and had had his first opera performed before he was 25.

The tune for which he will ever be remembered is *Rule Britannia*. The sentiments in it are now, sadly, outdated, but the infectious melody was part of a masque called *Alfred*.

He was appointed composer to the Drury Lane Theatre in 1744 and the University of Oxford gave him an Honorary Doctorate of Music 15 years later. Strangely, the tag of 'Doctor' seems to have stuck to Arne. Although many musicians have been similarly honoured over the years it is only Arne who invariably seems to be referred to as 'Doctor'.

ARNOLD Laleham, Sy., December 24,1822
Matthew Liverpool, April 15, 1888
Poet All Saint's Churchyard, Laleham

101, Mount Street, W1, 1848
2, Chester Square, SW1 (LCP 1954) 1858-1868

The eldest son of Dr. Arnold of Rugby School who did much for the English Public School 'image' and 'muscular christianity', Matthew was educated at Winchester, Rugby and Balliol College, Oxford; graduating from there *cum laude* in 1844. He became a Fellow of Oriel College in the following year.

From 1847 to 1851 he was secretary to Lord Lansdowne and then appointed Lay Inspector of Schools. He travelled up and down Britain visiting the (relatively) few schools within the State system and was most diligent, honest and painstaking in this rather mundane task.

During part of this inspectorial period (1857-1867) he was also Professor of Poetry at Oxford; his first volume of poems, *The Stray Reveller,* having appeared in 1849. This book included his most famous poem, *The Forsaken Merman.*

In 1883 he was granted a pension of £250 by the government and in that year undertook a lecture tour of America. An American journalist described his platform manner as, '...an elderly macaw picking grapes off a trellis'. This was in Detroit and Arnold had a sufficient sense of humour to quote the line in a letter to his daughter.

Though only 65 he collapsed and unexpectedly died in a Liverpool street, having possibly overexerted himself by jumping over a small gate.

AROUET	Paris, November 24, 1694
François Marie ('Voltaire')	Paris, May 30, 1778
Dramatist and Satirist	Pantheon, Paris

10, Maiden Lane, WC2 (P) 1728

'Voltaire' was the name he gave himself in 1718, for reasons which are still unknown. He began in the law but the profession disgusted him and he turned his hand to poetry. His influential godfather, the Abbé de Chateauneuf, introduced him into the most elevated circles of Parisian society but his unguarded tongue soon got him into trouble. He was twice imprisoned in the Bastille where he wrote the play, *Oedipe*, which was well received in England.
Exiled from Paris, he came to London and stayed here for nearly two years. Whilst in town he met the niece of Isaac NEWTON. ('Voltaire' was in Westminster Abbey for Newton's funeral on March 28, 1727). The unpublished memoirs of Newton, written by the niece's husband, John Conduit, contained the anecdote of the Newtonian theory of Gravity being inspired by a windfall apple. It was 'Voltaire' who gave this simple story a wide circulation. He also met Lord CHESTERFIELD, the Herveys and Sarah, Duchess of Marlborough. He dedicated his *Henriade* to Queen Caroline and in 1729, when allowed back to France, he took with him the substance for his *Letters on the English*. He grew rich as a result, initially through shares purchased in a government lottery and by speculation in corn 'futures'.
Cardinal Dubois (1656-1723) in his memoirs wrote, 'Voltaire is a long diaphanous body, yet he does not let you easily read the bottom of his thought. His lean, pale and bony face is marked by a look of mockery, all the more perfidious in that it finds expression in fair words. He has a perpetual epigram on his pinched lips, whether he is speaking to a prince or a lackey.' Dubois, 1656-1723, was at one time the Prime Minister of France as well as being a Cardinal.

ARUNDEL STREET, Strand, WC2   *Piccadilly line to Aldwych (Monday to Fridays only), otherwise Circle or District lines to Embankment*

Here stood Arundel House, town house of the Dukes of Norfolk, whose own castle in Sussex is at Arundel. The family owned this area from the mid 1500s. It was bought from the executors of Lord Thomas Seymour, who had been given it by King Henry Vlll after *he* had seized it from the Bishop of Bath and Wells!

12, Coventry PATMORE, in the 1840s.
29, Howard PAYNE, 1825-1827.

ASHLEY GARDENS (Victoria)
off Ambrosden Avenue, SW1   *Victoria, District and Circle lines to Victoria*

The family name of Lord Shaftesbury is Ashley-Cooper. The man who became Lord Shaftesbury in 1851 had already made his name (in a number of directions) as Ashley-Cooper and was still known by that style when these streets were developed around 1850.

48, Mrs Patrick CAMPBELL, 1895. Less that two years previously she had her first real success with *The Second Mrs. Tanqueray*.
140, Marie BELLOC-LOWNDES, 1904-1909. The novelist sister of Hilaire BELLOC.

ASQUITH
Herbert Henry
(1st Earl of Oxford and Asquith)
Prime Minister

Morley, Yorks., September 12, 1852
Sutton Courtenay, Oxon., February 15, 1928
Sutton Courtenay

20, Cavendish Square, W1 (LCP 1951) 1894-1922
44, Bedford Square, WC1, 1922-1928

Son of a cloth manufacturer, Asquith progressed through Oxford and the Bar to Westminster as a Liberal MP for Fife. He became Home Secretary, under GLADSTONE, in 1892.

When CAMPBELL-BANNERMAN resigned in. 1908, Asquith became Prime Minister. His ministry was a troubled one: the 'Irish Question' nearly unseated him, but World War One began and there were greater problems to face. These were such, politically, that Asquith was forced to form a Coalition Government in May 1915. But even that ran aground and he resigned in December 1916. He never regained his lost position and, after an election defeat in 1925, he was offered (and accepted) a peerage. Before his troubles as Prime Minister, it was becoming more and more evident that he was drinking too much. CHURCHILL, who was not, as we know, a teetotaller, noted that Asquith was at his best in the Commons until dinner time, 'But thereafter...!' The comment was made after his behaviour in the House during the Committee stages of the Parliament Bill when Asquith was too drunk to stand up and make a speech.

In 1877 Asquith married Helen Melland (1855-1891) daughter of a Manchester surgeon. They had four sons and one daughter. When Mrs. Asquith died, Asquith was truly grief-stricken. However, when still at the Home Office in 1894, he married the 30-year-old Margot Tennant, daughter of the wealthy baronet, Sir Charles Tennant ('The Bart').

She married Asquith in St George's Church, Hanover Square, W1 and the names of GLADSTONE, ROSEBERRY and BALFOUR, together with Asquith's appeared on the marriage register. Probably no other marriage had ever claimed three guests who were ex-Prime Ministers whilst the groom was to become Prime Minister. He had two children by Margot, Elizabeth in 1897 and Anthony ('Puffin') in 1902.

On the whole his second marriage was happy, but in 1912, the Prime Minister fell headlong in love with Venetia Stanley. This, '...dark-eyed girl...with aquiline good looks and a masculine intellect', was just 25. She was the daughter of Lyulph, 4th Baron Stanley of Alderley (1839-1925) and she became a willing target of a *bombardment* of letters from Asquith. Sometimes he was writing to her three times a *day* and, more than once, actually from the Cabinet Room in 10 Downing Street. He told her far too much but luckily she was most discreet and no harm was done. Over 500 of these letters survived. None of *her* letters remain and in 1915 she married a rich Jew, Edwin Montagu (1879-1924).

ASTAFIEVA
(Princess) Serafine
Ballet Dancer

1876
September 13, 1934

152, Kings Road, SW3 (LCP 1968) 1918-1934

The Princess came to England with Diaghilev in 1910, as a dancer in his company. In 1913 she left the public stage altogether and established a school in the King's Road. She lived 'over the shop' and became very much a Chelsea inhabitant.

Many of the great names from English ballet circles learnt under her critically expert eye. Three of the most famous of these must be Dame Margot FONTEYN, Anton Dolin (real name Patrick Healey-Keay, who studied with the Princess when he was still a teenager) and 'Markova', whose real name was Marks. Born in 1910, she was made a DBE in 1963, so her full, correct title would be: Dame Lilian Alicia Marks. Five years before he died Sergei Diaghilev, then 52, came to see the 14-year-old Alice Marks dancing in the School here.

ASTOR New York, March 31, 1848
William Waldorf October 18, 1919
(1st Viscount Astor) Cliveden
Millionaire

Lansdowne House, Berkeley Square, W1
4, St James's Square, SW1, 1912-1942

Astor came to England from America in 1890 because he thought the Britain of those days was, as he put it, 'Fit for a gentleman to live in'; his grandfather having been a farm labourer in Germany for the first 20 years of his life.

Astor spent his considerable wealth (both inherited and money that he himself had generated) lavishly, but money alone was not an 'open sesame' to the tightly closed ranks of the English upper classes. In London he bought the *Pall Mall Gazette* and the *Observer* and ran this paper empire from offices he built near the Temple. He also bought Cliveden, a beautiful country house, built by BARRY on the banks of the Thames. The large estate which surrounded it was totally enclosed and some wag gave him the nickname of 'Walled-off Astor'!

Astor's son (also William Waldorf) inherited his father's title and *his* son, William Waldorf III became the 3rd Viscount Astor in 1952; dying just seven years later when he was only 45.

'William III's' mother was the redoubtable Nancy, nee Langhorne, born in Virginia in 1879. She was a legend and, amongst other less public claims to fame, was the first woman actually to *sit* as a Member of the House of Commons. She took her seat in the Commons on December 1, 1919.

ATTWOOD London, November 23, 1765
Thomas London, March 24, 1838
Musician St Paul's Cathedral

17, Cheyne Walk, SW3, where he died

Attwood was one of the few English pupils of MOZART and, at the age of 31, became the organist at St Paul's Cathedral. Appropriately he is buried directly below the organ there. At one time he was also the organist to the Chapel Royal. He was one of the founders of the Philharmonic Society in 1813, which gave its first concert on March 8 of that year.

After his death his post at St Paul's was taken by John GOSS, who lived just along the Walk, at number 3.

AUDEN York, February 21, 1907
Wystan Hugh Vienna, September 28, 1973
Poet Kirchstetten, Austria

43, Chester Terrace, SW1, 1930

Auden was a doctor's son, educated at Gresham School, Holt and Oxford. In 1935 he married Thomas Mann's daughter, so that she could travel on a British passport (a marriage of 'convenience' suitable to both partners, as Auden was one hundred percent homosexual and Erika Mann was a lesbian.)

He migrated to the United States in 1938 and eventually took out citizenship there. But he moved around Europe in the 1930s, mostly in Germany (perhaps because German boys were much to his taste) and then in Spain during their sad, civil war. Though he was not *officially* a Communist, he served as a stretcher bearer on the 'losing' side.

Auden's earlier poems certainly reflected the bitterness of the 1930s and he has frequently been referred to as 'a poet of the Thirties'. His work transcends such a constrictive 'label' and his reputation as a poet is internationally honoured.

He spent his last years in Austria and he is buried in the churchyard in the village where he died. He is honoured by an engraved stone on the floor of Westminster Abbey in 'Poets' Corner'.

AUSTEN
Jane
Author

Steventon, December 16, 1775
Winchester, July 18, 1817
Winchester Cathedral (North aisle).

9, Henrietta Street, WC2, 1813 and 1814
23, Hans Place, SW3 (P) 1814 and 1815

It is hard to believe that little Jane Austen, the author of those wonderful novels, should have been buried in Winchester Cathedral in 1817 with a brass plate over her grave which makes no mention *whatsoever* of her ever having written a thing, let alone six novels which were truly works of art. On August 12, 1854, when Jane Austen had been dead for 37 years, MACAULAY, having just read *Hard Times* by DICKENS *and* a book of Pliny's letters, wrote in his diary for that day: 'Read *Northanger Abbey:* worth all DICKENS and Pliny put together. Yet it was the work of a girl.' Time has caught up with her original mourners and in the Cathedral today there is a side window near her tomb, which extols her *literary* virtues.

Jane was a shy and retiring daughter of the Rector of Deane and Steventon in Hampshire and had her first novel, *Sense and Sensibility* published in 1811, followed by *Pride and Prejudice* in 1813, *Mansfield Park* (1814) and then, in 1816, *Emma, Northanger Abbey* and *Persuasion* were both published posthumously.

AVENUE ROAD, NW8
Jubilee line to St John's Wood

The definition of 'Avenue' is, '...a wide and handsome street usually bordered by trees', a very apt description of Avenue Road, even today. It was first opened up in the 1830s.

64, Herbert SPENCER. He lived here in the 1880s and 1890s with his two unmarried sisters.

AVONMORE ROAD, W14
District line to Olympia (this station is only open when there is an exhibition on at Olympia, next nearest is West Kensington, served by the District line)

The origin of this road is not now known. The Yelverton family in Ireland bore the Viscountcy of Avonmore from 1795, when the 1st Viscount was Lord Chief of the Irish Exchequer. The 6th and last Viscount died, aged 44 in 1910, without heirs, so the title of Avonmore became extinct. There appears to be no connection between those Avonmores and W14, however.

9, Charles Kegan PAUL, 1902.
51, Sir Edward ELGAR (LCP 1962) 1890-1891. Elgar took a three-year lease in March 1890 and moved in on March 24.
54, Sir Compton MACKENZIE, 1891-1900. During part of this time, 'Monty' was a pupil at St Paul's School which, then, was just along the road.

B

BACON
Francis (1st Baron Verulam)
Philosopher

London, January 22, 1561
London, April 9, 1626
St Michael's Church, St Albans

1, Grays Inn Square, WC1, for nearly 50 years

Son of Nicholas Bacon, Lord Keeper to Queen Elizabeth, Francis went to Trinity College, Cambridge and took up the law. He became a Member of Parliament for Melcombe Regis in 1584 and urged for stronger measures against Catholics, a course of action destined to appeal to the 'Virgin Queen'.

In 1606 he married Alice Barham. The following year, he was appointed Solicitor General and in 1618 he became Lord Chancellor. However, only three years later he was found guilty of 'corruption and neglect' and heavily fined. Saved from incarceration in the Tower and the fine being returned to Trustees for Bacon's own eventual use, all by intercession of King James I, Bacon devoted the rest of his life to literary matters and philosophical study. His principal work was *The Advancement of Learning* and he intended to create a new philosophical system which, in many ways, differed from Aristotelian philosophy. In the purely literary field his most important published works are his essays, the first of which had been published in 1597.

John Evelyn, in his description of Bacon, wrote that, 'He had a delicate, lively eye...like the eye of a viper'.

Bacon died of pneumonia following a cold he was supposed to have caught when he stuffed a chicken's carcase with snow in Pond Square, Highgate. (Snowing in London, in April?) If so it must have been one of the earliest experiments in deep freeze. The 'ghost' of the unfortunate *fowl* is supposed to haunt the Square still!

A bronze statue of Bacon by F.W. Pomeroy, was erected in Gray's Inn, South Square, in 1912.

BADEN POWELL
Robert Stephenson Smythe
(1st Baron)
Founder of the Boy Scout movement

London, February 22, 1857
Africa, January 8, 1941
Kenya

6, Stanhope Street, W2 (now 11 Stanhope Terrace) here born
9, Hyde Park Gate, SW7 (LCP 1972) 1861-1876
15, Knightsbridge (then 8, St George's Place) SW7, 1878-1902
32 (now demolished) Princess Gate, SW7, 1902-1904

Educated at Charterhouse, 'B.P.' passed the Army Examination with such distinction, that he went into the 13th Hussars in India. Quite an achievement, as his family had no sort of military tradition attached to it – indeed, the family had a long literary background.

He was the Officer Commanding the British Army in Matabeleland (then a Bantu part of British South Africa) and was in command of Mafeking until its relief on May 17, 1900. (Which event introduced the word 'Maffick' into the language, meaning to celebrate uproariously, based upon the outbreak of the general public in London when news of the relief came through.)

Baden Powell founded the Boy Scout Movement in 1908; boys were taught the principles of bushcraft, drawing upon his experiences in the outback. In 1913, after a shipboard romance, he married Olave Soames, who was 32 years younger than himself. Despite the disparity of ages, their marriage was idyllically happy. When the Baden-Powells moved out of London early in the 1900s their address was: Pax Hill, Bentley, Hampshire. (Their telephone number was 8 – just 8!)

A granite statue of B.P. by Donald Potter stands outside the Scout Headquarters on the north west corner of Queen's Gate and the Cromwell Road SW7. The weary, balding, morose figure shown by the sculptor, could hardly be even a reflection of the Baden-Powell who began an International movement 54 years before this statue was put up.

BAGNOLD
Enid
Author

October 1889
London, March 31, 1981

13, Hyde Park Gardens, SW7, 1920s
29, Hyde Park Gate, SW7, 1930-1950s

In private life the author of the best-selling novel, *National Velvet* (1935) was Lady Jones. In 1920 Enid Bagnold married Roderick Jones, aged 43, who had been knighted two years earlier. Sir Roderick was head of *REUTER'S News Agency* in Britain and, by all accounts, foul to work for. Sir Roderick was not the first man to enjoy Miss Bagnold's physical favours. Frank HARRIS had told her that, 'Sex is the gateway to life' and so, as Miss Bagnold herself wrote, 'I went through the gateway in an upper room in the Cafe Royal' (a restaurant, still functioning, at the Piccadilly end of Regent Street. It is doubtful, however, if today any of their 'upper rooms' are available for casual letting.) HARRIS was a boastful, sexually swaggering man, who sometimes came near to greatness. In his own, written-for-the-money-and-no-mistake autobiography, he gallantly (unusually so) makes no reference to the *defloration* of Enid.

But long after the HARRIS *affaire* she was to find fame with *National Velvet*, which lived again on the screen in 1944. The leading part was played by an almost unknown, 12-year-old girl called Elizabeth Taylor. Miss Bagnold also wrote at least two very successful plays: *The Chalk Garden* in 1956 and *The Chinese Prime Minister* five years later.

BAIRD
John Logie
'Father of Television'

Helensburgh, Scotland, August 13, 1888
Hastings, June 14, 1946

22, Frith Street, W1 (LCP 1951) 1925-1927

Beginning in Glasgow, at which University (founded 1451) he had studied for his engineering degree, Baird set up a business to make and sell a sort of 'thermal' sock. The 'Baird Undersock Company' did not flourish and he moved on to boot polish, then honey and one or two more non-starters.

The principles of television had been more or less accepted since the 1880's and Baird, now ill as well as poor, came south to Hastings, on the Channel coast, to develop the idea. He borrowed £200, moved up to London and started to work in the Frith Street attic. On October 2, 1925 he transmitted his first television picture. It was of his odd-job boy, William Taynton. The following spring, Baird, even poorer than ever, invited some members of the Royal Institute to a demonstration of his process.

He 'sold' the BBC his 240 line, mechanically scanned system. But when the Corporation actually began a regular television service in 1936 (the first experimental television programme went out from Broadcasting House on August 21, 1932) they adopted a rival 405 line, electronically scanned system, which had been developed elsewhere. Meanwhile poor Baird,

without any financial backing, struggled on alone. It practically broke his heart, but his inventive spirit never deserted him. At the time of his death he was working on Colour TV and stereophonic sound.
'Television?' said C.P. Scott (1846-1932; who became editor of the *Manchester Guardian* at the age of 26) 'television? No good will come of this device. The word is half Greek and half Latin.'

BAKER STREET, W1 and NW1

Bakerloo, Jubilee, Metropolitan and Circle lines to Baker Street (numbers 2-134 inclusive are in postal district W1, being south of the Marylebone Road, north of it the postal district is NW1)

William Baker leased land from the Portman estate here and began to develop the street after having acted as agent for other Portman family holdings. The next generation of Bakers were knighted.

20, Richard RUSH, 1817-1825, at a rent of 450 guineas (£472.50) per annum.

21, This house was owned by John Morris and sold to his executors in 1840. Morris's son, Dr. Malcolm MORRIS, gave details of the house to CONAN DOYLE in 1886. DOYLE examined the property (then still a private house) and turned it into '221B Baker Street', the house owned by 'Mrs. Hudson' who had 'Sherlock Holmes' and 'Dr. Watson' as lodgers. The real 21 had three long drawing-room windows at the front of the house, but DOYLE cut one out in order to 'disguise the house'.

47 (formerly 64) Lord CAMELFORD a barmy aristocrat, killed in a duel in 1804, aged 29. Camelford was a cousin of William PITT, the Prime Minister.

61, Elizabeth Vigée LEBRUN 1802-1805. She went back to her native France where she, like Marie Tussaud, had not seen eye to eye with the French administration of the day.

68 (formerly 31) Lord LYTTON was born here in 1803.

120 (formerly 14, York Place) William PITT, 'Pitt the Younger' (LCP 1949) 1802-1806. His niece, the eccentric Lady Hester STANHOPE, kept house for him. She was 23 years old (he was 43) and he, '...came to regard her with almost a father's affection'.

186, here is **CHILTERN COURT NW1**

Flat 97, Arnold BENNETT lived here from 1930 until the following year, attended by his mistress, he died in the flat.

Flat 47, H.G. WELLS was living here in 1930.

226, Sarah SIDDONS lived for many years in a cottage on this site. She took a lease on the house in 1817 and then added a studio-cum-workroom, '...for her modelling'. She died here on June 8, 1831.

BALCOMBE STREET, W1

Bakerloo line and BR to Marylebone

The land around here was owned by the Portman family and it is just possible that somehow Balcombe was a corruption (or a transliteration) of Batcombe, a village in Dorset owned by the family.

65, Richard WAGNER, 1855.

BALDWIN

Worcester August 3, 1867
Stanley (1st Earl Balwin of Bewdley) Astley, December 14, 1947
Prime Minister   Ashes in Worcester Cathedral (near the West entrance)

93, Eaton Square, SW1 (LCP 1969) 1913-1924

After schooling at Harrow, followed by Trinity College, Oxford, Baldwin went into the prosperous family iron business. Seventeen years later he was elected Conservative MP for Bewdley (a small town on the river Severn). In 1916 he was Parliamentary Private Secretary to BONAR LAW, Chancellor of the Exchequer; five years later he was President of the Board of Trade and then Chancellor himself. Law resigned in 1923 and, much to the surprise of many, Baldwin became Prime Minister.

King George V asked Baldwin to form a Government on May 22. In October of that year Baldwin made a particularly stupid remark about Home Trade. The Press demanded, as only the Press can, that Baldwin should go to the country again and seek a new mandate. Baldwin shuffled round to the Palace to ask a furious King to dissolve Parliament and call another election. On November 16, 1923 Parliament was dissolved. At that moment Baldwin had a majority of 73 *over* all other parties. After the Election he found himself with a majority of 99 *against* him. During the five months in office he had relied upon the support of the 150 National Liberals in the House. Baldwin, commenting upon this reversal of fortune, said, 'Whatever else I have done I've smashed the Liberal Party!' Many political commentators think that Baldwin's unnecessary Autumn election put the Labour Party on its feet.

His next hurdle was the General Strike in 1926. On May 1 of that year, the miners all over the country came out on strike. At the end of three days the whole of Britain was out. It only lasted until May 12, but the miners stayed out. They maintained their action until November 19, when, impoverished after six months' loss of earnings, they went back on the employers' terms. With the Labour Party gaining strength a Coalition Government was forced and Baldwin was Lord President of the Council during the four years (1931-1935) of the uneasy Coalition.

His career was ended by the 'Abdication Crisis'. Together with Cosmo Lang (1864-1945) Baldwin felt that King Edward VIII should not marry Mrs. *Simpson* In the end, the King stepped down from his throne on December 11, 1936 and Baldwin faded out. He was made an Earl in 1937.

Harold NICOLSON said that Baldwin, '...used to scratch himself continuously and made strange movements with his head with half-closed eyes like some tortoise half awake, smelling the air, blinking, snuffly and neurotic.'

BALFE Dublin, May 15, 1808
Michael William Rowney Abbey, Herts., October 20,
Composer 1870
Kensal Green; Square 74, Row 2
(memorial tablet in Westminster
Abbey)

12 (then 7, Upper Seymour Street) Seymour Street, W1 (LCP 1912) 1861-1865

Balfe made his debut as a violinist when he was only nine and came to London six years later. By this time he was composing music seriously and one of his first works to be performed was *La Perouse* (The Peruvian Girl) which, with a ballet sequence incorporated in it, was staged in Milan.

By 1825 he was studying in Italy under Paer, Rossini and Galli. In 1827 he travelled north and sang Italian opera in Paris with great success. The Parisians liked his rich and flexible baritone.

Back in England in 1833, he was appointed conductor of the London Italian Opera Company and probably conducted his most famous work, *The Bohemian Girl*, in 1843. He was successful financially and bought himself Rowney Abbey in Hertfordshire, where he died.

He composed many songs but the one which must have been sung the most, before all sorts of different audiences, is probably *The Harp that Once Through Tara's Halls*.

BALFOUR Whittinghame, Scotland, July 25, 1848
Arthur James (1st Earl) Woking, March 30, 1930
Prime Minister

4, Carlton Gardens, SW1 (his town house for most of his adult life)

Whilst an undergraduate at Cambridge in the 1860s, Balfour's epicene looks earned him a number of unfavourable nicknames; such as, 'Miss Balfour', or 'Pretty Fanny'. He had gone up to Cambridge after five years at Eton – the 'nursery end' of so many British Prime Ministers. Politics were in his blood – his mother was a sister of Lord Robert Cecil, 1830-1903, *quondam* Prime Minister (and also an Old Etonian). In 1874, Balfour became MP for Hertford and for two years he was private secretary to his uncle, Lord Salisbury. In 1879 Balfour's book *Defense of Philosophic Doubt,* which argued the case of intellectual liberty in the face of scientific dogma, attracted attention to the young and up-and-coming politician.

Not long after, he joined Lord Randolph CHURCHILL's so called 'Fourth Party', but despite this and his apparent indolence, he rose up through the ranks of the Tory party, becoming Leader of the House of Commons in 1892 and Prime Minister ten years later, where he remained until 1906.

He resigned in 1922 and was created an Earl. He never married and so the earldom died with him. Both GLADSTONE and DISRAELI were supposed to have disliked him and Lord BEAVERBROOK was heard to say that, 'Balfour was a hermaphrodite: *no* one ever saw him naked'!

BANKS
London, February 13, 1743
(Sir) Joseph Isleworth, June 19, 1820
Botanist Parish Church, Isleworth

32, Soho Square, W1 (LCP 1938) 1777-1820.

Educated successively at Harrow, Eton and Christ Church, Oxford the young Banks sometimes attracted the wrong sort of notice from his mentors. One report on him said that, '...he was so immoderately fond of play that his attention could not be fixed to his studies'.

However, as he grew older he grew more studious and (having always inclined to the study of botany) he went off to Newfoundland on a 'field trip' in 1766. Two years later he set off with Captain COOK around the world in a ship that Banks equipped from his own pocket. In 1778 he was elected President of the Royal Society, a post he held for 41 years. In 1781 he was created a baronet.

It was thanks to Banks that the bread fruit was taken from Tahiti to the West Indies and mangoes brought from Bengal.

It was said that Banks conditioned his body for tropical exploration by spending longer and longer periods in a room where the temperature could be raised progressively. Banks claimed that eventually he could tolerate a temperature of 211° Fahrenheit (99.4° Centigrade) and his body temperature never 'mounted above normal'.

BARHAM Canterbury, December 6, 1788
Richard Harris ('Thomas Ingoldsby')London, June 17, 1845
Author and poet St Martin's Without, Ludgate

51, Great Queen Street, WC2, 1821-1824

He was the son of a 'country gentleman' who had the boy educated at St Paul's School in Hammersmith. When he was 14, returning to the school by coach, he was involved in an accident that left his right arm permanently crippled. So badly was it damaged that amputation was thought to be the only way of saving his life. Luckily the doctors tried an experiment whereby the arm was fixed back on, and together, using a contraption of 'catgut and silver rings'. From St Paul's he went up to Brasenose College, Oxford. He was ordained in 1813, held various livings thereafter, eventually ending up with a minor Canonry at St Pauls.

In 1819 his first published work appeared – a novel called *Baldwin* which (as the *DNB* puts it) '...fell dead from the press'.

He is remembered as the author of the *Ingoldsby Legends,* which appeared separately in *Bentley's Miscellany* and were published collectively in three series from 1840. The *Legends* are a series of comical episodes, full of wit and grotesque imageries. One of the finest editions was published with colour illustrations by Arthur RACKHAM in the early part of the 20th century.

BARRIE	Kirriemuir, Scotland, May 9, 1860
(Sir) James Matthew	London, June 20, 1937
Author and playwright	

8, Grenville Street, WC1, 1888
15, Old Cavendish Street, W1, 1892
14, Gloucester Walk, W8, 1892
133, Gloucester Road, SW7, 1900-1902
100, Bayswater Road, W2 (LCP 1961) 1902-1909
1/3, Robert Street, WC2, 1909-1937

His father, a weaver, saw to it (as many honest Scots will) that James had as good an education as possible and recognized that, from his earliest years, his son wanted to write.

In 1883, Barrie joined the *Nottingham Chronicle* and established links with the press in London. Soon he came further south to the capital and kept alive by free-lancing, selling articles on a number of subjects to a variety of publications.

He married an actress called Mary Ansell in 1896, but it was not a happy union. Barrack-room psychiatrists might well argue that Barrie had a latent 'Oedipus Complex'. In 1896 he published *Margaret Ogilvy* which was a tribute to his mother. Probably he had a low sexual drive and what drive was there, was probably of a homo rather than heterosexual nature. The marriage fell to bits completely in 1905 when Barrie's gardener told him that Mary, by then in her forties, was having an *affaire* with Gilbert Cannan, a 24-year-old barrister. Barrie challenged his wife with this allegation; she did not deny it and asked for a divorce.

In 1898 Barrie's novel, *The Little Minister,* was dramatized and staged most successfully. It earned him over £80,000 in the next 40 years. His greatest success was *Peter Pan,* however, in 1904. It goes on year after year as a children's play. 'Peter Pan' even has a statue in Kensington Gardens. The sculptor was George Frampton, who used the actress Nina Boucicault (daughter of the playwright Dion Boucicault, who died in New York in 1890, aged 68) as a model. The statue was erected in 1912 – Nina was 44 years old when Frampton sculpted the piece. *Officially* the donor of the statue remains anonymous but Barrie was supposed to have had the statue put up in the gardens overnight, so when the children (usually with their nannies) came to play, they might have supposed 'the fairies' had put it there. Unofficially, Barrie commissioned and paid for the statue himself.

BARRY	Westminster, May 25, 1795
(Sir) Charles	Clapham, London, May 12, 1860
Architect	Centre nave, Westminster Abbey
	(Houses of Parliament on brass grave covering)

39, Ely Place, EC1, 1820-1827.

Barry's triumph, the Houses of Parliament, can be seen by all as one of the finest pieces of 19th century 'Gothic'.
On October 16, 1834, a quantity of wooden tally sticks – which were used as a form of account by the Exchequer – were taken to the House of Lords for burning in the furnace there. The system became overheated; within hours the whole building was ablaze. Parliament, 24 hours later, lay a smouldering ruin. Untouched only were the Westminster Hall and the Jewel Tower. Barry was appointed architect and the foundation stone of the present building was laid in 1840; the House of Lords Chamber was finished in 1847, the Commons three years later, the Clock Tower, which houses the *bell* called 'Big Ben', in 1858 and the Victoria Tower at the opposite end of the building, then the largest square tower in the world, in 1860. The whole building, still called a 'Palace', has over 1,000 rooms, 100 or more staircases and the ground area covered is more than 8 acres (3.2 hectares).
Barry's chief assistant in this vast enterprise was Augustus PUGIN, who was only 28 when the foundation stone was laid. Pugin died mentally unbalanced, in 1852 and Barry himself never saw the building entirely finished. It was his son, Edward Middleton Barry (1830-1880) who took over where his father left off. Barry's second son went into the Church and eventually became the Bishop of Sydney. The other two sons, Charles (1823-1900) and John (1836-1918) both became architects. John, who later became Sir John WOLFE-BARRY, built Tower Bridge.
Charles Barry also designed the Traveller's Club in Pall Mall and the building was finished in 1832. The Club was founded in 1814 by Lord *Castlereagh* the son and heir of the first Marquess of Londonderry.

BARTON STREET, SW1   *District and Circle lines to Westminster*

Barton Street (and Cowley Street off it) were both built by an actor called Barton Booth in the 1720s. There is a statue of Barton Booth in Westminster Abbey sculpted by William Tyler (died 1801) in 1772. Booth's wealthy family owned land at Cowley, near Uxbridge in Middlesex.

1,   Marie BELLOC-LOWNDES, 1922-1929 and again from 1942-1947. In 1946 she took in paying guests and charged them £5.00 a week for bed and breakfast.

8,   John MASEFIELD, 1901. He began to make up the selection of poems which was published in 1902, called *Salt Water Ballads*.

9,   Marie BELLOC-LOWNDES, 1909-1922. Here she wrote *The Lodger*, published 1913; a mystery story based upon the 'JACK the RIPPER' murders in Whitechapel in 1888. It became a best seller and was made into a film.

10, Grant RICHARDS, 1890. He had two rooms in the house (actually the whole of one storey) and paid seven shillings (35p) a week rent, plus four shillings (20p) for 'Attendance'. This was maid service, some basic laundry and breakfast.

14, T.E. LAWRENCE (LCP 1966) 1922, 1923 and 1929. Lawrence (alias 'Lawrence of Arabia', 'Ross' and 'Shaw') used to stay in this house which was owned by Sir Herbert Baker (1862-1946) an architect who remodelled – disastrously – the Bank of England building in Threadneedle Street.
Lawrence lived in the attic and here, working at night, he wrote *The Seven Pillars of Wisdom* which was published in 1926. Here too he ordered the 19-year old John Bruce to give him 'ritual' beatings. This is just another unexplored chapter in Lawrence's strange history. It would seem from all the evidence he was a masochist.

BASEVI
George Ely,
Architect

London, 1794
October 16, 1848
Ely, in a chapel at the eastern end of
the Cathedral

17, Savile Row, W1 (LCP 1949) 1829-1845

Basevi was a pupil of Sir John SOANE who was the architect of the original, surviving lower portions of the Bank of England. Also collector of curious bits and pieces in his house(s) in Lincoln's Inn Fields. As a young man Basevi spent three years studying in Italy and Greece, there gaining a good understanding of the principles of Classical architecture.

One of his greatest works is the Fitzwilliam Museum in Cambridge. (Viscount Fitzwilliam, the 7th and last who, in 1816, bequeathed a collection of books, paintings and manuscripts, together with £100,000, made up of 'South Sea Bubble' dividends.) Work began on the building in 1847.

Additionally he laid out quite a lot of 'Belgravia' and produced a number of 'Gothic' churches in London. He fell to his death from a scaffold in Ely Cathedral, when he was surveying the fabric of the Church.

His paternal Aunt Mary was the mother of Benjamin DISRAELI.

BAYLIS
Lilian Mary
Theatrical Manager

Marylebone, May 9, 1874
Stockwell, November 25, 1937
her ashes scattered in East London
Cemetery, she specified; '...no grave
and no memorial'

19, Nottingham Street, NW1, here born.
6, China Walk, SE11
27, Stockwell Park Road, SW9 (LCP 1974) 1937

Before she was nine, Lilian was appearing in charity concerts, playing piano duets with Libbie (Elizabeth) her mother. She practised four or five hours a day under the martinet eye of John Tiplady Carrodus (1836-1895) who had led the orchestra – he was a violinist – at Covent Garden for 25 years. She became quite well known and, by 1889, she was advertised in the musical press as: 'Miss Lilian Konss-Baylis, violinist, pupil of J.T. Carrodus...visits and receives pupils for violin...'. In 1891 they were off to Cape Town on a musical tour - five of them: Papa, Mamma, Lilian, Willie and tiny Ethel. The promoter of their tour went bankrupt and they set out in South Africa on a tour of their own arranging. By 1892 they were in Johannesburg.

In 1897 Emma CONS, Lilian's Aunt, paid for Lilian and little sister Ethel to come back to London. Lilian was to help her aunt with 'The Old Vic' which she had leased on one of her charitable (and successful) actions to brighten the life of the poor. Lilian worked hard and not long after Aunt Emma's death in 1912, she was appealing for funds to keep the 'Old Vic' going as a regular theatre, even though it was outside London's 'theatreland' even then. She had been reasonably successful when the War began and she ran a Shakespeare Season from October 1914 to April 15, 1915 at the theatre (even playing through Zeppelin raids).

BAYSWATER, W2

Central line to Queensway

Probably a literal adaptation of the 'watering place' of a powerful Anglo-Norman called Bayard (or Baynard).

100, Sir James BARRIE (LCP 1961) 1902-1909. The Barries were living here when the gardener told Barrie of his wife's unfaithfulness. On a happier note, it was in this house that Barrie wrote *Peter Pan*. The house was always referred to as 'Leinster Corner'.

BAYSWATER TERRACE, W2

15, George DU MAURIER in 1887 and again in 1890.

BAZALGETTE	Enfield, March 28, 1819
(Sir) Joseph William	Wimbledon, March 15, 1891
Engineer	

17, Hamilton Terrace, NW8 (LCP 1974)

Sir Joseph Bazalgette (pronounced BAZELLJET) designed London's sewage system, which was completed in 1865. The system was designed to serve the needs of a city with a population of around two million and, with very few *radical* alterations, this same system is dealing with the waste products produced by seven million. Before Bazalgette, parts of London were malodorous (not least the Thames outside the Houses of Parliament!) and, in places, a great hazard to health.
Some of his other works, so familiar to Londoners and visitors to London, are the Victoria, Chelsea and Albert Embankments, which created road beds for many previously unusable miles. These works began in 1863 and were virtually complete ten years later. To build the stretch of the Embankment immediately south of Charing Cross, Bazalgette had to 'push the river' back some 130 yards (118 metres). By narrowing the river considerably it increased the flow, tidally, both up and down stream. London never saw the Thames freezing up, as it used to so, sometimes for weeks on end, after this lessening of the river's width.

BEARDSLEY	Brighton, August 24, 1872
Aubrey Vincent	Menton, France, March 16, 1898
Artist	Menton

32, Cambridge Street, SW1, 1899-1890
57, Chester Street, SW1
114 Cambridge Street, SW1 (LCP 1948) 1893
10/11, St James's Street, SW1, 1895.
19, Campden Grove, W8, 1896

WILDE claimed to have *invented* Beardsley; Roger FRY called him the 'Fra Angelico of Satanism'. But Bearsdley invented himself and one of the last letters he wrote was to his publisher, Lionel Smithers, imploring him to destroy some drawings of his that Smithers had kept. Beardsley having been received into the Catholic Church on March 31, 1897. The drawings were once intended for the *Lysistrata of Aristophanes.*
His father never seemed to exert much effort in earning a wage and his mother became a governess in London, teaching the piano and French, a language in which Aubrey became fluent. He was sent first to a preparatory school at Hurstpierpoint, then to one at Epsom and, in the winter of 1884, became a boarding pupil at the Brighton Grammar School. He was always frail – tuberculosis had been diagnosed when he was only five and he was piteously thin. He left school when he was 16 and came to London where he earned a living as a clerk in the Guardian Life Insurance Company. By 1890 he was totally bored by office life and thought he would exploit his talent for drawing. Edward BURNE-JONES saw his work and encouraged Aubrey to go to evening classes at Westminster School of Art.
Then luck came. John Dent, the publisher, was in Frederick Evans's bookshop explaining to Evans how he needed a black and white artist to work on a new edition of Sir Thomas Malory's *Le Morte d'Arthur* (the original of which had been printed by William Caxton in 1485). Beardlsey walked into the shop, was introduced to Dent and left having been commissioned to do the work. Eventually it was to take him 18 months and he grew very tired of it.

He had met WILDE in 1891 and produced illustrations for *Salomé*. It appeared in 1893 and he was paid 50 guineas (£52.50). The two men gradually came to dislike each other so that in 1894, when Henry HARLAND and John LANE offered Aubrey the editorship of *The Yellow Book,* Beardsley accepted the job providing there would be *no* contributions in it from WILDE. Life became hectic; he was obliged to work at night (and a myth sprang up that 'nobody had actually seen Aubrey drawing'). He moved in Café Royal 'Society' and was able to keep his end up in witty conversation and repartee.

BEATON   London, January 14, 1904
(Sir) Cecil Walter Hardy   Wiltshire, January 18, 1980
Designer, photographer   Broad Chalke, Wilts.

8, Pelham Place, SW7, 1946-1980

The writer of Sir Cecil's *Times* obituary wrote that Beaton was, '...one in a line of inspiring pioneers during the first century of an infant art'. He had launched himself on his photographic career whilst still a schoolboy at Harrow and by 1929 – only seven years later – '...only Queen Mary and Virginia WOOLF of the subjects he had aspired to had eluded his lens'.
He had a contract with Conde Nast (the publishers of *Vogue*) and he became a very close friend of Wallis SIMPSON. He was the 'official photographer' at her wedding (in France in 1936) to the man who had given up the throne of England for love of her.
Beaton did not stop at weddings or photography. He took up stage design and his triumph in this demanding field was when he won the Nieman Marcus 'Oscar' for his superb work on the film version of *My Fair Lady* in 1963. He became one of the very few good friends of Greta Garbo and there was often talk that one day they might marry, but Beaton was certainly *not* of the marrying kind.

BEATTY   Nantwich, Ches., January 17, 1871
David (1st Earl)   London, March 11, 1936
Admiral of the Fleet   St Paul's Crypt

Hanover Lodge, Regents Park, NW1 (LCP 1974) 1912-1924
17, Grosvenor Square, W1, where he died

Beatty first saw active service in the Sudan, then in the China War of 1900, by which time he was a captain.
In 1914 he sailed into Heligoland Bight and sank three German cruisers. The following year he sank the battleship *Blucher* and in 1916 he took a leading part in the much discussed Battle of Jutland. In 1919 he became First Sea Lord, was made an Earl (his full title was Earl Beatty of the North Sea) awarded the Order of Merit and granted £100,000 by Parliament. (Between January 1884 and April 1919 he served on 23 different ships.)
Beatty was quite seriously ill in November 1935, but, against his doctors' wishes, he insisted on attending the funeral of King George V on January 28, 1936. It was too much for him and he was dead in six weeks. There is a bronze bust of Beatty in Trafalgar Square. It is by William MacMillan and was placed there in 1948.

BEAUFORT   Ireland, May 27, 1774
(Sir) Francis   Brighton, December 17, 1857
Admiral and hydrographer

31, Harley Street, W1, 1812
11, Gloucester Road, SW7, 1836

Beaufort left school when he was only 14 and was virtually self-educated.

Nevertheless he rose to be a Vice-Admiral and Hydrographer to the Royal Navy from 1829-1855. His name lives on in the *Beaufort Scale* which calibrates and defines the strength of the wind.

He married Alicia Magdalena Wilson and they had one son. In 1834, Alicia died and his two unmarried sisters kept house for him. In his private (and coded) journal Beaufort 'confesses' to having had an incestuous relationship with his 57-year-old sister in 1836. Not long after, he married again and in his second wife, Honoria Edgeworth, he found an affectionate partner for his last few years.

BEAUFORT STREET, SW3 *District line to West Brompton*

Until 1867, this was Beaufort Row, which had taken its name from the Beaufort House Sir Hans SLOANE had had demolished in 1737. The house occupied practically half the lower (river) end of the street and once was owned by Sir Thomas More. Later it was bought by Henry, Duke of Beaufort. More lived in the house from 1520 until 1535, the year he was beheaded.

20, Charles MORGAN.

29, Roger FRY, 1892-1896 (house since demolished). A poet called Trevelyan, who was six years younger than Fry, lived here with him. They were sometimes looked after by their maid, Harris. When they were not, it was usually because Harris was drunk again.

31, Charles RICKETTS and Charles SHANNON, 1894. Here they began the Vale Press. The inside walls were distempered yellow and hung with Hokusai prints. Oscar WILDE saw the walls and commented, '...*and* you have yellow walls; so have I – yellow is the colour of joy!' (The upper half of the walls of the hall in Wilde's Tite Street house were yellow.)

BEAUMONT STREET, W1 *Circle, Metropolitan, Bakerloo and Jubilee lines to Baker Street*

This street lies across part of the land that made up the Marylebone Gardens. At the end of the 18th century the lease expired and Sir Beaumont Hotham acquired a building lease.

4, John Richard GREEN (LCP 1964) 1869-1876. Here he began work on his *Short History of the English People*. The desk ('poor old writing-desk') at which Green wrote his History was, '...dear from many an association, had been clothed in light blue with lines of red. When I re-entered my rooms for the first time, my artistic friends had just begun covering it with black dragons!' The house was demolished in 1924.

7, Roger FRY from his marriage in 1896 until April 1897 when the Fry's went to Italy as Helen Fry had pleurisy and needed a warmer climate.

38, Walter Savage LANDOR in 1794. He had just been 'sent down' (ie expelled) from Oxford University for shooting a pistol at someone whose politics he did not care for!

BEAVERBROOK
Canada, May 25, 1879
William Maxwell Aitken (1st Baron) London, June 9, 1964
Newspaper magnate

13, Cleveland Row, SW1 ('Stornoway House') 1929 for many years

Three men who dominated the English press in this century have all hailed from the other side of the Atlantic. Beaverbrook and Roy THOMSON (later Lord THOMSON of Fleet) from Canada and Lord ASTOR from New York.

Beaverbrook, who was born plain Max Aitken, made his fortune in Canada by the time he was 30. He managed to tie up the cement manufacturers in one, for him, prosperous cartel. The 'Beaver's' father was a presbyterian minister, but Max's horizons were set far beyond the pulpit. He came to England, entered politics, became Private Secretary to BONAR LAW and was given a knighthood in 1911. He was an 'observer' on the Western Front in 1916 (when it was *not* 'All Quiet…') and wrote *Canada in Flanders* in 1917. LLOYD-GEORGE made Beaverbrook Minister of Information and upped his knighthood to a Baronetcy.

The War over, Beaverbrook turned his attentions to Fleet Street, bought control of the *Daily Express* and made it into one of the most widely read newspapers in the world. He started the *Sunday Express* in 1921 and bought the London *Evening Standard* eight years later. At the same time he started what was to be a relentless campaign for the rest of his life, boosting the British Empire and extolling *Imperial Preference*.

When CHURCHILL became Prime Minister in 1940, he made Beaverbrook responsible for the stimulation of the 'plane building industry. It was Beaverbrook's forceful brilliance which was in part responsible for getting the *Hurricanes* and *Spitfires* into the air in time to save Britain only a few months later.

BECKFORD	Soho Square, W1, October 1, 1760
William Thomas	Bath, Avon, May 2, 1844
Author, Millionaire	Wolcot Cemetery, Bath

4, Devonshire Place, W1, 1810
22, Grosvenor Square, W1

As a ten-year-old, William inherited £1.5 million from his father, *plus* an annual income of £70,000 (from Jamaican investments). His mother, who was the granddaughter of the 6th Duke of Abercorn, was over possessive about her son and he was not sent away to school as was usual for boys of his class.

At the age of 19 William was staying at Powderham Castle in Devon and fell head over heels in love with the 11-year old the Hon. William Courtenay who was his host's only son. Despite this rather irregular infatuation, Beckford married the 20-year-old Lady Margaret Gordon, daughter of Lord Aboyne in May 1783. In October 1784 'on the verge' of being made Lord Beckford of Fonthill (Fonthill was his estate in Wiltshire) Beckford and his wife, who had just had a miscarriage, were again guests at Powderham Castle. Beckford was caught actually in bed with 'Kitty' Courtenay! Beckford denied any impropriety but 'Kitty' confessed (or was made to confess) to committing sodomy and Beckford left for the Continent in a hurry; saying 'goodbye' to the House of Lords.

He roamed Europe until 1796, when he came back to England and began to rebuild Fonthill. In 1786 he had published a *Gothic* novel called *Vathek*; a story about a sadistic young caliph, who sold his soul to the devil. Its style owes something to 'Voltarian' influence, Beckford having met AROUET ('Voltaire's' real name) *before* the 'Kitty' scandal.

BEDFORD GARDENS, W8	*Central, Circle and District lines to Notting Hill Gate*

Built in the 1830s and probably named after the 7th Duke (John) and Duchess of Bedford, who at that time lived in what is now Duchess of Bedford's Walk.

5, Richard LE GALLIENNE, early 1900s. By this time a widower.
27, Sir William (later Lord) BEVERIDGE, 1921. At this time he was a Director of the London School of Economics.

73A, C. DAY-LEWIS moved in here with Jill Balcon on September 19, 1950 (together with his 5,000 books). He married Jill in the following April.

BEDFORD PLACE, WC1   *Piccadilly and Central lines to Holborn*

The Place is one of the 70 or so street names which indicate one time (or present) ownership by the Russells, which is the family name of the Dukes of Bedford. This Place was built up between 1801 and 1805.

14, Edward JENNER, 1806-1807. He moved here, as an economy, from Hertford Street, W1.

14, Mary Ann CLARKE, 1808. By this time her liaison with HRH the Duke of York was at an end.

28, T.S.ELIOT lodged here in 1914.

34, Richard LE GALLIENNE, 1894-1900, just after the death of his first wife, Mildred. They had only been married for three years.

BEDFORD SQUARE, WC1   *Piccadilly and Central lines to Holborn*

The Russells (the family name of the Dukes of Bedford) were given large parcels of land in the Bloomsbury area. The first gift was in 1552 for 'services rendered' to the Crown and they had a further windfall, by marriage, in 1669. More than 70 streets around here were given Bedford/Russell associated names, but much of the land they once owned has had to be sold – the largest lumps in 1913. Bedford Square was part of the 'windfall lot', when the 4th Earl's grandson married Rachel, daughter of the 4th Earl of Southampton, whose family had been given the Manor of Bloomsbury by King Henry VIII. In 1760, Bedford Square was so rural that the Duchess of Bedford of the day used to invite guests to Bedford House, '...to take tea and walk in the fields'.

1, Weedon GROSSMITH, 1902-1919 – from the year he was 49 until his death.

11, Henry CAVENDISH (P 1904) 1786-1810. He lived here off and on almost as a hermit until his death in March 1810.

12, Sir George SMART, 1864-1867, where he died on February 23, 1867.

17, A.J.A. SYMONDS, 1928-1933. He lived here above the head office of the 'First Edition Club Limited' which he had founded. He had a flat on the second floor. The sitting-room was filled '...with shagreen and silver furniture...a square light fitting flush with the ceiling cast a cold aquarium light upon the room'.

31, Sir Edwin LUTYENS, 1914-1919.

35, Thomas WAKLEY (LCP 1962) 1828-1848. For 12 years of his time here he was an Independent Radical MP for Finsbury.

41, Sir Anthony HOPE HAWKINS (LCP 1976) ('Anthony Hope') 1903-1917. For part of his stay here H.H. was writing for the Ministry of Information.

42, William BUTTERFIELD (LCP 1978) 1886-1900. He still kept on 4, Adam Street (into which he had moved in 1842) as offices for the rest of his life.

43, Sir Seymour HICKS, 1901-1908.

44, Lady Ottoline MORELL, 1906. '...and there used to be a great lady in Bedford Square who managed to make life seem a little amusing and interesting and adventurous. So I used to think when I was young and wore a blue dress and Ottoline was like a Spanish galleon, hung with golden coins and lovely silken sails.' So wrote Virginia Woolf, who was nine years younger than Lady Ottoline.

44, Herbert and Margot ASQUITH, 1921-1929. Their scale of entertaining in this house was limited by the fact that their dining-room could only seat ten with any comfort. Asquith died in 1928, but Margot stayed on another year.

51,   John Passmore EDWARDS, 1860s.
51,   Robert BRIDGES lived here with his mother, 1877-1881.

BEECHAM	Lancashire, April 29, 1879
(Sir) Thomas	March 8, 1961
Conductor	Brookwood Cemetery, Surrey

12B, St. George Street, W1, 1961

Beecham was educated (at Rossall, then Oxford) using the fortune his father had made by making and marketing 'Beecham's Pills – worth a guinea a box'. He did not have any intensive *musical* training, but in 1906 he appeared at the Wigmore Hall as the conductor of the New Symphony Orchestra.

Before long he was an impressario and producer, performing over 50 works hardly heard in Britain in the early 1900s. He presented Diaghilev's Russian Ballet in London and, in 1932, was principal conductor at Covent Garden. Eleven years later he was conductor at the Metropolitan, New York.

He was first married to Utica Welles in 1916 and in 1944 got married a second time to Betty Humby, a pianist. When he was 80 he married the 27-year-old Shirley Hudson in Zurich. Beecham publicly admitted that this third marriage was 'preposterous'. In between times he conducted love affairs as well as orchestras. For many years he was a *most* intimate friend of Lady 'Emerald' CUNARD. She was generous with her husband's money, helping Beecham out quite frequently. (He was the most unbusiness-like person imaginable.)

BEERBOHM	London, August 24, 1872
(Sir) Maximilian Henry	May 20, 1956
Artist, novelist and wit	Crypt of St Paul's

57, Palace Gardens Terrace, W8 (LCP 1969) here born
19, Hyde Park Place, W2, 1893
77, Sloane Street, SW3, 1893
48, Upper Berkeley Street, W1, 1898-1909
31, Southwick Street, W2, 1915
115, Ebury Street, SW1, 1917
41, Tavistock Square, WC1, 1936

'The Incomparable Max!' writer and caricaturist; half brother to Sir Herbert Beerbohm TREE, was conventionally educated at Charterhouse School, then on to Merton College, Oxford. In his *Going Back to School* one can find: 'Not that I had any special reason for hating school. Strange as it may seem to my readers, I was not unpopular there. I was a modest, good-humoured boy. It is Oxford that has made me insufferable.' He was a slight, dandy, little man with a high-domed forehead, and slicked-down hair. He sometimes gave the impression that he was laughing *at* people rather than *with* them.

He was a brilliant essayist and a cartoonist, who knew when (and how) to mock and when merely to amuse. His first volume of essays, entitled (very Beerbohmishly) *The Works of Max Beerbohm,* was published in 1896. Some of the essays it contained had previously appeared in the ill-fated *Yellow Book.* Max succeeded G.B. SHAW as music critic of the *Saturday Review* and wrote the column until 1910, when he married Florence Kahn, an American actress.

Florence died in 1951 (they had had no children) and he married his wife's dearest friend, Elizabeth Jungman. Less than three years later Lady Beerbohm had a heart attack in her bath and died instantly. She was not found for a week.

BEITH
(Sir) John Hay ('Ian Hay')
Soldier, playwright, author

April 17, 1876
September 22, 1952

21, Bruton Street, W1, 1921-1930
21, Cadogan Square, SW3, 1930s
47, Charles Street, W1, 1936-1945
49, Berkeley Square, W1, 1945-1952

Having been educated at Fettes (in Scotland) and Cambridge, after graduating Beith went back to Fettes as a language master for a few years. He saw a lot of active service in the First World War and was awarded the Military Cross for bravery.

He was already slightly known as an author as he had published *Pip* in 1907, but real fame arrived on the publication of *The First Hundred Thousand* in 1915. This best seller was about KITCHENER's army and was wildly popular.

BELGRAVE SQUARE, SW1   *Piccadilly line to Hyde Park Corner*

All the houses in the square were finished and occupied by 1837. Someone once described the old 'turret ships' of the British Navy as, 'a side of Belgrave Square going out for a sail'.

5,   the Earl of SHAFTESBURY. He died here in 1885, as did a predecessor, Sir George Murray in 1846; Murray was Quarter Master General to the British Army during the Peninsular War, 1808-1814.
5,   'Chips' CHANNON, 1936-1958. The dining-room was an exact copy of one in the Amalienburg Palace in Munich. It was designed by Boudin of Paris and called 'the lovliest room in London'. The Channons sometimes used the service of gold plate which Napoleon gave to his sister, Pauline Borghese (1780-1825).
24,   Henry HALLAM, died here in 1859. Since the 1930s it has been the Spanish Embassy.
37,   George BASEVI, architect for many of the houses around the Square, signed his name on the side of the portico.

BELGRAVIA

All the 'Belgraves' derive from a small village in Cheshire, which name the first Earl Grosvenor (1731-1802) who owned Belgrave, gave to this part of London. Grosvenor is the family name of the Dukes of Westminster. When he was made a Viscount, he chose Belgrave for his title. The family still own literally hundreds of acres of prime land in Mayfair, Belgravia and Pimlico.

BELLOC
Hilaire Joseph Pierre
Author, politician, poet

La Celle-Ste. Cloud, July 27, 1870
Guildford, July 16, 1953
Church of Our Lady and St Francis,
West Grinstead

104, Cheyne Walk, SW3 (LCP 1973) 1900-1905

Belloc's father was a French lawyer, who died in 1872. Before he went up to Balliol College, Oxford (where he matriculated in 1893) he fleetingly joined the French Navy, spent a year in the French Army and then wandered about the United States living on his (and other people's) wits. He chose to become a British citizen in 1902 and four years later was elected as a Liberal MP for Salford, an industrial constituency, near Manchester.

Whatever else can be said about some of his many literary efforts, he will remain enshrined as the poet of *The Bad Child's Book of Beasts* published in

1896, and *More Beasts for Worse Children* in the following year. This is a sample:

> 'The Whale that wanders round the Pole
> Is not a table fish.
> You cannot bake or boil him whole
> Nor serve him in a dish'.

In 1902 he published *The Path to Rome* which sold well. In 1934 Pope Pius XI (1857-1939: Pope from 1922) conferred on him the rank of Knight Commander of the Order of St Gregory the Great. His thanks for the honour was to ask why, '...should I accept an 'honour' from some greasy monsignor?' He thought the Bible was a lot of 'yiddish folklore' and that Christ 'was a milksop'.

BELLOC-LOWNDES   1868
Marie Adelaide   November 14, 1947
Author

140, Ashley Gardens, SW1, 1904
9, Barton Street, SW1, 1909-1922
1, Barton Street, SW1, 1922-1929, and again from 1942-1947

Marie, Hilaire's sister, married Frederick Lowndes on January 9, 1896. He worked in 'The Morgue' of the *Times* and was in charge of that sombre department for many years. It was really a very good job for him as he was almost totally deaf.

She was a great little 'fixer-up' of people and things and she enjoyed nothing so much as a good discussion about aberrant sexual habits in general and those of her friends in particular.

In 1913 she published a book called *The Lodger* which placed her firmly on the map. The novel was based on the 'JACK the RIPPER' story/myth/case. Not only were the book sales rewarding, she also enjoyed an income from the film that was made of it.

BENEDICT   Stuttgart, November 27, 1804
(Sir) Julius   London, June 5, 1885
Musician   Kensal Green; Grave No. 29,757,
     Plot 65

2, Manchester Square, W1 (LCP 1934) from c.1845 until he died here

Benedict, the son of a Jewish banker, studied music at Dresden under Hummel and WEBER. He lived there for a few years, came to London in 1835 and became a British citizen as soon as possible. Three years later he was conductor at Drury Lane and he stayed there during the years of the composer BALFE's greatest popularity.

His conducting 'records' have perhaps never been equalled. He conducted at *every* Norwich Festival from 1845 to 1878 and the Liverpool Philharmonic's concerts from 1876 to 1880 (both dates inclusive).

BENNETT   Hanley, Staffs., May 21, 1867.
Enoch Arnold   London, March 27, 1931
Author   Burslem Cemetery, Burslem, Staffs.

7, Halsey House, Red Lion Square, WC1, 1908
12B, St George Street, W1, 1919-1921
75, Cadogan Square, SW3 (LCP 1958) 1921-1930
Flat 97, Chiltern Court, 186, Baker Street, NW1 (east side) from 1930 until he died here.

Bennett, having studied at London University, became a solicitor's clerk. But the literary world attracted him and he took a step towards it in 1893, when he became the assistant editor of the magazine *Woman* and later became editor of it.

By 1900 he was living in Paris, returning to England in 1908 when his book *Old Wives' Tale* was published. It became an instant success and in 1910 he produced *Clayhanger* This was to be the first of a series of novels set in the 'Five Towns' (Tunstall, Burslem, Hanley, Stoke-on-Trent and Longton. Actually there were six; the one omitted by Bennett, as he felt five 'more artistic' than six, was Fenton. All are now suburbs of Stoke-on-Trent.) The Five Towns were drab and grimy – and not much better now: a grimy part of London, Clerkenwell, was the setting for his 1923 novel, *Riceyman Steps*. These novels were in marked contrasts, as far as their backgrounds went, to his first book, *The Grand Babylon Hotel*, written in 1902 when he was living at Fontainebleau.

BENTHAM   Stoke, Nr. Plymouth, September 22,
George   1800
Botanist   Kew, September 10, 1884

25, Wilton Place, SW1 (LCP 1978) from 1861 until his death.

George's father, Sir Samuel, was JEREMY BENTHAM's brother and, when he was 26, George became secretary to the great philosopher for a few years.

Sir Samuel was a naval architect who worked for Catherine II of Russia and, as a boy, George spent two years in St Petersburg (today Leningrad). He was a precocious child and was skilled in Latin by the time he was five. He was never sent to school and was fundamentally very shy in any case, so he became a withdrawn young man. In 1834, however, he married a daughter of Sir Harford Brydges.

Bentham's greatest legacy was his work on *General Plantarum,* which occupied him for over 25 years; the first part appearing in 1862 and the final portion (Vol III) in 1883. He worked with the great Sir Joseph Hooker and it consumed all his energy. He did, however, publish more than *120* other papers and memoirs in his lifetime.

BENTHAM   London, February 15, 1748
Jeremy   London, June 6, 1832
Philosopher   (He has not buried, but his skeleton is
                        in University College)

19, Petty France, SW1

Bentham's father was a city attorney who sent the boy to Westminster School where his progress was so rapid, he entered Queen's College, Oxford when he was only 12. The precocious Jeremy qualified, but never practiced, as a lawyer, being much more interested in the theory of law rather than in the application of it. He reasoned that law should be socially useful. Like Priestly or Hutchinson he believed that all actions are right if (and *only* if) they promote '...the happiness of the greatest number.'

Bentham travelled extensively in Europe and Russia between 1785 and 1788. In 1792 his father died and Jeremy inherited a considerable fortune. In 1808 he met James MILL, who was 25 years younger than he. Despite this difference in age, a *rapport* was established and they founded a philosophically radical group which called itself the 'Benthamites'. MILL was also with Bentham in founding University College, a non-sectarian institution – unlike, then, Oxford or Cambridge.

In his will Bentham stipulated that his skeleton (clothed) should be preserved in the University of his founding. This was carried out and the skeleton and his mummified head can, apparently, still be seen by the morbidly curious.

BENTINCK STREET, W1   *Central line to Bond Street*

Hans Willem Bentinck was a *very* particular friend of the sexually ambivalent King William III. Hans was the envoy who had arranged the marriage of William to Mary, daughter of King James II. In due course Bentinck was rewarded with the Earldom of Portland.

5, in a flat, owned by Victor Rothschild, to be found over the offices of the magazine *The Practitioner,* Guy BURGESS lived. As did Anthony (later Sir, then, later on again, *not* Sir) BLUNT in 1940-1941. Goronwy Rees (a writer, a friend of Burgess) wrote in 1941 that the comings and goings in the flat showed an '...almost tropical flowering of sexuality... Watching, as if in a theatre, the extraordinary spectacle of life as lived by Guy. I felt rather like a tired business man who had taken an evening off to visit a strip-tease club.'

7, Edward GIBBON (LCP 1964) 1773-1784. He called it, 'the best house in the world' and lived here with a staff of Mrs. Ford, the housekeeper, a butler, a cook and four maids. There was also a parrot and a Pomeranian dog called Bath, the '...delight of my life, pretty, impertinent and fantastical'. Here Edward wrote most of *The Decline and Fall of the Roman Empire* (published between 1776 and 1788).

9, Harold NICOLSON rented a room here in 1919.

17, Sir James MACKENZIE (P) when he was a consulting physician to the London Hospital in Whitechapel.

18, Charles DICKENS. On February 11, 1833, he had a delayed (by four days) 21st birthday party here.

BENTLEY   London, July 10, 1875
Edmund Clerihew   London, March 30, 1956
Journalist and author

30A, Marlborough Hill, NW8, 1934-1938
10, Porchester Terrace, W2, 1939-1956

Edmund, a London newspaper journalist, wrote a detective novel, *Trent's Last Case*. It appeared in 1913 and in it 'Philip Trent', the first *realistic* fictional detective, makes his appearance.

But Bentley is remembered more widely as it was he who gave the 'Clerihew' to the world. This is a verse form he invented and the first 'Clerihew' leapt into being when Bentley was still a 16-year old schoolboy. It ran:

> 'Sir Humphrey Davy
> Detested gravy
> He lived in the odium
> Of having discovered sodium.'

The distinctive feature of a clerihew is a pair of rhyming couplets humourously characterizing real (usually) people in which the second line rhymes with the name of the person who is the subject of the clerihew itself. G.K. CHESTERTON once wrote of the '...severe and stately form of free verse known as the clerihew.'

BERKELEY SQUARE, W1   *Piccadilly, Jubilee and Victoria lines*
                                                       to Green Park

John Berkeley was the son of Sir Maurice Berkeley of the village of *Bruton* in Somerset. Berkeley, a devoted Royalist, won a battle for King Charles at *Stratton* in Cornwall. The King created him Baron Berkeley of Berkeley. Come the Restoration in 1660, the Baron, now wealthier through marriage, bought large parcels of land in and around Piccadilly.

3, Henry JAMES, when visiting London with his parents in 1855.

11, Horace WALPOLE, from 1779 until he died here in 1797.

19, Colly CIBBER, from 1750 until he died here in 1757.

28, Sir Robert SMIRKE, 1842. At this time he was still working on the South Colonnade of the British Museum.

36, Lord NORTHCLIFFE, early 1900s.

45, Robert, Lord CLIVE (LCP 1953). Clive bought this house in 1761. On November 24, 1774 he died in it. He was depressed, addicted to opium and it has usually been thought that he was a suicide. His niece, the Countess Waldegrave was living here in 1800 and the house stayed in the possession of Clive's descendants until 1937. It is one of the few mainly original buildings in the Square.

49, Ian Hay BEITH ('Ian Hay') from 1945 to 1952.

50, George CANNING (LCP 1979) in 1806-1807. He was on his way up the political ladder having become Under Secretary of State by this time.

54, Lansdowne House stands on the site. It is occupied by a section of the War Office. It was here, in 1774, Joseph PRIESTLY discovered oxygen.

54, Waldorf ASTOR rented the house on this site in 1894. He paid 25,000 dollars (then c.£5,000) a year for it.

54, Gordon SELFRIDGE followed ASTOR. The dining room, as he had it made, is now installed in the Metropolitan Museum in New York.

BERLIOZ	Grenoble, December 11, 1803
Hector	Paris, March 8, 1869
Composer	

58, Queen Anne Street, SW1, 1851

Berlioz went to the Paris Conservatoire in 1826 and soon after fell in love with a *Shakespearian* actress called Harriet Smithson. She inspired his *Symphonie Fantastique* and was to become his wife. In 1830 he won the *Prix de Rome* and spent two years in Italy – *Harold en Italie* in 1834, was one result of this extended visit.

Apart from music, Berlioz published seven books, including a treatise on orchestration and an autobiography. In 1851 he was in London to judge the musical section of the Great International Festival Exhibition which was held in the specially built 'Crystal Palace' in Hyde Park. It was the brainchild of Queen Victoria's beloved husband, Prince Albert and the ground on which stands his stupendous monument opposite the Albert Hall, was once covered by the Exhibition. Berlioz's task was not very exciting and he found it monotonous.

Berlioz's forehead was furrowed by the time he was 30 and his thick hair was, '...a large umbrella...projecting like a moveable awning over the beak of a bird of prey'. He was of medium height, but had a long, angular body so that, when sitting down, '...he seemed much taller than he [actually] was.'

In 1854, Harriet (aged 54) died, but within two years Berlioz married a second time, '...a rather mediocre singer called Martin' [sic] 'Recio', who really hindered him musically. However, when she died in 1862 he was grief-stricken.

BERNARD STREET, WC1   *Piccadilly line to Russell Square*

Bernard Street runs into Coram Fields and a Sir Thomas Bernard (1750-1818) was the Vice-President of the Foundling Hospital, established by Thomas Coram in 1739. Around the end of the 18th century the Hospital was low in funds, but potentially rich in undeveloped property (56 acres – 22.6 hectares). Despite an outcry, Sir Thomas pushed through a 'development' programme which enabled the Foundling Hospital to survive.

39, Peter ROGET, 1808-1843. It was here, from a semi-basement room, that Roget, watching movements outside through slatted blinds, first got the idea of 'moving pictures'.

48, Roger FRY, 1927-1934. He spent the last seven years of his life here.

BERNERS STREET, W1

Central and Northern lines
to Tottenham Court Road

William Berners, of Wolverstone Hall in Suffolk, owned an estate occupying some land north of today's Oxford Street in the middle 1700s.

8, John OPIE, 1792-1807. This was his last house in London and he was living here when he was elected to the Royal Academy.

8, George Du MAURIER, 1860. He moved in here not long after completing his studies in Paris.

13, Henry FUSELI, 1804. He moved here soon after opening his own gallery in Pall Mall.

35, Sir William CHAMBERS, from about 1786, until his death in 1796. Chambers gave great encouragement to the young John BACON by buying Bacon's gesso relief of *Aeneas Fleeing from Troy* and installing it over the mantelpiece in his sitting room.

54, In 1810 Theodore HOOK played a practical joke on a Mrs. Tottenham who lived here. Hook ordered some 200 items (and a variety of services) to be delivered to her – including doctors, barbers and undertakers – all at the same time. Mrs. Tottenham was *not* amused.

71, S.T. COLERIDGE (LCP 1966) 1812-1813. It was here he really began to try to shake off his opium addiction. He was finally 'rescued' by Dr. James Gillman and taken to live with the Gillmans at Highgate, where he remained until his death 19 years later.

BETJEMAN
(Sir) John
Poet Laureate

August 28, 1906
Trebetherick, Cornwall, May 19, 1984
St Enodoc Church, Cornwall

29, Radnor Walk, SW3, 1970s

Betjeman's first memories were of Highgate; 'Sheep were driven up the hill – I suppose they must have come from the old Caledonian market in Islington. And I remember an old lady selling brandy balls in the street outside. London was so different then – so quiet...'

In 1933 he married Penelope Chetwode, daughter of Field Marshal, Sir Philip Chetwode GCB, OM, GCSI. One can imagine the Field Marshall *not* being amused at having a *poet* as a son-in-law. And more especially as at a dinner party at the Chetwode's, Betjeman wore a black bow tie with his dinner jacket *of course* – which had a clockwork motor which could rotate the tie, rather like an aeroplane propeller underneath the, even then, pretty jowly Betjeman chin.

Betjeman had not always been a 'full time poet'. In 1937, for instance, he was working in Shell Oil's publicity department and, together with the British artist, John Piper (who wrote of him in an obituary, 'He was a lover of the human spirit') produced a *Shell Guide Book* of Cornwall. Sir John had also worked in the film division of the Ministry of Information under Sidney (now Lord) Bernstein.

Sir John had a stroke in 1981 and he was by then a wheel chair invalid, as a result of Parkinson's disease. He had a heart attack in the autumn of 1983, but recovered remarkably well (because, he claimed, his Teddy Bear, called Archibald Ormsby-Gore, was 'rushed to his bedside'). These attacks, together with his 77 years were finally too much and he died, peacefully, in his sleep.

BEVERIDGE Rangpur, India, March 5, 1879
William Henry (1st Baron) Oxford, March 16, 1963
Economist

27, Bedford Gardens, W8, 1921
94, Campden Hill Road W8, 1929
3, Elm Court, Middle Temple, EC4, 1935

Of Scottish descent, Beveridge was educated at Charterhouse and Balliol College, Oxford. After graduating, Beveridge taught law and was for a time leader writer on the *Morning Post*.
However, his memorial is in the *Beveridge Report* which he titled *Britain without Want, Disease, Ignorance, Squalor*. This report, published on December 1, 1942, effectively laid the foundation for Britain's 'Welfare State'. No report, before or since, has so changed the nation. It is a testimony to those in power that such a report, whose very purpose was to re-shape the future, was published when Britain was within an ace of being obliterated by Fascism. (It was rumoured that both Adolf Hitler and his crippled mouthpiece, Joseph Goebbels, read the report with interest!)

BINYON Lancaster, August 10, 1869
Lawrence Robert Reading, March 10, 1943
Poet and print expert

8, Tite Street, SW3, 1900
17, Cowley Street, SW1, 1904

Binyon's father was a vicar who sent the boy to St Paul's School in London and from there he went on to Trinity College, Oxford and won the Newdigate Prize. After university, Binyon joined the British Museum staff in 1893 and rose in those rarified ranks to become the Keeper of the Prints – a most responsible post.
He published his *Followers of William Blake* in 1925 but only three years later he was writing, 'I long in my heart to get away from the Museum and write a magnum opus, cherished for 20 years or more'.
Binyon lectured in Japan in 1930 and in 1933/34 he was Charles Eliot Norton Professor of Poetry at Harvard University, during which period King George V appointed him to be a Companion of Honour.

BLAIR Motihari, India, June 25, 1903
Eric Arthur ('George Orwell') London, January 21, 1950
Author All Saints Church, Sutton Courtenay, Berks.

23, Mall Chambers, Notting Hill Gate, W11, 1918
50, Lawford Road, NW5 (LCP 1980) August 1935
111, Langford Court , Abbey Road, NW8, 1941
27B, Canonbury Square, N1 (P) 1945-1947

Blair was educated at Eton which often surprises people, as an author (as 'Orwell' of course) he was so often thought of as 'working class'. After Eton he went back east and served from 1922 to 1927 with the Imperial Indian Police in Burma. His experiences there are reflected in *Burmese Days* which was published in 1934.
After Burma he lived 'on the breadline' in London and Paris: sometimes he was a tutor, a schoolteacher or a bookshop assisstant. His *Down and Out in Paris and London,* which was published in 1933, is a very revealing book. He became involved in the Spanish Civil War in 1936 where he was wounded fighting for the Republicans, so after that, came *Homage to Catalonia* in 1938. In 1945, with peace being declared, came his *Animal Farm*. Had he not

written another word this satire on dictatorship would have earned Blair a place in the history of English Literature. It certainly established the name of 'Orwell' widely, but *Blair* remained unknown.

In 1936 he married Eileen O'Shaughnessy. She was 31 and had a Second Class Honours degree in English, after having won a scholarship to St.Hugh's College, Oxford. In 1931 she had become the principal of 'Murrells Typing Agency' in Victoria Street, SW1. She was also an agnostic. So was Blair; but they married on June 9 in the Parish Church of Letchworth. They adopted a boy in 1944 and christened him Richard Horatio. In March 1945, Blair, as a War Correspondent acting for the *Observer*, was on his way into Germany. He was in Cologne when the *Observer* had to send him a cable telling him that Eileen had died on March 29 in a Newcastle Hospital, during an operation thought to be routine, but in fact for stomach cancer.

Over Christmas 1945, Blair and his son spent the holiday in Merionethshire with Arthur and Marianne KOESTLER. A fellow guest was Sonia Brownwell who was Cyril CONNOLLY's beautiful secretary. She and Blair had had a very fleeting *affaire* he had proposed to her and she said no: he was 42, she 27.

On September 3, 1949 he went into University College Hospital in Gower Street. He had a private room (for which he paid £17 a *week*). David Astor had long been a good friend and Blair wrote to him from his sick bed saying Sonia thought they ought to get married. The marriage took place by special licence on October 13. Orwell could not go on to the reception, so David Astor organized a wedding luncheon at the Ritz and a menu of the lunch, signed by all the guests, was taken to him in the hospital. It was arranged that Blair should be flown to Switzerland for treatment. On January 18, 1950 he made a new will but, three days later, he was dead.

BLAKE	London, November 28, 1757
William	London, August 12, 1827
Poet, artist, mystic	Bunhill Fields, under an upright stone on the right of the path on the west side

28, Poland Street, W1, 1785-1791
28, Broad Street, Golden Square, W1
31, Great Queen Street, WC2, c.1803
3, Fountain Court (now 103/4 The Strand) WC2, from 1821 until he died here.

Blake's father was a hosier and did not even bother to see that William went to school. As soon as he was old enough he was apprenticed to James Basire (1730-1802) an engraver. For Basire, Blake made many close studies of parts of Westminster Abbey and this early, practical knowledge of the *Gothic* influenced his later style. When he was nearly 30 he developed his own techniques and began printing his own poems using coloured illustrations, which he claimed his recently dead brother, Robert, had shown him in a vision. The first of these wonders, *Songs of Innocence,* appeared in 1789.

By 1793, married to the illiterate Catherine Boutcher, he settled in Lambeth. She married him in 1782, but less than two years later she could not only read *and* write; she helped him to make his prints and engravings and actually bound up the copies of his *Songs of Innocence.* He produced an engraved edition of his prose work, *Marriage of Heaven and Hell,* in 1790 but it attracted little or no attention. He was persuaded by a minor poet, William Hayley, to move down to Felpham, on the Channel coast of Sussex. Here he worked spasmodically for a number of different patrons, but before too long, was back in London and was befriended by a group of younger artists, like Varley, Calvert and Samuel PALMER. Together they formed a group, styling themselves as 'The Ancients'.

Songs of Experience appeared in 1764 and contains the inscrutable and unforgettable, *Tiger! Tiger! burning bright!* Blake was an individualist and more than just a little eccentric. He was also a nudist ('a child of God') and probably better remembered now as an artist than a poet. But, in Blake's view, the two art forms were inseparable.

BLANDFORD SQUARE, NW1   *Bakerloo and BR lines to Marylebone*

Another part of the Portman estate. Sir William Portman bought his Marylebone estate in 1553 and died two years later.

9,   Olive SCHREINER, 1885-1886. It was two years since her first novel, *The Story of an African Farm,* had been published and she had begun to move in literary circles.

16,   George Henry LEWES lived here with Mary Ann EVANS ('George Eliot') from 1860 to 1863. Here she wrote *Romola* and *Felix Holt* – generally considered to be her finest work.

38,   Wilkie COLLINS lived here with his widowed mother in the late 1840s.

BLESSINGTON   Clonmel, Ireland, September 1, 1789
(Countess) Marguerite   Paris, June 4, 1849
Society woman   Chambourcy

11, St James's Square, SW1, 1818-1830
Grove House, Kensington Grove, SW7, 1835-1849

Born plain Margaret Power, she was married against her will when she was only 15 to Maurice St Leger Farmer. He was a sot and died a drunkard's death when he fell out of a high window in the Middle Temple. Before this happy event, however, Margaret had gone off to live with a Mr. Thomas Jenkins in Hampshire. Through Jenkins she met the (then) Viscount Mountjoy. His father died in 1816 and he became the Earl of Blessington. Margaret (actually, by now *Marguerite*) married him in 1818 when Jenkins conveniently died.

The Blessingtons toured Europe *en prince* meeting Lord BYRON and other poets and intellectuals. In 1829 Marguerite's husband died – he was only 47 – and she came into a substantial fortune. Seven years before she had met 'the Last of the Dandies', the 21-year-old Count D'ORSAY. Two years before Blessington's death D'Orsay was married to Blessington's 15-year-old daughter, by a previous marriage, Lady Harriet Gardiner.

Back in London D'Orsay left his 'Child bride' – probably the marriage was never consummated – and lived next door to his ex-wife's step-mother – Marguerite! Tongues wagged, but Marguerite went on indulging the Count and getting through her Blessington inheritance so quickly, that before long Grove House was being plagued by bailiff's men. Eventually, with creditors in pursuit, she and D'Orsay fled to Paris. Her freedom was short lived: two months of Paris was too much and she died, not yet 40, of apoplexy.

BLIGH   Tyntan, Cornwall, September 9, 1754
William   Lambeth, December 7, 1817
Sailor   St Mary's Church, Lambeth

100, Lambeth Road, SE1 (LCP 1952) 1794-1813

Bligh sailed with Captain James Cook (1728-1779) at 18 and 15 years later was himself a Captain in command of the *Bounty.* His crew mutinied and Bligh, together with 18 loyal crew members, were set adrift in the Pacific. 4,000 miles later Bligh landed at Timor. (The mutinous crew had sailed *Bounty* to Pitcairn Island. Here they settled and their descendants live there till this day.)

The story of the *Bounty* has enjoyed a romantic reputation in its varied retelling, but Bligh was involved in *another* little- noticed mutiny. In 1808 he was Governor of New South Wales and the insurgents there actually held him prisoner for nearly two years in his own 'colony'. (The officer who had arrested Bligh was brought back to England, found guilty at a trial and cashiered.)

BLOMFIELD ROAD, W9 ('Little Venice')

Bakerloo line
to Warwick Avenue

For no good reason named after Charles James Blomfield (1786-1857) the Bishop of London. Blomfield was a fine classical scholar and was known for his editions of *Callimachus* and *Euripides*.

13, Nancy MITFORD, 1939, when she was still (just) Mrs. Peter Rodd. In 1984 a house on the north side of Blomfield Road – facing the canal – with six bedrooms, three bathrooms and all the 'accompanying bits and pieces', was up for sale. The price asked was £475,000.

BLOOMSBURY

Bloomsbury embraces a medieval Manor, stretching from what is now the Euston Road, in the north, to High Holborn, in the south; from Tottenham Court Road, in the west, to Southampton Row on the east. The Earl of Southampton acquired the Manor in 1545 and his descendants, the Dukes and Earls of Bedford, added to the estate by inspired marriages. Though much of the family's holding has been sold off, the Bedford/Russell influence is all-pervading in the area. As a *name* Bloomsbury derives from *Blemund's Bury,* the 'Manor House of Blemund'.

BLOOMSBURY PLACE, WC1

Central and Piccadilly lines to Holborn

3, Sir Hans SLOANE from 1695, after his marriage until 1742. He then acquired...

4, next door (LCP 1965) to house his collection of 'antiquities' which, after his death, was to be the nucleus of the collection in the British Museum.

BLOOMSBURY SQUARE, WC1

This Square, Russell Square and Bloomsbury Place were designed by Humphrey Repton; 1752-1818.

14, Richard BRIGHT, 1820-1829. This house is one of the few original houses left. Bright, still a bachelor, in 1820 was nominated to be a member of the Royal Society. He married and lived here with his first wife, Martha, who died in January 1824. His second wife, Eliza, came here not long after their wedding in 1826. Luckily, she liked the house; in it was a large drawing room, a 'book-lined' study (at the back of the house) and the dining room had been altered so that her mother's Irish dresser could be accommodated in it.

20, Gertrude STEIN, with her brother, Leo, lodged here in 1902.

28, Lord MANSFIELD (who also later lived at 29). This house was destroyed in the 'Gordon Riots' of 1780. Mansfield and his wife, both disguised, escaped from their blazing house and fled to their house at Kenwood (in Highgate, NW6).

29, Herbert SPENCER, 1862-1864.

29, Sir Edwin LUTYENS, 1898-1914. Lutyens, a gregarious man, was an occupant of this house (in great contrast to the reclusive SPENCER).

31, Sir Anthony PANIZZI, c.1856, when he was devizing the cataloguing systems of the British Museum.

45, The town house of the 2nd, 3rd and 4th Lord CHESTERFIELDS (P1907).

On the north side of the Square is a bronze statue of Charles James FOX (be-toga'd and beseated) by Sir Richard WESTMACOTT. It was erected here in 1816, ten years after Fox's death.

BLUNT London, September 26, 1907
Anthony Frederick London, March 26, 1983
Art expert (and traitor) Cremated at Putney

5, Bentinck Street, W1, 1940-1941
45, Portsea Hall (on the sixth floor)
Portsea Place, W2, 1960s until he died here

Blunt's father was the Vicar of St John's Church, Paddington and sent Anthony to Marlborough College, Wiltshire, in 1920. From there he went up to Trinity College, Cambridge and, while still an undergraduate, joined the Communist Party. (Already in the party was another homosexual called Guy BURGESS.)

Rather surprisingly Blunt joined Military Intelligence in 1940 (but the Russians were then *supposed* to be Britain's allies). The War over, Blunt blossomed out into the diffuse world of 'Fine Art', eventually becoming Surveyor of the Queen's Pictures in 1952; prior to which he was Director of the COURTAULD Institute. He stayed here until 1972, when he was appointed advisor to the Royal Collection. Four years later he was knighted. Late in 1979 Andrew Boyle wrote a book called *Climate of Treason*, which exposed Blunt's complicity and, indeed, initiative in treasonable activities and his friendships with Burgess, Maclean and Kim Philby whilst still at Cambridge.

Blunt shared his Portsea Place flat with John Gaskin who, 14 years his junior, was left the bulk of Blunt's estate. This turned out to be worth £858,121 – a figure which surprised many. After a few legacies, Gaskin received over £840,000, of which £500,000 was the estimated value of Poussin's painting *Rebecca at the Well*. The copyright notes, art history books and photographs were left to the Courtauld Institute and his architectural drawings went to the National Art Collection Fund.

BLUNT Petworth House, Kent, August 17,
Wilfrid Scawen 1840
Traveller and scholar Crabbet Park, September 10, 1922

15, Buckingham Gate, SW1 (LCP 1979) 1890s

Blunt's family background was impressive. He was sent to Stonyhurst, a Roman Catholic boy's Public School and then to Oscott, before joining the Diplomatic Service in 1859. He travelled extensively in the Middle East and left diplomacy when he was 30 years old, a passionate advocate of Egyptian nationalism.

His support for Irish nationalism came next. His belief in the Irish Land League was so fervent that in 1888 he was jailed. It was in that year he tried to enter Parliament. On a more spiritual level he wrote verse, some political, but some charming poems of love. On a more *physical* level he was a renowned sexual athlete and wrote with some knowledge on these matters.

BOLINGBROKE	(Baptized) Battersea, October 1, 1678
Henry Saint-John (1st Viscount)	Battersea, December 12, 1751
Politician	St Mary's Battersea (in the
	family vault)

21, Golden Square, W1, 1704–1708

Henry was sent to Eton and then up to Christ Church, Oxford. He travelled around Europe, on the traditional 'Grand Tour', but all one knows of the itinerary is that in 1699 he was in Milan. In 1700 he married Frances, a co-heiress of Sir Henry Winchcomb's fortune. The marriage made Bolingbroke wealthy, but not happy and they soon parted company.
In February 1701 he took his seat, as Member of Wootton Basset, in the Commons. His great friend, HARLEY, was Party Leader and when he was made Secretary of State in 1704, Bolingbroke became Secretary for War. In 1708 both he and Harley quit Parliament as the Whig party, with Marlborough and Godolphin leading it, were in power. One of Bolingbroke's political coups was the signing of the Treaty of Utrecht on April 11, 1713 effectively ending the war with France, which had been dragging on since 1702. Bolingbroke was a Stuart man and plotted against Harley until, in 1712, he outmanoeuvered Harley (now Lord Oxford) and, probably with the help of Mrs. Masham, Queen Anne's favourite, Harley was forced to quit on July 27, 1714.
Queen Anne died a few days later and, not seeing eye-to-eye with the new Hanoverian King of England, George I, Bolingbroke finally left London (suddenly and disguised) and fled to France. He had been created a Viscount in 1712 and now, in disgrace (and *in absentia*) he was impeached by WALPOLE for high treason.
In France Bolingbroke plotted with James II's elder son, 'The Old Pretender', for the overthrow of England's German (and Protestant) King.
He never really tried for a political comeback and he died in Battersea after, what must have been for him, nine long years. At his death he left all his manuscripts to David Mallet, the Scottish poet.

BOLSOVER STREET, W1 *Metropolitan and Circle lines to Great Portland Street*

Bolsover was a subsidiary title given to Augusta Cavendish-Bentinck in 1880 as Baroness Bolsover of Bolsover Castle, Derbyshire and devolved upon her stepson, the 6th Duke of Portland. The Dukes of Portland owned much of the land in the area.

8, David WILKIE, 1805–1812 (in his day, this was Norton Street). He had just come to London and in 1806 had his first picture hung in the Summer Academy. It was called *The Village Politicians*. WILKIE'S mother came to live with him here a year or so later.
39, Edward FITZGERALD, 1848–1850. This was before he had begun to learn the Farsi (the language of Persia).

BOLT COURT, EC4 *Central line to Chancery Lane*

A tavern called the Bolt-in-Tun stood on the South side of Fleet Street opposite this court. The Tavern (Number 64, Fleet Street) was named after Prior Bolton who was instrumental in restoring the Church of St. Bartholomew in West Smithfield. On the Prior's tomb there is a *rebus*. Bolton's *rebus* shows a 'bolt' – a crossbow arrow, passing through a 'tun' (a 252 gallon; 145 litres, wine cask).

7, Samuel JOHNSON from 1756 to 1777, when he moved to:
8, where he died in the back room of the first floor. He paid a rent of £40

and it was here he wrote his *Lives of the Poets*. Behind the house was a garden, '...which he took delight in watering; a room on the ground floor was assigned to Mrs. Williams and the whole of the "two pair of stairs" floor was made a repository for his books, one of the rooms thereon being his study'.

BOLTON GARDENS, SW5

2, Beatrix POTTER, 1866-1913. Where the Bousefield Primary School now stands was the back garden of the Potter's house. Here, too, is the burial ground of *Mrs. Tiggy Winkle*, Beatrix's hedgehog pet.

31, Sir Edwin Arnold (LCP 1931) from 1861 until his death here in 1904.

BOLTON STREET, W1   *Piccadilly, Jubilee and Victoria lines to Green Park*

This little street (not to be confused with The Boltons, SW10) was built on land owned by the Duke of Bolton, beginning about 1700. In 1708 it was described as, '...the most westerly street in London'.

3, Henry JAMES, 1876. He paid two and a half guineas (£2.65p) a week for a first floor flat. He wrote of it, 'I have excellent lodgings in this excellent quarter, a lodging whose dusky charms – including a housemaid with a prodigious complexion but a demure expression and the voice of a duchess – are too numerous to repeat'.

11, Fanny BURNEY (by this time Madame d'Arblay) (P 1885) 1818.

12, Winston CHURCHILL and his brother John Henry ('Jack', then 28 years old) in 1908, in which year Winston became engaged to Clementine Hozier. 'Jack' Churchill was born in Dublin in 1880. He, like his six-years older brother, went to Harrow, and fought in the South African War.

THE BOLTONS, SW10   *District line to West Brompton*

The land here was owned by a William Bolton at the beginning of the 16th century. Rather confusingly all his male descendants were christened William and successive 'Williams' sold off bits of the land, generation after generation, until 1864, when the Boltons began to be developed.

5C, Vyvyan HOLLAND died here in 1967.

27, Sir Francis BURNAND, 1904.

28, Douglas FAIRBANKS, Junior.

BONOMI	Rome, October 9, 1796
Joseph ('The Younger')	London, March 3, 1878
Sculptor and draughtsman	Brompton Cemetery

76, Great Titchfield Street, W1

Despite being born in Rome and having a father called Giuseppe, Joseph Bonomi *was* an Englishman. He specialized in archaeological drawings of Egyptian and Assyrian relics and, in 1852, published a book on *Ninevah and its Palaces*.

BOOTH	Liverpool, March 30, 1840
Charles	Gracedieu Manor, Whitwick,
Shipowner and social reformer	November 23, 1916
	Thringstone, Leics.

6, Grenville Place, SW7, 1889
24, Great Cumberland Place, W1, 1889-1905

Charles and his brother formed the Booth Steamship Company (in Liverpool). The rewards were agreeably great. In 1875, Charles settled in

London and, after 18 years of study and inspection – touched by compassion – he published *Life and Labour of the People of London* (1903).

This work, so much ahead of its time, was the prototype of social surveys that would soon be commissioned elsewhere. Booth was made President of the Royal Statistical Society in 1893, a Privy Councillor in 1904 and was elected a Fellow of the Royal Society. There is a tablet in his memory in the crypt of St Paul's. It is the work of Sir Charles Nicholson and was unveiled in 1920 by Sir Austen CHAMBERLAIN.

BORROW George Henry *Author*

East Dereham, Norfolk, February 16, 1803 Oulton, Suffolk, July 30, 1881 Brompton Cemetery (in the same grave as his mother)

17, Great Russell Street, WC1, 1830

Borrow's father was an army recruiting officer and this meant that if the family were to stay together they had to be prepared to move house quite frequently. (Perhaps *nomadism* was inculcated in him as a child.) He had the better part of his education in Edinburgh, where his linguistic ability was looked on favourably. His first job was back in his home county; in Norwich, as a solicitor's clerk.

The *wanderlust* was on him and he was very soon off on his travels, principally in Europe. Everywhere he went he was able to pick up more than the usual smattering of the language of the country he was visiting. He was most taken with the real Gypsies and actually produced a *Romany Dictionary*.

He got a job as an agent for the Bible Society, travelling Spain, and his experiences appeared in book form as *The Bible in Spain,* in 1843, which met with good notices. In 1851 he scored a literary bulls-eye with *Lavengro* billed as a novel, but really only a thinly disguised autobiography. The full title is, *Lavengro, the Scholar – the Gypsy – the Priest. Lavengro* in the Gypsy tongue meant a 'philologist'. This is what the Norfolk gypsy, Ambrose Smith, used to call Borrow as a boy.

BOSWELL James *Biographer*

Edinburgh, October 29, 1740 London, May 19, 1795

22, Poultry, EC2
22, Gerrard Street, W1, 1775 and 1776
56, Great Queen Street, WC2, 1786-1788

MACAULAY wrote of James Boswell that, he was '...one of the smallest men that ever lived, and he has beaten them [biographers] all... Servile and impertinent, shallow and pedantic, a bigot and a sot.'

But without Boswell we almost certainly would not know as much as we do about the great Samuel JOHNSON. Boswell 'bumped' into Johnson in Tom Davies' bookshop in Russell Street (WC2) on May 16, 1763 and, in the following year, Johnson actually went with Boswell to Harwich to say goodbye to his new, young (24) friend, on his way to Utrecht. By persistence (or gate crashing) Boswell managed to scrape an acquaintance with both 'Voltaire' (AROUET) and ROUSSEAU and enlarge his circle of literary and intellectual friends.

He took Johnson north of the border, right up to the Hebrides. Scotland did not impress itself on Johnson's mind favourably. In fact, the Scotsman Boswell, recorded Johnson's words commenting upon their visit as being, 'Norway, too, has noble wild prospects; and Lapland is remarkable for prodigious noble wild prospects. But, Sir, let me tell you, the noblest

prospect which a Scotchman' [sic] 'ever sees, is the high road that leads him to England!'
One of their mutual acquaintances calculated that Boswell had met with Johnson 256 times. Between such times, Boswell made time to marry Margaret Montgomerie in 1769. She died twenty years later, having borne him six children. By this time Boswell was very nearly 50 and 'the drink had got its hold on him'. However, his death five years later was not directly the result of the Demon Drink, but was compounded by the plague. He had been weakened by venereal disease as well.

BOULT
(Sir) Adrian Cedric
Conductor

Chester, April 8, 1889
February 23, 1983

38, Wigmore Street, W1
53, Welbeck Street, W1, 1962-1975

In 1920 Boult produced a handbook called, *A Handbook on the Techniques of Conducting* and there can have been few men as well qualified as he to do so. He went to Westminster School and then Christ Church College, Oxford, where he was President of the Oxford University Musical Club in 1910. He joined the staff of the Royal Opera in 1914, became Director of the Birmingham City Orchestra for six years in 1924 and then again in 1959; was Director of Music for the BBC, conductor of the BBC Symphony Orchestra from 1930-1950 and of the London Symphony Orchestra from 1950-1957.

BOW STREET, WC2
Piccadilly line to Covent Garden

Supposedly so called because historian John STRYPE described the street as, 'running in the shape of a bow'. This was in 1720 and the area was first developed in 1637.

6, 'Peg' WOFFINGTON, 1750. It would appear that she lived here with David GARRICK and Charles MACKLIN simultaneously!
19 and **20** (LCP 1929). The plaque here is a very wholesale affair. It records that at one time or another Henry FIELDING, his brother John Grinling GIBBONS, Charles MACKLIN, John Radcliffe (1650-1714) Charles Sackville, Earl of Dorset (1536-1608, poet and statesman) and, finally, William Wycherley (1640?-1716) a dramatist of mixed fortunes who, at the age of 64, married a young girl so as to deprive his own nephew of his inheritance. 'Serve him right', however, as he died 11 days later.
During GIBBONS' day the house fell down! This was on the night of January 22, 1702.
Radcliffe lived here from 1687 to 1714 and the houses were finally taken down in 1732 to make way for the new Covent Garden Opera House.

BRACKEN
Brendan (1st Viscount)
Politician, editor

Killmallock, Ireland, 1901
August 8, 1958

11, Lord North Street (merely North Street until 1936) SW1, 1929
8, Lord North Street, SW1, 1933-1958

> 'Brendan Bracken has lost his hat
> Which is really nothing to wonder at;
> For Brendan's head grows at such a rate
> That yesterday's hat won't fit his pate.'

Bracken had left his hat in Leslie Hore-Belisha's rooms at the House of

Commons in June 1932. (Leslie Hore-Belisha, 1st Baron Hore-Belisha, 1893-1957, was a West of England Jew who became first Chairman of the National Liberal Party in 1931.) The following day Bracken's hat was handed back to him with the anonymous four lines of doggerel, quoted above, pasted into the crown.

Bracken was a 'mystery man', conceited and self-sufficient, who frequently encouraged any rumour that he thought might, if believed, increase his standing. One such bit of gossip was that he was Winston CHURCHILL's illegitimate son! 'Clemmie' Churchill had no love for Bracken at *all*. Randolph Churchill, very *definitely* Winston's son, added, 'Mummy won't call him Brendan because she's *so* afraid he might call her Clemmie!' However, there certainly was a strong *political* relationship between Churchill and Bracken. Bracken became an MP in 1929 and rose to become Minister of Information in the critical years between 1941 and 1945. After this he passed 'upstairs' to the Upper House as First Lord of the Admiralty, continuing to make and collect enemies all the way. He was made a Viscount in 1952.

Bracken's physical appearance was also rather extraordinary, with thick, carrotty-red hair and badly discoloured teeth. Many Americans could be counted as unfriendly to him and one such once said, 'Everything about the man is phoney: even his hair, which looks like a wig, is his *own!*'

BRIDGES Walmer, Kent, October 23, 1844
Robert Seymour April 21, 1930
Poet Laureate

52, Bedford Square, WC1, 1877-1881

Eton College is long on Prime Ministers and politicians, but a bit short on poets. Bridges is the obvious exception. After he left Eton he went up to Corpus Christi College, Oxford and eventually qualified as a doctor for St Bartholomews in London. In one year he claimed to have seen 30,490 patients there.

He retired from medecine before he was 40, having had three volumes of lyrics published successfully. He settled in Berkshire, turning out three plays during the 1890s and a narrative poem called *Eros and Psyche*. In 1907 he retired even further and went to live at Boar's Hill, Oxford and really produced very little. In 1929, however, he published *The Testament of Beauty* (on his 85th birthday). This is generally regarded as his masterpiece, '...enshrining the wisdom of his long career.' Five years after he went to live at Boar's Hill, Sir Walter Raleigh (not THE Sir Walter Raleigh, but Sir Walter Alexander Raleigh, who died, aged 61 in 1922, an English scholar, critic and essayist) visited Bridges in November 1912 and found, '...Bridges is delightfully grumpy. He mentions thing after thing which is commonly believed and says that *of course* it is not so. He's *always* right. His intellect has been so completely self indulged that it now cannot understand rubbish.'

BRIGHT Bristol, September 28, 1789
Richard London, December 16, 1858
Physician Kensal Green (according to
 biographers)

14, Bloomsbury Square, WC1, 1820-1829
11, Savile Row, W1 (LCP 1979) 1830-1858

Bright studied medecine at Edinburgh, Berlin, London *and* Vienna becoming a member of Guy's Hospital staff in 1820.

Seven years later he published *Reports of Medical Cases* in which he traced to the source in the kidneys, the morbid condition, now known as 'Bright's Disease' (*Morbus Brightii*).

BRITTAIN Newcastle, December 29, 1893
Vera March 29, 1970
Author

19, Glebe Place, SW3, 1935
4, Whitehall Court, SW1, 1960

Immediately after Oxford, Vera Brittain went on to become a nurse in all the horrors of the First World War. This searing experience formed the background to part of her book *Testament of Youth,* which was published in 1933. In fact more than 25 of her books were published, but it was *Testament of Youth* that continued to sell. The literary agent (who was shrewd enough to take the book to GOLLANCZ who published it) used to refer to it privately as *Testicles of Youth*; though, as he said, '...it was by no means all balls'.

BRITTEN Lowestoft, November 22, 1913
Benjamin (1st Lord) Aldeburgh, December 4, 1976
Composer Aldeburgh

559, Finchley Road, NW8, 1935-1937
45A, St Johns Wood High Street, NW8, 1943-1946.
22, Melbury Road, W14, 1948-1953
5, Chester Gate, NW1, 1953-1958
59, Marlborough Place, NW8, 1958-1965

Britten probably inherited his musical talent from his mother, who was a competent amateur singer, rather than from his father, who was a dentist. By the time he was five years old, little Benjamin had already begun to compose music.
When he was at the Royal College of Music (and not at all happy) he met Peter (now Sir Peter) Pears. This was in 1937, Peter Pears was 27 years old and Britten three years younger. Britten spent the rest of his life with Pears and died in his arms (literally).
They both went to the States in 1939 and, for a short while, shared a house with W.H. AUDEN in Brooklyn. Britten wrote much music especially suited to the quality of Pears' singing voice. Among his great operas, *Billy Budd* stands out, together with *Death in Venice,* based on a story by Thomas Mann, whose son, 'Golo', Britten and Pears knew.

BROMPTON

The name of a village 'just outside' London which used to be divided into two hamlets, Old and New Brompton. Today there are still the Old and the New Brompton Roads. The origin of *Brompton* is obscure but it has been suggested that it derives from the bush, broom *Cytisus Scoparius* which grew extensively here.

BROMPTON SQUARE, SW3

The Square dates from 1830.

21, Francis PLACE (LCP 1961) 1833-1851. Here he drafted 'The People's Charter' in 1838. He moved in here with his second wife after they had been married for three years.

BROOK STREET, W1 *Central line to Bond Street*

The 'brook' was the Tyburn which once flowed over the land here. The Tyburn is now an underground sewer. It surfaces once where it feeds a lake in Regent's Park.

25, Sidney SMITH, 1835.

25 (then number 57) George Frederick HANDEL (LCP 1952) 1720-1759. He rented the whole house for £30 a year and in it he wrote *The Messiah*. Just 11 days after hearing it performed, he died here, in April 1759.

69 (now the Savile Club). It was the house of Sir William HARCOURT who shot himself on the main staircase. Harcourt was nicknamed 'Lulu' and when he lived here, the waspish Max BEERBOHM described the furnishings as 'Lulu Quinze'!

72 (then 25) Edmund BURKE lived here when Paymaster General in 1782.

72, Lady Randolph CHURCHILL. She was burgled here: the thieves took many valuables including gifts from King Edward VII (when he was Prince of Wales).

74, Sir William GULL, 1870-1890.

BROOKE   Rugby School, August 3, 1887
Rupert Chawner   Skyros, Greece, April 23, 1915
Poet   On Skyros

5, Raymond Buildings, Gray's Inn, WC1, on numerous occasions between 1907-1914.

Brooke was the second of three brothers and was born at Rugby School where his father was a Housemaster. Rupert was educated there and went up to King's College, Cambridge in 1905. After university he settled at the Old Vicarage in Grantchester, a village just outside Cambridge. ('Stands the' [Grantchester] 'Church clock at ten to three? And is there honey still for tea?') He made friends easily and soon had a wide circle of literary and political acquaintances. Of those older ones, Edward (later Sir Edward) MARSH was probably the most devoted – and helpful. Marsh was smitten by Rupert's classic good looks as well as the young man's poetry. Brooke knew the poets, W.H. DAVIES, Walter de la Mare and W.W. Gibson; politically, he knew the ASQUITH's well.

In 1911 Brooke was made a Fellow of Kings College and, with Harold MONRO, planned an anthology of *Georgian Poetry* (Georgian in that King George V came to the throne in 1910). In 1913 Brooke travelled extensively in the Far East and then came the First World War. In 1914 he was commissioned into the Royal Naval Divison at Antwerp. By 1915 he was on his way to the Dardanelles (where he stood a good chance of being killed in that bloody corridor) but *en route* he contracted septicaemia and died on the island of Skyros; the fabled 'Isle of Achilles' and was buried there.

BROOKE STREET, EC1   *Central line to Chancery Lane*

Named after Fulke Greville, Lord Brooke, a friend of Sir Philip Sidney. At Brooke House in September 1628, Lord Brooke's valet, thinking he had been left out of his lordship's will (one wonders why he thought he ought to be *in* it) stabbed his master to death.

4 (today) but 39, in 1770. On August 25 of that year, Thomas CHATTERTON poisoned himself with arsenic in an attic room, having moved here from a relative's house in Shoreditch early in June. The painting of the scene by Henry Wallis (in the Tate Gallery) was actually painted in the attic.

The house has gone, but between 1916 and 1925 it was used as a place for storage for the Prudential Assurance Company, whose mammoth red-brick pile dominates the skyline of the western end of Holborn. '...the last house in Brooke Street which forms one side of the square. The house is at right angles to St. Alban Church and, as I remember, it was entered by a door round the corner in a little alleyway...' (P).

BROPHY
June 12, 1926
Brigid Antonia
Author

Flat 3, 185, Old Brompton Road, SW5, 1960-1980s

Miss Brophy's father, John, a Liverpudlian, ran away at the age of 15 to join the British Army in the First World War. He survived that to become an author and write a number of novels, two of which had Liverpool backgrounds. He died, aged 66, in 1965. She must have inherited her father's literary streak. Her first book, *The Crown Princess,* appeared in 1953 and numerous books and plays have followed.

She and her husband, Michael Levey, jointly produced a book titled, *Fifty Works of Literature We Could Do Without.* He was appointed a Director of the National Gallery in 1973, and in 1981 was knighted, so Miss Brophy's proper and formal address is actually Lady Levey.

BROWNE
Kennington, June 15, 1815
Hablôt Knight ('Phiz')
West Brighton, July 8, 1882
Artist
North side of the *Extramural Cemetery* Brighton

99, Ladbroke Grove, W11, 1874-1880

Using the pseudonym of 'Phiz', Browne became widely known as the illustrator of Dickens' works starting with *Pickwick* in 1836. He also illustrated work by Robert Smith Surtees (1803-1864) and Francis Smedley (1818-1864).

His christian name of Hablot had a rather curious origin. Three days after he was born, the British Army under the Duke of WELLINGTON defeated the Emperor Napoleon at the Battle of Waterloo. One of Browne's sisters was actually engaged to a Captain Hablôt in the French army, and this fiancé was killed at the battle. So Miss Browne's little brother was christened as a sort of walking memorial to the death of one of Britain's enemies!

BROWNING
Durham, March 6, 1806
Elizabeth Barrett
Florence, June 30, 1861
Poet
Protestant Cemetery, Florence

99, Gloucester Place, W1 (LCP 1924) 1835-1838
50, Wimpole Street, W1 (LCP 1937) 1838-1846
13, Dorset Street, W1, 1855-1856

Born Elizabeth Moulton in 1806, Elizabeth's first home was Coxhoe Hall in the county of Durham, but she spent her girlhood years in Hertfordshire in a house called Hope End. She was a precocious child and was supposed to be reading Homer in the original before she was 10! When she was 15 she fell from her pony so injuring her spine that she was obliged to lie on her back for years. Her father, who was a tyrannical despot, changed the family's name from Moulton to Barrett and, after Mrs. Barrett died in 1826, Elizabeth and her father moved to London. Her translation of *Prometheus Bound* appeared in 1833 and *The Seraphim and other Poems* was published in 1838. Mary Russell MITFORD described her when she was 31, '...a slight delicate figure, with a shower of dark curls falling on each side of a most expressive face; large, tender eyes, richly fringed by dark eyelashes and a smile like a sunbeam'. Anne THACKERAY said that Elizabeth, '...rarely laughs but is always cheerful and smiling.'

She was a poet of merit and, at the time of her marriage, was better known than Robert. They settled first in Pisa, then went onto Florence, where they took a floor of the Palazzo Guidi. Elizabeth, in sympathy with the Italians fighting for their freedom, published, *Casa Guidi Windows* in 1851. In 1850 she had published *Poems* containing the *Sonnets from the Portugese,* which were not translations at all but poems of love from a wife to her husband. Robert used to call her, 'my little Portuguese'. As her health failed she kept on writing poetry but after only 15 years of an idyllically happy marriage she died of 'consumption' in Robert's arms.

BROWNING
Robert
Poet

Camberwell, May 7, 1812
Venice, December 12, 1889
Westminster Abbey in 'Poet's Corner'

26, Devonshire Street, W1, 1850
13, Dorset Street, W1, 1855-1856
19, Warwick Crescent, W2, 1862-1887.
19, De Vere Gardens, W8 (P) 1887-1889

Browning's first published poem, *Pauline*, appeared in 1833 to be followed by *Paracelsus* in 1835. Both won critical acclaim but made little impression on the public. The first work of his really to do so was *Men and Women* in 1855, by which time he and Elizabeth had more or less settled in Florence.

BRUMMELL
George Bryan ('Beau')
Wit and dandy

Westminster, June 7, 1778
Caen, March 30, 1840
Caen

42, Charles Street, W1, c.1792
4, Chesterfield Street, W1, 1799
22, Chesterfield Street, W1, 1810
24, South Street, W1, after 1810
13 (now demolished) Aldford Street, W1, 1813

The 'Beau' was the grandson of a 'gentleman's gentleman' and the son of Lord NORTH's private secretary. George was educated at Eton and then, briefly, at Oxford.
He came of age in 1799 and into an income of £4,000 – a fortune for a bachelor in 1800. He became an arbiter of fashion for the *ton* of the day. The tying of his cravat could take as long as an hour and even 'Prinny', the Prince of Wales, obeyed the Beau's sartorial dictate.
Unfortunately he fell out with the Prince, and so with society and, being a compulsive gambler, fell deeply into debt. In 1816 he fled across the Channel and his last days of shambling decay ended in a Caen asylum. At the time of his death he had a bank balance of just eightpence (3p).

BRUNEL
Isambard Kingdom
Engineer

Portsmouth, Hants, April 9, 1806
London, September 15, 1859
Kensal Green: Square 41, Row 1

98, Cheyne Walk, SW3 (LCP 1954) 1808-1825
18, Duke Street (St James's) SW1, 1836-1859

As a young man, Brunel spent two years in the College Henri Quatre in Paris, before entering his father's firm in 1828. The father, Marc, was busy at the time building the Thames Tunnel and Isambard helped him with its design. Later he branched out on his own with the dramatic suspension bridge spanning the Avon Gorge at Clifton, a suburb of Bristol. The work had been put out for architectural tender in October 1829 and 22 designs were submitted. Nothing came of this and a second design competition was started in 1831. Brunel won on a design which would produce a bridge with a span of 630 feet (192 m) weighing 1,468 tons, all at a height over the Avon river of 220 feet (67 m). He actually used the chains from the old Hungerford Bridge in London. The bridge was finally officially opened on December 8, 1864.

Brunel's genius turned to the surface of the water. He built the *Great Western,* which became the first British steam ship to cross the Atlantic. This was followed by the *Great Eastern,* the largest vessel ever built (then). It was launched at Millwall, E. London, in 1858: it was over 692 feet (212 m) long and had a displacement of 27,000 tons.

There is a bronze statue of Brunel, erected in 1877 at the junction of Temple Place and the Victoria Embankment. Brunel, holding a pair of dividers, was sculpted by Baron Marochetti and the Portland Stone screen behind the figure was designed by Norman Shaw.

BRUNSWICK SQUARE, WC1   *Piccadilly line to Russell Square*

Brunswick was a name popular with builders and property speculators when, in 1795, the *smelly* Caroline of Brunswick came to England to marry the equally awful Prince of Wales (later Prince Regent in 1811; then King George IV in 1820.) Despite the fact that 'Prinny' spent most of the wedding night in a drunken coma in the fireplace, a daughter, Princess Charlotte (1796-1817) was born to the Princess of Wales at Carlton House, Pall Mall on January 7, 1796. (Charlotte was to marry Prince Leopold of Saxe Coburg on May 2, 1816.)

1,   George William RUSSELL ('AE') in 1934, self-exiled from Ireland and dying of cancer.

26,   E.M. FORSTER. He lived here from 1929-1939.

32,   John LEECH, 1848-1854.

38,   Duncan GRANT, in 1911, painted a mural on the wall of the ground floor sitting room.

There is a statue of Thomas Coram in the Square adjoining the site of the *Foundling Hospital* he established. Coram was born at Lyme Regis, in Dorset, about 1868. He died in London on March 29, 1751. His statue is by William MacMillan and was erected here in 1937. Coram's likeness was taken from HOGARTH's portrait of him.

BRUTON STREET, W1   *Central line to Bond Street*

John Berkeley (of Berkeley Square) came from the village of Bruton in Somerset. His father fought valiantly if unavailingly for King Charles I and was eventually rewarded by Charles II with many parcels of land in and around Berkeley Square. Bruton Street was built originally about 1721.

11,   Anthony EDEN, as a little boy, between 1903 and 1904.

17,   This house had, for many years, been the London house of the Strathmore family. At 2.40 am on April 21, 1926, the Duchess of York, wife of the second son of King George V, Prince Albert, gave birth to a daughter here. Just over ten years later the girl's Uncle David abdicated from the throne of England and the girl, Princess Elizabeth Alexandra Mary, became heir to the throne. On February 6, 1952 she succeeded as Her Majesty Elizabeth II.
On July 1st, 1929 – the Yorks having moved – Norman HARTNELL gave a post-election party here for the defeated Conservatives. Lady Eleanor Smith, daughter of Lord BIRKENHEAD, led a white pony up the staircase. Nancy MITFORD was just one of the many 'Bright Young Things' who came to 'drink, dance and drive their fears away'.

The house was destroyed by a bomb on October 7, 1940 and the site, rebuilt, is now occupied by the First National Bank of New York.

21, 'Ian Hay', 1921-1930.
30, Eddie MARSH, 1873-1876, as a baby, and later at ...
36, from 1880-1885.

BRYANSTON

Is a large village in Dorset owned by the PORTMAN family. Their country seat here has been a boys' public school since 1928.

BRYANSTON SQUARE, W1   *District, Metropolitan or Circle lines to Edgware Road or Central line to Marble Arch*

1, Mustapha Pasha RESCHID (LCP 1972) in 1839, when he was the Turkish Ambassador in London. The house, designed by Joseph Parkinson was built in 1811.
25, Lord MORAN, 1970s.
34 (in Flat 8) Lord SAINSBURY 1970s.
35, James BRYCE, in March 1889, when he became engaged to Elizabeth Ashton.

BRYANSTON STREET, W1

13, John BUCHAN, 1910-1912. This was a time when he was a literary adviser to the publishing house of Nelson and he was obliged to make monthly trips to Edinburgh.
30, the 4th Earl of LONSDALE died here 'unofficially' in 1882. He had installed a 'female companion' in this house. His body was smuggled back to his house in Carlton House Terrace to 'die more properly'.

BRYCE   Belfast, N. Ireland, May 10, 1838
James (1st Viscount)   Sidmouth, Devon, January 22, 1922
Diplomat

35, Bryanston Square, W1, 1889
54, Portland Place, W1, 1914
3, Buckingham Gate, SW1, 1922

Though born in Ireland, Bryce was educated at Glasgow High School and afterwards at Trinity College, Oxford. He graduated in 1862 with a *Double First*.

Five years later he was called to the Bar and, in 1870, became Regius Professor of Civil Law at Oxford in which post he stayed until 1893. In 1907 he was appointed British Ambassador in Washington and remained there until 1913. He came back to England and, in 1914, he was created a Viscount. (He had already been awarded the Order of Merit in 1907.)

He was a firm believer in Home Rule and, among other serious books, wrote *The American Commonwealth,* which was published in 1888.

BUCHAN   Perth, Scotland, August 26, 1875
John (1st Lord Tweedsmuir)   Montreal, February 11, 1940
Author and Diplomat   His ashes lie in the Church of St
                                 Thomas Canterbury, Elsfield, Oxon

40, Hyde Park Square, W2, 1907-1910
13, Bryanston Street, W1, 1910-1912
76, Portland Place, W1, 1912-1919

Buchan, the eldest son of a Free Church minister, went, via a bursary, to Glasgow University, then, with a scholarship, to Brasenose College, Oxford, to the Bar of the Temple and finally joined Lord MILNER's staff in South Africa in 1901.

By 1903 he was back in England as a barrister, specialising in tax cases. He had already begun to have some works published and, in 1906, he joined Nelson's, the Edinburgh publishers, as their literary adviser. He continued to live in London but had to make monthly trips to Scotland. He married Susan Grosvenor, granddaughter of Lord Ebury and a relative of the super-rich Westminsters (and also of the WELLINGTON's). In 1918 he was appointed Director of Intelligence for the Government and ten years later entered Parliament as Member for the Scottish Universities.

In 1935 he was appointed Governor General of Canada and created Baron Tweedsmuir. He was popular in Canada, but in 1938 his health became undermined and he died in office.

BUCHANAN Stony Batter, Pa, April 22, 1791
James Wheatland, Pa, June 1, 1868
15th President of the United States

56, Harley Street, W1, 1853-1856

Buchanan entered Congress in 1821 and ten years later was posted to Russia as minister, coming back to the States two years after, to enter the Senate, where he remained until 1845 when he became Secretary of State. After a three-year tour of duty in London he returned to Washington to be elected to the Presidency in 1857. He held the office for just one four-year term.

He was by training, a lawyer, by instinct – a politician. In Russia he negotiated the first commercial treaty, he settled the Oregon boundary question (the State was admitted to the Union in 1859). He was a Democrat, fiercely *opposed* to the freedom of the slaves and supported the idea of making Texas a slave state.

BUCKINGHAM

The Palace itself, which is responsible for the naming of so many proximate streets, originates with John Sheffield, Duke of Buckingham in 1702. (*This Duke of Buckingham, is not to be confused with Charles Villiers, who was created Duke of Buckingham by his Royal lover, King James I, in 1623.*) Sheffield had built a brick mansion facing what is now the Mall which was finished by 1708. Buckingham's third wife, Catherine Darnley (by repute, yet *another* bastard child of King James II) lived in the house after her husband's death until her own in 1743. The house was purchased by King George III in 1761 for £21,000 and eventually became a Royal Palace, the first monarchical occupant being Queen Victoria in 1837. (She moved in on July 13, 1837 and, for the first time in her life, had a bedroom to herself.)

BUCKINGHAM GATE, SW1 *Victoria, District, Circle*
and BR lines to Victoria

Originally this was called St James's Street as the gate from the Palace into St James's Park was here.

3, Viscount BRYCE. His widow continued to live here after his death in 1922.
15, Wilfrid Scawen BLUNT (LCP 1979) in the 1890s.
16, W.E. GLADSTONE, 1890.
21, Joseph SEVERN, 1820s.

At the entrance to 65, there are bronze busts of the Hon. Charles ROLLS and Sir Henry ROYCE. They are both by William MacMillan and were erected here in 1978.

BUCKINGHAM PLACE, SW1

4,   Samuel MORSE, 1811.

BUCKINGHAM STREET, WC2   *Jubilee, Bakerloo and Northern lines*
                                                        /   to Charing Cross

This Buckingham development *was* entirely involved with Charles Villiers,
1st Duke of Buckingham, the beloved of King James I. Villiers' town house
was here and the Watergate, designed and built by Inigo Jones (1573-1651)
today stands high and dry in the Victoria Embankment Gardens at the
bottom of the street. The position of the 'gate' gives one some idea of the
width of the River Thames at the beginning of the 17th century.
Buckingham was assassinated at Portsmouth on August 23, 1628 (by John
Felton, 1595-1628). His profligate son (George, 1627-1688) finally had to sell
up, but not before he had developed the area and named four turnings off the
Strand: *George* Court, *Villiers* Street, *Duke* Street, and *Of* Alley. Of Alley,
alas, no longer exists; it was built in 1675.

9,   Peg WOFFINGTON, all too briefly.
12,   Samuel PEPYS (LCP 1947) 1684-1688. The house's original staircase is
          still there ('...and so to bed').
14,   PEPYS moved here in 1688. The house remained more or less as Pepys
          knew it until 1791 when the present building was put up (LCP 1908).
14,   Robert HARLEY, Earl of Oxford, 1701-1714.

BURDETT-COUTTS   London, April 21, 1814
Angela Georgina (1st Baroness)   London, December 30, 1906
Millionairess   Westminster Abbey

80, Piccadilly, W1, here born

1, Stratton Street, W1, practically all her adult life and died here
Baroness Burdett-Coutts' grandfather, the banker Thomas Coutts (1735-
1822) married his brother's maidservant and they had three daughters. All
three of these girls made excellent marriages. Fanny married the Marquess of
Bute; Susan married Lord Guildford and Sophia married Sir Francis Burdett,
Angela's father. In 1811 Coutts' wife became mentally unbalanced and
remained so until her death in 1815. Coutts had by then fallen in love with an
actress called Harriot (sic) Mellon, who, aged 40, was more than 30 years
younger than he. A fortnight after his first wife died Harriot became Mrs.
Coutts. Seven years later he was dead and Harriot inherited his entire
fortune. She wore her widow's weeds becomingly enough and then in 1827
married William de Vere, 9th Duke of St Albans, who was 20 years younger
than her. They lived happily together until she died in 1837. To the
amazement of everyone, she left her now immense fortune to her first
husband's granddaughter Angela Burdett, still, at 23, unmarried. The Duke
liked Angela and as his companion, he took her 'on tour'. (Her income was
around £80,000 a year.) Their cavalcade as they travelled was vast. They
even had *two* doctors in the retinue, in case one was taken ill.
At one time it was thought that she might marry the Duke of
WELLINGTON who was then about 78 and she 37. The Duke had written
her over 850 letters but in one advised her not to throw herself away on an
old man.
In her lifetime she gave away personally well over £3 million and was
generally full of 'good works'. In 1871 she was given a peerage – the first
woman ever to have been so rewarded. Ten years later she astounded society
by marrying an American, William Ashmead-Bartlett, who had been her
secretary. She was 67: he, 27! Queen Victoria was appalled at the
'unsuitability' of the marriage and referred to Angela as 'a silly old woman'.
In fact she was only five years older than the Queen.

BURGESS
Guy   Botkin Hospital, Moscow, September
Defecting Diplomat   1, 1963

5, Bentinck Street, W1, 1940-1941

Burgess and his fellow employee, Donald MacLean, both employed by HM
Government, hit the headlines all over the world when they fled from
Britain and turned up in Moscow in 1951.

MacLean was married to an American girl who subsequently joined her
husband in Moscow. But Burgess was an alcoholic and homosexual
bachelor. His pursuit and courtships of young men were quite well known.

Brian Howard, an Old Etonian (and, at one time, rich) homosexual, who
was a failure despite good looks, good education and good breeding, told
Harold Acton that Burgess's 'equipment' was '...gargantuan – what is
known as a *whopper* my dear!'

Neither Burgess nor MacLean could tell the Russians many secrets and so,
after the Russians had got from them all that was valuable, the British pair
were put on one side. Burgess, no longer of any use, slithered down the
slope propelled by booze and boredom to a sordid and hardly remarked
upon death.

BURGOYNE   c.1722
(Sir) John   London, June 4, 1792
Soldier and dramatist   Westminster Abbey

10, Hertford Street, W1 (LCP 1954) 1770 until he died here

Burgoyne entered the Army when he was only 17 and not long after eloped
with the daughter of the Earl of Derby. No forgiveness for this act was
forthcoming and the Burgoynes were obliged to live abroad for seventeen
years until her father, the 11th Earl, died.

He became a Member of Parliament and, restored to favour, was sent as a
soldier in 1774 to the troublesome Colony of America. He was in command
of the troops which took Ticonderoga in July 1776 but he was also in
command when obliged to surrender to the 44 years old General Gates at
Saratoga on October 11, 1777.

His (not very distinguished) military career ended as a Lieutenant-Colonel
and from the sword, he took to the pen. In 1781 he wrote a comic opera
called *The Lord of the Manor,* but his real hit was *The Heiress* in 1786, despite
one critique which ran, 'Every reader of the Heiress will mark the striking
parallelisms between many passages in it and the *School for Scandal*'. Which
play, by SHERIDAN, was first produced in 1777.

BURKE   Dublin, January 12, 1729
Edmund   Beaconsfield, July 9, 1797
Philosophic politician   St Mary and All Saints, Beaconsfield

72, Brook Street, W1, for many years
37, Gerrard Street, W1 (P 1876) 1787-1790

Had Burke been a little more influential at the time when America was
separating itself from Britain, it is possible the United States and Britain
might still be enjoying the sort of relationship enjoyed by, say, Canada and
Britain. Burke's speeches on *American Taxation* in 1774 and *Conciliation with
America,* a year later, were sound both politically and philosophically, but
the Marquis of Rockingham (through whom Burke originally entered
Parliament in 1765) had been ousted by the serenely stupid Lord NORTH.

BURKE London, November 16(c), 1886
Thomas London, September 22, 1945
Novelist Golders Green

33, Tavistock Square, WC1, for some years until 1934

Orphaned early, Burke, a real East End Cockney, was working in an office when he was 15 and had already sold his first story by the time he was 16. Then he went to work for a second-hand bookseller.

His first collected work of his own stories, *Nights in Town,* appeared in 1915. This was followed by *Limehouse Nights* the next year. Then followed a series of books, each one drawing upon his first hand experiences in London, especially of the East End and 'Chinatown'.

In 1930 he moved west a little and published *Living in Bloomsbury* (a very explicit title).

Burke produced some books of verse and several novels, one of which, *The Wind and the Rain* (1924) is largely autobiographical.

BURNAND London, November 29, 1836
(Sir) Francis Cowley Ramsgate, April 21, 1917
Quondam editor of Punch

27, The Boltons, SW10, 1904

After Eton, Burnand went into the law and was called to the Bar in 1862. He was writing plays in his spare time – the first one being written at Eton when he was 15 – and one or two of them were taken up commercially. He had not yet determined what he really wanted to do. He had actually been to Cuddesdon Theological College with a view to becoming a priest. He did not take orders but became a convert to Catholicism.

Being a good Catholic he fathered six sons and five daughters as well as over 120 plays, principally comedies. He once co-operated with W.S. GILBERT in a musical adaptation of John Maddison Morton's (1811-1891) farce, *Box and Cox*. Gilbert once asked Burnand if the editor of *Punch* had any *jokes* sent in. 'Hundreds' said Burnand. 'Why don't you print any of them?' retorted Gilbert.

BURNE-JONES Birmingham, August 28, 1833
(Sir) Edward Coley London, June 17, 1898
Artist Rottingdean Churchyard, Sussex

17, Red Lion Square, WC1, 1856-1859
62, Great Russell Street, WC1, 1861-1865
41, Kensington Square, W8, 1865-1871

Burne-Jones went up to Exeter College, Oxford, with a view to joining the Church. However, he met William Samuel MORRIS who persuaded him to turn to painting. D.G. ROSSETTI was the next to influence him. Later, on a visit to Italy, he stayed in Venice and Milan and he convinced himself that he really should be an artist. In Italy again, later, he met John RUSKIN and his career burgeoned.

Mythological and medieval matter became his chosen subjects for painting and later he became more influenced by the Italian 15th century painters – especially by Botticelli. One of his greatest paintings, *King Cophetua and the Beggar Maid,* hangs in the Tate Gallery. R.H. Wilenski wrote of Burne-Jones' technique that sometimes he made his lines, '...flow like the silvery melodies of Chopin'.

BURNETT Manchester, November 24, 1849
Frances Eliza Hodgson Plandome, Long Island, New York,
Author October 29, 1924
 God's Acre, New York

63, Portland Place, W1 (LCP 1979) 1893-1898

Papa Hodgson was an ironmonger, who was so unsuccessful in the north of England, he emigrated to the south of the United States – to a log cabin in Knoxville, Tennessee, when Frances was 16. She began to have her stories published in 1866 and, years later, claimed she had *never* had a manuscript of hers rejected – lucky *indeed*! When she was 24, she married Dr. Swan M. Burnett and moved with him to Washington four years later. The marriage was unsuccessful and they were divorced in 1898, by which time she was back in England. Later she married a Mr. Stephen Townshend, but that union finished almost as soon as the knot had been tied.
After London, she tried living in Kent, but this did not suit her, so she went back to America and settled in Long Island. Her nickname was 'Fluffy' and certainly her best remembered book, *Little Lord Fauntleroy* (published 1886) was sufficiently sickly to have been written by someone called 'Fluffy'! She wrote over 40 more novels, but the only one which seems to have survived, even if not intact, is *The Secret Garden* in 1911.

BURNEY Lyme Regis, June 13, 1752
Frances ('Fanny', Madame d'Arblay) Bath, January 6, 1840
Novelist Walcot, Nr. Bath

50, Poland Street, W1, as a child in the 1750s
89, Half Moon Street, W1
63, Lower Sloane Street, SW1, 1814-1816
11, Bolton Street, WC1 (P 1885) 1818
22, Mount Street, W1, 1838-1839
29, Grosvenor Street, W1, 1839

Little 'Fanny' Burney was an endearing and morally upright figure in the decaying court circles of King George III in his later, deranged years.
She had actually written a novel before she was 15, but burnt it, in case her step-mother found it. Ten years later she published (anonymously) *Evelina, or a Young Lady's Entrance in the World*. She was paid £15 for it! (Samuel JOHNSON was reputed to have learnt the book 'by heart' as he was so fond of it.)
In about 1777 she was appointed Second Keeper of the Queen's Robes (of Queen Caroline, wife of poor King George III) and was paid £200 a year for being a superior sort of Lady's maid. The atmosphere at Court must have been stupefyingly dull and the boredom of it all must have been beyond description as the King's illness became worse and worse.
On July 31, 1798 Fanny married General d'Arblay, a French military emigré. They had a son who became a priest. All three – *Notre Chère Trio* as Madame d'Arblay called them, lie buried near Bath.

BURY STREET, SW1 *Piccadilly, Jubilee and Victoria lines*
 to Green Park

Henry Jermyn, who died in 1684, followed King Charles I and exiled himself during the Commonwealth. He was rewarded by Charles II with the Earldom of St Albans and a large field behind St James's Palace. Jermyn became the 'Founder of the West End'. Bury Street (part of his development, built up c.1672) was named after his country house at Bury St Edmunds in Essex. The Historical Register for 1735, however, asserts that Bury Street was named after '...Berry, a half pay officer, and landlord of most of Berry Street, St James's. He was above 100 years old and had been an officer in the service of King Charles the First.'

1, Joseph HAYDN, 1794-1795. It was in this year that Haydn formed an attachment with Mrs. Rebecca Shroeter of 6, St James's Street, Buckingham Gate. She copied out music for him and gave him presents of soap! She was probably in her 40s; Haydn was 62. (Details are lacking of other services she may have supplied to 'My H.'.)

19, Tom MOORE, 1826.

19, Sir Edward CARSON, 1893. One year previously he had been elected as MP for Dublin University.

33, Tom MOORE 1814. BYRON wrote to his publisher, Murray, on July 11, 1814, asking him to send proofs of *Lara* to Moore, '...tonight, as he leaves town to-morrow and wishes to see it before he goes.'

37, George CRABBE, 1817.

BUTLER   Langar, Notts., December 4, 1835
Samuel   London, June 18, 1902
Author

15, Clifford's Inn, EC4, 1864-1902

Butler's grandfather (1774-1839) an eminent divine, was Bishop of Lichfield. Young Samuel, however, was always quarrelling with his father (also a clergyman) who sent the boy to Shrewsbury School, then on to St John's College, Cambridge and, as he found the thought of taking holy orders repugnant, he put 12,000 miles between Papa and himself and became a sheep farmer in New Zealand.

In 1872 his book, *Erewhon* was published and fame began. *Erewhon* is an anagram for 'nowhere' and so, really, *Utopia*. Butler had been back in London since 1864 and for a while studied painting and a painting of his, called *Mr. Heatherly's Holiday* is gathering dust *somewhere* in the cellars of the Tate Gallery.

BUTTERFIELD   London, September 7, 1814
William   London, February 23, 1900
Architect   Tottenham Cemetery

4, Adam Street, WC2, 1850s
42, Bedford Square, WC1 (LCP 1978) 1886

Butterfield was one of the first English architects to introduce colour into both ecclesiastical as well as domestic buildings. He remodelled a number of London churches (often *not* for the better) but one of his largest real creations in London is All Saints Church, Priory and School in Margaret Street (not far from Oxford Circus).

Out of London; he produced some buildings for the public school at Winchester and, most notable of all, Keble College, Oxford. The uncompromising Victorian architectural style he imparted to these buildings does not blend well with most of the longer established Colleges in the city.

BYRON   London, January 22, 1788
(Lord) George Noel Gordon   Missolonghi, Greece, April 19, 1824
Poet   Family vault, Church of St Mary
                             Magdalen, Hucknall Torkard, Notts.

16, Holles Street, W1, here born
24, Holles Street, W1
16, Piccadilly, W1, 1805
8, St James Street, SW1, 1812
Albany, Piccadilly, W1, 1814

Byron's father was a ne'er-do-well Captain who died before he was 35, having squandered most of the family fortunes. Young Byron (and his mother) spent his early years in squalid lodgings in Aberdeen, Scotland. His mother was a loud-mouthed and vulgar woman and so, considering the characters of both his parents, it is not really surprising that Byron was a little *wayward*.

In 1798, his uncle, 'The Wicked Lord', died and Byron succeeded to the title and a *small* fortune. Some of this was spent on his school fees at Harrow and then at Cambridge, where he spent most of his time in dissipation, rowing and (oddly) boxing.

He published *Hours of Idleness* whilst still up at Trinity: it was given a bad press. In 1809 he travelled in Portugal, Spain and Greece, but was back in London by 1811 to take his seat in the House of Lords. The following year the first two cantos of his *Childe Harold* were published and '...he woke up one morning to find himself famous'.

He married Annabella Milbanke in 1815, but the marriage was strained from the beginning and exacerbated by Byron's sometimes demented behaviour and poverty (the Bailiffs were regular visitors at Byron's London home). Their joint life was over in 1816 and Byron left England, never to return. Sometimes with the SHELLEYs, sometimes alone, he travelled in Switzerland and, for a while, settled in Genoa. Canto 3 of *Childe Harold* appeared in 1816 and Canto 4 two years later. Byron then took up the highly emotive cause of Greek liberty and went to Greece in 1823, only to die there from fever the following year.

Before he married, Byron had had a passionate love *affaire* with 27-year old Caroline Lamb, wife of William Lamb (later Lord MELBOURNE, the Prime Minister). Marriage did not regulate Byron's sexual antics and it was Caroline who said Byron was 'Bad, mad and dangerous to know'. Certainly, he was diverse, if nothing else, sexually. Quite apart from his mistresses, he has been accused of incest with his married half-sister, Augusta Leigh (an event which resulted in the birth of a daughter, Medora, on April 14, 1814.) It is also thought he loved a homosexual choir boy, called John Edleston, in 1805. This fair-haired, dark-eyed chorister inspired Byron with a '...violent, though *pure* love and passion', and was the 'most romantic period of my life'.

Many are the guesses over Byron's behaviour in and out of the bedroom but there have been as many over *which* of Byron's feet was 'club-footed' (*talipes equinus*). Very likely the answer was given by his great friend John Trelawny. Not long after the poet died, Trelawny went into the room where, '...lay the embalmed body of the Pilgrim,' [Byron] 'more beautiful in death than in life...I uncovered the Pilgrim's feet: both his feet were clubbed and his legs withered to the knee – the form and features of an Apollo with the feet and legs of a sylvan satyr.'

The Byron motto is *Crede Byron* – Trust Byron; which is probably the *last* thing one should have done.

There is a bronze statue of Byron inside Hyde Park on a traffic 'island' at the Hyde Park Corner end, more or less where Number 13 Piccadilly Terrace was to be found, the house where Byron spent most of his short, married life. The figure was sculpted by Richard C. Belt and was erected here in 1880. The poet is sitting on a 57 ton, 57.9 tonnes, slab of *rosso antico* marble donated by the Greek Government.

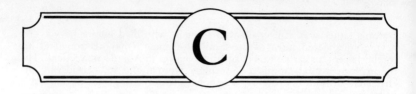

CADOGAN

All the street names in Chelsea in which the name Cadogan appears derive from Sir Hans Sloane's son-in-law. Sloane was Lord of the Manor Chelsea (although he was a doctor of medicine) and he had two daughters. The younger Miss Sloane married Lord CADOGAN of OAKLEY, a descendant of Cadwgan ap Elystan and their son Charles (1728-1807) was Viscount Chelsea. The Cadogan family motto is, 'Qui Invidet Minor Est' – He who envies is the inferior.

CADOGAN GARDENS, SW3   *Piccadilly line to Knightsbridge*

2,   Lily LANGTRY, 1888.
21,   John Hay BEITH ('Ian Hay') in the 1920s.
85,   Alfred NOYES, in the 1920s. Whilst they were here his first wife died. There is a memorial to Mrs. Noyes in the central aisle of Holy Trinity Church.

CADOGAN PLACE, SW3

18,   Lord Alfred DOUGLAS, c. 1880.
30   (previously 3) Mrs. Dorothy JORDAN (LCP 1975) 1812-1814, after her final parting from her lover, the Duke of Clarence (who was to become King William IV in 1830).
44,   William WILBERFORCE died here on July 29, 1833 (LCP 1961) having moved here three weeks before. A month later slavery was abolished in Britain, a cause to which he had devoted his life. The inside of the house has been little changed since the 1830's but an extra storey was added in 1850.
85,   Margaret OLIPHANT from about 1890 until her death in 1897.
On the north side of the gardens is a piece of statuary entitled *The Dancers*. This bronze by David Wynne, was erected here in 1975.

CADOGAN SQUARE, SW3

Part of the Square used to be the Princes Cricket Club Ground

60,   Denis WHEATLEY.
75,   Arnold BENNETT (LCP 1958) 1921-1930. Here he completed *Riceyman Steps* 1923. In 1926, his mistress, Dorothy Cheston, moved in; Bennett's wife steadfastly refusing to divorce him even though Dorothy had had a daughter by him in April. She was called Virginia.

CALDECOTT	Chester, March 22, 1846
Randolph	Augustine, Florida, February 12, 1886
Artist	

46, Great Russell Street, WC1 (LCP 1977) 1872

Caldecott's father was one of the founders of the Institute of Accountants and did not 'hold with' young Randolph's wanting to paint or draw. He sent the boy to learn his trade in a Shropshire bank.
Nevertheless, in 1871, Caldecott came up to London to study art and also, somehow, managed to retain his income from the bank. Before 1873 he really settled down and 'became a serious artist'. In 1875 he illustrated

Washington IRVING's *Sketch Book* and it was this commission that established him.

Never very healthy; in his late thirties he suffered a bad attack of rheumatic fever and thought he would live in a kinder climate. He was commissioned by the *Graphic* to make sketches of American life and he and his wife set off for the sub-tropical climes of Florida. The journey was too much for him and he died in Augustine, not yet 39 years old.

CAMBRIDGE STREET, SW1   *Victoria, Circle and District lines to Victoria*

A Grosvenor (and so the Duke of Westminster) family development of the 1830's and 1840's, before they became *Ducal*. Probably with an eye to retaining the approval of the Royal family the Grosvenors named a number of streets after Hanoverian sprigs. *Cambridge* was the Duke of Cambridge, youngest son of King George III, who died in 1850, aged 76.

21,   Mary Ann EVANS (alias 'George Eliot') 1853–1854. This was just before she went off to 'live in sin' with George LEWES.

32,   Aubrey BEARDSLEY, 1889–1890, at this time he was still working in an insurance office in the City.

114,   Aubrey BEARDSLEY (LCP 1948). Here he made the drawings for Malory's *Morte d'Arthur* and for Oscar WILDE's *Salomé*. His drawing-room was darkened by heavy curtains, but eventually one could see that the walls were painted a deep orange and, '...heightened by a faint all-pervading scent, which made the air sweet and heavy'.

Lord CAMELFORD, see PITT, T.

CAMPBELL	Kensington, February 9, 1865
Beatrice Stella	London, April 9, 1940
Actress	Pau, France

15, Tedworth Square, SW3
48, Ashley Gardens, SW1, 1895
33, Kensington Square, W8 (P) 1900–1921
64, Pont Street, SW3, 1928–1940

'Mrs Pat' (as she came to be known, almost universally) had an English father and an Italian mother – and probably inherited from them the worst traits of each of the two nations involved. She was 19 when she married Campbell (who died in South Africa 16 years later). She first appeared on the stage in 1888 but she had to wait another five years for her triumphant success in *The Second Mrs. Tanqueray* by Sir Arthur PINERO.

She was to play 'Eliza Doolittle' in G.B. SHAW's play, *Pygmalion,* and formed a lasting and platonic friendship with that half charlatan, Irish genius. (Many of their letters, to and from, have survived. They are a delight.)

In 1914, 'Mrs. Pat' married George CORNWALLIS-WEST, some nine years younger than herself. The marriage with CORNWALLIS-WEST did not work out and 'Mrs. Pat' went on, pretending time stood still. But not even for her would it do so and she became rather troublesome with playwrights and theatre managers. But, game as only a real 'trouper' seems able to be, she made a film (her first) called *Riptide* when she was 68. Her last years were sad and she died an unbeautiful wreck, leaving only £225.

CAMPBELL Edinburgh, March 8, 1708
John London, December 28, 1775
Historian Brunswick Square

20, Queen Square, WC1, 1757-1775

Much respected as an intellectual and a more than capable writer, Campbell
also knew how to play as well as work. James BOSWELL records that
Campbell once drank 13 *bottles* of port in one sitting! (Yet his liver lasted out
for nearly 70 years.)
Samuel JOHNSON (who often visited him in Queen Square) said that
though Campbell never actually *entered* a church, he always doffed his hat
should he pass one. 'This', wrote Johnson, 'shows that he has good
principles.'
In 1742 Campbell's *Lives of British Admirals and other Eminent British Seamen,*
etc. began to appear. It was very successful and ran to three editions in his
lifetime. (This was despite Campbell's dislike of the sea and his *complete*
ignorance of maritime matters!)

CAMPBELL Durban, October 20, 1901
Roy Lisbon, April 22, 1957
Poet

17, Campden Grove, W8, from 1949 for some years

Campbell was the 4th child of a successful doctor and in 1922 met Mary, the
daughter of another successful and wealthy doctor. Within a week they were
living together and not much later were married. She was 24; he 21. The
marriage could not have been expected to have been a raving success. *She*
was head-over-heels in love with *Mrs.* Harold Nicolson (Vita Sackville-
West!) and Campbell 'had trouble' with alcohol: but *somehow* Mary and he
managed to produce two daughters.
Even sober, Campbell was a braggart and able to make enemies easily. From
his *Home Thoughts in Bloomsbury*:
> 'Of all the clever people round me here
> I most delight in me-
> Mine is the only voice I care to hear
> And mine the only face I like to see.'

CAMPBELL Glasgow, July 27, 1777
Thomas Boulogne, June 15, 1844
Poet Westminster Abbey

2, Piccadilly, W1, 1803
30, Foley Place, W1, 1804
62, Lincoln's Inn Fields, WC1, 1828
30, Langham Street, W1, c.1830-1840

Campbell compiled *The Annals of Great Britain from George II to the Peace of*
Amiens and, after a spell in Germany, came back to London and published
Specimens of British Poety in 1818. Of his own poetry the best known is
probably, *Ye Mariners of England*.
One of the permanent memorials to him is the work he undertook towards
the end of his life, in bringing about the foundation of London University.
He thought that what he had achieved in *this* direction was truly important
and the only *real* event in his own 'life's little history'.
Campbell had married his second cousin, Matilda Sinclair; they had two
sons, one died in infancy; his wife died in 1828 and their surviving son went
insane.
The statue of Campbell in Westminster Abbey was made by William Calder
Marshall (1813-1894) in 1855.

CAMPBELL-BANNERMAN   Scotland, September 7, 1836
(Sir) Henry   London, April 22, 1908
Prime Minister

6, Grosvenor Place, SW1 (LCP 1959) 1877-1904
29, Belgrave Square, SW1, 1905-1908

Entering Parliament in 1868, Campbell (Bannerman was added later under the terms of the will of his maternal uncle, Henry Bannerman) was a 'convert' to Home Rule for Ireland and later on was pro–Boer.

He was Prime Minister from December 1905-1908, when ASQUITH became Prime Minister and he died only 18 days later. He had not been well, having suffered quite a severe heart attack just after having addressed a political meeting in Bristol in November 1907.

He had married Charlotte Bruce in 1860 but there were no children. In a funeral oration on Campbell-Bannerman in the House of Lords, Lord Tweedmouth (according to *Hansard*) said that his fidelity to his wife, Charlotte was, '...all the more remarkable as she was not a woman of any particular attraction'. What he is really supposed to have said was that, 'she was an ugly old bitch'.

CAMPDEN

The first Lord Campden began life as Baptiste Hickes in 1551. He became a prosperous mercer in Cheapside and at one stage he was lending the improvident King James I money and took some of the interest in the form of a title in 1628. The story is that Baptiste beat Sir Walter Cope (who died in 1614) at cards so overwhelmingly that Cope settled the debt by handing over large chunks of property in what is now the rich and Royal Borough of Kensington. Hickes had chosen the title of Campden for his Viscountcy, apparently after a small village called Campden in Gloucestershire in the West of England, probably out of sentiment. Baptiste/Campden had a house built for him on his ground, so luckily gained. Today Camden Flats on the corner of Sheffield Terrace and Hornton Street cover part of the foundations of Campden House.

CAMPDEN GROVE, W8   *Central, District and Circle lines to*
                                          Notting Hill Gate

13,   Arthur Reed ROPES ('Adrian Ross') c.1880s, not long after he had come down from Cambridge.
17,   Roy CAMPBELL, 1949. The house was, '...always identifiable by the two bay trees flanking its front door'. Campbell used to say of them, 'You can't do without them' [bay leaves] 'in good cooking – I put into my cooking what ought to go into my poetry'.
19,   Aubrey BEARDSLEY, 1896. Desperately ill from tuberculosis which was to kill him less than two years later, he was forbidden to work whilst here.

CAMPDEN HILL GARDENS, W8

19,   Dame Marie RAMBERT, 1946.
20A, Ford Madox FORD lived here, poverty-stricken, in the 1920's. Wyndham LEWIS moved in after him.
23   (in the ground floor flat) Anatoly ZOTOV and his wife, Nina; from December 1981 to December 1982, when he was declared *persona non grata* and given a week to leave the country.

CAMPDEN HILL ROAD, W8

29,   Sir Henry NEWBOLT died here on April 19, 1938.

80, Ford Madox FORD and his mistress, Violet Hunt (LCP 1973) 1913-1919.

96, Cecil DAY-LEWIS, 1953-1957. His second child, Daniel, by his second wife, Jill Balcon, was born here.

CAMPDEN HILL SQUARE, W8

9, John STUART (LCP 1962) from 1865 until he died here the following year. He lived here (gradually going blind) with relatives.

16, Charles MORGAN.

CANNING	London, May 11, 1770
George	Chiswick, August 8, 1827
Prime Minister	Westminster Abbey (North Transept)

37, Conduit Street, W1
50, Berkeley Square, W1 (LCP 1979) 1806-1807

Canning's father, who had 'married beneath his station' died, poverty-stricken, when George was only one year old. His uncle, Stratford Canning, generously paid for his nephew's education at Eton and, after that, for three years at Christchurch, Oxford.

As a supporter of PITT, Canning entered Parliament as Member for Newport in the *Isle of Wight*. Within two years he became an Under Secretary of State, still not 26 years old. In 1800 he married Joan Scott, sister of the Duchess of Portland, who brought with her a dowry of £100,000 – which must have helped.

Canning was setting sail for India, to take up the post of Governor-General, when CASTLEREAGH committed suicide and Canning was called back to become Head of Foreign Affairs. Lord LIVERPOOL was Prime Minister (and had been since June 16, 1812) but five years after the (unexplained) death of Castlereagh, Liverpool was stricken by paralysis and, on April 30, 1827, Canning became Prime Minister at the head of a Tory Government. A powerless Government, however, and Canning, overcome by such a burden, died less than four months later.

His statue by WESTMACOTT stands on the north-west corner of Parliament Square. Unsuitably clad in a toga, with some sort of scroll in his left hand, poor Canning was originally placed in Palace Yard in 1832. For some reason he was transposed to his present site in 1867; still looking distinctly chilly.

CARLILE	Brixton, January 14, 1847
(Prebendary) Wilson	September 26, 1942
Divine	

34, Sheffield Terrace, W8 (LCP 1972) 1881-1891

Carlile first came to London as curate of St Mary Abbot's Church, Kensington in 1880. Two years later he resigned his holy orders and founded the Church Army. This organization is *not* to be confused with the Salvation Army (founded by William Booth in 1865) but Carlile admitted to borrowing a number of ideas and procedures introduced by the Salvation Army.

CARLTON

All the 'Carltons' lie on the site of the house and gardens belonging to Lord Carlton. In 1709 Queen Anne leased a plot of land to Henry Boyle, Baron Carlton, for 31 years at £35 per annum. Carlton died childless in 1752 and the property passed to his nephew, Richard Boyle. *This* Boyle was also Lord Burlington, an architect. *He* eventually gave it to his mother, who passed it onto Frederick, Prince of Wales ('Poor Fred') father of King George III, in 1732. Frederick died in 1752 and *his* widow, Augusta, stayed on in Carlton House. At that time it was still a smallish brick building, but in 1783, the Prince of Wales ('Prinny') took it over and instructed Henry Holland to renovate it. The chief feature of Holland's design was the Corinthian portico. When the 'new' Carlton House was demolished in 1826, the portico columns were preserved and then incorporated into the façade of the National Gallery in Trafalgar Square.

CARLTON GARDENS, SW1

Jubilee, Northern and Bakerloo lines to Charing Cross

1, NAPOLEON III, 1839-1840.

2, Lord KITCHENER (LCP 1924) 1914-1915. The house was owned by Lady Wantage. Here Kitchener devised the recruitment poster, 'Your Country Needs *You*' campaign at the beginning of the First World War.

4, Lord PALMERSTON (LCP 1907) 1846-1855.

4, Viscount CURZON, 1896. His first daughter, Irene, was born here on January 20, 1896.

4, A.J. BALFOUR's town house (c.1870-1930) it was rebuilt in 1933.

4, General DE GAULLE during the Second World War. The plaque is in French, but the GLC are going to add an English one.

6, W.E. GLADSTONE, 1848-1856. His father had given him the lease of the house, 'in consideration of a natural love and affection I have for my son'.

CARLTON HOUSE TERRACE, SW1

1, Viscount CURZON (LCP 1976) lived here from 1905 until he died here on March 20, 1925. The house was bought for Curzon by his father-in-law, Levi Leiter, a wealthy American who was a partner in the Marshall Field business and had a daughter, Mary. Curzon finally married Mary in 1895. The meticulous Curzon supervised *every* aspect of the domestic arrangements and the decoration for the house. He even had cork pads fixed to the back rests of any non-upholstered chairs so they would not mark the walls if pushed back against them!

2, The Duke of Devonshire's house. In 1922 it was let to Lord NORTHCLIFFE. By this time the Press baron had gone completely 'ga-ga' and was living in a little hut on the roof. It was here he died on August 14, 1922.

11, W.E. GLADSTONE (LCP 1925) 1856-1875. This house was actually on part of the site of the Prince Regent's Carlton House.

13, W.E. GLADSTONE (again!) 1839-1848. Gladstone was very loyal to this area as it was an easy walk for him to the Houses of Parliament across St James's Park.

14 and 15, the town house of the Earls of LONSDALE. The corpse of the 4th Earl was brought here by cab in February 1882 as he had very inconsiderately expired in his mistress's house on the other side of Hyde Park! When his brother, the 5th Earl (who lived here for 62 years) took over the property, the entire first floor of *both* houses was one gigantic ballroom.

20, Sir Gilbert PARKER, 1904. Here he wrote *Old Quebec, a History*.

CARLYLE SQUARE, SW3
Piccadilly, District and Circle lines to South Kensington

Originally this was Oakley Square after the courtesy title in the Cadogan family. It was changed in 1972 to Carlyle in honour of Thomas CARLYLE who, though a Scotsman, had lived in Cheyne Row since 1834. In the 18th century the Square was a market garden owned by a Mr. Hutchings who, in 1771, had his house burgled and the occupants of it murdered by four Jews, all of whom were hanged. In 1796, stags were actually hunted in the area.

2, Sir Osbert SITWELL. He moved here in the spring of 1920 and stayed for 40 years. In the house he had a table; its marble top resting on two bronze lions which had come from a *chiffonier* in Carlton House, the Prince Regent's London home.

14, Alfred North WHITEHEAD, in the 1920s. He was living here when he won the first James Scott Prize in 1922.

24, Ruth DRAPER, May 1933. 'London is lovely – the parks a dream – and I have a darling house.' (In 1934 she seriously considered buying the house and 'doing it over'.)

41, Vyvyan HOLLAND from 1929; for some years. Here he used to give dinner parties where superb wines were served to *really* appreciative guests and knowledgeable *oenophiles.*

CARLYLE Dumfriesshire, December 4, 1795
Thomas Chelsea, February 4, 1881
Philosopher Ecclefechan, Scotland

24 (formerly 5) Cheyne Row, SW3, 1834 until he died here. It is now a Carlyle Museum, owned by the National Trust.

Carlyle was the second son of a stonemason. After his preliminary schooling, he went on to Edinburgh University where he excelled in geometry. By 1813 he had begun to study intending to become a Church of Scotland Minister. He tried teaching but found his heart was not in it, neither was it in mathematics, the law *nor* the Church.

In 1821 he met the 20-year-old daughter and heiress of Dr. John Welsh of Haddington. Five years later he and Jane were married. During their five-year courtship, Carlyle came south to London and stayed there until his *Life of Schiller* was published in 1825. From then on he was practically always busy on books, essays or articles. The book that really established him both as an historian and a philosopher was his *French Revolution,* published in 1837. By this time Jane and he were settled in Cheyne Row and he began his largest work, *The History of Frederick the Great.* It took him 14 years to complete and appeared from 1858 to 1865.

He was always hyper-sensitive to noise and had had a supposedly sound proof room built at the top of the house, but it did not effectively shut out the normal domestic noise which irritated him so much.

There is a bronze statue of Carlyle, seated, in the little Cheyne Gardens between Cheyne Row and the Chelsea Embankment. It was the work of Sir Joseph Boehm and was erected in 1882.

CARRINGTON Hereford, March 29, 1893
Dora de Houghton Hungerford, March 11, 1932
Artist

16, Yeomans Row, SW3, 1916
70, Frith Street, W1, 1917
3, Gower Street, WC1, 1917
41, Gordon Square, WC1, 1920
37, Gordon Square, WC1, 1920

Carrington – she always preferred to be called by her surname only – was one of the 'Bloomsbury Set' (if such a 'set' existed.) She was a competent artist and she moved in artistic circles. In 1916 she met Lytton STRACHEY and, eventually, lived with him, despite Strachey being totally homosexual and she being married to Ralph Partridge (in 1921). She also had love *affaires* with Mark GERTLER, Gerald Brennan and Bernard Penrose. Her pet names for Strachey were 'Bugger-wug' or 'rat Husband' (*such* a pet).

After Strachey died in January 1932, Carrington became distraught: everyone thought she had got over his premature death – he was not yet 52 – but less than two months later she shot herself.

CARSON   Dublin, February 9, 1854
(Lord) Edward Henry   Ramsgate, October 10, 1935
Solicitor General

19, Bury Street, W1, 1893
39, Rutland Gate, SW7, 1899
5, Eaton Place, SW1, 1922-1935

Son of a Dublin architect, Carson was educated entirely in Ireland, finishing off with a degree from Trinity College, Dublin. He had been called to the Irish bar in 1880 and to the English bar in 1894. He was one of the most successful lawyers ever. In 1899 his fee book earnings were over £20,000 and he is said to have refused other briefs which would have been worth £30,000 to his practice.

Carson was *violently* opposed to Home Rule for Ireland and it was he who organized the Ulster Volunteers (nicknamed 'Carson's Army') to oppose the creation of an Irish Sovereign State. He was Solicitor General (of England) 1900-1906: Attorney General in 1915 and First Lord of the Admiralty two years later. He was made a life peer and chose Lord Carson of Duncairn as his title.

CARTE   Greek Street, W1, May 3, 1844
Richard D'Oyly   London, April 3, 1901
Impressario

71, Russell Square, WC1 (pre-1888)
4, Adelphi Terrace, WC2, 1888-1901

D'Oyly Carte was responsible for staging all GILBERT and SULLIVAN's operas and he also built the Savoy Hotel. The Gilbert and Sullivan partnership, off stage, was rancorous and Carte really did very little to pour oil on the troubled duo. He usually was not on speaking terms with one or other of them (Gilbert was the most cantankerous of the three). But the operas were a success in every sense and the company formed by Carte for staging them, lasted until 1981.

CASSON   May 23, 1910
(Sir) Hugh Maxwell
Architect

35, Victoria Road, W8, until 1980
60, Elgin Crescent, W11, from 1980

Casson began in practice as an architect in 1937. The firm still flourishes wonderfully in 35, Thurloe Place, SW7. Interestingly the largest, newest and nearest building, the centre for the Ismailis – the followers of the Aga Khan – is designed by Casson. Its be-marbled exterior, facing the Victoria and Albert Museum, has *not* won wholesale acclaim. *Per contra* Casson described Aston Webb's Victoria and Albert building as, 'Clumsy, overcooked and confused'. When the Second World War began, Casson's talents were soon utilized as a camouflage officer in the Air Ministry.

Casson has served on a number of diverse committees: he was a member of the Royal Danish Academy and, nearer home, a member of the Royal Mint Advisory Committee since 1972.

He has published a number of books on buildings, both from the technical and historical points of view. He also provided the delightful line drawings to Joyce GRENFELL's little book, *Nanny Says* (1972).

CASTLEREAGH
(Viscount) Robert Stewart
Politician

Dublin, June 18, 1769
Foot's Cray, Kent, August 12, 1822
(by suicide)

18, St James's Square, SW1, 1815-1822

His father was a landed Irish landowner and his wealth was partly responsible for his being raised to the rank of Viscount in 1796. In 1816 he was created Marquess of Londonderry, just five years before he died. He spent nearly £60,000 on getting Robert a seat in the House of Commons as member for County Down. Robert polled 3,114 votes and came second to Lord Hillsborough. Down was a 'double member' seat and by the standards possible in the 18th century, the poll was a heavy one. However, rich though the family might have been, the outlay of sixty thousand pounds reduced their fortune so much that they were never as rich after the election ever again. He became an MP in the Whig cause but 'crossed the floor' to join PITT, who became his 'hero'. Despite this political coat-turning he lost office in 1801.

He was Foreign Secretary in Lord LIVERPOOL's Government (Prime Minister, 1812-1827) and did much to combat the apathy of the coalition against Napoleon. He was due to attend the Congress of Vienna when he committed suicide by cutting his throat with a penknife.

His friends had worried over his moodiness and unusual lapses of memory. Even the often obtuse King George IV thought it rather odd, when Castlereagh told him that he feared he was to be arrested on the same charge as the Bishop of Clogher (on a charge of homosexual behaviour with a soldier in July 1822, in a back room of a tavern. Both were arrested. The Bishop was given bail and fled the country. The unfortunate soldier was sent to prison.) 'I'm mad,' said Castlereagh, 'I know I am mad'. He had recently asked his doctor as to the *precise* location of the jugular vein and there can be no doubt that he killed himself when his balance of mind was disturbed. The cut on his throat, apparently, was 'skilful and expert'.

CAVENDISH
Henry
Natural Philosopher

Nice, October 10, 1731
London, March 10, 1810
All Saint's Church, Derby

11, Bedford Square, WC1 (P) 1786-1810

Henry, the reclusive son of Lord Cavendish, was the first scientist to create water from its constituent elements by purely inductive experiment. He had been educated in Hackney, then Peterhouse, Cambridge (the oldest college there) but came down without a degree. He inherited a very substantial sum of money from an uncle and so was able to spend the rest of his life in scientific research.

Sir Joseph BANKS said of him that, '...he probably uttered fewer words in the course of his life than any man who has lived to four score years.' His library was four *miles* away from his house so he need not see people coming to take books from it and he communicated with his servants almost exclusively in writing.

As might be imagined, he never married but when he died, this 'Founder of Pneumatic Chemistry' left over one million pounds to his relatives.

CAVENDISH PLACE W1

*Bakerloo, Central and Victoria lines
to Oxford Circus*

The Place, Cavendish Square, Old and New Cavendish Streets were developed by Edward Harley about four years after he had married Henrietta Cavendish in 1713. She was a descendant of the Dukes of Newcastle.

2, Quintin HOGG at the time of his death in 1903.

14, George STREET (LCP 1980) 1870. It was when he was living here that he began to think about the plans for the Royal Courts of Justice in the Strand. He never lived to see the final pile, which eventually had over 1,000 rooms.

CAVENDISH SQUARE, W1

The Square was laid out in 1718 but building was held up by the number of financial failures following the 'bursting of the South Sea Bubble'.

As the South Sea Bubble is mentioned under various headings, a few words of explanation might be useful. 'South Sea House' used to stand at the north-east end of Threadneedle Street and housed the business of 'The Governor and Company of Merchants of Great Britain trading to the South Seas and other parts of America'. They floated a scheme for which Harley – the 2nd Earl of Oxford – was principally responsible in 1711, to fund a floating debt of £9,177,967 and the purchasers would become stockholders in a company which would have the monopoly of the trade with Spanish South America. At the same time the company offered to take over the National Debt. £100 shares in the company rapidly increased to £890 and then finally over £1,000 each. Speculation in the company was frantic, but then Spain refused to enter into commercial relations with Britain and the 'bubble burst'. Hundreds of families were bankrupted by 1720.

5, Captain (sic) Horatio NELSON and *Mrs*. Nelson in 1787.

5, Quintin HOGG (LCP 1965) 1885-1898.

8, Sydney SMITH, 1804. He was a preacher at Coram's Foundlings Hospital at this time.

12, Wilkie COLLINS lived here with one of his numerous mistresses from 1859-1864.

15, Sir Jonathan HUTCHINSON (LCP 1981) 1874-1913. He was appointed President of the Royal College of Surgeons whilst living here.

19, William HEINEMANN, the founder of Heinemann's publishing house in 1890, lived here between 1914-1918.

20, H.H. ASQUITH (LCP 1951). This house was given to Margot Asquith by her father (the 'BART') when she married ASQUITH in 1894. The Asquiths gave their last dinner party in this house in March 1922. They put the house up for sale at £30,000. It was not an easy house to run and in the Asquith's day, the meals had to be carried from the kitchen across an *open* courtyard and then into the house itself! They had an indoor staff of 14 *plus* a coachman and a stable boy.
In 1907 Raymond Asquith thought that the house was, '...quite uninhabitable. Margot's nurse' [presumably the nursemaid for his half brother and sister] 'is still there, which means I have to sleep in the bathroom. Also all the servants are new and mad. There is one man who has socks which chirp like crickets all through dinner and another who hands one brown sugar with the partridges instead of bread crumbs.'

20, Lady 'Emerald' CUNARD rented the house from the Asquiths in 1916 and when Asquith lost the premiership in that year – and so had to quit 10 Downing Street – Lady Cunard insisted that Margot Asquith had back her own bedroom and sitting room while Lady C. lived on the floor above.

35, Dr. Victor HORSLEY, 1891.

32, George ROMNEY, 1777-1799. He painted many portraits of Emma HAMILTON (whom he adored) in this house. This was before her involvement with NELSON. Sir Joshua REYNOLDS, in many ways a rival of Romney, could not stand the younger artist and used to refer to him as 'That man in Cavendish Square'. It is estimated that Romney produced over 2,000 paintings, sketches and drawings while he lived here. The house had been built for Francis Cotes, RA, who died in it in 1770, aged 45.

The statue on the south side of the Square is that of Lord William Bentinck (1802-1848) a bronze by Thomas Campbell (1790-1858) and was erected here in 1851.

CAYLEY (Sir) George *Aviation Pioneer*	Scarborough, Yorks., December 27, 1773 Brompton Hall, Yorks., December 15, 1857

20, Hertford Street, W1 (LCP 1962) 1840-1848

In 1808 Cayley designed and *flew* a glider having a wing area of about 300 square feet (27.87 square metres) and by so doing was really the inventor of the first heavier-than-air 'flying machine'. In 1853 he designed a glider which actually carried a 'pilot'.

More down to earth, he designed *caterpillar treads* for a sort of tractor; a very sophisticated telescope and also produced designs for some very advanced artificial limbs.

CECIL Edgar Algernon Robert (1st Viscount Cecil) *Creator of the League of Nations*	September 14, 1864 November 24, 1958

100, Grosvenor Road, SW1, until 1922
16, South Eaton Place, SW1 (LCP 1976) 1923-1958.

Cecil was the third son of the 3rd Marquess of Salisbury and in the First World War had worked for the Red Cross, and afterwards was made assistant Secretary of State for Foreign Affairs.

Having seen so much of the bloody horrors of war at first hand he produced a document, which effectively became the first draft of the Covenant of the League of Nations. ·The League came into being on January 10, 1920 and at one time had 60 member-nations. It ground to a halt as America would not join – though Woodrow Wilson worked hard for the League – and Russia was excluded by the League itself. Its last plenary meeting was on April 18, 1946 and it had been more than replaced by the inauguration of the United Nations on October 24, 1945. Despite the failure of 'his' League, Cecil wholeheartedly supported the United Nations.

CHADWICK (Sir) Edwin *Sanitary Pioneer*	Manchester, January 24, 1801 East Sheen, Surrey, July 6, 1890 Old Mortlake Cemetary

9, Stanhope Terrace, W2 (P)

Chadwick had been called to the Bar in 1831, but he always had the interests of the (too numerous) poor of London, especially the unbelievably awful unhygenic conditions, under which they were obliged to live, at heart.

He had become a close friend of Jeremy BENTHAM who left Chadwick a substantial portion of his extensive library, when he died in 1832. Chadwick gave up the law and got himself appointed as an assistant commissioner working on the 'Poor Laws'.

In 1847 he expanded his brief and pressed for a proper and separate drainage system to be created for London. This was put in hand and by 1865 an efficient system (which is substantially the same today in the central London area) was constructed under the engineer, Sir Joseph BAZALGETTE. Chadwick also brought about beneficial alterations in the sanitary rules of practice for the Indian Army.

CHALLONER Lewes, September 29, 1691
(Bishop) Richard London, January 12, 1781
Divine Milton, Nr. Abingdon, Berkshire

44, Old Gloucester Street, WC1 (P) from 1780 until he died here

A Catholic, Challoner was made Bishop of Debra, having been over 25 years at the English College at Douai, a Roman Catholic University 18 miles south of Lille. Challoner was at Debra from 1740 to 1758 when he was appointed Vicar Apostolic in London.

It was a bad time for Catholics. Lord George Gordon (1751-1793) fanned the flames of religious intolerance and stirred up feelings in London to such an extent that on June 8, 1780 troops had to be called in to deal with rioters. Gordon was tried for his part in the unrest (they have been known ever since as the Gordon Riots) but was acquitted through lack of evidence. Prudently, Challoner moved up to Highgate during the height of the rising.

In 1750 he had published the *Rheims New Testament* and the *Douai Bible with Annotations*. This latter is the version used by the majority of English-speaking Catholics. Challoner produced a number of other pieces of Catholic literature, many becoming standard works on their subject and quite a few still used 200 years later.

CHAMBERLAIN Birmingham, March 18, 1869
Arthur Neville Heckfield Park, Nr. Reading,
Prime Minister November 11, 1940
  Cremated at Golders Green (plaque in
  South aisle, Westminster Abbey)

35, Egerton Crescent, SW3, 1920-1922
37, Eaton Square, SW1 (LCP 1962) 1923-1935

Neville Chamberlain was the son of Joseph CHAMBERLAIN by his second wife, Florence. He was to become MP for the Ladywood division of Britian's second largest city, Birmingham, from 1918-1929. Without any political fire-works, he rose steadily through the ranks until he became Prime Minister of a Coalition Government on May 28, 1937.

In 1938 Hitler was threatening Europe with his territorial demands and on September 29 of that year, Chamberlain went to Munich to meet Hitler, Daladier and Mussolini. He came back to England to announce that there would be 'peace in our time'. Less than a year later Britain and Germany were at war. By May 1940 the Nazis had thrust their all-conquering army through Europe. Chamberlain was under too great pressure and he resigned on May 10, leaving CHURCHILL in control.

CHAMBERS Stockholm, 1726
(Sir) William London, March 8, 1796
Architect

53, Berners Street, W1, c.1786-1796

Stockholm born, of Scottish parents, Chambers was entirely brought up in

England. His greatest surviving work is Somerset House. This massive building of Portland stone was begun in 1776 and so called because it covers the site of the palace of 'Protector' Somerset, built between 1547 and 1552. Edward Seymour, born c.1506 and beheaded in London on January 22, 1552, was created Duke of Somerset in 1546. He was the brother of Jane Seymour, Henry VIII's third wife, and uncle to the boy King, Edward VI. He played a leading part in his short reign. The courtyard of Somerset House, into which the main entrance in the Strand leads, measures 310x350 feet (94x106 metres). The river frontage is 800 feet (243 metres) long and rests on 'massive arches with vermiculated rustication' (Pevsner).

Chambers was a tall, aristocratic man with refined Gallic tastes who behaved like an aristocrat, especially in his job as Treasurer of the Royal Academy where he made even the autocratic President, Sir Joshua REYNOLDS, seem humble.

CHANDOS STREET, W1

Bakerloo, Victoria and Central lines to Oxford Circus

James Brydges, 1st Duke of Chandos and Edward Harley were the first real 'property developers' in this area. Chandos, however, had invested quite heavily in the 'South Sea Bubble' and his losses on it made it necessary to curtail his property plans.

8, Washington IRVING, 1829-1832, when he was assistant to the American Ambassador of the day.

CHANNON
(Sir) Henry ('Chips')
Politician (inter alia)

March 7, 1897
October 7, 1958

21, St James's Place, SW1, 1935
5, Belgrave Square, SW1, 1936-1958

Channon was a socialite of American origins who married the wealthy Lady Honor Guinness (of 'Guinness is Good for You' brewing fame). He was put into the safe Tory parliamentary seat of Southend by the Iveaghs (the ennobled form of Guinness) and, in due time, this kept-warm seat passed on to his son Paul.

Nancy CUNARD was staying at the Ritz in Paris just after the First World War when she met Channon, 'hanging about'. In her diary she wrote that the 'young Chips Channon' was, 'an *odious* little snob, American'.

Despite Honor (and Paul) Channon was one of London's wealthy homosexuals and his wealth enabled him (sometimes) to buy sexual favours where those favours would otherwise have not been forthcoming.

CHANTREY
(Sir) Francis Legatt
Sculptor and benefactor

Norton, Derbyshire, April 7, 1781
London, November 25, 1842
Norton

24, Curzon Street, W1, 1806

Orphaned as a very young boy, Chantrey worked as a farm labourer and then, in 1797, was apprenticed to a wood carver and gilder in Sheffield. When he was 21 he gave Ramsay, the carver to whom he was apprenticed, the last £50 he owned to cancel his indentures, even though he only had six months of his apprenticeship left to serve.

He painted portraits of Yorkshire worthies but came south to London after visiting Ireland (where he caught a fever which left him almost entirely bald). He married his cousin Mary Ann Wale either in 1807 (according to the *Dictionary of National Biography*) or 1809 or 1811: there seem to be three separate authorities. Whichever the year, Mary Ann brought with her a fortune of £10,000, with which he bought ground and built two houses and a studio.

He made a statue of King George IV, who, on seeing it complete, is supposed to have said, 'Mr. Chantrey, I have reason to be obliged to you, for you have immortalized me'. This statue is one of two of George IV at Windsor Castle. Chantrey made two others, one is in Brighton and the other is an equestrian statue of the King, which was intended to be put on *top* of the Marble Arch! The Arch was then in front of Buckingham Palace where the Queen Victoria Memorial group now stands. Commonsense and judgement altered that decision and the piece now stands at the north-east corner of Trafalgar Square.

CHARLES STREET, W1
Piccadilly, Jubilee and Victoria lines to Green Park

Built on Berkeley family land by the 5th Baron Berkeley about 1742. The Baron had a brother and an Uncle who had both been christened Charles.

6, John RUSKIN lived here briefly not long after his marriage to 'Effie' in 1848.

18, John HOPPNER, from 1784 until he died here in 1810, when he was only 52 years old.

18A, Ruth DRAPER 1927. She rented the apartment here for just a few months for one of her (practically annual) tours of England.

20, the 5th Lord ROSEBERRY was born here in 1847 (LCP 1962). It is altogether fitting that a plaque should be here as it was he who suggested that the London County Council should have an 'historical department' to commemorate famous houses with distinctive plaques.

33, Sydney SMITH, 1836-1839. In November 1835 he wrote that he had bought, '...a house in Charles Street (lease for 14 years)...for £1,400 and £10 per annum ground rent'.

34, Gugliemo MARCONI, 1906-1907, by which time his invention of the 'wireless' was well established.

43, 'Beau' BRUMMEL, as a boy, c.1792, when he had just started at Eton.

47, John Hay BEITH ('Ian Hay') 1936-1945. From 1939 to 1945, Beith was director of Public Relations at the War Office.

On the north side of Charles Street was a tavern, called, in full, 'I am the only running footman'. There is a story that George MORLAND could only settle his bill here by painting a new inn sign for the landlord.

CHARLOTTE STREET, W1
Northern line to Goodge Street

Named in honour of Queen Charlotte (Charlotte of Mecklenburg-Strelitz) the plain but fecund consort of King George III. She married George in 1761 when she was 17. She had 15 children by him and died at Kew, two years before her demented spouse, in 1818.

3, Theodore HOOK was born here in 1788.

15, David GARNETT had rooms here in 1939. A year later the house was destroyed in an air raid.

63 (then 35) John CONSTABLE from the autumn of 1822 until he eventually died in the house in 1837. In 1826 he had taken a house at Well Walk, Hampstead where his wife and children lived. She died in 1828 and though he kept on the Hampstead house he lived mostly here.

81, Sir Robert SMIRKE (LCP 1979) 1833-1842, during which time he was engaged on building the vast British Museum.

85 (in his day 63) Daniel MACLISE, 1835-1836. In 1836 there was a fire in the house and John CONSTABLE (at 35, opposite) finding that one of the servants in MACLISE's house had left her life savings in her garret room, went into the burning building and recovered the poor woman's money.

101, Dr. Victor HORSLEY in 1882 when he shared lodgings with a fellow doctor, Charles Bond.

CHATTERTON	Bristol, November 20, 1752
Thomas	London, August 25, 1770
Poet and forger	Shoe Lane Workhouse Burial Ground

4, Brooke Street, EC1, from the middle of June 1770 until he committed suicide here.

Chatterton was the posthumous son of a Bristol 'writing master' and his mother kept a Dame's School but sent the boy to Colston's Blue Coat School (where he was judged to be a dull student). He began his true poetical career in 1764 with a poem he called *Apostate Will*. Not long after he found some genuine 15th century documents in the Church of St Mary Redcliffe not far from his home. He began to write the 'works' of a monk he called Thomas Rowley, whom he made out to be a friend of a (genuine) Bristol notable called William Canynge (who, despite the different spelling, was claimed as an ancestor by George CANNING, Prime Minister in 1827). Chatterton actually sent the bogus *Historic of Peyncters of England bie Thomas Rolie* to Horace WALPOLE, who was, for a time, deceived. Chatterton also sent other 'examples' to a London publisher called Dodsley, who was not so easily deceived.

The boy was apprenticed to John Lambert, a Bristol attorney, on July 1, 1767 but they did not suit each other at all and Thomas eventually came up to London in April 1770.

He achieved nothing in London; he first stayed in Shoreditch with relatives but came to Brooke Street in June 1770 and here, with no money, no encouragement and little hope, he killed himself by drinking arsenic. It is extraordinary to think that a boy, before he was 18 years old, could have produced (forged or not) works of the quality he exhibited. His *Rowley* poems are truly the work of genius and one can only hope that he gained some comfort by seeing his piece, *Elinoure and Juga* published in his lifetime – he was not 12 when he wrote it.

CHELSEA

The name is probably derived from the Saxon word *ceosol*, which described the gravel formation of the banks of the Thames. John Norden (1548–c.1620) a map maker, wrote that, 'Cheselsey was called from the nature of the place whose strand' [ie river bank] 'is like the Chesel'. Geologically that is probably so but Quentin Crisp, who was quite pleased to be referred to as one of the 'stately homos of England', once wrote that Chelsea is the *one* area of London, '…in which you can behave *so* badly with so little risk'.

CHELSEA EMBANKMENT SW3
District or Circle lines
to Sloane Square

The Embankment was built by Sir Joseph BAZALGETTE. It was finished in 1874, the year he was knighted. It involved (*inter alia*) the reclamation of 10 acres (4.04 hectares) of land from the Thames.

9 (once called 'TURNER's Reach') the Marquess of RIPON (LCP 1959) 1890-1909. The Marquess lived here for the last 19 years of his life.

14, Peter USTINOV, 1949-1953. When he came here he had just reached the last stages of his divorce from his first wife, Isolde; he lived on here until a short while before he took on wife Number Two, Suzanne Cloutier.

CHELSEA PARK GARDENS, SW3

96, Sir Alfred MUNNINGS (P 1960) 1920-1960. Onto the house, Sir Alfred had built a large studio.

CHELSEA SQUARE, SW3   *District and Circle lines to Sloane Square*

This used to be called Trafalgar Square: leading off Manresa Road, both being Spanish place names. Trafalgar Square changed to Chelsea in 1937.

18, Ethel SANDS, 1944-1962. It was to this house in June 1961 that Aldous HUXLEY came to tea. Another guest that day was Enid BAGNOLD, who had not seen Huxley for many years. She introduced herself and said, '...you were an odious little boy'. To which Huxley replied, 'I'm odious still'.

51, Ethel SANDS, 1937. This house, originally built in 1938, was destroyed by bombing in 1941.

CHESHAM PLACE, SW1   *Piccadilly line to Knightsbridge*

William Lowndes (1652-1724) a political wheeler-dealer made a lot of money from (and speculation in) the home counties and then moved into town and concentrated on high class property, first in Soho and later in what is now loosely termed 'Belgravia'. The family had a house at Chesham in Buckinghamshire.

25, Moreton FREWEN, 1896-1900.

25, Sir George Sitwell, father of EDITH OSBERT and Sacheverell (1860-1943) took this house in 1900 'for the season'. John Singer SARGENT painted the Sitwell family portrait here.

36, Syrie MAUGHAM, 1936. She moved here after selling the Chelsea house when her marriage to W. Somerset MAUGHAM finally failed. Cecil BEATON took over the flat when Syrie went to Paris (to live in a small flat on the Place Vendôme) in 1939.

37 (until 1852 it was numbered 32) Lord John RUSSELL (LCP 1911) 1841-1870. He had the house built for him and he became Prime Minister for the first time five years after moving in. Lady Russell felt that the post taxed his 'naturally feeble frame'. Despite such wifely fears he lived to be Prime Minister again and did not die until he was 86.

CHESTERFIELD	London, September 27, 1694
Philip Dormer Stanhope (4th Earl)	London, March 24, 1773
Statesman	Originally in the Grosvenor Chapel, South Audley Street, then at Shelford, Notts.

45, Bloomsbury Square, WC1 (P. 1907)
Chesterfield House, South Audley Street, W1, where he died

A supporter of WALPOLE, Chesterfield was MP for St Germains, in Cornwall, from 1715 to 1722 and then for Lostwithiel until 1723 and succeeded his father, the 3rd Earl, in 1726. In that year he was made Ambassador to the Hague. Later he changed his politics, supported Pelham and was appointed Lord Lieutenant of Ireland in 1746.

Outside the world of politics he had many literary friends: Swift, POPE and JOHNSON (who once wrote him a stern letter rebuking him for his failure as a patron). Chesterfield's place in literature must be given to his *Letters*. There were addressed to his 'Godson and Successor' (in fact, his bastard son, Philip) giving him practical advice on the etiquette and deportment required of an aristocratic youth in the mid-18th century. Chesterfield can have had little useful advice from *his* father. His *grandfather* the 2nd Earl was a rake, given to gambling and 'exceeding wildness' and was once imprisoned in the Tower for duelling. The *Letters* were never practically effective as 'godson' Philip, a poor, wet thing, died young.

The Chesterfield Motto was: *A Deo et Rege* – From God and King.

CHESTERFIELD STREET, W1   *Piccadilly line to Hyde Park Corner*

Philip Dormer Stanhope, 4th Earl of Chesterfield, built a magnificent house here and moved into it on March 13, 1749. Its gardens covered today's Chesterfield Street and more. It was built by Isaac Ware on ground belonging to Lord Crewe. In his *Letters* to his son (see CHESTERFIELD above) Chesterfield refers to the 'Canonical Pillars' of the house. A pun intended, as the pillars came from Lord CHANDOS's house, Canons, at Edgware.

4,   'Beau' BRUMMEL 1799-1810. It was in this house that the Prince Regent, '...began to blubber when told that Brummel did not like the cut of his coat'.

6,   Catherine WALTERS ('Skittles') c.1860-1872. When she moved in here, she had money problems and was in between lovers.

6,   Somerset MAUGHAM (LCP 1975) 1911-1919. The house has been completely rebuilt since Maugham's day.

CHESTER (in 'Belgravia')

The SW1 'Chesters' are very distinct from the Regent's Park variety. These lie on land owned by the Dukes of Westminster and Westminsters, who, apart from owning an incredible amount of land in London, own large bits in and around the Cathedral City of Chester.

CHESTER SQUARE, SW1   *District and Circle lines to Sloane Square*

It began to be built up in 1840.

1,   Sir Ralph RICHARDSON, 1950s.

2,   Matthew ARNOLD (LCP 1954) 1858-1868. '...a house in Chester Square. It is a very small one but it will be something to unpack one's portmanteau the first time since I was married.'

8,   Mrs. Neville CHAMBERLAIN, widow of Neville C., Prime Minister, died here in February 1967.

14, Harold MACMILLAN (created Earl of Stockton in 1984) lived here from 1922-1929.

24, Mary SHELLEY (née Godwin) (P 1977) SHELLEY's second wife died here in 1851. Shelley's mother had lived here previously.

CHESTER TERRACE, SW1

43, W.H. AUDEN, 1929. He was in London as a tutor to an eight-year old boy, called Peter Benenson (who, some years later, founded Amnesty International). AUDEN was *supposed* to be staying with the boy's aunt, Manya Harari, in Bayswater.

57, T.S. ELIOT, 1926. Whilst he was living here, ELIOT became a member of the Church of England.

CHESTERTON   London, May 29, 1874
Gilbert Keith   Beaconsfield, June 14, 1936
Author

32, Sheffield Terrace, W8 (P) here born and lived until 1881
1, Edwardes Square, W8, 1901-1904

Chesterton left St Paul's School in 1892 and went on to the Slade School of

Art. He began writing for periodicals whilst still at the Slade and some of his best essays appeared in *The Bookman The Speaker* and, later on, in his own *GK's Weekly* which he started in 1925. The *Weekly* was originally his brother Cecil's magazine called *New Witness*.

He joined the Catholic Church in 1922 having recognized which way his religious feelings had been heading for some years. In 1911 the first of many detective stories featuring 'Father Brown' appeared. John O'Connor (later Monsignor) a Bradford priest who received G.K.C. into the Church of Rome, was the original on whom 'Father Brown' was based.

In 1908 he published *The Man who was Thursday,* which is thought by some to be the prototype of almost every spy story since.

He was (literally) an enormous man, very quick witted, but *very* absent minded. Apropos his feeding habits, Chesterton wrote in his *Autobiography* that he had '...never been anything so refined as a *gourmet*; so I am being a glutton. My ignorance of cooking is such that I can even eat the food in the most fashionable and expensive hotels in London.'

CHEYNE

Charles Cheyne, Viscount Newhaven (c.1624–1698 and sometimes spelt *Chiene*) bought the Manor of Chelsea, so becoming Lord of the Manor, in 1657. Cheyne Walk and Cheyne Row had begun to be built before his son, William, sold the Manor to Sir Hans Sloane in 1712.

CHEYNE ROW, SW3
District and Circle lines
to Sloane Square, then quite a long walk

21, James McNeil WHISTLER 1890-1892. A magazine journalist of the 'Society' page reported that, 'All through the summer Mr. Whistler holds a kind of reception every Sunday afternoon in the garden at the back of his house. You meet all sorts of conditions of people there – men of light and leading in the world of art and literature: tenth-rate daubers who adulate him, and whom he takes pleasure in constantly snubbing...'

24 (until 1877, No.5) Thomas CARLYLE (P) from 1834 until he died here in 1881. In May 1834 Carlyle wrote to his wife, Jane: 'The house is eminent, wainscotted to the very ceiling. Broadish stairs, massive balustrade thick as one's thigh. Three stories, everyone three apartments in depth. Front and back dining rooms. On the whole a massive, roomy sufficient old house with places, for example, to hang, say, three dozen hats or cloaks on and as many crevices and queer old shelved closets as would gratify the most covetous Goody. Rent £35. I confess I am strongly tempted.'

The house was purchased in 1895 as a sort of 'shrine' to Carlyle and the German Emperor, Queen Victoria's grandson, donated £100 toward the purchase price.

30, William DE MORGAN, 1872-1881. Here he built a firing kiln in his back garden and acquired the art and technique of tile glazing.

The houses numbered from 16 to 34, inclusive, were built in 1708.

CHEYNE WALK, SW3

Numbers 3 to 6 were built in 1717/18.

3, Sir John GOSS, 1850s. During the period he lived here, Goss was the organist at St Paul's Cathedral.

4, Daniel MACLISE died here in 1870.

4, Mary Anne Evans ('George Eliot') (LCP 1949) 1880. She died in this house only a few weeks after moving in and just a few months after she married John Cross.

10, Count Alfred D'ORSAY, early 1830s.

10, David LLOYD-GEORGE, 1924-1925.

13, Ralph VAUGHAN-WILLIAMS, pre-1914.

14, Bertrand RUSSELL, early 1900s. While here he published his brilliant *Principles of Mathematics* which established his reputation while he was still not yet 30.

16, Dante Gabriel ROSSETTI (LCP 1949) 1862-1882. In his time this was known as 'Tudor House'.

17, Thomas ATTWOOD died here in 1838.

17, Naomi MITCHINSON, 1919-1923. The dining room was on the ground floor and above it was an 'L'-shaped room which had two tall windows overlooking a balcony. In 1921 the Mitchinson's added another storey with dormer windows to make room for the first two of their (eventually) five children.

27, 'Bram' STOKER, in 1878, soon after his marriage to Florence Balcombe (1858-1937) an Irish girl and a daughter of an Army Officer. George DU MAURIER thought her one of the three most beautiful women he had ever seen. In 1882 Stoker saw a man leap into the Thames from a steamboat. Stoker leapt in after him and got the would-be suicide ashore. He took the insensible man into the house and, for the want of a better, or a more easily accessible, surface, laid him out on the dining room table, where, rather ungratefully, the man expired. Knowing nothing of all this drama, Florence Stoker came into her dining room to find the table laid-up with a corpse. (She never felt the same about the house after that.)

60, Thomas SHADWELL, the Poet Laureate died here in 1692.

74, James McNeil WHISTLER lived here for a year or so before dying in this house in July 1903.

91, Charles CONDER, 1904.

93, Mrs. GASKELL (LCP 1913) was born here in 1810. The house was then in Lindsey Row. Her mother, Mrs. Stevenson, died not long after Elizabeth's birth and so the infant was taken to Knutsford Cheshire, to be brought up by an aunt. Knutsford was the model for 'Cranford' made famous by her novel of that name which appeared in 1853.

93, William Bell SCOTT, 1860, having recently (and unhappily) married Mary Letitia Norquoy.

96, James McNeil WHISTLER (LCP 1925) 1866-1878. Here he painted the famous portrait of his mother which now hangs in the *Louvre*. WHISTLER delighted in giving dinner parties but as his means became more restricted he took to inviting guests to breakfast.

104, Walter GREAVES (LCP 1973) 1855-1897, who, with his brother, was frequently used as unpaid help by WHISTLER, who lived just along the road.

104, Hilaire BELLOC (LCP 1973). He moved here from Oxford and spent a lot of his time in nursing his future constituency in Salford and, after five years here, was elected to Parliament in 1906. He also wrote his *The Path to Rome* here. It was published in 1902.

104, James LEES-MILNE was here for some years until 1945. The house was badly damaged by bombs in the Second World War.

109, P. Wilson STEER (LCP 1967). He lived here for 40 years and, '...painted in the best bad taste'. He died in the house in 1942.

119, J.M.W. TURNER (P) from 1846 until his death here in 1851. He died 'without a groan' in his tiny bedroom overlooking the Thames. It was a foggy, December morning but, as he died, the sun broke through and shone full on his face. He had been known in the locality as 'Admiral Booth'. The house has been enlarged since 1851, but then, the undertakers could not get the coffin up the stairs and so the corpse had to come down to it.

131, Katherine MANSFIELD, 1910-1911. The previous year (1909) she had just got rid of her husband, Charles Bowden – having lived with him exactly one *week* and before she left this house she had become the mistress of Middleton MURRY.

CHOPIN
Frédéric François (or Frydeyk)
Pianist and composer

Zelazowa-Wola, Poland, March 1, 1809
Paris, October 17, 1849

99, Eaton Place, SW1 (P 1949) on June 23, 1848
4, St James's Place, SW1 (LCP 1981) 1848

His French father had settled in Poland and encouraged little Frederic in his music. Precociously, the boy first played in public when he was only just eight years old and he was 16 when he published his first composition, *Rondo in C Minor*. He studied at Warsaw until he was 20. He became known and almost lionized in Vienna and in 1831 moved on to Paris. He was a great hit but the various demands on him both musically and physically undermined his health.

Most of his compostions were for the piano but he did work orchestrally. He produced two concertos for piano and orchestra and in his short life found time to produce some 50 mazurkas, 27 *études,* 25 *preludes* 19 nocturnes, 13 waltzes and other pieces, not forgetting his funeral march.

Outside the Festival Hall on the South Bank is a piece of sculpture from which the head of Chopin sprouts, set on a black marble base. It is the work of a Polish sculptor; Kubica (b.1936). Its cost was largely covered by Polish citizens living in Britain.

CHRISTIE
Agatha Mary Clarissa
Author and playwright

Torquay, September 15, 1890
Wallingford, Berks, January 12, 1976

Sheffield Terrace, W8

Her father, F.A. Miller, was an American and she was almost entirely educated by her English mother. In her late teens she did go to school in Paris for a few terms.

In 1914 she married Colonel Archibald Christie by whom she had a daughter and soon after Mrs. Christie was working in a Torquay hospital while the Colonel fought in France. The marriage did not work out well after the War and they finally divorced in 1928. Just two years before the divorce Agatha Christie became involved in a real life mystery as intriguing as any she had devised for her 'thrillers'. In her first book, *The Mysterious Affair at Styles,* published 1920, she introduced 'Hercule Poirot, her little, pompous Belgian detective. Five more appeared and the sixth, in 1926, was *The Murder of Roger Ackroyd,* which really established her reputation.

On December 3, 1926 she disappeared! On the 4th her 'two-seater' was found, crashed, not far from her home at Newlands Corner, Surrey and one of her gloves was found in a nearby bush. On December 14 she was found (not only alive, but well) in a hotel in Harrogate, 200 miles away. During the ten days absence, for which no satisfactory explanation has been given, she was 'sighted' frequently once, even, on a London bus disguised as a man!

In 1930 she and her daughter Rosalind were travelling abroad when they met the archaeologist Max MALLOWAN. She married him in the same year and when in England they lived mostly at their attractive Devonshire home, Greenaway House, Churston Ferrers. Mallowan was knighted in 1968 and so she became Lady Mallowan.

She published over 70 books, the last being *Rule of Three* in 1962, but her most incredible work must be her play, *The Mousetrap*. This slight, murder mystery opened on November 25, 1952 at the Ambassadors Theatre. After 8,862 performances, it moved to the St Martin's on March 25, 1974 and on July 22, 1980 it had clocked up 11,500 performances.

CHURCHILL	Brooklyn, January 9, 1854
(Lady) Randolph	Blenheim Palace, June 29, 1921
Politician's wife	Bladon, Oxfordshire

35A, Great Cumberland Place, W1, 1896–1914
32, Dover Street, W1, 1914
72, Brook Street, W1, 1916
8, Westbourne Street, W2
For previous addresses see Lord RANDOLPH

Jennie was one of the three beautiful daughters of Leonard Jerome (1818-1891). Jerome was a rich 'self-made' American business man and proud of it.
Miss Jerome and her sisters came to England and the eldest girl, Clara, married Morton FREWEN; Jennie (the middle sister) married Lord Randolph CHURCHILL, the 3rd son of the 7th Duke of Marlborough, in 1874 and Leonie, the youngest, married Sir Jack Leslie.
Lady Randolph was much admired by a number of well-to-do gentlemen, not the least of whom was HRH Albert Edward, Prince of Wales. She was a loving mother, but there are letters from Winston (then at Harrow) chiding Jennie for not coming to see him. However, when he went into politics, she was indefatigable in promoting her son. Winston once told ASQUITH that his mother, '...had left no stone unturned, no cutlet uncooked' on his behalf and she '...lobbied and lunched for him'.
Jennie was 41, but certainly did not look it and men still flattered her and she them. She married George Cornwallis-West in 1900. He was 16 days older than Winston! Predictably the marriage failed and CORNWALLIS-WEST went on to marry, unhappily, twice again, before committing suicide in 1951. Jennie married again; this time, Montagu Porch, who was 23 years younger than herself, and nearly three years younger than his stepson. Porch died, aged 87, in 1963.

CHURCHILL	Blenheim Palace, Oxon, February 13,
(Lord) Randolph Henry Spencer	1849
Politician	London, January 24, 1895
	Bladon, Oxon.

1, Curzon Street, W1
48, Charles Street, W1, 1874–1878
29, St James's Place, SW1, 1878–1880
2, Connaught Place, W1 (LCP 1962) 1881–1892
50, Grosvenor Square, W1, where he died

Lord Randolph was the third son of the 7th Duke of Marlborough. John Churchill was owner – and builder – of Blenheim Palace, victor of the battle of that name on August 13, 1704 and created Duke of Marlborough by a grateful Queen Anne. There was little chance that Randolph would inherit the Dukedom (or the money that went with it) and so he went into politics, secure that he would not have to go to the Upper Chamber when the 7th Duke died, which he did in 1883.
In 1880 he made himself politically conspicuous by forming a group that came to be called 'The Fourth Party'. Some people saw him as a potential leader of a (changed) Conservative Party and so eventually Prime Minister. In the event he got as far as Leader of the House of Commons but resigned the position in 1886.
He had become increasingly fractious and harder and harder to deal with. A

long sea voyage was 'prescribed' and off they sailed; but, as the ship approached the Far East, Lord Randolph became totally deranged and actually dangerous. The Churchills hurried back to England but death was obviously near. The last month of his life was spent in Grosvenor Square where, '...he lingered pitifully until very early on the morning of 24 January the numbing fingers of paralysis laid that weary brain to rest.' Sadly, those 'numbing fingers' were the terrible symptoms of tertiary syphilis.

CHURCHILL
(Sir) Winston Spencer
Prime Minister

Blenheim Palace, Oxon., November 30, 1874
London, January 24, 1965
Bladon Churchyard, Near Blenheim (between his parents)

105, Mount Street, W1, 1904-1906
12, Bolton Street, W1, 1908
2, Sussex Square, W2 (P) 1920-1925
Flat 11, Morpeth Mansions, Morpeth Terrace, SW1, 1938
28, Hyde Park Gate, SW7, 1945-until he died here

Winston was sent to Harrow School where he was *not* a distinguished scholar. Lord Randolph's pedigree was long but his purse was short and so Winston could not hope for a commission in one of the 'crack' regiments where ample private means were essential for officers.

When he was 19 he *did* go to Sandhurst though he was below their physical minima for entry. Presumably the family name counted for something and he passed in as an Officer Cadet. When he passed out he was gazetted to the 4th Hussars and went overseas with two African postings, where, at Omdurman he fought hand-to-hand with the Dervishes.

In the Boer War he became a Press Correspondent, his first official connection with literature. He was captured by the Boers, but escaped, and there was a price of £25 on his head. Returning safely to England he followed Lord Randolph's footsteps and went into politics. He was elected MP for Oldham as a Conservative, but had differences with that party and 'crossed the floor' to join the Liberals in 1906. Four years later he was Home Secretary. During the First World War in the Admiralty, he was made a scapegoat for the bloody failure at the Dardanelles.

Legends gather about great men, but in the case of a giant like Churchill, the legends are usually greater and usually less believable. One such story is that Churchill had a small green budgerigar, which sat on the almost bald Churchillian pate and shared the great man's whisky. Appealing as this anecdote may be, Mr. Fogg Elliot of Forham in Essex (who described himself as 'Purveyor of Budgerigars to the late Winston Churchill') said the *true* story was that the bird was a *blue* and quite large, cock budgerigar called Toby. Toby did *not* touch whisky – only port! And, in the household pecking order, Toby took precedence over Rufus, Churchill's poodle, as the bird travelled *with* Winston and Rufus was allocated space in the following car.

There is a bronze statue of Churchill by Ivor Roberts-Jones, which was erected in Parliament Square in 1973. He looks over towards his beloved House of Commons. On June 21, 1955, Oscar Nemon's statue was unveiled at the Guildhall. The model who 'stood-in,' so that Nemon could sculpt the body, was a notorious old *queen* called Gerald Hamilton, then 67, who had the same measurements as the Premier. Ironically Hamilton had twice been interned on Churchill's orders for expressing Pro-German sympathies. Hamilton was also supposed to have been the original of 'Mr. Norris' of Christopher ISHERWOOD's, *Mr. Norris Changes Trains* published in 1937.

CIBBER　　　　　　　　　　London, November 6, 1671
Colley　　　　　　　　　　　　London, December 12, 1757
Actor and Poet Laureate　　　Danish Church, Whitechapel, E1

17, Southampton Street, WC2, 1714-1720
19, Berkeley Square, W1, from 1750 until he died here

By the time Cibber (pronounced 'sibber') was 17 he was serving as a private soldier, but at 20, he was on the stage. Later he played in his own adaptation of Shakespeare's *Richard III* and for some years afterwards, Cibber's version was preferred to the original! Generally his plays, and there were to be more than 30 of them, had little success. When he was appointed Poet Laureate in 1730, an official sinecure, Alexander POPE in his *Dunciad* attacked Cibber savagely. In Book One; Cibber was 'Bayes', in the 'reign of Dulness'.

CITY ROAD, EC1　　　　　　　　　　*Northern line to Old Street*

For once a logical name! The road connected the City of London to the (then) village of Islington. The road was finished and officially opened on June 19, 1761. The man responsible for the work was a Mr. Dingley who modestly declined the honour of having the thoroughfare named after him. Nearby, however, are Dingley Road and Dingley Place which *were* named after him.

47,　John WESLEY (LCP 1926). Here John Wesley died on March 2, 1791. Today the house is open to the public. He is buried in the chapel, for which he laid the foundation stone on April 1, 1777. On laying it, Wesley said, 'Probably this will be seen no more by any human eye, but will remain there till the earth and the works thereof, are burnt up'.

CLARENCE GARDENS, NW1　　　　*Bakerloo and BR lines*
to Marylebone

Another 'Royal': this Clarence was Prince William, Duke of Clarence who became King William IV in 1830. (A number of public houses are called the *Duke of Clarence*; in practically all cases they were named after William. Naming pubs after 'Royals' has died out. Indeed, permission was not given when one of the breweries asked the Palace if they could name one of their pubs, 'The Prince of Wales' – after HRH Prince Charles.)

2A,　W.H. DAVIES, pre-1914.
9,　T.S. ELIOT, 1923. Here his wife, Vivienne, lay in an, '...abyss...a helpless and unspeakable wreck of drugs, fear and semi-paralysis for a whole year.'

CLARENCE GATE, NW1

That part of Baker Street which today runs north from the Marylebone Road used to be called Upper Baker Street. This is no longer so but in the early part of the 19th century, houses were numbered in Upper Baker Street, but often referred to as being either 'Regent's Park' or 'Clarence Gate'.

Mrs. SIDDONS lived from 1812-1831 at 27 Upper Baker Street. Here in March 1821 (though long retired from the stage) she gave a reading from *Macbeth*. Benjamin HAYDON was at it and he wrote, 'It is extraordinary the awe this wonderful woman inspires. After her first reading the men retired to tea. While we were all eating toast and tinkling cups and saucers, she began again. It was like the effect of a Mass bell at Madrid. All noises ceased; we slunk back to our seats like boors, two or three of the most distinguished men of the day, with the very toast in their mouths, afraid to bite.'

CLARGES STREET, W1

Piccadilly, Jubilee and Victoria lines
to Green Park

This street was built up around 1717 and named after Sir Walter Clarges, a nephew by marriage of General Monk (1608-1670) who was the architect for the Restoration of the Monarchy in 1660, when he was created Duke of ALBERMARLE. Clarges was *probably* the son of a politician called Sir Thomas Clarges (who died in 1695). Sir Thomas lived in Clarges House, which in 1708 became the home of the Venetian Ambassador to London.

11, Emma HAMILTON, 1804-1806. NELSON's brother, William (a Doctor of Divinity, 1757-1835) was dining here when news was brought to him that Parliament had voted *him* £100,000, '...on account of his brother's services'!

12, Lord NORTHCLIFFE (then still Mr. Harmsworth) 1894. At the time he had financed a Polar Expedition and amongst the stores he provided for the journey were five *tons* (5.51 tonnes) of 'Cod Liver Oil Biscuits' for the dogs and, amongst greater delicacies, 500 pounds (226 kilogrammes) of 'delectable sardines and tomatoes'.

40, James Russell LOWELL, 1884. This was the last year of his tour-of-duty as the (27th) Minister for the United States at the Court of St James's.

40, Ronald FIRBANK was born here in 1886.

46, Charles James FOX (LCP 1950) 1803-1804. It was during these years that Fox was trying to persuade PITT to break off the hostilities with France.

CLARK
Kenneth MacKenzie (1st Lord)
Art Historian

London, July 13, 1903
Kent, May 22, 1983

32, Grosvenor Square, W1, here born
30, Portland Place, W1, 1938
5, Gray's Inn Square, WC1, 1938-1940
B5, Albany, Piccadilly, W1, 1975

Clark was educated at Winchester and Trinity College, Oxford and, after graduating, spent two years in Italy with Bernard Berenson. Berenson said, many years after Clark had been with him, something to the effect that he, Berenson, '...would *only* accept Clark's statement, opinion or identification of pictures whose provenance was in doubt'. For years Berenson's identification of a painting was *the* hall-mark in the world of art. Latterly there have been a number of stories that Berenson was *not* quite such a Simon-pure picture authority after all. So, perhaps Clark, was also not 100% infallible?

Berenson or no, Clark had a magnificent career. He was Director of the National Gallery, Fine Art Keeper at the Ashmolean Museum in Oxford, Surveyor of the King's Pictures and a trustee of the British Museum. It was on TV that Clark became a national *somebody*. His series, *Civilization* on BBC; opened hundreds of thousand of *philistine* eyes. His deceptively casual manner, his marvellous exposition – without ever 'talking down' – seemed to make 'Art' no longer an expensive and mysterious branch of intellectual interest.

Clark was not considered scholarly by *every* critic, but there was one work of his which is unassailably brilliant. Owen Moreshead, the Librarian at Windsor Castle in 1927, asked Clark if he would undertake the task of cataloguing the superb Leonardo da Vinci drawings in the Royal Collection. It took three years but of it Clark wrote that, 'The Catalogue remains my only claim to be considered a scholar'. A modest, gentle statement from a man who was not always publicly modest.

CLARKE
(Sir) Edward George
Barrister

London, February 15, 1841
Staines, April 26, 1931

15, King William Street, EC4, here born
71 (then 38) Moorgate Street, EC2, 1858
37, Russell Square, WC1, 1894–1900

Clarke's father was a jeweller in the City and Edward was born 'over the shop'. He rose above his middle class background, was a very successful (and honourable) barrister and became the Solicitor General. By his own account his average earnings for ten years were, '...more than 10,000 guineas (£10,500) a year'.

He became a Member of Parliament in 1886. As his salary was only £6,000, he was given a knighthood in recompense. Clarke stayed in the post for a (then) record six years. Unlike many members of the legal profession, he was a vociferous tee-totaller.

CLARKE
Mary Ann
Royal Mistress

London, c.1776
Boulogne, June 21, 1852

62 (then 18) Gloucester Place, W1, 1803
9, Old Burlington Street, W1, 1807
11, Holles Street, W1, 1808
14, Bedford Place, WC1, 1808
18, Portman Square, W1, 1813

As a young woman, Mary Ann married a bricklayer, but set her sights higher. She became the acknowledged mistress of HRH, the 40-year-old, Duke of York, second and favourite son of King George III.

The Duke, Commander-in-Chief of the Army, was involved by his witty, pretty Mary Ann in a 'commissions for sale' scandal. Mary Ann was prepared to let it be known that she could arrange, for a price, Army Commissions. There was very nearly a major scandal. As it happens, though the Duke was certainly *not* without blemish, he was not trafficking in this market.

Mrs Clarke 'retired' to write: a book she called *The Rival Princes*. Not long after its publication she was obliged to spend some nine months in prison for libels contained in those memoirs. The book appeared in two volumes in 1810. She had another pot boiler ready and she was supposed to have been paid £10,000 in 1813 – and a pension of £600 pa – *not* to publish it. Obviously Mrs Clarke passed on some of her writing talent; Daphne DU MAURIER is her direct descendant.

CLARKSON
Willy
Theatrical Costumier

1861
London, October 13, 1934

41–43, Wardour Street, W1 (LCP 1966) 1905–1934

Willy, who was not 5 foot (1.5 metres) tall, very bandy and as *camp as a row of tents,* went into his father's wig making business. He always dressed in striped trousers and morning coat and was *always* available to customers of his shop, over which he had lived since 1905. When his business was *really* booming he had been known to have 10,000 wigs out on hire during the Christmas season. Some of the wigs had been hired for *criminal* use and Clarkson used to boast that Dr Crippen and Charles Peace (both murderers) were amongst his clients.

Clarkson often used to recount, with glee, how he had superintended some of the amateur theatricals put on in Windsor Castle. He once recounted how, at the Castle, he had to make a dash for one of the very few lavatories, which was near the makeshift stage. He did not lock the door of the lavatory on which he was ensconced, '...and *then* just as I 'ad settled down, as it were, the 'andle turned and 'oo should enter but 'er Majesty 'erself! Now, now Vicky, don't take on. It's only little Willie Clarkson sitting on 'is own initials.' She went away, quite quiet, you know...'

CLEMENS   Florida, Missouri, November 30, 1835
Samuel Langhorne ('Mark TWAIN') Redding, Ct., April 21, 1910.
Author and humourist

30, Wellington Court, SW7, 1897

Samuel's father was a feckless grocer, who died when his son was only 12. On leaving school, Sam became a journeyman printer and, by the time he was 19, he had already lived in New York and Philadelphia. He went back to Missouri to train as a river boat pilot. The men who took the soundings as they went up river would call out 'Mark Three', 'Mark Twain' and so on, for the pilot's guidance and Clemens adopted 'Mark Twain' as his pen-name. (There was a Mississippi River pilot called Isiah Sellers who was born in 1802 and died in 1864. He wrote articles which were published by the *New Orleans Daily Picayune* over Sellers' chosen pen-name, 'Mark Twain'. As far as one can ascertain Clemens did not use *his* 'Mark Twain' until after the Civil War and he had become the editor of the *Nevada Enterprise*. So it would seem he had not been truly original.)
The American Civil War ended (on May 26, 1865) and Samuel moved to the far West to become a gold miner. In San Francisco, he met Bret HARTE, who was only nine months younger than he. In this year a New York paper published his first story. This was *The Celebrated Jumping Frog of Calaveras Country* and the trail seemed set for him to be a comic writer. Four years later *The Innocents Abroad* (based upon a Mediterranean holiday) was published and then 'Twain' went back to Missouri, married Olivia Langdon there and they lived at Hartford from 1871-1891.

CLEMENTI   Rome, 1752
Muzio   Evesham, Worcs., March 9, 1832
Musician   Westminster Abbey Cloisters

128, Kensington Church Street, W8 (LCP 1963) 1820-1823

Clementi's father was a silver embosser who made vases and the like for use in Church. When Muzio was 13 he caught the eye of an Englishman, called Peter Beckford, who undertook the education of the boy in the future and brought him back to his home in Dorset. Clementi had studied in Rome under both Carpani and Santarelli and had written a Mass for four voices before he was 14.
In London he took the principal interest in a firm of music publishers and, for a time, devoted himself exclusively to business. He made a second tour, in 1808, with his pupil Field, and they got as far as St Petersburg (now Leningrad). In Berlin he married and the Clementis travelled south to Italy. She died giving birth to a son. (The boy was very much his father's pride and joy, but lost his life, being accidentally shot with his own pistol.)
The Philharmonic Society of London was founded in 1813 with Clementi's considerable help and he presented them with two of his own symphonies.

CLEVELAND ROW, SW1   *Piccadilly, Jubilee and Victoria lines*
                                                    to Green Park

Barbara Castlemaine (1641-1709) was created the Duchess of Cleveland by her Royal lover, King Charles II. She became, by him, the mother of the Dukes of Cleveland, Grafton and Northumberland. Barbara made life very difficult for the King, but her house here was conveniently placed both to St

James's Palace and Whitehall Palace, where Charles lived when in London. Later her house was, '...severed into several houses, the chief of which is now inhabited by the Earl of Nottingham'.

5, Theodore HOOK, c.1825. Not long after he had been released from prison where he had been wrongly held on a charge of speculation whilst a civil servant in Mauritius. He paid £200 per annum rent and had the house redecorated for £2,500.

13 (Stornoway House) Lord BEAVERBROOK for many years after 1929. By 1967 it was the offices of Firth Cleveland Limited.

CLEVELAND STREET, W1 *Northern line to Goodge Street*

One of Barbara Castlemaine's bastards by King Charles II was Henry Fitzroy, Earl of Euston, later, in 1675, Duke of Grafton. He married an heiress who inherited land in the Tottenham Court Road area and Fitzroy developed some of it. His mother was created the Duchess of Cleveland by the King.

7, Dante Gabriel ROSSETTI, 1848. Rossetti, Holman HUNT and MILLAIS founded the Pre-Raphaelite Brotherhood in this year.

15, Walter SICKERT rented rooms here in 1884.

19, On July 4, 1889 a male brothel was discovered by the police in this house. Young, underpaid telegraph boys used to come here and allow themselves to be 'used' by homosexual men; some of the clientele being very top drawer. The Duke of Clarence – again! – was supposed to be a paying visitor. However, a great friend of Royalty who definitely *was* a cash customer, was the 38-year old Lord Arthur Somerset, who managed the Prince of Wales's stables at Marlborough House and Sandringham. He was allowed to leave the country and he only came back to England (to his mother's funeral) once in 37 years. The house's tenant and the brothel keeper, a man called Hammond, fled (or was allowed to flee) the country.

22, Charles DICKENS, 1830. He gave this address (though·it was then part of Norfolk Street) when applying for British Museum book privileges.

141, Samuel MORSE (LCP 1962) 1812-1815. Not everything in London pleased Morse. In a letter home from this address, he wrote, '...the cries of London...are very annoying to me as, indeed, they are to all strangers...they all appear to be cries of distress'.

CLIFFORD STREET, W1 *Central line to Bond Street*

The Earl of Burlington married a Lady Clifford and bought land on the north side of Piccadilly in the middle of the 17th century. His nickname was 'Richard the Rich' as Lady Clifford had brought a considerable fortune into the marriage.

8, WILLIAM of ORANGE. This 21-year old Dutch pipsqueak stayed here in 1813/14 with a view to becoming engaged to be married to Princess Charlotte, only daughter of the Prince Regent and so heiress presumptive to the English throne. Charlotte, however, had other ideas and sent him a letter to this house rejecting his suit. William wrote back, resigned, saying, 'hoping that you shall never feel any cause to repent of the step you have taken, I remain, Yours sincerely, William'.

CLIVE
Catherine Rafton ('Kitty')
Actress

London, 1711
Twickenham, December 6, 1785
Twickenham Church Yard

59, Great Queen Street, WC2, 1743-1747

Daughter of William Rafton, a Jacobite lawyer from Kilkenny in Ireland, Catherine made her stage début in 1727, having been given a part by Colley CIBBER. It was not long before she established a reputation as a comic actress.

Success, however, did not attend her marriage to George Clive, a barrister, in 1731 and they soon went their separate ways. She stayed on the stage for nearly 40 years and off it she had many friends; like WALPOLE, who gave her the use of a house near his own, Strawberry Hill at Twickenham.

Her last performance was opposite GARRICK on April 24, 1769. GARRICK called her by the pet name of 'Pivy'. After she had settled down in her house at Twickenham, he wrote to her from Drury Lane frequently. He used to call her house 'Clive's-Den'.

CLIVE
Robert (Baron Clive of Plassey)
Soldier and Statesman

Styche, Salop, September 29, 1725
London, November 22, 1774
St Margaret's Church, Moreton Say, Salop

45, Berkeley Square, W1 (LCP 1953) from 1761 until he died here

Clive was the eldest of a lawyer's 13 children; the family being long-established and well thought of in Shropshire. Altogether young Robert was sent to four different schools and, at most of them, proved to be, '...a better fighter than a scholar'. When he was 18 he was packed off to India. By the time he reached Madras (where he was a penniless office drudge) he tried to shoot himself. *Twice* the pistol's mechanism failed and Clive took this to be some sort of sign that there *was* a role for him to play in life.

From then on his life became as exciting as could be imagined. In 1744 a war had broken out between the French and English in India and in 1747 he was commissioned as an ensign in the East India Company's service. During the 'Second' War with the French (1751-1754) he captured Arcot and then defended it against recapture by a large French force aided by the troops under Raja Sahib. He came home briefly and returned to India as Lieutenant-Governor of Fort St David. In 1756 he commanded an expedition against the Nawab of Bengal and avenged the tragedy of the 'Black Hole of Calcutta'. (On June 20, 1756, 146 British prisoners were forced by the troops of the Nawab Siraj-ud-Daula into the garrison strong room at Calcutta which was only 18 feet square – 1.67 square metres. By the next morning 123 Britons were dead.) On June 23, 1757 at the Battle of Plassey the British scored a complete victory over the Indian forces and Clive elevated Mir Jaffier (1691-1765) to the throne. Clive was appointed Governor of Bengal in 1758; defeated the Dutch at Chinsura the year following, but ill health forced him to return to England in 1760, when he was given an Irish peerage.

He had a second stint in Bengal from 1765 to 1767 but his health broke down again. He was a complete ruler and his pay was such that he could bring back to England the wherewithal to afford him an income of over £40,000 a year. He never returned to India and in London his critics were numerous and vocal. Clive suffered from increasing depression and was dosing himself heavily with opium. He was quite addicted and practically every history book states that Clive committed suicide by giving himself an overdose of drugs.

At the St James's Park end of King Charles Street, SW1, there is a bronze statue of Clive by John Tweed. It stands on a limestone and grey granite pedestal, on the south side of which is a bas-relief of the Siege of Arcot, 1751: on the east, The Eve of Plassey, 1757 and on the north, the Grant of Bengal, Behar and Orissa. Tweed finished the statue in 1912 and temporarily it was placed in the gardens of Gwydyr House, Whitehall, being finally placed in its present site in 1916.

COBDEN
Richard
Free Trader

Midhurst, Sussex, June 3, 1804
London, April 2, 1865
Lavington, Sussex

38, Grosvenor Street, W1, 1856
23, Suffolk Street, SW1 (LCP 1905) he lodged here for a few months and
died here.

Son of a bankrupt Sussex farmer, Cobden was sent to a sort of 'Dotheboys
Hall' in Yorkshire, but left when he was 15 and came back to London to
work in his uncle's warehouse. It was not long before he became a travelling
salesman for the firm.
He set up on his own, selling calico in 1828 and moved north to Manchester.
He visited America eight years later and, as a result of this trip, produced
two pamphlets advocating free trade and non-aggression with Russia. He
lectured up and down the country and in 1841 was elected as Member of
Parliament for Stockport. His political activities took up so much time that
his business suffered and, before long, it was ruined. However, the
staggering sum of £80,000 was raised for him by public subscription and, in
1847 he bought the Sussex farm at Midhurst where he had been born. He
was a vigorous supporter of the 'North' in the American Civil War (he did
not live to see it end) and he arranged a commercial treaty with France in
1860.
There is a badly eroded marble statue by W. and T. Wills, erected at the
northern end of Hampstead Road, in Camden Town in 1868. It cost £320
and the *largest single contributor was NAPOLEON III*. It stands where the toll
bar stood until 1866.

COCHRANE
Thomas (10th Earl of Dundonald)
Admiral

Annsfield, Scotland, December 14,
1775
October 31, 1869
Westminster Abbey

Hanover Lodge, Outer Circle
Regent's Park, NW1 (LCP 1974) 1830-1845
Cochrane was the eldest son of the 9th Earl of Dundonald, who had spent
the family fortune on chemical experimentation. So he joined the Navy
when he was 18, not the usual course for the son and heir in aristocratic
families. By 1800 he was given command of a sloop in which he took over
50 Spanish and French ships, as 'prizes', in 15 months.
A year before the Battle of Waterloo, Cochrane was accused of falsely
reporting the death of the Emperor Napoleon to his own speculative gain.
He was imprisoned for a year, fined, expelled from the Royal Navy and
turned out of the House of Commons where he had been a member since
1806.
After his release he accepted an invitation to organize the Chilean navy, early
in 1818, but quit the job after many disagreements and joined the Brazilian
fleet. He was in command of it by 1823, but resigned his post after he had
been accused of insubordination. So, gathering his gold braid about him, he
upped and joined the Greek Navy in 1827!
Eventually he was exonerated from guilt in the case of the 'Napoleon
Rumour' and the Order of the Bath was bestowed on him in 1832.
The family motto was *Virtute et Labore* – by courage and labour. Cochrane
was also created the Marquess of Maranham in Brazil in 1824.

CODY   Leclair, Iowa, February 26, 1846
William Frederick   Denver, January 10, 1917
Showman   Lookout Mountain, Denver

86, Regent Street, W1, 1887

Isaac Cody used to claim descent from King Milesius, the Celtic King of
Spain whose family invaded Ireland, establishing the first Irish Kingdom.
That genealogy, however, did not prevent him from being stabbed to death
by an employee of his brother, Elijah, whilst Isaac was speaking against
slavery at an informal public meeting. William Frederick was only ten years
old, but after his father's death, largely had to take care of himself.
Eventually he became a United States Government Scout and earned the
nickname of 'Buffalo Bill' after he had been awarded a contract by the
Kansas Pacific Railway Company to supply buffalo meat to their labourers.
In honouring the contract Cody killed over 4,200 buffalo in eighteen
months.
In 1872 he became a member of the Nebraska Legislature and five years later
he had put together a travelling 'Wild West Show' which played extensively
'before the Crowned Heads of Europe' before coming to London in 1887.
His show packed Earls Court Exhibition Hall and its popularity almost
outshone the celebrations being held in Britain to commemorate the Golden
Jubilee of Queen Victoria that year. The public's first show had an audience
of 30,000 – a packed house – and three days later the old Queen herself was
given a command performance.
The town of Cody, Wyoming covers part of the ranch that 'Buffalo Bill'
once owned.

COLEFAX   1872
(Lady) Sybil   London, September 22, 1950
Society Hostess

Argyll House, 211, Kings Road, SW3, 1922-1937
19, Lord North Street, SW1, 1937

Lady Colefax was the widow of Arthur Colefax, a famous jurist and she
became one of the noted hostesses of her day. There was a rather unkind
story about how she had begun to establish herself as one. She was alleged to
have invited G.B. SHAW and H.G. WELLS – on postcards – to dine with
her, writing that each man was eager to know the other. She was a small
woman – though larger than Emerald CUNARD – and Bernard Berenson,
who knew her at the turn of the century wrote that she, '...looked like a
young begum. Something un-European in her looks. Strange, for both her
parents were ultra-Nordic.'

COLERIDGE   Ottery St Mary, Devon, October 21,
Samuel Taylor   1772
Poet   Highgate, N6, July 27, 1834
                                   St Michael's Church Crypt, Highgate,
                                   N6

21, Buckingham Street, WC2, 1799
Mitre Court, Fleet Street, EC2, 1810
55, Frith Street, W1
14, Addison Bridge Place, W14 (LCP 1950) 1818

Fired with revolutionary views, but suffering from lack of funds (even
revolutions have to have money) Coleridge left Jesus College, Cambridge
where he was a *sizar* and joined the 15th Dragoons under the name of 'Silas
Thomkyn Comberback'. As he could not master the art of riding a horse
and, anyway, his pseudonym was seen through, his brothers bought him
out of the Army and he went back to Cambridge in 1794. In Bristol, the

same year, he met Robert Southey (who was born in Bristol in 1774) and they planned a 'Utopian' Community on the banks of the Susquehanna River. The scheme, like most schemes of that ilk, came to nothing.

Coleridge had generous friends in Bristol, amongst them Thomas Poole, who lent Coleridge and his new bride, Sarah (née Fricker – Southey's sister-in-law) a 'honeymoon' cottage at Nether Stowey in Somerset. Here they met William and Dorothy WORDSWORTH and from their association grew a new style of English Poetry. In 1798 they published *Lyrical Ballads,* which opened with Coleridge's *The Ancient Mariner* ('It is an ancient Mariner, And he stoppeth one of three').

His natural melancholia was worsened by his growing addiction to opium. Despite the drug he went with the Wordsworths to Germany in 1804 and later (strangely) became Secretary to the Governor of Malta.

In 1818 he was taken by a surgeon, John Gilman, to Highgate. By this time, drugs had brought him to the verge of madness. The good doctor kept him in his house and managed to reduce Coleridge's dependence on drugs. Though he never gave them up altogether, he was brought to a stage where all he needed was a small, regular and manageable dose.

COLLINS	London, W1, January 8, 1824
Wilkie William	London, W1, September 23, 1889
Author	Kensal Green; Square 141, Row 1

11, New Cavendish Street, W1 (P) here born
38, Blandford Square, W1, in the late 1840s
12, Cavendish Square, W1, 1859-1864
17, Hanover Terrace, NW1, 1860
65, Gloucester Place, W1 (LCP 1951) 1868-1876 and 1883-1888
82, Wimpole Street, W1, where he died

Wilkie Collins was one of six sons and he had some of his education at Highbury, in London, and some in Italy where the family lived from 1836-1839. He began in law but soon moved into literature and in 1860 published *The Woman in White,* which T.S. ELIOT once described as, '...the first and the greatest of English detective novels'. Collins produced a number of other books, mostly forgotten today, but in 1868 he produced *The Moonstone* and this brilliant work featured 'Sergeant Cuff' who really was the grandfather and prototype of *all* fictional detectives.

Collins never married. He probably had little time to do so as he had a number and variety of mistresses; often more than one at a time. He had children by quite a few of them and he always treated his mistresses (whether cast-off or not) and his little bastard brood, generously and with kindness.

During the last years of his life he suffered agonies from 'rheumatic gout' and became addicted to opium. By the time of *The Moonstone* when he was nearly 44 years old, he was taking enough opium daily, '...to put a dinner party of 12 under the table'.

John Lothrop MOTLEY met Collins in the 1860s and described him as: 'A little man, with black hair, large white forehead, large spectacles and, small features. He is very unaffected, vivacious and agreeable'.

COMPTON-BURNETT	Pinner, Middx., June 5, 1884
Ivy	London, August 27, 1969
Author	

97, Linden Gardens, W2, 1926-1929
5, Braemar Mansions, Cornwall Gardens, SW7, 1960-1969

After a 'private' education, Miss Compton-Burnett read Classics at London University. Her first book, *Pastors and Masters* was published in 1925 and, thereafter, a flood of rather similar titles with similar content, appeared at regular intervals. They were very popular with so-called 'Middle Class' readers, who probably identified themselves in the ever rolling stream. The critics, collectively, were not kind, but the books sold well despite their diatribes and, in 1955, her *Mother and Son* won the Tait Black Memorial Prize.

When she was 40 years old, she was 'plump and bosomy, with streaky grey-brown hair, the shape of a mob-cap, kept in place with a string – which colour and shape never varied for 40 years'. Both she and her constant companion, Margaret Jourdain, were *compulsive* food gobblers. Apparently Ivy used really to get down to the business of eating, '...her legs splayed apart and her skirt hitched above her knees.'

CONDER London, October 10, 1868
Charles Virginia Water, Surrey, April 9, 1909
Artist

1, Pembroke Cottages, Edwardes Square, W8, 1899
11, Stafford Terrace, W8, 1899
14, Wellington Square, SW3, 1902
91, Cheyne Walk, SW3, 1904

Though born in London, Conder started to paint at 17, in Australia. In 1890 he moved from 'down under' to Paris, where, amongst other artists, he became friendly with Henri Toulouse-Lautrec. Conder and the stunted little French aristocrat shared a common interest in the bottle.

He finally settled in London and married a girl called Stella Maris in 1902. Around that time he was producing paintings of the fantastic and also became a specialist in decorating silk fans in water colours.

CONDUIT STREET, W1 *Central, Bakerloo and Victoria lines*
to Oxford Circus

There used to be a pump house at Conduit Mead. Conduit Street began to be built up about 1718. This was part of a fresh water supply system, which had been operating since the 1400s.

6, Harriet MARTINEAU, 1832. She stayed here when she first came to London.
14 and 15, the Hon Charles ROLLS at the time of his death in an aeroplane accident in 1910.
37, George CANNING, 1802-1803.

CONNAUGHT January 13, 1883
(Prince) Arthur Frederick Patrick September 12, 1938
Albert
Relatively Royal

54, Mount Street, W1, 1913
41, Belgrave Square, SW1, 1923-1928

Prince Arthur was the second child and only son of HRH the Duke of Connaught (1850-1942) and Princess Louise of Prussia. His grandmother was Queen Victoria, as the old Duke was the Queen's third son.

The Prince married the Duchess of Fife in 1913, another relative. She was a daughter of the Princess Royal, whose father was King Edward VII; so her *great* grandmother was Queen Victoria! All rather complicated but suffice it to say they were some sort of cousins. They only had one son, Prince Alastair, Earl of MacDuff who was born on August 19, 1914, five days after the First World War began.

CONNAUGHT PLACE, W2   *Central line to Marble Arch*

Named after Connaught House, built here in 1808 for George III's nephew who, as well as being the Duke of Gloucester, was also the Earl of Connaught. In 1819 the ground rent on a typical house in the Place was between £40 and £80 a year. The rent for a mews cottage behind the Square was around £2 a year!

2,   Lord Randolph CHURCHILL (LCP 1962) 1883-1892. This house was one of the first (if not *the* first) private houses in London to be lit by electricity in 1883.

CONNAUGHT SQUARE, W2

15,   Fanny KEMBLE, 1877.

CONNOLLY   Whitley, Nr. Coventry, September
Cyril Vernon   10, 1903
Author, journalist and critic   November 11, 1974

80, St Georges Square, SW1, 1926-1927
11, St Leonard's Terrace, SW3, 1927
26A, Yeomans Row, SW3, 1927-1928
312A, King's Road, SW3, 1930

It was Connolly who wrote: 'Imprisoned in every fat man, a thin man is wildly signalling to be let out'. Inside Connolly was an internationally famous author trying to be let out and so justify his early promise. Evelyn WAUGH (b. October 28, 1903) and Eric BLAIR ('George Orwell'; b. June 25, 1903) were close in age to him and established themselves to be authors whose works are read long after their death. Someone wrote that Connolly was:

> 'At Eton with Orwell, at Oxford with Waugh,
> He was nobody after and *nothing* before.'

It is an unkind but telling couplet.

Connolly wrote two thinly disguised autobiographical books; *Enemies of Promise* and *The Unquiet Grave* in 1944. From the latter one can find his own description of himself; 'A fat, slothful, querulous, greedy, impotent carcass; a stump, a decaying belly washed up on the shore'.

After Oxford he became a journalist and was a regular contributor to journals such as the *New Statesman*. In 1939 he and Stephen Spender established a literary magazine called *Horizon*. It lasted ten years until the vogue for such magazines evaporated. From 1952 until his death he was the main book reviewer for the *Sunday Times*. He described himself as '...a hack in his element'. He was also literary editor for the *Observer* 1942-1943.

CONRAD   Mohilow, Poland, December 3, 1857
Joseph   Sittingbourne, Kent, August 3, 1924
Novelist   Roman Catholic Cemetery,
                        Canterbury, Kent

17, Gordon Place, WC1, early 1900s

When Conrad was only three, his father was exiled to Northern Russia. Not long after his mother died and the (in effect) orphaned boy was brought up at Cracow by an uncle. In 1874 he went to Marseilles and became a sailor. He and three companions were involved in a small smuggling ring. This phase of his life is reflected in his book, *The Mirror of the Sea*, which was published in 1906.

In 1886 he obtained his 'First Mate's ticket' and became a British subject. In a short while he was Captain of a river steamer in the Belgian Congo. One of

his greatest books, *Heart of Darkness*, draws upon this phase of his life.
In 1895 E.V. LUCAS ('Evoe' of *Punch*) was introduced to Conrad in the
Restaurant d'Italia in Old Compton Street, Soho, by Edward Garnett (father
of David GARNETT). Lucas recalled that Conrad's eyes were brilliant, he
spoke with a very strong foreign accent and his sentences were 'very badly
constructed' as he talked. His accent remained 'exotic' until the end of his life
– which is not really *too* surprising considering he did not really *speak*
English until he was nearly 40.

CONSTABLE	East Bergholt, Suffolk, June 11, 1776
John	London, March 30, 1837
Artist	Hampstead Church Yard

50, Rathbone Place, W1, 1801
49, Frith Street, W1, 1811 (then to Keppel Street for five years)
63 (formerly 35) Charlotte Street, W1, 1822
79, Charlotte Street, W1, where he died

With TURNER, Constable is regarded as the finest English landscape
painter, if not for all time, then certainly of the 19th century. Though he
showed artistic talent, early in his life, he did not come to London until he
was 19 and did not start at the Royal Academy Schools for another four
years. His first picture to be hung at the Academy was in 1802 and in this he
had been advised by Benjamin WEST.
His *View on the Stour* (1819) and his *Hay Wain* the following year (the latter is
now in the National Gallery) won Gold Medals at the Paris Salon of 1824
and the admiration for his work there spread back across the Channel.
(Eugène Delacroix, 1798-1863, to be hailed as a leader of the French
'Romantic' School of painting, admired Constable's painting wholeheartedly.)
Constable said of his love of the country, 'the sound of water escaping from
mill dams, willows, old rotten planks, slimy posts and brickwork I love
such things. These scenes made me a painter.'

COOK	Melbourne, Derbyshire, November
Thomas	22, 1808
Travel Agent	July 19, 1892

59, Great Russell Street, WC1, 1863-1879

The company, founded by Cook and at one time the largest organization of
its kind in the world, really began because Cook was a tee- totaller. In 1841
he chartered (in the nomenclature of the travel business today) a whole
passenger train for a temperance outing from Leicester to Loughborough.
Seeing the potential, it was not long before he expanded his original idea
until the 'Cook's Man' really meant something and was a familiar figure – in
his peaked cap and blue uniform – at railway stations and hotels, half way
round the world. Cooks catered for the introduction of paid holidays for the
working classes, soon to be made a *right* and for the growing affluence of the
middle classes. They had the time, and the money, but lacked the experience
or initiative to make travel arrangements for themselves and their families
abroad. So Cooks did it all for them.

COOPER	Norwich, February 22, 1890
Alfred Duff (1st Viscount Norwich)	'at sea', January 1, 1954
Diplomat	Belvoir Castle

90, Gower Street, WC1, 1929

Cooper, after Eton, Oxford and the Grenadier Guards (the first Regiment of

Footguards) in the First World War, became a Conservative Member of Parliament in 1924. By 1935 he was Secretary of War and one of a group of politicians who saw the Nazi Movement as a threat to Britain, if not the world. In 1938 – then First Lord of the Admiralty – he resigned in protest against CHAMBERLAIN's ('Peace with Honour') appeasement policy.

When CHURCHILL came to power in 1940 he made Cooper Minister of Information. Just before the end of the war, Cooper was sent to Paris as British Ambassador, then probably *the* top Diplomatic post. He only stayed there until 1947.

COOPER	Burlington, N.J., September 15, 1789
James Fenimore	Cooperstown, N.Y., September 14,
Author	1851

33, St. James's Place, SW1, March–May 1828

Cooper came from a wealthy Quaker family, his father being a judge, and James went to Yale University in 1803. From that ivy-clad institution he was expelled 'for an escapade' in 1806 and he then joined the Navy.

In 1811 he married Susan de Lancey of New York, resigned his commission and settled down to become a country gentleman. His first book, *Precaution,* was published in 1819 and was anything but a success. Neither were the 32 books which followed! Then, in 1826, *The Last of the Mohicans* appeared and, as an author, he was on his way. He was appointed United States Consul at Lyons, in France and here he made the acquaintance of Marie Joseph Paul Yves Roch Gilbert Motier, Marquis de Lafayette. During his brief stay in England he met Walter Scott.

The Deerslayer (which appeared in 1841; the last of the *Leatherstocking Tales* of which the *Mohicans* is the second) is the other book for which Cooper is most widely remembered.

COPLEY	Boston, Mass., July 3, 1737
John Singleton	London, September 9, 1815
Artist	Highgate Cemetery

12, Leicester Square, WC2, 1776–1784
25, George Street, W1, 1784–1815

Copley's father was an Irishman who emigrated to America not long before Copley was born. By the time he was 16, young John was painting portraits for money and in 1755 George Washington sat for him. This was the year he saved the remains of Edward Braddock's army, where 63 of Washington's 86 fellow officers were killed near Fort Dusquesne.

Copley came to England in 1774 having previously sent over some of his work for the Royal Academy. He was commissioned to paint portraits of King George III and Queen Charlotte. Having done so, he set off for Italy, where he spent the next two years. He was elected to the Royal Academy in 1783. The previous year an American, Elkannah Watson (1750-1802) had won a £100 bet on the Relief of Gibraltar (by a British force, under Lord Heathfield, on September 13, 1782). Watson decided to spend his winnings on a portrait of himself by Copley. Copley set the figure against a seascape background, showing a ship leaving for America, '...carrying the news of the Independence of that country'. On December 5, Watson dined with Copley and afterwards they went down to the House of Lords, at Westminster, to hear King George III formally announce the existence of the *United States of America.* They went back to Copley's studio and there, Copley painted in the 'Stars and Stripes' on the flag of the ship in the painting's background. This was the first time 'Old Glory' (a nick-name given to the American flag in 1831 by a skipper from Salem called William Driver, according to hearsay) was 'hoisted' in England!

CORELLI	London, May 1, 1855(?)
Marie	Stratford-upon-Avon, April 21, 1924
Novelist	Stratford-upon-Avon Cemetery

47, Longridge Road, SW5 (P) 1883-1899

Some mystery surrounds Marie Corelli's forbears. No birth certificate has been found for her, but she was almost certainly the child of a journalist and one-time editor of the *Illustrated London News* Charles MacKay, and Ellen Mills. 'Marie', like 'Corelli', is a flight of fancy and she may well have been plain Minnie MacKay. She also had a ne'er-do-well half brother called Eric. Detractors of Marie Corelli (and they were legion) spread rumours that Eric had had an incestuous connection with his half-sister. Miss Corelli's old foe, Edmund Gosse, told a friend of this spiteful rumour: 'How *absurd*', said his friend. 'Yes, isn't it,' replied Gosse, 'Why, everybody *knows* she is his *mother!*'

Marie had trained for a musical career, but in 1886 she published *A Romance of Two Worlds* and nine years later her *Sorrows of Satan* made her the best selling female novelist in Britain. In 1896 her *The Mighty Atom* was top of the 'charts' and that book title found a new turn in the diary of Edith Sichel, writing to Lady Robert Sichel in 1914; 'At the dinner given to Anatole France', she wrote, 'I sate with WELLS' [H.G.] 'to the back of me and Marie Corelli (in pale blue baby-dress, a pink rose over the ear, an immense barrel-bulk, a *mighty* atom indeed!) to the side of me.'

CORK STREET, W1   *Piccadilly and Bakerloo lines to Piccadilly Circus*

The Earl of BURLINGTON, 'Richard the Rich' and his family, developed this area progressively. Burlington was the son of the 'Great Earl of Cork.'

11, Doctor ARBUTHNOT, lived here from 1724 until he died here in 1735.

15, George PEABODY. He had established himself as a banker in the City in the 1860s.

CORNHILL, EC3   *Central and Northern lines to Bank*

'Cornhill' was recorded even before the Norman Conquest of 1066. Cornhill is one of the twin hills of the City of London – the other being Ludgate Hill – but Cornhill was less populated; more fertile and so more suitable for the growing of corn and other like crops. A burgess of London, Edward Hupcornehill, lived here in 1115. In 1582 Peter Morris, a Dutchman, piped water from the Thames through leaden pipes to a number of houses nearby. The conduit he created was called 'The Standard'.

32, W.M. THACKERAY met Charlotte and Anne Brontë here.

119, George CRABBE lodged here in 1780. Whilst he lived here, Crabbe became suicidal. Had not Edmund BURKE helped him over the appealing note he had had, Crabbe well may have drowned himself.

'CORNWALL, Barry' see PROCTER, B.

CORNWALL GARDENS, SW7   *Piccadilly, District and Circle lines to Gloucester Road*

The development of this area was planned in 1862, the year Edward, Prince of Wales, became 21. His secondary title was Duke of Cornwall.

BRAEMAR MANSIONS

5, Ivy COMPTON-BURNETT, in the 1960s. She used to sprinkle broken glass on her window boxes to prevent her neighbours' cats from frollicking in these miniature gardens.

29, Hardy AMIES, 1983.

CORNWALLIS
Charles (1st Marquess)
Soldier

London, December 31, 1738
Ghazipur, India, October 5, 1805
Ghazipur

16, Grafton Street, W1, 1793

Cornwallis joined the Army in 1756 and saw some very active service at the battles of Minden, Vellinghausen and Wilhelmstadt. In 1775 he was promoted to Major-General and in the following February was sent with seven regiments to America where he joined Sir William Howe at Halifax and served with Howe in the campaign on Long Island. In September 1777 he won the Battle of Brandywine and occupied Philadelphia. He was promoted but, at Yorktown on October 19, 1781, he surrendered to George Washington's Army. Five years later he was appointed Governor-General of India.

In 1793 he resigned his Indian offices and came back to England. In 1795 he had a seat in the Cabinet as Master-General of the Ordnance and then Viceroy in Ireland which he 'ruled' all too firmly. He negotiated the Treaty of Amiens (signed on March 27, 1802) which afforded a shaky peace between Britain and France and three years later went back to India where he died and was buried.

COURTAULD
Samuel
Patron of the Arts

1876
London, December 1, 1947

8, Palace Green, W8, 1929
20, Portman Square, W1
12, North Audley Street, W1, where he died

'Sam' was a member of the Huguenot Courtauld family who gained their wealth from the firm of Courtauld, which was founded in 1825. The company were very involved in artificial fibres and to a great degree responsible for the British rayon and nylon industry as a whole. Samuel was Chairman of the organization for a number of years.

He and his wife, 'Lil', were generous hosts; both artistically and musically knowledgeable. His love of art found tangible expression over the years. In 1923 he gave £50,000 to the Tate Gallery to buy works of French 19th century painters. Courtauld had been buying French works, of the 1880-1900 period, extensively, and was very conscious that the major galleries in Britain had few, if any, French Post-Impressionist pieces. He presented his collection to the University of London (the Courtaulds were childless) and the whole collection was shown for the first time at the Tate in 1948.

He endowed the Courtauld Institute for the University of London and made over 20, Portman Square to them. The paintings can now be seen in Woburn Place, WC1 (Piccadilly Underground to Russell Square). The Gallery, admission free, is usually open on weekdays, 10-5, and 2-5 on Sundays.

COURTFIELD GARDENS, SW7
Piccadilly, District and Circle lines to Gloucester Road

The name derives from 'Courtefeld' which was the name of a large piece of land (or field) near Earl's Court. Its development began in 1873 and the name was conjured up for the benefit of property agents (probably) so that they could sell a bit of 'history' as well as bricks and mortar.

2, Ada LEVERSON, in the 1890s. The Leversons gave sanctuary to Oscar WILDE for the two weeks or so when he was on bail between the second and third trials in 1895.

39, Sir George SCOTT died here on March 27, 1878, having lived in the house for some years.

COVENT GARDEN, WC2   *Piccadilly line to Covent Garden*

When spelling was even less precise than it is today, some scribe could well have written 'Covent' for 'Convent'. In fact the area covered once by the old fruit and vegetable markets, *was* the Kitchen Garden for the Convent (or Abbey) of Westminster. Certainly monks worked the land from the early 13th century until King Henry VIII dissolved the monastery in 1536. Not long after, the whole area, lock stock and barrel, was given to the *Earl* of Bedford. (The Bedfords only became *Dukes* in 1694.) In 1913, the 11th Duke of Bedford sold the whole property to a clothing manufacturer called Mallaby-Deely for a reputed £1,750,000.

The square was almost certainly designed by Inigo Jones between 1631 and 1637 and though rather exotically called 'The Piazza' was the ancestor of the numerous London Squares all over the city, which add so much to its charm. Its original style owes something to the square at Leghorn, say the Italians: the French say it resembles the Place des Vosges. So thought Sorbiere in 1686.

12, Sir James THORNHILL lived here, followed by his son-in-law, William HOGARTH, until 1733. Later it became the Piazza Hotel which, as well as providing food, let off bedrooms upstairs on a very short term arrangement for country gentlemen who wished to explore the many delights of London a little more extensively.

15, Sir Godfrey KNELLER, 1682-1702, another favourite Court painter. By 1753, Charles MACKLIN opened the 'Piazza Coffee House' here.

COWARD	Teddington, Middlesex, December
(Sir) Noel	16, 1899
Entertainer	Jamaica, March 26, 1973

111, Ebury Street, SW1, until 1929
17, Gerald Road, SW1, 1929-1956

The 'Master' began life at Teddington (where the first lock of the Thames is situated) and ended up as a tax exile with homes in Switzerland and Jamaica. As a fourteen-year old, he appeared in 'Peter Pan'. He was truly a prodigy and his first play, the (then) daring *Vortex* written when he was 23, did big box office business in 1924 and for a number of years afterwards.

As a composer his songs were witty, their music sophisticated and both sometimes mocking. He *could* be serious. It is hard to imagine that the author of *Private Lives* playing the title role of 'Elyot Chase' in it in 1930, could be the author, actor and director of the intense war film, *In Which We Serve* in 1944. His touch was golden and he moved as easily in the upper echelons of international society as he did with his friends and equals in the world of entertainment.

He never married though his name was often linked with eligible women by the gossip columnists.

A memorial, black marble stone was set into the floor of Westminster Abbey to the memory of Noel Coward, the last line inscribed on it being the four words, 'A talent to amuse'. Her Majesty, Queen Elizabeth, the Queen Mother attended the simple ceremony of dedication in the Abbey on March 28, 1984. Joyce Carey, Evelyn Laye, Dame Anna Neagle and Sir John Mills laid bouquets of flowers at each corner of the stone.

COWLES	U.S.A., August 24, 1910
Virginia	France, September 16, 1983
Newspaper woman	

19, Chester Square, SW1, 1973-1983

Virginia was the daughter of Edward Spencer Cowles and in 1945 she married the 37-year old Aidan Crawley, who was a member of the Labour Government from 1950 to 1951, but crossed over to the Tories and sat for them from 1962-1968. He was also, at one time, Chairman of London Weekend Television. The Crawleys had two sons and a daughter.

She became a war correspondent in the Spanish Civil War and was later appointed as 'special assistant' to the American Ambassador in London in 1942 for just over a year. She was given an OBE in 1947.

In *Who's Who* she gave as her 'recreation'; politics. In addition to being very prominent socially she published a number of very skillful biographies on King Edward VII, Winston CHURCHILL, Kaiser Wilhelm and group studies of the Romanovs and the ROTHSCHILDS.

On their way to the South of France, their car, driven by Aidan Crawley, crossed a dual-carriageway between Bayonne and Bordeaux and struck another car. Virginia Crawley was killed and her husband suffered severe injury.

COWLEY STREET, SW1.

District and Circle lines to Westminster

Cowley and Barton Streets were both built up by Barton Booth, an actor (1681-1733). His family and he had a little money and owned a bit of property at Cowley, Nr. Uxbridge, 15 miles west of London. There is a monument in the Abbey to Booth (he died at Cowley) erected and paid for by his wife, who was the mistress of the 3rd Duke of Marlborough.

17, Lawrence BINYON, 1904. He was then working in the Printed Books Department of the British Museum.

COWPER
William
Poet

Great Berkhamstead, November 26, 1731
East Dereham, Norfolk, April 25, 1800
East Dereham

62, Russell Square, WC1, 1750-1754

Cowper, a son of the Rector of Berkhamstead, was sent to Westminster School in 1741 and, on leaving in 1749, he went in to the Inner Temple and was called to the Bar there in 1754. Nine years later his natural melancholy had become so set in that he was placed in a private asylum at St Albans. Though he did become more stable, he was given to fits of a suicidal nature and this mental imbalance found an outlet in religious matters and he eventually wrote 68 hymns, the most notable being:

> 'God moves in a mysterious way
> His wonders to perform;
> He plants his footsteps in the sea,
> And rides upon the storm.'

His hymns, though plentiful, are not his real claim to faim. By 1782 his mental health had improved and he had moved to Olney, in Buckinghamshire, where one of his neighbours was a Lady Austin who told him the story of John Gilpin which Cowper turned into the poem that practically every English school child has had to take note of:

> 'John Gilpin was a citizen
> Of credit and renown,
> A train-band captain eke was he
> Of famous London town.'

HAZLITT thought Cowper effeminate and Charles Greville (1794-1865) thought that Cowper had gone mad as he was a *hermaphrodite*.

CRABBE Aldeburgh, Suffolk, December 24,
George 1754
Poet Trowbridge, Wilts., February 3, 1832

37, Bury Street, SW1, 1817

Crabbe's father was a salt tax collector for the Government, but decided his son was to be a surgeon and sent him to London to study to that end. George, however, was squeamish, disliked medecine in general and surgery in particular. And who can blame him for that; in the days when the only 'anaesthetic' was a vast dose of brandy? He began to think about the literary world and ways and means to make a living from it. He was not initially successful and before long he was broke. He wrote a letter in desperation to Edmund BURKE, enclosing some samples of his talent. Burke, impressed, took the young man into his household.

In 1781 Crabbe's *The Library* was published which had favourable reviews but these were not encouraging enough. George then took Holy Orders and became domestic chaplain to the Duke of Rutland and went to live with the Rutland family at Belvoir (pronounced 'Beever'!) Castle, their country seat. From here he published *The Village*. This work, which really did establish Crabbe as a person of note in the well ploughed literary field, had been extensively revised by both Burke and Samuel JOHNSON. Not long after, Lord THURLOW presented Crabbe with two livings.

His last published work was *Tales of the Hall* in 1817 and for this, John Murray, his publisher, paid him *£3,000* (to include the copywright on his other existing poems).

Crabbe has sometimes been called the 'Poet of the Poor', and sometimes 'Pope in Fustian'. This latter being an allusion to Crabbe using heroic couplets in his works, as did Alexander POPE before him.

CRAIGIE Boston, Mass., November 3, 1867
Pearl Mary Teresa London, August 13, 1906
Author

7, Porchester Terrace, W2, late 1860s
24, Upper Woburn Place, WC1
56, Lancaster Gate, W2, 1900-1906

When she was one year old, Pearl Craigie's merchant father uprooted from America and transferred his business to London. So, though born near Boston, she was entirely English or European in upbringing, having been educated in London and Paris.

When hardly out of school she married Reginald Walpole Craigie. It was not a happy marriage and, though she had become a Catholic in 1892, she divorced Craigie in 1895.

In 1891, under her pen-name of 'John Oliver Hobbes' she had had her first novel, *Some Emotions and a Moral*, published in 1891 (perhaps the 'Emotions' were hers whilst preparing for her marriage and the 'Moral' was to be found in 1895?). She wrote a number of plays, the first being, *A Repentance*, which was put on at the St James's Theatre in 1899. She went on writing up to her death and her last novel, *The Dream and the Business*, was published posthumously.

CRANE Liverpool, August 15, 1845
Walter Horsham, March 15, 1915
Artist

13, Holland Street, W8 (LCP 1952) 1892-1915

Crane's father was a portrait painter and he brought his family down to

London when Walter was only 12. In January 1859, not yet 14, the boy was apprenticed to Lintons, a firm of engravers at 33, Essex Street, just off the Strand. The apprenticeship was for seven years and in that time Linton's moved back to their old premises at 85, Hatton Garden. Crane's father died of tuberculosis and the family moved to Argyle Square where an uncle had a house. Crane became a skilled craftsman and in the first few years of his working life he established himself as an illustrator of children's books. In fact, until Kate Greenaway and Ralph CALDECOTT appeared on the scene, he had the market practically to himself.

His skills were multiple, he designed wall papers, tiles (in the DE MORGAN manner) murals, books, decorative furniture and was, in every sense a *practical* artist – even if some of his designs look rather *impractical* to today's more austere tastes.

G.B. SHAW thought Crane a '...pleasant soul without a trace of quarrelsomeness which did no harm to the Labour Movement... The combination of art clique and Labour faction makes their society almost impossible. I never saw any of this in Crane.'

CRAVEN STREET, WC2

Bakerloo and Northern lines to Charing Cross

Originally it was called Spur Alley and was given its present name in 1742. Dame Elizabeth Craven bought the land in 1620 for her sons Thomas and William. (William turns up again in Craven Road, W2) Until the building of the Embankment – which began in 1862 – was finished in 1870, the street ended at a river bank coal-wharf. For some reason many lawyers lived and or worked in Craven Street. An 1837 *jingle* by James Smith who lived at number 27; ran:

> 'In Craven Street, Strand ten attorneys find place,
> And ten coal barges are moored to its base
> Fly, honesty fly! Seek some safer retreat,
> For there's craft in the river and craft in the Street.'

25, Herman MELVILLE, 1849. In 1836 Melville travelled from America to Liverpool as a cabin 'boy' on the *Highlander*. It was his experience on this trip that was the basis for his novel *Redburn,* which was published when he was here in 1849.

32, Heinrich HEINE (LCP 1912) 1827. He wrote, '...this overdriven London oppresses fancy and rends the heart'.

33, Mark AKENSIDE, 1759-1761. In the last year of his occupation here, Akenside was appointed physician to Queen Charlotte, consort of King George III.

36 (formerly 7) Benjamin FRANKLIN (LCP 1914) 1762-1775. The house belonged to a Mrs. Margaret Stevenson. He lived here off and on for over 12 years, sometimes bringing his son William and a negro slave with him. The house was built about 1730.

CROMWELL

The Cromwell Road, and the other Cromwells off it or near it, spring from the *legend* that Oliver Cromwell (1599-1685, Lord Protector of Britain 1649-1658) once had a cottage at the Earl's Court end of the road. His *son* Henry (1628-1674, who became Lord- Lieutenant of Ireland) married Elizabeth Russell, daughter of Sir Francis Russell of Chippenham in St Mary Abbot's Church, W14. Henry may have lived in Old Hale House, Brompton but Queen's Gate now runs over the site.

CROMWELL PLACE, SW7

Piccadilly, District and Circle lines to South Kensington

5, Sir John LAVERY (LCP 1966) 1899-1940. Here he painted a portrait of his second wife, Hazel, as she lay dying. She died, still in the house, on January 3, 1935.

7, Sir John Everett MILLAIS, 1862-1978. It was here he painted the *Boyhood of Raleigh,* which today is probably his best known work.

CROMWELL ROAD, SW7 *Directions as for Cromwell Place*

21, Sir Charles FREAKE (LCP 1981) 1860-1884. A speculative builder, he built this one-time imposing house for himself. It had a large ballroom at the back.

67, Lord Alfred DOUGLAS moved here with his family (but not the head of the family, the choleric 8th Marquis of Queensberry). 'Bosie' was only four at the time.

199, Lord SNOW, 1966-1975. He wrote *The Sleep of Reason* whilst here.

CROOKES	London, June 17, 1832
(Sir) William	London, April 4, 1919
Chemist	

20, Mornington Terrace, NW1

Crookes was pupil and then assistant to August Wilhelm von Hoffman at the Royal College of Chemistry for three years and from 1855 was the Chemistry lecturer at the Science College in Chester. In 1859 he established the magazine *Chemical News* and five years later was to become the editor of the *Quarterly Journal of Science* as well.

He became a Fellow of the Royal Society in 1863 and the French *Académie des Sciences* awarded him 3,000 francs and a Gold Medal. In 1913 he was President of the Royal Society. He was knighted in 1897.

It was Crookes who discovered the metal Thallium in 1861. (Thallium; from the Greek 'to bloom': atomic weight 204: symbol T1: found in iron and copper pyrites: rare, bluish-white in colour and extremely soft.) He improved the quality of electric lighting, invented the radiometer and the sphinthariscope in 1903; a device which detects the presence of radium salts. He was also a renowned authority on sanitation.

CROSLAND	Leeds, July 21, 1868
Thomas William Hodgson	London, December 23, 1924
Journalist	Finchley

48, Leicester Square, WC2, 1904

Crosland, a gloomy, taciturn child, was the son of an insurance agent. He began as a school teacher and wrote in his spare time. Like so many others of a like persuasion he gravitated to London, becoming a publisher's reader and then, later on, the editor of a journal called *The Outlook.*

In 1902 he published a book called *The Unspeakable Scot* which he alleged he wrote in one sitting. At about this time his visiting card read:

'T.W. CROSLAND, Jobbing Poet,
Orders executed with the greatest dispatch.
Terms: Strictly Cash.'

Not long after he became Assistant Editor to Lord Alfred DOUGLAS on a paper called the *Academy.* Their female factotum, wrote that, '...Crosland was invariably penniless...he influenced Lord Alfred most unwisely and led him into all sorts of difficulties'. (As if Douglas *needed* much leading!)

Siegfried Sassoon wrote in his private diary for April 19, 1922; 'Crosland! I lunched with him at Paganis in February 1914 (and hadn't set eyes on him since) and we ate a gargantuan meal of jugged hare and pêche melba. (Curiously enough paid for the lunch.) That was in the days of my innocence.' [Sassoon was then 28!] '...before Crosland and DOUGLAS began their infamous attacks on Robbie ROSS. At that time Crosland impressed me as being a sinister and powerful character. Today he merely looked shabby and bad tempered. ...And he wrote a cheap, sneering article on my war poems in November 1918. Poor, bombastic writer of dud cheques.'

CROWN OFFICE ROW, EC4   *District and Circle lines to Temple*

From the days of the Tudors, 'Civil Servants, Clerks of the Crown' had an office here. Indictments were framed in that Office right up to the 1880s.

2,   Charles LAMB was born here in 1775. He spent his early childhood in 'The Row'. Here he wrote, under his pen-name of 'Elia', of '...cheerful Crown Office Row, place of my kindly engender'.

CRUIKSHANK
George
Illustrator and cartoonist

London, September 27, 1792
London, February 1, 1878
Kensal Green (originally) then St Paul's

263, Hampstead Road, NW1 (P) 1850-1878

His father, Isaac (1756-1811) and his elder brother, also Isaac (1789-1811) were both caricaturists, but George, at one time, thought seriously of a maritime career. However, a publisher saw some of his work and had him illustrate a children's book, after which Cruikshank never looked back.

A publication called *The Scourge* (appropriately, considering its contents) provided Cruikshank with an outlet for his style, wit and mordant sense of humour. The magazine only lasted five years, but by then Cruikshank was established.

The Prince Regent (and his 'marital infelicities') was a frequent butt for Cruikshank's barbed style. Cruikshank, however, later had his own 'infelicities'. When his address was in the Hampstead Road where Mrs. Cruikshank lived, Papa C. was mostly at 31, Augustus Street, NW1, with his mistress, Adelaide Archbold, together with a litter of little Cruikshanks. Later and in a happier frame of mind, Cruikshank illustrated Charles Dickens' *Oliver Twist*. His water colour paintings also show the brighter side of the artist in him. He very rarely worked in oils.

In his sixties he began to show signs of mental distress. He started to claim that not only had he illustrated *Oliver Twist* he had *written* it as well!

CUNARD
(Lady) Emerald
Hostess

San Francisco, United States, 1872
London, July 10, 1948

20, Cavendish Square, W1, 1908
44, Grosvenor Square, W1, 1916
9, Grosvenor Square, W1, 1942

Christened Maud, Miss Burke was an heiress to a not inconsiderable gold-mining fortune. Failing to nab a Polish prince, she settled for Sir Bache Cunard and took her place in English society. The Cunard Line was founded by two brothers who once lived on the 250 acre island of Pabay Mor in the Outer Hebrides. The name of Cunard derives from two Celtic words, *Cuan Ard* meaning high seas. The commercial elbow was provided by Sir Samuel Cunard, born in Nova Scotia in 1787 and died in London in April 1865. The first voyage by the Cunarder *Britannia* from Liverpool to Boston was made July 4-19, 1840. Cunard was made a baronet in 1859 and Sir Bache was his grandson.

Maud Cunard decided that she should be called Emerald and so she was. Sir Bache was a countryman and an ardent rider to the hounds. Such diversions (and the people attracted to them) bored Emerald and she took up residence more or less permanently in London. They had only one child, a daughter, Nancy, who was to cause her socially clambering mother more than one headache.

Lady Cunard established a sort of non-intellectual *salon*; she was even able to lure the Prince of Wales into her toils. The greatest disappointment for Emerald must have been when Edward abdicated in 1935 and she did not have a *King* on her invitation lists.

LLOYD-GEORGE considered Lady Cunard 'a most dangerous woman'. Some times Lord CURZON used to call on her straight after a Cabinet meeting and tell her the latest from Number 10. Emerald was surprisingly discreet about such revelations – to the very considerable relief of the Cabinet!

CUNARD	Nevill Holt, Leicestershire, March 10, 1896
Nancy Clara	
Problem child	Paris, March 16, 1965
	Ashes in Père Lachaise Cemetery, Paris

5, Montagu Square, W1, 1946

'That hussy!' as H.H. ASQUITH referred to Nancy Cunard in October 1914 (an 18-year old 'hussy' at that.) Asquith was apparently quite worried that his youngest son, Cyril, might be attracted to her.

Nancy was the only child of Sir Bache Cunard and his American wife Maud ('Emerald'). Nancy was born at the country house which her father loved and her mother hated. Bache was 45 and 'Emerald' just 24. Nancy's education was sparse and took place as and where she happened to be. She became a fixture at 'high society' parties and often embarrassed other guests by her uninhibited tongue. She became great friends with another 'bohemian', Iris Tree, younger daughter of Sir Herbert BEERBOHM-TREE. She and Nancy lived rather squalidly in a studio in Fitzroy Street (Iris was a student at the Slade).

In 1916 Nancy made a disastrous marriage with an Australian soldier called Sidney Fairbairn. The marriage was really over before the World War One but it was not until 1925 that they were divorced.

She made many friends, many of genius, many to become famous and practically all of them rather raffish. In Venice in 1928 she met a negro jazz musician who had once been a piano player in a brothel. He was to become *the* one, long lasting relationship in her life. A jazz musician was bad enough, but a *negro!* Many doors were closed to her for good. Though her black man, Henry Crowder, meant much to her, she set out *determinedly* to sleep with other negroes when Crowder and she were in Paris.

She dabbled in practically every fringe form of 'intellectual' activity. She started a small printing/publishing company; she wrote some quite good poetry, but the pace of life caught up with her; too much drink, soon drugs and excessive sexual activity reduced her to a wraith. Half out of her mind and biting the hands which tried to feed her, she died in a public ward of a Paris hospital.

CURZON	Kedleston, Yorks., January 11, 1859.
George Nathaniel	London, March 20, 1925.
Diplomat and Viceroy	All Saint's Church, Kedleston

4, Carlton Gardens, SW1, 1897
1, Carlton House Terrace, SW1 (LCP 1976) from 1905 until he died here

Curzon was the eldest son of the Reverend Alfred Curzon, 4th Baron Scarsdale, who was, '...an old despot of the 18th Century'. George

Nathaniel had a fine record at Eton, but failed to get the expected First in Classics at Oxford. He was, however, elected a Fellow at All Souls in 1883. He entered Parliament as MP for Southport in 1886 and stayed there until 1887, when he took himself off to the Far East and gained a deep insight of that mysterious part of the world. By 1891 he was Under- Secretary for India and seven years later (when only 39) became Viceroy of India. He chose an Irish barony as this would not debar him from sitting in the House of Commons. Had he chosen an English title he would automatically forfeit his right to sit in the lower Chamber.

He was never an easy man to deal with and he was a turbulent Viceroy, though he did introduce measures and reforms for the good of the 'Sub Continent', established the North West Frontier Province and the partition of Bengal. However, he left India in 1905, a disappointed man.

He resurfaced in British politics as Lord Privy Seal in the Coalition Government of 1915 and entered the Cabinet a year later. He was then awarded the Order of the Garter. His was a strong position and he continued upwards very surely. When BONAR LAW resigned the Premiership, many people (*including* Curzon) thought that he would be asked to form a Government. King George V sent for BALDWIN instead: Curzon swallowed hard and accepted the post of Foreign Secretary, where he stayed until 1924.

In 1895 he had married Mary, the daughter of the very rich American, L.Z. Leiter, who lived at Dupont Circle, Washington. (Mary was born in Chicago on May 27, 1870.)

As a boy Curzon suffered from spinal curvature and when grown up still had to wear a corset like sheath which must have been uncomfortable and his rigid carriage was in part caused by this, making him appear to be more pompous than he really was. Despite this he was, '...a most passionate physical lover'. This evidence was supplied by Elinor Glyn (1864-1943) the author of the *daring* book, *Three Weeks,* in 1907. Some anonymous 'poet' wrote:

> 'Would you like to sin
> With Elinor Glyn
> On a tiger skin?
> Or would you prefer
>   To err
>   With her
> On some other fur?'

In 1915 Miss Glyn wrote a memoir on Curzon which contained some *very* candid observations!

Sir Bertram MacKennal's bronze statue of Curzon was placed almost opposite his front door at 1, Carlton House Terrace in 1931. Curzon is wearing his Garter robes.

CURZON PLACE, W1   *Piccadilly line to Hyde Park Corner*

George Curzon, the 3rd Viscount Howe (1724-1758; and not to be confused with George Nathaniel, 1st Marquess Curzon) gave his name to the Place and the Street. An ancestor of his, a Derbyshire baronet, Sir Nathaniel Curzon had bought the land hereabouts in 1699.

8,   Ruth DRAPER, 1951.

CURZON STREET, W1

1,   Lord Randolph CHURCHILL, 1876.
15,   Crewe House. It is the finest example of 18th century domestic architecture in London. It was built for Shepherd (hence Shepherd Market, just across the road) in 1735. It was sold to Lord Carhampton in 1750 and in 1818 J. Stuart-Wortley bought it for £12,000. In 1983 the

house (and suite of offices behind it) were put on the market and a price tag of £16-20 million put on them.

A happy occasion for this lovely house was in 1907. It was here that Winston CHURCHILL first met Clementine Hozier who was to become his wife in the following year.

19, Benjamin DISRAELI (First and last Lord Beaconsfield) died here in 1882 (LCP 1908). He had bought a seven-year lease on the house, financed by the profits of his novel *Endymion,* which was published in 1880.

24, Francis CHANTREY, 1806. He lodged here with his uncle and aunt, a Mr. and Mrs. Wade, servants of Mrs. D'Oyley who owned the house. She was very kind to Chantrey and it was from here (probably) that he went to his wedding in 1809. His wife brought with her a dowry of £10,000; a real fortune.

32, Rufus ISAACS, 1st Marquess of Reading died here in 1935 (LCP 1971).

33, Ronald FIRBANK, 1912.

D

DANBY, Frank, see FRANKAU, J.

DANCE
George (the 'Younger')
Architect
London, 1740(?)
London, January 14, 1825
St Paul's Cathedral

91, Gower Street, WC1 (LCP 1970) from 1790 until he died here

Dance learned his trade in his father's office and took the business over when his father died in 1768. Two years later he was involved in the rebuilding of Newgate Prison. He then rebuilt St Luke's Hospital but, as he grew older, he spent more and more time with 'Art' rather than 'Architecture'.

He was made Professor of Architecture at the Royal Academy but he does not seem to have given even one lecture! In 1815 he resigned as City Surveyor and spent the last few years of his life as an invalid in Gower Street. When *he* died, *then* died the last surviving member of the original 40 'Royal Academicians'. His father – Dance, 'the Elder', was the architect of the Mansion House in the City of London in 1739. In fact the elder Dance, who died in 1768, in his 69th year, was a far greater figure *architecturally* than his son George. He built the Churches of St Botolph's, St Luke's and St Leonard, all in the City of London and a number of secular buildings, including the Excise Office in Broad Street.

DARWIN
Charles Robert
Philosophic scientist
Shrewsbury, February 12, 1809
Hampshire, April 19, 1882
North Aisle, Wetminster Abbey

41, Great Marlborough Street, W1, 1836-1838
110, Gower Street, WC1 (LCP 1961) 1838-1842

Charles Darwin's *grandfather* was Erasmus DARWIN and his father, Dr. Robert Waring Darwin (1766-1848) was a General Practioner, even though he could not stand the sight of blood! Sometimes he exhibited almost psychic powers; he was very strictly tee-total, very tall and *very* fat. Charles's mother was born a Wedgwood and, in 1839, when Charles married, Emma, another Wedgwood became a Darwin. It was at Christ Church, Cambridge where Darwin's biological studies became serious. Having got his BA, Professor Henslow recommended him as a naturalist to go to South American waters aboard *HMS Beagle*. Darwin sailed on December 27, 1831 and he did not see England again for nearly five years. After he married Emma, he lived like a country gentleman in Kent. Here he evolved the theories which were to give him the fame he did not want. His basic theory was made public before he wished and, after a hectic few weeks of preparation, *The Origin of Species by Natural Selection* was published in November 1859. It was studied intensively in Britain and elsewhere and attacked from many quarters. The arguments, for and against, had been vociferous for 12 years when his *Descent of Man* was published in 1871, posing further complications for previously true believers.

DAVIES   Newport, Gwent, April 20(?), 1871
William Henry   Gloucestershire, September 26, 1940
Poet

2A, Clarence Gardens, NW1, pre-1914
18, Little Russell Street, WC1, 1914
14, Great Russell Street, WC1, 1917-1921

Davies's grandfather kept a public house in Newport and young William
was apprenticed to a picture frame maker, a job he did not find congenial.
When he was 22 he went to America arriving in New York with 10 dollars
in his pocket. He got himself around the country by 'train jumping'.
However, having crossed the border into Ontario, he made a clumsy 'jump'
and his right foot was cut off.
He came back to England and worked only fitfully; once as a pedlar, selling
shoelaces. In 1905 he was able to get a book of verse called *The Soul's
Destroyer* published. It caught the eye of G.B. SHAW; they became friendly
and SHAW was able to get him better known in wider circles. Davies was
lent a cottage in Sevenoaks, Kent, and here he wrote most of his most
successful book, *The Autobiography of a Super Tramp*. It was published in
1907 and fame followed. In 1925 he published another autobiography called
Later Days, but this seems to have been largely forgotten.

DAVIS   Philadelphia, April 18, 1864   ·
Richard Harding   Mount Kisco, N.Y., April 11, 1916
Author

118, Cheyne Row, SW3, 1907-1908

Davis was a very highly regarded war correspondent, but he also produced a
number of novels, short stories, plays and travel books (such as *Our English
Cousins* in 1894.)
He began as a reporter on the *Philadelphia Record* and in 1890 became editor
of *Harper's Weekly.* He 'covered' the Boer, Spanish-American, Japanese-
Russian and the First World Wars.
The short stories often had a very romantic flavour – Davis *was* a romantic
and he maintained the image by escorting the original of the 'Gibson Girl'.
(Charles Dana Gibson, 1867-1944, produced this idealized beauty in many
black and white drawings from 1896 on. His model was really his wife,
Irene. She was one of the Langhorne girls and Nancy, Viscountess ASTOR,
was her sister.)

DAVY   Penzance, Cornwall, December 17,
(Sir) Humphry   1778
Scientist   Geneva, May 29, 1829
                                   (Geneva – beside his widow's third
                                   husband)

28, Grosvenor Street, W1, 1820-1825
26, Park Street, W1, 1825-1829

Son of a Cornish wood-carver, Davy became a laboratory assistant in
Beddoes Pneumatic Institute at Bristol in 1798. He was lecturing on
Chemistry at the Royal Institution by 1801 and became its Director in 1805.
He discovered the decomposition of fixed alkalis in 1807, but the invention
for which he will evermore be remembered was the 'Miner's Safety Lamp'
in 1815. This device saved thousands of underground miners' lives and Davy
was given a baronetcy for this achievement in 1816.
In 1812 Davy had married Mrs. Apreece, who, though of a plain
appearance, was able to bring a substantial 'dowry' with her. After his death,
Lady Davy married again. This husband, her third, died before she did and

so she had spouse number three put beside spouse number two (H. Davy) in his tomb in Geneva. It would be interesting to think what the two ex-husbands might discuss on *Judgement Day!*

DAWSON
Bertrand Edward (1st Viscount)
Physician

Croydon, Surrey, March 9, 1864
March 7, 1945

23, Harley Street, W1, 1918
32, Wimpole Street, W1, 1921–1940

Dawson was the fourth of the seven children of a Croydon architect. He eventually became a Royal doctor extraordinary. He was physician to King Edward VII, George V, Edward VIII, George VI and Queen Mary.

He was one of the three doctors to sign the last, tragically simple bulletin on the health of King George V. He, after Frederick Willans and Stanley Hewett had signed, put his name to the statement issued from Sandringham House on January 20, 1936, at 9.25 in the evening. It simply read 'The King's life is moving peacefully towards its close'. Three hours later King George V was dead. At the bedside were Queen Mary, the Prince of Wales and the Dukes and Duchesses of York and Kent.

DAY-LEWIS
Cecil
Poet Laureate

Ireland, April 27, 1904
May 21, 1972
Stinsford, Dorset

73A, Bedford Gardens, W8, 1950–1953
96, Campden Hill Road, W8, 1953–1957
66, Torrington Square, WC1

Day-Lewis, though Irish born (where his father was a clergyman) was educated in England: at Sherborne School and Wadham College, Oxford. He set out as a teacher but soon abandoned this for a more concentrated literary life.

He married Constance King, the daughter of his old Headmaster, but that marriage was dissolved in 1951. His elder son (by Constance) Sean, has written that the family name *is* DAY-LEWIS, but Cecil dropped the hyphen 'as a gesture of inverted snobbery' in 1927. He re- instated the hyphen later as he did not like being plain 'Mr Lewis'!

Day-Lewis also wrote a number of very good detective novels under the pseudonym of *Nicholas Blake*. Blake was a family name on his mother's side and his second son was christened Nicholas. If poetry does not appeal, then try *A Question of Proof* (1935) or *Malice in Wonderland* (1940).

DEAN STREET, W1
*Central and Northern lines
to Tottenham Court Road*

This street first began to be built up in 1681 and may have been named as a compliment to the Dean of Chapel Royal, Bishop Henry Compton (1632–1713) who was very much involved in the building of St Anne's Church in Soho Square, into which Dean Street leads.

28, Karl MARX (LCP 1967). The plaque reads, 'Karl Marx lived here 1851–1856'. It should be 1850–1856. The bailiffs had thrown the Marxes out of their first home in London (in Anderson Street) . They had stayed for a short while at 64 Dean Street. At 28 they had just two rooms on the top floor. Here lived Marx, his wife, five children (the fifth Franziska being born in March 1851) and an English nurse for the confinement. One of the rooms Marx used exclusively as his 'study'. Their landlord was an Italian cook called Marengo.

75, Sir James THORNHILL, 1725–1730. It was from this house, on March

23, 1729, that William HOGARTH eloped with Thornhill's daughter. They were married at Old Paddington Church. 200 years later there still were wall paintings, dimly seen, for which tradition had Hogarth partially responsible.

78, Peg WOFFINGTON, 1740-1748.

DE GAULLE	Lille, November 22, 1890
Charles André Joseph Marie	Colombey des deux Eglises
Soldier and Statesman	November 11, 1970

4, Carlton Gardens, SW1 (P) 1940-1944 (the plaque is in French)

The General and Madame de Gaulle actually lived at 99, Frognal, Hampstead, NW3 during their four year stay in England. The building is now part of the Convent of Saint Dorothy.

De Gaulle, a very professional soldier, who fought through the First World War and was convinced thereafter of the dominant role the aeroplane would play in the future, became President of the Fifth French Republic in December 1958.

In June 1940, as France collapsed against the German onslaught, de Gaulle and some members of his staff managed to escape to England, where he became head of the 'Free French'. Never an easy man, even in triumph; in defeat he was sometimes almost objectionable.

He became head of a provisional French Government in 1958 when France was being considerably troubled by what were once her North African Colonies. de Gaulle came to power, almost as a dictator, in December. No person – including Napoleon – had held such authority before in French history.

When the European Common Market was broached, de Gaulle was adamantly opposed to Britain joining it. In 1965 he was narrowly re-elected as President after much student unrest and his attitude became haughtier than ever. He was forced to resign in April 1969.

DELAFIELD, E.M., see DASHWOOD, E.

DELANCEY STREET, NW1   *Northern line to Mornington Crescent.*

The Fitzroy family (the founding father of which was one of King Charles II's bastard sons by Barbara Castlemaine) owned land here and in 1795, leased or granted fields to one, James Delancey, who began to put up houses as quickly as he possibly could.

15, Charlotte MEW, 1928, not long before she committted suicide.

54, Dylan THOMAS, briefly, in 1951. By this time he was completely alcoholic.

62, Sir Oliver LODGE, 1874-1877. He lodged here whilst studying advanced mathematics.

DE LA RAMEE	Bury St Edmunds, January 7, 1839
Maria Louisa ('Ouida')	Viareggio, January 25, 1908
Author	51, Welbeck Street, W1, 1867-1883

11, Ravenscourt Square, W6 (LCP 1952)

'Ouida's' correct surname was probably Rame, and 'Ouida' was her own babyish attempts to pronounce Louisa. Her father was French and her mother English. In 1857 her father died and 'Ouida' came to London soon after. Around 1859 she met the novelist William Harrison Ainsworth (1805-1882). His first novel was published in 1834 and was followed by some 40 more. *The Tower of London* 1840 and *Old St Pauls* the following year, were his most popular. Ainsworth helped to launch 'Ouida' as an author. Her first novel to be published was *Held in Bondage* in 1863; to be followed at almost yearly intervals by similar works which were a bit racy and some positively swashbuckling. The most 'ouida-ish' of them all was *Under Two Flags* in 1867. She also wrote books for children.

DE MORGAN
William Frend
Artist and author

London, November 16, 1839
January 13, 1917

69, Gower Street, WC1, here born
30, Cheyne Row, SW3, 1872-1881
1, The Vale, SW3 (LCP 1937) 1887-1909
127, Church Street, SW3, 1910-1917

De Morgan's father, Augustus (1806-1871) came from a military family in Madras, but returned to England to go to Cambridge, from which he emerged as 4th Wrangler in 1827. (A 'Wrangler' at Cambridge is one who is in the highest of the three classes of honours in mathematics. Until 1909 there used to be the title of 'Senior Wrangler' for the best wrangler of the year, academically). He was to be Professor of Mathematics at University College, London.

William, born a Londoner, went to the Royal Academy Schools and began designing tiles and stained glass windows. Eventually he built a kiln and had a 'showroom' at the Orange House, Cheyne Row. The Pre-Raphaelites were his friends and he worked for a while with William Samuel Morris.

His little 'factory' closed in 1907, having run into money problems, but de Morgan had already become a successful author before the final crash. His first published work was *Joseph Vance* in 1906 and it was a success. Not only was it remarkable that the first novel of a 64-year old craftsman should become a best seller, but it was 230,000 words in length – every one in de Morgan's own hand in the manuscript.

A tablet by Halsey Ricardo to de Morgan's memory was unveiled in Chelsea Old Church by Reginald BLUNT in 1918.

DE QUINCEY
Thomas
Essayist

Manchester, August 15, 1785
Glasgow, December 8, 1859
West Churchyard, Edinburgh

61 (then 38) Greek Street, W1 (LCP 1909) 1802

De Quincey's father died when Thomas was very young and his early upbringing seems to have been taken care of by a tyrannical elder brother. He was schooled in the West of England, but, by 1801, he was back at the Manchester Grammar School. From there he ran away and lived in Wales, supported by a tiny allowance from his widowed mother. In December 1802 he came to London 'and led a very much hand-to-mouth existence. With backing from very good friends, he went up to Worcester College, Oxford. In the College vacations he usually came to London and, on one of these, he first tried opium.

With Oxford behind him, he expanded his literary acquaintances; he got to know COLERIDGE (13 years older and an opium addict too) WORDSWORTH, Southey and, later, Charles LAMB. By the time he was 28 years old, de Quincey was taking between 8,000 and 12,000 'drops' *daily*. But, by 1844, he had managed to reduce his daily intake of opium to six *grains*. At the peak of his addiction he had been known to 'consume as much as ten wine-glasses a day'. John Wilson, who had befriended him, took him up to Edinburgh and, in Scotland, de Quincey met Margaret Simpson, a farmer's daughter and married her in 1816.

His real literary claims to fame began in 1821, when his *Confessions of an Opium-Eater* was published in the *London Magazine*. Before long some of his lengthy articles were published quite regularly in *Blackwood's* and other similar magazines.

Unlike Coleridge, de Quincey had no Doctor Gilman to rescue him from drugged despair. However, de Quincey did gather all his works together – amounting to 14 volumes and these were published in a standard edition by Professor David Masson, a Scottish scholar (1822-1907) who also wrote a biography of de Quincey.

DERBY
(14th Earl)
Prime Minister

Knowsley, Merseyside, March 29, 1799 Edward Geoffrey Smith Stanley
Knowsley, Merseyside, October 27, 1869
Knowsley

10, St James's Square, SW1 (LCP 1910) 1837-1855

The first Lord Derby was Thomas, who actually placed the crown of King Richard III (slain at the Battle of Bosworth, August 22, 1485) on the head of Henry Tudor, who became King Henry VII. The Derbys have been King's men ever since. The 14th Earl succeeded his father in 1851; but until then he had been sitting in the House of Commons as Lord Stanley – the family name of the Derbys. His constituency was Stockbridge (in Hampshire) and he held the seat for 24 years.

Derby was Prime Minister, first in 1852 and again in 1858, but resigned on a vote of 'no confidence' in 1859. In 1863 he was *offered* the Crown of Greece but refused it. Still, a 'non-royal', he became Prime Minister of Britain again in July 1866 and lasted nearly two years, when DISRAELI became Premier. The tenants on his very large estates found him to be a good landlord and respected him all the more because he was a great sportsman. His racehorses were superb: from 1843 to 1863 horses carrying the Derby colours, won over £94,000 in prize money. (That truly great flat race, The Derby, was first run in 1790 and actually won by a horse called *Diomed* owned by Sir Charles Bunbury; but, luckily it was decided to call it 'Derby', rather than 'Bunbury'!)

The Derby motto is *Sans Changer* – Without changing.

DERBY
Edward George Villiers Stanley
(17th Earl)
Aristocratic diplomat

London, April 16, 1865
February 4, 1948

23, St James's Square, SW1, here born
36, Great Cumberland Place, W1, 1890s
Derby House, Stratford Place, W1, 1908-1948

Derby was probably the closest person (outside the Royal Family itself) to King George V. He was politically prominent and, having served as Secretary of State under three Prime Ministers, was certainly able to supply the King with, what today would probably be called, 'feedback'. He was also British Ambassador in Paris from 1918-1920: a critical time to be in the highest diplomatic post on offer.

In 1889 he married Lady Alice Montagu, a daughter of the 7th Duke of Manchester. They had three children, the heir Edward, Lord Stanley being born in 1894. The Derbys owned many thousands of acres and the Earl's annual income was around £300,000 – at a time when tax was almost non-existent.

Like his ancestors, he had an eye for a good race horse and his horses won the Derby (appropriately) three times. He was nicknamed the 'King of Lancashire' (the county in which rests the Derby country seat, Knowsley Park, at Prescot).

DE VERE GARDENS, W8

*District and Circle lines
to High Street Kensington*

Named after Aubrey de Vere, the first Lord of the Manor of Kensington. The Garden were built around 1875 but the de Vere family goes right back to Albericus de Ver, who came over with William the Conqueror (from Ver, near Coutance in Normandy). The Bishop of Coutance granted tenure of the Manor to Alberic and when the Bishop died in 1093, the de Vere's gained ownership of the estate. With the dissolution of the Monasteries, Kensington went to the Crown.

29, Robert BROWNING moved here in the Spring of 1887. He died in Venice only 18 months later and the funeral procession for his interment in Westminster Abbey started from this house.

32, J.K. STEPHEN, 1890. It is most likely that when living here he would have visited his eight-year old cousin Virginia Stephen (later Virginia WOOLF) just along the road at 22, Hyde Park Gate.

34, H.M. STANLEY, 1872-1874. Recently returned from Africa having found Dr. Livingstone (we presume).

34, Henry JAMES (LCP 1949) 1886-1902. Here he wrote *The Ambassadors* (1903). His brother, William, lived here in 1899 and again in 1900.

DEVONSHIRE PLACE and STREET, W1 *Bakerloo line to Regent's Park*

Both named after Dorothy Cavendish, daughter of the Duke of Devonshire who was married to the heir of the Harley's Marylebone estates. She was only 16.

DEVONSHIRE PLACE

2, Sir Arthur CONAN DOYLE had his first surgery here in 1882.

4, William BECKFORD, 1810, his last address in London.

10, Sir William ROTHENSTEIN, in the 1940s.

23, Field Marshall Sir Evelyn WOOD, 1896, soon to be made Adjutant-General of the Army.

DEVONSHIRE STREET

11, George PEABODY, 1837. His first house in London while he established himself as a banker.

26, Robert and Elizabeth BROWNING, July to September 1850, where they had a small, gloomy and expensive apartment.

DICK
(Sir) William Reid
Sculptor

Glasgow, January 13, 1879
October 10, 1961

10, Maida Vale, W9, his name goers until his death

Another instance of a Scotsman making his mark anywhere but in his own country, Dick was arguably one of the best known sculptors for the first half of the twentieth century. He became an ARA in 1928 and was knighted eight years later.

On an international scale his work can be seen on the Menin Gate: he sculpted the lion for this memorial of the First World War at Ypres. He was chosen to make the statue of President Roosevelt which now stands in the garden of Grosvenor Square. The cost of the statue was met by contributions from the British public, the most anyone was allowed to give was five shillings (25p). Another standing figure by Dick is the statue of King George V which is outside the east end of Westminster Abbey, opposite the House of Lords. In the City is his John SOANE on the Bank of England, a medallion of Lord GREY of FALLODON on the Foreign Office

Wall. In 1936 he gave his *Boy With Frog* fountain, a bronze, to Queen Mary's Gardens in the centre of Regent's Park.

DICKENS	Portsmouth, February 7, 1812
Charles John Huffam	Gad's Hill, Rochester, Kent, June 9,
Author	1870
	Westminster Abbey in 'Poets' Corner'
	(having no monument by his request)

4, Gower Street, WC1, 1823
10, Norfolk Street, Fitzroy Square, W1, 1829-1832
15, Fitzroy Street, W1, 1832-1833
18, Bentinck Street, W1, 1833-1834
21, George Street, Adelphi, WC2, 1834
15, Furnival's Inn, EC4, 1836-1837
48, Doughty Street, WC1 (LCP 1903) 1837-1839
1, Devonshire Terrace, W2, 1839-1849
9, Osnaburgh Street, NW1, 1849
Tavistock House, Tavistock Square, WC1 (P) November 1851-July 1860
3, Hanover Terrace, NW1, 1861-1862
16, Hyde Park Gate, SW7, 1862-February 1864
52, Gloucester Place, W1, 1864-June 1864
6, Southwick Place, W2, March 1866-1869.
5, Hyde Park, W2, January 1870

Dickens' father was a clerk in the Navy Pay Office and in 1817 moved the family to Chatham in Kent – then an important Navy town In 1822 they moved up to London and Dickens senior was soon arrested and clapped into Marshalsea Prison for debt. In May, after three months, he was released and they lived briefly in Camden Town, North London. (Some of the family experiences are recalled in *Little Dorrit*.) In March 1827, Dickens joined Ellis and Blackmore at 5, Holborn Court, Gray's Inn as a solicitor's clerk, but, two years later, having learnt shorthand, he had become a freelance reporter in *Doctor's Commons* and from there he graduated to be a newspaper reporter on an evening paper called the *True Sun*.

On December 1, 1833, his first story, *A Dinner at Poplar Walk* was published in the *Monthly Magazine*. This piece was later retitled, *Mr. Minns and his Cousin*. In February 1836, the first series of 'Boz' was published (sometimes he used 'Charles John Huffam' as a *nom-de-plume* rather than 'Boz'). On April 2 of that year he married Catherine Hogarth at St Luke's Church, Chelsea. *Pickwick* was being published in 20 monthly parts by Chapman and Hall. When Robert Seymour, the artist who was illustrating *Pickwick* committed suicide, Hablôt BROWNE took over the task, with very happy long-term results. (His pen-name was 'Phiz'.) The original scheme was re-arranged (by Dickens) and emerged as *The Pickwick Papers* in monthly parts during 1836 and 1837.

Dickens' popularity soared and novel after novel followed: many, like *Oliver Twist* being issued in 24 monthly parts. He made a hit in America with his 'readings' from his own works in May 1868 and from this one tour alone he *netted £20,000*.

As a novelist and a public figure he was supreme, but his relationship with Catherine deteriorated. She had borne him seven sons and three daughters. She was not able to cope with her husband's success and they separated in 1858. There were still novels to come and in 1859, he became editor of a weekly journal which he called *All the Year Round* – and took offices for it: 11, Wellington Street, just off the Strand. When he died (of cerebral haemorrhage) at his country house (Gad's Hill, in Essex, which he bought in 1856) he left behind one, unfinished novel, *The Mystery of Edwin Drood*.

DILKE   Chelsea, London, December 8, 1843
(Sir) Charles Wentworth   August 10, 1911
Politician

76, Sloane Street, SW3, 1911

Both Dilke's father, who was a Liberal politician and his grandfather (who was a journalist and a critic) were christened *Charles Wentworth*. So, until 1864, when grandfather Dilke died, there were *three* Charles Wentworth Dilkes 'in circulation'.
This Dilke graduated from Trinity Hall, Cambridge as head of the Law *Tripos* in 1866 and was called to the Bar. He then travelled widely in North America and Australia. His visits to these places were described in a book he published in 1868, called, *Greater Britain*. This same year he was elected as MP for Chelsea; a *Radical* who professed Republicanism. Despite this, there were many people who saw Dilke as a suitable successor to GLADSTONE.
In 1885 he married a widow, Mrs. Mark Pattison (née Strong) as his second wife. But, in the following year, his involvement in the divorce case of Mrs. Crawford, led to his political defeat and political retirement. His 'exile' was soon over and he was elected MP for the *Forest of Dean* in 1892.

DISRAELI   London, December 21, 1804
Benjamin (1st Earl of Beaconsfield)   London, April 19, 1881
Prime Minister   St Michael's, Hughenden, Bucks.

22, Theobalds Road (previously 6, Kings Road, Bedford Row) WC1 (LCP 1948) born and lived here until he was 13
6, Bloomsbury Square, WC1, 1828-1829
93, Park Lane, Gloucester Gate W1 (P) 1839-1880
2, Whitehall Gardens, SW1, 1875-1880
19, Curzon Street, W1, where he died

Disraeli was born a Jew but in 1817, his father, Isaac, instead of organizing a bar-mitzvah for him, had the boy baptized into the Protestant faith. Having put behind him his semitic origins he was able to embark on his chosen career of politics. (A practising Jew in the last century was not able to sit in Parliament, hold a commission in the Army or Navy, nor even go up to Oxford or Cambridge.)
In 1837 – the year of Queen Victoria's accession – Disraeli was elected an MP for Maidstone, Kent. He had already brought himself to the notice of the public as an author of five novels, the first being *Vivian Grey* in 1827.
He was never one to be overlooked and he rose up through the ranks, being Chancellor of the Exchequer three times and, crowning all, Prime Minister, for the first time in 1868 and again between 1874 and 1880. During this second term he was created Earl of Beaconsfield (he had a country house near this village).
Probably Disraeli's greatest coup was to secure the Suez Canal for Britain in 1875. The new route cut the sailing time to India dramatically and enabled England to open up the 'sub continent' very quickly. In 1876 he persuaded Victoria to add 'Empress of India' to her other titles.
Early in life Disraeli was far from well off and often in debt. This situation was happily resolved when he married the wealthy widow of Mr. Wyndham Lewis. (Lewis had been an MP and friend of Disraeli.) Mrs. Disraeli was a simple person and careful with the money she had. (On the day of their marriage she noted that there was £3,000 in her bank account and that her wedding gloves had cost two shillings and sixpence – 12½p.)
She adored her 'Dizzy' and her very simplicity had great charm. Once at a party the ladies, alone, had been discussing the beauty of the 'Classical nude figure'. She entered the discussion with; 'Oh, but you ought to see my Dizzy

in his bath!' She was raised to Viscountess Beaconsfield in her own right. She died in 1872 and was sorely missed by Disraeli.

Of London, Disraeli once wrote, 'it is a wonderful place...this London; a nation, not a city; with a population greater than some kingdoms, and districts as different as if they were under different governments and spoke different languages'.

On the coffin at Disraeli's funeral lay a wreath of primroses with a card in the Queen's handwriting (in itself a signal honour) saying; 'His favourite flowers from Osborne, a tribute of affection from Queen Victoria'. It was not surprising that most people assumed that primroses were *Disraeli's* favourite. April 19 became 'Primrose Day' and in 1883 'The Primrose League' was founded by 'The Fourth Party' (Sir Henry Drummond Wolff, Sir John Gorst, A.J. BALFOUR and their leader, Lord Randolph CHURCHILL. They existed largely to harass GLADSTONE.) What no one realized was that primroses were Prince *Albert's* favourite flower and the Queen had sent a sort of 'proxy tribute from the Beyond'! Indeed Gladstone at the dinner table not long after Disraeli's death suddenly said to his dinner companion, 'Tell me, Lady Dorothy' [who had been a good friend of Disraeli's] 'upon your honour, have you ever heard Lord Beaconsfield express any particular fondness for the primrose? ... No? ...the gorgeous Lily, I think, was more to his taste.'

There is a bronze statue of Disraeli, on the west side of Parliament Square between PEEL on *his* left and DERBY to the right. It is by Mario Razzi and unveiled on April 19 – 'Primrose Day' – 1883.

D'ORSAY

	Paris, September, 1801
Gillion Gaspard Alfred de Grimaud	Paris, August 4, 1852
Artistic dandy	Chambourcy

Gore House, Knightsbridge, SW7, 1836-1849

D'Orsay was the son of a French general and an Italian dancer, who came to London in 1821. Before this he had briefly been a member of the *Garde Royale* – and he the son of a Bonapartist general!

He met the BLESSINGTONS and they were mutually attracted to each other; before long there was a *ménage à trois* in St. James's Square. Blessington, a strange man, offered to make d'Orsay his heir if he would marry his (then 12 years old) daughter, Harriet Gardiner. Three years later this unlikely couple were married in Rome, but it is more than probable that the alliance was not consummated. Blessington died in 1829 and a household was set up consisting of the widow Blessington, her probable lover d'Orsay and d'Orsay's bride, who (in law) was Lady Blessington's stepdaughter!

D'Orsay lived a spendthrift's life and there came a time when he could only move out of his house on Sundays, that being the only day of the week when writs could not be served! The puritanical Thomas CARLYLE amusingly enough, rather 'admired' d'Orsay, as did *Mrs. Carlyle.*

Captain Gronow wrote of d'Orsay that, '...when I first knew him, he might have served as a model for statuary. His neck was long, his shoulders broad, and his waist narrow and though he was, perhaps, somewhat underlimbed, nothing could surpass the beauty of his feet and ankles. His dark, chestnut hair hung naturally in long, waving curls, his forehead was high and wide...he had full lips and very white teeth, but a little apart; which sometimes gave to the generally amiable expression of his countenance a rather cruel and sneering look, such as one sees in the heads of some of the old Roman Emperors.'

DORSET STREET, W1   *Bakerloo and BR lines to Marylebone*

South of the Marylebone Road it was once part of the Portman estate. The Portmans had large land holdings in the county of Dorset, in the West of England.

13, Robert and Elizabeth BROWNING, stayed here in 1855. Here she wrote *Aurora Leigh* and TENNYSON read his recently completed poem, *Maud*, to them.

22, Algernon SWINBURNE, 1865-1870. He wrote many of his poems here and here, too, the odd American trick horse-back rider, Adah Isaacs Menken, introduced herself to him and so began their (almost certainly platonic) friendship.

DOUGHTY STREET, WC1   *Piccadilly line to Russell Square*

The Doughty family had inherited property in Holborn from their forebears, the Brownlows. The Doughty's became extinct in 1826 and their land passed to Sir Edward Tichborne.

8, Sydney SMITH, 1803.

10, Charlotte MEW was born here in 1869.

14, Sydney SMITH (yet again!) (LCP 1906) 1803. He had just come south from Edinburgh, staying a short while at number 8. In 1804 he gave a series of lectures to the Royal Society for which he was paid £50. This relieved the very precarious finances of the family.

14, James AGATE, 1935.

42, Richard Le GALLIENNE, 1899: his daughter, Eva, was born here. Her mother was Le Gallienne's second wife.

43, Edmund YATES, 1854-1860. Yates wrote that Doughty Street was, 'A broad, wholesome street. None of your common thoroughfares to be rattled through by vulgar cabs and earth-shaking Pickford' [a furniture removers still in existence] 'vans, but a self-including property with a gate at each end, and a lodge with a porter in a gold laced hat with the Doughty arms on the buttons of his mulberry-coloured coat to prevent anyone, except with a mission to one of the houses, ever intruding on the exclusive territory.'

48, Charles DICKENS. His agents wrote to a Mr. Banks in March 1837 to the effect that their client was wishing to treat for the house on a three year agreement at £80 pa and that he was agreeable to painting the front drawing room and blind frames round the windows. (Attention was drawn to a ceiling which needed cleaning.) Here Dickens finished *Pickwick Papers* wrote the whole of *Oliver Twist* and nearly finished *Nicholas Nickleby*.

On June 9, 1925 it was first opened to the public as a Dickens' Museum. On September 21, 1983 the fully refurnished drawing room, the next room to Dickens' study, was reopened by Sir Anthony Jolliffe, Lord Mayor of London. The Heritage of London Trust gave £10,000 toward the cost. As far as possible they tried to restore the decorations as they were in Dickens' day. (Three rosewood chairs, a table and a cushioned chair, with plum-coloured upholstery which are in the room are known to have been owned by Dickens.)

DOUGLAS
(Lord) Alfred Bruce
Poet

Worcester, October 22, 1870
Brighton, March 20, 1945

67, Cromwell Road, SW7, 1880
18, Cadogan Place, SW3, c.1881

'Bosie' (a corruption of his adoring mother's nickname for him of 'Boysie') was a central figure in the events which led to the imprisonment for two years of Oscar WILDE. These two were introduced by Lionel JOHNSON in 1891. Wilde's star was in the ascendant and Lord Alfred was flattered to be known so well by one of the leaders of London's literary society. And Wilde was delighted to be fawned on by a very beautiful youth who was also the son of a Marquis.

On Wilde's release from prison in 1897 he was to be allowed £150 per annum from his wife's small fortune, *providing* he did not see 'Bosie' again. Within weeks the two were back together and living near Naples in a villa rented by Douglas! Their relationship had lost its passion but Douglas gave Wilde quite a large sum of money over the last four years of Oscar's life; and paid for Wilde's funeral.

Douglas had joined the Catholic Church and, as he wrote in his autobiography, gave up all homosexual practices. Indeed, he married Olive Constance who was on the point of marrying someone else. They had a son who was, tragically, mentally retarded. Douglas and Olive parted and she died of a cerebral haemorrhage in Hove on February 13, 1944.

Lord Alfred was a poet and though the purple passages of his life rather obscured his skill, he was a much better poet than might have been expected from a selfish and rather shallow man. His first book of poems, *City of the Soul* appeared in 1899. He also edited a magazine he had bought called *The Academy* from 1907-1910. In this he was helped, and sometimes hindered, by Thomas CROSLAND.

Douglas spent his last years at Hove, a Channel watering place linked with Brighton. He had very little money. In 1942, Henry 'Chips' CHANNON and Alan Lennox-Boyd called on him, at the suggestion of Lady Diana COOPER. They found him, '...very pathetic...alone, poor and almost friendless'. These two, together with Marie Stopes (1880-1958) and Evan Morgan, the 2nd (and last) Viscount TREDEGAR (1893-1949) clubbed together to pay Douglas's rent of £150 per annum. (Tredegar attended Douglas's funeral; as did the Marquis of Queensberry and a 21-year-old actor called Donald Sinden.)

DOUGLAS-HOME
July 2, 1903
(Sir) Alexander Frederick
Prime Minister

24, Roebuck House, Palace Street, SW1, 1960s
Alec Douglas-Home (pronounced Hume) like Quintin HOGG, gave up his title, so that he could sit in the House of Commons. He was the 14th Earl of Home, having inherited his father's title in 1951. In fact he was a Prime Minister without a *seat* at one stage. Historically not unusual, but, in 1963, with egalitarianism rife, it was thought better for the Conservative's party image that their *Leader* have a democratically elected seat, and a seat was found for him as a Unionist for Kinross and West Perthshire in November 1963. He was Prime Minister from October 1963 to October 16, 1964. That he was Prime Minister at all was a surprise, even to the political editors of the Press, let alone the bemused members of the voting public.

After Eton he was up at Christ Church College, Oxford, became a Member of Parliament in 1931 and Neville CHAMBERLAIN's Secretary at the time of the Munich 'crisis'. He was not in Parliament at all between 1945 and 1951, then he became Minister of State for the Scottish Office, Commonwealth Secretary (though by now in the House of Lords) Leader of the Upper House, and Lord President of the Council from 1957-1960.

The family motto is 'True to the End', which, patriotically is emblazoned in English.

DOURO PLACE, W8
District, Circle and Piccadilly lines
to Gloucester Road

The first Duke of WELLINGTON was created Baron Douro in the Napoleonic Wars (in 1809). Duoro, or Duero, is a river rising in the Spanish province of Soria which flows into the Atlantic near Oporto. Along part of its length lies the Spanish/Portuguese border. The heir to the Dukedom bears the courtesy title of Marquess Douro. Douro Place was developed about ten years before the death of the 'Iron Duke'.

6,   Samuel PALMER (LCP 1972) 1851-1861. Heartbroken after the death of his 19 years old son, Thomas, Palmer could not bear to stay in this house. His other son, Arthur, rather unkindly (and inaccurately) described the house as a, '...hideous little semi-detached.'

DOYLE   Edinburgh, May 22, 1859
(Sir) Arthur Conan   Crowborough, Sussex, July 7, 1930
Author   All Saints Churchyard, Minstead,
                                       Hants.

2, Devonshire Place, W1, 1882 (his surgery)

Like MAUGHAM and A.J. Cronin, both medical men who deserted their original calling and became rich and famous authors, Doyle became a doctor. He got his degree at Edinburgh and practised from 1882 to 1890, but never earned more than £300 a year in all those eight years. Even then he was busy with his pen. 'Sherlock Holmes' actually took his first bow in the Christmas issue of 1882 of *Beaton's Annual,* when he appeared in *A Study in Scarlet.* Ten years later the Strand Magazine published *A Scandal in Bohemia,* the first of 'Holmes's' short stories. From then on the pipe-smoking, violin-playing, heroin-injecting 'Holmes' was up and running, together with his amiable but thick companion, Dr. Watson, who was supposed to have been modelled on a Dr. Joseph Bell, under whom Doyle had once studied.

In his 40s Doyle got bitten by Spiritualism and in 1922 published *The Coming of the Fairies.* Much of his 'evidence' produced to show that fairies *did* exist, was derived from a series of 'spirit' photographs which were taken by a 15 years old girl, Elsie, and her nine-year-old cousin, Frances. Elsie's mother, a Theosophist, sent the photographs to Doyle and he sent the girls £20 in War Bonds. The pictures were elaborate fakes and neither girl felt like admitting the jape as they 'were sorry' for Doyle for accepting them and sorry, too, that his son had been killed in the War. They only revealed the fake details of how they had taken the snapshots years later: Elsie by this time was a Mrs. Hill and Frances, a Mrs. Griffiths. Doyle published the *History of Spriritualism* in 1926 and died still believing in fairies and the like.

DRAPER   New York, December 2, 1884
Ruth   New York, December 20, 1956
Entertainer   19, Edith Grove, SW10

122, Ebury Street, SW1, 1919
120, Ebury Street, SW1, 1920
9, Pembridge Gardens, W2, 1922
79, St Leonard's Terrace, SW3, 1926
18A, Charles Street, W1, 1927
28, Chapel Street, SW1, 1931
24, Carlyle Square. SW3, 1933
70, Lansdowne House, W1 (south side of Berkeley Square) 1937
11, Alexander Place, SW7, 1939
8, Curzon Place, W1, 1951
39, Hyde Park Gate (Flat 11), SW7, 1953

Ruth Draper, *diseuse* extraordinary, a granddaughter of Charles A. Dana, editor of the *New York Sun* made her début in 1915 and in May 1916 was 'a maid' in *A Lady's Name* at the Maxine Elliott Theatre in New York. Over the years she perfected the technique of the monologue, and she was able to keep an audience enthralled for a whole evening from an empty stage with only one or two 'props'. She performed in many places around the world but London was the most dear to her.

She was most generous with her money (her income was very handsome) and many, many English causes benefitted from her kindness. She was made a Commander of the British Empire and the insignia was given to her personally by King George VI, only weeks before his death from cancer in February 1952. The last performance she gave in London was before an all female audience – in Holloway Gaol!

DRAYCOTT PLACE, SW3

District and Circle lines
to Sloane Square

In 1825 Sir Francis Shuckburgh married Anna Marie Draycott. Sir Francis's home, Blackland House (and so, later, *Blacklands Terrace*) stood on the corner of what today are Draycott Avenue and Draycott Terrace. The area began to be developed in the first half of the 19th century.

25, Viscount JELLICOE (LCP 1975) 1906-1908. JELLICOE's second daughter, Myrtle, was born here in 1906. He was to have two more daughters before a much wanted son, George, was born on April 4, 1918.

DRIBERG
Thomas Edward Neil (1st Baron Bradwell-juxt-mare)
Politician and journalist

Crowborough, May 22, 1905
London, August 12, 1976

66, Frith Street, W1, 1927
5, Queens Gate Place Mews, SW7, 1935

Driberg, who professed to be a Socialist politically, was practically everything a *real* socialist despises. He had had a public school education (at Lancing in Sussex) he had worked on the *Daily Express,* a paper controlled by that hyper-Conservative, Lord BEAVERBROOK, he was a flagrant homosexual, and, to cap it all, he accepted a peerage.

Actually Driberg first entered Parliament as an 'Independent' but not long after joined the Labour Party officially and sat on their National Council from 1944 to 1974. Curiously, he married a Mrs. Ena May Binfield in 1951. She was some years older than he and presumably knew which side of the bed Driberg preferred. (As to sides of bed, see under 5, Queen's Gate Place Mews.) Driberg's autobiography, *Ruling Passions* is probably one of the frankest works in that genre *ever*. The 'ruling passion' was his search for and *finding* men for his sexual gratification.

He became Chairman of the Labour Party, but in 1980 a book written by Chapman Pincher (one time Scientific and Medical editor for the *Daily Express*) alleged that Driberg was an undercover agent for both the British *and* the Russian Secret Services! His code name was supposed to have been 'Crocodile' in the KGB 'Crocodile' was encouraged by Moscow to visit Guy BURGESS, the English defector and obtain the necessary information to publish a book about the flight of Burgess and MacLean in 1951. The book eventually netted Driberg some £60,000.

At one time Driberg used to write the gossip column in the *Express* over the *nom-de-plume* of 'Ian Paddock'. He nearly always wrote under the pressure of deadlines and often, at the eleventh hour, used to go round the office searching for gossipy items of (usable) social tittle-tattle. Eventually he came to be referred to as 'May-I-use-that' Driberg.

DRYDEN
John
Poet Laureate

Aldwinkle, Northants., August 9(?), 1631
London, May 1, 1700
Westminster Abbey, 'Poet's Corner'

44 (or 43?) Gerrard Street, W1, from 1686 till he died here

Dryden's maternal grandfather was a Northamptonshire vicar and his father was the third son of Sir Erasmus Driden (sic). He was sent to school at Westminster then on the Trinity College, Cambridge, settling in London in 1657 (and lived until 1663 in The Strand). In 1657 his poem *Heroic Stanzas on the Death of Oliver Cromwell* – who had died that year – met with considerable success.

In 1663, with the Monarchy restored, he married Lady Elizabeth Howard, daughter of the Earl of Berkshire. She died before him and he composed her epitaph. From it one can only assume that their marriage was *not* roses all the way. It ran: 'Here lies my wife, here let her lie; Now she's at rest, and so am I.'

He soon turned his hand to playwriting. His first effort was a failure, but *The Rival Ladies* in 1664 established his reputation. His greatest play was *All for Love* in 1678. It tells the story of Anthony and Cleopatra using the facts employed by Shakespeare in his *Anthony and Cleopatra* (which was written in 1607/08). None of Dryden's plays cashed in on the great wave of anti-puritanical immodesty which broke out soon after the end of eleven years of Republicanism.

Dryden became Poet Laureate in 1668, succeeding Sir William Davenant who had died on April 7 that year, aged 62. He was also appointed Historiographer Royal. With these two posts came honours and a pension of £200 per annum. But in 1686 Dryden became a Catholic. Out he was chucked from the Laureateship and all the other posts, real or imagined. Stopped, too, was his pension and much of any other income.

The last 14 years of his life, further soured by the appointment of his old enemy, Thomas SHADWELL, as Poet Laureate, were spent in reduced circumstances though his old friends, such as the Earl of Dorset, gave him quite liberal sums of money. He earned money from the stage for which he wrote six plays between 1690 and 1694. He also began to take advantage of the trend for classical translation which was becoming all the rage. In addition to his versions of Juvenal and Persius he produced an outstanding Virgil in 1607. His last work, *Fables Ancient and Modern,* published a few weeks before he died, extended to 11,700 verses!

In the aisle of the South Transept by St Benedict's Chapel, as one enters Poets' Corner, there is a fine bust of Dryden by Scheemakers, a Flemish/English sculptor (1691-1770). Dryden lies beside Chaucer, who had been buried here exactly 300 years before.

DUKE STREET (St James's) W1   *Piccadilly, Victoria and Jubilee lines to Green Park*

Duke Street was first mentioned by name on records dated 1673 and had been named after the Duke of York, who was to become King James II in 1685.

15, Thomas MOORE, 1833. His biography of Lord Edward Fitzgerald had recently been published. Previously he had stayed at 19 Duke Street in 1826 and twice before that at No.20 (in 1805 and 1811).

18, Isambard Kingdom BRUNEL from 1836 until he died here in 1859.

DU MAURIER   London, May 13, 1907
(Dame) Daphne
Author

24, Cumberland Terrace, NW1, 1910

Dame Daphne, the daughter of Sir Gerald du Maurier (and granddaughter of George du M.) inherited much from both these men and two books of biography; *Gerald* in 1934 and *The Du Mauriers* in 1937 are well worth reading. But, of course, it is not as a biographer she will be widely remembered. In 1936 came *Jamaica Inn* followed by *Rebecca* both were best sellers and spawned a number of films, as did *Frenchman's Creek* in 1942.
In 1932, Miss du Maurier married Lieutenant-General Sir Frederick ('Boy') Browning. They had one son and two daughters, who had a near idyllic childhood at Menabilly, in Cornwall. Sir Frederick became the Controller of HRH Princess Elizabeth's Household in 1947.

DU MAURIER   Paris, March 6, 1834
George Louis Palmella Busson   London, October 6, 1896
Author and Artist   Ashes in Hampstead Paris Churchyard

8, Berners Street, W1, 1860
70, 85 and 90 Newman Street, W1, 1860-1862
82, Grosvenor Street, W1, 1862
48 and 91, Great Russell Street, WC1 (LCP 1960) 1863-1868.
12, Earl's Terrace, W8, 1868
27, Gloucester Gardens, W2, April-July 1868
15, Bayswater Terrace, W2, 1887 and 1890
3, Stanhope Terrace, W2, 1893

Du Maurier's father was French and his mother English so that he was bilingual. For a short while he worked as a chemist at London University but in 1856 his father died and George went to Paris to study art. Nearly 40 years later he was to draw on his student experiences in Paris when he wrote his best selling novel, *Trilby*.
In 1859, however, he lost the sight in one eye and he found painting difficult, but he was able to draw (and draw beautifully) cartoons for *Punch*. Mostly his jokes were about upper class society and the standards of those people, their clothes and furniture are exquisitely set out for all today to see. His first cartoon was published in *Punch* in 1860 and he was a regular contributor for many years. In 1883, Henry JAMES wrote that, *'Punch* for the last fifteen years has been, artistically speaking, George du Maurier'.
On his tombstone are written the last lines of *Trilby*:
> 'A little trust that when we die
> We reap our sowing! and so – good bye.'

DUNCAN TERRACE, N1   *Northern line to Angel*

Possibly after Viscount Duncan of Camperdown (1731-1804). The British fleet gained a decisive victory over the Napoleonic Dutch Fleet at the engagement at Camperdown in 1797. Score: Dutch lost 9: British, nil.

64, 'Colebrook Cottage', Charles LAMB (LCP 1907) 1822-1827. Charles and his poor sister, Mary moved here a year after his *Essays of Elia* was published. The immediate area around the Terrace was a sort of 'red light' district but Lamb described the cottage as, '...a white house with six good rooms...you enter, without passage, into a cheerful dining room, all studded over and rough with old books and above is a lightsome Drawing room, 'full of choice prints. I feel like a great Lord, never having had a house before.' Behind the cottage was a 'spacious' garden complete with vines.

DURHAM PLACE, SW3

District and Circle lines
to Sloane Square

1794 is the first date recorded for the existence of this street. It takes its name from a 16th century building called Durham House which was only demolished in 1920.

3, 'Billy' Ritchie. W.M. THACKERAY's only grandson, born in 1878, was living here when his mother, Anne, died in 1919. 'Billy' had been educated at Sedbergh (a boys' public school in Yorkshire) and Trinity College, Oxford. He was articled to solicitors and in 1906 married Margaret Booth, daughter of Charles BOOTH. They had a son, James, in 1908, who was killed in the Second World War, and two daughters.

4, 'Bram' STOKER at the time of his death in 1912.

DUVEEN
Joseph (1st Baron Duveen of Millbank)
Art dealer

Hull, Yorks, October 14, 1869
London, May 25, 1939
Jewish Cemetary, Willesden

8, Kensington Palace Gardens, W8, 1937

Duveen was at Brighton College until he was nearly 17 and from that time, until 1939, he was constantly crossing and recrossing the Atlantic and became undoubtedly the greatest dealer in fine art (initially only paintings) of all time. He was a salesman *par excellence*; he was a psychologist and a showman. He established his business in Grafton Street and he had showrooms in New York and Paris. Duveen realized early on that many Americans were very rich and Europe had a lot of paintings for sale. The rich Americans were either ignorant of the world of art or slightly abashed by their extraordinary wealth (or both). Duveen began to cultivate these millionaires. He determined only to sell them the very best, at *his* prices and conduct *his* business in a way that would mean these wealthy men would only buy works of art from *him*.

His list of clients read like a transatlantic *Almanac de Gotha* and single handed he took hundreds of valuable and unique works of art out of Europe and into America. In London though, he is remembered gladly as he was a generous patron of the National Gallery and he had John Russell Pope design the elegant and beautiful hall which contains the Elgin Marbles in the British Museum. All this Duveen paid for personally.

E

EARL'S COURT

The De Veres came to England with King William the Conqueror in 1066 and were created by him Earls of Oxford. They probably never lived in the area, though their Court House was in Earls Court Road more or less where the Underground railway station now stands. On the same side as the station, a few steps to the south, is a charming, gated *cul-de-sac* rather mews-like, still called Old Manor Yard. The nobility and land owners in feudal days were, of necessity, judges and magistrates for their own 'manors', there being no police or federal judiciary. By the end of the 18th century the old Manor House had become a mere farm house and it was finally demolished in the 1870s.

EARLS TERRACE, W8

District and Circle lines to High Street Kensington.

4, Elizabeth INCHBALD lived here in 1812, 'as a boarder'. Money was very short and often she, '... would sit without fire in the winter till she cried with cold'. So wrote Leigh HUNT.

12, George DU MAURIER, 1868-1869. It was, '... a palace after 91 Great Russell Street'.

23, Sir Henry NEWBOLT, 1900-1910. The Newbolts had moved here from Victoria Road, not far away, but Sir Henry wrote that the new house, '...was not only more dignified with its Adam cornices and basket fireplaces, but it had two well proportioned drawing rooms, a dining room, ample enough to seat a fairly numerous party at table, a school room for children and a study for myself...'

EATON

All the 'Eatons' (spelt with an 'A', unlike Eton of Eton College) denote ownership by the immensely rich Duke of Westminster. His great country seat is Eaton Hall in Cheshire and the family still own large tracts of land in Cheshire, apart from real estate overseas, and, it is said, the Grosvenor Estate in London (despite the horrific possibility of death duties) has never sold a *freehold* unless it was to their eventual advantage.

EATON PLACE, SW1

District and Circle lines to Sloane Square

5, Lord CARSON, at the time of his death in 1935.

15, Lord KELVIN, at the time of his death in 1907.

16, William EWART (LCP 1963) from 1830 to 1838. He moved here not long after the house was built and left soon after his wife died. A plaque here is happily well-sited. It was Ewart who publicly proposed such a scheme in 1863. (His own plaque had to wait for 100 years!)

29, John LUBBOCK (afterwards Lord Avebury) (LCP 1935). He was born in this house in 1834 and spent the first six years of his life in it.

29 (now split up) Terence RATTIGAN lived in the penthouse here from April 1952.

36, Sir Henry WILSON was shot dead here, on his own doorstep, by two *Sinn Fein* murderers in 1922.

45, Frédéric CHOPIN gave his first recital in London in this house on June 23, 1845.

90, Victor GOLLANCZ, 1967. As a good socialist publisher, he was happy to accept a knighthood and live surrounded by capitalists nearly as rich as he. This was his last London address. He died in 1967.

EATON SQUARE, SW1

Begun in 1828; building went on until 1855. But, in April 1940, when the 'Blitz' over Britain – especially London – had not begun, it was noted that only *six* of the 118 houses were occupied. Thomas Cubitt was responsible for building the Square.

12, Sir Osbert LANCASTER, 1961-1976. He married, as his second wife, Anne Scott-James in 1967.

17, General, Sir William Knollys, 1870s. He was Controller and Treasurer to King Edward VII (when Prince of Wales) and father of Queen Alexandra's devoted companion, the *'inevitable Charlotte'*.

37, Neville CHAMBERLAIN (LCP 1962) 1923-1935. Two years later he moved into 10, Downing Street.

44, Prince METTERNICH (LCP 1970) May to September 1848. The house was owned by Lord Denbigh (1823-1892). The Duke of WELLINGTON called on the Prince every morning during his stay. Lord Minto's daughters; next door, used to play 'ceaselessly' on the piano and METTERNICH moved to Brighton.

80, George PEABODY (LCP 1976). He died in this house on November 4, 1909. The property was owned by Sir Curtis Lampson, a Trustee of the fund which PEABODY had established.

90, W.S. GILBERT, 1907-1911. While he lived here, his *Fallen Fairies* with music by Sir Edward German (1862-1936, originally, Edward German Jones) was staged. SULLIVAN had died in 1900 and the 'play' failed – it just was *not* GILBERT *and* SULLIVAN.

93, Stanley BALDWIN (LCP 1969) 1913-1924. In May 1923, Baldwin became Prime Minister for the first time and moved to 10, Downing Street. Later the property was used by the Nufffield Foundation and in 1970 acquired by Iranian interests. It burnt out completely under very mysterious circumstances ('There was a good view of the sky from the basement'.) It was virtually rebuilt and divided into three flats. The first one sold for £1 million; the second for £450,000 and the third, an apartment on two floors was being advertised in March 1984; the 62-year lease remaining was available for £1,260,000!

EATON TERRACE, SW1

25, The Earl of Snowdon (Anthony ARMSTRONG-JONES) was born here on March 7, 1930. By 1938, Lord Rosse (the 6th Earl) was here, having married Snowdon's mother in 1935, he then being 29, after she had divorced Snowdon's father, Ronald Armstrong-Jones.

55, Rosa LEWIS (or Edward Albert, HRH Prince of Wales) set up this establishment as a *house of convenience* at the end of the 19th century. In 1902 she moved to Jermyn Street and established the Cavendish Hotel (a house largely of *in*convenience).

EBURY STREET, SW1

*Victoria, District and Circle lines
to Victoria*

Pimlico (in which Ebury Street lies) was a wet, marshy area, traversed by many rivulets which percolated through to the Thames. The two sides of the Manor were bounded by the rivers Tyburn and Westbourne. In the Domesday Book this parcel of land was shewn as *EIA* meaning 'well watered', eventually evolving to EIABURY, then Ebury. Much of the Manor remained intact under one family ownership for centuries and Mary Davies brought it into the Grosvenor family in 1665 when she married Sir Thomas Grosvenor.

75, Thomas WOLFE, 1930-1931, whilst working on *Of Time and the River,* published 1935.

111, Noel COWARD, 1920s. His mother took in lodgers here to bring in *some* money, as father Coward seemed helpless in this important direction. Noel had the top back room. As he became more successful he took over the more expensive ground floor rooms. 'As I rose in the world,' he used to say, 'I went down in the house'. He was still nominally owner of the property in 1929.

115, Max BEERBOHM, 1917. The Beerbohms came back to England (from their Italian home) during the First World War, as they did in the Second.

120, Ruth DRAPER, 1920. 'I was very lucky in finding a sunny top floor room...a lovely big double room in front and I am so comfortably fixed...for one guinea (£1.05) a week'. The following year she stayed at No. 121.

121, George MOORE (LCP 1936) from 1911 until 1933 when he died here.

153, George MEREDITH, 1849, the year he had his first poem printed and *Chamber's Journal* published his *Battle of Chillian-wallah.* (A conflict between some 15,000 British troops and 23,000 Sikhs in January of that year. Although the British lost 2,400 men they claimed a technical victory.)

180, Wolfgang MOZART (LCP 1939) 1764-1765 (then the address was 5, Fields Row). Here he completed his *first* symphony, in E. Flat; K.16, at the ripe age of eight, when his, '...fingers could scarcely reach a fifth on the harpsichord'. Only 27 years were left to him after this visit to London, yet in his all too short life Mozart wrote 40 symphonies, 20 operas and operettas, 27 piano concerti, 27 string quartets, 7 violin sonatas, plus other concertos, songs, masses, quintets, trios and so on.

182, Harold NICOLSON, 1916-1920. His son, Nigel, was born here in 1917. His mother-in-law, Lady Sackville moved in here in 1920 having left her house at 34, Hill Street, W1.

EDEN   Bishop Auckland, June 12, 1897
Robert Anthony   January, 14, 1977
Prime Minister

11, Bruton Street, W1, 1903-1904
1, Mulberry Walk, SW3, 1929

Anthony was the son of an eccentric baronet, the well-to-do Sir William Eden. Sir William had a long and strange relationship with Rosa LEWIS and a long and acrimonious dispute with WHISTLER over the cost of a portrait of Lady Eden. Whistler won the final law suit and it caused Louis Henry May to publish a book entitled, *Eden versus Whistler. The Baronet and the Butterfly* (the Butterfly being a sort of 'trade mark' used by Whistler).
Eden went to Eton and straight from there into the carnage of the First World War. He was a captain at the age of 20, practically all the older officers in his regiment having been killed. He was awarded the Military Cross for bravery during the Campaign.
The war over, Eden went up to Oxford and gained a first class degree in Oriental Languages. This very considerable achievement was hardly ever commented on after he had gone into politics. He had a first class brain and good looks. He dressed well and the black homburg type of hat he usually sported is still called an 'Anthony Eden'.
He entered Parliament as Conservative member for Leamington Spa (in Warwickshire) in 1923 and was their member for 34 years. In 1935 he became Foreign Secretary – still only 38 years old, but he disagreed with Neville CHAMBERLAIN's appeasement policy and he resigned. 1940 found him as Winston CHURCHILL's Secretary of State for War and he

was really responsible for the establishment of the *Home Guard*.

After the war and the immediate, six-year Socialist Government, the Conservatives came back and Eden was again Foreign Secretary. Churchill made the mistake of staying too long in office, he was too old and ill and Eden only became Premier in April 1955. The following year the Suez Crisis blew up in Eden's face. During this agonizing period Lady Eden said, '...the last few weeks I have felt that the Suez Canal was flowing through my drawing room'. He had ordered British and French troops to occupy the Canal Zone. It was a bad decision; the United Nations condemned the British action and Eden resigned in 1957, a sick and sad man.

EDITH GROVE, SW10 *District line to West Brompton*

Edith Grove (and Terrace) were named after Edith Günter, one of the daughters of the famous Günter, the pastrycook, who made a fortune from his skills and developed a lot of property on the Chelsea/Fulham borders. The Grove was built up in 1878.

102, John MURRY and Katherine MANSFIELD, 1914. By this time she was Murry's mistress but she eventually married him (three addresses later) in 1918.

EDWARDES SQUARE, W8 *District and Circle lines*
to High Street Kensignton

The Holland family split up into the Hollands (of Holland House) and the Edwardes, who were to become the Barons of Kensington, and it was this limb which is commemorated here. The Square first appeared in 1813 (for greater detail about the Holland ramifications, see under HOLLAND).

Leigh HUNT wrote that the Square was '...the work of a Frenchman...he adapted the large square and the cheap little houses to the promenading tastes and poorly furnished pockets of the ensigns and lieutenants of Napoleon's army. It was allowable for French imagination in those days to run a little wild on the strength of Napoleon's victories'. (Students of history will not need to be reminded of the little skirmish at Waterloo – and the result of it – some two years after the Square was built.)

1, G.K. CHESTERTON, 1901-1904 immediately after his marriage to Frances Blogg.

7, Norman O'NEILL. He and his wife, Adine, moved in here after their marriage in July 1899. Probably the newly wedded CHESTERTONS were friendly with the newly wedded O'NEILLs.

19, Ugo FOSCOLO, 1818. To make it harder for his creditors to track him down he equipped himself (a quite usual Foscolian ploy) with a transparent *nom-de-guerre*; *Hugo Foscolo Esquire, 19 Edward [sic] Square, Kensington, près de Londres.*

The road – going – west then becomes South Edwardes Square and almost immediately one will find:

1, Pembroke Cottages, William ROTHENSTEIN lived here in 1898. He paid his landlord, '...a shrunken, little man, wearing stays and high-heeled shoes', £50 a year for the house and another £20 for the even smaller cottage, which Rothenstein used as a studio and, '...a garden of one's own in London, however small, is a precious thing'.

32, Leigh HUNT, 1840-1851. The Hunts had moved here from Cheyne Row.

EDWARDS Truro, Cornwall, March 24, 1823
John Passmore London, April 22, 1911
Philanthropist Kensal Green, Grave No. 42,954; Plot
161

51, Bedford Square, WC1, 1860s

John Edwards' life-long interest lay in establishing a true Free Library
System in Britain. Although he was not of affluent stock he managed to
make a very reasonable fortune for himself in publishing. He was one of the
early supporters of the Chartist movement and worked hard to make the lot
of the poor a happier one. He was vigorously opposed to both capital and
corporal punishment, the Crimean and the Boer Wars, the opium trade and,
of course, slavery.

Using his own money, he put 'his cash where his mouth was' and built 24
Free Libraries, even more hospitals and paid for countless horse drinking
troughs. He 'most respectfully declined the honour of a knighthood from
both Queen Victoria *and* King Edward VII (a record?). He died leaving only
some £47,000 of his cleverly garnered fortune.

He was a friend of sculptors, too; as he paid for 32 busts of eminent men
which were to be placed in, or on, public buildings.

EGERTON

The Hon. Francis Egerton was a trustee of Smith's Charity in the middle of
the 19th century when the 84 acres (34 hectares) owned by the Charity were
being developed. The names of some of the other trustees can be seen in this
part of London. Names like, Cranley Onslow, Sydney, Sumner, Walton,
Lennox and Pelham. The Charity was originated by Henry Smith an
alderman of the City of London. In 1627 he left his estate in trust for the,
'...relief and ransom of poor captives being slaves under Turkish Pirates'
(and a bit, too, to his poor relations). The last relation perished at the end of
the 18th century and the last case of a Christian slave under a Turkish pirate
was in 1723, so the Trustees had to look for other (acceptable) ways of
disposing of an income from the Trust of over £200,000. Much is spent on
country holidays for poor city children, hospitals and so on.

EGERTON CRESCENT, SW3 *District, Circle and Piccadilly lines
to South Kensington*

35, Neville CHAMBERLAIN, 1920-1922.
46, David FROST, 1966-1983. After his second marriage (to Lady Carina
Fitzalan Howard in March 1983) there was talk of selling the 53
remaining years of the lease. A modest £540,000 was thought
reasonable.

EGERTON, G. see BRIGHT, M.G.

ELGAR Broadheath, Worcester, June 2, 1857
(Sir) Edward Marl Bank, Worcs., February 23, 1934
Composer St Wulstan's Churchyard, Little
Malvern, Hereford

3, Marloes Road, SW7, 1889
51, Avonmore Road, W14 (LCP 1962) 1890-1891
37 and 38, St James's Place, SW1, 1929

Elgar's father was an organist and sheet music dealer but Elgar never had any
formal music lessons except for violin. When his father died young, Elgar
took over his post as organist at Saint George's Catholic Church in

Worcester. He was by now also conductor of the Worcester County Asylum Band.

He married Alice Roberts at the Brompton Oratory in 1889, but after two years or so moved back to Malvern more or less permanently. In 1900 his *Dream of Gerontius* won acclaim for him in England and Germany and his *Enigma Variations,* the following year, were even more successful and established him as the leading English composer of the day. He was Knighted in 1904 and given the Order of Merit. His wife died in 1920 and he really produced little or no music afterwards, but he was made Master of the King's Musick in 1924.

Elgar was commissioned in 1902 to write two pieces for the Coronation of King Edward VII. One was to be a Coronation Ode – *Crown the King with Life* and King Edward requested that words should be made to fit Elgar's trio melody from *Pomp and Circumstance March, Number 1.* The poet who was given the job of providing the words was Arthur Benson, brother of E.F. BENSON, sons of the Archbishop of Canterbury, Edward White Benson.

Elgar was popular with another faction of the community, far removed from music. He was a dedicated race-goer and the bookmakers practically followed him around the course, hoping to take his bets as he had an uncanny knack of picking the losing horse in nearly every race!

ELIA, see LAMB, C.

ELIOT, see EVANS, M.A.

ELIOT	St Louis, Mo, September 26, 1888
Thomas Stearns	January 4, 1965
Poet	St Michael's, East Coker, Somerset

5, Chester Row, SW1, pre-1914
28, Bedford Place, WC1, 1914–1915
Carlyle Mansions, Lawrence Street, SW3, – 1918
9, Clarence Gardens, NW1, 1923
91, Emperor Place, NW1, 1938–1940

Eliot's father, Henry Ware Eliot, was one of the founders of Washington University but Thomas finished his education at Harvard, the Sorbonne, then Merton College, Oxford. He settled in England just before the First World War and became a British citizen in 1939. He taught briefly at Highgate School and then went to work for Lloyds Bank in the City from 1919 to 1922. (In a, '...little room under the street. Within a foot of our heads when we stood were the thick, green glass squares of the pavement on which hammered all but incessantly the heels of the passers-by...'. Perhaps I.A. Richards, who wrote this description, should have written, 'passers-above'.)

In 1915 Eliot married Vivenne Haigh-Wood. He left her (eventually) in 1932 when she had to be admitted into the Northumberland House Nursing Home at Hastings, having been certified as insane. She behaved extraordinarily and there was a nervous tension whilst they were together that could have destroyed a lesser person than Eliot. Once she poured a 'soup tureen' filled with melted chocolate bars through the letter box of Faber and Faber, the publishers, at 24, Russell Square, WC1, of which company he was a director. Vivienne did not die until 1947.

In the same year as he began his ill-starred first marriage, Eliot had his first poem published; *The Love Song of Alfred Prufrock* appeared in the magazine, *Poetry.* In 1922 *The Waste Land* won the Dial Award, bringing him recognition (and 2,000 dollars). It was soon to be translated into French, German and Spanish. The same year he began the magazine *Criterion* which lasted until 1939. His field widened and fame spread with the play *Murder in the Cathedral* (1935), *Practical Cats* (1939) then, after the Second World War; *The Cocktail Party* in 1950 and *The Confidential Clerk* four years later.

In 1948, not only was he awarded the Nobel Prize for literature, but the nearly ultimate 'accolade'; the Order of Merit, which is an honour *personally* bestowed by the Sovereign.

On January 10, 1957, at 6.15 *in the morning* Eliot sprang a surprise by marrying his 30-year-old secretary, Esme Fletcher.

Eliot was very different from the 'Bohemian' figure most people seem to like their poets to be. (But those two poets who *were* 'Bohemian', Dylan THOMAS and Roy CAMPBELL, both of whom predeceased him, used to call him 'His Grace' and often borrowed money from him, which, incidentally, was always gladly given.) He always looked a little like a bank manager.

ELM PARK GARDENS, SW10   *District, Circle and Piccadilly lines*
                                                     to South Kensington

On the corner of the Fulham Road and Old Church Street is a public house called 'The Queen's Elm'. The legend of this name is that Good Queen Bess was strolling with Lord Burghley, who had a house not far away in Brompton when it began to rain. They took shelter under an elm tree and Her Majesty declared, 'Let this henceforward be called the Queen's tree'. On many old maps of Chelsea, 'a great elm' is clearly indicated at this spot. However, how far anecdote influenced cartography, is hard to say. The Gardens here were built on in 1876.

34   (Flat 8) Joyce GRENFELL, 1956. The main windows of her flat faced east, the kitchen and the bedroom faced west. Once the accommodation must have been the 'nursery floor' of two houses. At the end of the passage, a staircase led to two attic rooms and a second bathroom.

49,   Laurie LEE, 1964. The poet could often be seen in the 'Queen's Elm' itself. Sean Treacy, landlord of the pub from 1951, recalled; one December LEE came into the pub with a basketful of his book of poems, *A Bloom of Candles,* and was selling them off, signed, for three shillings and sixpence (17½p) telling customers that they 'were better than Christmas cards'.

58,   Sinclair LEWIS and his wife stayed here in 1923 and 1924, when the property was a private hotel.

EMERSON   Boston, Mass., May 25, 1803
Ralph Waldo   Concord, Mass., April 27, 1882
Essayist   Sleepy Hollow, Concord

63, Russell Square, WC1, 1833
142, The Strand, WC2, 1848

Emerson's father, a clergyman, died when Ralph was only eight and Mrs. Emerson was only able to keep herself and six children by taking in lodgers. She managed very well indeed and four of her brood went to Harvard. Ralph did not distinguish himself scholastically and in 1829 he was admitted as a pastor in the Unitarian Church. In this same year he married Ellen Louisa Tucker. Tragically, in two years, she was dead (only 19 years old) and, round about the same time, two of Ralph's brothers died. He resigned from the Church; certainly he must have thought God had given him a raw deal and in 1833 he sailed for Europe.

He 'landed in London at Tower Stairs' on July 30, 1833 and before long, he met LANDOR, COLERIDGE, WORDSWORTH and Thomas CARLYLE; his meeting with CARLYLE was to establish a friendship which lasted until CARLYLE died only 13 months before Ralph himself. Back again in America he earned a living as a lecturer and, in 1835, married Lydia Jackson. They settled in Concord where his mother now lived. He was beginning to establish a reputation as a philosopher, albeit a rather home-spun one, and some of his lectures were published in 1841-1844.

In 1848 he was back in Britain and lecturing. All the while he was gathering material for his book, *English Traits,* which was eventually published in 1856.

The *London Athenaeum* of February 17, 1855 said of Emerson that, 'It is better, we think, for a man to tell his story as Mr. IRVING, Mr. HAWTHORNE, or Mr. Longfellow does, than to adopt the style Emersonian – in which thoughts may be buried so deep that common seekers shall be unable to find them'.

He published a book of his poems in 1866 (his second) but before long his memory began to fail him and he sank into amiable, forgetful old age.

ENGELS   Barmen, Germany, September 28,
Friedrich   1820
Socialist   London, August 5, 1895

6, Macclesfield Street, W1, 1849-1850
121, Regent's Park Road, NW1 (LCP 1972) 1870-1894

Engels came to England in 1844 to act as an agent for his father's cotton business. The year before he had met MARX in Paris. He lived almost permanently in England and he wrote his *Condition of the Working Classes in England,* where it was published in 1844. The next task was to collaborate with Marx and the first fruit of their cooperation was the *Communist Manifesto* which appeared in 1848.

Compared to Karl Marx, Engels was prosperous and the Marx family benefitted not a little from Engels' generosity, since Marx was a hopeless home economist. As well as financially, Engels helped Marx with his English and translated a lot of Marx's writing for his English publisher. Between them, they founded 'scientific socialism'.

Marx's daughter, Eleanor, wrote of Engels in 1890, '...he bears his three score years and ten with great ease. He is vigorous in body and soul. He carries his six foot so lightly that one would not think he is so tall... His hair, on the contrary, is brown without a streak of grey... And although Engels looks young, he is even younger than he looks. He really is the youngest looking man I know. As far as I can remember he has not grown any older in the last twenty hard years.'

EPSTEIN   New York, November 10, 1880
(Sir) Jacob   London, August 21, 1959
Sculptor   Putney Vale Cemetery

18, Hyde Park Gate, SW7, 1928 until he died here

Epstein was a Russian Polish jew born in New York, who finally became a British citizen. He studied at the Ecole des Beaux-Arts in Paris and he was given his first English commission when he was 28. He was asked to produce 14 figures to stand on the outside wall of the second floor of 429 Strand (on the corner of Agar Street. The building is now *Zimbabwe House.*) Their reception was a taste of things to come for Epstein. They were branded as *indecent.* A religious society who had offices on the south side of the Strand changed their clear windows for semi-opaque so that the morals of their workers would not be undermined. The statues were of sandstone and originally depicted human beings in various stages of life.

Epstein was rarely out of the public eye. His work on the Medical Council Building in the Strand, his *Night and Day* on the Headquarters of London Transport in St James's Broadway (1929) and, most of all, his *Rima* on the Hudson Memorial in Hyde Park all caused outbursts and sometimes involved police protection. *Rima* was more than once bedaubed with paint.

ESTERHAZY
(Prince) Paul Anton Von Galantha
Diplomat and 'swell'

March 11, 1786
Ratisbon, Bavaria, May 21, 1866

11, Chandos Street, W1, 1815-1818 and 1830-1838

Paul was the son of Nikolaus von Esterhazy (1765-1833) who in turn was the grandson of Nikolaus Joseph von Esterhazy. They were rich aristocrats and Paul's father collected many magnificent works of art and was so well thought of by Napoleon in 1809 he was approached by Buonaparte to see if he might be willing to take the throne of Hungary.

Paul Anton was the Austrian Ambassador in London for many years up till 1842. He was a dandy, a *bon viveur*: his entertainments and his style of dress were on a princely scale. His appearance at Queen Victoria's Coronation in 1837 brought forth this doggerel:
> 'T'would have made you crazy
> To see Esterhazy
> All jewels from jasey [Regency *slang* for a wig]
> To di'mond boots.'

Before London, Esterhazy had been Ambassador in both Dresden and Rome and in the first faintly responsible Hungarian administration of 1848, he was Minister for Foreign Affairs.

The last years of his life were spent (for *him*) in poverty. His estates, though large, were no longer able to keep him in funds and so fiscal matters were placed in the hands of 'curators'.

EVANS
Mary Ann (Marian)
Author ('George Eliot')

Chilvers, Coton, Warks., November 22, 1819
Cheyne Walk, December 22, 1880
Highdale New Cemetery, Square 84

142, The Strand, WC2, 1851-1853
21, Cambridge Street, SW1, 1853-1854
16, Blandford Square, W1, 1860-1863
21, North Bank, NW8, 1863-1878
4, Cheyne Walk, SW3 (LCP 1949) here she died

Mary Ann's (or Marian's) father was a Warwickshire estate agent. He died in 1849, his wife having predeceased him and Mary Ann, at the age of 30 began to exercise her intellectual wings. She moved in such cultural circles as then existed in Coventry and in 1854 she produced a translation of *Essence of Christianity* which was to be the only book published under her own name. Her literary talent was noticed before she was 40 and *Blackwood's Magazine* printed her story *The Sad Fortunes of the Reverend Amos Barton* in 1857. She then set about producing the novels on which her fame has deservedly rested: *Adam Bede* in 1859, the *Mill on the Floss* in 1860 and *Silas Marner* a year later.

In 1854 she began to live with George Henry LEWES (1817-1878). He was a remarkably ugly man (and *she* was no beauty) from a stage family, who had started out to become a doctor. When he was 23 he had married Agnes Jervis of Darlaston Hall, Staffordshire who was his pupil. Being both a little highbrow and both a little literary they believed in sexual emancipation. She had three children by George Henry and two by Thornton HUNT. When George met 'George Eliot' Agnes was still inconveniently alive and so Marian and he stayed happy as lovers. 'George Eliot' was another sexual emancipist who had probably already been seduced by a publisher called Chapman and even before that by a Swiss, who was probably her model for the Reverend Mr. Casaubon, the old scholar in *Middlemarch – a Study in Provincial Life*, who Dorothea Brooke marries.

Lewes was already a literary success before fame came to his lover Marian, but as her reputation grew so did her income until it way outstripped his. Lewes could well have been a sort of catalyst. He died in 1878 and, grief stricken, she turned to John Walter Cross (1839-1924) who had been a friend to them both. She married Cross in May 1880, moved into Cheyne Walk and died there a few weeks later. Cross produced a three-volume biography of 'George Eliot' in 1885.

Photographs of her probably do her little justice but when LOCKER-LAMPSON met her in 1869, he found, 'Her countenance was equine – she was rather like a horse; and her head had been intended for a much longer body – she was not a tall woman'. So maybe the camera did not lie.

There is a plaque in the floor of 'Poet's Corner' in Westminster Abbey to her memory.

EWART
William
Politician

Liverpool, May 1, 1798
Devizes, January 23, 1869
Wiltshire

16, Eaton Place, SW1 (LCP 1963) 1830-1838

Ewart, the son of a Liverpool merchant was educated at Eton and Christ Church, Oxford and called to the Bar in 1827. After HUSKISSON was killed (in the first ever, anywhere, railway accident, in 1830) Ewart took over his Liverpool parliamentary seat in the House of Commons. He was an enlightened and active reformer for the abolition of hanging for a number of crimes and an outspoken advocate for the provision of *free* libraries for everybody. He was a prime factor in the formulation and passing of the Public Libraries Act of 1850.

He is important too, within the context of a book of this sort. In 1863 he suggested to Parliament that some sort of commemoration of the dwelling houses of the famous should be made: 'the places which have been the residences of the ornaments of their history cannot but be precious to all so-thinking Englishmen'. Parliament was characteristically deaf to Ewart's idea but the Royal Society of Arts established a committee the following year, to try and implement Ewart's scheme. The first ever plaque was placed on 24 Holles Street, W1; Lord BYRON's birthplace. The house has been long demolished and the site covered by a department store.

FAIRBANKS New York, December 9, 1909
(Sir, honorary) Douglas Elton
(Junior)
Actor

28, The Boltons, SW10, 1950-1970

Son of Douglas Fairbanks (Senior) and Anna Beth Sully, Fairbanks began as
a film actor when he was 14 and made his stage début in 1926. Father
Fairbanks died on December 12, 1939, aged 56, leaving a fortune of
£750,000. He was born Douglas Elton Thomas Ulman; his mother was Ella
Marsh and his father, Hezahiah Ulman. The Ulmans were divorced in 1884
and she assumed the name of her first husband, John Fairbanks. Douglas
Fairbanks, senior, took his name legally in 1900.
In addition to being the head of the Douglas Fairbanks Corporation,
Fairbanks, *Junior* held directorships in at least 20 other companies ranging
from hotels to 'Scripto' pens. He was Vice-President of a Committee called
'Defend America by Aiding the Allies' formed in 1939 when American
isolationist feeling was running high. The decorations and awards bestowed
upon him are testimony to Fairbank's courage.

FANTIN-LATOUR Grenoble, January 14, 1836
Ignace Henri Jean Théodore August 28, 1904
Artist

26, Golden Square, W1, 1880

His father, of Italian descent, was a landscape painter and gave him his first
lessons in drawing and painting. Later, Fantin-Latour went to the Ecole des
Beaux Arts and afterwards studied under Marc Gabriel Gleyre, where he
met Degas, Legros and WHISTLER.
He first exhibited at the Salon in 1861, visited London quite regularly and
exhibited at the Royal Academy. In England he became quite well known
for his rather 'pretty' floral pieces.

FAWCETT Salisbury, August 25, 1833
Henry Cambridge, November 6, 1884
Blind Politician Trumpington Church Yard

2, Gower Street, WC1, 1877-1883

Fawcett was the son of a prosperous business man and, after passing through
King's College School, London, Peterhouse and Trinity Hall at Cambridge
he graduated seventh Wrangler in 1856 and was elected a Fellow of Trinity.
He entered Lincoln's Inn and a brilliant career was forseen. His prospects (in
fact the prospects of a lesser man would have been 'nil') suffered, when he
was blinded in a shooting accident in 1858. Soon, however, he walked, rode,
skated and learnt to play cards and was practically a normal member of
Trinity. He became a specialist in political economy and his book on the
subject in 1863 sold 20,000 copies over the years. He was elected to the Chair
of Political Economy at Cambridge and in 1865 MP for Brighton.
Two years later he married the 20 year-old Millicent Garrett. He was
sufficiently radical (politically) to be viewed with disfavour by some
members of his own Liberal Party. In 1880, when Gladstone brought the
Liberals back to power, he gave Fawcett the Postmaster General's job (but

without a Cabinet seat). In that job he introduced: (a) postal orders, (b) sixpenny telegrams, (c) the Parcel Post, (d) increased facilities for life insurance and annuities, and (e) small savings using stamps. More simply, but with great effect, it was Fawcett who worked out and implemented the 'next collection is' changeable plaque on each pillar box.

There is a medallion to Fawcett in the Embankment Gardens behind the Savoy Hotel. It is by Mary Grant and forms part of a fountain, designed by Basil Champneys in 1886. There used to be a statue to Fawcett in Vauxhall Park but this was removed in 1955.

FAWCETT   Aldeburgh, Suffolk, June 11, 1847
(Dame) Millicent   London, August 5, 1929
Champion of Women's Rights

2, Gower Street, WC1 (LCP 1954) from 1877 until she died here.

Millicent (the younger sister of Elizabeth GARRETT ANDERSON) was the eighth child of Newson Garrett, a prosperous shipowner. Millicent and Elizabeth, each in their own way, advanced the status of British women; more even than the Pankhursts.

At 20 Millicent married Henry FAWCETT, MP, then 43 years old. Their marriage, tender but interdependent, lasted for 17 years.

Very soon after marriage she began what was to be her life's work – the introduction of unrestricted women's suffrage. In 1867 she made her first public speech. Apart from its substance, the fact that a woman should make a *public speech of any sort* except perhaps, in the case of a lady 'opening' a charitable fête, was commented upon in Parliament – '...two ladies, wives of Members of this House...had disgraced themselves...' at a public meeting. That meeting had been attended by J.S. MILL, Charles KINGSLEY, John Morley, Sir Charles DILKE, James Tanfield and Henry FAWCETT, all of whom risked the criticism which was sure to be levelled at them.

After Henry died in 1884, Mrs. Fawcett worked on tirelessly. In practically every session of *every* Parliament (save during War-time) for 50 years, a Woman's Suffrage Bill was introduced and, as consistently, thrown out. She dealt with these, almost technical, setbacks patiently and with good humour.

During the Boer War, the Government sent her to Africa to investigate the 'concentration camps' (a British 'invention') for Boer women and children. Mrs. Fawcett's report exonerated ('whitewashed' her opponents said) the camps' administration.

There is a memorial to Dame Millicent in the Chapel of the Holy Cross in Westminster Abbey.

FETTER LANE, EC4   *Central line to Chancery Lane*

'Fewtor' in Norman French (which was the 'official' language in upper class circles in England for many years after the Conquest of 1066) meant, 'an idle person'. The Lane enjoyed an unenviable reputation for 'fewtors'. In 1934 Paul Morand wrote in *A Frenchman's London* that; 'The tears of King Lear are London rain; Hamlet's black velvet suit with its buttons of cut steel is right in the Docks, and the green fog of the City is the tint of Othello, the crooked lanes of Whitechapel are the fingers of Shylock and Fetter Lane is one of Falstaff's bowels...'

15,   Clifford's Inn, Samuel BUTLER 1864-1902 had his rooms on the second floor on the north side of the staircase. The sitting room faced the courtyard in which there was a pump where he drew his water. At one time Butler wanted to have his ashes sprinkled in Clifford's Inn.

77,   Tom PAINE, 1790-1793. His *Rights of Man* was published while he was living here.

NEVILL'S COURT, off the Lane

14, Keir HARDIE from 1902 to 1911. He had also lived at No. 10 in 1914. During this period, houses built in 1663 were still standing. Hardie wrote, 'The silence and solitude of my London mansion is the envy of all who have seen it. Outside the barking of a dog is the only sound which disturbs the clammy night air. Despite the eighth of an acre of sloping roof the Toms and Tabbies keep a respectful silence.' Nevill's Court was said to be the oldest *inhabited* house in London.

FIELDING	Glastonbury, Avon, April 22, 1707
Henry	Lisbon, October 8, 1754
Author	In the English Cemetery, Lisbon

19-20, Bow Street, WC1 (LCP 1929)
15, Buckingham Street, WC2, 1753

Fielding was at Eton with both William PITT and Charles James FOX and not long after leaving there he began a love-affair with a wealthy, young woman who lived in Lyme Regis, Dorset. His father dealt with this matter by packing Henry off to Leyden to study law. Father then married again and stopped his son's allowance.

He came back to London and just remained in funds by writing lightweight and farcical plays. In 1735 he married Charlotte Cradock, who was not only beautiful, but brought with her a modest dowry. He was able to spend this all too quickly and so back to the *pot-boilers* again. Not long after he was actually managing a theatre in the Haymarket, where, if he wished, he could put on his own plays! This ended after he had satirized WALPOLE in one piece and the Licensing Act of 1737 was passed which required the approval of the Lord Chamberlain before any play could be publicly performed – a form of censorship, which lasted well into the 20th century.

Fielding went back to the Law, was called to the Bar and went out onto the Western Circuit (the name given to the journies through the counties made by the judges twice a year. There are six circuits in England, two in Wales and three in Scotland.) In 1742 Charlotte died and four years later he set tongues wagging by marrying Mary Daniel, who had been Charlotte's maid. Tongues were set wagging again when Mary gave birth to a child in February 1748, having only married Henry at St Benet's the previous November.

In 1749 his novel *The History of Tom Jones,* the book which immortalized him, was published. Fielding called it, 'a comic opera in prose'. *Amelia* appeared in 1751 but Fielding had become a sick man and, in the hope of a better climate improving his health, he set off for Portugal but died there very soon after his arrival.

FIRBANK	London, January 17, 1886
Ronald Arthur Annesley	Rome, May 21, 1926
Author	In the *Protestant* Cemetery, Rome (reburied Catholic Muncipal Cemetery, Verano)

10, Clarges Street, W1, here born
102, Queen's Gate, SW7, 1912
33, Curzon Street, W1, 1912
19, Old Square, Lincoln's Inn, WC2, 1914
48, Jermyn Street, SW1, 1919
49A, Pall Mall, SW1, 1922

Stories abound about Firbank, nearly as many as about that other flamboyant homosexual, Oscar WILDE; though they were very different characters. Wilde was gregarious (dangerously so) and extrovert, whereas Firbank was often painfully withdrawn.

Firbank was a novelist – where Wilde was a playwright. In 1918 Firbank's first novel, *Valmouth,* appeared. It was an English village phantasy and the 'hero' of the book, a homosexual, comes back home with a Negro bride. (*Valmouth* was turned into a musical stage show and was very *nearly* a success in 1958.)

As a Catholic, Firbank introduced Catholic themes into much of his work and he was also very attracted to negroes. Practically all his characters, nuns, kings, lesbians and society ladies were fantastic. In 1924 he published a book called *Prancing Nigger.* (Today, it probably would not be possible to parade such a title!) His last novel, *Concerning the Eccentricities of Cardinal Pirelli* was published in 1926. In it, the Cardinal dies in his own cathedral, pursuing (predictably) a pretty choirboy.

Harold NICOLSON described Firbank when he invented his character, 'Lambert Orme'. 'Orme' [Firbank] had '...a curved face, a boneless face, a rather pink face, fleshy above the chin'. 'Orme/Firbank's' gait '...was more than sinuous, it did more than undulate: it rippled. At each step a wave was started which passed upward through his body, convexing his buttocks...'

FISHER

(Admiral) John Arbuthnot (1st Baron)	January 28, 1841
	July 10, 1920

First Sea Lord

16, Queen Anne's Gate, SW1 (LCP 1975) 1909-1920

Fisher entered the Royal Navy as a 14–year-old and was a Lieutenant before he was 20. He saw action in the Far East and was First Sea Lord in 1904. He stayed in that post and assumed it again in 1914, for a year. It was Fisher who took the decision to 'scrap' the old ships and introduce *Dreadnoughts.* The first of these, in service by 1906, was of 17,900 tons – 18,200 tonnes – with turbine engines. The original ship of this name was in Queen Elizabeth I's Navy.

FITZGERALD

Edward	Woodbridge, Suffolk, March 31, 1809
	Merton, June 14, 1883
Poet and translator	St Michael's Church, Boulge, Suffolk

39, Portland Place, W1
7, Southampton Row, WC1, 1830
13, Great Coram Street, WC1, 1843
19, Bedford Square, WC1, 1844-1848
39, Bolsover Street, W1, 1848-1850
31, Great Portland Street, W1, 1856-1857

Coming from a reasonably wealthy family, Fitzgerald, after graduating from Cambridge, was not forced to earn a living. He was able to make friends where he would and he made good friends. (One such was THACKERAY who said that 'Old Fiz was among those he had loved best in the World'.)

Sometime around 1853 Fitzgerald began to learn and study the language of Persia (today Iran) and three years later he published – anonymously – a translation of *Jamis Salaman and Absal.* This (in the original by Omar Khayyam) contained 516 *rubaiyat* in the Calcutta version, the largest surviving copy left: Fitzgerald translated 101 of these from the original Persian. Each quatrain expresses a complete thought. Khayyam (who died in the first quarter of the 16th century, having been born in Nishapur perhaps some 50 years before) was not honoured in his native country, which accounts for the incomplete state of his surviving work, and he was hardly a name at all in Europe. Fitzgerald's *Rubaiyat* published in 1859, changed that and his name has been so closely linked with the Persian original that it might be a pardonable mistake to think that the piece was of Fitzgerald's own making throughout.

FITZROY

The children of the bitchy Barbara Castlemaine, later Duchess of Cleveland (born Villiers, 1641-1709) sired by King Charles II were given the surname of Fitzroy. The second son, Henry, was married as a child to Isabella, the only child of Lord Arlington, who left to her the estate around the Tottenham Court Road – some of the land stretching as far to the north as Highgate. She also had another estate called Euston, in Suffolk. Henry was given the Dukedom of GRAFTON and all these have found their way into street names in this area. Henry had not long to enjoy it. He was killed in combat when he was only 27.

FITZROY ROAD, NW1   *Northern line to Camden Town*

The road was developed between 1850 and 1880 and many of these original houses are still standing.

23, W.B. YEATS (LCP 1957) 1867-1873. He spent his 'teenage' years here with his family.

23, another poet, the American Sylvia Plath (1932-1963) lived through the cold winter of 1962/63 only to commit suicide here.

46, H.G. WELLS boarded here with his aunt from 1889-1891, during which time he was an assistant master at Henley House School in Kilburn.

FITZROY
Robert
Hydrographer and Admiral

Suffolk, July 5, 1805
London, April 30, 1865

38, Onslow Square, SW7 (LCP 1981) from 1854 until his suicide here.

Fitzroy had royal blood in his veins; his grandfather, the Duke of Grafton being the illegitimate child of Barbara Castlemaine by King Charles II. He went into the Navy and spent seven years surveying the coasts of Patagonia and Tierra del Fuego. He was appointed to command the *Beagle* in 1831 and was Captain when DARWIN made his famous voyage in it. Jointly, they published *A Narrative of the Voyages of HMS Adventure and Beagle* in 1839.
As a Vice Admiral, he was placed on the retired list in 1863, having previously been attached to the Meteorological Department of the Board of Trade; the Fitzroy Barometer was named after him. It was he who instituted the system of storm warnings which developed into daily weather forecasts. Upset by some of Darwin's theories about evolution and overworked, he became more and more depressed, finally committing suicide not long before his 60th birthday.

FITZROY SQUARE, W1   *Victoria and Northern lines*
                                                  to Warren Street

Development began in 1793.

21, Robert Cecil, 3rd Marquess of SALISBURY (LCP 1965) 1858-1862. Five years previously, when he was only 23 he had become an MP.

21, the Marquess of SALISBURY.

21, Maynard KEYNES and Duncan Grant.

29, G.B. SHAW lived here with his mother (LCP 1975) 1887-1898. Here he wrote *The Philanderer, Mrs. Warren's Profession, Arms and the Man,*

The Man of Destiny and *Candida*. He was saved from the self-imposed squalour of this house by marrying his 'green-eyed Irish Millionairess' (Charlotte Payne-Townshend) in 1898.

29, Virginia WOOLF and her brother Adrian Stephen in 1907. Henry JAMES said that Adrian, 'interminably long and dumb', walking with Virginia was like '...a giraffe beside an ostrich'. Vanessa had married Clive BELL and they stayed on at 46, Gordon Square. (Thoby Stephen had died of typhoid on November 20, 1906.) The ground floor of 29 was Adrian's study – he was 23, and just down from Cambridge. The first floor was the sitting room; it had a green carpet and red brocade curtains over the long windows which looked out onto the Square. They had a cook, a maid and Virginia's 'legendary' dog, Hans.

33, Roger FRY, 1933.

37, Ford Madox FORD, 1865-1881.

FITZROY STREET, W1

8, J.A.M. WHISTLER had a studio here.

8, Duncan GRANT, 1919. His studio here, '...rose without a ceiling to a rounded brown roof of timber so that it was like a big boat turned upside down'. Below his rooms lived an Italian family who restored furniture for a living. The studio had been used both by WHISTLER and SICKERT (Sickert used it in 1903). Whistler painted a portrait of C.E. Holloway in this room and a photograph of his painting was superstitiously passed on from tenant to tenant.

13, Charles DICKENS' family in 1832.

18, Roger FRY in 1918.

19, W.R. SICKERT, 1911-1913. Augustus JOHN had also used the studio here. Alfred Thornton, an artist who was born in the late 1860s, has recalled that Sickert, helped by Rutherston and Spencer Gore, a landscape painter who lived from 1878 to 1914, instituted the 'Saturday Afternoon At-Homes'. Augustus John, Lucian Pisarro – Camille Pisarro's eldest son, Harold Gilman (1876-1919) and Charles Ginner (1879-1952) were habitués of these functions.

56, Captain Matthew FLINDERS (LCP 1973).

FLAXMAN   York, July 6, 1755
John   London, December 7, 1826
Sculptor   St Giles-in-the-Fields

27, Wardour Street, W1, 1781-1787
7, Greenwell Street, W1, where he died

A puny child, John was taken by his father (also John, also a sculptor, born in Buckinghamshire in 1726, died in 1795) to London in 1765. His health *did* improve and he entered the Academy Schools in 1770. Five years later, now 20, John joined his father in working for the Wedgwoods, designing the *cameos* which decorated a lot of their 'Etruria' ware. (Young John was well thought of, enough to give *Wedgwood* advice.) When he was 27, Flaxman married Ann Denman, whose father made gunstocks in Whitechapel in the (even then) sordid area of Whitechapel. Sir Joshua REYNOLDS, a bachelor by choice, on hearing of the marriage, said to Flaxman, 'So, John Flaxman, I am told you are married. If so you are ruined for an artist'. And he meant it! The newly-weds went to Rome, intending to stay for no more than two years. They were to spend seven years, coming back to London in 1794 and in three years he was made an ARA and a full Academician in 1800. In 1810 he was appointed Professor of Sculpture at the Academy.

King George IV commissioned Flaxman to make drawings for sculptural embellishments on the façade of Buckingham House, which fat George was intending to make his Palace.

Of his many statues, some are still to be seen in London: in Westminster Abbey – an 1826 statue of John KEMBLE, Lord MANSFIELD, Captain James Montagu, William Buchan and George Johnstone. In St Paul's: Sir Joshua REYNOLDS and Captain Ralph Miller and, finally, in the Victoria and Albert Museum a terracotta self-portrait, dated 1779, and one of Miss Flaxman, dated 1772. (Mary Ann Flaxman, his sister, 1768-1833; worked as a governess and eventually was acknowledged as an artist in her own right. She lived with Flaxman and his wife and was buried beside them.)

FLEET STREET, WC2

Piccadilly line to Aldwych (Monday to Friday only)

The Anglo-Saxon word for creek or tidal inlet was 'fleet'. A river, rising at Hampstead, flowed into the tidal inlet of the Thames and part of its course crossed what is now Fleet Street at its Ludgate (eastern) end. Fleet Street was an important road even in Roman times and there was a substantial bridge across the 'fleet'.

1 (now a Bank) here stood the Devil Tavern in which Ben Jonson helped establish the Apollo Club. Shakespeare *could* have been a member of it. Certainly, later, PEPYS, Steele, Dean Swift (1667-1745) and ADDISON came here. Samuel JOHNSON once 'threw' an all night party in the Tavern in 1751.

Off Fleet Street are 34 alleys and courts which really can only be explored on foot. Starting on the north side of the street at Fetter Lane and moving east – towards St Paul's – you come first to:

CRANE COURT

9, saw off the first numbers of *Punch* Magazine and,
10, was the first office of the *London Illustrated News*.
Next, **Red Lion Court** then:
Johnson's Court named before Samuel JOHNSON, but he did live in it from 1756 to 1776.
St Dunstan's Court, Bolt Court, Hind Court and:
Wine Office Court
6, Oliver GOLDSMITH lodged here in 1760 and wrote most of the *Vicar of Wakefield* here.

FLEMING	London, May 28, 1908
Ian Lancaster	Canterbury, August 12, 1964
Author	St Andrew's Church, Sevenhampton, Wilts (in an unmarked grave)

16, Victoria Square, SW1, 1954-1964

Son of Major Valentine Fleming (MP for South Oxfordshire) and a member of a well-to-do banking family. Ian Fleming joined *Reuters* and 'covered' the trial in MOSCOW of six British engineers who had been arrested 'for spying'.
He then moved into the City and worked as a stockbroker. It was during this period that he became an avid and expert book collector. After an 'exciting' Second World War, he joined Kemsley Newspapers in 1945 – they then owned the *Sunday Times*. When THOMSON bought the paper Fleming left the group in 1952. He had a house built in Jamaica in 1946 and it was here that many of the *James Bond* books were written. The 'Bond Image' has spread around the world = daring, sexy, cool-headed, rich, in fact, everything a sort of super private eye *should* be. The first 'Bond' book, called *Casino Royale* (1st editions now very hard to come by) was published in 1953

and the last, *The Man with the Golden Gun,* was published posthumously. Fleming claimed that he wrote *Casino Royale* in two months, '...as a piece of manual labour to make me forget the horrors of marriage'. Fleming was not a great author, but there can be very few writers who have started an international 'industry'.

FLINDERS
Matthew
Explorer

Donnington, Lincs., March 16, 1774
London, July 19, 1814
St James's Gardens, Cardington Street

5, Stanhope Street, NW1, 1790
56, Fitzroy Street, W1 (LCP 1973) 1813-1814

His father, grandfather and great-grandfather were all surgeons but Matthew chose to go into the Navy. In 1796 he and George Bass (who is thought to have died in 1812) discovered the Straits between Tasmania and Australia. Five years late, Flinders was commissioned to circumnavigate Australia.

Having done so, he was on his way home (having been shipwrecked once) and put into Mauritius, a French colony on December 15, 1803 to find France and England were at war. He was detained there until 1810, only getting back to England in October. His book, *A Voyage to Terra Australis,* was published on July 19, 1814, the day he died.

The Flinders River, and the mountain range in South Australia are named after him. His survey of New Holland (one of the original names for Australia) which was begun in 1802, when he began his circumnavigation, still forms the basis of the Admiralty charts used today.

His grandson, Sir William Matthew Flinders Petrie (1853-1942) who lived at 5, Cannon Place, NW3 (LCP 1954) from 1919-1935, studied Stonehenge, then went to the Middle East to the Pyramids and the Temples of Gizeh. He held the Chair of Egyptology at London University from 1892 to 1933.

FLINT
(Sir) William Russell
Artist

Edinburgh, April 4, 1880
London, December 27, 1969

Peel Cottage, 80 Peel Street, W8 (P) 1924-1969

Flint, a Scotsman, came to London in 1900. He first worked as a medical illustrator, drawing leprous mutilation, Boers' bullet wounds and diseases of the eye – a far, far cry from the luscious pictures that were to gain him an international reputation. Three years later, Bruce Ingram (later Sir Bruce Ingram) commissioned Flint to produce two half page illustrations for a story by Max PEMBERTON, published in the Christmas issue of the *Illustrated London News* which Bruce Ingram was editing. The payment was to be at the rate of eight guineas (£8.40) a page.

Cassells, the publishers, gave Flint a good sum of money for illustrating Rider Haggard's adventure story, *King Solomon's Mines,* and on the strength of this coup, Flint married Sibylla Sueter (a girl he had used as a model – a fully dressed one, in a rented studio he had at 19, George Street, W1).

Flint was elected as an ARA in 1924. He was painting on the Gareloch, in Scotland. A friend told him of his election, having just heard it on 'the wireless'. (This was the first time that the radio had been used for announcing such a happening.)

In 1962, Flint was one of the nine Academy members to have work exhibited in the Diploma Gallery of the Academy in their own lifetime. The others are: BRANGWYN, JOHN, MUNNINGS, KELLY, Winston CHURCHILL, Dunoyer de Segonzac (in 1959 – Hon RA) Laura KNIGHT and John Nash (in 1967). Flint was knighted in 1947.

FLOOD STREET, SW3   *District and Circle lines*
to Sloane Square

Named after Luke Thomas Flood, a Justice of the Peace and a Treasurer of
the Chelsea Parish School. In that capacity he helped considerably in
advancing the education of the poor children of Chelsea. Before settling on
Flood Street, this road – which runs off the King's Road almost to the
Thames – had been called successively Pound Lane, Robinson's Row and
Queen Street.

19   (at the top, on the King's Road end) Margaret THATCHER,
1969-1984. (The shade of L.T. Flood may look down here unkindly.
Before Mrs. Thatcher emerged as leader of the Party and then Prime
Minister, she was principally known, when she occupied a much lesser
post in a Conservative Government, for cutting down the supply of
free milk to school children.)

FONTEYN   Reigate, Surrey, May 18, 1919
(Dame) Margot
Ballerina

19, Pelham Crescent, SW7, 1946

Dame Margot was born Margaret Hooker and was educated in a widespread
way: from Kentucky to Shanghai and a few places in between! She began
ballet lessons under Princess Serafina ASTAFIEVA in the King's Road and
made her first appearance with the Sadler's Wells Company (now the Royal
Ballet) on October 4, 1934, in *The Haunted Ballroom*. Since then she has
danced practically all the great Classical roles and at one time, her favourite
was 'Giselle'.
In 1955 she married Roberto Emilio Arias, then the Panamanian
Ambassador in London (b.1918). Not long after their marriage, Arias
became the target of political killers and was shot at close range by one of
these would-be murderers. He survived but the bullet had done irreparable
damage to the spinal system and he was left a paraplegic.
Her grace, elegance and intelligent beauty bring applause wherever she
appears. She has received many honours (her DBE in 1956) and honorary
degrees. Bearing in mind her tranquility and peacefulness, perhaps her most
inappropriate decoration was in 1960, when Finland invested her with the
'Order of the Finnish Lion'!

FORD   Surrey, December 17, 1873
Ford Madox   Paris, June 26, 1939
Man of letters

10, Airlie Gardens, W8, 1903
84, Holland Park Avenue, W11, 1907
80, Campden Hill Gardens, W8, 1920s

In 1923 Ford changed his name from Ford Madox Hueffer (his father was
Francis Hueffer or Franz Huffer, 1845-1889, a Westphalian music critic) to
Ford Madox Ford, which is rather confusing. He has been called the 'last of
the Pre-Raphaelites' and he once described himself as 'An Englishman
knowing a little bit about Good Letters'. A rather typically snobbish,
Ford-like remark.
His mother was the daughter of Ford Madox Brown, a Pre-Raphaelite, and
the sister-in-law of another; William Michael Rosetti. Ford founded the
English Review in 1908 and was its editor. He collaborated with Joseph
CONRAD on two novels, the first being *The Inheritors* in 1901 and his first
independent novel was *The Fifth Queen* in 1906. He claimed to have
'discovered' D.H. LAWRENCE and he *did* introduce Ezra POUND to the
English literary scene. (Pound once told Ford that, '...if he were placed

naked and alone in a room without furniture', he would be able to create *total* confusion in that room 'within the hour'.)
Actually for an untidy man Ford dressed quite elegantly and in the early 1900s always had a well brushed top hat, a high 'GLADSTONE' collar and white spats.
He wrote three volumes of autobiography, the last being *It was a Nightingale* in 1933. For some years his star waned but by the 1950s he seemed to come back into favour and his 1915 novel, *The Good Soldier,* was read by a totally different public 40 years after its original appearance.

FORSTER
Edward Morgan
Novelist

London, January 1, 1879
Coventry, June 7, 1970

26, Brunswick Square, WC1, 1929-1939

Forster apparently had a miserable time at his Public School, Tonbridge. He went up to King's College, Cambridge in 1897 and life became much more bearable. With Goldsworthy Dickinson, who was 15 years older than he, and, like him, homosexual, he founded the *Independent Review*. In 1934 Forster published a biography of Dickinson, who had died in 1932.
After Cambridge he went to Italy and his first two novels, *Where Angels Fear to Tread* (1905) and *A Room with a View* three years later, both have Italian settings. *Howard's End* appeared in 1910 and then he set sail for India. This journey was to be translated into his very successful *Passage to India* which won him the Femina Vie Heureuse and Tait Black Memorial prizes in 1925. His literary successes earned him a sizeable income and from the 1920s onwards he quietly and generously helped many people, both literary and not so literary.
As he grew older and older, his early friends were dying away, but the State recognized his growing, unsought-for, role of a sort of Grand Old Man of English literature and, in 1953, he was made a Companion of Honour, then given the Order of Merit in 1968.

FOSCOLO
Ugo
Poet

Zakinthos, Greece, January 26, 1778
Turnham Green, London, October 10, 1827
Florence (finally)

11, Soho Square, W1, 1816-1818
19, Edwardes Square, W8, 1818
22, Woodstock Street, W1, 1818
154, New Bond Street, W1, 1819
1, Wells Street, W1, 1826

Sometimes considered to be the 'Italian Lord Byron', Foscolo was obliged to leave Italy in something of a hurry and came to London full of publishing schemes and other grandiose ideas which, if lacking practicality, made up for that in their deviousness.
Before he decamped to London he had published a number of important works; *Ultime Lettere di Jacopo Ortis* in 1797, a romance; and a long lyric poem, *I Sepolcri,* in 1807. He also translated much of Homer.
At one stage he appears to have inherited money, from a Mrs. Emerytt, and some property and he set up house in London with his illegitimate daughter (who died in Manchester of tuberculosis when she was only 22).
He has a tomb in the parish church of Chiswick but his body was taken back to Florence in 1870 and lies in the Temple of Santa Croce.

FOUNTAIN COURT, EC4   *District and Circle lines to Temple*

On the right of Middle Temple Lane (as one goes down it from Fleet Street) is Fountain Court. The fountain, from which it takes its name was built in 1681. Even today almost tranquil; its peace inspired DICKENS to make this Court the place where 'John Westlock' met 'Ruth Pinch' in *Martin Chuzzlewit*. 'Brilliantly the Temple fountain sparkled in the sun, and laughingly its liquid music played...'

2, Arthur SYMONS, 1890 (on the top floor). 'The nights in Fountain Court were a continual delight to me. I lived chiefly by night and, when I came late, I used often to sit on the bench under the trees, where no one else ever sat at those hours.'
Ernest Dowson once visited him here at tea-time; then, '...later on we tried the effects of haschisch' [sic] '- that slow intoxication, that elaborate experiment in visionary sensations...'
Havelock Ellis stayed here in 1894 and W.B. YEATS in the following year.

3, (now 103/4 the Strand) William BLAKE lived from 1821 until he died here in August 1827.

FOX   Conduit Street, London, W1,
Charles James   January 24, 1749
Politician   Chiswick, September 13, 1806
   Westminster Abbey (North transept)

9, South Street, W1, 1792-1796
46, Clarges Street, W1 (LCP 1950) 1803-1804
9, Arlington Street, W1
13, Albermarle Street, W1

BURKE called Fox 'The greatest debater the world ever saw'; other persons might have said of him, 'The Greatest Gambler London ever saw'! In addition to being addicted to gambling, he could see off more bottles of wine at a sitting than anyone in the House, regardless of their politics. In the House, Fox was a Liberal and he *lived* liberally.
He was the third son of the first Lord Holland, went to Eton, followed by Hertford College, Oxford and, when only 19, he was MP for Midhurst in Kent. He spent most of his vacations burning the candles at every possible end, usually in Paris. He supported Lord NORTH who gratefully made him Lord of the Admiralty. Fox resigned from that post in 1772 and three years later North sacked him altogether. They formed an uneasy truce in 1783 and then the Coalition administration of the Duke of Portland ended in April. Here began the power struggle of Fox and the Tory, PITT.
Fox was totally against continuing the war with France and, when Pitt died in January 1806, Fox was called to office and was on the point of introducing an anti-slavery bill when he died suddenly at Chiswick House.
(It was said that on being told that the rip-roaring Charles was actually getting married, his uncle, Lord Holland, said, 'Well on *that* night perhaps the boy *will* be in bed'. Holland was a witty man and, as he lay dying in Holland House in June 1774, George Selwyn, a man about town, who had a fondness for viewing corpses, called on the moribund Earl. Holland was supposed to have said, 'If Mr. Selwyn calls again, show him up; if I am alive I shall be delighted to see him, and if I am dead, he would like to see me.')
Sir Richard WESTMACOTT's statue of Fox was put up on the east side of Bloomsbury Square in 1816. In his right hand Fox is holding a copy of the Magna Carta.

FRANKLIN Boston, Mass., January 17, 1706
Benjamin Philadelphia, April 17, 1790
Statesman Philadelphia

6, Sardinia Street, WC1, 1725-1726
7 (now 36) Craven Street, WC2 (LCP 1914) 1757-1770

His father was a tallow chandler and Benjamin was the tenth of his 17 children. (Some records have him as the youngest. This latter would accord more with his name of Benjamin.) Tenth or 17th, he was apprenticed when he was only 12 years old to his brother James in a printing house.

In 1726 he entered political life and, after only one year, was Postmaster of Philadelphia. He quarrelled with James and came to London where he worked as a compositor for two years. By 1727 he was back in Philadelphia, had set up his own printing firm and bought *The Pennsylvania Gazette* in 1729. He was almost entirely self-taught in French, Spanish, Italian and Latin. He also studied science and this led him to find out the nature of lightning – tying keys to kite strings in electric storms.

Franklin was one of the Committee which drew up the Declaration of Independence and was despatched that year to establish an *entente cordiale* with France, eventually helping to draft the Franco American Treaty of 1778.

The last six years of his life he remained principally in Philadelphia. He was troubled with gout for many years, added to which he suffered considerably from gall stones. In March 1790 he fell heavily downstairs and his 84-year old body was too tired to fight back. The city of Philadelphia gave him a magnificent funeral and even the rather cynical French Assembly noted the death of a great man and went into mourning for three days.

Franklin wrote his own epitaph. It ran:

'The Body
of
BENJAMIN FRANKLIN
Printer,
(Like the cover of an old Book,
Its contents torn out,
And stript of its Lettering and Gilding)
Lies here Food for Worms;
Yet the Work itself shall not be lost,
For it will (as he believed) appear once
More in a new
And more beautiful Edition,
Corrected and Amended
By the Author.'

FREAKE 1814
(Sir) Charles James 1884
Builder

21, Cromwell Road, SW7 (LCP 1981) 1860-1884

Had Freake been born in 1764, rather than in 1814, the chances are he would not have been able to come 'from nothing' to a position of wealthy eminence in the way that he did. The Victorian climate was just right for someone like Freake. His father was a coal heaver (maybe a publican) and in 70 years his son Charlie had worked his way up so that by the time he died he was a baronet, he owned a vast house in Kensington, his only son had been through Cambridge, his wife was the daughter of a member of the Honourable Corps of Gentlemen-At-Arms, his daughters had married into the aristocracy and, when he died, he left over £700,000. And all from speculative building.

His house in the Cromwell Road (which, naturally he built for himself) had a ballroom in which theatricals could be staged and no less a person than Edward Albert, Prince of Wales sometimes came. It was probably the pressure the Prince brought to bear on GLADSTONE caused Freake to be created a baronet in 1882. He elected to be sonorously styled as Sir Charles Freake, Bt., of Cromwell House Kensington and Fulwell Park.

Freake, almost entirely at his own cost, built the National Training School of Music in 1875. Today this freakish pink and white building immediately to the west of the Albert Hall in Kensington Gore is now the Royal College of Organists. Truly his progress was remarkable. He made the best of the opportunities in a period when expansion was on every hand and taxes were almost non-existent.

It was said of him, that he was 'the cleverest of all the speculating builders'. Probably Cubitt was cleverer but nobody could deny Freake's success.

FREWEN Northiam, Sussex, May 8, 1853
Moreton September 2, 1924
Entrepreneur

18, Chapel Street, W1, 1886
18, Aldford Street, W1, 1886-1892
25, Chesham Street, SW1, 1896-1900

Moreton's wife was Lady Randolph CHURCHILL's sister (one of the three daughters of Leonard Jerome, a New York millionaire) making Frewen a cousin of sorts to Winston CHURCHILL. Frewen senior was a land- owner on a vast scale and allowed his son to be educated 'privately' and afterwards sent him on to Trinity College, Cambridge. Moreton wanted to be a 'somebody' – anything – but whatever it was to be it must be on a large scale. He involved himself and others in a number of enterprises (almost always with other people's money) with invariably disastrous results, so that his nickname in the City was 'Mortal Ruin'. (Rudyard KIPLING, 12 years his junior, however, wrote of Frewen, *post mortem* that he was 'wholly a sahib'.)

When his eye was not on get-rich-quick schemes it was on the ladies and Lily LANGTRY was just one of the 'Professional Beauties' on whom his roving eye rested. Frewen wrote in his (very) private journal, 'Every woman I have enjoyed has been completely paralysed by the vigour of my performance'.

FRIESE-GREEN Bristol, September 7, 1855
William London, May 5, 1921
Pioneer of the cinema Highgate New Cemetery, East 1

136, Maida Vale, W9 (LCP 1954) 1888-1891

Friese-Green came up to London in 1885 and rented premises in Piccadilly to carry on his (largely at that time) unsuccessful experiments on 'moving pictures'. Eventually he developed his ideas so that celluloid could be used as the actual 'carrier' of the film and he 'shot' 50 feet of film (15 metres) showing people sunning themselves in Hyde Park. He patented this development in 1890 but success did not attend his ventures.

In all, poor Friese-Green took out over 70 patents; the most important being his 1889 camera. In 1888 the Photographic Society of Vienna awarded him the Daguerre Medal (after Louis Jacques Daguerre, 1789-1851, the French photographic pioneer) for his camera using paper film with perforated edges.

Having patented his camera, Friese-Green wrote to Thomas Alva Edison, describing the camera and suggesting it somehow be linked with Edison's 'Phonograph' and so make 'talkies'. It was 40 years before 'talkies' arrived commercially. He also had quite advanced ideas on stereoscopy, colour film, electrical *inkless* printing and the movement of distant objects by radio command ('Technicolor', 'Xerox' and the space programme!)

On his grave in Highgate are inscribed the words: 'William Friese-Green, the Inventor of Kinematography'. And so he was.

FRITH STREET, W1
Central and Northern lines to Tottenham Court Road

In 1677, Richard Frith, a bricklayer began developing about 20 acres of land in Soho. By 1683, however, he was bankrupt and was forced to give up all title to his so-nearly-ripe speculation. He never recovered and died, destitute, in 1695.

6, William HAZLITT (LCP 1905). In this house he wrote his four-volume *Life of Napoleon* and died here in 1830. The house was built in 1718.

18, Samuel ROMILLY was born here in 1757.

20, Wolfgang Amadeus MOZART, 1764. The eight-year old Mozart, his father and sister lodged here. Their landlord's name was Thomas Williamson.

22, John Logie BAIRD (LCP 1951) 1925-1927. On October 2, 1925 in an attic in this house, the office boy, William Taynton, was made to sit in front of Baird's 'Camera' and so became the first person in the world to 'appear on television'. On January 26, 1926, Baird showed a group of eminent scientists his device.

49, Mary Russell MITFORD, c. 1820.

49, John CONSTABLE, 1811.

55, S.T. COLERIDGE stayed here with his friend, Basil Montagu.

60, Lytton STRACHEY spent a week here with Dora CARRINGTON in July 1917.

64, Charles MACREADY, 1843-1851.

66, Tom DRIBERG, 1927. He rented a top floor room for seven shillings and sixpence (37½p) a week.

FROST
April 7, 1939

David Paradine

TV 'Personality'

46, Egerton Crescent, SW3, 1975-1983, until just after second marriage

At one time Frost seemed to BE television. His features appeared 'on the box' at all hours.

From grammar school he went on to Caius College, Cambridge. Frost joined the 'Footlights', a dramatic group within the University, and was editor of the magazine *Granta*.

He was in a feature position in the BBC programme, *That Was The Week That Was* (TWTWTW) in 1962-1963; a programme that created a whole new TV world for British audiences – *and* for the BBC. Adapted and re-shaped for American TV, this was Frost's first trans-Atlantic leap.

Backwards and forwards he shuttled across the Atlantic with amazing frequency and built up a following (and a fortune) all the while. The rest of the 'media' speculated about his love life and had him married off to any available woman practically week by week. He spiked all their guns by marrying Lyn, widow of Peter Sellers, six months after Sellers' death. It lasted as many months and the Frosts divorced in July 1982.

The same year Frost and others bid for, and were awarded, the contract for TV AM – television before breakfast. Their first programmes went out on February 1st, 1983; within weeks they were in trouble despite the 'Whiz kid', Peter Jay, being Chairman of the outfit. On March 19, Jay resigned and Jonathan Aitken, MP, wealthy, 40-year old great-nephew of the wealthier Lord BEAVERBROOK took over.

On the following day Frost married Lady Carina Fitzalan Howard, daughter of the 17th Duke of Norfolk, Premier Earl of all England, his title having been handed out in 1483. Family motto – *Sola Virtus Invicta* – Virtue alone is unconquerable. Frost was born a Methodist and Lady Carina a Catholic so Frost's second marriage ceremony, and her first, was as ecumenical as possible.

FROUDE James Anthony *Historian*	Dartington, Devon, April 23, 1818 Kingsbridge, Devon, October 20, 1894 Salcombe Cemetery

5, Onslow Gardens, SW7 (LCP 1934) 1873-1892

Froude's father was a Devonian Archdeacon who sent young James up to Westminster for his schooling and, after that, to Oriel College, Oxford. In 1842 he was elected a Fellow of Exeter College and he took Deacon's orders in 1844. For a time he was attracted to the 'High' Church under NEWMAN but he decided to turn his back both on his Fellowship and the Church of Rome and devote himself to literature and, especially, history.
He wrote for *Fraser's magazine* and, for a short time, was editor of it. History came first, however, and in 1856, the first two volumes of his *History of England* were published. (Ten more volumes were needed before the work was completed in 1869.)
In 1874 and again the following year he visited the South African colonies on an official Government mission and reported his findings in a publication called *Two Lectures on South Africa*.
His purely historical writing tended to be too subjective but, as Thomas CARLYLE's executor, he eventually produced a fine biography of the Scottish philosopher in 1884.
Froude was a tall (5 feet 11 inches: 1.8 metres) distinguished man. Sir Edgar Boehm made a bust of him which Froude thought 'atrocious'.

FRY Roger Eliot *Artist*	Highgate, London, December 14, 1866 London, September 9, 1934

29, Beaufort Street, SW3, 1892-1896
7, Beaumont Street, W1
18, Fitzroy Street, W1, 1918
48, Bernard Street, WC1, 1927-1934

Son of the celebrated jurist, Sir Edward Fry (1827-1918) Roger went to Clifton College and then on to Cambridge. It was to be Fry who was largely responsible for bringing the works of the Post-Impressionists (and, in particular, Cezanne) into the British artistic world. In 1910 he arranged the first London exhibition of the 'school'. He was a more than able artist himself but his *forte* (and a commercial one) was the design of household artefacts. In 1913 he founded the 'Omega' workshops which were to produce everyday products to good designs and of first-class workmanship. When he was 30 he married Helen Combe, who was older than he and had no money. The marriage was soon troubled and finally ruined by her mental instability. He spent five years with the Metropolitan Museum of New York (five not very happy years) and then came back to England in 1910 to edit the *Burlington Magazine*.

FULHAM

In about AD 700 there was a Saxon village on the banks of the Thames called FULANHAM, which could be translated as a 'HAMM' – a bend in the river, the village belonging to a Saxon satrap called Fulla. It will be seen that there is a long, curving bend in the Thames between Putney and Chelsea bridges. The northern foreshore of this bend still lies within the Borough of Hammersmith and Fulham.

FULHAM ROAD, SW3 and SW10

Low numbers, take District, Circle or Piccadilly lines to South Kensington; high numbers, District line to Fulham Broadway

18   (formerly 2, Onslow Terrace) Giuseppe MAZZINI, late 1850s, early 1860s, when he spent his time rallying support from Italians in London to create a real Italian Republic.

454,   J. McNeil WHISTLER moved here with his mistress, Maud, who gave birth to their first child in this house. Maud Franklin, who used to call herself 'Mrs. Whistler', was described by an American artist called John M. Alexander, as, '...not pretty, with prominent teeth, a real British type'. The house was rather startlingly decorated and referred to sometimes as 'The Pink Palace'.

454,   Henri GAUDIER-BRZESKA (LCP 1977) 1912-1914. He lived here with his mistress, Sophie. He had added her surname, Brzeska, to his own. From here he left for the army and was killed in action in 1915.

FUSELI   Zurich, February 7, 1741
Henry   Putney, April 16, 1825
Artist   St Paul's crypt (between the graves of
                        REYNOLDS and OPIE)

100, St Martin's Lane, W2, 1779-1785
37, Foley Street, W1 (LCP 1961) 1788-1803
7, Great Queen Street, WC2, 1803
13, Berners Street, W1, 1804

When he was 20, Fuseli was a priest in holy orders though he never followed the vocation. He moved to Berlin as an artist where his work caught the eye of the British Ambassador of the day, who recommended that he come to London. He arrived in the capital in 1765 and was encouraged in his work by no less a person than Joshua REYNOLDS. In 1770 he moved to Italy for further study and became engrossed in the works of Michelangelo.

In London he was a great friend of William BLAKE who, though 16 years younger than Fuseli, influenced him considerably. In their turn, later on ETTY, HAYDON, Landseer and CONSTABLE all studied under Fuseli.

He formed an attachment for William GODWIN's wife, Mary Woolstonecroft, about which Godwin wrote at some length after Mary's death in 1797.

On June 30, 1788, Fuseli married Sophia Rawlins of Bath. (She may have been one of his models.) She had a quietening influence on him and he re-established contacts in the world of Art and was elected a member of the Royal Academy, beating BONOMI to that honour, much to the obvious annoyance of Joshua Reynolds. He was elected Professor of Painting to the Academy in 1799. The same year he opened a gallery of his own in Pall Mall with an exhibition of 47 of his paintings.

G

GAINSBOROUGH
Thomas
Artist

Sudbury, Suffolk, 1727
London, August 2, 1788
St Anne's Church, Kew

82, Pall Mall, 'Schomberg House', SW1 (LCP 1951) from 1774 until he died here

Gainsborough came to London in 1740 to work as an engraver but went back to his native Suffolk (perhaps disenchanted?) six years later. In 1752 he established himself as a painter of portraits and most of his output consisted of 'heads and half-lengths' of the local worthies in Ipswich. Anxious to get a better social class of 'sitter', Gainsborough went to fashionable Bath in 1760. He was kept busy there, his style altered slightly and he began sending his paintings to the Royal Academy for showing. Fourteen years later he returned to London and settled in Pall Mall. His style had now developed to a fine degree and his polished best can be seen in his full length portrait of Mary, Countess Howe, which today hangs in Kenwood House in Highgate. His growing success came to the eyes of the Royal family and today, HM Queen Elizabeth *personally* owns 34 of his paintings.

GALSWORTHY
John
Playwright and novelist

Combe, Surrey, August 14, 1867
London, January 31, 1933
Ashes scattered on Sussex Downs,
memorial Highgate New Cemetery,
West VI

3, Palace Street, Buckingham Gate, SW1, 1894
Cedar Studios, Glebe Place, SW3
14, Addison Road, W14, 1905-1912
1A, Adelphi Terrace, Robert Street, WC2, 1912-1918

Galsworthy's father was a well-to-do solicitor who sent the boy to Harrow (where he excelled on the football field). He went on to study law and was called to the Bar of Lincoln's Inn, but this did not prevent him from taking an extensive tour of the Far East, where he met Joseph CONRAD and a lifelong friendship was started (despite Conrad being ten years older than Galsworthy and from a *very* different background).
His first publication was a book of short stories in 1897, followed by the novel, *Jocelyn* the year after and *Villa Rubein* in 1900. In 1905 he married the divorced wife of his cousin, A.J. Galsworthy, but the marriage was anything but a success.
The Man of Property was the first of a sequence of novels that came to be called *The Forsyte Saga*. The 'Forsytes' went on until *Swan Song* in 1928. (The BBC made a series called the *Forsyte Saga* which had the great British public glued to the little silver screen Sunday night after Sunday night. It was so popular that vicars altered the time of their evening service to accomodate the mania.)
Galsworthy refused a knighthood but accepted the Order of Merit in 1929. In 1932 he won the Nobel Prize for Literature. Bearing in mind the background of his upper-middle class wealth plus the very considerable sums which his pen earned for him, it is maybe a little surprising that in his will in 1933 he was only 'worth' £88,587.

GALTON   Birmingham, February 16, 1822
(Sir) Francis   Haslemere, Surrey, January 17, 1911
Explorer and scientist

42, Rutland Gate, SW7 (P) (LCP 1959) from 1858 until six months before his death

A man of wide interests with an intelligent appreciation of all of them, Galton has been sometimes called 'The Founder of Eugenics'. He was a grandson of Erasmus DARWIN and so his interest in eugenics could well have been an inherited trait. He was a qualified doctor (ex- King's College, London) and in his lifetime won and had bestowed upon him many varied awards.

In 1850 he set out for Africa and for two years explored Damaraland, the land of the Hottentot and Ovamboland, a Bantu country. He was for many years on the Council of the Royal Geographical Society and a member of many geographical and anthropological learned bodies.

He founded (and funded) the laboratory for Eugenics in University College, London (the 'godless' University). Criminology interested him and he originated the process of composite portraiture by assembling the facial features of criminals from eye-witness evidence. He also paid much attention to identification from fingerprints. Finger printing is an older science than generally supposed. J.E. Purkinje, a physiologist, read a paper before the University of Breslau on the subject in 1823. Alphonse Bertillon (1853-1914) introduced the definitive science of fingerprinting in 1880. The first official use of a fingerprint as proof of identity in America was Gilbert Thompson's thumbprint on the geological survey of New Mexico in 1882 to prevent the forging of commissary orders.

GARRICK   Hereford, February 19, 1717
David   London, January 20, 1779
Actor   Westminster Abbey, 'Poet's Corner',
                                             his wife (d. 1822) is in the same grave

27, Southampton Street, WC2 (P) 1747-1772
5, Adelphi Terrace, WC2, from 1772 until he died here

Garrick's father was a captain in the army and sent David to school in Edial, where he was one of the *three* pupils of Samuel JOHNSON. Johnson was only eight years older than Garrick and when schoolmastering proved a financial failure, Garrick and his ex-teacher set off for London.

This was in 1737 and at that time Garrick's brother was a wine merchant and David joined him as a partner in the business, but in less than four years he was on the stage. Fame came to him when he was playing in *Richard III* at the Drury Lane and after this he hardly ever looked back. He became joint-patentee at Drury Lane in 1747 and retired from the stage when he was 69

He married a dancer from Vienna, a Catholic girl called Eva Marie Violetti who lived to be nearly 100. They married on June 22, 1749 and he settled £10,000 on her and gave her 'pin money' of £70 a year. She gave up her career and devoted herself to her husband. Though he was a compulsive hoarder no letters from either of them to each other exist. (Perhaps there *were* none as they never spent even one day apart in over 30 years!) Unlike many 'theatricals', Garrick managed money well and left £120,000 in his will, a quite staggering amount for the 18th century.

Garrick was the last actor to be buried in Westminster Abbey and his death moved his old school teacher and friend, Sam Johnson, to say that Garrick's death, '...eclipsed the gaiety of nations'.

Over the door of 27, Southampton Street is a bronze medallion of Garrick, set into a terracotta surround, made by H.C. Fehr in 1901.

GASKELL Chelsea, September 19, 1810
Elizabeth Cleghorn Alton, Hants, November 12, 1865
Author Brook Street Chapel, Knutsford,
Ches.

93, Cheyne Walk (then Lindsey Row) SW3 (LCP 1913) here born
25, Lower Brook Street, W1 1829

At the age of one, her mother having died, Elizabeth was taken up to Knutsford and was brought up by an aunt. Her father was a Unitarian Minister and, in 1832, she married another one; the Reverend William Gaskell (1805-1884). The Gaskells moved to Manchester and were there for practically the rest of her life. She had four children but her only son died only a few months old.

It has been said that she wrote her first book, *Mary Barton,* as a sort of 'therapy' after the boy's tragic death. This first novel was published anonymously. Other books (under her own name) appeared: *Ruth* and (her most famous) *Cranford* in 1853. Lord HOUGHTON thought it, '...the finest piece of humoristic description that had been added to British literature since Charles LAMB'.

GAUDIER-BRZESKA St Jean de Braye, October 4, 1891
Henri Neuville St Vaast, June 5, 1915
Sculptor Killed in action

454, Fulham Road, SW6 (LCP 1977) 1912-1914

A 'Vorticist' sculptor, he was, until 1910, just Gaudier. He then met Sophie Brzeska in Paris and joined his name to hers.

He won a scholarship to Bristol to study art and was provided with funds to continue studying there. In London he became a close friend of Ezra POUND – a leading 'Vorticist' and contributed to the magazine *Blast.* He had begun a head of Pound in 1914, but at the outbreak of the First World War, he joined the French Army and was killed when charging the Germans at Neuville.

Enid BAGNOLD, who was two years older than Gaudier-Brzeska, said that he was '...a hard, disagreeable little creature, with a curious, rattling voice like a machine-gun and a complete unawareness of when he was being a bore'.

GAY Barnstaple, Devon, September 16,
John 1685
Poet and dramatist London, December 4, 1732
Westminster Abbey, in 'Poet's Corner'

16, Lawrence Street, SW3, 1712-1714

Coming from a 'good, but decayed family' and orphaned even from that, Gay came up to London and was apprenticed to a silk merchant, a post he did not like. In 1711 he published *Rural Sports* which he dedicated to Alexander POPE and so established a lifelong friendship with the 'Bard of Twickenham'.

By 1728 Gay had become famous and well-to-do as his *Beggar's Opera* opened in London and had a run of 63 performances – a 'smash hit' by the standards of the day. The music was by Christopher Pepusch (1667-1752) a German/English composer, who was born in Berlin, came to London when he was about 30 years old and played the harpsichord at Drury Lane.

Gay rather rested on his laurels after his *coup* and, being by nature rather indolent, he was content to live in the household of the Duke of Queensberry, at the Duke's expense. In 1715, Gay had produced a book of poems called *Trivia, or the Art of Walking the Streets,* which sheds some quite amusing, poetical light on some of the seamier aspects of early 18th century London street life.

'As a poet, he cannot be rated very high', wrote JOHNSON of Gay, 'He was, as once I heard a female remark, "of a lower order".' Certainly Gay faded away for nearly 200 years until *The Beggar's Opera* was revived in 1920 with musical re-arrangements by Frederick Austin (who was born in London in 1872). Then, in Berlin in 1928, Kurt Weill's *Die Dreigroschenoper* ran for 2,000 performances and came to London in concert form as *The Beggar's Opera* again. There must be many people familiar with 'Mac the Knife' who don't realize John Gay began it all. On his tomb are inscribed his own words:

> 'Life is a jest, and all things show it;
> I *thought* so once, and now I know it.'

GEORGE STREET, W1 *Central line to Bond Street*

The George remembered in this little street, leading out of Hanover Square on the south side, is George I, who had been on the throne for three or four years when this was developed c. 1719.

3, Madame de STAEL, c.1812. Before she established herself and her 'salon' in Argyll Street.

9, R.B. SHERIDAN, 1803-1805. His playwriting days over, Sheridan was an MP while here and in 1806 became secretary to the Navy.

15, Tom MOORE (LCP 1963) 1799-1801. His lodging here was, '...a front room up two pairs of stairs...for which I pay six shillings (30p) a week...a poor emigrant Bishop occupied the floor below me. The other day I had soup *bouilli* rice pudding and porter for nine pence ha'penny (3p).'

24, Nathaniel HAWTHORNE, September 1855, with his wife and their son, Julian. This visit to the capital confirmed to him all, '...his book knowledge which had made London the day dream of my youth'. Mrs. Hawthorne died in London in 1871 and was buried at Kensal Green. On her grave her daughter, '...planted some ivy that I had brought from America, and a periwinkle from Papa's grave'.

25, John Singleton COPLEY, 1784-1815. Afterwards the house was lived in by his son, who was to become Lord Lyndhurst. Copley had bought the house originally from Lord Fauconberg. Lyndhurst was still living here in 1850 (he died, aged 91, in 1863). He also had a little house called Walnut Tree Cottage in Fulham, which was demolished in 1857.

64, Sir Morell MACKENZIE, 1862.

GERALD ROAD, SW1 *District and Circle lines to Sloane Square*

Origin quite unknown. Though it is part of the Grosvenor Estate there do not seem any likely Grosvenors called Gerald after whom the road could be named and no territorial reasons either.

17, Noel COWARD, 1925-1956. On November 27, 1930, Harold NICOLSON and his wife, Vita came to an after-theatre supper here '...and on to supper with Noel... An elaborate studio. Noel very simple and nice. He talks of the days when his mother kept lodgings' [at 111 Ebury Street] 'and he himself had a top back room. Gradually he began to make money and took the top floor for himself, finally descending to the first floor and ejecting the lodgers. "As I rose in the world I went down in the house". Completely unspoilt by success. A nice eager man.'

GERRARD STREET, W1

The family name of the Earls of Macclesfield was Gerard [sic] and they owned a plot of land on the south side of what is now Shaftesbury Avenue, which was walled in and used as a Military parade ground. The area began to be developed commercially about 1680.

22, JOHNSON's biographer, James BOSWELL lodged here in 1775 and 1776.

30, David GARNETT's 'Nonesuch' Press was here.

35, Fanny KEMBLE lived here before she went onto the stage to earn money to bolster the family's finances.

37, Edmund BURKE (P 1876) 1787-1790. By this time, just still *in* politics, but *out* of favour.

43, John DRYDEN, 1686(?) until he died here in May 1700 (P 1875). The plaque is on No. 43 but it is more than probable that Dryden lived and died in No.44, '...the 5th door on the left coming from Newport Street'.

GIBBON	Putney, April 27, 1737
Edward	London, January 16, 1794
Historian	St Mary and St Andrew's Church,
	Flitching, Sx.

7, Bentinck Street, W1, 1773-1783
76, St James's Street, SW1, from 1793 until he died here

Grandfather Gibbon was one of the Directors of the 'South Sea Bubble'. When it 'burst' his losses were serious but enough of the family fortune remained to send Edward to Westminster School then to Magdalen, Oxford. He stayed there 14 months, 'idly and unprofitably': which is perhaps not surprising as he was only 15 years old when he went up! Despite his short stay at Oxford it was time enough for him to become a Roman Catholic. His father, a devout Protestant, became alarmed and packed the boy off to Puritanical Switzerland. Edward, having embraced Rome, now embraced Suzanne Curchod, a Swiss miss. Father Gibbon thought their possible union to be impossible and demanded that Edward and Suzanne should be separated. Edward 'sighed like a lover, obeyed like a son'. Suzanne (1739-1796) married Jacques Necker (1732-1804) and produced a daughter who was to become Madame de STAEL.

In 1770 his father died leaving a tangled estate and Gibbon left the family home of Buriton and came to live in London. He set to work and the first volume of the *Decline and Fall of the Roman Empire* was published in 1776 and Volumes Two and Three in 1781. By 1783 Gibbon was back in Switzerland and worked on *The Decline* practically every evening. On the night of June 27, 1787, the final words were written and the last three of the six volume 'set' were published in 1788.

In 1761 Gibbon visited a surgeon in Southampton seeking treatment for a grossly swollen left testicle. Thirty years later he was writing to Lord Sheffield about a recurrence of this problem as his scrotum was enlarged to such a degree that the swelling was obvious through his breeches and his gait was altered. On November 14, 1793 his doctor drew off eight *pints* (4.5 litres) of a clear, watery fluid from the testicle. Ten days later, a second puncture was made and a further six *pints* (3.4 litres) of fluid were withdrawn. Soon he developed fever and, on January 13, 1794, 12 more *pints* of fluid (6.8 litres) were drawn off. Three days later he was dead.

GIBBONS Rotterdam, April 4, 1648
Grinling London, August 3, 1721
Wood Carver St Paul's Church, Covent Garden

19-20, Bow STreet, WC2 (LCP 1929)

Gibbons had come to London before he was 20 and was 'discovered' by John Evelyn (whilst carving a crucifix) in 1671. Sir Peter LELY had also taken notice of him and so had the architect, Hugh May. These three men recommended young Gibbons to Sir Christopher WREN.

He was unsurpassed for his wood carvings of flowers, fruit, small animals and cherubs. His work in London is most easily seen in the carving on the choir stalls in St Paul's.

Gibbons, or very often artists in his employ and his apprentices, worked in stone and bronze for tombs. An example is the marble to Cloudesley Shovell in Westminster Abbey, or the very fine statue of King James II outside the National Gallery. His carving can be seen in profusion at Windsor and Hampton Court Palace; the best examples of his purely domestic work are at Petworth House in Sussex (Lord Egremont's country seat).

GIBBS Kensington, May 1, 1877
(Sir) Philip Armand Hamilton March 10, 1962
Author

36, Holland Street, W8, 1908
8, Sloane Gardens, SW3, 1920s-1930s
6, Sloane Gardens, SW3,
43, Cadogan Gardens, SW3,
33, Cliveden Place, SW1, and,
4, Lyall Street, SW1, these last four taken for short winter lets

Gibbs' father had actually been born *in* Windsor Castle. Later he was a devoted Civil Servant and Queen's Messenger. The Gibbs family was made up of six boys and two girls. One of the boys, Cosmo, who used Hamilton, the family name, as a surname became a very successful playwright.

Gibbs was educated privately and was journalistically precocious, becoming literary Editor for the *Daily Mail* when he was only 20. His novel, *The Street of Adventure* published in 1909, informatively reflects his life and times in Fleet Street.

In the War, Gibbs became a brilliant 'front-line' correspondent and his experiences appear in his, *Realities of War* published in 1920. In that year he was awarded the KBE, so becoming Sir Philip.

GILBERT London, November 18, 1836
(Sir) William Schwenk Harrow, November 29, 1911
Dramatist and versifier His ashes are buried in the Church of
St John the Evangelist, Stanmore

17, Southampton Street, WC2, here born
39, Harrington Gardens, SW7, 1894-1898
90, Eaton Square, SW1, 1907-1909
52, Pont Street, SW3, 1909-1911

Gilbert was at Kings' College, London and for five years thereafter was a clerk in the Privy Council office. He was called to the Bar in 1864 but met with no success in the profession of law. However, all this time he was writing humorous verse over the pen name of 'Bab', some of them being published in *Punch*.

In 1871 he met SULLIVAN and their now inseparable 'double act' came into being. Richard D'OYLY CARTE was the theatrical catalyst and, that year, the first Gilbert and Sullivan operetta, *Trial by Jury* was performed.

More combined operettas followed, all of which were well received by both public and the critics. Their *Gondoliers* was the first work to be played at the Savoy Theatre, designed by C.J. Phipps for D'OYLY CARTE in 1881. Carte built the Savoy Hotel more or less on top of the theatre in 1889. The architect was T.E. Collcut.

Gilbert was not an easy man to get on with: he and Sullivan once quarrelled so badly over who should share the cost of a new carpet in the theatre that they were not on speaking terms for weeks, and only three more operettas were written after this petty squabble. D'Oyly Carte was usually somewhere in the middle and had to wave olive branches at both sides.

Gilbert built himself a mock Tudor mansion just north of Harrow, which he called 'Grimsdyke'. It was designed by Norman Shaw. In the grounds Gilbert had a lake 'built'. Two females got into trouble in the water and Gilbert went in after them. The exertion was too much for a 75-year old and he died of a heart attack. (What anybody was doing in the water in an English *November* leaves one puzzled.)

Just by Hungerford Bridge, in the wall of the Embankment, is a medallion of Gilbert by Sir George Frampton, put up here in 1913. Gilbert, in profile, looks even grumpier than usual. At the bottom of the memorial is Gilbert's coat of arms, a very unusual inclusion in commemorative sculpture.

GILBERT STREET, W1   *Central line to Bond Street*

This little street began life as James Street in 1730. Around 1830 the name was changed to Gilbert for no known reason. Perhaps it was thought there were too many James Streets. Even today there are two in the West End.

23,   P.G. WODEHOUSE, 1924. The previous year his *Leave it to Psmith* and in 1924 *Ukridge* was published.

GISSING   Wakefield, Yorks, November 22, 1857
George Robert   St Jean de Luz, December 28, 1903
Author

7K, Cornwall Residences, Marylebone Road, NW1, 1884-1887

Gissing was at Owen's College, a Quaker boarding school in Manchester, but left under some sort of cloud and was packed off to America. He was back in England by the time he was 20 and had begun on the first of what was to be 30 novels.

His experiences in Boston, Mass., and the time he nearly starved to death in Chicago, are reflected in his book, *Grub Street* which caused quite a sensation when it was published in 1891. (Grub Street was first referred to as 'Grobstrat' in 1217. JOHNSON, in his dictionary wrote, 'Grubstreet. The name of a street in London much inhabited by writers of small histories, dictionaries and temporary poems; whence any mean production is called Grubstreet'. In 1829, by request of the residents, the street was re-named 'Milton Street'.) Gissing left England to live on the Continent for a while, which neither dispelled the rather pessimistic views on life he held, nor did it save his two marriages.

Later in life he became very friendly with H.G. WELLS but Wells once described him as a 'humourless prig'.

GLADSTONE
William Ewart
Prime Minister

Liverpool, December 29, 1809
Hawarden, Ches., May 19, 1898
North-west transept, Westminster
Abbey (beside him lies his wife)

L2, Albany, Piccadilly, W1, 1832-1839
13, Carlton House Terrace, SW1, 1840-1848
6, Carlton Gardens, SW1, 1848-1856
11, Carlton House Terrace, SW1 (LCP 1925) 1856-1874
73, Harley Street, W1 (P 1908) 1876-1882
16, St James's Street (now Buckingham Gate) SW1, 1890
10, St James's Square, SW1 (LCP 1910) 1890-1898

Until Harold WILSON appeared on the political scene, Gladstone had held the record for being Prime Minister four times (1868, 1880, 1886 and, finally, in 1892, when he was 83 years old).

Gladstone – the 'Grand Old man' as he came to be called – was from a well-to-do family and educated, first at Eton, followed by Oxford, where he was prominent in the affairs of the Union. Soon after coming down he was elected as Member of Parliament for Newark. He was a powerful orator and he dominated the Liberal party for over 30 years.

In 1850 Gladstone's income was £5,100 (and the average wage for an agricultural labourer was £26 a year). There are few, if any, photographs – in an era when photography was all the rage – of Gladstone, which shows his left hand clearly. In September 1842, when cleaning a shotgun, he managed to fire it, damaging his left index finger so badly that it had to be amputated.

Gladstone and his wife Catherine (1812-1900) felt a very genuine and Christian concern for 'fallen women'. London in their time had a quite amazing number of street-walkers and his opponents tried to make political capital out of his interest in prostitutes. The magazine *The Lancet,* founded in 1823 for the medical profession by Thomas WAKLEY, alleged that in 1867 there were 6,000 brothels in London which provided jobs for 60,000 women.

Gladstone rates *two* statues in London. One is by Albert Bruce-Joy and erected in Bow Churchyard – which today is hardly more than a glorified traffic island in the East End. The other and more imposing one is by Sir William Hamo THORNYCROFT in 1905. It is a free-standing bronze, a little west of the entrance to the Church of St Clement Dane, which lies in the middle of the Strand, just opposite the Law Courts.

GLEBE PLACE, SW3

*District and Circle lines
to Sloane Square*

Glebe land is land belonging to the church and what is now Glebe Place used to belong to St Luke's Rectory (in Sidney Street) until the reign of Queen Elizabeth I. The Reverend Charles Kingsley, father of Charles, George and Henry KINGSLEY came to St Luke's having been given the living by 2nd Lord Cadogan in 1836.

19,   Vera BRITTAIN, with her friend, Phyllis Bentley in 1935.

44,   Charles CONDER had a studio here. Having been trained in Australia he could perhaps feel at home as it was said that more than 30 Australians lived close by.

45,   'Cedar Studios'. John GALSWORTHY lived here for a short while and his life during that period is reflected in young 'Jolyon's' story in the *Forsyte Saga.*

53,   Walter SICKERT had a studio here before 1894.

53,   William ROTHENSTEIN, 1890-1901. In 1892 he had his first Paris exhibition which he shared with CONDER.

GLOUCESTER PLACE, W1 *Bakerloo, Circle, Metropolitan and Jubilee lines*
to Baker Street

King George III created his favourite brother, Prince William, the Duke of Gloucester in 1764 and the Place began to be developed in that year.

48,   John GODLEY (LCP 1951) lived here from 1852, until he died here in 1861.

57,   Charles DICKENS, from February to June 1863. He had just come back from a visit to Paris with Georgina Hogarth and Mamie Dickens. Georgina, 1827-1917, was the youngest of the three Hogarth sisters. Dickens had married the eldest, Catherine, in 1836, when she was 21. She died in 1879.

62   (formerly 18) Mary Ann CLARKE, in 1803. Her Royal lover, HRH the Duke of York, was second in succession to the English throne. He gave her £500 for a 'housewarming present' for this house.

65   (formerly 90) Wilkie COLLINS (LCP 1951) from 1868-1876, and again, from 1883-1888. Here he began to write *The Moonstone* – probably the first *detective* story ever published. By this time he had become addicted to opium and was taking *massive* doses of the drug.

74,   the Barrett family. Later they moved to 50, Wimpole Street and from there, their daughter, Elizabeth, eloped with Robert BROWNING.

99,   where the said Elizabeth lived from 1835 to 1838 (LCP 1924).

117   (until 1929 No.65) Sir Gerald KELLY, from 1915 until he died here in 1972. His father had died in this house in 1918. Afterwards Kelly built a large studio in the garden. In 1955, property values (or, at least, *costs*) had soared and Kelly had to sell a few things to retain the property. He sold 34 lots of furniture, which realized £1,277 and eventually raised the money. He had the top floor turned into a separate self-contained flat and the large front door, at street level, was divided in two and another staircase constructed.

GLOUCESTER ROAD, SW7   *District and Circle lines*
to Gloucester Road

Named after Maria, the widow (but only as a result of a clandestine and not valid marriage) of the Duke of Gloucester. In 1805 she built herself a villa, on a site where today, Stanhope Mews stands. The villa (in which George CANNING later lived) was called after her, but it was demolished in 1856.

11,   Sir Francis BEAUFORT, in 1836, after his second marriage, to Honoria Edgeworth.

133,   J.M. BARRIE, 1900-1902. This was his home before moving to Bayswater.

153,   Lady RITCHIE, 1877. In this year Anne (W.M. THACKERAY's daughter) married Richmond Ritchie, who was 17 years younger than she.

GLOUCESTER SQUARE, W2   *Central line to Lancaster Gate*

So called because the Duke of Gloucester's house was built near here in 1808. He was also Earl of Connaught which accounts for Connaught Place, Square and Street nearby.

35,   Robert STEPHENSON (LCP 1905) from 1847 until he died here in 1859. The house was completely rebuilt in 1936. In Stephenson's time his drawing room was more like a museum full of clocks and a number of scientific instruments.

GLOUCESTER WALK, W8

Central, District and Circle lines
to Notting Hill Gate

Queen Anne, who came to the throne in 1702, aged 37 and died in 1714, married Prince George of Denmark in 1683. He was an amiable, roly-poly drunkard and by him she became pregananT 17 (at least) times. Most of these children were still born and she had a number of miscarriages. Their only child to live at all was a hydrocephalic boy, who was given the title of Prince William, Duke of Gloucester. While her sister, Queen Mary II was on the throne, Anne lived in Campden House (the 'country' air was considered to be better for poor little William, but despite that he died before his 12th birthday). Gloucester Walk now, runs along what, more or less, was the drive up to Campden House. William had an eleventh birthday party on July 25th, 1700, fell ill – believed to have been small pox, was 'bled, blistered and cup't, tho to no purpose' – and died on the morning of July 30. His death finally sealed the end of the Stuart dynasty.

14, James BARRIE, 1892. His novel, *The Little Minister,* had appeared the previous year and he had become a minor literary figure.

21, Count Eric STENBOCK, 1890-1894. The house was described by Arthur SYMONS as being, '...rather out of the way, on a row of houses where degenerates live'.

GODLEY Ireland, 1814
John Robert London, November 17, 1861
Politician

48, Gloucester Place, W1 (LCP 1951) from 1853 until he died here

Sometimes known as the 'Founder of New Zealand', Godley received a good formal education, firstly at Harrow, then Christ Church, Oxford and was called to the Bar, but he never practised law.

He became managing director of the Canterbury (NZ) Association whose object was to establish a Church of England colony which was to draw its members from all walks of Protestant life. The first settlers began to arrive in New Zealand about the end of 1850 and Godley became a sort of 'Governor' for two years. He once said, 'I would sooner be governed by a Nero on the spot than a board of angels in London'.

GODWIN Wisbech, Cambs., March 3, 1756
William London, April 7, 1836
Philosopher In St Pancras Church Yard, but
'removed by railway', now St Peter's
Church Yard, Bournemouth

25, Chalton Street, NW1, December 1792
17, Evesham Buildings, Chalton Street, NW1, April 1797.
41, Skinner Street, EC1
165, The Strand, WC1, June 1822

William, the son of a Presbyterian Minister, was initially educated in a Presbyterian School in Hoxton, N1, with a view to joining the Ministry. Though William's views altered and he was rejected by Homerton Dissenting Academy in April 1773, he entered Hoxton Dissenting Academy in September of that year. He preached, after graduating from Hoxton in May 1778, in various Suffolk villages but came to live in London in April 1782. He turned his back on religion and entered into the literary life. He was to meet and influence poets like WORDSWORTH, SHELLEY, COLERIDGE and others.

In 1797 he made his first marriage to Mary Wollestoncraft (whose biography he later wrote). He had lived with her before marriage but the marriage itself

was pitifully short. She died on September 10, 1797, having given birth to their daughter, Mary, only eleven days before. (Mary was to marry Percy Bysshe Shelley on December 30, 1816. *Their* daughter, Clara, was born on September 22, 1817.)
Godwin married Mary-Jane Clairmont ('tough and irritable') in 1801. Mary-Jane already had a daughter and she had another by Godwin.

GOLDEN SQUARE, W1   *Piccadilly, Bakerloo and Jubilee lines*
to Piccadilly Circus

Building was started in 1674 on land which had previously been known as Gelding Close. It has been suggested that the *gentry* for whom the houses were being built might feel a little emasculated and perhaps the first occupants themselves changed *gelding* for *Golden*. However, in the *London Gazette* of 1688, there are references to Golden Square and in a street map in the reign of William and Mary (1688-1702) 'Golden' Square is shown.

11,   Angelica KAUFFMANN, 1767. In this year she married 'Count de Horn', who was actually only a valet.

19,   Lady MONTAGUE, c.1737, just before going to settle in Venice.

21,   Henry St John BOLINBROKE, 1704-1708, when he was Secretary of War. 23 and 24, these two houses made up the Portuguese Embassy and so here the Marquess of Pombal (1739-1744, Ambassador to Britain) lived (LCP 1980) 1699-1782. He encouraged trade with Britain and was a driving force in rebuilding Lisbon after the earthquake of 1775.

26,   the house of Edwin Edwards, where, in 1880, FANTIN-LATOUR stayed. 'The house, built in the 18th century, was sheltered by trees whose branches dropped from the gardens of the Square in cascades of heavy foliage towards the lawn, growing as profusely as they do in Holland.'

31   (rebuilt 1931) John HUNTER (LCP 1907) 1763-1770. Hunter found it difficult to earn enough from his medical practice here.
In the Square is a white painted, lead statue of King George II by John Van Nost the elder. It was brought from the Duke of Chandos's house at Canons in 1753.

GOLDSMITH   Pallas, Co. Longford, November 10,
Oliver   1728
Playwright and poet   London, April 4, 1774
                              Temple Church courtyard

6, Wine Office Court, EC4

Oliver was the fifth of seven children of the Reverend Charles Goldsmith (who obtained his first preferment in the Church at Kilkenny – when Oliver was two). The boy was first taught by the village schoolmaster, and after more schooling at Athlone and Edgworthtown went up to Trinity College, Dublin, as a *sizar* in 1744: the fees being paid by relatives. Here he was '...very idle, extravagant and occasionally insubordinate', and did not get a BA until February 1749. His father dead, Goldsmith was helped out by a maternal uncle, the Reverend Thomas Contarine who wanted him to go into the Church. But Oliver refused, so Uncle Contarine gave him money to study law in London. In Dublin Goldsmith spent the lot in gambling! Uncle gave him more money and sent him off to Edinburgh to study *medecine* in 1752. Two years later Goldsmith left University there and went to Leyden, where he stayed for a year studying chemistry under Gaubins and anatomy under Bernard Siegfried Albinus during the day, and frollicking most of the night. He left Leyden on foot, with no money and one clean shirt, travelled widely (somehow) and was back in London in the autumn of 1756. He appears to have been an apothecary's assistant and then actually practised as a doctor. However, he did not pass an examination set by the College of Surgeons.

In 1761, while under arrest, Goldsmith wrote *The Vicar of Wakefield*. Though the work was not published until 1766, he was given £60 for it. *The Traveller* appeared in 1765, as did the *Hermit*. Covent Garden staged his *Good Natured Man* in 1768 and a year later his *Deserted Village* was published. In 1770 he was appointed Professor of Ancient History at the newly established Royal Academy of Painting. 1773 saw his greatest, and most permanent, triumph on the stage, *She Stoops to Conquer*. JOHNSON said of it that he knew '...of no comedy for many years that has so much exhilarated an audience...'. His book *History of the Earth and Animated Nature* appeared in 1774. He had been given an advance of £850 but he had gambled it (or given it) away within weeks. He died soon after in poverty.

When his friends heard of his death, REYNOLDS 'laid down his brush' and BURKE wept. Johnson wrote the epitaph for the monument raised to Goldsmith by his friends: it ran, *Nullum tetigit quod non ornavit* – He touched nothing he did not adorn.

GOLLANCZ	London, April 9, 1893
(Sir) Victor	London, February 8, 1967
Publisher	

42, Ladbroke Grove, W11, 1953
90, Eaton Place, SW1, 1964-1967

Though Jewish the Gollanczes sent Victor to St Paul's School, which is a Church of England establishment. In 1911 he went up to Oxford, New College where he won the Chancellor's Prize for Latin verse.

For a short while, he was a master at Repton (a boys' public school in Derby, founded in 1557) but 'went out on his own' in 1928 and set up a publishing business.

In 1936 he founded 'The Left Book Club' which played a very real part in the establishment of the Socialist Party, especially in middle class families. He worked very hard before and during the Second World War helping Jewish people to get out of Europe, yet, when the war was over, he worked as hard doing what he could to save the German people from death by starvation. He was also a vigorous opponent of capital punishment and an active antagonist of nuclear weaponry.

Luckily in 1965 his Socialist principles were sufficiently elastic to allow him to accept a (deserved) knighthood.

GORDON SQUARE, WC1 *Metropolitan and Circle lines to Euston Square*

Yet another part of the Bedford estate. John, the 6th Duke, took as his second wife, Georgiana, who was the granddaughter of the Duke of Gordon. 'Gordon Square', wrote Virginia WOOLF, '...is like nothing so much as the lions' house at the Zoo. One goes from cage to cage. All the animals are dangerous, rather suspicious of each other, and full of fascination and mystery.'

37, Duncan GRANT and Vanessa BELL; from here they moved to 39.
37, David GARNETT (in the basement) 1929.
42, Gordon HAKE, 1840 and 1841.
46, after Sir Leslie STEPHEN's death in 1903, his four children, by his second wife – Vanessa, Thoby, Virginia and Adrian moved in here in October 1904. Thoby organised 'literary' Thursday evenings. They were strictly *male* affairs. Virginia (later WOOLF) wrote that the 'abstractness and simplicity of No. 46...were largely due to the fact

that the majority of young men who came there were not attracted by young women'.
Later, Clive BELL lived here, as did Duncan GRANT, 1914-1916.
46, John MAYNARD KEYNES (LCP 1975) 1916-1946. Pablo Picasso once came to a party given by the Keynes here.
47, Henry D. TRAILL, 1880s.
50, Arthur WALEY, 1930 and 1955-1960.
50, Clive BELL, 1929 and early 1930s. He painted a great mural in the drawing room and Francis MEYNELL, who moved in in 1936, added gold wallpaper 'columns' on either side of it to contain 'these disorderly elements'.
51, Lytton STRACHEY (LCP 1971) 1919-1924. It is now London University's Publication Department.
57, Bertrand RUSSELL, 1918-1919. Divorced from his first wife, Alys, he married Dora Black two years after he left Gordon Square.

GORDON STREET WC1

1, William MORRIS with Edward BURNE-JONES in 1856.
9, Charlotte MEW, for most of her life (1869-1928). The house was destroyed by a bomb in 1940.

GORELL	April 16, 1884
Ronald Barnes (3rd Baron)	May 2, 1963
Man of letters	

11, Catherine Street, Buckingham Gate, SW1, 1920s
31, Kensington Square, W8, 1930-1950
15, Callcott Street, W8, 1959-1963

Gorell's father had been created Lord Gorell of Brampton in 1909. He was President of the Probate, Divorce and Admiralty Division of the High Courts. He died in 1913 and his title passed to his eldest son, who was killed in 1917, aged 35. He had no sons and so the title fell to Ronald who became the 3rd Baron.
Gorell was the editor of the *Cornhill* magazine from 1933-1939, an author in his own right and he sat on numerous Committees which existed to further a wide variety of aims. He had qualified as a barrister and had a distinguished record in the war, being awarded the Military Cross in 1917. He had also been, at one time, on the editorial staff of the *Times* and Parliamentary Secretary to the Air Ministry in 1921/22. (His 'range' was wide. In 1920 he had been National President for the Council for Combating Venereal Disease.)

GOOSSENS	London, May 26, 1893
(Sir) Eugene Aynesley	Hillingdon, June 13, 1962
Musician	

1, Wetherby Gardens, SW5, 1929
76, Hamilton Terrace, NW8, 1962

Eugene, a noted violinist, was the father of this Eugene who became principal conductor to the Carl Rosa Company. He studied music in Bruges and London and rose to be associate conductor with Thomas BEECHAM. Later he became well known in America and, on the 'other side of the world', was appointed Conductor to the Sydney Symphony Orchestra in Australia. Musically, he was of considerable influence 'down-under'.

GOSS	Fareham, Hants., December 27, 1800
(Sir) John	London, May 10, 1880
Organist	Kensal Green, Grave No. 27,370; Plot 75

3, Cheyne Walk, SW3, c.1872–1876

Goss was a 'link' in one of London's chains with W.A. MOZART. Goss who had been a pupil of Mozart's in Vienna, was appointed organist in St Paul's Cathedral on the death of the incumbent organist. Goss held the Cathedral post for 34 years, which meant St Paul's had had only *two* organists between 1796 and 1872.

Goss retired from the St Paul's post only eight years before his death and was knighted in that year. He wrote some 'dignified' (*vide Scholes* in his *Dictionary of Music*) church music and two of his anthems are occasionally heard today: *O, Taste and See* and *The Wilderness.*

GOUGH SQUARE, EC4

District and Circle lines to Blackfriars

Named after Nicholas Gough, a printer, which was probably why Sam JOHNSON moved here. There was a John Gough, a printer, working between 1528–1556, who *may* have been an ancestor of Nicholas. This 16th century Gough seems to have spelt his name variously – Gowghe, Gowgh or even Gouge.

17, Samuel JOHNSON (P) 1749–1759. Here, with six clerks working in the garret, the great Dictionary was compiled. It appeared in two volumes in 1755 and was not really financially successful.
Johnson had to pay eight shillings eight pence (43p) a year for street lighting, 56p annually for the 'Watch' and 25p for 'scavengers'. When he moved in.
In 1910 when the house was in a disgracefully dilapidated state, Cecil Harmsworth (to become the 1st Baron Harmsworth in 1936) bought it for the nation and the house is now open to the public as a museum of *Johnsoniana.*

GOWER STREET, WC1

Metropolitan and Circle lines to Euston Square

All once part of the Bedford estate; John Russell, the 4th Duke of Bedford (1710–1771) once English Ambassador to France, married Gertrude, daughter of the 1st Earl Gower (who was ennobled in 1746).

Described by Peter Cunningham in 1850 as, 'A dull, heavy street of third rate houses, but well inhabited'.

2, Dame Millicent FAWCETT (LCP 1954) from 1877, till she died in this house in 1929.

3, Luke HANSARD, 1808–1810. He had been the sole proprietor of *Hansard* (the daily Parliamentary report) for a decade when he moved here.

4, Charles DICKENS, 1823. The rent was £40 a year and it was here that Charles's poor mother tried to start a school. 'Nobody ever came to the school, nor do I recollect that anybody ever proposed to come...'

7, John MILLAIS was living here with his parents (it was then numbered 57) and he helped found the Pre-Raphaelite Brotherhood with Holman HUNT and D.G. ROSETTI at this time.

10, Lady Ottoline MORELL, 1910–1933. She wrote in 1910, 'I have found the dearest little doll's house'.

14, Sarah SIDDONS, 1784–1789. She was at the height of her fame during this period, having been on the stage for nine years.

14, Anthony 'HOPE' (real name, Anthony Hope HAWKINS) 1921–1925.

27, P.M. ROGET, 1800, for a few months only; when training to be a doctor.

54, Sir Samuel ROMILLY, 1798-1802. Two years after he moved from here to Russell Square he was appointed Solicitor General.

69, William de MORGAN was born here in 1839.

73, D.H. LAWRENCE, 1925. He and Frieda had recently come back from Australia, via New Mexico. The *Plumed Serpent* was published in 1926.

83, John MILLAIS, 1851. The John RUSKINS visited him here and this was the first time MILLAIS had met Mrs. Ruskin – Effie – who was to be married to him (after her marriage to RUSKIN was legally finished).

90, Duff and Lady Diana COOPER, 1929. Whilst living here he was a Member of the House of Commons, and had been for five years.

91, George DANCE ('the Younger') (LCP 1970) 1790-1815.

106, Edward POYNTER, 1866-1868. He had not long been back from studying art in Paris. Sometime after POYNTER left, Simeon Solomon lived here, briefly.

110, Charles DARWIN (LCP 1961) 1838-1842. Nothing remains of the house. The building that covers the site today is the Biological Sciences Building of University College, happily called DARWIN HOUSE.

129, Louis KOSSUTH, 1858-1859. He had now been living (in exile) in London for nearly seven years.

183, Giuseppe MAZZINI (LCP 1950) 1837-1840. Like KOSSUTH, just down the street, Mazzini was an exile in London (from his beloved Italy). For some obscure reason he chose to use the name of *Hamilton* as his 'cover' (as they say) but the game tended to be given away as his rooms here were openly used as a sort of Italian patriots' Recruitment Office.

GRAFTON STREET, W1   *Piccadilly, Victoria and Jubilee lines*
to Green Park.

Henry, Charles II's son, by his longest lasting mistress, Barbara Castlemaine, Duchess of Cleveland, was eventually created Duke of Grafton. His son, the 2nd Duke, was living round the corner in Bond Street in 1701. Before 1723, Grafton Street used to be called Ducking-Pond Row.

15A, Sir Henry IRVING (LCP 1950) 1872-1899. He lived on the 2nd and 3rd floors (over what today is Asprey's shop) '...in the confusion and neglect of order in which the artistic mind delights'.

16, Algernon SWINBURNE, 1860. He had just left Oxford (without a degree) and he worked here on his first (and unsuccessful) play *The Queen Mother*.

GRAHAME   Edinburgh, March 3, 1859
Kenneth   Pangbourne, Berks., July 6, 1932
Author   St Cross Churchyard, Oxford

16, Durham Villas, Campden Hill, W8, 1907

Kenneth was the third of four children of an Edinburgh lawyer. His mother died in 1864 and, heartbroken, his father sent the children to live with his mother-in-law at Cookham Dene, on the Thames in Berkshire. The children only saw their father once again.

The four little Grahames were shuffled around amongst willing (*and* unwilling) relatives, but Kenneth liked best to be near the Thames and in the countryside through which it meandered. He was sent to school at St Edward's in Oxford, a city he came to love and eventually hold out hopes he could settle in. Perhaps attend one of its Colleges. However, his Uncle John had other ideas and 'placed' his young nephew as a 'gentleman clerk' in the Bank of England in Threadneedle Street in the City of London. It nearly broke Kenneth's heart, but he knuckled under and stayed with the Bank. By the time he was 40, he became Secretary to the Bank (an important position he held for eight years).

By then, his books, *The Golden Age* (in 1895) and *Dream Days* in 1898, were literary successes. To the amazement of practically all who knew him, he married Elspeth Thomson and they had one son, Alaistair. Master Graham, nicknamed 'Master Mouse', listened avidly to the stories his father told him at bedtime and, in 1908, Grahame published a sort of *omnium gatherum* of these bedtime recitals as *The Wind in the Willows*.

This delightful, whimsical book became one of the best-sellers in the children's book market ever. It has never been out of print since 1908 and still has an *average* general sale of 80,000 copies a year. The copyright expired on January 1, 1983 and 'new' editions were all ready to meet the demand. All are illustrated, the original book was not. Twenty years after the first edition, Grahame wanted Arthur RACKHAM to illuminate it. RACKHAM was too busy and, happily, the job fell to Ernest Shephard, who had illustrated the *Winnie the Pooh* books for A.A. MILNE. The drawings for the *Wind in the Willows* were masterpieces. (The story of 'Master Mouse' was less happy and Alaistair Grahame was dead before he was 20.)

MILNE later dramatized *The Wind in the Willows* and produced the play *Toad of Toad Hall* which is a hardy British Christmas-tide theatrical annual, year after year.

GRANT Inverness, 1885
Duncan James Corrowr Scotland, May 7, 1978
Artist

8, Fitzroy Street, W1
37, Gordon Square, WC1

Grant's father was Lady STRACHEY's youngest brother, thus Grant and Lytton STRACHEY were cousins. (If Lytton had had his way they would have been lovers, too.) As Major Grant had to be in India, Duncan was 'boarded' in the Strachey's Lancaster Gate house and he went as a day boy to St Paul's School in Hammersmith. Lytton wrote to Maynard KEYNES, saying 'I have a sort of adoration' [for Duncan] and to Clive BELL, 'I have fallen in love hopelessly and ultimately', [hopelessly, yes; ultimately, *no*]. KEYNES himself was to become Duncan's lover and they lived together in Fitzroy Square. Grant also had a liaison with Vanessa BELL and lived with her until her death in 1961.

Grant went to the Westminster School of Art in 1902 and spent nearly three (undistinguished) years there. His mother took him to Italy in 1904 where he 'found' Piero della Francesca (c.1415-1492). An aunt provided him with enough money to study in Paris and he joined the studio of Jacques-Emile Blanche. Blanche moved in elevated circles; he knew Marcel Proust and was a devoted Anglophile. Grant took a studio himself, in the Rue Delambre in Montparnasse, in 1907. He met – and disliked – Wyndham LEWIS. He was strongly influenced by *Les Fauves* and contributed to the second Post-Impressionist Exhibition in 1912.

D.H. LAWRENCE described Grant as 'a dark-skinned, taciturn Hamlet of a fellow'. Ottoline MORELL thought him 'shy, vague and nice-looking' and he had, 'the rare secret of eternal youth'.

At the age of 90 he was still painting busily and nipping up to London for exhibitions and cocktail parties!

GRAY'S INN, WC1 *Central line to Chancery Lane*

This is the fourth of the great *Inns of Court* and, in the reign of King Edward I (1272-1307) the Manor House and lands of Reginald de Gray were here. In 1505 Lord Gray de Wilton leased the manor to Hugh Denny, his heirs and assigns for £6.13s 4d (£6.66) a *year!* From him it passed into the hands of the Prior of East Sheen, but at the Dissolution of the Monasteries, it became (conveniently) the property of the Crown and was handed on to students of the law (at the same rental). Francis BACON was responsible for the layout of the gardens, c.1600.

GRAY'S INN PLACE, WC1

3, Eddie MARSH, 1899-1903, where his devoted housekeeper, Mrs. Elgy, used to cater for him and the many good-looking young men of artistic or literary pretensions and budding genii, with whom MARSH surrounded himself.

4, SUN YAT SEN, or SUN WEN, (P) 1895. He was living here before being 'kidnapped' by Chinese opponents to his philosophies.

GRAY'S INN SQUARE, WC1

1, Sir Francis BACON lived here for nearly 50 years. His apartments were destroyed by fire in 1684.

5, Lord CLARK, 1938-1940. His rooms looked out over the garden and the mulberry tree supposedly planted by Sir Walter Raleigh (1552-1618). The dining room only held six people. In September 1940 a bomb 'blew out' the two bottom floors, leaving the Clark's bedroom hanging in mid-air. (The blast had blown them out of bed.)

6, Sir Samuel ROMILLY (P) 1778-1791. He was living here when he was admitted to the Bar, at 21 in 1778.

GREAT CASTLE STREET, W1 *Central, Bakerloo and Victoria lines to Oxford Circus*

The road was built over the grounds of a public house called the 'Castle' which fronted on Oxford Street.

6, Samuel JOHNSON took lodgings here soon after coming to London and wrote his poem, *London,* here in 1738. When not writing he spent some of the time visiting the daughters of Admiral Cotterell who lived in the house opposite. Joshua REYNOLDS also used to visit the Cotterels and this is where Johnson and he first met.

GREAT COLLEGE STREET, SW1 *District and Circle lines to Westminster*

Along the north length of this short street ran the wall of Westminster College (or School). Originally the College was entirely a part of the establishment of the Church and certainly by the late 1400's scholars were at their lessons in or around this street.

15, the 9th Duchess of MARLBOROUGH, 1922, a year after her marriage to the Duke.

25, John KEATS, 1819. He moved from here so that he could be near his beloved Fanny Browne in Hampstead. Two years later he was dead.

GREAT CUMBERLAND PLACE, W1 *Central line to Marble Arch*

Named after the unattractive Royal Duke, William Augustus, Duke of Cumberland, younger son of King George II. He earned the nick-name of 'Billy the Butcher' when he gave orders after the English victory over the Scottish at the Battle of Culloden (April 16, 1746) that wounded Scottish soldiers should be put to death rather than taken prisoner.

24, Rt. Hon. Charles BOOTH, 1899-1905. The family's nick-name for their house was 'Cumbersome'.

37A, Lady Randolph CHURCHILL, 1895; widowed 'Jennie' moved into this seven-storeyed house, complete with its own library, shortly after Lord Randolph's death (when only 46 years old). Later, her sister, Clara Frewen, took the house opposite (Number 39A) and not long after that, the third 'Jerome girl', their sister Leonie, took Number 10. The wags began to call the street, 'Lower Jerome Terrace'.

37, Rupert HART-DAVIS, for four months in 1924. He later wrote, '...it was a charming house, containing, to my delight, nine hundred carefully catalogued books'.

48, George BOOTH, 1906-1910, who took over the house from a friend of the family.

51, Edward HULTON, 1911-1919. 'A long, low, dark-brown eighteenth century building.' It was 'sinking' at one end to such an extent that Edward could, '...run a toy motor down the red linoleum on the nursery floor'. Hulton, senior, had concealed electric lighting installed in the dining room, behind a cornice. Probably the first example of its kind in London.

GREAT GEORGE STREET, W1   *District and Circle lines to Westminster*

Named (so say) after a tavern called the 'George' which had been here since the early 1500s.

12, Thomas Babington MACAULAY, 1839. He was Independent MP for Edinburgh whilst living here.

25, in 1824 Lord BYRON's body lay here while it was argued whether he should (or *could*) be buried in Westminster Abbey – he was not.

GREAT JAMES STREET, WC1   *Central line to Chancery Lane*

The DOUGHTY family owned land in the Holborn area, much of it inherited from their BROWNLOW ancestors. Descendants of the Doughty's were helped in the eighteenth century by JAMES Burgess, hence GREAT JAMES.

3, Algernon SWINBURNE, 1872-1875 and 1877-1878. George MOORE once went to visit him here in 1877 and went upstairs to the first floor and found himself '...in a large room in which there was no furniture except a truckle bed. Outside the sheets lay a naked man, a strange, impish little body it was, and about the head, too large for the body, was a great growth of red hair'. This was Swinburne. He was probably drunk again. E.F. Benson also produced a story that Watts-Danton – the man who 'rescued' Swinburne eventually and took him off to live in Putney for the rest of his life – visited Algernon at No.3 and found him naked – again! – and 'performing a Dionysiac dance all by himself in front of a large looking glass'. No *wonder* Swinburne's father, the Admiral, was worried.

5, E.V. LUCAS, late 1890s.

22, Arthur WALEY 1920s. During this period he was Assistant Keeper of the Department of Prints and Drawings at the British Museum, just five minutes walk away across Southampton Row.

24, Dorothy SAYERS, 1923-1957. Dorothy Sayers kept this house on even though she lived mostly in the country. This was her town address when she gave birth to an illegitimate son in January 1924 and, two years later, when she married Oswald Fleming (*not* the boy's father). Her first detective novel *Whose Body?* was published in the year she moved here.

26, George MEREDITH lived here with his father in the 1840s.

GREAT MARLBOROUGH STREET, W1   *Central line to Oxford Circus*

Named after John Churchill, the first Duke of Marlborough and built about 1698 and so actually some six years *before* his triumph at Blenheim. He was not a Duke until 1702. By 1722, however, Defoe was writing that the street, '...though not a square, surpasses anything that is *called* a street, in the magnificence of its buildings and gardens, and inhabited all by prime quality.'

41,   Benjamin HAYDON, 1808-1817, still, as always, in *debt*.
41,   Charles DARWIN lodged here in 1836.
54,   Sarah SIDDONS, 1790-1802.

GREAT ORMOND STREET, WC1   *Central and Piccadilly lines to Holborn*

Probably the street was named after James Butler, who was created Duke of Ormonde by King Charles II. The street was not begun before the Duke's death in 1688 and, by 1708, it was 'a street of fine new buildings'; by 1734 it was '...beyond question, one of the most charming situations about town...'.

23,   John HOWARD (LCP 1908) 1770-1789.
34,   William ARCHER, in the 1890s, and, by this time, a respected theatrical critic.
38,   Wyndham LEWIS and the 'Rebel Art Centre', in 1914.
41,   William SAMUEL MORRIS brought his new wife here, in 1859.
45,   Lord Chancellor Edward THURLOW, 1771-1792. On the night of March 24, 1784; thieves scaled the garden wall and forced the iron bars of a kitchen window. They found their way to the Chancellor's study and took the Great Seal of England from his writing table. The thieves were finally apprehended, but not before they had melted down the Seal (which was of silver) and many important public documents were held up until a new Seal could be made.
50,   Lord MACAULAY, 1823-1829. In 1825 he first began his long lasting relationship with the *Edinburgh Review*.

GREAT PORTLAND STREET, W1   *Bakerloo and Circle lines to Great Portland Street*

Named, like its parallel, Portland Place, after the Dukes of Portland whose family were the landowners in the area. The Place was developed around 1778 and the Street not long after.

31,   Edward FITZGERALD, 1856-1857. While here he was working on his translation of the poetry of Omar Khayyam.
35,   Leigh HUNT, 1812-1813. From here Hunt moved to prison for two years. He had made a published reference to the Prince Regent ('Prinny') calling him a 'Fat Adonis of Fifty' – actually he was 51. Hunt was prosecuted for libel.
91,   in 1826 the house was owned by Sir George SMART, the organist. Carl Maria VON WEBER died here on June 3, 1826. The 'Creator of Romantic Opera', was only 40 years old (P).
122   (formerly 47) James BOSWELL (LCP 1936) from 1788 until he died here in 1795, aged 55. His wife, Margaret was dead and one of his daughters was housekeeper for him. He must have been a bit of a handful by this time. In 1790 he was thrown into the Watch House for 'crying the hour in the streets'. Boswell was practically an alcoholic and he defended the charge by saying that he was 'teaching the Watchman how he *ought* to cry the hours'; that they should emphasize the word 'two', so: 'Past *two* o'clock and all's well', not, '*Past* two o'clock and all's well'.

GREAT PULTENEY STREET, W1 *Piccadilly, Bakerloo lines to Piccadilly Circus*

Once called *Knaves' Acre* this land was owned by Thomas Pulteney in the late 16th century. By 1720 the Pulteneys had grown rich and William Pulteney became Earl of Bath. There is a Pulteney Bridge in Bath, that gracious city in the west of England. Part of the London land had been *demised* to a carpenter called Thomas Beake – hence Beak Street, hard by – but in 1808 the rest of the estate passed to Sir Richard Sutton, a remote relative who was descended from Lord Lexington. One can find Lexington Street running parallel with this one.

18, Joseph HAYDN, lived here in 1791/92 in a '...charming and comfortable, but very expensive lodgings'. Here he wrote six of the 'Salomon' symphonies. London weather did *not* appeal to HAYDN. The fog was so thick, he wrote, '...that you could spread it on bread'.

GREAT QUEEN STREET, WC2 *Central line to Holborn*

Built about 1630 and supposed by some to have been named after Queen Anne of Denmark; consort of King James I of England. However, Anne died in 1619 and it is more probably named after her daughter-in-law, Henrietta Maria (of France) who married Anne's second son Charles, who became King Charles I in 1625, when Anne's husband died. Inigo Jones is supposed to have designed the street originally and to have left a little niche in the middle house of the street, intended to have standing in it a statue of Queen Henrietta. *Whichever* Queen *was* honoured, this street was a fine one and considered by some, to have been the first 'regular street in London'.

7, Henry FUSELI, 1803 who, though only 38 years old, was white-haired.

31, William BLAKE was living here about the same time as FUSELI.

51, R.H. BARHAM ('Thomas Ingoldsby') 1821-1824, still probably licking his wounds after the failure of his novel, *Baldwin* published about 18 months before moving here.

55/56, Richard Brinsley SHERIDAN 1770-1790. During part of this time, 'Sherry' was involved in politics.

59, 'Kitty' CLIVE, 1743-1747. During this period she was solely an actress and did not have any jealous husbands in tow.

63, John OPIE, 1783-1791, here he painted *The Schoolmistress* which is now in the Lockinge Collection.

GREAT RUSSELL STREET, WC1 *Central and Northern lines to Tottenham Court Road*

Once Bedford – family name Russell – property, it was built up around 1670 and, by 1700, it was in a '...very handsome, large and well built street, graced with all the best buildings in Bloomsbury...and the prospect of the pleasant fields up to Hampstead and Highgate'.

14, W.H. DAVIES, 1916-1922. His *Autobiography of a Super Tramp* an enormous success, he had been in receipt of a Civil Pension for five years.

17, George BORROW, 1829.

24, Nathaniel HAWTHORNE, 1857.

36, Arthur MACHEN, 1893. His rooms were in the garret, '...a *real* garret, with a sloping roof and a dormer window – looked out on Dyott Street, the last remnant of the old *rookery* of St Giles'. The rooms, including tea and a bread and butter breakfast, cost ten shillings and sixpence (52½p) a week. After he married, he moved along the street to number 98.

46, P.M. ROGET, 1800.

46, George Du MAURIER, 1862. This was just before his marriage to Emma Nightwick. The rooms were over the 'Pear's Soap' Shop and he had three rooms on the second floor, for which the rent was 25 shillings (£1.25p) a week. He also had a studio on the ground floor back, for which he paid £25 a year.

46, Randolph CALDECOTT (LCP 1977) 1872. Soon after, he won fame for his illustrations of Washington IRVING's *Sketch Book* in 1875.

59, Thomas COOK, 1863-1879.

77, Thomas WYATT (LCP 1980) for many years until he died in 1880.

89, John KEMBLE, 1808-1820.

91, George DU MAURIER (LCP 1960) 1863-1867.

101, Percy B. SHELLEY and also at 90 in 1816.

106, Augustus PUGIN (P) 1822-1823. Co-designer and architect of the Houses of Parliament.

109, Sir Christopher WREN.

109, William HAZLITT stayed here with his brother in 1804. He finally left here for good in 1807.

GREAT TITCHFIELD STREET, W1 *Bakerloo, Victoria and Central lines to Oxford Circus*

The land here was owned by the Dukes of Portland and a subsidiary title in the family is the Marquess of Titchfield (which is a Hampshire place name).

3, Peter Mark ROGET, 1800. At this time he was still training as a doctor.

GREAVES
Walter
Artist

Chelsea, July 4, 1846
November 23, 1930

10 (afterwards 3) Lindsey Row, SW3
104, Cheyne Walk, SW3 (LCP 1973) 1855-1897
525, Fulham Road, SW10, 1897
38, Lillie Road, SW5, 1919-1922

Walter and his brother Henry were the sons of a local Chelsea boat-builder and the young men used to row WHISTLER here and there on the Thames. Walter, in particular, was used as a sort of unpaid servant to Whistler, but Walter absorbed some of the techniques used by the volatile American artist. In no way imitative of Whistler's style, Greaves became a 'primitive' painter of some quality. In his lifetime he enjoyed no reputation at all but in the 1960s he was 'discovered' and both his paintings, *Chelsea Regatta* and *Boat Race Day, Hammersmith Bridge* are now recognized as works of skill and intelligence.

GREEK STREET, W1 *Central and Northern lines to Tottenham Court Road*

Probably named after the Greek Church built near here for Greek refugees who had come to England, having fled from the Turkish rule under Kiuprili Viziers in the 1670s. The church was in Hog Lane, St Giles; which today is the site of the St Martin's School of Art in the Charing Cross Road. There was a back entrance into the church from what is now Greek Street.

12, Coventry PATMORE in the 1820s, when he was still living in his father's (P.G. Patmore's) house.

60, Sir Thomas LAWRENCE, 1787-1814.

61, (then 38) Thomas DE QUINCEY (LCP 1909) in 1802, after he had run away from his school in Wales, when he was only 17. It was then that the Soho prostitute, Anne, who he met in Soho Square, saved him practically from death by starvation. The house was a dirty, neglected place owned by an attorney called Brunell-Brown, who was himself up to his eyes in debt and usually went from his house to his office by stealth (and often in the dark) to dodge the baillifs, who were hunting him down. de Quincey told Brunell-Brown a little about his own problems and the out-of-luck landlord allowed him breakfast and any room in the house that might be empty, for nothing!

GREEN
John Richard
Historian

Oxford, December 12, 1837
Menton, March 7, 1883

4, Beaumont Street, W1 (LCP 1964) 1869-1876

Green spent the first 25 years of his life in Oxford. He was educated at Magdalen College School there and became a scholar at Jesus College. He took Holy Orders and became incumbent in the east end of London, in a poor parish at Stepney.
In 1868 he became Librarian in Lambeth, but his always precarious health gave way and the diagnosis was tuberculosis. During a period of convalescence he wrote the *Short History of the English People,* which was first published in 1874. It became immediately popular particularly as it was written in a way readily understandable to people with limited education. In 1877 the work was expanded and in the next three years was brought out in four volumes.

GREGORY
Maundy
'Honours Broker'

Southampton, July 1, 1877
Paris, September 28, 1941
Ivry-Paris New Cemetery

10, Hyde Park Terrace, W2, 1930s

Gregory was a 'man from nowhere' who claimed friends in high places and could fix up those anxious to receive honours with them; but, at a *price*. A knight bachelor cost only £10,000, but he wanted £40,000 for a baronetcy. The difference being that a baronetcy is an hereditarial honour. LLOYD-GEORGE certainly broke new ground with his wholesale distribution of honours and titles. Newspaper magnates, beer potentates began moving 'up into Debrett'. On his last day in office, LLOYD-GEORGE offered the 4th Marquess of Bute, The Most Ancient and Most Noble Order of the Thistle, which is restricted to only 16 Knights of the Order at one time, beside Royalty, and was founded by James II in 1687. Bute refused it. If, and to what extent, LLOYD-GEORGE used Gregory is not known.
He had offices at 38, Parliament Street, SW1 and he went there by taxi every morning, but never by the same routes every day, 'for security reasons'.
Though he was homosexual he shared a flat with Edith Rosse, who died under mysterious circumstances in 1932, leaving Gregory £18,000. He arranged her funeral and the burial plot he chose was the graveyard of Bisham Church just up the river Thames from Marlow. Significantly he chose that part of the graveyard which was *below* the flood level of the river. In April 1933 her body was exhumed but the waters had washed away any traces of the poison it had been thought to contain.

GRENFELL February 10, 1910
Joyce Irene November 30, 1979
Comédienne

149, King's Road, SW3, 1939-1946
114, King's Road, SW3, 1946-1956
Flat 8, 34, Elm Park Gardens, SW10, 1956-1979

In 'real life', Miss Grenfell was Mrs. Reginald Pascoe (she married in 1929.) She had no children which made some of her dialogues fascinating as well as extremely funny. She wrote all her own material and some of the pieces in which she is a 'kindergarten' teacher, having to deal (as it were) with a host of misbehaving four- and five-year-olds, makes one marvel at her powers of 'close observation'.
She was the Radio Critic on the *Observer* for three years and moved into actually performing on radio after she had been encouraged to develop an entirely amateur skill of mimicry. She joined Farjeon's *Little Revue* in 1939. It opened at the Little Theatre on April 21, and the music was by Walter Leigh. She travelled extensively, often dangerously, during the Second World War to entertain the troops and then, when peace returned, she went into Noel COWARD's *Sigh no More*.

GREY April 25, 1862
Edward (1st Viscount Grey of September 7, 1933
Fallodon)
Politician

1-3, Queen's Gate, SW7 (LCP 1981) 1906-1912
37, Smith Square, SW1, 1929

After Winchester College he went on to Balliol College, Oxford. Grey succeeded to his grandfather's baronetcy in 1882. Three years later he became Liberal Member of Parliament for the English/Scottish border town of Berwick-on-Tweed. He had a small part in Lord ROSEBERRY's Government, but when CAMPBELL-BANNERMAN formed a Cabinet in December 1905, Grey became Foreign Secretary. In 1913 he was to achieve much in the Balkan Peace negotiations. It was really Grey who was behind the secure alliance between Britain, France and Russia and prompted that alliance to realise the natural enemy of these three countries was Germany. 1914 proved him right and, on August 3, Germany having declared war on France, Grey said, 'the lamps are going out all over Europe; we shall not see them lit again in our lifetime'. (Luckily Grey did not live to see September 3, 1939, when the 'lamps began going out' all over the *world*.)
In 1919 he spent three months in Washington as Ambassador, to talk about the problems arising from the peace begun in 1918. When he came back to England he was elected Chancellor of Oxford University. He was made a Viscount in 1916, having declined an earldom.
He married his first wife, Dorothy, in 1885 (her father rejoiced in the name of Shallcross Fitzherbert Widdrington). Lady Grey was driving herself in her own pony carriage on February 1, 1906, when she was thrown out of it. She landed on her head and died soon after without recovering consciousness. His second marriage, in 1922, was to Pamela, widow of the 1st Baron Glenconner, who had died in 1920. Both marriages were childless.
The Grey family motto was *De bon vouloir servir le roy* – willing to serve the King.
In 1937 Grey's old friend BALDWIN unveiled a stone plaque made by REID-DICK set into the wall of the Foreign Office, near the steps.

GROSSMITH
Walter
Author

London, June 9, 1853
Weedon London, June 14, 1919

1, Bedford Square, WC1, 1902-1919

Weedon and his brother, George wrote *Diary of a Nobody*. It appeared in chapter form in *Punch* and was eventually published in one volume in 1892. It is a minor classic 'exposing' the pretensions of Charles Pooter, a lower middle-class clerk in the City and takes a close look at late Victorian suburban smugness and its *mores*.

GROSVENOR

The Duke of Westminster is probably the richest Englishman in Britain today. Grosvenor is the family name of the Westminsters and, since the end of the 18th century the family has owned vast tracts of London covering practically the whole of north Mayfair, most of 'Belgravia' and practically all Pimlico.

All the streets owned by the Grosvenors around Grosvenor Square in W1 and many in Pimlico bear names from Grosvenor family connections or land holdings.

GROSVENOR PLACE, SW1
Circle, District, Victoria and BR lines to Victoria

6, Sir Henry CAMPBELL-BANNERMAN (LCP 1959) 1877-1904. While living here, he moved swiftly up the Liberal ladder, becoming leader of the party in 1899.

13, Lady Ottoline MORRELL, 1898. She lived here with her half brothers, Lord Henry Cavendish, then 32 (and married to the daughter of the Earl of Bective) Lord William Cavendish, 33 and Lord Charles Cavendish who was 30. Ottoline was 25.

18, Algernon SWINBURNE, early 1860s. He had just come down from Oxford, without a degree.

25, Mrs. Humphrey WARD, 1881-1900. When she lived here, her husband worked for the *Times*.

35, Nubar GULBENKIAN, 1929, when he was Commercial Attache to the Persian Legation.

GROSVENOR ROAD, SW1
Victoria line to Pimlico

32, Lady Ottoline MORELL, 1902, not long after her marriage to Philip Morell.

41, Sidney WEBB, 1904. Whilst here he was a 'Progressive' member on the London County Council.

100, Viscount CECIL, until 1922. He was living here when his pet brain child, 'The League of Nations' was being formed.

GROSVENOR SQUARE, W1
Central line to Bond Street

The Dukes of Westminster, family name Grosvenor owned some 100 *acres* (40 hectares) around here, Grosvenor Square being part of their West One estate. In 1725 an ancestor, Sir Richard Grosvenor (d.1732) gave instructions to John Alston, a Pimlico gardener, to lay out six acres (2.4 hectares) of the family holding here. The cost was £350.

3 (Flat 30) John G. WINANT, 1941-1942. 'The flat', he wrote, 'has been my workshop and my living quarters. There are few men in British public life, whether in Government or in the armed forces, who have not stepped in at some time...'

5, 6 and **7,** Sir Jeffry WYATVILLE made substantial alterations to these houses between 1809 and 1816. Samuel WYATT altered No. 10 in 1802 and completely reconstructed No. 45 for Lord Petre between 1801 and 1806.

6, W.H. PAGE, 1913-1918 (P) whilst United States Ambassador in London.

9, Lady CUNARD ('Emerald') 1942. After which she moved in to the Dorchester Hotel, almost for the rest of her life.

10, Lord ROCKINGHAM, he was Prime Minister in March 1782: on July 1, 1782 he died here.

12, Lord LYTTON. This was his address in London when he died in 1873, having lived here for four years.

17, Admiral BEATTY, from August 1925 until his death in March 1936.

20, here were the Headquarters of Dwight D. Eisenhower from January to March, 1944 (P).

22, William BECKFORD, c.1800. He was visited here by Lord NELSON and Emma HAMILTON (whose husband, Sir WILLIAM, was Beckford's second cousin.)

24, the Earl of SHAFTESBURY was born here in 1801.

30 (later 35) John WILKES died here in 1797. He also had a house at Kensington *and* another on the Isle of Wight.

The American Embassy, surmounted by its massive bald-headed eagle now occupies the whole of the west side of the Square. It was completed in 1960. The architect, Eero Saarinen (1910-1961) went to the States with his father from their native Finland in 1923. A 99-year lease was bought from Grosvenor Estates (business arm of the Duke of Westminster's ever-expanding property portfolio) in September 1950 by the American Government.

50, Frances, Dowager Duchess of Marlborough, widow of the 7th Duke. Her son, Lord Randolph CHURCHILL, died here on January 24, 1895.

Today, a bronze statue of a cloaked Franklin Delano Roosevelt stands on the north side of the Square. He faces south and was sculpted by Sir William REID DICK. It was unveiled by F.D.R.'s widow, Eleanor, in 1948. The cost of the statue was met by public subscription. The maximum contribution from any one person was five shillings (25p) and the money needed was donated in a few weeks.

GROSVENOR STREET, W1   *Central line to Bond Street*

16, Mrs. George KEPPEL, 1922-1928. In the summer of 1924 she let the whole house to Mrs. James Corrigan, a *very* wealthy American. In July Mrs. Corrigan gave a dinner for 104 guests. (The house had been converted for the evening into *Une Jardin des Perroquets Verts*.) Many people unkindly wondered how Laura Corrigan managed to move so quickly in such exalted circles. It was put about that the rent charged by Mrs. Keppel included the use of her address book! Laura Corrigan had started out (it was said) as a telephone girl. Be that as it may, she married James Corrigan, who was Chairman of the Corrigan-McKinney Steel Corporation. He died in January 1928 and left her 60 *million* dollars.

28, Sir Humphry DAVY, 1820. He was living here when he became President of the Royal Society.

29, Fanny BURNEY in 1839, not long before her death.

38, Richard COBDEN, 1856. Whilst he and his wife were lodging here, their son was at school in Weinheim, 14 miles from Heidelberg, Germany. He died suddenly of scarlet fever and, due to bungling, the Cobdens were not even told of the boy's illness until he was buried.

49, the *Sesame Club* where Dame Edith SITWELL used to stay on and off for a number of years.

60, Anne ('Nance') OLDFIELD, the actress died in this house on October 23, 1730.

75, Clementine CHURCHILL (née Hozier) was born here on April 1, 1885.

82, George DU MAURIER in the 1860s.

GROTE	Clay Hill, Kent, November 17, 1794
George	London, June 8, 1871
Banker and historian	Westminster Abbey

3, Buckingham Palace Road, SW1
12, Savile Row, W1 (LCP 1905) from 1848 until he died here

Grote's grandfather, Andreas, came from Bremen and was one of the founders of the banking house of Grote, Prescott and Co. in January 1766. His eldest son, George (by a second marriage) married Selina Peckwell, who descended from a Huguenot family, the De Blossets of Touraine.

Selina herself handled young George's education to a great extent though he did go to Sevenoaks Grammar School and, when only ten, went to Charterhouse, which was then under the Headmastership of Dr. Raine, FRS (1760-1817). Grote stayed at Charterhouse for six years where he was friendly with a boy with the strange name of Thirlwall Connop. Connop, 1797-1875, became Bishop of St David's and his own history of Greece was superceded by Grote's in 1846. At sixteen, his father, having no 'faith in Universities', put him to work in the family bank. Privately, young George taught himself German, Italian and French.

In 1814 he first met Harriet Lewin of Bexleyheath, whose father was of 'private means'. Grote married Harriet in 1820 and their first home was a house actually attached to the bank in Threadneedle Street. In 1822 he began to make a special study of Greek History. The Grote's only child died a week after its birth and Harriet Grote was left ill and probably averse to any more attentions from her husband.

Between 1825 and 1827, Grote was deeply involved in the foundation of London University. In 1830 his father died and Grote inherited land in Lincolnshire and Oxfordshire valued at £40,000. In 1833, he entered Parliament as one of the members for the City of London. He stayed so for eight and a half years until June 1841, when he decided to retire from both politics and banking and devote himself to his *History of Greece* (after a year's travelling in Italy). In March 1846, the first two volumes appeared, to acclaim. In the biography of her husband, Mrs Grote wrote '...I became, for once, witness of a state of feeling on his part approaching gratified self-love, which at times would pierce through that imperturbable veil of modesty habitually present with him'. The third and fourth books appeared in 1847; fifth and sixth in 1849; seventh and eighth, 1850; ninth and tenth, 1852; eleventh, 1853; the twelfth – and last – in 1856.

GROVE END ROAD, NW3   *Bakerloo line to Maida Vale*

So called because it *starts* where Lisson Grove *ends*.

31, W. Reid-Dick (1879-1962). He sculpted the figures of King George V (at the east end of Westminster Abbey and facing the Houses of Parliament) and of Franklin Delano Roosevelt in Grosvenor Square. Dick was living here in 1929.

44, Sir Laurence ALMA-TADEMA (LCP 1975) from 1886 until his death in 1912. He built what was an unusual house for the day on the base of an 18th century building. The house has now been subdivided into flats and all the little *oddities* have gone.

GUILDFORD STREET, WC1 . *Piccadilly line to Russell Square*
In 1792 this part of London was being wholeheartedly developed and in this year Lord North, hardly the most enlightened of Prime Ministers, died. He had a subsidiary title of the 2nd Early of Guildford and some developer misguidedly named this bit after him, perhaps hoping for better things from the following generation.

35, Algernon SWINBURNE was 'rescued' from this house in October 1876 by Theodore WATTS-DUNTON and taken off to the pastures of Putney.

38, 'Eddie' MARSH was born here in November 1872.

77, Sydney SMITH lodged here in 1803.

116, Olive SCHREINER lodged here in 1882, whilst being treated in a nearby hospital. She paid 26 shillings a week (£1.30) rent.

GUIZOT   Nîmes, October 4, 1787
François Pierre Guillaume   Normandy, September 12, 1874
Politician

20, Pelham Crescent, SW7, 1848-1849
Guizot studied law in Paris when he was only 18 but soon entered the political scene; was elected to the Chamber of Deputies in 1830 and, as Ambassador, came to London in 1840.
He was recalled to Paris to become chief adviser to King Louis and as such must necessarily have been involved in the King's downfall. They both escaped to London. After the *coup d'état* Guizot withdrew from politics entirely and spent the rest of his life with historical studies. His *Histoire de France racontée à mes petits enfants* told the story of his country up to 1789 and was extended up to 1870 by his daughter, Madame Guizot de Witt.

GULBENKIAN   June 2, 1896
Nubar Sarkis   January 10, 1972
Millionaire

35, Grosvenor Place, SW1, 1929
70, Arlington House, Arlington Street, SW1, 1964
Flat 8, 55, Park Lane, W1, 1972
Nubar, the only son of Calouste ('Mr. 5%') Gulbenkian and Nevarte, (née Essayan) was first married in 1922 to Herminia Feijoo; secondly to Dore Freeland in 1928 and, lastly in 1948, to Maria de Ayala, but by none of his wives did he have children.
His education was as top-drawer English as money could buy: Orley Farm Preparatory School, followed by Harrow then Trinity College, Cambridge. His shrewd old father, whose income from oil was almost incalculable, trusted nobody and made sure little Nubar was not spoiled by too large an allowance. So, after a little work with Royal Dutch Shell, then the French Ministry of Supply, he came into father's oil business in 1925 and worked there (nominally) for 30 years.
He bought a country house (The Old House, Hoggeston, Nr. Bletchley) to be near good fox hunting country. The sight of a monocled Armenian with a silk hat and an *orchid* as a buttonhole on his 'pink' coat joining in with the *county*, was a sight for the sore eyes of gossip columnists.
In London he used to be driven about in what was basically a black London cab, but fitted, however, with a Rolls Royce engine, real carriage lamps and gilt basket work decoration on the body. It was made for him in 1965 and on his death seven years later there were only 7,000 miles (11,265 kilometres) 'on the clock'. It was bought for an American museum, but in 1982 it was back in England and for sale at £38,500. The man who wanted this price for

it was Minas Khachadourian, who, as his name suggests, was Armenian. One little touch that would be worth something by itself was a *Lalique* crystal mascot of a boar's head that lit up at night!

GULL
(Sir) William Withey
Physician

Colchester, December 31, 1816
? London, January 29, 1890
? Thorpe-le-Soken, Essex

74, Brook Street, W1, 1870–1890

Gull was the youngest of eight children, brought up in poor circumstances by their widowed mother. (His father was a barge owner who died in 1827.) By diligence, William managed to pass into Guy's Hospital and qualified from there as a doctor in 1841.

In November 1871, the 29-year old Prince of Wales appeared to be dying of typhoid (the disease which killed his father, Prince Albert, almost exactly ten years earlier.) The Prince was at his Norfolk house at Sandringham and, *somehow* Gull was brought from London to treat the Heir to the throne. Unlike his father, as the crisis of the disease approached, the Prince was raving; he flung his pillows about (one, so flung, knocked his wife, Princess Alexandra, to the ground!)

'That's all right old Gull', the invalid shouted, 'one more teaspoonful...'. The Prince was mending by December 14. 'Dear Bertie had been on the very *verge* of the grave', wrote Queen Victoria. Gull had cured the Prince, over the head of the established Royal Physician, Sir William JENNER; he was given a baronetcy in 1872 and he became a *society* doctor.

At his death Gull left the amazingly large sum of £344,000. This is probably the largest fortune ever amassed by any British doctor (or surgeon) *solely* from the wages of healing.

GUTHRIE
Thomas Anstey ('F. Anstey')
Author

London, August 8, 1856
London, March 10, 1934

7, St George's Court, SW7, here born
16, Duke Street Mansions, Grosvenor Square, W1, 1904
24, Holland Park Road, W14, from 1921 until he died here

Guthrie's father had a prosperous tailoring business and sent his son to Trinity College, Cambridge after providing him with a good educational base. After Cambridge Guthrie was called to the Bar in 1881. The following year, his book *Vice Versa* (in which the roles of a schoolboy and his pompous father are reversed) was a considerable success and Law went out of the window. He originally wanted to use the pen name of Thomas Anstey but the compositor mistook the 'T' for an 'F' and so 'F. Anstey' he became.

For 43 years he was on the staff of *Punch* and at one time wrote the column in the magazine which was called *Voces Populi*. He also published three more novels, the most successful of which was *The Brass Bottle,* in 1900. His autobiography, *A Long Retrospect,* was published posthumously.

GWYNN (or GWYN)
Eleanor ('Nell')
Royal Mistress

Hereford, February 2, 1650
London, November 13, 1687
St Martin-in-the-Fields

79, Pall Mall, SW1, 1671–1687

'Nell' graduated from the streets of Covent Garden to its stage and from there to the bed of King Charles II, by whom she had (at least) one son, Charles Beauclerk, who later was the Duke of St Albans.

The King's last words were popularly supposed to have been, 'Let not poor Nellie starve' and she remained pretty faithful to his memory. She once rejected a potential lover scornfully, saying, 'Shall a dog lie where the deer once couched?' (For *once* Charles's brother, James II, behaved honourably and saw to it that Nellie did *not* starve.)

The King was most certainly not her only lover. Not long before her royal patronage, her lover had been Lord Buckhurst. She was a warm hearted girl and had been in receipt of charity more than once. It has been suggested that it was she who urged Charles to build the Royal Hospital, which building by Christopher WREN survives today.

On October 5, 1667, Samuel PEPYS went 'To the King's house: and there going in met with Knipp' [a married actress, who was on the stages of London in the 1760s] 'and she took us up into the tiring rooms; and to the womens' shift where Nell was dressing herself and was all unready, and is very pretty, prettier than I thought.'

HAIG
Douglas (1st Earl Haig of Bemersyde)
Field Marshall

Edinburgh, June 19, 1861
London, 1928
Dryburgh Abbey, Scotland

21, Prince's Gate, SW7, where he died

In 1914 Haig took the 1st Corps of the British Expeditionary Force to France and he succeeded Sir John French as Commander-in-Chief of the British Forces in December 1915.

Haig's strategy was considerably hampered by the failure of the French Army; particularly after the Nivelle offensive in 1917. He was also bedevilled by the frequent interference of LLOYD-GEORGE. Eventually Haig's strategy was forced through and, though hundreds of thousands of soldiers (on both sides of the trenches) were killed, his plan triumphed and was to lead to the defeat of the German forces in 1918.

An equestrian statue of a hatless Haig was erected in Whitehall, opposite the Banqueting House in 1937. It was sculpted by A.F. Hardiman. Apart from the solecism of Haig's hatlessness, equestrian experts were quick to point out (letters to the *Times* and so on!) that no *real* horse could have stood up, or even moved, if its hooves were in the position Hardiman had put them.

HAKE
Thomas Gordon
Physician and Poet

Leeds, March 10, 1809
January 11, 1895

42, Gordon Square, WC1, 1840-1841

Medically, Hake was extensively educated; at St Georges Hospital at Hyde Park Corner, Edinburgh and Glasgow. Eventually he 'put up his plate' in Brighton.

In 1849 his poem *Vales* was published. It was published again in William Ainsworth's magazine under the title of *Valdarno*. There it attracted the attention of Dante Gabriel ROSSETTI and it was not long before Hake became a member of the 'Pre-Raphaelite Brotherhood'.

He had four more collections of poems published and, in 1892, his autobiography, *Memoirs of Eighty Years,* appeared. Despite the rather unimaginative title it is informative and still readable.

HALDANE
Richard Burdon (1st Viscount)
Statesman

Edinburgh, July 30, 1856
Cloan, August 19, 1928

3, Whitehall Court, SW1, 1905
28, Queen Anne's Gate, SW1, 1907-1928

Haldane was educated at Edinburgh and Göttingen. He was called to the Bar in 1879 and in the same year he entered Parliament as a Liberal. His income after one year at the Bar was £31.10s 0d (31.50); the following year it had more than *trebled* (£109) but by 1884 it was still only £1,100. He decided the Bar was not for him. His social life was active and he was friendly with a fellow Scot, Margot Tennant, later to become Mrs. Asquith, and her 'intellectual' group, the 'Souls'.

Having turned his back on the details of law he applied himself to politics.

He was to be Secretary of State for War and, in that post, found the Territorial Association ('part-time soldiers'). This totally volunteer force was to save Britain's bacon in both 1914 and 1939. He became Lord High Chancellor of England in 1912, having been created a Viscount (1st and last, because he never married) in 1911. At the end of his Chancellorship, King George V awarded him the Order of Merit in 1915.

HALF MOON STREET, W1   *Piccadilly, Victoria and Jubilee lines*
to Green Park

There used to be a tavern here called the *Halfe Moone at Mayffair* which was still standing in 1780: the Street itself was practically built up by 1730. The area must have been prosperous because Mrs. Winter, who kept the tavern, died in September 1759 and left over £8,000 (which she willed to her 'poorest relations').

7,   Henry JAMES, 1869. His apartment was on the ground floor and, '...the fading daylight reached it in a sadly damaged condition'.

40,   William HAZLITT, 1827-1829. His four-volume biography of Napoleon was published in this period. It was *not* a success.

44,   Robbie ROSS, c.1910-1918. The house was owned by Nellie Burton. Ross, a bachelor, only had rooms here. In 1921, a young man called Holloway shot himself, rather than face up to some sort of scandal involving his diplomatic appointment. He 'chose' Nellie Burton's *bathroom* in which to do it. Nellie found him dying on the floor wrapped in *her* bath towel. 'Why?' complained Nellie afterwards, reasonably enough, 'Why couldn't he have gone out and done it in the *Park?* – instead of damning me?' (Green Park faces Half Moon Street at its Piccadilly end.)

HALIFAX   April 16, 1881
Edward Frederick Lindley Wood   December 23, 1959
Diplomat (1st Earl of the 2nd creation)

7, Kingston House North, Princess Gate, SW7, for some while until his death in 1959

Halifax was the only son of the 2nd Viscount Halifax, quondam Groom of the Bedchamber to HRH the Prince of Wales. He had married Lady Agnes Courtenay, daughter of the 11th Earl of Devon in 1869 (see William BECKFORD) and they lived at 79, Eaton Square, SW1, in 1897.
Edward Frederick, as Baron Irwin (created in 1925) was Viceroy of India from 1926-1931 and Foreign Secretary under Neville CHAMBERLAIN from 1938 to 1941. He was then posted to Washington where he was a well-liked and respected British Ambassador until 1946. In 1944 he was made an Earl and awarded the Order of Merit, two years later.
In 1909 he married Lady Dorothy Onslow, daughter of the 4th Earl of Onslow. They had three sons, one of whom was killed in action in 1942. Lady Dorothy had been a Lady of the Bedchamber to Queen Elizabeth, consort of King George VI, from 1937 until the appointment to Washington.
The rather smug English version of the Halifax motto is; 'I like my choice'.

HALLAM   Windsor, July 9, 1777
Henry   Penshurst, Kent, January 21, 1856
Historian   Clevedon, Somerset (now Avon)

67, Wimpole Street, W1 (LCP 1904) 1817-1841
24, Belgrave Square, SW1, where he died

Hallam practised as a barrister until his father died, leaving him sufficient money to allow him to spend all his time on historical research and writing. As an historian, his '...knowledge of original sources was unequalled before his day'.

He was a quite extraordinarily fast talker and had a justified reputation as a 'brick-dropper'. Sidney SMITH said of him, 'And there was Hallam with his mouth full of cabbage and contradiction'. Despite his ineptitude socially, he was once regarded as the founder of the 'Critical School of History'.

There is a statue of Hallam in St Paul's Cathedral, sculpted in 1863 by William Theed, the 'Younger'.

HALLAM STREET, W1

*Bakerloo and Circle lines
to Great Portland Street*

Named after Henry HALLAM (see above) the historian and father of Arthur Hallam, beloved of TENNYSON.

110, Dante Gabriel ROSSETTI (LCP 1906). In 1828, when Dante was born here, this house was 38, Charlotte Street. It was renumbered to 110, demolished in 1928 and a block of flats, called Rossetti House, erected. The plaque is on the corner of Devonshire Street.

HAMILTON
Emma (née Lyon)
NELSON's mistress

Great Neston, Cambs, May 12, 1765
Calais, January 15, 1815
Calais

7 (old numbering) Wigmore Street, W1, 1791
23, Piccadilly, W1, 1800-1803
11, Clarges Street, W1, 1804-1806
36, Albermarle Street, W1, 1810
150, Bond Street, W1, 1813

Emma Hamilton has been seen by some as a combination of Cleopatra and Helen of Troy. She only resembles the former in that they both loved men whose place is sure historically. In fact, Emma was on the short side, rather dumpy, had a blotchy complexion (*and* she sometimes smelled!).

Despite all this she married Sir William Hamilton at St Marylebone Parish Church on September 6, 1791. Sir William, a widower, was 35 years older than she. But Emma's fame rests entirely on the love affair with Horatio NELSON, which spread over 12 years, only ending with his death at Trafalgar in 1805.

They met in Naples, where Sir William was envoy, but their grand passion really began after the Battle of the Nile in 1798. She had two children by Nelson, the elder, Horatia, was born in London on January 30, 1801. Horatia was secretly placed with a lady in Little Tichfield Street, W1, until Sir William died in 1803 and only then, in the May, was she baptised. The younger daughter, Emma, was born in the autumn of 1803, but died in March 1804.

Sir William viewed his wife's liaison with Nelson very complacently. So complacently in fact, they established a *ménage à trois* in a house that Nelson bought at Merton, just a few miles south of London. Nelson left her the house and £2,000 and a £500 annuity (the house was valued at £12,000). In 1810, 'Old Q', the 4th Duke of Queensberry, died aged 86 and left her another £510 per annum. Despite not being too badly off, Emma got deeper and deeper in debt, gambling to try and pay her debts. She was obliged to leave England and spent the last two years of her life comparatively impoverished in Calais.

HAMILTON Scotland, December 13, 1730
(Sir) William London, April 6, 1803
Amiable Cuckold

7 (old numbering) Wigmore Street, W1, 1791
23, Piccadilly, W1, 1800–1803

Hamilton claimed that he began life 'with an ancient name and £1,000'. He remedied the latter by marrying a lady of '...very large property, as well as amiable and agreeable character', (a rare combination in any age.) Hamilton was 25 when he married for the first time.

He was made a Knight of the Bath in 1771 and a Privy Councillor in 1791. In that same year, Hamilton, then 61, married Amy Lyon at Marylebone Parish Church. Amy was 26 years old and was to become better known as EMMA HAMILTON. (Actually in the reports of her marriage to Sir William she was described as 'Emily Harte'.) Afterwards they moved back to Naples and met Horatio NELSON in 1793. The rest, as they say, is history. In an appreciation of Hamilton published 35 years after his death his second marriage was listed and the obituarist went on, 'Sir William appears however to have maintained an unblemished character except in his weak indulgence of his licentious wife'.

HAMILTON TERRACE, NW8 *Jubilee line to St John's Wood*

Harrow School owns a large amount of property in this area. It had been given to the school by John Lyon, who founded Harrow in 1571. Originally Lyon intended that the income deriving from the London properties should be used for maintaining the Harrow Road. At the time the Terrace was being built, one of the Governors of the school was Charles Hamilton.

17, Sir Joseph BALZAGETTE (LCP 1974).

20, Sir George MACFARREN (P 1895) who died here in 1887 aged 74, having been blind for the last 20 years of his life.

20, William STRANG (LCP 1962) from 1900 until his death in 1921. The KIPLING edition which carried his illustrations was published while STRANG lived here.

23, Stephen POTTER, 1968, after his second marriage (to Heather Jenner).

62, Sir Arthur PINERO, 1896. By this time he was an established playwright, largely due to his *The Second Mrs. Tanqueray* – with Mrs. Patrick CAMPBELL in the lead.

76, Eugene GOOSENS. This was his London address at his death in 1962.

98, Brian JOHNSTON, 1968, near enough to Lord's Cricket Ground, to make it easy to get there for the cricket commentaries he broadcast for the BBC.

HAMPSTEAD ROAD, NW1 *Northern and Victoria lines*
to Warren Street

In the charter of King Edgar (944–975) the first king, incidentally, of *all* England, Hampstead was 'Hamstead' – a home. The 'p' was inserted much later on. In the middle ages much of Hampstead belonged to the Bishops of London and travellers were subjected to a toll to pass through. The only remaining evidence is the toll house opposite the Spaniards Inn at the edge of the Heath.

83 (then 10) David WILKIE painted his *Blind Fiddler* (now in the Tate Gallery) in this house in 1806.

165, Emmeline PANKHURST. The Pankhursts lived over their shop (which sold 'artistic objects with which housewives could beautify their homes') in 1886.

225, Alfred TENNYSON stayed here briefly in 1849/1850.
263, George CRUIKSHANK (P 1885) 1830-1878. By this time he was mentally unbalanced. He spent most of his time with his mistress, Adelaide Archbold at 31, Augustus Street, just around the corner.

HANDEL	Halle, Prussia, February 23, 1685
George Frederick	London, April 14, 1759
Musician	Westminster Abbey (in 'Poet's Corner')

25, Brook Street, W1 (LCP 1952) c.1712 until he died here

Handel first came to London in 1710 to superintend the production of his opera, *Rinaldo* (performed in London for the first time in March 1711). He came back to the capital in 1712 and never left it again, apart from 'holiday visits' to Germany. Queen Anne died in 1714 and George, Elector of Hanover, came to the throne. As Handel had exiled himself from Germany only two years before, he was really *persona non grata* with the new, German speaking, King George I of Great Britain.
During 1735 Handel conducted 15 Oratorio concerts in London, but two years later he suffered a stroke. He rallied well and in the next five years he composed *Saul* (1739) *Israel in Egypt* in the same year and the *Messiah,* which was first performed in Dublin in 1742. (The *correct* title of the oratorio is just *Messiah* without the definite article preceding it.) There were seven more operas to come (including *Samson*) but his sight failed altogether around 1751. At his death he left the not inconsiderable sum of £20,000; half of it to be put into a fund for 'decayed musicians'.
Handel was a large eater. Once he dined alone in a tavern, having ordered dinner for *three*. 'Is de tinner retty?' he asked after a little while. 'As soon as the company comes'. answered the waiter. 'Then,' said Handel, 'pring up de tinner prestissimo. *I* am de company.'

HANOVER

The Whig party was exultant in 1714 when Queen Anne *was* dead and George, Elector of Hanover, crossed to England to be crowned King George I in Westminster Abbey on October 20, 1714. Lord Scarborough, the 2nd Earl, who died in 1740, celebrated the Protestant succession by building Hanover Square and Princes Street (also, what is now, St George Street).

HANOVER SQUARE, W1   *Central line to Oxford Circus*

Built up in 1717/1718, the Square was known first as 'Hanover Square Street'. It was suggested that the Tyburn Gallows – then more or less on the site, today, of the Marble Arch – be moved and so, '...removing any inconveniences or annoyances that might be occasioned to that Square or the Houses thereabouts.'

3, Charles DICKENS rented a room here in 1861.
12, Mary SOMERVILLE, 1818-1827. Her second husband, Dr. William Somerville, was appointed to sit on the Army Medical Board, after he and Mary had been married for four years. A previous occupant of this house was Sir James Earle, a surgeon, who died here in September 1817. The freeholder was General, Sir Arthur James Talbot and, after the Somerville's occupancy, the property was mortgaged to the 2nd Earl Harewood (ancestor of George HAREWOOD, 7th Earl).
17 (in her day 15) Mrs. JORDAN. The original ceilings in this house were the work of Angelica KAUFFMANN.

21, Prince TALLEYRAND (LCP 1978) 1830-1834, when he was Louis Philippe's Ambassador in London.
26, Thomas WOLFE lodged here in the Spring of 1935.
The statue on the south east of the Square is of William PITT, the Younger. The bronze, made by Sir Francis CHANTREY, was put up here in 1831; 25 years after Pitt's death. It cost £7,000 and was put on its plinth between 7 and 8 in the morning. The workmen were at their breakfast and a group of 'Reformers' threw a rope over the statue and tried to pull it off its pedestal. The statue, however, had been well bolted down so the anarchistic attempt failed.

HANOVER TERRACE, NW1   *Bakerloo, Metropolitan and Jubilee lines to Baker Street*

This Hanover is three generations after the previous Hanoverian entry. It was part of the development of Regent's Park and the family's dynastic name was pressed into use.

3, Charles DICKENS wrote *Great Expectations* here during 1860.
7, Harold PINTER, 'eking' out a living in the 1960s.
10, Ralph VAUGHAN WILLIAMS 1953-1958.
13, H.G. WELLS, from 1936 until he died here in August 1946. When he moved in, the house was, '...old, tumbledown, on the borders of Regent's Park'. The *number* of the house appealed to WELLS and, to tempt superstition even further, when bombs were falling, almost incessantly in the 'Blitz' of 1940, '41 and '42, he had the numeral '13' painted very large on the front door!
17, Wilkie COLLINS, with his widowed mother, in 1860.

HANS

All the 'Hans' and all the 'Sloanes' derive from Sir Hans SLOANE (1660-1753) who was Lord of the Manor of Chelsea from 1712 until his death. He was also the first medical doctor to be given a Knighthood (in 1710).

HANS CRESCENT, SW1   *Piccadilly line to Knightsbridge*

Until the 1880s this was known as Exeter Street.

4, Prince Louis MOUNTBATTEN, 1901, when he was working at the Admiralty, he was still Prince Louis BATTENBURG then.

HANS PLACE, SW1

22, Viscount MELBOURNE.
23, Jane AUSTEN (P) in November 1814 and again in 1815. Her banker and beloved brother, Henry, lived here. Jane wrote that the house was delightful and, '...the garden is quite a love. I am in the front attic which is the bedchamber to be preferred'. In October 1815 Henry was very ill and Jane nearly wore herself out nursing him.
25, Letitia Elizabeth LANDON ('L.E.L.') was born here in 1802. In due course she was sent to school only three doors away at number 22.
Both 22 and 25 have been completely rebuilt since their day.
33, Mary Russell MITFORD came to live here almost immediately after leaving school. She was here from 1805-1820.
41, P.B. SHELLEY, 1817. His wife, Mary, gave birth to a still born child here. The house has two more storeys addded to it since the Shelleys were here.
44, Margaret OLIPHANT, 1880s. By this time she was writing books like *The Beleagured City*; very different stuff to her earlier and poorer work.

HANSARD　　　　　　　　　Norwich, July 5, 1752
Luke　　　　　　　　　　　　London, October 29, 1828
Printer　　　　　　　　　　 St Giles-in-the-Fields, Holborn

In Great Turnstile, WC2, 1774
4, Gower Street, WC1, 1808-1810

Hansard gave the name to the publication in which the business transacted in the House of Commons is recorded, *verbatim,* every day when members are sitting.

He came from East Anglia and joined a business man called Hughes, who was printer to the House. Hansard became his manager in 1774 and took over the whole business in 1798. The Parliamentary work stayed with Hansard until 1889, yet the name, *Hansard* only appeared on the title page in 1892. In that year Reuter's Telegram Company published the reports; then Eyre and Spottiswode published them for a year or so until 1894. Other firms handled the work after this, but they are now a regular publication produced by Her Majesty's Stationery Office (HMSO). Their showrooms at 49, High Holborn, WC1 (on the corner of Brownlow Street) are only a stone's throw from Great Turnstile, where Hansard first lived in London.

HANSOM　　　　　　　　　York, October 26, 1803
Joseph Aloysius　　　　　　　London, June 29, 1882
Architect　　　　　　　　　 St Thomas of Canterbury, Fulham

13, Neville Terrace, SW7, 1863-1867
25, Thurloe Street (formerly Alfred Place) SW7, 1867
27, Thurloe Street, SW7, – 1872, and again in 1882
27, Sumner Place, SW7 (LCP 1981) 1873-1877
399, Fulham road, SW10, where he died

Hansom was an architect who designed the neo-classical Town Hall in Birmingham, St Aloysius's Church in Oxford and the Roman Catholic Cathedral in Plymouth.

But his name lingers on. In 1834 he took out a patent on a 'suspended axle' for a cabriolet and so the *Hansom Cab* was born. 'Hansoms' were still in regular use in London up until the First World War.

HARCOURT　　　　　　　　Nuneham Park, Oxon., January 31,
Lewis Vernon (1st Viscount)　 1863
Politician　　　　　　　　　 London, February 24, 1922
　　　　　　　　　　　　　　 Nuneham Park

69, Brook Street, W1, where he killed himself

Politically; Harcourt had some success, having been *Commissioner of Works* from 1905 to 1910; Colonial Secretary, 1910-1915 and then back to *Works* for another year.

He married a wealthy American girl, Mary Ethel Burns of New York and they had a son and three daughters. Socially he was on the 'up and up', having been made a Viscount in 1917.

However, in 1921, another sort of love seems to have crept in. This (if one believed the gossip of the day) was that a certain Edward James, an Eton schoolboy and Harcourt, were more than just 'friendly'. Harcourt shot himself on the stairs of his Brook Street house. *Officially* he had, '...died of heart failure', in his sleep.

Harcourt was nicknamed 'Lulu' (or 'Lou-Lou') and frequently moved in more 'Bohemian' circles than has come to be expected of an ex-Commissioner of Works. Lytton STRACHEY's sad, mixed-up 'girl friend', CARRINGTON wrote in a letter in 1916, 'Last Thursday the arch-bugger Lou Lou Harcourt came to supper with us at Brett's studio' [Dorothy Brett daughter of Lord Esher, then 43 years old] '...a terrible long creature tightly buttoned in a frock coat all the way up and then a face bulging out all pink and very tight above his collar. Really a nightmare of a face'.

HARDIE	Holytown, Scotland, August 15, 1856
James Keir	Cummock, Scotland, September 26,
Politician	1915

14, Nevill's Court, off Fetter Lane, EC4, 1902-1911 and then:
10, Nevill's Court, EC4, until 1914

Hardie's mother, Mary Keir (or Kerr) produced Master James before she had received the formal blessing of a church marriage. The father's name was William Aitken, a local collier. Three years later Mary married David Hardie and James took his surname.
Keir Hardie began work at the age of eight and had a number of different jobs in the depressed areas around Glasgow, but by 1867, he was down the coal mines and worked in them until 1879.
He stood for Parliament in 1888 but was defeated. Four years later he was elected Member for West Ham South (in London) and he stayed in the Commons for three years. He later represented Merthyr Tydfil (in Wales) founded the *Labour Leader* and, in 1903, handed the publication over to the Independent Labour Party. He was an outspoken Pacifist and his attitude during the Boer War cost him too many votes and he lost his seat.

HARDY	Upper Bockhampton, Dorset, June 2,
Thomas	1840
Novelist and poet	Dorchester, January 11, 1928
	Ashes in Westminster Abbey, near
	DICKENS, his heart in the family
	tomb at Stinsford, Dorset

8, Adelphi Terraace, WC2, 1862-1867

In 1866 the Midland Railway was building St Pancras Station and bringing its passenger line into the terminus, under and behind, what was to be one of the architectural glories of 'Railway Gothic'. The railway engineers decided that they would not tunnel under the Grand Union Canal (as the Great Northern and London and North Western had done to Kings Cross and Euston) but run the tracks on a bridge *over* the canal. This required the use of land occupied by the very full and old St Pancras graveyard. A.W. BLOMFIELD was put in charge of this rather ghoulish task and he sent his assistant to superintend the operation, to make sure the corpses were removed reverently. Once the assistant and Blomfield found two skulls in one coffin. The sight moved the assistant to write:

'O, Passenger, pray list and catch
Our sighs and piteous groans,
Half stifled in this jumbled patch
Of wrenched memorial stones!

We late-lamented, resting here,
Are mixed to human jam,
And each to each exclaims in fear,
"I know not which I am!"'

The poetical assistant was the 26-year old Thomas Hardy. He had been apprenticed to an ecclesiastical architect in Dorchester from 1856 to 1861; in 1862 he came to London and studied under Sir Arthur Blomfield. In 1863 he actually won a medal awarded by the Institute of British Architects. During the day he worked with Blomfield and on most week nights went to evening classes at King's College.

But his literary self simmered secretly and in 1865 he had his first piece published. *Chamber's Journal* printed his *How I Built Myself a House*. In 1871 he published (at his own expense) a murder story called *Desperate Remedies*. In 1874, came *Far from the Madding Crowd*. His success gathered strength and, by 1886, he was an established novelist and had moved back to his native Dorset, having built himself a house called 'Max Gate', near Dorchester. *Tess of the D'Urbevilles* was written here in 1891 and, in 1895, came *Jude the Obscure*. It aroused such hostile criticism (and disgust) that Hardy never published another novel.

He became absorbed in poetry and his greatest work in this field was the long, epic drama, The Dynasts, which contained three parts, 19 acts and *130* scenes, all in blank verse. It began to appear in 1904 and was completed four years later.

HARLAND   St Petersburg (?), March 1, 1861
Henry   San Remo, December 20, 1905
Editor

144, Cromwell Road, SW7, 1894

Kensington Palace Mansions, De Vere Gardens, W8, 1895-1905

Harland always maintained that he had been born in Russia, but some used to say, for 'St Petersburg, read Brooklyn'. (They were probably right.) He was educated in Rome, Paris and at the Divinity School at Harvard University.

In 1884 he married Aline H. Merrian, a musician who later turned her talents to journalism and the Harland critics used to call her 'Penny-a-line'!

In December 1893, Aubrey BEARDSLEY wrote to Margery Ross (Robert ROSS's sister) that she, '...will be vastly interested to hear that Harland and myself are about to start a new literary and artistic Quarterly. The title has already been registered at Stationers Hall and on the scroll of fame. It is the *Yellow Book...* . The publication will be undertaken by John LANE and the price will be five shillings' (25p). The first two issues appeared in April and July 1894, before Lane and his partner Elkan Matthews dissolved their partnership, but the *Yellow Book* was doomed. Oscar Wilde was sent to gaol for homosexual offences in April 1895 and the *Yellow Book* quite unfairly, was thought to be tarred with a pervert's brush. In fact, by the express wish of Beardsley, WILDE never contributed to the magazine at all.

HARLEY   Bow Street, WC2, December 5, 1661
Robert (1st Earl of Oxford) London, May 21, 1724
Prime Minister   Brampton Bryan, Hertfordshire

14, Buckingham Street, WC2, 1701-1714

Harley, a Whig, entered Parliament in 1689 and by 1701 he was Speaker and Secretary of Trade in 1704. His cousin, Abigail Masham, proved a very useful relative, for she was the favourite of Queen Anne, a role she 'took over' from Sarah Churchill, Duchess of Marlborough. In 1707 she married Samuel Masham who was created Baron Masham five years later. The year before, Abigail, an intelligent, scheming but, unfortunately, very plain woman indeed, had been given charge of Queen Anne's privy purse.

Despite having friends both in court and in Government, Harley was obliged to resign his offices, as a result of his secretary being convicted of 'treasonable correspondence'. Harley then began to plot for the downfall of the Whig party. As a result the 1st Earl of Godolphin (c.1635-1712) who had been created an Earl in 1706, after being premier and Lord High Treasurer since 1702, was toppled. The Marlboroughs 'fell' and Godolphin with them. Harley became Chancellor of the Exchequer and party leader. He survived an attempt to murder him (by a deranged Frenchman wielding a pen-knife) and was made Earl of Oxford.

HARLEY STREET, W1   *Bakerloo line to Regents Park*

Edward *Harley* the son of Robert Harley married Lady *Henrietta Cavendish* thereby acquiring another large estate for the family. He began to develop parts of the holding around 1720 and practically every street was given a name associated with either his family or his wife's. (All the words printed in italics in this preamble are examples of this policy.) His father-in-law was *Holles* whose wife was the daughter of Viscount *Mansfield* and Baron *Ogle*. She was heiress to estates at *Welbeck, Clipstone, Carburton* and *Bolsover*. Harley himself became the 2nd Earl of *Oxford* in 1724 (as a main title, with the subsidiary titles of *Wigmore* and *Mortimer*). His only daughter, *Margaret* married the 2nd Duke of *Portland* who was also the Marquess of Titchfield and of *Bulstrode and Viscount Woodstock*. So it went on, marriage after marriage, generation after generation, until his great great granddaughter married Viscount *Ossington*.

CAVEAT. Certain street numbers in Harley Street are difficult to find *in* Harley Street. A Harley Street address confers such *cachet* to a doctor or medical practice, that they all try to get in on the act. For example: '90A and 93A Harley Street' are actually around the corner in Weymouth Street. Numbers 112A, 114A, ll5A and 117A Harley Street' are *all* in Devonshire Street!

6,   Sir Frederick TREVES.

8,   Dr. Malcolm MORRIS, 1887 on. The whole of the ground floor was taken up with Morris's surgery and waiting room. The family had lunch and breakfast in the 'breakfast room', which looked out on to the coal cellar well and 'area' steps.

11,   The Duke of WELLINGTON. At this time he was just Sir Arthur Wellesley and from this house he set off to fight the Peninsular Wars in 1808.

15A, Sir Arthur PINERO (LCP 1970), 1909-1934.

19,   Sir Morell MACKENZIE. In 1870 *Dr* Mackenzie took the lease of the largest house in the street. The lease stipulated that he spend £3,000 (or more, 'if need be') on refurbishing it. On the ground floor were two consulting rooms and a dispensary. On the first floor were a pair of 'handsome drawing rooms' which stretched the width of the house.

23,   Lord DAWSON of PENN, 1930s.

31,   Sir Francis BEAUFORT, 1812-1821. He moved into this house – a gift from Lestock Wilson – after he had married Alicia Wilson in 1812.

38   (formerly 13) Bryan PROCTER ('Barry Cornwall') from about 1840 to 1861 when he moved to Weymouth Street.

41,   Katherine MANSFIELD (then K. Beauchamp) 1901-1906, when she was a student at Queen's College.

45   (formerly 67) Allan RAMSAY. Here he painted a portrait of Queen Charlotte, consort of George III. The Crown Jewels and Regalia were all brought here to his studio.

45,   J.M.W. TURNER, 1803-1811, having lived at 51 (formerly 64) in 1800. He built a gallery which was 70 feet long by 20 feet wide (21.3 x 6 metres).

56,   James BUCHANAN (1791-1868) who was the 15th President of the United States, was living here when United States Minister in London. Nathaniel HAWTHORNE called on him here on September 12, 1855;

he wrote, 'The Ambassador [Buchanan] seems to intend some little state arrangements; but, no doubt, the establishment compares shabbily enough with the legations of other great countries and with the houses of English aristocracy. A servant not in livery (or in a very unrecognizable one) opened the door...'

73, William Ewart GLADSTONE (LCP 1908) 1876-1882. In April 1880, Gladstone became Prime Minister for the second time. In his study here, a visitor noticed that Gladstone had a toy figure of his political rival, Benjamin DISRAELI; '...something like a clown', hanging from a bell.

86, Henry NORTHCOTE, 1st Earl of Iddesleigh, in the 1880s.

108, Elizabeth LONGFORD (Lady Pakenham) was born here in 1906. Her family, the Harmans, were still at this address until 1959.

133, Sir James MACKENZIE, 1907-1925.)

135, Stephen POTTER, 1945-1950.

141, Lord HORDER (d. 1955) doctor to Royalty and lesser mortals. Made a Lord in 1933.

HARRINGTON GARDENS, SW7   *Piccadilly, District and Circle lines to Gloucester Road*

The 11th Earl of Harrington sold part of an estate in South Kensington that his family had owned since the early 16th century. The land he sold eventually became Harrington Road and Gardens, STANHOPE Gardens (the family name) PETERSHAM Place, because they were also Viscounts Petersham and ELVASTON Place, because that was the name of the family castle in Derbyshire. In 1850 the family had about 90 acres in South Kensington and today, even after the sort of sell-offs already described, they still retain over 25 acres (10 hectares).

39, Sir William GILBERT (LCP 1929) 1884-1890. The house was built for him, designed by Ernest George. The extensive use of terra-cotta was attributed by Charles Booth to a masons' strike. In addition to central heating and a telephone, the house was supposed to have 26 bedrooms, '*each* with its own bathroom'!

HARRIS
Frank
Editor and poseur

Galway, February 14, 1856
Nice, August 26, 1931
British Cemetery, Caucade, G Row,
No 11, Grave Grave No 1

33, The Strand, WC2, 1911

Harris was *probably* born in Galway of Welsh parents. *Probably* (when he was about 14) he sailed for America where at different times he was a bootblack, hotel clerk, cow puncher and even *may* have studied Law in Kansas and been admitted to the American bar. Some one once asked Max BEERBOHM if Harris *ever* told the truth? Max thought for a moment and then replied, 'Sometimes; don't you know...when his invention flags.'

Certainly he did come to London and became editor (in turn) of the *Fortnightly Review, The Saturday Review* and *Vanity Fair*. He had a very real and very deep knowledge (and love) for Shakespeare.

When he was 'in funds' he was quite recklessly generous. He championed Oscar WILDE in 1895 when society turned their collective backs on the witty Irishman. He entertained WILDE in Paris and in the South of France when Oscar was a pariah. Harris was friendly with G.B. SHAW over quite a long period and that Irishman did *not* suffer fools gladly.

In the last few years of his life Harris resorted to a number of ploys to keep some sort of income coming in. He produced an autobiography, challengingly entitled, *My Life and Loves* which for a time had the invaluable advertising feature working for it, in that it was banned. Even if half his stories were true and one could only believe part of the remainder, one must admire Harris's sexual stamina.

Shaw's wife, Charlotte burned the first volume of *My Life and Loves*. (This perhaps is not surprising as she married Shaw a virgin and died one. They had agreed that there would be no sexual intercourse.) After Harris's death, Shaw sent his widow, Nellie, a cheque and in return she sent him more of Harris's work, in proof form. Shaw himself, destroyed these. On the day of publication, *My Life and Loves* sold 27,000 copies and all the royalties went to Nellie; she died, in dire financial straits, in Nice, on March 25, 1955.

HARRISON	Faulby, Yorks., March 31, 1693
John	London, March 24, 1776
Horologist	Hampstead Paris Churchyard

Summit House, Red Lion Square, WC1 (LCP 1954) 1752 until he died here

Harrison's father was a carpenter and John followed him into that trade but he was always interested in clocks and chronometers. In 1714, an Act of Parliament was passed offering cash prizes of £10,000, £15,000 and £20,000 respectively for a method of ascertaining longitude within 60, 40 or 30 miles. In 1735 Harrison came up to London with a timepiece he had constructed and got eminent men (such as Edmond Halley of 'comet' fame) to vouch for its accuracy. In 1761 Harrison sent his son William with his chronometer on a King's ship to Jamaica. On his arrival at Port Royal the watch was found to have been five and one tenth seconds out. That is an error of 18 nautical miles in 3,000 miles covered (equivalent of 20.72 land miles or 33.3 kms). Another test was made in 1765 and eventually, after another Act was passed, Harrison was awarded £20,000.

HART-DAVIS	London, August 28, 1907
(Sir) Rupert Charles	
Publisher	

79, Victoria Road, W8, here born
3, Stanhope Street, NW1, 1908
8, Wilton Street, SW1 (for two months) 1924
35, Great Cumberland Place, W1 (for four months) 1924
36, Soho Square, W1 (over his office)

Hart-Davis has written of himself: 'I am reasonably certain that biologically speaking, Richard Hart-Davis was not my father...and, when the mother herself is uncertain who fathered her children, as my mother told Duff [her brother Duff COOPER, later Viscount NORWICH] she was, nothing is left but fascinating conjecture.' Be *that* as it may; Hart-Davis writes of the man (who was accepted as his father) who, when 81 took a fortnight's holiday in Eastbourne, accompanied by a 24 years old waitress, called Iris, who posed as his niece!

Hart-Davis can probably speak with some sort of authority on matrimony as he has been married four times. First, in 1929 to Peggy Ashcroft (now Dame Peggy) the marriage was dissolved. Second, to Catherine Borden-Turner in 1933; third, to Ruth Ware (widow of Oliver Simon) in 1964 and wife number four was June Clifford (widow of David Williams) in 1968. By Catherine (wife No 2) he had two sons and one daughter.

HARTE
Bret
Author

Albany, New York, August 25, 1836
Camberley, Surrey, May 5, 1902
St Peter's Churchyard, Frimley, Sy

109, Lancaster Gate, W2, 1894
74, Lancaster Gate, W2 (LCP 1977) 1895 (the plaque is here because he was supposed to have died here. Other authorities have him dying in Surrey. This latter version is supported by the *Encyclopaedia Brittanica*.)

His paternal grandfather was Jewish and both English and Dutch blood were in Harte's veins. His father was a schoolmaster who took care of his son's intellectual, if not his financial, well-being. Young Harte left school when he was only 13 and was financially independent when he was 16. He went west to California to join his mother in 1853 and tried his hand at one or two different jobs, ending up as a compositor with the San Francisco *Golden Era*. He had already begun to write, but in 1864 he became Secretary of the Californian Mint! Four years later he was the Editor of the *Overland Monthly*. In one issue he printed his own story *The Luck of the Roaring Camp*, became a literary figure and went east to New York ('by popular request') in 1871.

Lionization has its problems and, before long, Harte was broke. Influence got him a job in Crefeld (Germany) as United States Commercial Agent. He left the States, never to return, in 1878.

HASTINGS
(Sir) Patrick
Lawyer

London, March 17, 1880
London, February 26, 1952

9, Young Street, W8, 1902–1908
26, Victoria Road, W8, 1908–1918
111, Park Street, W1, 1929
2, Berkeley House, Hay Hill, W1, from 1938 until he died here.

After active service in the Boer War, Hastings was called to the Bar and after only 15 years he was a King's Council in 1919.

Politically, a Socialist, he became Attorney General in the 1924 Labour Government. He was MP for Wallsend, which constituency has *always* returned a Labour candidate.

In the Courts his two most famous cases were of Vaquier in 1924 and Rouse in 1931. Out of Court and Parliament he also was a playwright with some success: *Scotch Mist* in 1926 and *The Blind Goddess* in 1947. They both had good runs in the West End.

HASTINGS
Warren
Colonialist

Churchill, Oxon., December 6
Daylesford, Worcs., August 22, 1818
Daylesford Church

40, Park Lane, W1, 1786

At 18 Hastings went out to India as a clerk in the East India Service and by the time he was 29, had worked his way up to be a member of the Calcutta Council. By the time he was 40, he was Governor of Bengal and in 1774 was made the (first ever) Governor General of all India. One of his first acts was to expel Rajah Chait Singh, the Zemindar of Benares, and, in the following year, confiscated the land and the jewels of the Nawab of Oudh. (The chief city of Oudh being Lucknow.)

He had enemies in the Council from the very first and one of Hasting's chief problems was the shaky state of finances in Bengal. He put the two chief ministers of the state on trial for embezzlement, but the case failed. A corrupt official, Nand Kumar, who had conducted the case and brought charges of corruption against Hastings in 1775, was tried and executed on forgery offences. Doubts were raised over Hasting's own position and that of the Chief Justice, Sir Elijah Impey (1732-1809). In 1777, serious efforts were made to depose Hastings but the Supreme Court intervened on his behalf.

In 1777 Hastings married again; his first wife, a sailor's widow, had died in 1761 and in 1769, on the ship sailing from England to India, Hastings had met the Baron and Baroness Imhof. The Baroness was suffering from Baronial neglect and she eventually divorced him and married Hastings on August 8, 1777. Mrs Hastings lived on until 1837 and was buried beside Warren in Daylesford Church, as was her son, General, Sir Charles Imhof, who died in 1853.

At home his behaviour was the subject of a Parliamentary enquiry and, after an investigation, he was impeached at the bar of the House of Lords and his trial, on charges of corruption whilst Governor General, began in Westminster Hall on February 13, 1788. It ended with his acquittal, seven *years* later, on April 23, 1795! He had proved that he was innocent of all charges against him, but his defence had cost him his entire savings of £80,000. The East India Company behaved generously and Hastings retired to Daylesford in Worcestershire. In May 1814 the 82-year old Hastings was given further and final proof of his integrity by being made a Privy Councillor. Old age was showing, but he kept going until April 1818. In July 1818 he was very unwell: he was 'cupped' but there was little else that could be done. He was no longer able to swallow and so really starved to death.

HATCHARD	1769
John	Clapham, June 21, 1849
Bookseller	

173, Piccadilly, W1, 1797-1801
190, Piccadilly, W1, 1801-1810

Fourteen-year old John Hatchard was apprenticed to a printer called Bensley, whose premises were just off the Strand. When he had formally finished his training there, in October 1789, he joined a Mr. Payne of Castle Street. The National Gallery now covers the area today.

Married by now, Hatchard took a shop at 173, Piccadilly at a rent of £40 per annum and paid £31.00 for the 'goodwill'. From the very start he prospered and soon moved along Piccadilly to better premises at 190, in which the firm still operates and enjoys the privilege of being the Queen's bookseller.

| **HATTON GARDEN EC1** | *Metropolitan and Circle lines to Farringdon* |

Named after Sir Christopher Hatton (1540-1591), once Chancellor and also once the *blue-eyed-boy* of Queen Elizabeth I. Her Majesty lent him the money to develop some 14 acres (5.6 hectares) around ELY PLACE, where Hatton died, and the street names in the area today still reflect the existence of a rich man's Manor House and the cultivation which was part and parcel of such an establishment; Vine Street, Plum Tree Court, Saffron Hill and even perhaps, Cowcross Street!

5,   Giuseppe MAZZINI. A plaque on the building (once) read, 'In this house Giuseppe Mazzini, the apostle of modern Democracy, inspired Young Italy with the idea of unity, independence and regeneration of his Country.' Below the inscription, in *bas-relief* were two clasped hands.

13,   Mary ROBINSON, 'Perdita', in 1775.

HAWKINS

(Sir) Anthony Hope   London, February 9, 1863
('Anthony Hope')   July 8, 1933
Author

41, Bedford Square, WC1 (LCP 1976) 1903-1917
14, Gower Street, WC1, 1921-1925

Hawkins' father, a clergyman, was the first boy to be entered for Marlborough School in 1843 and, in due course, he sent his son there (in 1876). On leaving school, young Hawkins took up the Law and was called to the Bar in 1887. He did not really care for his profession but he practised until November 1893.

On November 28th, 1893 he was walking back home to St Bride's Vicarage, when the idea of 'Ruritania' came to him. The following morning he wrote the first chapter of *The Prisoner of Zenda* in rough and the first draft of the whole book was finished on December 29! The *Prisoner* was published in 1894 and four years later its sequel, *Rupert of Hentzan* once again took the bookstalls by storm.

Hawkins/Hope wrote and had published five more novels and also produced a book of reminiscences in 1927 called *Memories and Notes*. He visited America frequently and, in 1903, he married Elizabeth Sheldon, a New York girl, daughter of Charles H. Sheldon of that city.

In 1918 he was knighted (really for no *particular* reason) and in the middle 1920's he moved out of London to live in Surrey – in Tadworth, where he became rather a *squirearchical* figure. His books, especially the *Ruritanian* pair, sold well, but at his death, he only left £29,000.

HAWTHORNE

Nathaniel   Salem, Mass., July 4, 1804
Author   Plymouth, New Hants., May 18, 1864
                                      Concord, Mass.

24, George Street, W1, 1855
24, Great Russell Street, WC1, 1857-1858

Son of a sea captain, who died when he was only four, Nathaniel lived a solitary life and, being slightly lame, found it hard to compete with his fellows. He was an avid reader as a result. His formal education was completed at Bowdoin College (where one of his contemporaries was Longfellow, even though Hawthorne was three years his senior). He began working for the Customs service but he did not find the work congenial and turned his attention to literature. His first novel, *Fanshawe* was published anonymously in 1828.

In 1841 he joined a Socialist community started by the Transcendental Club at Brook Farm, but left it, disillusioned before a year had passed. In 1842 he married Sophia Peabody and they set up house (once lived in by EMERSON) in Concord. In this one-time manse, Hawthorne began to write seriously. *Mosses from an Old Manse* appeared in 1846 and then four years later, his greatest book, *The Scarlet Letter*. Rather strangely he was offered the post of American Consul in Liverpool: equally strangely, he accepted. The offer probably came to him through the influence of his friend Franklin Pierce, who was the 14th President of the United States. Whatever the reason, Hawthorne was Consul in Liverpool from 1853-1857, then came to live for a year in London.

HAY, Ian see BEITH, J.H.

HAYDN   Rohrau, Lower Austria, March 31,
Joseph   1732
Composer   Vienna, May 31, 1809
                  Bergkirche, Eisenstadt (finally)

45, High Holborn, WC1, in 1791, for a few days
18, Great Pulteney Street, W1, January 1791 – June 1792
1, Bury Street, W1, February 1794 – August 1795

Outside London, Haydn travelled in England quite extensively. He particularly liked Oxford; and Oxford him. The University made him a Doctor of Music. He wrote Symphony in G, number 92, which was performed when he was in Oxford to receive his degree. Since then it has always been known as the *Oxford Symphony*.

Haydn's father was a wheelwright and his mother, a cook; both were musically inclined. Haydn was a choir boy in the Cathedral in Vienna, until his voice 'broke' and he then earned a few pfennigs teaching music. In 1761 his luck began to turn and he became the *Maestro di Capella* of the extremely rich, Prince Esterhazy (1714-1790) and stayed in that position, nominally, for the rest of the Prince's life. Under this patronage Haydn began to compose music (and took the opportunity to hunt and fish on the Prince's estates).

Johann Peter Salomon, born in Bonn in 1745; a violinist and concert organizer who had settled in London in 1781, arranged that Haydn should come to England to give a series of concerts and MOZART (24 years younger than Haydn) should follow on after him. Alas, poor MOZART was dead by that December. 1791 was a critical year for Haydn. He travelled to London and gave six of his *Twelve Grand Symphonies*. These were Breitkopf numbers 93-104 (of Breitkopf and Hartel, an important music publishing house in Leipzig, established in 1542). His Symphony No 7 in D is often called his *London* though there seems to be no real reason for calling it so. He came again to London in 1794 and Salomon guaranteed him £1,550 for 12 concerts.

A year before his death a group of eminent musicians gave Haydn a 76th birthday present in Vienna. At a special concert a performance of his *Creation* (1798) was given. Beethoven, who was then 38 and had studied under Haydn but fallen out with him over his C Minor Piano Trio, knelt and kissed Haydn's hand.

In all Haydn composed 116 symphonies, 83 violin quartets, 60 piano sonatas, 15 masses, 4 oratorios, 14 operas, 42 duets and more than 200 concerti and *divertissements*. Beautiful as his music was, Haydn, physically, was anything but. Short – even for his age, today he would be thought hardly more than a dwarf – he had stubby legs, a face deeply pitted by small pox and, later in life, he became very self-conscious about a tissue growth (probably some sort of *polypus*) which grew out from the end of his already long, aquiline nose.

HAYDON
Benjamin Robert
Artist

Plymouth, January 26, 1786
London, June 22, 1846
St Mary's Churchyard, Paddington
(but, as a suicide, just out of hallowed
ground)

342, The Strand, WC1, 1804
3, Broad Street, Carnaby Market, Marlborough Street, W1, 1805
41, Great Marlborough Street, W1, 1808-1817
116 (formerly 22) Lisson Grove, NW8 (LCP 1959) 1817-1822

Haydon was not altogether a 'satisfactory' painter. He set out with perhaps too much 'message' and not enough 'technique'. He tried to 'redeem English painting by producing historical and religious works rather in the *Grand Manner* preached at one time by REYNOLDS. His name became firmly linked with the Romantic Movement and both WORDSWORTH and KEATS were his friends. Wordsworth once wrote a sonnet to him. T.B. MACAULAY wrote that Haydon was like, 'The vulgar idea of a man of genius. He had all the morbid peculiarities which are supposed by fools to belong to intellectual superiority – eccentricity, jealousy, caprice, infinite disdain for other men; and yet he was as poor and commonplace a creature as any in the world'.

And not only that, he was chronically in debt and spent many hours dodging baillifs. Friends helped him financially, even Sir Robert PEEL and Sir Walter Scott sent him money. Despite this generosity it all became too much for him and he killed himself. Like many suicides, it was the act of a coward, as he left a penniless wife with their small children to support and over £3,000 worth of debts. He left all his papers to Elizabeth Barrett BROWNING.

HAZLITT
William
Essayist

Maidstone, April 10, 1778
London, September 18, 1830
St Anne's Churchyard, Soho

288, High Holborn, WC1, 1788
139, Long Acre, WC2
12, Rathbone Place, W1, 1799-1803
109, Great Russell Street, WC1, 1804-1807
34, Southampton Buildings, WC2, 1807-1811
19, Petty France, SW1, 1811-1819
9, Southampton Buildings, WC2, 1820-1824
40, Half Moon Street, W1, 1828
6, Frith Street, W1, where he died

Hazlitt's father, a Unitarian Minister, took his family to America in 1783, returning to England two years later and became a pastor at Wem in Shropshire, where William started school. In 1793 he began to study at the Unitarian College in Hackney. To his father's annoyance he did not want to enter the ministry and chose to study drawing, going to do so in Paris in 1802. He painted a number of portraits but gave up Art and in 1803 was back in London as a 'literary adventurer'.

He was, by nature, quarrelsome and COLERIDGE thought him '...singularly repulsive – brow hanging, shoe contemplative, strange'. He got to know dear little Charles LAMB. Mary Lamb had a friend called Sarah Stoddart who Hazlitt married in 1808 and took off to Wiltshire. They were back in London by 1811 and lived in the same house as MILTON once lived. The marriage failed and they were divorced in 1822 and he remarried in 1824. His second wife was a widow, a Mrs. Bridgewater, who had £300 a year of her own. (No one seems to know, however, what her maiden name was.) They went to Italy where the second Mrs. Hazlitt left her new husband. Perhaps she found out about Sara Walker, a tailor's daughter from

Bristol. Sara lived in the same lodgings as Hazlitt in Southampton Buildings. It was an unrequited affair and the only lasting effect was that the whole, sad, little episode inspired him to write *Libor Amoris*.

Hazlitt wrote a life of Napoleon – a four-volume work and hardly, in the 1820s, one would have thought, a popular subject with English readers. (In any case the publishers went bankrupt, owing Hazlitt £500.)

According to his grandson, Hazlitt's last words were, 'Well, I've had a happy life…'. One would hardly have thought so.

HEATH
Edward Richard George
Prime Minister

Broadstairs, Kent, July 9, 1916

F2, Albany, Piccadilly, W1, 1965

Heath was a scholar at Balliol College, Oxford, just before the Second World War and came into politics after it, in 1950. His 'intake' was part of a new look for the Conservative party. R.A. Butler began the change from fuddy-duddy, died-in-the-wool Tories with his recruitment of youngish intellectuals from a much broader – and 'lower' – social base with his 'One Nation' style of members in Parliament.

Heath was appointed Chief Whip in 1955 and in 1960 became Lord Privy Seal and chief negotiator for Britain's entry into the Common Market. He was not really successful because of DE GAULLE's *implacable* resistance to British membership. The Germans, however, gave him the 'Charlemagne Prize' for having a good try.

July 1965 found him heading the Party and in 1970 he came to power as Prime Minister at the head of a jubilant administration.

He is a musician and has been invited to conduct first class orchestras more than once; he is an author and an owner of a succession of expensive yachts, all called *Morning Cloud*. *Morning Cloud V* was up for sale in 1981 for about £100,000. It eventually was bought by a Manhattan banker, Larry Huntington (who renamed it *Denali*) for about £50,000 in 1984.

HEINE
Heinrich
Poet

Dusseldorf, December 13, 1797
Paris, February 17, 1856
Montmartre, Paris

32, Craven Street, WC1 (LCP 1912) 1827

Heine, of Jewish antecedents, was born Chaim Harry Heine and all his life he had a sort of love/hate relationship with Germany, its institutions and the people. He was 29 when his work *Die Harzreise* (Trip in the Harz Mountains) was published with some success.

In October 1834 he met and fell in love with Eugénie Mirat, a Parisienne, who was a shoe-shop saleswoman. His infatuation with Eugénie was overwhelming and, despite all well-meaning advice to talk him out of it, he married Eugénie in 1841 and she outlived him by 27 years.

About four years after his strange marriage he began to suffer from an increasingly debilitating spinal infection. It kept him bedbound for the rest of his life. He used to refer to his sickbed, gloomily, as his 'mattress grave'.

HEINEMANN
William
Publisher

Surbiton, Surrey, May 18, 1863
London, October 5, 1920

33, Lower Belgrave Street, SW1
19, Cavendish Square, W1

Heinemann founded his publishing house in 1890 and it was not long before the business was profitable and expanding. He had a good list of authors, which included: R.L. Stevenson, KIPLING, H.G. WELLS, GALSWORTHY, MAUGHAM and J.B. PRIESTLEY.

One of Heinemann's first publications was WHISTLER's *Gentle Art of Making Enemies* (a subject in which WHISTLER could easily claim to be an expert) and it became one of his best-sellers. In addition to a good string of British authors, Heinemann brought Ibsen, Maeterlink and Tolstoy's work to England.

HENRIETTA STREET, WC2   *Northern line to Leicester Square*

The street was named after Henrietta Maria, the French wife of King Charles I. She was daughter of Henry IV of France, born 1609, married Charles in 1625, was widowed in 1649 and died, near Paris, on September 10, 1669. Laid out in 1631, it was originally intended that it should be an 'up-market' shopping street. At one time there were five public houses in it.

19, Ugo FOSCOLO, 1827. Here, mortally ill, he was moved into an apartment, which was clean, airy and had plenty of fresh water.

HEREFORD ROAD, W2   *Central line to Queensway*

The Ladbroke family (of Ladbroke Grove) leased some of their land to a W.H. Jenkins, whose son, a lawyer, William Kinnaird Jenkins, set about developing it. He owned land in the County of *Hereford* (on the English/Welsh border) and the 'Welsh connexion' crops up a number of times in this area (for example; *Denbigh, Newton, Garway, Ledbury, Bridstow, Chepstow* and *Monmouth*).

71, Guglielmo MARCONI (LCP 1954) 1896-1897. A Patent, dated July 2, 1892 (number 12,039) opens thus: 'I, Guglielmo Marconi of 71, Hereford Road, Bayswater, in the County of Middlesex, do hereby declare the nature of this invention to be as follows: According to this invention electrical actions or manifestations are transmitted through the air, earth or water by means of electric oscillations of high frequency.' So, here radio began.

HERSCHEL
(Sir) John Frederick William   Slough, Berks., March 7, 1792
Astronomer   Hawkhurst, Kent, May 11, 1871
     Westminster Abbey (north aisle near NEWTON)

56, Devonshire Street, W1, 1824-1827

John (the son of Sir Frederick, who had begun life as an oboeist in the Hanoverian Guards band, and who, later, discovered the planet Uranus) was sent to Eton and then up to St John's College, Cambridge where, in 1813, he was the Senior *Wrangler*.

He followed in his father's final footsteps and, in 1848, was President of the Royal Astronomical Society. He discovered over 500 nebulae and really pioneered celestial photography. The first Observatory was established by Herschel at the Cape of Good Hope. Between 1834 and 1838 an up-to-date record of the Southern Skies was accurately prepared.

HERTFORD STREET, W1   *Piccadilly line to Hyde Park Corner*

Charles Seymour, Lord Hertford, 6th Duke of Somerset (1662-1748) nicknamed 'the Proud', lent his name to a tavern here in 1744 and the street is named after the Hertford Tavern. It was built up by 1764 and in 1791 there were 38 houses in the Street, with rents ranging from £30 to £250 a year and 'rates' on each house from £5 to £51.

10, Angelica KAUFFMAN, 1766. She came to London from Switzerland for the first time in this year.

10, General Sir Richard BURGOYNE (LCP 1954) from 1771 until he died here in 1792.

10, Richard Brinsley SHERIDAN (LCP 1955) 1795-102.

14, Edward JENNER for three years after 1803 until the cost of living in an unnecessarily fashionable street forced him to move.

20, Sir George CAYLEY (LCP 1962) 1840-1848. The façade of the house is late 19th century, but much of the interior is as it was in Cayley's day.

26, Robert JENKINSON, 2nd Lord Liverpool, 1818. For the previous three years he had worked hard to help rehabilitate France after the Napoleonic Wars.

31, John Lothrop MOTLEY, 1859. His book *Rise of the Dutch Republic* published in 1856, was still in 'the best-sellers' list.

36, Edward Bulwer LYTTON, 1831-1834. In 1831, he became MP for St Ives and wrote most of *The Last Days of Pompei* while here.

41, Sir Max PEMBERTON 1929. He had just been given his knighthood when he moved here.

47, Sydney SMITH, 1824. This was the fifth of *twelve* homes which Smith had in London at one time or another.

HERZEN (or Hertzen)	Moscow, March 27, 1812
Alexander Ivanovich	Paris, January 21, 1870
Political theorist	

1, Orsett Terrace, W2 (LCP 1970) 1860-1863

Imprisoned at the age of 22, in his native Russia (for his revolutionary and socialist beliefs) Herzen managed to escape to Paris in 1847 and he had settled in London by 1851.

As ever, the British suffered one more political exile whose gratitude took the form of finding fault with his 'adoptive country' and he established the *Free Russian Press* in Regent Street and his review, *The Polar Star,* began to appear in 1855, followed by *The Bell,* which appeared every month for nearly ten years. (Some copies were even smuggled into Russia from time to time.)

Russian visitors came to visit Herzen at Orsett Terrace. Tolstoy and Bakunin in 1861 and Dostoyevsky the following year.

Herzen sometimes used the pseudonym 'Iskander' – the Turkish form of Alexander.

HICKS	St Helier, Jersey, 1871
(Sir) Seymour Edward	April 6, 1949
Actor, manager	

53, Bedford Square, WC1, 1901-1908

As a 16-year old, Hicks made his stage debut in Islington. From then on he never looked back and became one of the most popular stage comedians of the day. He also wrote a number of plays (*for* himself). The best remembered were *The Man in Dress Clothes* and *The Gay Gordons*. The latter was a musical which opened at the Aldwych in September 1907, the music was by Guy Jones. Hicks was knighted in 1935.

HIGH HOLBORN, WC1   *Piccadilly and Central lines*
to Holborn (Kingsway)

The *Hol-Burne* river flowed down the valley, now spanned by the Holborn
Viaduct, into the River Fleet. Its existence made a dramatic change (for the
good) for traffic problems in and out of the City. Queen Victoria 'opened' it
in 1869; its cost was over £2½ million.

23,   William MARSDEN lived here in 1816 as an apprentice to a surgeon
called Dale.
45,   Franz Joseph HAYDN, in January 1791. This was the house of his
publisher John Bland, who died in the same year.

HILL   London, 1838
Octavia   Westerham, August 13, 1912
Social Reformer

190, Marylebone Road, NW1, 1904–1912

Octavia and her elder sister, Miranda (1836–1910) were granddaughters of
Dr. Southwood Smith, a pioneer in sanitarian reform and their early
attention had been drawn to the housing conditions of those less fortunate
than themselves.
With the help of John RUSKIN, Octavia purchased the 56-year lease of
three houses in the very poorest part of the parish of Marylebone. These
houses were repaired and subdivided into apartments of two rooms each.
The Hills collected the rents themselves. This was very unusual. The poor
rarely, if ever, saw the owner of the slums in which they lived. If they were
lucky, they only saw his agent; if they were unlucky they saw the bailiff.
Her first three-house experiment was so successful she bought six more
houses and treated them similarly. These, too, proved that philanthropy
need not equal poverty and other landlords asked the Hills to act for them.
Notably the Church of England Commissioners who, after the Crown and
the railway companies, were Britain's largest landlords. Much of their
property was in poor sections and encouraged the very behaviour which the
Church condemned whilst they accepted the rent from them without query.
Octavia published *Homes of the London Poor* in 1875 and she was one of the
founders of the National Trust.

HILL   Kidderminster, Worcs., December 3,
(Sir) Rowland   1795
Postal pioneer   Hampstead, August 27, 1879
Highgate Cemetery (West VI)

1, Orme Square, W2 (LCP 1907) 1839–1844

For the first few years of his working life, Hill was a school teacher and his
disciplinary methods were widely acclaimed. He was also one of the
founders for the 'Diffusion of Useful Knowledge' in 1826. He was interested
in the schemes of the socialist, Robert Owen and he took a very active part
in the colonization of southern Australia.
In 1837 he published *Post-Office Reform* in which was recommended a low
and uniform postal rate, prepaid by stamps. On January 1, 1840 the 'penny
post' came into being. Fifteen years later, an investigation was made into
postal accounts and it was found that the 5th Duke of Grafton was still being
paid £4,700 by the Post Office. This sinecure dated back to King Charles II
who died in 1685!
The Liberal Government of 1846 made Hill the Secretary to the Postmaster
General and in 1854 Secretary to the Post Office. Hill established 'book post'
and the money-order system.
There is a granite statue to Hill, which cost £1,800, by Onslow Ford.

Originally erected in front of the Royal Exchange in 1882, today it stands, more appropriately, outside the main Post Office in King Edward Street, EC1.

HILL STREET, W1   *Piccadilly, Victoria and Jubilee line*
to Green Park

This street, together with Hay's Mews and Farm Street, all owe their names to the actual farm owned by Lord Berkeley in the 1690s. The ridge between Hyde Park and the (now submerged) River Tyburn was called 'Aychille' – the Tyburn was sometimes referred to as 'Ayebrook'. Hill Street began to be built up in the 1750s.

35, Lady ASTOR, widowed in September 1952, gave the great house Cliveden to her son Bill and moved in here.

38, was built in 1725 and was once the home of PITT, the 'Younger'. It is now the *Naval* Club. The Club, established in 1945 and so, *not* to be confused with the Naval *and* Military Club established in 1864 and now housed at 94 Piccadilly. There is a connection in historical sentiment between the two, however. The Naval and Military's premises were once the home of another Prime Minister; Lord PALMERSTON.

39, Thomas WYATT made alterations to this house for the 2nd Earl of Durham. Much later, Alec WAUGH had a three-roomed flat in this house (in 1935). They had a 'very modern architect' fit it up with '...concealed lighting, built in settees and tables.'

HINDE STREET, W1   *Central line to Bond Street*

Jacob HINDE married Heiress Anne Thayer, who had a dowry of £40,000 in 1775. Hinde had leased land in what is now Regent's Park and probably farmed it. Anne Hinde brought more land into the family and development of Hinde Street, Thayer Street and Jacob's Wells Mews began in 1775.

6, Herbert SPENCER, lodged here in 1862-1863.
20, Rose MACAULAY, from 1941 until her death in 1958.

HOBBES, J.O., see CRAIGIE, P.M.

HOGARTH   London, November 10, 1697
William   London, October 26, 1764
Artist   Chiswick Churchyard

12, Covent Garden, WC2, pre-1733.
30, Leicester Square, WC2, from 1733 until he died here. His widow retained the house until her death in 1789.
He also had a 'country house', now called 'Hogarth House'; today a Hogarth Museum, open to the public (P 1749-1764). It is on the main route to London Airport, on the left just after a traffic roundabout, as one *leaves* London.

His father, a school teacher, apprenticed young William to a silver engraver and not long after that he began to study painting under Sir James THORNHILL. Here he was to consolidate his position by eloping with THORNHILL's daughter in 1729. They were married 'privately' in Old Paddington Church. In the National Gallery there is a painting by Hogarth called *Sigismunde,* which shows the Old Church clearly.
He had begun to paint the sort of pictures for which he would find fame, in his early 30s. He was an acute observer of the social scene, a gift he developed splendidly in his eight narrative paintings called *The Rake's Progress* in 1734. (Today, open to all, free, these can be seen in the Soane

Museum at 13 and 14, Lincoln's Inn Fields.) Another *genre* set, *Marriage à la Mode,* was bought by a Mr. Lane of Hillingdon in Middlesex. He paid £126 for them. The six are now in the National Gallery.

By the time he was 54 years old (in 1751) some critics believe that he had passed his artistic prime. A little while before he had experimented with political cartooning – a popular pastime of the day – and his butts were usually PITT and WILKES, who he depicted as war-mongers. In June 1757 he became Serjeant Painter to King George II, succeeding his father-in-law, THORNHILL who had resigned the post. He was only paid £10 a year but 'certain perquisites' made the post worth over £200 a year.

There is a stone bust of Hogarth by Joseph Durham which was put up in Leicester Square in 1875. It may seem to be a little insignificant for so great an artist, but – as Hogarth was only five feet (1.52 metres) tall – a full length statue might appear a little odd!

HOGG	London, February 14, 1845
Quintin	London, January 17, 1903
Philanthropist	St Marylebone Cemetery

5, Cavendish Square, W1 (LCP 1965) 1885-1898
2, Cavendish Place, W1, 1903

Hogg was the son of a prosperous City business man, Sir James Weir Hogg (1790-1876) a director of the East India Company. As a young man he travelled widely in America and in the East and West Indies. He was a fine sportsman and, amongst other achievements, captained the Old Etonian Football Club for seven years, during which time they were *never* beaten.

His lasting fame can be seen at 309, Regent Street, W1 – he founded the Polytechnic Institute and he actually died *in* it – of 'accidental suffocation'. His son, Douglas McGarel Hogg (1872-1950) a politician, was created Viscount Hailsham in 1929. On January 3, 1929 Hailsham, then 57, married 35-year old Mrs. Mildred Laurence. The marriage ceremony was performed by the Dean of Westminster in the Abbey. His 21-year old son, Quintin, was 'best man'.

In Langham Place – at its southern end – is a statue to the first Quintin Hogg, seated with a boy on each side of him. The statue by George Frampton was erected in 1906. The inscriptions on the pedestal were added at a later date.

HOLLAND	London, November 3, 1886
Vyvyan Beresford	London, October 10, 1967
'Literary bon-viveur'	41, Carlyle Square, SW3, 1929

5C, The Boltons, SW10, where he died

Oscar WILDE had two sons; the elder boy, Cyril, was killed fighting in the First World War. The younger son was christened 'Vyvyan' but his name was often spelt 'Vivian'. After Wilde's disgrace in 1895 Constance Wilde (1857-1898) took the boys abroad. They all adopted the surname of Holland, which was the middle name of her older brother, Otho Holland Lloyd (1856-1943).

Vyvyan's childhood was troubled and often unhappy. (He recorded it faithfully and touchingly in his book, *Son of Oscar Wilde.*) As an adult he became an expert on food and wine. On August 29, 1939 he attended a revival of his father's superb comedy *The Importance of Being Earnest.* It was at the Comedy Theatre and starred John Gielgud, Margaret Rutherford and Edith EVANS. After the performance, Holland was reported as saying; 'I really found it most amusing. I feel quite proud of the old boy'.

HOLLAND PARK

Probably only the Grosvenor family (the Dukes of Westminster) has 'christened' more London streets than the families originally connected with Holland House.

Briefly: the Lord of the Manor, Sir Walter Cope, built Cope Castle in 1605. This 'Castle' eventually became Holland House. Cope's wife was Dorothy Grenville, whose forbears had owned Kensington during the reign of King Henry VIII (1509-1547). The Copes had one child, Isabel, who was to marry Henry Rich, Earl of Holland. Their son Robert, later Earl of Warwick, had two surviving children; Lord Edward, whose widow was to marry (so unwisely) Joseph ADDISON and Lady Elizabeth, who married into the Welsh family of Edwardes. They were descendants of the Lords of Radnor, who had settled in the county of Pembroke, in the west of Wales. Villages in the area are remembered in Kensington, in street names: Marloes, Nevern, Pennant, Penywern, Philbeach, Templeton, Trebovir and the like.

Lady Elizabeth's son sold Holland House to Henry Fox, the first Lord Holland (1705-1774) and then the 'tribes' split up. One lot, the Edwardes, were created Barons of Kensington and the Foxes of Holland House, the Hollands. When the 4th Lord Holland died in 1849, his property passed to a cousin called Henry Fox Strangeways, who was also Lord Ilchester and Baron of Woodford! He owned land at Abbotsbury and Melbury in Dorset – and their names creep onto the Kensington maps. His descendants sold Holland House to the (then) London County Council in 1951, the building itself having been grievously damaged by German bombs. (Kensington suffered quite badly between 1940 and 1945 from enemy action. 33,340 houses were hit by bombs, 4,000 of them being completely destroyed. Mercifully, despite high material damage, only some 400 civilians were killed.)

HOLLAND PARK ROAD, W14   *Central line to Holland Park*

12, 'Leighton House' – Frderick, Lord LEIGHTON (LCP 1958) from 1866 until he died here in 1896. This (internally) exotic house was built for Leighton by George Aitchison. It is now open to the public (Monday to Saturday, 11-5) and well worth a visit, especially anyone interested in Arabic and Moorish design.

24, Thomas GUTHRIE ('F. Anstey') lived here from 1921 until he died here in 1934.

HOLLAND STREET, W8   *District and Circle lines*
                              to High Street Kensington

This street, named after the Hollands of Holland House, came into being around 1801 and was originally called Parson's Yard.

13, Walter CRANE (LCP 1952) 1892-1915. After much searching the Cranes happened to walk past this house and noted its 18th century brick front. Inside, they were to find, '...instead of the usual squeezy passage, a square hall with a fireplace in it.' The back garden ran down towards St Mary Abbot's Church. At their meals, Crane, his wife and their three children all sat, '...on one side of a long table like people in early Italian paintings...every available place' [in the house] 'was filled with china, pewter and brass, Indian idols, carved figures, plaster casts'.

36, Sir Philip GIBBS, c.1908. The house was built about 1830. In his day a tailor called Colton lived opposite.

37, Marguerite Radclyffe-Hall, 1929. She lived here with her lover, Una (Lady Troubridge, 1887-1963). Una married Admiral, Sir Ernest Troubridge in November 1907 but in 1915 she met Radclyffe-Hall and they became lesbian lovers. She died of cancer in Rome and left some £100,000 to the 'Poor Clares'.

HOLLES STREET, W1 *Central, Bakerloo and Victoria lines to Oxford Circus*

Named after Edward Harley's father-in-law, John Holles, Duke of Newcastle. He had bought the Manor of Marylebone in 1710 and through his daughter, Henrietta, it passed by marriage to the Harley estate.

3,   Anthony TROLLOPE, 1872-1873. *The Eustace Diamonds* one of his political, rather than clerical novels, was published while he lived here.

11,   Mary Ann CLARKE, 1808. Two years later her book of memoirs, which she must have started to write here, appeared and she had to spend nine months in gaol for the libels her book was said to contain.

16,   Lord BYRON was born here in 1788. The site was swallowed up by part of the John Lewis store. He was christened at the nearby Church of St Marylebone. Later he lived at number 24.

HOLLIS December 2, 1905
(Sir) Roger Henry October 26, 1973
Quondam Head of British Secret Service

6, Campden Hill Square, W8, 1950s-1960s

Hollis was educated at Clifton College and went up to Worcester College, Oxford but came down without a degree. He worked first for the British American Tobacco Company in Shanghai, returning to Europe in 1936 to be treated for tuberculosis. Three years later he joined MI5 and became Director General of it in 1956, retiring from Government Service altogether (having been knighted in 1960) in 1965.

That should have been the end of the story but in March 1980, suggestions were made in the Press that for most of his career he was actually an agent for the Russians! The evidence offered seemed quite convincing but there was no proof or sign that Hollis was a traitor.

Sir Harold Acton recorded in his memoirs that when he met Sir Roger, Hollis impressed him as being 'somewhat drunken'.

HOME Edinburgh, June 3, 1912
William Douglas
Playwright

35, South Eaton Place, SW1, 1937-1939

Though the full and younger brother of Sir Alec DOUGLAS-HOME (alias Lord Home of the Hirsel) William prefers to be known as W.D. Home. Like brother Alec, he was sent to Eton and went to Oxford (New College) where he got his BA and then went on to the Royal Academy of Dramatic Art. He is one of the minority of playwrights who has acted professionally.

Politically 'Independent' he has contested two seats in England and two in Scotland and, predictably, been beaten four times. His fame rests on his plays. His greatest successes are probably: *The Chiltern Hundreds* (with Cecil Parker and that loveable old rogue, A.E. Matthews in the roles of butler and crusty employer), *The Reluctant Debutante* and *Lloyd George Knew My Father*. On October 25, 1944, Home, then a Captain, was sentenced to be cashiered and imprisoned for a year, for failing to obey an order during the Normandy landings in June 1944. As a result of his prison spell, Home wrote *Now Barrabbas,* which opened at the Boltons Theatre on February 13, 1947.

HOOD   London, May 23, 1799
Thomas   Finchley, London, May 3, 1845
Poet   Kensal Green; Square 74, Row 1

31, Poultry, EC2 (P) here born
1-2, Robert Street, WC2

Though born a Londoner, Hood's father was a Scottish bookseller. When he was only 13, Thomas began work in a counting house but soon showed signs of tuberculosis and was despatched to Dundee in Scotland. When that danger seemed over he came back to London and worked with his uncle who was an engraver.
In 1821 he became a sub-editor on the *London Magazine* and it was here he met DE QUINCEY, LAMB and HAZLITT. Four years later he published *Odes and Addresses to Great People* and followed that up in 1826 with *Whims and Oddities*. In 1829 he began the *Comic Annual* and this lasted for nine years. Then in *The Gem* he published his great poem, *Eugene Aram*.
Not long after his publisher went bankrupt and Hood's earlier tubercular troubles returned. For a while he lived abroad, hoping for better health and a lower cost of living. In 1840 his friends raised sufficient funds for him to be able to afford a return to London but his health was irreparably impaired. Despite what was to be a crippling illness he seemed to work as hard as ever and in 1843 his best remembered poem, *The Song of the Shirt,* appeared (anonymously) in *Punch.*

HOOK   London, September 22, 1788
Theodore Edward   London, August 24, 1841
Author   All Saints, Fulham High Street

3, Charlotte Street, W1, here born
5, Cleveland Row, W1, c.1825

Hook was the son of an organist who was 'resident musician' at both Marylebone and Vauxhall Gardens. Despite the relatively low social position Hook senior occupied, Theodore went to school at Harrow. A precocious boy, he had written 13 comic melodramas by the time he was 18 and was a witty conversationalist.
In 1812, for no apparent reason, he was appointed Accountant General for Mauritius. Hook stayed here for five years and then 'irregularities' in his book-keeping (or as Hook described it: 'disorder of the chest') was suspected. He was sent back to England, prosecuted (the sum involved being £12,000) and sent to prison. Later the speculation itself was shown to be the work of one of Hook's staff and he was freed, but still found guilty of gross mismanagement.
He became editor of *John Bull* – a high-Tory journal and also edited the *New Monthly Magazine.* He published a number of novels, the first being, *Sayings and Doings* in 1826; the last, *Gurney Married,* in 1838. His combined incomes were substantial, for the day, but Hook was a hopelessly bad money manager and, broken in health, he died penniless in Fulham before he was 53.

HOOVER   West Branch, Iowa, August 10, 1874
Herbert Clark   New York, October 20, 1964
31st United States President   West Branch, Iowa

39, Hyde Park Gate, SW7, 1902-1918

Hoover's father, Jesse, was a blacksmith and was of Swiss-German stock. Herbert was the second of three children who had the intelligence to graduate from Stanford University, California, with an AB in 1895. Before he died, 69 years later, he was to be awarded 85 honorary degrees from

around the world. He was the first United States President (1929-1933) to
have been born west of the Mississippi. He was an orphan before he was
eight and was brought up by uncles. His first job was as a gold miner; paid
two dollars per ten–hour night shift, seven days a week. He travelled to
China in 1899 – having been working for a British firm, Bewick Moreing in
Australia. He travelled to Tientsin via California, getting married to a
banker's daughter, Lou Henry (1874-1944) on the way. The Hoovers were
involved in the siege of Tientsin in the Boxer Rebellion in 1900.
The first ballot in 1928 made him Republican candidate for the Presidency
and he was in the White House the following year. Just in time for the Wall
Street Crash, followed by the worsening of the Depression in 1931. His
Presidency became linked with hard times for the country and, in 1933,
Franklin Roosevelt and his 'New Deal' swept into power. (From 1933 to
1953, Hoover was the only living ex-American President.)

HOPE, A. see HOPKINS, A.H.

HOPPNER Whitechapel, London, April 4, 1758
John London, January 23, 1810
Painter St James's Chapel, Hampstead Road

18, Charles Street, W1, from 1784 until he died here

Hoppner was trained as a chorister in the Chapel Royal and was later granted
an allowance by George III to study art at the Royal Academy Schools. This
gave rise to the rumour that the King sired Hoppner. It is unlikely but the
story has never been officially denied.
In 1789 he was appointed as Portrait Painter to HRH the Prince of Wales
('Prinny'). Certainly he was very much in the social swim as a result of this
appointment and in 1795 he was elected to the Academy.

HORNTON STREET, W8 *District and Circle lines*
to High Street Kensington
Some doubt about its origin but probably named after the builder of part of
it.
56, Sir Charles STANFORD (LCP 1961) 1894-1916. His long running
operatic success was being played in the West End whilst he lived here.
Who today, however, remembers *Shamus O'Brien*?

HORSLEY Kensington, London, April 14, 1857
(Sir) Victor Alexander Haden Mesopotamia, July 16, 1916
Physician Mesopotamia

101, Charlotte Street, W1, 1882-1891
25, Cavendish Square, W1, 1891
33, Seymour Street, W1, 1892-1900
80, Park Street, W1, 1900

Horsley qualified as a doctor in 1880 when LISTER's teaching regarding
antisepsis was only just beginning to take root; but, by the time he died only
36 years later, Horsley was almost regarded as the founding father of brain
surgery. The first operation carried out by Horsley was on May 25, 1886. A
22-year-old Scotsman had been injured in a street accident as a boy. His skull
was fractured and he was a victim of continuous fits. In the first two weeks
as a patient in the National Hospital, where the operation was carried out, he
had 2,870 seizures. Horsley's diagnosis was, 'a scar involving the hinder end
of the superior frontal sulcus'. He removed the scar to the depth of 0.787
inches (two centimetres) the patient's mental state improved and the seizures
(or fits) stopped. On June 9 of the following year Horsley carried out

(successfully) the first operation in England, to remove a tumour from the spinal cord. The patient, a Captain Gilbey, a regular soldier, had suffered agonizing pain for three years.

In other fields, sociologically important, he was also ahead of his time. He fought for LLOYD-GEORGE's National Insurance Scheme and he advocated sex education in the schools to try and combat the scourge of venereal disease.

HOUSMAN   Bromsgrove, Worcs., July 18, 1865
Lawrence   February 20, 1959
Author, playwright

77, York Mansions, Prince of Wales Drive, SW11, 1900

Lawrence was the younger brother of A.E. Housman (of *Shropshire Lad* fame) and went to school in Bromsgrove, coming south to London in about 1882 to study art in South Kensington. He actually began as an illustrator; then added poetry, illustrated by himself. The first such volume was *Green Arras* published in 1895.

Ten years later he blossomed into drama and *Little Plays of St Francis,* which was made up of a number of episodes in the life of the saint of Assisi. His best remembered work of all, is the play *Victoria Regina,* which opened in London in 1937, the hundredth anniversary of the accession of Queen Victoria. This was followed up in 1945 by *Happy and Glorious,* dealing with Victoria's 60 years on the throne. ('Send her victorious/Happy and Glorious/Long to reign over us/God save the Queen', being the last lines of the first verse of the *British National Anthem.*)

When he was 71, he published his autobiography which he called *The Unexpected Years.* An unusual number of unexpected years were to be his, as he did not die until he was 93.

HOWARD   Hackney, September 2, 1726
John   Kherson, Russia, January 20, 1790
Prison Reformer   Dophinorka, Russia

23, Great Ormond Street, WC1 (LCP 1908) 1777-1789

John's father was a well-to-do upholsterer who died when his son was not very old, but was able to leave him sufficient money for the boy to travel extensively, visiting, for instance, Lisbon not long after the great earthquake there in 1756. On his way home, the ship in which he was travelling was captured by a French privateer and he was thrown into a prison in Brest. This taste of two different sorts of confinement made him think deeply about prison reform in general.

Eventually released, he came back to England, married for the second time (his first wife, very much older than he, having died before he had set off for Lisbon) and settled at Cardington in Bedfordshire, of which county he was appointed Sheriff in 1773. Not long after he travelled at length in England to preach prison reform. As a result, two Acts were passed, one of which provided for fixed salaries for jailers and the other tried to establish reasonably hygenic standards for prisoners in gaols throughout Britain.

Still concerned with prison reform, in 1778 Howard set off for Holland (re-visiting the *Rasp Houses* there) and on through Europe. After returning to England in 1780 he finally went to Russia. He had, however, '...proceeded no farther than the Crimea, when a rapid illness, which he himself believed to be an infectious fever, caught in prescribing for a lady, put an end to his life...'

There is a medallion of Howard, it is said he refused to sit for a statue, over the door of Wormwood Scrubbs Prison in Du Cane Road, Hammersmith, one of London's largest prisons. Howard faces a medallion of Elizabeth Fry.

In St Pauls Cathedral there is a more than life size statue of Howard by John BACON, sculpted in 1795. This was the *first* effigy to be placed in the Cathedral since the re-building began in 1670.

HOWLAND STREET, W1
Northern and Victoria lines to Warren Street

Elizabeth Howland, the only daughter of John Howland of Streatham (a suburb of London, south of the Thames) married Wriothesley Russell, a son of Lord Russell, whose family own the land here. Wriothesley was made Baron Howland of Streatham on June 13, 1695.

25, Paul VERLAINE and his boy friend, Arthur RIMBAUD, 1872-1873.

HUGHES
Thomas
Author

Newbury, Berks, October 20, 1823
Brighton, March 22, 1896

41D, Park Street, W1, in the 1840s, afterwards at 113, 33 and finally, number 40 in the same street

After Rugby School Hughes went into law and eventually rose to be a County Court Judge. In 1857, he published a work of fiction called *Tom Brown's School Days*. The school is Rugby and often 'Tom Brown' *is* Thomas Hughes. Practically any one the least familiar with the English language has heard of – and often read – *Tom Brown's Schooldays* yet probably 90% who know the name of the book, would be hard put to it to name the author. Hughes published a sequel, *Tom Brown at Oxford* in 1861, but it is scarcely heard of at all today.

Hughes also wrote biographies of Alfred (the 'Great') Bishop Fraser and MacMillan, the publisher. With F.D. MAURICE he helped to found a working men's settlement for the Christian Science Movement in the Tennessee Mountains; it was called 'Rugby'.

HULTON
(Sir) Edward George Warris
Magazine proprietor

Harrogate, Yorks., November 29, 1906

51, Great Cumberland Place, W1, 1911-1919
50, Upper Brook Street, W1, 1919
42, Hyde Park Gate, SW7, 1953-1975
Flat 3, 22, St James's Square, SW1, 1975
215, Cromwell Road, W14, 1977
95, Peel Street, W8, 1983

Hulton's father (also Sir Edward) was the proprietor of the London *Evening Standard*. After Harrow he went on an Open Scholarship, to Brasenose College, Oxford (no mean feat in itself) was called to the Bar of the Inner Temple and practised on the South Eastern Circuit.

He became Chairman and Managing Director of Hulton Publications which once published the *Picture Post,* Britain's first (and last) topical illustrated weekly magazine.

HUMPHREYS
(Sir) Travers
Judge

1867
February 20, 1956

41, Norfolk Square, W2, 1869-1895

Humphreys was called to the Bar in 1889 and only six years later was one of Oscar WILDE's defence counsels in the case that finished the career of that flamboyant playwright.

He figured prominently in many a sensational trial after the Wilde case: the Seddons', Bottomley's and Sir Roger Casement's – the traitor who was found guilty of high treason and executed in 1916. In 1928 he was made a judge and one of his last (and perhaps most bizarre) cases was the trial of John George Haigh, the 'acid bath murderer' in 1949. He, too, was executed: he probably murdered six people in all and developed a taste for human blood – literally; he drank it!

HUMPHREYS
Travers Christmas
Buddhist Barrister

London, February 15, 1901
London, April 13, 1983

7, Royal Crescent, W2, here born
37, South Eaton Place, SW1, 1933-1942
58, Marlborough Place, NW8, here he died

As Senior Prosecutor for the Crown, Humphreys was a leading figure in many high powered trials, none more famous than his prosecution of Timothy Evans. Evans was found guilty (and hanged) in 1950 for the murder of his infant daughter. Subsequently he was (belatedly) officially pardoned! The scene of the crime was 10, Rillington Place (now Ruston Close, W11). It is almost certain that a fellow tenant in that evil house killed the child and also killed a number of women that he had 'picked up'. Humphreys came from legal stock and his unusual Christian name of 'Christmas' had nothing to do with Noël; it was a name in the family, sometimes he was irreverently called 'Xmas' but more sympathetically and widely, just 'Toby'. At school he was converted to Buddhism and in 1924 he founded the 'London Buddhist Lodge' and was president of it. Later, it became the 'Buddhist Society', Humphreys retaining the presidency of it – a position he held for 50 years. One of the books he wrote was entitled *Buddhism* and it sold over half a million copies.

Less well known; he was President of the Shakespearian Authorship Society which firmly avows that the Earl of Oxford wrote *all* the plays and the poems (*not* Bacon or the 'Man of Stratford'). He also wrote – and published – several volumes of poetry which are more creditable than most of the poetical works which part-time poets normally seem to produce. He married Aileen Irvine, a Yorkshire doctor's daughter in 1927 but they had no children. He left estate to the value of £299,560 and his Marlborough Place House to the Zen Trust.

HUNT
James Henry Leigh
Poet and Editor

Southgate, October 19, 1784
between Putney and Hammersmith whilst travelling home on August 28, 1859
Kensal Green, Square 121, Row 3

35, Great Portland Street, W1, 1812-1813
13, Lisson Grove, NW8, 1815
10, Upper Cheyne Row, SW3, 1818
22 (formerly 4) Upper Cheyne Row, SW3 (LCP 1905) 1833-1840
32, Edwardes Square, W8, 1840-1851

Hunt's brother John was a printer who founded a paper called *The Examiner*. For 13 years, James was its editor and the paper came to be regarded as the voice of Liberal (political) opinion. The Hunts were drawn into contact and friendship with such people as BYRON, MOORE, SHELLEY (at whose unofficial cremation in Italy, Hunt was present in July 1822) and lovely little Charles LAMB.

In 1813 Hunt referred to the Prince Regent ('Prinny') as a 'Fat Adonis of 50' and was prosecuted for libel. He was sent to prison for two years. (This was just one of three prosecutions for 'political offences', against the brothers Hunt.) On his release from prison in 1815 Hunt, his wife and their seven children went to Italy, but after Shelley's death they were more or less forced to accept Byron's hospitality in Pisa.

This was not a happy state and they came back to London in 1825. A contemporary of Hunt commented on his writings about London (after the publication of Hunt's *The Town,* which began to appear in April 1834) that '...Hunt had illumined the fog and smoke of London with a halo of glory and peopled the streets and buildings with the life of past generations'.

HUNT   London, April 2, 1827
William Holman   London, September 7, 1910
Artist   St Paul's Cathedral

59, Cheyne Walk, SW3
18, Melbury Road, W8, where he died

Holman Hunt has at times been confused with another artist called William *Henry* Hunt, who was 37 years older (and died when William *Holman* was 37). The other Hunt was a water colourist and a still-life exponent, specializing in flowers and fruit. He was nicknamed 'Bird's Nest Hunt' to distinguish him from his younger, but to become much more famous, namesake.

Hunt was one of the founders of the 'Pre-Raphaelite Brotherhood' of artists in 1848. His statement of the aims of the Brotherhood was to '...find genuine and serious ideas to express, direct study from nature in disregard of all arbitrary rules and to envisage events as they must have happened rather than in accordance with the *rules of design'*.

HUNTER   East Kilbride, Scotland, February 13,
John   1728
Physician   London, October 16, 1793
     (originally in St Martin-in-the-Fields,
     reinterred in Westminster Abbey in
     1859)

31, Golden Square, W1 (LCP 1907) 1763-1770
28, Leicester Square, WC2, c.1780-1793.

John began training with his elder brother, ten years older than he, and was, for a time, physician extraordinary to Queen Charlotte (Consort of King George III). In 1759 he had some sort of nervous breakdown, joined the Army as a Staff Surgeon and travelled in Portugal with the troops. (One might well think surgery in Army circles in 1760 would *cause* a nervous breakdown.) However, by 1763 he was back in London and three years later appointed surgeon extraordinary to the King.

In 1785 he began to build a medical museum, complete with lecture rooms. He was certainly a pioneering doctor as exampled by his experimentation on curing aneurysm (a dilation of an artery due to excessive blood pressure) by surgical means.

Always a quick-tempered man, Hunter was in St Georges Hall when something annoyed him and '...a spasmodic seizure took place, of which he died'.

Over the years he assembled a collection of medical specimens and oddities – he had more than 10,000 items at the time of his death. This fascinating museum was bought by the Government in 1795 and presented to the Royal College of Surgeons. Tragically the whole collection perished in 1941 in the London 'Blitz'.

There is a stone bust of Hunter by Thomas Woolner, dating from 1874, in

Leicester Square. A bronze bust by Sir Alfred Gilbert, made in 1893, is now in the St George's Medical School at Tooting, South London. The College of Surgeons paid for another bust of Hunter in Queen Elizabeth II's Jubilee Year of 1977. It was erected in the south west corner of Lincoln's Inn Fields (the College being in the south east corner of the Square) in 1979. It was made by Nigel Boonham, who used the death mask of the beardless Hunter and the REYNOLD's portrait of the Doctor, as models.

HUSKISSON	Worcestershire, March 11, 1770
William	Eccles, Lancs., September 15, 1830
Politician	Liverpool

28, St James's Place, SW1 (LCP 1962) 1804-1806

A capable politician but an unlikeable man whose way of leaving this life was more important than his living of it. He became the first man in the *world* to be killed by a railway train. He was President of the Board of Trade and was at the official opening of the Liverpool and Manchester Railway line and somehow fell under the engine (*The Dart*). He died later from his injuries.

There is a statue of Huskisson, in a most unlikely toga, opposite St George's Square, Pimlico in a little public garden by the Thames. It was sculpted by John Gibson and belonged originally to Huskisson's widow, but she gave it to Lloyds in 1848 where it stood in the Underwriting Room; presumably to remind them of the risks involved in insuring the lives of politicians while standing on stations. Lloyds (no doubt with relief) gave it to the London County Council and it was planted on the river bank in 1915.

HUTCHINSON	Selby, Yorks., July 23, 1828
(Sir) Jonathan	Haslemere, June 23, 1913
Surgeon and scientist	

15, Cavendish Squre, W1 (LCP 1981) 1874-1913
22, Chenies Street, WC1, 1913

One of Hutchinson's less enviable claims was that he had seen *over one million cases of syphilis* in his working life. However, if one uses simple mathematics then the claim is not only unenviable, but untrue. If, say, he had seen his first case of VD when he was 22, which leaves him 63 years before he hung up his stethoscope forever, he would have had to have seen 44 cases *every day*; 365 days a year, non-stop!

His name is perpetuated in a symptom of congenital syphilis. Some syphilitics have their permanent incisor teeth narrowed and notched by the infection. These are now known as 'Hutchinson's Teeth'. Such teeth combined with Keratitis – inflammation of the cornea – and middle ear disease, were referred to as 'Hutchinson's Triad'.

Hutchinson was President of the Royal College of Surgeons in 1889 and a member of the 1884 Royal Commission on Small Pox Hospitals. For all this he was awarded a knighthood in 1908.

HUXLEY	Godalming, Surrey, July 26, 1894
Aldous Leonard	California, November 22, 1963
Author	Compton Cemetery, Surrey

27, Westbourne Square, W2, 1909-1917
155, Westbourne Terrace, W2, 1921
144, Prince's Gardens, SW7, in the 1920s
4, Ennismore Gardens, SW7, 1961

Aldous, grandson of Thomas Henry HUXLEY (and brother of Sir Julian Huxley) was schooled at Eton, followed by Balliol College, Oxford. Here

HUXLEY   Ealing, London, May 4, 1825
Thomas Henry   Eastbourne, June 29, 1895
Biologist   Finchley Cemetery

41, North Bank, NW1, 1851
14, Waverley Place, NW8 (demolished 1855)
38 (formerly 4) Marlborough Place, NW8 (LCP 1910) 1872-1890

An insatiable reader, Thomas became a medical apprentice when he was only 13 and, in 1845, took a Medical Degree at Charing Cross Hospital. He was appointed surgeon aboard HMS *Rattlesnake* which had been commissioned to survey the Torres Strait. The passage, which separates Australia from Papua, discovered by Torres in 1606, is a dangerous 90 miles (144 kilometres) wide. Huxley kept in touch with the Linnaen Society during this *antipodean* journey and was made a member of the Royal Society when just 26.

He was recognized as a most eminent biologist and was President of the Royal Society in 1883. Huxley became an ardent supporter of Darwinian theories, not long after DARWIN's *Origin of Species* was published in 1859. Thus influenced, Huxley was to alter the teaching in schools throughout Britain and he sat on a number of Commissions which were looking at biological and scientific subjects then being taught in Britain's schools.

HYDE

An early 13th century manuscript refers to the land covered today by Hyde Park as 'HIDA' then part of the Manor of EBURY. One *hide* was a usual measurement of land then, being the amount of ground that could be tilled by one plough in one 'agricultural year'. Usually it worked out at about 120 acres. Excluding Kensington Gardens, Hyde Park today covers about 390 acres.

Henry VIII had it enclosed for his own private hunting and it remained private until James I opened it to the public.

HYDE PARK CORNER, W1   *Piccadilly line to Hyde Park Corner*

Apsley House (actually number 149, Piccadilly). The site was originally granted to Henry Bathurst, Baron Apsley (1714-1794) who was made Lord Chancellor by George III in 1784. It was bought back by the government in 1815 and presented to the Duke of WELLINGTON. In 1830 the Crown sold its interest in the property to the Duke for £9,350. Wellington lived here from 1816 until his death in 1852 and part of the house is still used privately by the family. The remainder is open to the public as a museum of 'Wellingtonia' (weekdays 10-6 and Sundays 3-6).

Apsley House was usually referred to as 'Number 1, London' as it was the first house a traveller would come to after passing the old turnpike gate on London's western boundary.

Facing the house is an equestrian statue of Wellington by Sir Joseph Boehm and this, together with the four soldiers at the corners of the pediment: a Grenadier, a Black Watch Highlander, a Welsh Fusilier and an Inniskilling Dragoon, was erected in 1888. The Duke is astride his great war horse, 'Copenhagen'. This beast was seven years old at Waterloo and lived on for another 21 years after that decisive battle. When he died in 1836, he was buried – with full military honours! – in the garden of Stratfield Saye, Wellington's country house, about eight miles south-west of Reading in Berkshire.

Students of horse flesh can also see 'Copenhagen' and his ducal owner outside the Royal Exchange and *inside* St Paul's. The Exchange statue was begun by CHANTREY, who died when he had hardly finished the preliminary models and the piece was finished by Henry Weekes. The Duke himself was present at the statue's unveiling in 1844. (Possibly he was not too pleased, as there are no stirrups, or saddle on the horse!)

HYDE PARK GATE, SW7
Circle and District lines to High Street, Kensington

Rather confusingly, Hyde Park Gate faces Kensington Gardens.

9, Lord BADEN-POWELL (LCP 1972) 1861-1876. Originally this house was numbered 1 and 2, being built around 1845 by J.F. Hansom. Baden-Powell's father – a clergyman – died in 1860 leaving his widow (who was his third wife) with ten children. She bought the property in 1860 for £6,200.

16, Charles DICKENS lodged here in 1862.

18, Sir Jacob Epstein (P) from 1929 until he died here in 1959.

22, Sir Leslie STEPHEN (LCP 1960) from 1879 until he died here in 1904. The house originally had five storeys. Two more ('...of atrocious design', according to Quentin BELL), were added for nurseries. There were eight children all told. One of these eight, Virginia WOOLF, described the 'master bedroom' on the first floor as '...the sexual centre of the house'. Not without just cause as four of those eight children were conceived in that bedroom; Vanessa, Thoby, Virginia and Adrian. Their mother, Julia, died, aged 48, in that same room.

28, Sir Winston CHURCHILL. He bought the house after his Party's defeat in 1945. Previously it had been owned by a jockey called Seracold. Clementine Churchill had seen it first and, in the Spring of 1945, wrote to her daughter, Mary, now Lady Soames, 'Yesterday I took Papa to see the little house I covet. He is mad about it. So now I must be careful not to run him into something which is more than he can afford'. A few years later No 27 became available and the two houses were made into one. In 1950 it was let to the Spanish Ambassador for five years after which the Churchills moved back into it. In 1965 Dr. Leonard Simpson paid £102,500 for the property.

29, Enid BAGNOLD, 1930s-1950s. Her drawing room was created out of the stables by Sir Edwin LUTYENS. In 1948 Enid Bagnold (or, more properly Lady Jones) used to keep a Jersey cow in the back garden, which produced about two gallons of milk a day. The Epsteins usually used up the surplus.

39, Flat II, Ruth DRAPER, 1953.

42, Sir Edward HULTON. On March 5, 1953, Sir Edward gave his nephew, Jocelyn Stevens, a coming-of-age party here. The downstairs rooms had been fixed up to look like a saloon bar. In June 1956, Stevens married Jane Sheffield and Uncle Edward again provided his house for their reception.

HYDE PARK PLACE, W2
Central line to Lancaster Gate

3, 9th Duchess of MARLBOROUGH, 1902 (when still just Gladys Deacon of Boston).

5, Charles DICKENS, spring 1870. Here he worked on his eventually unfinished novel, *Edwin Drood*.

19, Max BEERBOHM, 1893.

HYDE PARK SQUARE, W2

21, Ada LEVERSON, as a child, 1863-1885. Her father, Samuel Beddington, was a health crank. No one was allowed to *touch* money ('full of germs') and only white wine or barley water was offered to drink.

40,   John BUCHAN, after his marriage to Susan Grosvenor in July 1907.
They left the house in 1910.

HYDE PARK STREET, W2

5,   Cecil BEATON's parents were living here in 1925. They gave a dance
for him on January 13, for his 21st birthday.

5,   Philip Guedella, novelist, 1929. Here he wrote *The Duke,* his
biography of Wellington. The house was 'Regency' and the walls lined
with Napoleonic relics and BEERBOHM drawings.

12,   W.H. SMITH (LCP 1966). This was his first married home in 1858
and is now the sole survivor of the mid-19th century houses which
used to be on both sides of it.

HYNDMAN	London, March 7, 1842
Henry Mayers	Hampstead, November 22, 1921
Socialist	9, Queen Anne's Gate, SW1, 1900–1903

2, Pump Court, The Temple, EC4, 1904

Hyndman published *England for All* in 1881 and in it he expounded his
pronounced Marxist views. He has sometimes been referred to as 'The
Father of English Socialism'. Like all too many 'textbook socialists' he came
from a wealthy family, who sent him up to Trinity College, Cambridge.
Turning his back on his privileged past, he went on to found the Social
Democratic Federation, having been deeply influenced by the Paris
Commune.

He nearly always wore a formal and expensive frock-coat and a well brushed
'topper'. He used to 'twit' the crowd who came to hear him speak (often on
Sundays at Hyde Park Corner) for working so hard just so *he* could afford to
dress so well!

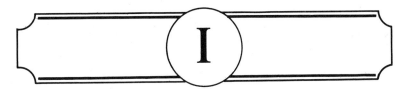

INCHBALD
Elizabeth
Actress and author

Stanningfield, Suffolk, October 15, 1753
London, August 1, 1821
St Mary Abbots, Kensington

163, Strand, WC2, c.1780

Born Elizabeth Simpson, a farmer's daughter, she left home before she was 19 and became an actress in London. Though good looking, she had a speech impediment which obviously would restrict her theatrical chances. She married Joseph Inchbald, an actor, in June 1772 and for about seven years thereafter, she was in provincial repertory.

Inchbald died and Elizabeth produced plays before writing her own. The most successful of these, in 1785, had the strangely modern sounding title of *I'll Tell You What*. She also wrote novels, mostly of the romantic nature and *A Simple Story*, published in 1791, enjoyed good sales. It tells the story of a *flirt* called Miss Milner and has all the ingredients of an 18th century romance, complete with brutal ravishers and priests who turn out to be Lords.

Charles LAMB was wont to refer to Elizabeth and Letitia Barbauld as, 'his two bald authoresses'. (Anna Letitia Barbauld was born in 1743, a sister of John Aikin, a school teacher in a boys' academy. She married Rochemont Barbauld, a French dissenting minister, who had a school in Suffolk. She died in 1825, having produced *Hymn in Prose for Children* in 1781, a few other works and a 50-volume collection of British novelists with her own introductory essay in 1810.)

INGOLDSBY, T. see BARHAM, R.H.

INNER TEMPLE LANE, EC4.   *District and Circle lines to Temple*

Inner Temple Lane is one of the two surviving entrances to the original *Temple* of the Knights Templar. Their Temple, based upon the Temple of Solomon in Jerusalem, was consecrated in 1185. The 'Order' was suppressed in 1307 as a result of a number of trumped-up charges (as well as some quite valid ones) and the property was gradually taken over by the legal profession, who are obviously better able to defend themselves against the sort of allegations made against the Knights Templar.

1, Samuel JOHNSON, 1760-1765. 'His library at this time was contained in the two garrets over his chambers, where the son of Barnaby Lintot [a prosperous publisher, 1675-1736] had his warehouse.'

4, (overlooking Hare Court, named after Sir Nicholas Hare – who died in 1557 – who paid for the building. Hare was a noted judge who seemed to specialize in cases of treason.) Charles LAMB, 1811. 'I have two rooms on the third floor and five sleeping, cooking and etc. rooms on the fourth floor. In my best room is a choice collection of the works of HOGARTH...' [on his walls] '...my best room commands a Court, in which there are trees and a pump, the water of which is excellent cold, with brandy.'

IRVING
(Sir) Henry
Actor manager

Keinton Manderville, Somt., February 6, 1838
Bradford, October 13, 1905
Westminster Abbey in 'Poet's Corner'

87, Newgate Street, EC1
15A, Grafton Street, W1 (LCP 1950) 1872-1899
17, Stratton Street, W1, 1904
27, Gilston Road, The Boltons, SW10, 1905

Irving became the first 'theatrical' to be given a knighthood (in 1895) and so he led the growing trend for actors to become socially *respectable*. He began life as John Henry Brodribb and his career, as a clerk, having been educated at Dr. Pinches' school in George Yard, Lombard Street. In September 1856 he trod the boards (for the first time using the name Irving) playing the part of the Duke of Orleans in Bulwer LYTTON's *Richelieu*. By 1864 he had progressed to *Hamlet*; but his first great success was in *The Bells* by Leopold Lewis, which opened at the Lyceum on November 25, 1871. It ran for 150 performances, was revived at the Queens with Irving in the leading role and then was brought out again with Henry Baynton in Irving's part in September 1924. Then again, with Sir John Martin Harvey in 1933.

In 1869 he married Florence O'Callaghan, by whom he had two sons and a daughter. From 1878 to 1902 he managed the Lyceum Theatre with Ellen TERRY (who was heard to say at his funeral: 'How Henry would have loved it!'). He was essentially a romantic actor, but today his affected style would probably produce cat-calls from the gallery.

He was attacked by pleurisy in 1899 and he never really recovered from it. Towards the end of his life he was using 500 handkerchiefs *each week* to catch the phlegm he was continually coughing up. His last appearance on a London stage was in Sardou's *Dante* at the Drury Lane, opening on April 30, 1903. (His son Laurence had translated it from the French.) He died in Bradford during a provincial tour two years later.

There is a bronze statue of Irving by Sir Thomas Brock, behind the National Portrait Gallery, which has been gazing up the Charing Cross Road since 1910.

IRVING
Washington
Man of Letters

Tarrytown, New York, April 3, 1783
'Sunnyside', N.Y., November 28, 1859
Sleepy Hollow

38, Norfolk Street, WC2, 1805
4, Mount Street, W1, 1824
8, Chandos Street, W1, 1829-1932.

Having studied the law, Irving came to Europe in 1804, returning to New York and being called to the Bar in 1806. His father was a native of Orkney Island. Irving senior had established a prosperous business and had opened a branch of it in Liverpool. Washington Irving inherited the undertaking, but by 1815 it was so unrewarding that he began to look to literature for support.

The Legend of Sleepy Hollow, though not his first published work, appeared in 1820. This tale of *Rip Van Winkle* was one of a number of stories contained in *The Sketch Book of Geoffrey Crayon, Gent*. His reputation established, Irving went on to produce *Tales of a Traveller*, which appeared in four parts in 1824. His income fairly secure, he went to live in Madrid. One of his historical novels, *The Alhambra*, published in 1832, caught the Spanish imagination and today one can find 'Cafe Washington Irving' in Granada; in which town the Palace of the Alhambra lies. Later he was given the honorary (very) post of Secretary to the US Embassy in London, the

Minister of the day being Martin VAN BUREN. (The diplomatic post in London being held by a *Minister:* the first Ambassador was Thomas F. Bayard in 1893). Oxford University gave Irving an honorary degree in 1831. Now, after nearly 17 years of roaming, he went back to the States in 1832 and built himself a house on the Hudson River which he called 'Sunnyside', in which, by now practically a national hero, he expired at the age of 76. He never married.

ISAACS	London, October 10, 1860
Rufus Daniel (1st Earl of Reading)	London, December 29, 1935
Lord Chief Justice	Cremated at Golders Green

32, Curzon Street, W1 (LCP 1961) from 1910 until he died here

Son of a Jewish fruit trader, Isaacs left school at the age of 14 and was generally considered to be a bit of a tearaway. He got on to the floor of the Stock Exchange, but was 'hammered' (ie thrown out) with debts of £8,000 in 1884. Yet, against practically all odds, he rose to be the first Marquess created since WELLINGTON was created Marquess of Wellesly in 1813, the youngest QC of his time, a Liberal Member of Parliament, Lord Chief Justice in 1913 (for eight years) and then appointed Viceroy of India in 1921.
As a lawyer in practice, Isaacs prosecuted the poisoner Seddon and, as Judge, tried Sir Roger Casement for treason (qv Travers HUMPHREYS). His list of acquaintances and friends included LLOYD GEORGE, his 'fellow Viceroy' CURZON, Mahatma Gandhi, Woodrow Wilson, Winston CHURCHILL, Pierre Laval and the Duke of Windsor.
In 1918 he served as Ambassador Extraordinary in Washington, having been created an Earl the year before. In 1887 he married Alice Cohen, who was very much a figure in her own right and was made a Dame (GBE civil) in 1920. They had two sons and two daughters, the elder son and heir, Gerald, carrying the courtesy title of Viscount Erleigh, who lived at 65 Rutland Gate, SW7, in 1924 having married Violet, daughter of Sir Alfred Mond ten years previously.

ISHERWOOD	Disley, Ches., August 26, 1904
Christopher William Bradshaw	United States, 1976
Novelist	

26, Redcliffe Road, SW10, 1926–1927
19, Pembroke Gardens, W8, 1930s

Isherwood's father was killed at Ypres in 1915 and his widowed mother brought him up during a very taxing period in Britain, especially for those who were 'middle class'. However he went to Repton and then to Corpus Christi College, Cambridge.
His first novel, *All the Conspirators,* was published when he was 24 and was followed in 1928 by *The Memorial.* In 1933 he went to Berlin (where the pound was strong, the mark weak and the boys willing) and taught English there until 1937, then travelled around Europe as the clouds of war gathered and grew darker. In Berlin he had met a boy '...with a face like a ripe peach' who appears as 'Otto Nowak' in Isherwood's book, *Goodbye to Berlin,* in 1939. After 'Otto' (and so many others) came 17-year old Heinz who travelled with him, then was imprisoned by the Nazis for evading army conscription, compounded with homosexuality.
W.H. AUDEN, three years younger (but as involved sexually) wrote three plays with Isherwood and then they both went to China, from which journey emerged *Journey to a War* published in 1939.

JACK
'The Ripper'
Murderer

? August 15, 1857
? December 3, 1888

?9, Kings Bench Walk, EC4, 1880s

The mystery of 'Jack-the-Ripper's' real identity not only baffled the entire police force of London but has also been fruitful ground for amateur detectives and literary criminologists ever since. The accusing finger has been pointed at various times to practically the highest in the land, the Duke of Clarence eldest child of HRH Edward, Prince of Wales (and so heir presumptive to the throne) right down, across a broad list of suspects, to a down-and-out Polish slaughterman.

One person many thought the 'Ripper' *might* have been was J.K. Stephens, who at one time was actually tutor to the Duke of Clarence. Other candidates were the prisoner, Thomas Neill Cream; the wife-murderer, George Chapman; a deranged midwife ('Jill-the-Ripper'?); a vengeful and unbalanced doctor, who was seeking to expatiate his son's syphilis contracted from a whore.

Certainly, between August and November 1888, six prostitutes (or women of *very* easy morals) were horribly murdered and indescribably mutilated in the East End of London. Five of these poor creatures were found dead and 'gutted' in the street and a sixth woman was found dead in a ground floor room of a sordid house.

Probably no one will *ever* know who the 'Ripper' really was and, of course, anybody having had the least possible connection with the case is long since dead and gone. However, it was the opinion of some that this 'monster' was none other than a mild young man called Montague John Druitt.

Druitt was the son of a surgeon in Wimborne (in Dorset) and had been a scholar at Winchester. From there he went up to New College, Oxford, where he got his BA in 1880 and entered the Middle Temple on May 17, 1882. His chambers were at 9, Kings Bench Walk. There is no room in a book of this nature to explore the 'whys and wherefores' of the 'Ripper Mystery' but the assembled evidence against Druitt looked very compelling. He was last seen alive on December 3, 1888 and probably committed suicide on that day or soon after. He was in his 32nd year.

JAMES
Henry
Author

New York, April 15, 1843
London, February 28, 1916

3, Berkeley Square, W1, 1855
10, Marlborough Place, NW8, 1855
7, Half Moon Street, W1, 1869
3, Bolton Street, W1, 1876
34, De Vere Gardens, W8 (LCP 1949) 1886-1902
21, Carlyle Mansions, Lawrence Street, SW3, from 1913 until he died

James's father was a theological writer and sufficiently wealthy to enable him to travel to Europe for holidays *en famille* and implant in Henry a love of the 'Old World' and London especially. Henry's 'formal' education was patchy ending with a rather half-hearted study of law at Harvard.

Critical experts in James's works say that his *style* falls into three distinct, consecutive periods, irreverently labelled by Philip Guedella as: James I, James II and the 'Old Pretender'!. Probably the last of his novels, *The Ambassador*, which was published in 1903, remains his best novel. His writing was circumlocutory, with a plethora of commas, and is, today, a very acquired taste.

He never married and he became a British citizen in 1915. He felt that this was the least he could do to show whose side he was on in the First World War. (The conflict was well on into the disastrous and bloody second year and it was not until April 6, 1917 that Woodrow Wilson declared war on Germany.)

In the 'Honours' list of New Years' Day, 1916, James was awarded the Order of Merit by King George V. The medal was brought to his bedside as by, this time, he was mortally ill. His sister-in-law, Alice, was with him when he died. His last words were, 'Tell the boys to follow, to be faithful and to take me seriously'.

JELLICOE Southampton, December 5, 1859
John Rushworth (1st Viscount) London, November 20, 1935
Admiral of the Fleet St Paul's Crypt

25, Draycott Place, SW3 (LCP 1975) 1906-1908
80, Portland Place, W1, 1929
19, Prince's Gardens, SW7, 1935

Son of John Henry Jellicoe, salt water ran in young Jellicoe's veins. He first saw active service in the Egyptian War of 1882. He led the overland relief party to Peking in the Boxer Rebellion of 1900 and was quite severely wounded. Not long afterwards he made an especial study of gunnery.

It was Jellicoe and FISHER (1st Baron of Kilverstone) who favoured the adoption of the *Dreadnoughts* and submarine tactics, thus putting the Royal Navy in an advantageous position over the growing German fleet by the time the First World War started in 1914. On the evening of May 31, 1916, Jellicoe (as Commander-in-Chief of the Grand Fleet) managed to catch up with the reluctant German Navy and the Battle of Jutland was joined. The Germans disappeared into the fog and so it was hardly a total victory for the Royal Navy, who suffered substantial losses. Nevertheless it was a psychological victory and the German Fleet never set out again in full force for the rest of the war. Jellicoe was awarded the Order of Merit and soon after made First Sea Lord.

In 1920 he was appointed Governor General of New Zealand where he stayed for four years. In 1925 he became an Earl and was President of the British Legion from 1928 to 1932.

He had married Gwendoline Cayzer in 1902 and they had daughters in 1903, 1908, 1910 and 1913 and then, in 1918, a *son*, who succeeded to the Viscountcy in 1935.

There is a bronze bust of Jellicoe by Sir Charles WHEELER on the north wall of Trafalgar Square. On one side of him is his contemporary, BEATTY and on the other, Admiral Cunningham (1883-1963).

JENKINS Abersychan, November 11, 1920
Roy Harris
Politician

33, Ladbroke Square, W11, 1964-1980
2, Kensington Park Gardens, W11, 1980

Jenkins was Chairman of the Oxford University Democratic Socialist Club when he was up at Balliol College, reading 'PPE' (Philosophy, Politics and Economics). Oxford, even in the late 30s, must have seemed a long day's march from the Abersychan Grammar School, where he received his secondary education.

In the Second World War he served in the Royal Artillery and was demobilized as a Captain in 1946. In 1945 he had contested the Parliamentary seat of Solihull (Birmingham) as a Socialist, but, despite the massive Labour victory in that year, he was not elected. He was given the safe Labour seat at Stechford (also a Birmingham constituency) in 1950 and from then on, the way was 'up'. He was Chancellor of the Exchequer in 1967 and handled that office for three years. He was the Chairman of the Labour European Committee and a President of the United Kingdom Council for the European Movement. Very much a man *for* the Common Market, he went on to be 'our man in Brussels'. Here he was paid such a high salary and has such advantageous tax advantages that he really could *not* be blamed for not coming home as an avowed Socialist. Instead he led a new party, the 'Social Democrats.'

JENKINSON	June 7, 1770
Robert Banks (2nd Lord Liverpool)	London, December 4, 1826
Prime Minister	Hawkesbury, Warwicks.

26, Hertford Street, W1, 1818

Educated at Charterhouse, then Oxford, Jenkinson went to Paris and actually witnessed the capture of the Bastille on July 14, 1789. In 1790 he became a Member of Parliament; six years later he began to use his courtesy title, Lord Hawkesbury and was appointed as Master of the Mint. From there to a rather undistinguished period at the Foreign Office (being held responsible for the failure to evacuate Malta. According to the Treaty of Amiens; a peace treaty signed on March 27, 1802, between Britain on one side and France, Spain and the Batavian Republic on the other, Malta was to be restored to the Knights of St. John.) In 1804 he was transferred to the Home Office and also became Leader of the House of Lords.

In 1808 he succeeded his father as Lord Liverpool and was made Prime Minister in 1812, a position he held for only 22 months.

JENNER	Berkeley, Glos., May 17, 1749
Edward	Berkeley, Glos. January 26, 1823
Medical 'pioneer'	St Mary's Church, Berkeley

14, Hertford Street, W1, 1803
14, Bedford Place, WC1, 1806-1807

Jenner studied medicine for three years in London, then returned to his native Gloucestershire in 1773. He built up a thriving general practice but early on, he had become convinced that vaccination of cowpox in humans would provide immunity to the widespread, disfiguring and often fatal disease of small pox. Work here did not progress smoothly and there were many sceptics in the medical and lay professions. The vital experiment that was to prove Jenner's beliefs conclusively was made on May 14, 1796. Still vaccination was mistrusted but, at a conference held in London, over 70 eminent physicians and surgeons signed a declaration of confidence in the efficacy of the vaccine and from then it did not take too long for the treatment to gain acceptance on practically a world-wide basis.

In 1802 Jenner was given a grant of £10,000 in recognition of his work and by 1807 when vaccination had begun to prove itself, the Government gave him a further grant of £20,000.

A bronze statue of Jenner was made by W. Calder Marshall. Originally it was in Trafalgar Square, but in 1862 it was moved to the Water Gardens in Kensington Gardens at the top end of the Serpentine.

JERMYN STREET, W1   *Bakerloo and Piccadilly lines to Piccadilly Circus*

Named after Henry Jermyn, Lord St Albans (d.1684). He had been a staunch monarchist and went into exile with Charles I's widow, Queen Henrietta Maria in 1643. Charles II rewarded Jermyn with a title and a goodly parcel of land in this area. Jermyn Street was built up from about 1667.

27, W.M. THACKERAY, 1843-1845. By this time his marriage was effectively over as his wife, Isabella (née Shaw) had become mentally unbalanced.

48, Ronald FIRBANK, 1919. His first novel, *Valmouth* appeared just after he left here.

58, Sydney SMITH, 1825. By this time he was very much a 'social lion'.

81, Tom MOORE, 1825. It was about this time that MOORE, having come into possession of BYRON's diaries (a year after the poet's death) destroyed them entirely, as their contents shocked him so much!

81, 82 and **83,** Rosa LEWIS's hotel (the original *Cavendish*) stood here. She began the business in 1902 and her little empire lasted nearly 50 years.

87, Sir Isaac NEWTON, 1700-1709. Newton had lived at 88 for three years before moving next door. Whilst he lived here he was Master of the Mint, at a salary of £1,500, which was sufficient to afford him his own carriage and maintain six servants. The house was completely rebuilt in 1915.

JEROME   Walsall, May 2, 1859
Jerome Klapka   June 14, 1927
Author   St Mary's Churchyard, Ewelme, Oxon.

29, Queen Square, WC1
41, Belsize Park, NW3, 1927

Jerome was the son of a Nonconformist preacher in the Midlands. His almost surrealistic middle name was given to him in memory of Gyorgy Klapka (1820-1892) a Hungarian general who, when in exile, often visited the Jeromes.

The family moved to Poplar, a not very salubrious London suburb and Jerome became a railway clerk at Euston Station.

He also tried his hand at reporting, school mastering and even tried the stage. In 1889 he struck gold with his book, *Three Men in a Boat* which sold a million copies (alas 'pirated') in America alone. Three years later he became joint editor of the monthly magazine *The Idler*. It lasted 19 years, finally folding in 1906.

Of his plays, his most successful was *The Passing of the Third Floor Back*, which appeared in 1908. In the First World War, then 55 years old, Jerome was an ambulance driver.

Too many 'pirated' copies of his successful books meant a very considerable loss to Jerome's income and at his death his estate only amounted to £5,478.

JOHN   Tenby, S. Wales, January 4, 1878
Augustus   Fordingbridge, Hants., October 31,
Painter   1961
     Fordingbridge

20, Fitzroy Street, W1
28, Mallard Street, SW3 (LCP 1981) 1916-1929
49, Glebe Place, SW3, 1935-1938
33, Tite Street, SW3, 1940

John was always a 'bit larger than life'. At the Slade School of Art he was thought to be the most brilliant pupil of his day. He was always the leader –

not always successfully, but he was certainly one of the most talked about citizens in 'London's Bohemia'.

A story was circulated that as an adolescent John had exhibited no artistic inclination, let alone brilliance, until one day, when swimming near his home town of Tenby he dived too deeply into shallow water, struck his head on a rock and was hauled out unconscious. He recovered fully, but from that day onwards he was an artist of enviable talent. Whether the story is true or not, John never contradicted it.

When he was not actually painting, he was either drinking or womanizing (or both). He sported a piratical red beard which James AGATE 'classified' as one of the four 'legitimate Cafe Royal' beards. The other three belonging to G.B. SHAW, Thomas BEECHAM and Cifford Bax. John was a painter of society portraits and never (well, *hardly* ever) compromised his talent with the wish of the sitter to be painted as flatteringly as possible. One of his best portraits was one of his wife (a long-suffering woman) which is in the Tate Gallery entitled, *The Smiling Woman*. He was one of the few (perhaps, the only?) artist to be elected to the Royal Academy (1928) resign from it on a matter of principle (1938) and be re-elected (1940). He was awarded the Order of Merit in 1942.

In October 1939 John accepted a commission to paint a portrait of HM Queen Elizabeth (wife of King George VI; she was 39 years old). The first sitting was to be on October 30. John failed to turn up and sent a telegram to the Palace to say he 'was suffering from the influence'. Not long after sittings *did* begin, the ever considerate Queen allowed her staff 'just to leave a bottle of brandy' in a cupboard not far from his standing easel.

JOHN ADAM STREET, WC2

Bakerloo, Jubilee and Northern lines to Charing Cross

This street was only part of a carefully planned, carefully designed project by the brothers ADAM. The whole development was called ADELPHI (qv). The Adams obtained the lease of what had been Durham House in 1768 and they began to build elegant streets on raised arches on the sloping land between what is now the Strand and the Thames. The river then, was appreciably wider at this point than it is now. There is also a Robert Adam Street, named after the second eldest brother. Another Robert Adam Street is in MARYLEBONE as Robert designed Home House in PORTMAN SQUARE.

16, Thomas ROWLANDSON (LCP 1950). He lived in the basement here from about 1793 for two years; '...a dismal uninhabited place and likely to remain so'. In 1800 he had moved up in the world, *literally* and was living in an attic of this same house.

JOHNSON
Samuel
Lexicographer and savant

Lichfield, Staffs., September 18, 1709
London, December 13, 1784
Westminster Abbey ('Poet's Corner')

6, Great Castle Street, W1, 1738
17, Gough Square, EC4 (P) 1749-1759
1, Inner Temple Lane, EC4
7, Johnson's Court, EC4, 1765-1776
Bolt Court, EC4, where he died

Johnson's father was not a very prosperous bookseller and, though Samuel was educated locally, he did go up to Pembroke College, Oxford, but had to leave without a degree when father's funds ran out.

He started to work for a publisher in Birmingham and, in 1735, he met and married Elizabeth Porter, a widow 20 years older than he. Despite the disparity in their ages and 'Tetty' (her affectionate nickname) being no match for his intellect, the marriage was happy. When she died in 1752, Johnson grieved for her. She had capital of about £800 which was a great comfort to them both and financed Johnson's venture at Edial.

The next chapter in Johnson's career was to start a private school in Edial (west of Lichfield). This venture was *not* successful and practically the only pupil was David GARRICK and in 1737 they set off together for London.

In 1747 he issued a prospectus for his *Dictionary of the English Language* and not long after began a magazine he called *The Rambler*, which he wrote almost entirely himself and did not last long.

His mother died and the story is that Johnson sat down and wrote his one and only novel, *Rasselas*, in seven days to raise enough money for her funeral. In 1763, James BOSWELL, a rather loose-living son of a minor Scottish aristocrat, was introduced to Johnson and Boswell was to hang on Johnson's every word, persuade him to travel to the 'Western Isles', be his general friend, and, eventually, biographer.

It was SMOLLETT who christened Johnson 'The Great Cham of Literature' and it was *Goldsmith* who said of him, '...that he had nothing of the bear, but the skin'. The observant (and irreplaceable) Fanny BURNEY described the 'Great Cham' as being, '...very ill- favoured! Yet he has naturally a noble figure – tall, stout, grand and authoritative; but he stoops horribly; his back is quite round; his mouth is continually opening and shutting as if he were chewing something...'

Obviously Johnson's *Dictionary* is today quite out of date, but an unchanging memorial to Johnson's intellectual and literary genius is his *Lives of the Poets*. These occupied ten volumes and were published between 1779 and 1781.

Dr. Johnson's Museum is at 17 Gough Square. It was opened in 1914 and is open daily all the year round (except Sundays) – 11-5.

Percy Fitzgerald presented the bronze figure of Johnson, which he made in 1910, to London. It stands in the Strand, at the eastern end of the Church of St Clement Danes. It shows Johnson, book in hand, gazing towards Temple Bar and the City he loved. The inscription on the plinth reads: 'Critic, essayist, philologist, biographer, wit, poet, moralist, dramatist, political writer, talker.'

JOHNSTON　　　　　　　　　Little Berkhamstead, June 24, 1912
Brian Alexander
Cricket buff and broadcaster

35, South Eaton Place, SW1, 1938-1939
98, Hamilton Terrace, NW8, 1969-1982
43, Boundary Road, NW8, 1982

The family coffee-importing business was sufficiently prosperous to send Johnston to Eton, then to New College, Oxford for his BA. In the Second World War he served in the Guards and, when peace broke out, he joined (almost by chance) the British Broadcasting Corporation.

He is a keen cricketer and it has been the cricket commentary on radio that has given him a world wide and deserved reputation. He is given to punning and nicknaming his fellow workers in the medium. Some of his sallies from the commentary box bring forth anguished groans.

JONES　　　　　　　　　　　Shropshire, February 9, 1845
(Captain) Adrian　　　　　　　　January, 24, 1938
Sculptor

147, Church Street, SW3 (P) 1892-1938

Jones had a rather strange caree: and background for someone who became a professional sculptor. He was educated at Ludlow Grammar School and then spent 23 years in the Army as a *veterinary* surgeon.

When he turned to sculpture, after more than two decades of dealing with sickly horses he always used to work in the long cavalry cloak he had worn in his Army days.

His most noted (and most noticeable) piece of work is the *Quadriga* – a memorial to King Edward VII – on top of Decimus Burton's triumphal arch that stands between Apsley House and the top of Constitutional Hill.

Jones's other easily seen sculpture is the statue of the 2nd Duke of Cambridge (1819-1904) grandson of George III and Commander in Chief of the British Army, 1856-1895. The statue shows the Duke in full Field Marshall's dress and is mounted on a block of Dartmoor granite. It stands in the middle of Whitehall with the statue of Lord HAIG a little down wind of him.

JORDAN Waterford, Eire, c.1762
Dorothy Ste. Cloud, France, July 3, 1816
Actress Richmond Parish Church

14, Somerset Street, W1, 1791
17, Hanover Square, W1
30, Cadogan Place, SW3 (LCP 1975) 1812-1814

Dorothy Bland (as then she was) became the mistress of the Duke of Clarence, third son of King George III (later to be King William IV) when she was about 27 years old. By that time she had been on the stage for 14 years and had had three illegitimate children by Richard Ford and a daughter by Richard Daly. She was a successful actress – in comedy and HAZLITT thought, '...her smile had the effect of sunshine.'

By her Royal lover she had ten more children, who all took the surname of Fitzclarence. They proved an unruly lot, even though their Royal father gave them not a little help and all sorts of titles.

The Duke was permanently hard up – a real 'Georgian' trait – and Dorothy Jordan often sent him small sums of money when she was 'touring' the provinces. Their liaison was forcibly broken up in 1811 but the Government of the day was not ungenerous. Despite a large 'hand out', she was still (or again) in trouble financially and she quickly crossed to France in 1815. She became mentally unbalanced and less than a year later she was dead.

KAUFFMANN
Angelica Maria Anna
Artist

Coire, Switzerland, October 30, 1741
Rome, November 5, 1807
Sant'Andrea della Fratte, Rome

10, Hertford Street, W1, 1766
38, Suffolk Street, SW1, 1767
11, Golden Square, W1, 1767
7, Park Street, W1, 1780

The Oxford *Companion to Art* rather dismissively describes Kauffman as '...a Swiss decorative painter'. Strictly speaking, this is probably nearer the truth than to have called her an *artist*.
Nevertheless, when she first came to London in 1765, her work (and she) attracted admiration. She was friendly with Joshua REYNOLDS – not the easiest position to be in – and was actually one of the Founding Members of the Royal Academy in 1786. Mary Moser, who died in 1819, was another of the 36 Royal Academicians. It is interesting that two women should be amongst the very first Academicians; women in the 1770s were very much 'second class citizens'. The next female into the Academy, and then only as an Associate, 'ARA', was Annie L. Swynnerton in 1922, a gap of over 150 years.
In November 1767 she was married clandestinely to a man claiming to be 'Count de Horn'. It transpired that he was only a valet but, because they had been married as Catholics, a deed of separation had to be obtained from Pope Clement XIII. Luckily, 'Count de Horn' died in 1768 and, free again, Angelica married Antonio Zucchi. Zucchi, an artist, a fellow Academician and a Venetian, was 55 when they married and he died 12 years before her in 1795.

KEAN
Edmund
Actor

London, November 4, 1789
Richmond, May 15, 1833
St Matthias's Church, Richmond

12, Clarges Street, W1, 1816-1824

Kean's mother was Nance Carey, the granddaughter of Henry Carey (1690-1743). The Careys sometimes claimed kinship with the aristocratic Savile family – Savile Row was named after the Earl of Burlington's wife, Dorothy Savile. As a youngster Edmund became a cabin boy, but not for long and he gave up shipboards for stage boards and became a 'strolling player'.
When he was only 21 he married Mary Chambers, an Irish actress, who was a little older than he. They had two sons, Howard and Charles. It was a rocky marriage, nevertheless and Kean's extramarital adventures and his gargantuan appetite for alcohol were too much and she left him. Her departure was no doubt hastened as a Mr. Cox had sued Kean for having 'criminal conversation' with his wife, Charlotte. Kean was ordered to pay the outraged Cox £800 damages. Meanwhile Mrs. Cox jumped into bed with one of her husband's employees, called (rather engagingly) Whatmore. Theatrically his early career was more successful than his matrimonial trials. He toured in the provinces and made his 'West End' début at Drury Lane in 1814, playing the part of 'Shylock' and became an overnight hit (COLERIDGE said Kean's 'Shylock' was, '...like reading Shakespeare by

flashes of lightning'.) Success followed, but always at risk, for he was chronically unpunctual and frequently the worse for drink. In 1826 he went to America for nearly a year but was welcomed back to England by his English audiences. The success was too much for him. His health broke down completely and he died a sad, sodden, syphilitic wreck at Richmond.

KEATS London, October 31, 1795
John Rome, February 23, 1821
Poet Protestant Cemetery, Rome

76/78, Cheapside (Bird-in-the-Hand Court) 1816-1817
25, Great College Street, SW1, 1819

Keats' father kept a livery stable (above which, John was born). After schooling at Enfield, in Middlesex, he was apprenticed to a surgeon in Edmonton (not far from Enfield) and became a medical student. Qualified, he was doing quite well as a doctor, but his mind was always on 'higher things'. He had friends who painted, he adored the music of MOZART and gradually poetry became his consuming passion.
Leigh HUNT was a neighbour of his and introduced him to SHELLEY. Encouraged by these attentions, Keats produced his first volume of poetry in 1817. Though it was not a publishing success, Keats quit medecine for good. He was, facially, rather beautiful and, though only five feet tall (1.52 metres) he tended to be pugnacious and certainly was no coward. In the summer of 1818 he went on a walking tour of Scotland, but it had to be curtailed as his tubercular condition was worsening. Nevertheless, he was back in London to nurse his younger brother, Tom, who died of TB in December 1818.
Keats moved 'uphill' to Hampstead and (typically) fell in love with a near neighbour, Fanny Brawne, who did not respond to his romantic passion. By 1820 he had to realize he had not long to live and set off for Naples, hoping the Italian climate would benefit him. His artist friend, Joseph SEVERN, two years older than he, was with him and stayed with him until he died in Rome the following year.
Keats lies in the Protestant Cemetery in Rome. On his tombstone are his own lines: 'Here lies one whose name was writ in water'.

KELLY London, April 9, 1879
(Sir) Gerald Festus London, January 1, 1972
Artist

117, Gloucester Place, W1 (originally 65) 1915-1972

Kelly, a clergyman's son, went to Eton, followed by Trinity Hall, Cambridge. Then, that was a rather unusual educational background for someone who really *was* an artist. He went on to Paris to study painting and he became friendly with Dégas, Renoir, Monet, Rodin and Cézanne. He painted in France, then Spain; then, thousands of miles away to the east, in Burma.
He was to become one of the oldest (and one of the few) *friends* of Somerset MAUGHAM and he painted him many times. Kelly's sister, Rose (against the wishes and hopes of her family) married the 'Satanist' Aleister Crowley. As could be predicted, the marriage did not prosper and, after a divorce in 1909, Rose married a doctor of medecine rather than her last 'witch-doctor'. Kelly married Lilian Ryan in St Michael's Church, Paddington (where his father had been curate) in 1920 and, though they were from very different backgrounds, they adored each other and she became his favourite model. She was beautiful and 'Jane', as Kelly called her, became the subject of a

clerihew written by the architect of that poetical form, E.C. BENTLEY. It
ran:

> 'Mr. Gerald Kelly
> Never paints Joan or Nelly
> When at each show one sees Jane
> One can only gasp, "Again".'

KEMBLE London, W.1., November 27, 1809
Frances Anne ('Fanny') London, January 15, 1893
Actress Kensal Green, Grave No. 11981, Plot 5

35, Gerrard Street, W1
29, Soho Square, W1, 1822-1825
18, Orchard Street, W1, 1847
29, King Street, SW1,, 1848
99, Eaton Place, SW1,, 1852
15, Connaught Square, W2, 1877

Fanny came from real Thespian stock. Her father was the actor Charles
(1775-1854) her mother Maria Teresa de Camp, an actress (1774-1838) her
paternal grandfather was Roger Kemble, an actor, originally from Hereford
(1721-1802) who married Sarah Ward, an actress; both of whose parents
were 'theatricals'.

Actually, Fanny only went on to the stage to try and restore the family
fortunes which had dwindled to nothing as a result of Charles's lessee-ship
of Covent Garden. Luckily she was a great hit when she made her début as a
suitably young 'Juliet' at the Garden in October 1829. For four more years
she appeared on the London stages, then went with her father to America.
She met and married Pierce Butler (1807-1867) in 1834. He was a wealthy
Philadelphian, deriving a great deal of his income from slave-worked land.
Slavery was abhorrent to Fanny and it was their different attitudes over this
emotive subject that was to break up their marriage. They had quite a long
period of separation and then divorced in 1848.

KEMBLE Prescott, February 1, 1759
John Philip Lausanne, February 26, 1823
Actor Lausanne; in a cemetery on the Berne
Road

89, Great Russell Street, WC1, 1808-1823

As a 15-year old Kemble was sent to Douai College with the intention he
should afterwards enter the church. Kemble, however, turned his back on
the cloth, joined his father's (Roger, 1721-1802) touring company and made
his acting début in January 1776 as 'Theodosius' in Wolverhampton. He had
to wait for seven more years before, as *Hamlet* he appeared at the Drury
Lane.

In 1802 he became manager of Covent Garden and caused a riot (literally) in
1809 when he raised the prices of admission to the new theatre, which
replaced the one burnt down in 1808. The disturbances have always been
referred to as the 'OP Riots' ('Old Price').

As a tragic actor, Kemble was superb (as was his sister, Sarah SIDDONS)
but he rather 'hammed' the comedy roles. In 1802, at Drury Lane, he was
earning £56.14.0 (£56.70.) a week, a very considerable sum for those days.
In 1803 he somehow raised £23,000 capital and bought a one-sixth share of
'The Lane' from William Lewis. (Lewis, who was born about 1748 and died
in 1811, was nicknamed 'Gentleman Lewis', though his father was a linen
draper on Tower Hill.)

KENNEDY
John Fitzgerald
34th President of America

Brookline, Mass., May 29, 1917
Dallas, November 22, 1963
Arlington Cemetery, Virginia

14, Prince's Gate, SW7, 1939

'JFK' was the second of Joseph Patrick Kennedy's nine children. Joseph (1888-1969) was the wealthy Ambassador for the United States in London, when Britain stood alone against the *Axis* powers. Kennedy believed that the Germans would soon overrun London as they had done the rest of Europe. He left Britain on October 3, 1940. As he left he told the Press, 'I have been through it all and I have the greatest respect for Londoners'. But they had little for him. One eminent American medical man once said that in the States (too) '...Joseph Kennedy was hated; *gleefully*'.

John Kennedy produced a book in 1940 called *Why England Slept*. It dealt with the unready state of the United Kingdom when it declared war on Germany on September 3, 1939. (Probably his father helped him a little, in producing the publication.) Certainly Henry Luce, proprietor of *Time Life* and *Fortune* magazines, thought the book so good he wrote a laudatory preface for it. John K. had had a year at the London School of Economics which was ended by a disabling attack of jaundice in 1936. He then went on to Harvard, where his elder brother, Joseph, was already enrolled. In his sophomore year he suffered a spinal injury whilst playing Rugby (*à la Americaine*) football which was to affect him to his death.

In the garden of 1, Park Crescent, off the Marylebone Road, is a bust of Kennedy, unveiled by his brother Robert (killed by Sirhan Bishava Sirhan) and the youngest Kennedy, Edward. The sculptor was an American of Lithuanian origin, Jacques Lipchitz. The London bust is actually a copy and other copies have been placed in the Library of Harvard and in the Library of Congress. The cost of the London copy was met by donations (maximum £1 per donor) paid into a fund organized by the *Daily Telegraph*. It is in a happy place for any memorial and especially for Kennedy, a gregarious man, as it stands in the garden of the International Students' Hostel.

KENSINGTON

In the Domesday Book, produced for King William the Conqueror (who reigned 1066-1087) there was a village shown here as *Chenesitun* and the main road of the village was more or less the Kensington High Street of today. The road, then obviously a Norman one, may actually have been laid down originally by the Romans, six or seven hundred years before the Conqueror crossed the Channel.

KENSINGTON CHURCH STREET, W8 *Central, District and Circle lines to Notting Hill Gate*

In this street today there are over 60 antique shops of varying reliability as to the provenance of the goods they sell and little is left of the original houses. The top (north) part used to be known as 'Silver Street' and the southern end, by St Mary Abbot's Church, as 'Church Lane'.

108, Angela THIRKELL and her new husband, MacInnes rented this, then pretty, house in 1911. They lived here until 1914 when their second child was on the way.

128, Muzio CLEMENTI (LCP 1963) 1820-1823. When he was living here he was concentrating on muscial composition. He sold the house to William Horsley, a musician who was friendly with Mendelssohn who visited the Horsleys here quite frequently. Horsley's son, John, lived on in this house for 65 more years, until 1903. He was an artist with the jokey nickname of 'Clothes-Horsley' and has been credited with designing the very first *English* Christmas card.

KENSINGTON GORE, SW7

District and Circle lines to High Street, Kensington

'Stage Blood' is a joking name for Kensington Gore, though this Gore has no sanguine connection. A 'gara' in Old English meant a 'triangle' and what is now the Gore was one side of a triangular piece of land owned for centuries by the City of Westminster even though the land itself lay in the parish of Kensington.

Where the Albert Hall stands used to be Gore House (and **Albert Hall Mansions** now cover part of the grounds). In 1808 William WILBERFORCE came to live here and enlarged the house quite considerably. In the garden WILBERFORCE used to '...sit and read...as if I were two hundred miles from the great city'. He left the house in 1821.

In 1836 Lady BLESSINGTON and her aristocratic French gentleman companion came to live in some style. The Count D'ORSAY had a little cottage adjoining the Gore House wall.

KENSINGTON PALACE GARDENS, W8

District, Circle and Central lines to Notting Hill Gate

This road (which is still a private one, for 'residents, their visitors, their dogs and their servants' – note order given) was once the kitchen gardens for Kensington Palace. It was laid out as a residential street in 1843. Overtly prosperous, it is sometimes referred to as 'Millionaire's Row'. The nickname is ironic as the Russian Embassy is housed in numbers 5, 10, 13, 16 and 18; the last two are described officially as annexes.

6 and 7, Thomas WYATT built these (and the North Gate lodges) for John Blashfield between 1844 and 1846. Blashfield went bankrupt, but Wyatt went on to finish South Gate lodges in 1849 and numbers 25 and 26, which he had started for Blashfield.

8, Lord DUVEEN of Millbank, 1937. He also had a New York home at 15, East 91st Street and kept a permanent suite at Claridges, W1.

18, Baron Paul Julius de REUTER from 1867 until his death in 1899.

18, Viscount LEE of Fareham from 1922 to 1929. He bought the lease for £10,000 and sold it for £15,000 to...

18, Lionel Rothschild, who began moving in on July 20, 1927. He brought with him the panelling from his bedroom in his house in Park Street, W1. Then there were another 39 bedrooms to furnish here.

KENSINGTON SQUARE, W8

Circle and District line to High Street Kensington

In 1681 this was just 'The Square'. Seven years later it became King's Square. This *may* have been King James II, after whom King Street (now Derry Street was named). A few years after, King William III bought Nottingham House and, with WREN, turned it into Kensington Palace. In 1705 John Bowack (an English topographer active at the beginning of the 18th century) remarked that the Square, '...for beauty of buildings and worthy inhabitants exceeds several noted Squares of London'.

3, Alexis SOYER, 1850s.

7, Margot ASQUITH, 1945 (Lady Oxford and Asquith). 'Margot now lives with one servant in a beautiful old house...'. She died here on July 28, 1945.

17, Sir Hubert PARRY (LCP 1949) from 1887 until his death in 1918.

18, John Stuart MILL (LCP 1907) 1837-1851. Here he had a 'charming library and an immense herbarium'.

21, Lord Ronald GORELL 1920s to the late 1950s. He had been editor of the *Cornhill* magazine since 1933.

33, Mrs. Patrick CAMPBELL (P). She first saw Isadora Duncan and her brother Raymond dancing on the grass of the Square in front of her house. The house was built in 1695 and 'Mrs. Pat' lived here from 1900 to 1921.

36,37, TALLEYRAND-PERIGORD, 1793. This was after he was President of the French Assembly but before the fall of Robespierre.

41, Sir Edward BURNE-JONES, 1856-1866, '...they moved the furniture including the Webb dining table and the little painted piano to 41, Kensington Square. There was nothing but gardens then between the Square and the narrow countrified Kensington High Street. No. 41 was on the north side and the light was poor, but there was a garden big enough to play bowls in on summer evenings and it was quiet'.

KEPPEL	1868
Alice	Italy, September 11, 1947
Royal mistress	Protestant Cemetery, Florence

16, Grosvenor Street, W1, 1922-1928

Alice was the daughter of Admiral, Sir William Edmonstone (the 4th Baronet, who died in 1888) and the youngest of his six daughters. In 1891 she married the Hon. George Keppel who was then a Lieutenant in the Gordon Highlanders. In 1894 the Keppels had a daughter, who they christened Violet.

Mrs. Keppel met Edward, Prince of Wales in the late 1890s and for the last twelve years of the life of that hedonistic monarch, she was his most intimate and trusted friend. Unlike many mistresses she was of such quality and understanding that everybody *really* liked her – even the Queen. On his deathbed, Mrs. Keppel was allowed to visit the dying King with Alexandra's blessing.

Charles Hardinge, later created Baron Hardinge of Penshurst, ten years older than Alice; one time Viceroy of India, Permanent Secretary for Foreign Affairs and (later) Ambassador in Paris wrote that Alice Keppel had, '...wonderful discretion and...was an excellent influence' on the King. Margot Asquith, one of the bitchiest of commentators of the social scene, said that the King's mistress was, '...a plucky woman of fashion, human, adventurous and gay, who, in *spite* of doing what she liked all her life, has never made an enemy'. Praise indeed from *la* Margot.

(One of her husband's ancestors; a Keppel, the first Duke of Albermarle, was physically attractive to King William III of England. Once, *taxed* on the details of her friendship with King Edward VII; Mrs. Keppel told her interrogator briskly, 'Of *course* I went to bed with him *and* it was not the first time a Keppel was in a King's bed'.)

The Edmonstone motto was, 'virtus aucet honorem' -Virtue adds to honour. Perhaps Alice felt that *lack* of virtue added *much* more to honour.

KEYNES	Cambridge, June 5, 1883
John Maynard	April 21, 1946
(1st Baron Keynes of Tilton)	Firle, Sussex
Economist	

3, Gower Street, WC1, 1916
49, Gordon Square, WC1, 1916-1946

The 'Bloomsbury Group' (so called) attracted a lot of differing people, most of whom had artistic or literary skills or tastes. Keynes was quite a central figure to this *coterie*, but he was an economist of brilliance. During the First World War he worked in the Treasury and was its representative at the Peace Conference (from which he resigned on matters of principle). In 1919 he published *The Economic Consequences of the Peace* which established him as a figure of economic vision and brilliance on an international scale. In 1942 he was made a Baron; he had been a director of the Bank of England since 1940. It was he that led the British Delegation at the 1945 Bretton Woods Conference and negotiated the American Loan in Washington.

He was educated at Eton and King's College, Cambridge (where he was a contemporary and lover of Lytton STRACHEY who was some three years older than he). He became a Fellow of the College and, at one time, was Bursar there.

Privately he was almost exclusively homosexual though he married Lydia Lopokova (who was a year older than he) in 1925. She had been with the Diaghilev Ballet and Keynes helped her to form the 'Vic-Wells' company. She outlived him and was living in Sussex as late as 1975.

Strachey and he came into competition for the love of Duncan GRANT. He was a cousin of Lytton's and five years his junior. Keynes 'won' and his relationship with the highly sexed Grant lasted over the years. Leon Edel, in his *Bloomsbury, a House of Lions* (1979) neatly summed up the Keynes/Grant involvement. He wrote 'From this time on, and for many years, Duncan Grant and Maynard Keynes – the economist who was an artist in his field, and the painter who knew the economy of art – shared homes and travelled together.'

Nicknames were all the rage in the literary dovecotes of that era and Lytton's choice of name for Maynard was 'Pozzo de Bongo'.

KING'S BENCH WALK, EC4 *District and Circle lines to Temple*

Crown Office Row leads through from Middle Temple Lane to King's Bench Walk, which is in the Inner Temple. Originally it was a shady, tree-lined footpath in front of the Office of the Court of the King's Bench. The original building burnt down in 1677.

4, Sir Harold NICOLSON, 1930-1945. Though not a barrister, Nicolson lived here during the week while Vita, his wife, lived at their country home of Sissinghurst Castle in Kent. The flat here had a good sized living-room and a small lobby, two bedrooms, 'kitchenette' and a bathroom. The rooms were wainscotted and Vita had had the living-room painted in an 'old ivory' colour.

5, Lord MANSFIELD, before 1756 (when he was still plain Mr. Murray, a Scottish lawyer).

8, George MOORE, 1896. His greatest novel, *Esther Waters* was two years behind him and *Evelyn Innes* was still two years away.

KINGSLEY	Dartmoor, Devon, June 12, 1819
Charles	Eversley, Hants., January 23, 1875
Novelist	St Mary's Church, Eversley

56, Old Church Street, SW3 (LCP 1979) 1836-1860

Before becoming a curate at Eversley, Kingsley had graduated from Magdalene College, Cambridge with a Classical First degree. Eventually he became Rector of the village and spent the rest of his life there.

The Water Babies published in 1863, established him as a children's author of note and was the first of his many books. Another still remembered, is *Westward Ho* (1855) but books like *Yeast* (1848) and *Alton Locke*, seem to have sunk altogether.

He was deeply interested in the problems of the less privileged classes and, with F.D. MAURICE, involved himself in social problems. together they both worked hard to try and make the lot of poor people a little more bearable.

In 1869 he was made a Canon of Chester and of Westminster four years later. All his life he was hot-tempered, highly strung and combative but was profoundly religious, favouring the school of 'Muscular Christianity' extolled by the 'great doctor' Arnold of Rugby School.

KINGS ROAD, SW3

District and Circle lines to Sloane Square
(all right for the low numbers but
buses do go right along the road from the station,
look for one marked PUTNEY)

King Charles made the road part of his 'official' route from his Whitehall Palace to his Palace at Hampton Court. The road had to be quite heavily guarded – especially the stretch which is Eaton 'Square' today. Entrance could only be gained if one held a ticket which bore the emblem of the Crown. This system lasted until the reign of King William IV (1830-1837) who had the whole road made fully public.

149, Joyce GRENFELL, 1939-1956. Here she had the '...luxury of a box room'. She also had the luxury of Mrs. Gabe, her housekeeper for 18 years.
152, Princess Seraphine ASTAFIEVA (LCP 1968) 1918-1934. The house was her home and she also continued her ballet school here. One day in 1924, Serge Diaghilev came to watch one of her pupils, the 14-year old Alice Marks, who was to become Dame Alicia Markova.
211, Lady COLEFAX, one of London's great 20th century hostesses lived here from 1922-1937. Invitations to her dinner table were eagerly sought. At one of these occasions, Gertrude LAWRENCE was very late in arriving and, on entering the dining room, gave a sweeping, full court curtsey to one man already at the table, thinking him to be H.R.H. the Duke of Kent. She was later very embarrassed to be told he was a columnist on the *Daily Express*.
213 and **215** were built as a pair in 1720.
213, Somerset MAUGHAM, late 1920s. Here his wife, Syrie, created the 'all white drawing room' for the first time.
213, Sir Carol REED, 1948-1978.
215, Thomas ARNE, early 1770s, in the last years of his life.
215, Ellen TERRY (LCP 1951) 1904-1920. During her time here, her third marriage failed and she had begun to decline mentally and physically.

KING STREET (St James's) SW1

Piccadilly, Jubilee and Victoria lines
to Green Park

The street was developed in 1673 by its owner, Henry Jermyn, who dedicated it to his benefactor, King Charles II.

1C, NAPOLEON III, 1848. He lived here with his mistress, Elizabeth Howard, to whom he used to refer as, 'My landlady'.
8, is Christies, the great art auctioneers. The firm was founded by James Christie (1730-1831) who carried on the business and whose grandson, Sir William Mahoney, was Astronomer Royal from 1881 to 1910. Sir William died in 1922, aged 77.

KIPLING
Joseph Rudyard
Author

Bombay, December 30, 1865
London, January 18, 1936
Westminster Abbey; 'Poet's Corner'

43, Villiers Street, WC2, 1890-1892

Kipling's father was an ordained Methodist minister but had also been an art student and, in the months before Rudyard was born, he had a post in the Bombay School of Art. Rudyard was named after a lake in Staffordshire, where his father first met his bride-to-be, Alice MacDonald.

Rudyard was sent back to England in 1871 and lived with a couple in Southsea (whom he came to loathe) but spent holidays with the BURNE-JONES family in Fulham. (His maternal aunt had married Edward Burne-Jones.) Mrs. Kipling came back to England in 1877 and saw for herself how unhappy Rudyard was in Southsea and the following year he was sent as a boarder to the United Services College at Westward Ho! in Devon. (The School was later immortalized by Kipling in his *Stalky and Co.* published 1899.)

In 1882 Kipling went back to India and worked for a newspaper in Lahore (his father now being curator of the museum there). Kipling was really a brilliant journalist and between 1887 and 1889 he published over 70 short stories, many of which later appeared in his *Plain Tales from the Hills.*

His novel, *The Light that Failed* (1891) was written in Villiers Street, Kipling having come back to London in 1889.

Money was coming in and he took a trip around the world. He came back via Vermont, United States, met Caroline Starr Balestier in 1892 and married her. He did not find his in-laws congenial and he was on particularly bad terms with Caroline's reprobate brother, Beatty.

He bought a house in Vermont called 'Naulakha' and it was here he wrote the *Jungle Books.* In 1895 he was offered the Poet Laureateship on TENNYSON's death but he declined the offer. Alfred Austin took the post. Without doubt he was the worst Poet Laureate Britain ever had and there is good cause for believing he was Britain's worst poet altogether.

KITCHENER
Horatio Herbert (1st Earl)
Field Marshall

Ballylongford, Eire, June 24, 1850
Lost at sea, June 5, 1916
No grave, but a memorial chapel in St Paul's

44, Phillimore Gardens, W8, 1875-1878
17, Belgrave Square, SW1, 1888-1914
2, Carlton Gardens, SW1 (LCP 1929) 1914-1916

As a 21-year old, Kitchener went into the Royal Engineers and three years later was on the Palestine Survey, which kept him busy until he was sent to Cyprus on another survey in 1882.

In 1890 he was appointed Sirdar of the Egyptian Army, a post he held for nine years and, in 1898, he was raised to the peerage and chose the nicely alliterative title of Kitchener of Khartoum. the title was awarded after the battle of Omdurman on September 2, 1898, when the Khalifa was overwhelmingly defeated by the Egyptian force under Kitchener, so winning back the Sudan for Egypt.

His next post was Commander-in-Chief of the British Army in the Boer War, in its closing stages. A grateful government awarded him £50,000 (in the days when a pound sterling meant something) gave him a Viscountcy, the Order of Merit and appointed him Commander-in-Chief in India.

By 1914 he was made Secretary for War and he re-organized the Army and its recruitment methods. In June 1916 he set off in *HMS Hampshire.* The ship struck a mine off the Orkneys and Kitchener was one of the many who drowned.

John Tweed's statue of Kitchener was placed on the south side of Horse Guards' Parade in 1926. There is also a small bust of him on the first floor pediment of the building at 73, Knightsbridge.

KNELLER
(Sir) Godfrey
Artist

Lübeck, August 8, 1646
London, October 19, 1723
In the garden of his house near
Hounslow now Kneller Hall and the
Royal School of Military Music

15, Covent Garden, WC2 1682-1702
55, Great Queen Street, WC2, 1703-1723

Born Kniller (and christened Gottfried) he studied in Amsterdam and Italy before coming to London in 1676. Four years later he was appointed Court Painter. By 1691 he had become sufficiently anglicized to be given a knighthood by King William III and, in 1715, George I made him a baronet. (In all, ten reigning sovereigns sat to Kneller.)
He was an arrogant man, yet he often had 14 'sitters' a day in his large London studio. He amassed a considerable fortune, though lost some of it in the 'South Sea Bubble' affair. Many members of the 'Kit-Kat' Club were painted by Kneller and a number of these portraits can be seen in the National Portrait Gallery in Charing Cross Road.

KNIGHT
(Dame) Laura
Artist

Nottingham, August 4, 1877
London, July 7, 1970

1 and 2, Queens Road, NW8, 1919

Dame Laura was a great admirer of the circus and she sometimes travelled and lived with circus people, many of her works reflect this lifelong interest. She married Harold Knight (also an artist) in 1903. He was elected to the Royal Academy and she, too, joined those illustrious ranks; the first full female Academician elected since Angelica KAUFFMAN and Mary Moser. For some time the Knights lived and worked at Newlyn in Cornwall. A picture of that period, *Spring in Cornwall*, was bought by the Chantrey Fund in 1936 (the year she became an Academician). In 1965 she became the first woman ever to be given a retrospective exhibition at the Academy.

KNIGHTSBRIDGE, SW1 *Piccadilly line to Knightsbridge*

During the reign of Edward III (1327-1377) this area was called 'Knyghtbrigg' and orders were given that the slaughtering of all animals for the London meat trade must be carried out to the west of this place. Later the spelling 'Kingesbridge' occurs. Certainly there was a bridge here; over the river Westbourne, which still runs into Hyde Park's Serpentine Lake. There is also a record of a 'Sir H. Knyvet' who, on being attacked by footpads on the bridge, killed the leader of the gang. This story was recorded by the county historian, John Norden in 1593.

70, Charles READE, 1868-1882. Mrs. Seymour, an actress, kept house for him here from 1868 until her death in 1879. This part of Knightsbridge used to be called St George's Place.

79, Sir Godfrey TEARLE, 1929. In this year he was playing 'Captain Banner' at the Arts and then, in July, went on tour playing 'Tice Collins' in *This Thing Called Love*.

KNOBLOCK
Edward
Dramatist

New York, April 7, 1874
July 19, 1945

G 2, Albany, W1, 1914-1935

Knoblock had been given a European education but was a Harvard graduate.

He came to England again in 1897 and wrote a number of quite successful plays, the best of which was probably *My Lady's Dress* in 1914. Actually Knoblock, a homosexual, would hardly have been interested in a lady's dress.

He achieved great success with the play *Kismet*, based on Sir Richard Burton's (*bowdlerized*) *Arabian Nights*. This musical play brought him in touch with Arnold BENNETT and together they wrote *Milestones* (from which Bennett made £16,000 in just one year). He then co-operated with J.B. PRIESTLEY on a dramatization of Priestley's *Good Companions*. He also worked with Beverly NICHOLS (who would have been *much* more to his taste than Priestley) on a play called *Evensong*. He became a British citizen in 1916.

KOESTLER Hungary, September 5, 1905
Arthur London, March 3, 1983
Author

8, Montpelier Square, SW7, from 1965 until he (and his wife) committed suicide here

Koestler's native tongue was Hungarian, but as a result of his education at the Vienna Polytechnic and afterwards at the University there (he left in 1926) he chose to write in German. As a journalist he began, excitingly enough, as the only reporter with the Graf Zeppelin Arctic Expedition in 1931. After this cold start he toured Asia for two years and then joined the Communist Party in Russia resigning from it in 1938.

In 1936 he reported on the Spanish Civil War for the London *Evening News* and was actually condemned to death by the Fascists, spending 100 days in the condemned cell, expecting each day to be his last. (In 1937 he wrote *Spanish Testament* in German.) Eventually he was 'exchanged' for another prisoner as a result of intervention by the British Government. He travelled, it is said, using the 'passport' and papers of a mythical Swiss taxi driver.

September 1939 found him in France and then imprisoned in the vile camp at Le Vernet. He was released in 1940, joined the French Foreign Legion, deserted them and finally made his way back to England, where he joined the Pioneer Corps ('the lowest form of animal life') in April 1941. His prison camp ordeal was the subject for the first book he wrote in English. It appeared in 1941, entitled, *Scum of the Earth*.

His first real success was the novel, *Darkness at Noon*, translated (with his collaboration) by Daphne Hardy. It was a book that analysed the different sorts of Communist psychology and describes some of the methods used to make a man 'confess' to crimes he has not committed. *Arrival and Departure* was his first *novel* in English, which probably deserves more success than its sales figures indicate. His last published work was *Bricks to Babel*, which was a large selection from his own non-fiction pieces.

His first marriage to Dorothy Asher in 1935 ended in divorce in 1950. He then married Marianne Paget but that, too, ended in divorce in 1953. Finally he married Cynthia Jefferies. Both he and Cynthia were members of 'EXIT', voluntary euthanasia society and she became vice-president of it in 1981. She was 56 when she died.

KOSSUTH Monok, Zemplin, September 19, 1802
Lajos (Louis) Turin, March 20, 1894
Hungarian Patriot Pest

129, Gower Street, WC1, 1858-1859

Kossuth, a lawyer, had been a Deputy in the 'Diet' in Pressburg, but in 1837 he published a small revolutionary news-sheet and was imprisoned for his trouble. Released three years later, he became editor of a very radical newspaper and leader of the party in Opposition. He demanded an independent Hungary. In 1848 he became provisional Governor of the country.

He disagreed with Arthur Gorgel (1818-1916) the Commander-in-Chief and fled to Turkey where he was again imprisoned in 1849.

British and American 'influences' were brought to bear, he was released and came to London in 1851. When Hungarian affairs became relatively settled in 1867, Kossuth went to live in Turin. He was now in his late forties and his naturally curly hair was beginning to thin and Kossuth, believing that it was hard hats that caused baldness, took to wearing cloth caps (a Hungarian Keir HARDIE?). He spoke, wrote in and read six European languages fluently.

The dome of St Paul's once dominated the City's skyline, today
'high rise' buildings reduce its majesty.

Top: Both Browning and Byron compared the canal here to Venice. Now popularly referred to as 'Little Venice', the name only seems to have been used since 1945.

Above: Carlton House Terrace, designed by Nash was finished in 1832. It covers the site of the Prince Regent's palatial Carlton House.

Opposite: A backwater of bustling Kensington High Street, Kensington Square still affords a little peace. Mrs Patrick Campbell first met a barefooted Isadora Duncan dancing on the grass here.

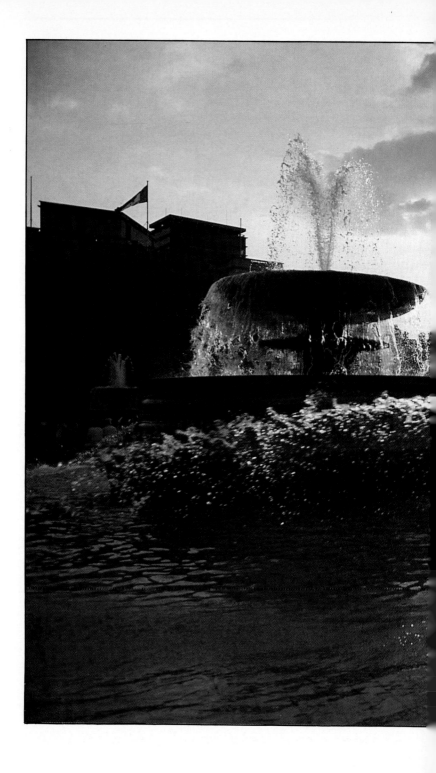

The National Gallery commands the north side of Trafalgar Square. In front of
it fountains play and the crowds feed strutting pigeons throughout the day.

Above: Lord Kitchener lived briefly at 2 Carlton Gardens. In front of the house, King George VI looks down onto the Mall.

Right: Prime Minister Canning surveys Parliament Square. The statue fell over in Westmacott's studio and crushed fellow sculptor, Vincent Gahagan to death in 1832.

Opposite: Looking towards the Houses of Parliament from the South Bank across Westminster Bridge the tall St Stephen's tower houses the great bell, 'Big Ben'.

Above: Once rudely nicknamed 'The Kensington Gas Works', the Royal Albert Hall faces the Albert Memorial across Kensington Gore.

Right: Until the Chelsea Embankment was finished in 1874, the River Thames lapped the front gardens of these houses in Cheyne Walk.

LADBROKE

All the 'Ladbrokes' are named after the Ladbroke family, who were large landowners in the North Kensington area from the 17th to the 19th centuries.

LADBROKE GROVE, W11   *Central line to Holland Park*

9,   James POPE-HENNESSY, from 1942 until he was murdered here. In 1960 the Duke and Duchess of Windsor came to visit him here. He had been their guest in France in 1959, gathering material for a book.

42,   Victor GOLLANCZ, 1929-1953. He had started his own publishing company the year before he came to live here.

99,   Hablôt BROWNE ('Phiz') 1874-1880. Before leaving this house, two years before he died, Browne burnt all the letters he had received from DICKENS, whom he had known for 44 years, Charles Lever and Harrison Ainsworth.

LAMB
Charles ('Elia')
Essayist

London, February 10, 1775
Edmonton, London, December 27, 1834
All Saints' Church, Edmonton (by sister Mary, the grave is under a paved enclosure S.W. of church)

2, Crown Office Row, EC4 (P) here born
45, Chapel Street, Pentonville, NW1, 1800
34, Southampton Buildings, WC2, 1809
4, Inner Temple Lane, EC4, 1811
20, Russell Street, WE2, 1817-1822
64, Duncan Terrace (Colebrook Cottage) N1 (LCP 1907) 1822-1827

One of the most felicitous of English writers, poor Lamb had a most unhappy life. His father was secretary to Samuel Salt (died 1792) one of the Benchers of the Inner Temple and there was enough money in hand in the Lamb household, in 1788, to send young Charles to Charterhouse (where he formed a life-long friendship with COLERIDGE). After school Lamb went to work in the South Sea House where his elder brother, John, was a clerk. From here he went on to India House; remaining there for 33 years and, at the age of 50, was retired on a two-thirds pension. The year he began at India House, Samuel Salt died and his father's income came to an abrupt halt. So Lamb, his father, mother and his beloved sister, Mary, who was ten years older than he, were obliged to live frugally. (Brother John appears to have given no help.) In 1796, Mary Lamb, suddenly insane, killed her mother with a table knife, for apparently no reason, and had to be put into an asylum.
Henceforth Charles gave up thoughts of marriage and devoted his life to caring for Mary. She was released from the asylum and came to live with him. (She is the 'Cousin Bridget' of his *Essays*.) She never totally recovered her mental balance and sometimes had to be re-incarcerated. Times were hard, money was scarce and Mary's intermittent breakdowns worried Charles tremendously.

Then in 1807 Lamb was asked by W. GODWIN to help him with his 'Juvenile Library'. It was a happy alliance and it resulted in the justly famous *Tales from Shakespeare*. Charles worked on the tragedies and Mary on the comedies.

In 1818 he began to produce essays for the *London Magazine*. These were to become the *Essays of Elia*. (Elia was a fellow clerk in India House.) The first book appeared in 1823 and the second, *The Last Essays of Elia* ten years later. By the time the Lambs had moved out to Edmonton, Mary's breakdowns became frequent and more distressing. Lamb, too, was not in the best of health and one day when out for a walk, tripped and slightly hurt his face. The wound developed into erysipelas and it was this from which he died. Poor Mary lived on, unhappily for another 13 years.

In Giltspur Street, across the road from the Old Bailey, is a restored watch house. On it is a bust of Lamb by Sir William Reynolds-Stephens. Originally the piece stood outside Christ Church, Newgate, which was badly bombed in 1941. The bust was placed in its present niche in 1962. There is also a fibreglass statue by Margaret Wrightson in Inner Temple Gardens. It was placed there in 1971.

LAMBERT   London, August 23, 1905
Constant   August 21, 1951
Composer

15, Percy Street, W1, 1936
197, Albany Street, NW1, 1947-1951

Son of a successful portrait painter, Lambert was studying at the Royal College of Music when Serge Diaghilev asked him to write music for a ballet. The result, *Romeo and Juliet*, was first performed in 1925. Later, Lambert was a conductor for the Sadler's Wells Ballet, but he was by no means narrowly traditional. He was as appreciative of jazz as he was of Elizabethan music.

He was a very heavy drinker and alcohol was to cause much trouble towards the end of his short life. His first marriage had foundered and, in 1947, he married Isobel Nicholas, a painter and a stage designer. He had a nice line in wit and once described himself as the '...only Francophil English composer-conductor, the son of an Australian painter from St Petersburg, who worked on the Trans-Siberian railway, who himself can play *God Save the King, literally* by ear'. Lambert used to hold his nose and force his breath through a punctured ear drum – the sounds made being recognizably the National Anthem. Once, however, his wit did not come 'up to scratch': he met Lytton STRACHEY at a party and re-introduced himself to the bearded, Bloomsbury *guru* '...don't you remember, Mr. Strachey?...it was four years ago'.

'Quite a nice interval, I think, don't you?' replied STRACHEY.

Lambert was also an astute music critic, but of his own music the most lasting pieces are probably *Summer's Last Will and Testament* (1936) a choral and orchestral setting of lyrics from a play of that name written by Thomas Nash in 1593 and *Rio Grande*, a setting of a poem by Sacheverell Sitwell, which had its first performance in London in 1929.

LAMBERT   Leicester, March 13, 1770
Daniel   Stamford, July 21, 1809
'Professional Fat Man'   St Martin's Stamford Baron, Leics.

53, Piccadilly, W1, 1806

At his peak, Lambert weighed 739 pounds (336 kilogrammes) and was 102 inches (259 centimetres) around his 'waist'. He was an insomniac and only drank water. His waistcoat is in the King's Lynn Museum, Norfolk.

He took rooms at 53, Piccadilly '...next Albany nearly opposite St James's Church'. Here he put himself on show and the admission charge was one shilling (5p). Big as he was, by today's standards of obesity, he was positively sylph-like. In 1980, John B. Minnoch weighed in at 1,400 pounds (635 kilogrammes).

LAMBETH ROAD, SE1   *Bakerloo line to Lambeth North*

Lambeth *may* have been from the Saxon 'lamhithe', a port or harbour where lambs and sheep were loaded and unloaded. Lambeth North was given by William the Conqueror's sister, Goda, to the See of Rochester and these lands were exchanged with Canterbury in 1197.

100 (once 3, Durham Place) William BLIGH (LCP 1952) from 1794 until his death in 1817 The house was built in 1794 and the Blighs were its first occupants.

LANCASTER   Notting Hill, August 4, 1905
(Sir) Osbert
Cartoonist

10, Addison Crescent, W11, 1938
12, Eaton Square, SW1, 1961-1976
78, Cheyne Court, Royal Hospital Road, SW3, 1977-

Practically every day since January 1, 1939, the *Daily Express* has printed a 'pocket' cartoon. Lancaster launched the idea (just a newspaper column wide cartoon) having seen French versions of this miniature *idée*. BEAVERBROOK agreed to its English version and for years Lancaster's creation, 'Maudie Littlehampton' with her pop-eyes and her aristocratic family have (truly) been on the front page of an otherwise fairly pedestrian London daily.

In some respects Lancaster poked fun at his own circle of friends and, indeed, probably relations. He was educated at Charterhouse and then Lincoln College, Oxford. He was attached to the British Embassy in Athens in 1944 and (amongst other things) is adviser to the Greater London Council's Historic Buildings Board.

LANCASTER GATE, W2   *Central line to Lancaster Gate*

The complications surrounding even *ordinary* titles are involved; but the Royal complications are really *tortuous*. Suffice it, therefore, to say that the British sovereign is, by tradition, the Duke of Lancaster. This series of Lancasters are a way (a roundabout one) of naming something after the reigning sovereign. Here the 'Lancaster' was Queen Victoria. (A real problem can occur in the Savoy Chapel. Should the National Anthem be played, one must not sing 'God save the Queen', but, 'God bless the Duke of Lancaster'. Try it.)

56, Mrs. Pearl CRAIGIE, in 1906, the year she died. Her pen name was 'John Oliver Hobbes'.

69, Lytton STRACHEY, 1884-1909. The house was put up for auction in May 1907. It did not reach the reserve price insisted upon by Lady Strachey and it was sold privately (for an undeclared sum) in September.

74, Bret HARTE (LCP 1977) from 1895, until he died here in 1902. He lived with his secretary (and mistress) Mrs. Marguerite Van Velde. Previously he had lived for nearly ten years at Number 109. This house was built in 1887 by Sancton Wood.

94, the house was rented by a rather mysterious American millionaire called George Wood but Sir John French (later Lord YPRES) lived here almost throughout World War One.

LANDON London, August 14, 1802
Letitia Elizabeth ('L.E.L.') South Africa, October 15, 1838
Author

25, Hans Place, SW3, from birth until 1820

Her father, who came from a prosperous county family, largely impoverished by the 'South Sea Bubble' fracas, was a partner in Adair's Army Agency in Pall Mall.

As a child she got to know William Jordan, a Scottish journalist, who in 1820 was editor of the *Weekly Gazette*. He was the first to publish her work – the poem, *Rome* – and she became the *Gazette's* principal book reviewer. Her first novel appeared in 1821, called *The Fate of Adelaide* and her next, *The Improvisatrice*, which ran to six editions, in 1825.

She was now earning something like £2,500 a year and so was of considerable help to her rather down-on-their-luck family. She was a woman of spirit and she embarked on a talked about romance with a brilliant, but drunken journalist, called (aptly) Maginn, who was nine years older than she. The scandal caused her to break off her engagement with John Forster and, 'on the rebound', she married the Governor of the Cape Coast Castle, George MacLean, in June 1838. They set sail for Africa on July 5 and on October 15 she was found dead in her bedroom with an empty bottle (which had contained prussic acid) beside her. It was said a jealous ex-mistress of MacLean's had wreaked her vengeance and the matter rather drifted; no formal finding of suicide, murder or accident being proved.

LANDOR Warwick, January 30, 1775
Walter Savage Florence, September 17, 1864
Dilettante Florence

38, Beaumont Street, W1, 1794

From Rugby School Landor went up to Oxford, where he was nicknamed 'The Mad Jacobin' and behaved so badly he was 'rusticated'. Oxford really was the beginning of a life full of troubles (usually self-inflicted ones). He was quick tempered, violently prejudiced against anyone or anything which did not suit him immediately. He quarrelled with his father, a Warwickshire doctor but (luckily) was reconciled with him before 1805, when the doctor died and left the 30-year old Walter a considerable fortune. Three years later he was in Spain to fight against Napoleon but, unlike so many 'altruistic patriots', he actually *did* see some fighting.

When he came back to England he married Julia Thuillier, bought Llanthony Abbey and had his tragic play, *Count Julian* published, all in 1811. Predictably he was soon quarrelling with everybody (including his wife). He left England in a huff, travelled through France to Italy and stayed at Como for two years. Here he 'insulted' the local authorities, travelled south to Florence and settled there in 1818 for the rest of his life. He worked on his *Imaginery Conversations* published in five volumes (two in 1824, the third in 1828 and the last two in 1829).

Landor once wrote to the Bishop of St Davids, offering to pay for the restoration of the church at Llanthony where he and Julia had been married. The Bishop sent no answer and Landor wrote again, that, 'God alone is great enough for me to ask anything of twice'. The Bishop replied by return of post.

LANE   Bristol, September 21, 1902
(Sir) Allen   July 7, 1970
'Penguin' publishing pioneer

8, Lancaster Gate, W2, c.1930

Lane was a nephew of John LANE and, until 1919, was Allen Williams, when he changed to Lane by Deed Poll. Uncle John took him into his publishing house at Bodley Head which had had a very successful run for nearly 50 years.

Allen Lane was innovative and it was he who really brought 'paperbacks' into the world in 1935. The first *Penguin* paperbacks sold at sixpence (two and a half new pennies). Lane's brain child altered the world of publishing (a very foot-dragging industry, even now) all over the world.

Young Lane was also responsible for introducing two authors (to the public at large) who were scandalous in 1936 and probably not entirely acceptable today. Lane published *Ulysses* by James Joyce and, later, D.H. LAWRENCE's *Lady Chatterly's Lover* (qv Lawrence).

LANE   Putford, Devon, March 14, 1854
John   February 3, 1925
Publisher   St Nectan's Church, Hartland, N.
                                           Devon

37, Southwick Street, W2, 1885-1890
G 1, Albany, W1, 1890s

A railway clerk from Devon, Lane met Elkin Mathews, another Devonian and they established the publishing house 'The Bodley Head'. (Named after Sir Thomas Bodley, yet another Devon man, born in Exeter in 1545 and died in London in 1613. He opened the Bodleian Library in Oxford, one of the greatest libraries in the world, on November 8, 1603. It had been originally established in 1445.) The 'Bodley Head's' first publication was a book of poems by Richard LE GALLIENNE in March 1889, called *Volumes in Folio*.

Lane had a 'great eye' for the ladies and someone had nicknamed him 'Petticoat Lane'. Nevertheless he married a wealthy American widow in 1894 and they lived 'happily ever after'. (He did, in fact, have protruberant, as well as roving, eyes and sported a small, well-trimmed beard.)

LANG   Selkirk, March 31, 1844
Andrew   Bangory, Scotland, July 20, 1912
Author

1, Marloes Road, SW7 (LCP 1959) 1876-1912

After really rather an extended education (Edinburgh Academy, St Andrew's University, Glasgow University and, finally, Balliol College, Oxford) Lang was made a Fellow of Merton College, Oxford.

In 1875 he married and then, like so many sensible Scotsmen, he left Scotland and settled with his new wife in Kensington. He made his living with his pen and his first, published work was *Ballads and Lyrics of Old France* in 1872, followed by *Ballads in Blue China* in 1880.

Twenty-eight years and 59 books later he published a book entitled, *A Defence of Walter Scott*, though one might well think that Scott would have not needed much *defending* in the early part of the 20th century. Lang's versatility extended from translations of Theocritus (1880) to a series of Fairy Tale books and a *Book of Romance* in 1902. In 1890 he wrote a book which *tempted* Providence. It was *How to Fail in Literature*.

LANGHAM STREET, W1

*Bakerloo, Central and Victoria lines
to Oxford Circus*

This street and Langham Place were bought by Sir James Langham from the 4th Lord Foley, who, 'by debauchery, extravagance and gaming', had dissipated the family fortunes by 1814.

30, Thomas CAMPBELL, c.1830-1840. It was during this period that he was working his hardest to establish London Unviersity.

40, Edmund MALONE (LCP 1962) from 1779 to 1812. Only his death prevented another edition of Shakespeare, intended to supersede his own edition of 1790.

48, Ezra POUND, 1908. This was his first fixed address since he had come to London two years before.

LANGTRY

Lily (or Lillie)
'Professional Beauty'

Jersey, October 13, 1853
Monte Carlo, February 12, 1929
St Saviour's, Jersey

12, Norfolk Street, W1, 1877
2, Cadogan Gardens, SW3
18, Pont Street, SW3, 1880s
18, Albert Mansions, W8, 1882
21, Pont Street, SW3 (LCP 1980) 1892-1897

Born Emilie Charlotte Le Breton on the island of Jersey in the Channel Islands, where her father was Dean, Lily managed to escape from the restrictive net of a rather small and narrow-minded community, by marrying the rich but ineffectual Edward Langtry in 1874.

The Langtrys came to London and soon her striking good looks gave them the run of London's socially select *salons*. Lily was to have discreet *affaires* with a number of men (usually married ones) and she found herself right at the very top of the tree when she woke up in the bed of 'Bertie', Prince of Wales and heir to the Throne. Many people believed that the daughter which Lily had, some months later, had been fathered by the Prince, but in fact the girl's father was another Prince (not so lofty) Prince Louis of Battenberg, father of Lord Louis MOUNTBATTEN. The child was trained to call Lily, 'Aunt'. Eventually she married and had a daughter, who grew up to be Mary Malcolm, one of the first TV 'personalities'.

Lily reached the stage when she needed a different scene and went *on* the stage. She was no Sarah Bernhardt but her performances earned justifiable applause. Her nickname of the 'Jersey Lily' did not come from her stage ventures but as a result of having had her portrait painted by MILLAIS.

Langtry, who had remained in the background for years, died in 1897 and Lily then married Gerald de Bathe in 1899. She was 46 and Gerald was 28. He became the 5th baronet in 1907. At the time, her address was Cornwall Lodge, Cornwall Terrace on the edge of Regent's Park.

Despite the fact that practically anyone on the stage was thought to be immoral and having had a number of 'extramarital liaisons', Lily somehow seemed to be able to keep above malicious gossip. The Press was not always kind and one yellow sheet of the day reported that, 'Mrs Langtry has lost her parrot...That the lady possessed such a bird we were unaware, but we knew she had a cockatoo'.

LASKI

Harold Joseph
Political 'philosopher'

Manchester, 1893
1950

5, Addison Bridge Place, W14 (LCP 1974) 1926-1936

Laski came from a Manchester Jewish family and was educated at

Manchester Grammar School (founded in 1515 and considered as a boys' 'Public School', a fact which, later in life, Laski would have called 'élitist'). He went up to New College, Oxford and when the First World War broke out, he was lecturing at McGill University in Montreal. In 1916 he travelled south to Harvard for four years, then Amherst in 1917 and finally Yale. (A very ivy league circuit for a minor revolutionary.)

In 1920 he joined the teaching staff of the London School of Economics and was Professor of Political Science there by 1926. He was held in the highest esteem by his peers and almost 'revered' by his pupils. He believed in individual freedom though the downfall of the Labour Government in 1931 made him harden his views and he took a considerable step to the left (politically). Labour got back to power in 1945 and in that year Laski became Chairman of the Labour Party, but only for a year.

LAVER	Liverpool, March 14, 1899
James	London, June 3, 1975
Man of letters and critic	

11, Wellington Square, SW3, 1935-1940s and 1950s
4/10, The Glebe, SW3, 1975

From the Liverpool Institute Laver went on to New College, Oxford, where he won the Newdigate Prize for his poem on *Cervantes* in 1921. The following year he came up to London and was appointed Assistant Keeper of the Print Room at the Victoria and Albert Museum. Five years later he was the Keeper.

He published a number of books of art criticism and on the history of English costume. He later became Art Director of the Working Men's College in Camden Town. This rather unlikely sounding Directorship had previously been held by RUSKIN, BURNE-JONES and Dante Gabriel ROSSETTI.

Laver retired from the 'V and A' in 1959. The Second World War had, of course, intervened; in 1940 Laver was 41 and he became a Civil Servant. At one stage he worked in a Department which dealt with the affairs of 'Escheated Estates of Intestate Bastards'.

LAVERY	Belfast, March 16(c), 1856
(Sir) John	January 10, 1941
Artist	Putney Vale Cemetery

5, Cromwell Place, SW7, 1899-1941

Lavery was, at first, a disciple of the 'Glasgow School' of painting. Before moving to London, having studied in Paris, his work had become influenced by Impressionists and WHISTLER.

He became a fashionable portrait painter, but the promise he had held, '...was not fulfilled as in later life he succumbed to the facile lures of a society portrait painter'. He was awarded one of those 'facile lures'; a knighthood in 1918. In 1921 he was elected to the Royal Academy and was President of the Royal Society of Portrait Painters for nine years.

LAW	New Brunswick, September 16, 1858
Andrew Bonar	London, October 30, 1928
Prime Minister	Westminster Abbey, in the centre of the Nave

24, Onslow Gardens, SW7 (LCP 1958) 1921-1928

Law, born in New Brunswick, became an iron merchant in Glasgow. He also made thereby, a modest fortune. He became a Unionist MP in 1900 and Unionist Leader after BALFOUR, staying in the House of Commons until

1911. He was a member of the War Cabinet, Chancellor of the Exchequer from 1916-1918, Lord Privy Seal in 1919 and 'retired' in March 1921. Though undoubtedly ill, he was prevailed upon to make a 'political come-back' and was Prime Minister from October 1922 until May 1923.

LAWRENCE Eastwood, Notts., September 11, 1885
David Herbert Vence, France, March 2, 1930
Author Eastwood Cemetery

44, Mecklenburg Square, WC1, 1917
73, Gower Street, WC1, 1925

Lawrence's father was a coal miner working in one of the many coal mines to be found in the Nottingham area in the 19th century. His mother was a school teacher and, as a young man, Lawrence followed in her footsteps and became a school master (a very poor one) in Croydon. When he was 26, he found a publisher for *The White Peacock* and its success was sufficiently encouraging for him to lay down the cap and gown and pick up the pen.
In 1915 his novel, *The Rainbow*, was suppressed as obscene. Sex features in most of Lawrence's work and, had he only written *Lady Chatterly's Lover*, he would be remembered for that. The book was banned in Britain and the United States. *Penguin Books* printed it in 1960 and *dared* the Director of Public Prosecutions to take them to court. So he did. *Penguin* had lined up a galaxy of literary witnesses to swear that the novel had real merit. *Penguin* won the day and released over 200,000 copies to make it the best-seller they had ever had.
Sir Osbert SITWELL only met Lawrence once (in Italy) and wrote, '...what a fragile and goatish little saint he was: a Pan and a Messiah: for in his flattish face, with its hollow, wan cheeks and rather red beard, was to be discerned a curious mingling of satyr and ascetic...'. The doctors could discern from '...those hollow, wan cheeks' tuberculosis and it was T.B. which killed him.

LAWRENCE Bristol, May 4, 1769
(Sir) Thomas London, January 7, 1830
Artist St Paul's Cathedral crypt

60, Greek Street, W1, -1814
24 (then 29) Old Bond Street, W1
65, Russell Square, WC1, where he died

Lawrence's father was a West Country inn keeper and Thomas was a true artistic prodigy from *any* social class. At the age of 12, he had his own studio in Bath. He entered the Royal Academy Schools when he was 18 and it was not until then that he first began to paint in oils. Two years later he was commanded to paint a portrait of Queen Charlotte, Queen Consort of King George III. The painting is now in the National Gallery. It could not have been an easy commission. The Queen, who was 45 years old, had had her *15th* child six years previously, having had her first in 1762, when she was only 18 years old and her last, Princess Amelia, nineteen years later in 1783. Even when young she was really *very* plain.
When Hoppner died in 1810, Lawrence was considered to be the finest living painter of portraits. In 1810 the Prince Regent sent Lawrence off to Europe to paint portraits of the most eminent persons of the Allied nations who had joined together to defeat the Emperor Napoleon. This series of paintings now hangs in the Waterloo Chamber of Windsor Castle. The Prince rewarded Lawrence with a knighthood. Soon after, Benjamin WEST died and Lawrence was elected as President of the Royal Academy.

LAWRENCE   Tremadoc, August 15, 1888
Thomas Edward   Dorset, May 13, 1935
Middle Eastern hero St Nicholas's Church, Moreton,
                     Dorset

14, Barton Street, SW1 (LCP 1966) 1922-1929

Lawrence was one of the enigmas of 20th century Britain. He was a small man, physically, though he showed that his small frame had tremendous reserves of strength. He always seemed to have a chip on his shoulder and, if the chip was not easy to find, he would soon work out a way to invent one. Part of his complex may have been caused by the knowledge of his illegitimacy; his father's name was Chapman. Later in life he may have suffered disappointments which would have meant little to another, less 'prickly' man. He went to Oxford High School and on from there to Jesus College, where he formed a taste for archaeology. He worked with Sir Flinders PETRIE for two years until 1914. The First World War began in August that year; Lawrence started to work for British Intelligence and also helped the Arab tribesmen to revolt against their Turkish oppressors. By 1918 he was nearly a legend and was awarded a DSO and the CB. (It was *said* he had refused a knighthood *and* a Victoria Cross.) He was elected a Fellow of All Souls College, Oxford – an honour he *did* accept.
Engines had become one of the great loves of his life and he had bought a powerful 'Brough Superior' motor cycle which was his pride, love and joy. It was to kill him when he overturned it on an apparently totally clear length of straight road in Dorset.

LAWRENCE STREET, SW3   *District and Circle lines*
                                 to Sloane Square

Named after the wealthy Lawrence family who lived in nearby Lawrence House in the 16th and 17th centuries. The widow of Sir Thomas Lawrence sold the lease of her house to Anne, Duchess of Monmouth in 1712. This *lady* born in 1651, was also the *Duke* of Buccleugh. In 1663 she had married the fourteen-year old James, Duke of Monmouth. He was the bastard son of Charles II by Lucy Walters (so she said). James was beheaded on Tower Hill in July 1685.
On the corner of Cheyne Walk is a block of flats called **Carlyle Mansions**.

Flat 19, T.S. ELIOT was here during the First World War. He shared it with John Hayward (1905-1965). Hayward was crippled and confined to a wheel chair, yet he kept in the literary swim and, at one stage, was editorial adviser to the *Book Collector* magazine. He lived on here until his death. Altogether, he was not a very prepossessing man and his face was marred, '...by a really horrifying lower lip'.

Flat 21, Henry JAMES died here in 1916. As he lay dying, Edmund GOSSE came to see him to tell him that King George V had made him a member of the exalted Order of Merit. James did not rally to Gosse's whispered news and Gosse tip-toed out. When he had gone James said quite cheerfully to the maid 'Kidd, take away the candle and spare my blushes'.

16, John GAY, 1712-1714, acting as the Duchess of Monmouth's secretary.

16, Tobias SMOLLETT (LCP 1950) 1747-1762. Having given up medecine, Smollett moved here and his successful novel, *Roderick Random*, was published the following year. He also (probably) wrote *Peregrine Pickle* and *Sir Launcelot Greaves* here as well.

LEAR
Edward
Artist and Poet

London, May 12, 1812
San Remo, Italy, January 29, 1888
San Remo

197, Albany Street, NW1, c.1830s
17, Stratford Place, W1, 1850-1852
30, Seymour Street, W1 (LCP 1960) 1857-1858 (in his day 16, Upper Seymour Street)

Lear's fame tends to rest on his delightful *Book of Nonsense* published in 1846. Much of this was originally produced to amuse the children of the Earl of Derby. Lear was staying at Derby's vast mansion, Knowlsey House, near Liverpool, as he had been commissioned by the 13th Earl of Derby to paint a number of paintings of beasts and birds in the Earl's collection for a book on the Knowsley Menagerie. Lear was a fine draftsman and had begun his career as a 19-year-old with the Zoological Society.

His health was never good and, in 1837, he left England in search of a kinder climate. He earned a little money as a drawing teacher in Rome. For a brief time he instructed Queen Victoria in drawing on one of his flying visits to England. When he was over 60, the Viceroy of India, Lord Northbrook, a friend of his, invited him to visit the 'sub-continent'. Lear accepted and brought back fine work painted on this visit.

VIGEE-LEBRUN
Marie-Louise Elizabeth
Artist

Paris, April 16, 1775
Paris, March 30, 1842

61, Baker Street, W1, 1802-1805

Madame Vigée Lebrun had been Mademoiselle Vigée until she married J.B.P. Lebrun, a Parisian picture dealer; a nephew of the historical painter, Charles LeBrun (1619-1690).

She had been a favourite at the Court of Louis XVI and a friend of Marie Antoinette. Come the Revolution she left France hurriedly in 1789 and lived in Italy for a while, returning to Paris in 1801. She did not like Napoleon either, so she set herself up in London. Her work appealed to English society and she painted portraits of both the Prince of Wales and Lord BYRON. She charged 200 guineas (£210) for a three-quarter length portrait.

LECKY
William Edward Hartpole
Historian

Dublin, March 26, 1838
London, October 22, 1903

38, Onslow Gardens, SW7 (LCP 1955) from 1874 until he died here

Lecky graduated from Trinity College, Dublin in 1959 as a BA and two years later published four brilliant essays on Swift, Flood, Gratton and O'Connell. He also produced a nicely balanced *History of England in the 18th Century*, between the years of 1878-1890.

In 1895 he had become an Ulster Unionist Member of Parliament for Dublin University, though he had stopped championing the cause of Irish Home rule, which he had supported previously. He was made a Privy Councillor in 1897 and had the Order of Merit bestowed upon him; he was one of the first so honoured as the Decoration had only been devised by King Edward VII in 1902.

LEE   Bridport, Dorset, November 11, 1868
(1st Viscount) Arthur   July 21, 1947
Politician

22, Elsham Road, W14, 1874-1900
84, Chesterfield Street, W1, 1902-1914
2, Abbey Gardens, SW1, c.1914-1918
18, Kensington Palace Gardens, W8, 1922-1927

Lee's most solid monument is 'Chequers' ('Chequers Court' in full) the
country house which he gave to the nation to be used as a 'retreat' for the
Prime Minister of the day. It is a Tudor mansion set in an estate of some 700
acres (283 hectares) in the Chiltern Hills, about three miles from Princes
Risborough. Lee gave it in 1917 and LLOYD-GEORGE was the first Prime
Minister to use it in 1921. The gift included a rich collection of Cromwellian
portraits and relics.
He was the son of an impecunious parson and had an unhappy childhood.
He overcame many of his drawbacks and passed out top of his year at the
Royal Military Academy, the training school for Army officers, at
Sandhurst in Berkshire. He served with the British Expeditionary Forces in
France in 1914/1915.
On a visit to the United States he met Ruth Moore, a wealthy heiress and
they were married on Christmas Eve in 1899. Politically he was a Liberal –
and so supported Lloyd-George; privately, he bought and sold works of art.

LEE   Slad, Gloucestershire, June 26, 1914
Laurie
Poet

49, Elm Park Gardens, SW10, 1964-1984

Lee's first published success was a prose rather than a poetical work; his
'autobiographical' *Cider with Rosie* in 1959. Its fame was such that it almost
became a 'cult' book. Ten years later he published, *As I Walked out One
Midsummer Morning* an overt autobiography. In it he tells of his first days in
London; a country boy just up from the rural west of England, '...yet to me,
when off duty, London offered a well-heeled idleness, even on £2.5s 0d
(£2.25p) a week. After paying for my lodgings, I had £1 to spend, which
could be broken up in a hundred ways. A tot of whisky cost sixpence (2p) a
pint of beer fourpence halfpenny (2p) cigarettes were elevenpence (5p) for
20. The best seats in the cinema cost ninepence to a shilling (5p) or I could
climb to the gallery for threepence (1p).'
His first collection of poems, *The Sun My Monument*, was published in 1944.
Cider with Rosie, already mentioned, won the W.H. Smith Annual Literary
Award in 1960. (It was the second one to be awarded. In 1959 *Voss*, by
Patrick White, won the first ever prize.) Some of Lee's other poetical works
are, *My Many-Coated Man* (1955) and *The Bloom of Candles*.

LEECH   London, August 29, 1817
John   London, October 29, 1864
Illustrator   Kensal Green: Square 6, Row 1 (beside
                                           W.M. THACKERAY)

32, Brunswick Square, WC1, 1848-1854
28, Bennet Street, SW1
6, The Terrace, W14, 1854-1864

Leech's father, though a man of some culture, kept a coffee shop on Ludgate
Hill, over which John was born. He was sent to Charterhouse School, only a
short walk away, when he was 13 and there he met THACKERAY. Some

accounts make them out to be firm friends at school but the novelist was seven years older than Leech and a friendship there would be unlikely. Even more so when one knows Leech left Charterhouse when he was only 16 and was apprenticed to a surgeon, called (appropriately?) Whittle. Medecine was not to his taste and he only stayed with Whittle for two years. When he was 18 he published *Etchings and Sketches* by 'A. Pen Esquire'. This, however, did not make his fortune.

His first illustration appeared in *Punch* in 1841 and he was to contribute 3,000 for *Punch* alone (including some 600 cartoons) before he died. He also illustrated *The Ingoldsby Legends* and Surtees' *Handley Cross* novels. Dickens said that Leech's drawings were '...always the drawings of a gentleman'. Certainly his satire was of the gentlest sort.

LEES-MILNE
August 6, 1908
James
Adviser to the National Trust

104, Cheyne Walk, SW3, for some years until 1945
17, Alexander Place, SW3, 1945

Lees-Milne's family were wealthy, but socially not in the first flight and his father sent him to Eton where he '...did not excel'. Incredibly his father enrolled him in a typewriting school where he was the only male student. After that ordeal he went up to Magdalen College, Oxford, where he '...just got a degree'.

After graduating he worked for three years for Lord Lloyd, whom he respected and admired and then for Sir Roderick Jones at Reuters, whom he did not. In common with practically anybody who came across Sir Roderick, Lees-Milne could not stand Jones and eventually took the advice of Stanley BALDWIN, whom he met by chance at a country house week end and resigned before he gave Jones the pleasure of sacking him.

LE GALLIENNE
Liverpool, January 20, 1866
Richard
Menton, France, September 14, 1947
Culture enthusiast

34, Bedford Place, WC1, 1894–1900
5, Bedford Gardens, W8, early 1900s

The Le Galliennes were of Channel Island stock, but Richard's father had been in Liverpool from the early part of the 1800s and he worked for a brewery. Richard, having finished schooling in Liverpool, wanted to be a journalist and/or a poet. Neither of these possibilities appealed to papa who articled the lad to a firm of Liverpudlian accountants (the articles were to run for seven years). Maybe Le Gallienne senior was not all Philistine as he took his son, in December 1883, to hear Oscar WILDE lecture on his recent tour in America.

In 1887 Le Gallienne had a small collection of his poems privately printed in Liverpool, calling them *My Ladies Sonnets*. He spent a holiday in London that September and he must have given Wilde (who by this time was married and living in Tite Street) a copy of his *Sonnets*.

Le Gallienne, obviously more determined than ever to live a cultural life, came to London in 1889 and shook the dust of Liverpool off forever. He got a job as private secretary to Wilson Barrett, literary critic of the *Star*, a London evening newspaper, but for some reason had his office in the Princess Theatre in Oxford Street.

LEICESTER SQUARE, WC2
*Piccadilly and Northern lines
to Leicester Square*

Once covered by Leicester Fields, this site was where the 2nd Earl (a descendant of Sir Philip Sidney, 1554-1586) was allowed to build his mansion here, *providing* he left a green area where the local peasants could dry their washing. He finished his house in 1631, when he was 36 years old. A later developer of the Square was a man who styled himself as 'Baron Grant' (real name Gottheimer, 1830-1899). Between 1872 and 1874 the 'Baron' spent some £28,000 on the creation of the Square more as it appears today. (He claimed his 'Barony' had been given to him by the King of Italy.) Somehow he was elected MP for Kidderminster, Worcs. and bought the *Echo* newspaper. He had a fittingly baronial house in Kensington. However his circumstance altered for the worse and he eventually died, poor and forgotten in Bognor on the south coast.

12, John Singleton COPLEY, 1776-1784. Copley had his studio here, having arrived in London in 1774 from America.

28, John HUNTER, c.1780-1793, the year he died. After his death the Government of the day bought the house for £12,000.

29, John TRUMBULL, 1808, another American painter. He married in London eight years previous to moving here.

30, William HOGARTH died here in 1764. He probably took this house in 1732, when he also had lodgings in Isleworth. The house was the last but two on the east side of the square. In Hogarth's time there were still fields about. Outside the house was a cork bust of Van Dyck (or Vandyke, born Antwerp, March 22, 1599 and died London, December 9, 1641). Hogarth made this quaint piece and gilded it. There are contemporary prints showing the *Golden Head* made by Bowles in 1753. Dr. John HUNTER at one time lived next door to number 30.

47 ('Fanum House', the head office of the Automobile Association today) Sir Joshua REYNOLDS died in his house on this site in 1792, having lived here since 1761. 'His study was *octagonal* some twenty feet long, by sixteen broad and about fifteen feet high. The window was small and square and the sill nine feet from the floor. After his death a firm of auctioneers bought the house.

48, T.W.H. CROSLAND, 1904. He wrote *The Lord of Creation* here.

In the centre of the Square is a statue of Shakespeare, which is a copy by Giovanni Fontanta (1821-1893) of Peter Scheemakers' (1691-1781) statue of the *Bard* in Westminster Abbey. The pedestal on which Shakespeare stands together with the dolphins and fountains were designed by Sir James Knowles (1831-1908). The four statues on the corners are all of one time residents in the Square, N.W. REYNOLDS by Henry Weekes (1874), N.E. HUNTER by Thomas Wollner (1874), S.E. HOGARTH by Joseph Durham (1874) and S.W. NEWTON by W. Calder Marshall (1874).

LEIGHTON Scarborough, Yorks., December 3,
Frederick (1st Baron) 1830
Artist London, January 25, 1896
  St Paul's Cathedral

Leighton House, 12, Holland Park Road, W14 (LCP 1958) from 1866 until he died here

Leighton was the son of a prosperous Scarborough doctor and he set the boy to study art seriously when he was very young. Dr. Leighton would appear to dominate Frederick's life. It is all the sadder to think that this despotic father lived to 1892, only four years before the death of the son he persecuted. Leighton's artistic education took place in Rome, Florence, Frankfurt, Berlin, Paris and Brussels. In Frankfurt he studied under E.J. von Steinle (1810-1886).

His first picture in the Academy of 1855, a *quattrocento pastiche* he called *Cimabue's Madonna Carried in Procession*, was bought by Queen Victoria. He settled in London in 1860, was elected a full Academician in 1868 and

President in 1878. Eight years later he was made a baronet and a peer (the first artist ever to have been so honoured) only a few days before he died. He did not, therefore, arrange a motto for himself with the College of Heralds. Leighton House is now a museum, open every weekday from 11-5. The gardens are open from April to September. The front hall of the house is spectacularly Arabic. Admission is free.

L.E.L., See LANDON, L.E.

LETHABY	Barnstaple, Devon, 1857
William Richard	London, July 17, 1931
Architect	Westminster Abbey Cloisters

111, Inverness Terrace, W2, 1931

As an architect Lethaby, a pupil of Norman Shaw, tried always to follow the precepts of William Samuel MORRIS. He was as opposed to the 'scrape-off-the-dirt' school of thought (when used in Westminster Abbey) as Morris was in 1892. Lethaby's books on the Abbey, published in 1906 and 1925 are as good as any on the subject. (This is the view of Nikolaus Pevsner, whose views on London and its architects are better than most.) Most of Lethaby's surviving work was on country houses and one office block in Birmingham.

LEVER	Bolton, September 19, 1851
William Hesketh (1st Lord	London, May 7, 1925
Leverhulme)	Port Sunlight, Lancs.
Soap millionaire	

Lancaster House, The Mall, SW1, 1912-1925 (formerly Stafford House and, originally York House)

Sixteen-year old William left school in Bolton and started work as an apprentice in his father's grocery business. He was paid one shilling (5p) a week. He and his brother expanded the business and in 1886 went into soap making, using vegetable oils rather than tallow. He called the product *Sunlight* and he prospered.

When he died 40 years later his business had grown into an international conglomerate called Lever Brothers, capitalized at £50 million and employing nearly 100,000 workers.

He was made a Baron in 1917 and a Viscount in 1922. Among many charitable activities he founded a School for Tropical Diseases at Liverpool University (he had many business interests in Africa) and gave Lancaster House to the Nation. He died at his house, 'The Hill', North End in Hampstead, NW. His coffined body was placed 'in state' in the Art Gallery he had built at Port Sunlight and more than 30,000 people came to pay their last respects.

LEWES	London, April 18, 1817
George Henry	London, November 28, 1878
Journalist and critic	Highgate Cemetery, East IV (behind 'George Eliot's' grave)

16, Blandford Square, W1, 1860-1863
21, North Bank, NW8, where he died

Lewes was the grandson of a once quite well-known comedian, Charles Lee Lewes (1740-1803) but George Henry had no inclination for the stage. He began his working life in a Russian merchant's office, tried medecine (but found he could not stand the sight of blood) and then went off to Germany for two years. Back in London he scraped a living writing for various journals and for *Penny's Encyclopaedia*. He was a fine dramatic critic and in 1875 published *Actors and the Art of Acting*. His most substantial and long lasting work was his life of Goethe (1749-1832) which was published in 1855.

His marriage had produced four children, but not happiness and in July 1854, all pretences of holding it together ended. He met 'George Eliot' (Mary Ann EVANS) and this intellectual but irregular union lasted for 24 years – until his death.

LEWIS　　　　　　　　　　　Ely Place, London, April 21, 1833
(Sir) George Henry　　　　　　London, December 7, 1911
Solicitor

88, Portland Place, W1, 1896-1911

Lewis was admitted as a solicitor in 1856 and eventually became senior partner in the firm of Lewis and Lewis (of 10, 11 and 12 Ely Place, Holborn). He was to become solicitor to the 'Establishment'.

He was the repository of all sorts of secrets, often sexual, of the 'Upper Crust' (including *some* of those of the then Prince of Wales).

Lewis was Jewish, had a long nose, balanced by 'Dundeary Whiskers', and always sported a monocle and an ultra-glossy silk top hat.

LEWIS　　　　　　　　　　　Sauk Centre, Minnesota, February 7,
Harry Sinclair　　　　　　　　1885
Novelist　　　　　　　　　　　Rome, January 10, 1951
　　　　　　　　　　　　　　　Sauk Centre

58, Elm Park Gardens, SW10, 1923 (at this time it was a hotel)

Lewis's father was a doctor and sent Harry to Yale where his academic career rather took second place as Sinclair became more and more involved in journalistic activities. His first novel was *Our Mr. Wrenn* published in 1914, but it was *Main Street* six years later which brought him fame and fortune. Over half a million copies sold in America alone. In 1922 *Babbitt* appeared, a satirical novel about the American business man. (The noun 'babbitt' is still sometimes used to describe a middle class American philistine.)

He refused the Pulitzer Prize in 1926, but accepted the Nobel Prize for Literature in 1930, so becoming the first American citizen to be so honoured. When he came to London in 1933 he was described as being, '...tall, reddish, clean-shaven with raw, red skin and blotchy eyes almost popping out of his head. He is drink sodden, his stomach has gone to pieces and he has shingles. He is just over 40' [infact he was 48] 'and looks over 50.' So Bruce Lockhart wrote on meeting him.

LEWIS　　　　　　　　　　　London, September 26, 1867
Rosa　　　　　　　　　　　　　London, November 29, 1952
Cook and hotelier　　　　　　Putney Vale Cemetery

55, Eaton Terrace, SW1 (until 1902)
The Cavendish Hotel, Jermyn Street, SW1, 1902-1951

Rosa was the 5th child of William and Eliza Ovenden and she was brought up in Leyton in north east London where she was born. William was a watch maker and was neither well or badly off. Rosa rose up through the ranks of being 'in service' in very ordinary middle class households, but she took every opportunity to learn as much as possible about cookery. Eventually she became one of the best thought of cooks of her time both in England and America.

As a sideline she set up a household where rich and aristocratic gentlemen could entertain their *petites amies*. To add to her 'respectability' she married

Excelsior Lewis, who was a rather drunken butler. Even sober he was of little account. The house which Rosa so discreetly and expertly managed was sometimes visited by HRH the Prince of Wales.

Eventually she bought (or had bought for her) the Cavendish Hotel in Jermyn Street. Here she 'reigned' from 1902 until not long before her death 50 years later. The Cavendish had cost £5,000 for the lease, goodwill, fixtures and fittings. It covered numbers 81, 82 and 83 Jermyn Street.

LEWIS	Maine, November 18, 1884
Wyndham Percy	March 7, 1957
Author, artist, crank	Kensal Green (though no record exists)

27, Redcliffe Gardens, SW10, 1920
61, Palace Gardens Terrace, W8, 1920s
33, Ossington Street, W2, 1920s-1930s
4 (formerly 31) Percy Street, W1, late 1930s

Born of English parents in America, he was brought back to England and, in 1897, sent to Rugby School. In 1902 he was studying at the Slade School of Art and then into the Artillery to fight an undistinguished World War One. After it was all over, he and Ezra POUND founded the magazine *Blast*, which was (some thought mercifully) short-lived. Lewis's first novel, *Tarr*, had been published in 1918 and his novels after that have sometimes been described as, '...part novel, part essay...but all satire'. He also painted and it was thought that his paintings had been executed '...by a mailed fist in a cotton glove'.

His Kensington studio was, '...haunted by pallid hens' and overrun with mice. At one time Lewis became convinced that Roger FRY and Clive Bell (Virginia WOOLF's brother-in-law) roosted on his studio roof, to 'spy on him'.

LINCOLN'S INN, WC2   *Central line to Chancery Lane*

The Black Friars (Dominicans) settled here in 1221, before they moved (or, more accurately, *were* moved) to the area which today is at the City end of Blackfriars Bridge. The Earl of Lincoln was appointed by King Edward I (reigned 1272-1307) to enquire into alleged scandals connected with the Inns of Court (Lincoln's Inn having become an Inn of Court in about 1300). The Earl's town house stood on part of the grounds of the Inn.

4, Stone Buildings William Pitt (the 'Younger') for a year in 1779/80.
61, William Charles MACREADY, 1832-1837. In his last year here he took over the management of Covent Garden.

OLD SQUARE

So named after 'New Square' was built in 1682.

1, in a three storey building (then called Gatehouse Court) William MURRAY (later Lord MANSFIELD) began his law studies, in about 1728.
2, Lord CAMPBELL, 1800-1804.
8, Lord BROUGHAM, 1820.
19, Ronald FIRBANK, 1914, 'in a *tiny* flat'.

LINCOLN'S INN FIELDS, WC2

This 'square' is the largest in London and has often had its layout (wrongly) attributed to Inigo Jones. It was laid out in 1618 and it was erroneously claimed that the 'square' of the Fields was the same as the 'square' of the Great Pyramid of Egypt. However, the base of the Pyramid is 821 by 625 feet (250 by 190 metres) and Lincoln's Inn is 764 square feet (71 square metres).

3, Ramsay MACDONALD, 1896-1916. His wife, Margaret, a compassionate woman, died here in 1911. On the north side of the Fields is a bronze of Mrs. MacDonald which was placed above a seat here in 1914. The sculptor was Richard Goulden.

12, 13 and **14,** Sir John SOANE. He died in number 13 on January 20, 1837, but because of the influenza epidemic, was not buried in St. Giles's Churchyard until ten days later. He had designed number 12 for himself in 1792 and lived there before designing 13, twenty years later. The three houses now form a fascinating museum, open to the public (free of charge). The incredibly varied collection is much as SOANE laid it out originally.

50, Dante Gabriel ROSSETTI, 1862.

55, Sir William BLACKSTONE, 1768 and 1780.

59, Spencer PERCEVAL, 1796-1807 (LCP 1914). At the end of his occupancy here he had risen to be Chancellor of the Exchequer.

60, Alfred, Lord TENNYSON, in 1842 and 1846.

61, Thomas CAMPBELL, 1828-1837 and again later, until 1841.

LIND	Stockholm, October 6, 1820
Jenny ('The Swedish Nightingale')	Malvern, November 2, 1887
Singer	The Cemetery, Great Malvern, Worcs

189, Old Brompton Road, SW5 (LCP 1909) 1876-1886 (formerly 1, Moreton Gardens)

Of a poor Swedish family, Jenny Lind rose to international fame and her 'Nightingale' nickname was affectionately given. She studied singing in Paris but her first concert performance was in Stockholm on March 7, 1838, in the part of Agatha in *Der Freischutz*. She did not sing in London until 1847 and in America in 1850. (P.T. Barnum organised an 'auction' of three-dollar seats and such was her reputation that up to 225 dollars were bid for places in the audience.)

There is a memorial to Jenny and her husband (who died in 1907) in the 'Poet's Corner' in Westminster Abbey, below the monument to Handel.

LINDEN GARDENS, W2 *Central, District and Circle lines to Notting Hill Gate*

A house called Linden Lodge, which had a fairly large garden used to stand in this area.

42 (formally number 1) William MULREADY, 1827-1863. The artist John LINNEL often stayed with the Mulreadys.

42, Sylvia PANKHURST, 1910. In her day there seemed to be something called Cambridge Lodge Studios here.

97, Ivy COMPTON-BURNETT, 1926-1929. She lived here with Margaret Jourdain.

LISSON GROVE, NW8 *Bakerloo line to Edgware Road*

This is probably a corruption of 'Lill's Tun' meaning a farm owned or cultivated by a Saxon yeoman called Lill. There was a Manor of Lilestone (mentioned in the Domesday Book) which used to belong to the Priory of St John of Jerusalem.

13, Leigh HUNT lived here after he was released from a two-year prison sentence, meted out to him for having libelled the Prince of Wales in 1815. P.B. SHELLEY came to stay with him here in 1817. The house has now disappeared.

116 (formerly 22) Benjamin HAYDON (LCP 1950) 1817-1820. The house had been built in 1808 by Charles ROSSI. It was in this house on December 28, 1819 that KEATS was introduced to WORDSWORTH at the 'Immortal Dinner'.

LISTER	Upton, Essex, April 5, 1827
Joseph	Walmer, Kent, February 10, 1912
(1st Baron Lister of Lyme Regis)	West Hampstead Cemetery
Physician	

12, Park Crescent, W1 (LCP 1915) 1877-1902

Lister was the second son of Joseph Jackson Lister (1786-1869) of Upton in Essex, a Fellow of the Royal Society and a microscopist. Young Joseph graduated from London University in 1847, but in the Arts, then, in 1852, as a doctor, becoming a Fellow of the Royal College of Surgeons in that same year.

He became house surgeon to James Syme, whose daughter, Agnes, he married in 1852. Then he became a surgery lecturer at Edinburgh – then Regius Professor of Surgery at Glasgow – then back to Edinburgh as Professor of Clinical Surgery in 1869. He held the same post at King's College Hospital, London from 1877-1893 and was President of the Royal Society from 1895-1900. By then he was already a baronet (created in 1883) and he was made Baron in 1897. Actually he was a terrible old snob and his greatest hour must have been in September 1871. Queen Victoria's doctor (or, at least *one* of her doctors) Dr. Marshall, sent a telegram from Balmoral requesting Lister's immediate attendance on the Queen. Her Majesty was suffering from a painful abscess in her left armpit. Lister hurried to Scotland and found the Royal armpit in a bad way. He counselled immediate action: to open up the inflamed parts. HM asked Lister that the area, '...be 'frozen' as I bear pain so badly'. Sir William Jenner, who was physician in ordinary to the Queen, administered chloroform (to which Her Majesty was no stranger, as anaesthesia had been used on her in all of her nine confinements) and Lister cut into the by now six inch (15 cms) abscess. Relief under the Royal limb was felt immediately. Subsequently he used to boast that he was the only man in the world, '...who has ever stuck a knife into the Queen'.

His motto was *Malo mori quam foedari* – Death rather than disgrace.

In the middle of the road in Portland Place, at the north end, is a bronze bust of Lister by Sir Thomas Brock. It stands on a large granite plinth, the whole piece being erected here in 1924. There is also a medallion of Lister, also by Brock, in the North Aisle of the Choir of Westminster Abbey.

LITTLE RUSSELL STREET, WC1   *Central and Piccadilly lines to Holborn*

Originally built about 1670 and was named after the family name of the Dukes of Bedford who had inherited this land as part of Bloomsbury Manor.

7, George BORROW, 1830. This was after that period of his life when he was roaming with the gypsies.

18, W.H. DAVIES, 1914. His *Autobiography of a Super Tramp* had been published some seven years previously, but he was still enjoying the 'Lionization' he received from it.

LIVERPOOL (Prime Minister, 1770-1828) see under JENKINSON, R.B.

LLOYD-GEORGE
David (1st Earl of Dwyfor)
Prime Minister

Manchester, January 17, 1863
Ty Newydd, near Llanystumdwy,
Wales, March 26, 1945
Ashes buried in Westminster Abbey

10, Cheyne Walk, SW3, 1924-1925
2, Addison Road, W14, 1928-1938

His parents were Welsh and, though he spent the first two years of his life in Manchester, his father died in 1865 and his widow took her family back to Llanystumdwy, near Criccieth in Wales where they lived with an uncle, Richard Lloyd, who took the boy's education in hand. He implanted the seeds of Welsh nationalism in David and showed him the value and power of oratory.

Lloyd-George became a solicitor and then moved into politics, soon becoming Liberal Member of Parliament for the Carnarvon Boroughs. By 1905 he was President of the Board of Trade and was responsible for the passing of the Merchant Shipping Act in 1906. Two years later he was Chancellor of the Exchequer and it was under him the foundations of the Old Age Pensions and National Insurance schemes were laid, only to be thrown out by the House of Lords, which brought about a constitutional crisis. Up till 1914 Lloyd-George was always thought to be a pacifist, but in 1915 he was appointed Minister of Munitions and eventually succeeded ASQUITH as Prime Minister of the Coalition Government in 1916, which office he held until 1922. (Adolf Hitler – who was a private in the German Army, 1914-1918 – said that it was 'Lloyd-George who won the War'.)

Anyone having read a little about ASQUITH's 'extra-marital' love life who was puzzled by Asquith's behaviour, must be astounded by Lloyd-George's. Lloyd-George took his secretary, Frances Stevenson, as his mistress on February 21, 1913; a daughter was born to them on October 4, 1929 and the lovers were married at Guildford Registry Office on October 23, 1943 after the death of Lloyd-George's long suffering wife.

LODGE
(Sir) Oliver Joseph
Physicist

Penkhull, Staffs., June 12, 1851
August 22, 1940

62, Delancey Street, NW1, 1874-1877

Oliver Lodge studied at the Royal College of Science and at University College, London. In 1881 he was appointed Professor of Physics at Liverpool and in 1902 he was the first Principal of Birmingham University. He was knighted in the same year. He was a pioneer of wireless telegraphy and he had become a Fellow of the Royal Society in 1887. One of his books, published in 1897, was entitled *Signalling Across Space without Wires*.

LOHR
Marie
Actress

Sydney, Australia, July 28, 1890
January 21, 1975

Flat 8, 199, Sussex Gardens, W2, 1946-1975

Marie's father, Lewis J. Löhr, was at one time treasurer of the Melbourne Opera House and she made her first stage appearance at four. She waited until she was a mature eleven years old before appearing in London at the Garrick Theatre. Also on that night (December 14, 1901) Beerbohm-Tree was in the cast of *Shock-Headed Peter* with her.

She married Val Prinsep's son, Anthony Leyland Val Prinsep by whom she had one daughter before divorcing him in 1928.

LONG ACRE, WC2

Piccadilly and Northern lines to
Leicester Square

This 'Long' acre is not a land measurement, but the older understanding of the word 'acre' as a field. *Longacre* was a long, thin field beside the Convent Garden. Henry VIII pinched it from the Church in 1536 and in 1552, gave it to John Russell, Earl of BEDFORD. At one time it was known as Elmes Street.

137, John DRYDEN. On the night of December 8, 1679, Dryden was severely beaten up near here by thugs thought to have been hired by the Earl of Rochester (1647-1680).

139, William HAZLITT lodged here with his brother when he first came to London in 1798.

LONGFORD

London, August 30, 1906

(Countess of) Elizabeth
Author and biographer

108, Harley Street, W1, here born
18, Chesil Court, Chelsea Manor Street, SW3, 1950-1980s

Elizabeth Pakenham's (her married name) father was an eminent opthalmologist called Harman and the Harman family 'lived over the shop' in Harley Street.

In the summer of 1927, Hugh Gaitskell took Elizabeth Harman to a party at the Cafe Royal, in Regent's Street (and still there) to celebrate the graduation of Frank Pakenham from Oxford (New College). Frank and Elizabeth had met once at a Commemoration Ball a few months previously. He had discreetly retired to a small room in the College to sleep off the immediate effects of having had too much to drink. She had come across this 'sleeping beauty' and awoken him with a full kiss on his lips. It must have been a pleasant awakening, as the austere *Times* had not long before written that her beauty and wit '...linger with the potency of Zuleika Dobson in the memories of contemporaries'.

She has written a number of superb biographies, one of the finest being her biography of WELLINGTON; *Years of the Sword* in 1969. Writers' ink runs in the family veins. Her three sisters-in-law, Pansy (who married Henry Lamb, the artist) Mary and Violet all became authors (and Violet 'doubling-up' by marrying the writer Anthony Powell). Of the eight Longford children Antonia (Mrs. Hugh Fraser, then Mrs. Harold PINTER) Thomas, Judith, Rachel and Kevin all have used a pen professionally and well.

LONGFORD

London, December 5, 1905

Francis Pakenham (7th Earl)
Politician

7, Great Cumberland Place, W1, here born
18, Chesil Court, Chelsea Manor Street, SW3, 1950-1980s

With generations of money, breeding, an Eton and Oxford education behind him, and Tory friends 'in high places', Lord Longford became a Catholic and a Socialist. In his political career he has been Lord Privy Seal, First Lord of the Admiralty and Leader of the House of Lords. Outside Westminster he is Chairman of the publishing firm, Sidgwick and Jackson (who, ironically, were the publishers of Edward HEATH's book, *Sailing*).

Outside both these pursuits is his zealousness in lost or unpopular causes. He is a sort of professional lifter-of-lame-dogs-over-stiles. He investigated pornographic films and live shows on stage – going to Denmark to study them more closely. He supported the plea that a woman, Myra Hindley, who was found guilty of obscene murders of children on the Yorkshire moors and imprisoned, should be allowed parole if not release.

The Longford motto is: *Gloria Virtutis Umbra* – Glory is the shadow of virtue.

LONGRIDGE ROAD, SW5

Piccadilly, District and Circle lines to Earls Court

Longridge was the name of one of the Welsh estates owned by the Edwardes family who were major land owners in this part of Kensington. It was established in 1872.

33, Ellen TERRY was living here from 1877 and 1888. At one stage she lived with Charles Kelly, her second, but not long-lasting, husband.

39, Marie CORELLI (P) 1883-1899. Here she wrote the best seller of all her novels, *The Sorrows of Satan*, which was published in 1895. Her widowed father lived here as well.

LONSDALE
Saint George Henry (4th Earl)
Aristocrat

October 4, 1855
London, February 8, 1882

30, Bryanston Street, W1, where he died

Son of the great (literally, he weighed over 300 pounds or 136 kilogrammes when he died) 3rd Earl, Henry was the holder of the title for only six years. The manner of his dying caused complications, as he died in Bryanston Street in a house he had taken for his mistress (qv Bryanston Street). George Henry's death saved his younger brother Hugh (who became the 5th Earl) not a little embarassment, as on that very day the bailiffs had moved in on him and his wife, Grace (née Huntly). With the title came a very considerable income, so Hugh was able to start again, debt free.

The Lonsdale family motto is, *Magistratus indicat virum* – The magistrate shows the man.

LONSDALE
Hugh Cecil (5th Earl)
Sporting Earl

London, January 25, 1857
April 13, 1944

21, Wilton Crescent, SW1, here born
14 and 15, Carlton House Terrace, SW1, 1882-1944

Lonsdale's grandfather (who, incidentally, was not a Lord Lonsdale) established a record having sat as a member in the House of Commons for Westmoreland for 55 years and *never* made a speech in the Chamber. Hugh's records were more sporting. He knocked out John L. Sullivan, the American and world heavy-weight boxing Champion, he walked 100 miles (160 kilometres) in 17 hours and 21 minutes in June 1878 (an average of 5.76 miles per hour). He was the first President of the Automobile Association in 1905. The distinctive 'house colour'; yellow of the club, derives from the colour of the Earl's livery. All his coaches, then cars, were yellow and he was nicknamed, affectionately, 'The Yellow Earl' because of this. (King Edward VII was once heard to comment that Lonsdale was '...almost an Emperor, but not *quite* a gentleman'.)

The Sport of Boxing remembers the Earl to this day as the *Lonsdale Belt* is still one of the greatest prizes of the canvas ring.

At one time the income of the Lonsdales was over £200,000 a year, principally from coal mining. (Hugh was spending over £3,000 a year on cigars alone.)

His wife (Lady Grace Gordon, daughter of the 10th Marquess of Huntly) was childless and after she had recovered from a rather complicated miscarriage they probably never slept together again. He had a number of love affaires, one of the most constant being his liaison with Violet Cameron, whose Opera Company he financed. He had a daughter by Violet and they were installed in a house in St John's Wood.

LORD NORTH STREET, SW1

District and Circle lines
to Westminster

SMITH Square was built in 1725 and this street was merely the north entrance to the Square and so called, logically, North Street. In 1936 the London County Council 'ennobled' it, for reasons best known to themselves. If it *was* after Lord North himself, why choose someone who was the worst Prime Minister Britain ever had? There *are* streets named after him, North Court off Tottenham Court Road, North Mews, off the Gray's Inn Road and Guildford Street, WC1, he was also Earl of Guildford.

5, Sir Harold WILSON, 1970s. This was one of three houses (plus a holiday bungalow in the Scilly Isles) owned by this fair-shares-for all Prime Minister.

6, Compton MACKENZIE, 1890s – early 1900s. When the MacKenzies first moved here 'Monty' was still at St Paul's School, Hammersmith.

8, Brendan BRACKEN in 1933, having lived at number 11 in 1929.

19, Lady COLEFAX. On September 27, 1939, the Duke and Duchess of Windsor lunched here. They had travelled secretly to London a few days previously (the Second World War having started on September 3) together with their old friend Major 'Fruity' Metcalfe and three spoilt and yappy Cairn terriers called 'Pookie', 'Preezi' and 'Detto'.

LOUDON
John Claudius
Gardener

Cambuslang, Scotland, April 18, 1783
London, December 14, 1858
Kensal Green, Grave No.4547; Plot No.74 (his wife, who also died in 1858, is beside him)

4, Chapel Street, SW1, 1803
3, Porchester Terrace, W2 (LCP 1953) 1823

Loudon's wife Jane, whom he married in 1830, was very much part of the business and she worked at it very hard to keep it going. Jane was 24 years younger than her husband but died in the same year as he.

When Loudon signed the contracts for the Porchester Terrace house his *Encyclopaedia of Gardening* had been published and he was established as an expert designer of greenhouses and conservatories as well as gardens.

LOW
(Sir) David Alexander Cecil
Cartoonist

Dunedin, New Zealand, April 7, 1891
London, September 19, 1963

33, Melbury Court, W8, 1963

Low came to London from New Zealand (via Australia, where he had worked on the *Bulletin*) in 1919 having been offered a job on the *Star*. (Not the *Star* of today, which is a tabloid daily morning paper). He found life very different in Fleet Street, but he persevered.

In 1920 he sent a cablegram to a Miss Madeline Kenning of Auckland, saying; 'Will you marry me?' prepaying address and one word in reply. Madeline cabled 'Yes' and, in due course, they were married in St. Paul's Church, Covent Garden in front of his sister (who had come over with him in 1919) her (new) husband and two friends, plus the officiating priest, Father Adderley.

By 1927 he had moved into the BEAVERBROOK 'camp' and was working on the London *Evening Standard*. The 'Beaver' made him an offer which he would have been foolish to turn down (Low now had two daughters to support). Beaverbrook and his papers were totally Tory but shrewdly he never let political views get in the way of hiring talent. Low was a Socialist and so was Tom DRIBERG and so was poor sad little 'Vicky', a brilliant cartoonist who was to kill himself.

LOWELL	Cambridge, Mass., February 22, 1819
James Russell	Cambridge, Mass., September 2, 1891
Academic diplomat	

10 and 31, Lowndes Square, SW1, at various times between 1881 and 1884
40, Clarges Street, W1, 1884

A 'son of the manse', Lowell graduated from Harvard in 1838 and had published two volumes of poetry before he was 22. Together with HAWTHORNE, POE and John Greenlead Whittier (the Quaker poet, 1807-1892) he edited *The Pioneer*. In 1855 he succeeded Longfellow as Professor of Modern Languages and Literature back at Harvard. In the Civil War, Lowell was an ardent abolitionist and worked unsparingly for freedom's cause.

Though he had never been officially involved in politics he was appointed United States Minister of Spain in 1877 and then promoted to a Ministerial post in London from 1880-1885. Lowell wrote to a friend on July 25, 1885 that, 'I am as fond of London as Charles Lamb. The rattle of a hansom shakes new life into my old bones and I ruin myself in them'.

LOWER BELGRAVE STREET, SW1   *Circle, District, Victoria and BR lines to Victoria*

All part of the Westminster estate, Belgrave being a village in Cheshire owned by the family. The 1st Duke of Westminster, Hugh Lupus Grosvenor (1825-1899, Dukedom created in 1874) had eight sisters who altogether collected ten husbands between them: Duke of Northumberland (Eleanor's), Earl of Macclesfield (Mary's), Lord Wenlock (Elizabeth's), Baron Leigh (Caroline's), Sir Michael Shaw-Steward (Octavia's), Sir Archibald Campbell and Philip Frank Esquire (Agnes's), Baron Muncaster and Hugh Lindsay Esquire (Jane's) and lastly Thomas Guest Esquire (Theodora's).

46, the home of the 7th Lord LUCAN. For the savage attacks and the intrigue which began here on the night of November 7, 1974, see LUCAN.

LOWNDES

William Lowndes, who died in 1724, was a *nouveau riche* politician from the county of Buckinghamshire. The real origin of his wealth is rather obscure but he used a large portion of it buying property, at first in Soho (where now Lowndes Court is, off Carnaby Street) and then moved west to Knightsbridge and bought more. His great grandson, together with Charles Lyall, built Lowndes Square in 1837, then Lowndes Street and Place and Lyall Street not long after. Lyall's mother was Harriet and the Lowndes had come originally from Chesham. All these names can be seen in this immediate area.

LOWNDES SQUARE, SW1   *Piccadilly line to Knightsbridge*

10   (formerly 31) James Russell LOWELL, 1881-1885, when he was American Minister at the Court of St James's. Before this he had lived for a short while at 37, Lowndes Street. By 1929 the house had become the Belgian Embassy.

Lowndes Court (on the south side of the Square).

Flat 5, Sir Oswald MOSLEY. This was the Mosley's last address in London. Soon after 1964 they moved to France more or less permanently.

LUBBOCK
John (1st Baron Avebury)
Politician

London, April 30, 1834
May 28, 1913

29, Eaton Place, SW1 (LCP 1935) here born and spent his first seven years

Leaving Eton when he was not yet 15, Lubbock went into his father's bank, Robarts, Lubbock and Company and was made a partner in the concern in 1856, when he was just over 21 years old.

In 1870 he was elected as Liberal Member of Parliament for Maidstone (the county town of Kent). His parliamentary career was successful and he brought about a number of Acts intended to make the lot of the 'working classes' more endurable: the Bank Holidays Act of 1871 and the Shop Hours Act of 1889, to name but two. Outside banking and Westminster, he was a dedicated researcher in Natural History – especially the habits of ants and bees. (DARWIN was a country neighbour of his and encouraged him greatly.)

LUCAN
Richard John (7th Earl)
Man-about-Town and?

December 18, 1934

5, Eaton Row, SW1
46, Lower Belgrave Street, SW1, 1974

Lucan's ancestor, the 3rd Earl, was almost solely responsible for the gallant fiasco of the Charge of the Light Brigade at Balaclava on October 25, 1854. (Disaster runs in the Lucan blood.) He inherited his title when he was 30 years old, having married Veronica Duncan the year before. They had one son (Lord Bingham, born September 21, 1967) and two daughters.

On the night of November 7, 1974, *someone* broke into the house in Lower Belgrave Street and battered the Lucan nanny, Sandra Rivett, to death in the basement. That *same* person inflicted severe head injuries to the Countess. Lady Lucan was able to get out of the house, staggered – covered in blood – to the nearby pub and raise the alarm.

Lord Lucan disappeared that same night and the Police felt their enquiries after Lucan were deliberately frustrated by his cronies and friends. No one has *officially* seen him since. (Every year, *Who's Who* continues to show him as if he *is* still alive.)

The Lucan family motto is *Spes Mea Christus* – Christ is my hope. If Lucan is still alive then He *is* practically his only hope.

LUTYENS
(Sir) Edwin Landseer
Architect

London, March 29, 1869
London, January 1, 1944
St Paul's Cathedral

29, Bloomsbury Square, WC1, 1895
6, Grays Inn Square, WC1, 1896
16, Onslow Square, SW7, 1896
31, Bloomsbury Square, WC1, 1914 (now the London School of Hygiene and Tropical Medicine)
13, Mansfield Street, W1 (LCP 1922) from 1923 until he died here

Lutyens has more than once been called the greatest English architect since

Wren. Certainly his range was wide; from the beautiful (and deceptively sophisticated) Cenotaph in Whitehall to the Viceroy's House in New Delhi, where his father-in-law, Lord LYTTON, had been Viceroy from 1876-1880. He also designed a number of country houses which were built on a realistic scale – in contrast to his Roman Catholic Cathedral in Liverpool.

In 1926 he designed the British Embassy in Washington. His first house design was a red brick house in Surrey but as he grew older his designs clearly owed much to Palladian and Georgian influences.

He was President of the Royal Academy in 1938 and awarded the Order of Merit in 1942. He had been knighted in 1918.

LYTTON	London, May 25, 1803
(Lord) Edward George Earle Bulwer	Torquay, January 18, 1873
Author and politician	Westminster Abbey

68 (formerly 31) Baker Street, W1, here born
36, Hertford Street, W1, 1831-1834
12, Grosvenor Square, W1, 1868-1873

Born Edward Bulwer (he assumed the name of Lytton when, through his mother Elizabeth Barbara Lytton, 1773-1843, he inherited her Knebworth estate in Hertfordshire). He was the youngest son of General Earl Bulwer (176-1807). He was only 17 when he published *Ismael and other Poems* and, when up at Cambridge, he won the Chancellor's Gold Medal for his poem on *Sculpture*. Perhaps poetry absorbed too much of his time as he could only get a pass degree.

Much of what he has written is now forgotten, but two of his books, at least, have lasted, *Eugene Aram* (1832) and *The Last Days of Pompei* (1834).

As well as producing some 18 novels and much dazzling poetry, Lytton wrote three plays. *The Lady of Lyons, Richelieu* and *Money*, this last in 1840. He was obviously not admired by *all* his poetical peers. TENNYSON once described his as the 'padded man who does not wear stays'.

LYTTON	London, November 8, 1831
Edward Robert (1st Earl) ('Owen	Paris, November 24, 1891
Meredith')	Knebworth, Herts
Diplomatic poet	

36, Hertford Street, W1, here born

Having been educated at Harrow and Bonn, Lytton became secretary to his uncle, Sir Henry Bulwer (1801-1872) who was created Baron Dalling and Bulwer, but was almost always referred to as Sir Henry. Lytton was with him in Washington DC and afterwards in Florence.

Subsequently Lytton held a number of diplomatic posts in Europe, then was appointed Viceroy of India in 1876. Four years later he relinquished this post and was made an Earl. Politics had not lost him and in 1887 he was made Ambassador in Paris.

Despite his high flown diplomatic career, Lytton thought of himself more as a poet than a 'man-of-affairs' even though he had little literary success. His despatches from India, however, were always admired for their literary excellence.

The Lytton motto was: *Hoc Virtutis Opus* – This is the work of valour.

MACAULAY   Rugby, August 1, 1881
(Dame) Rose   London, October 30, 1958
Author

7, Luxborough Street, W1, 1930s
20, Hinde Street, W1, 1941–1958

Dame Rose (she was made a Dame of the British Empire in 1958) spent much of her early childhood in Italy, though her father was a Cambridge lecturer. She, however, completed her formal education at Oxford and her first novel, *The Valley of the Captives*, was published in 1911 when she was still up at Oxford.

In 1913 *The Lea Shore* won a publishers' prize of £1,000 and the last of her novels, *The Towers of Trebizond*, won the James Tait Black Memorial Prize in 1956.

She had a deceptively frail appearance; she was, infact, remarkably robust and was an all-year-round swimmer.

MACAULAY   Leicestershire, October 25, 1800
Thomas Babington (1st Baron)   Kensington, December 28, 1859
Historian   Westminster Abbey, in 'Poet's Corner'

50, Great Ormond Street, WC1, 1823–1829
8, South Square, WC1, 1829–1834
12, Great George Street, W1, 1839–1940
F 3, Albany, W1, 1846

Thomas was the son of Zachary Macaulay (1768–1838) a West Indian merchant, a member of the 'Clapham Sect' and, to his great credit, a passionate anti-slaver. Thomas was educated privately and went up to Trinity College, Cambridge and became a Fellow there in 1824. He was brilliant in Classics but not very good in Mathematics, so he did not get a first class degree. He twice won the Chancellor's medal for English verse and was awarded a prize for Latin declamation.

His first published effort appeared in *Knight's Quarterly* magazine and he soon formed an understanding with the *Edinburgh Review* and was one of its most regular contributors for more than 20 years. In 1825 the *Review* printed his article on John MILTON. This established him in the literary world but in later years he found fault in that famous essay. He soon became quite a literary lion and the drawing-rooms of London were opened to him. Through the influence of Lord Lansdowne (the 3rd Marquis, 1780–1863) Macaulay became the MP for Calne, in Wiltshire. He entered the House of Commons when that chamber was debating the Reform Bill. His skills were soon recognized and he was sent out to India as legal adviser to Supreme Council in Bengal. His salary (in 1834) was £10,000; in today's terms a salary of this size would have the purchasing power of nearly half a million.

Five years later he began on *The History of England* and, in 1839, became MP for Edinburgh and was Secretary for War for two years. In 1842 his *Lays of Ancient Rome* were published with tremendous success at all levels.

In 1847 (by now out of politics) he settled down on his *History* in earnest and in 1848 the first and second volumes were published and, after another political whirl, volumes three and four appeared in 1855. They were immensely successful and he was given a peerage in 1857, becoming Baron

Macaulay of Rothley. He 'retired' to 'Holly Lodge' where eventually he was to die.

There is a statue of Macaulay in Westminster Abbey. It was sculpted by Nevil Northey Burnard, (1818-1878). Burnard was a native of Cornwall and his early work attracted the attention of his Member of Parliament, Sir Charles Lemon, who got him a place in CHANTREY's studio.

MACDONALD	Lossiemouth, Scotland, October 12,
James Ramsay	1866
Prime Minister	(Mid-Atlantic) November 9, 1937

3, Lincoln's Inn Fields, WC2, 1896-1916

Whilst still at school MacDonald became an avowed Socialist and on leaving the Dramie Board School he became a member of the Independent Labour Party. In 1884 he had come to London and worked for 12s 6d (62½p) a week as a clerk. He was secretary to the ILP from 1900-1911, twice Leader of it (1911-1914 and 1922-1931). He was also a member of the London County Council (now the Greater London Council).

He had been in the House of Commons as MP for Leicester since 1906. He was opposed to Britain entering the First World War, he lost his seat at Leicester in 1918 and failed to get back in for East Woolwich in 1921. In 1922 he came back into the Commons for Aberavon (Wales) and Labour members now outnumbered the Liberals at Westminster. The Conservatives were defeated in the House on June 21, 1924 and the following day King George V called upon MacDonald to form a government. It was a minority government and MacDonald depended upon the goodwill of the sinking Liberal Party. It could not, and did not, last. He was back in Opposition on November 4, 1924 – even though the Labour Party had attracted over a *million* more votes.

In May 1929 another General Election gave Labour 290 seats, Conservatives 259, Liberals 57, and Independents 9.

Unluckily for MacDonald, the world was heading for a massive industrial slump with Britain leading the way down. He was forced into an uneasy coalition called a 'National Government' in 1931 but he handed over to Stanley BALDWIN (Conservative) in 1935. MacDonald was finished and his health gave way. He was advised to go to a warmer climate and have a complete rest. He died in mid-Atlantic on his way to South America.

MACFARREN	London, March 2, 1813
(Sir) George Alexander	London, October, 1887
Musician	Hampstead Cemetery

24, Villiers Street, WC1, here born
20, Hamilton Terrace, NW8 (P) where he died

Having studied at the Royal Academy, he became a Professor there in 1834 and Principal of it in 1875 (succeeding Sir William Sterndale BENNETT, who died on February 1 of that year).

He wrote several operas, well thought of then but now largely forgotten. What he is remembered for, is his work on musical theory.

On September 4, 1844 he married Clarina Thalia Andrae in St Marylebone Church. She was a professional singer from Lübeck and actually made her début in the small part of a page in his opera, *Charles the Second* in October 1839.

His eyesight began to fail when he was in his forties and he was totally blind for the last 27 years of his life.

MACHEN Caerlon-on-Usk, March 3, 1863
Arthur Beaconsfield, December 15, 1947
Author

36, Great Russell Street, WC1, 1893, then, after marriage, to number 98

Machen's father was a clergyman and (as is so often the case with the clergy, even today) a not very affluent man. Young Arthur spent a solitary childhood and a fairly austere one.

Coming up to London he started out as a publisher's clerk, tried his hand at teaching and actually joined Benson's company as an actor in 1902. By this time he had already published two novels, *The Great God Pan* in 1894 and *The Three Impostors* two years later.

When he was 50 he joined the staff of the, now defunct, *London Evening News*. His story of the *Angel of Mons* appeared and was widely accepted as fact. In August 1914 the 3rd and 4th Divisions of the 'Old Contemptibles' were harried continuously during their retreat from Mons. Despite heavy losses, those that survived the withdrawal believed they had been saved by divine intervention. This was the basis of Machen's story. He romanticized it and gave the incident a vision of St George clad in white and his angels, holding back the German Army with flaming swords. He also published *The Memoirs of Casanova*, translated and bowdlerized.

MACKENZIE West Hartlepool, January 1, 1883
(Sir) Compton Edward Montague Scotland, November 30, 1972
Author

54, Avonmore Road, W14, 1891-1900
6, Lord North Street, SW1, early 1900s
E 1, Albany W1, 1912

Both his mother and father came from theatrical families and his sister Fay Compton became an actress. He was educated at St Paul's School in Hammersmith (now removed to Barnes, the original site covered by a rash of 'Council' flats) and afterwards went on to Magdalen College, Oxford. At university he was a member of the Dramatic Society there – OUDS. He began in law at the Inner Temple and soon was writing in his spare time. A play of his, *The Gentleman in Grey* was staged in 1907. Then, in 1911, came his first novel, *The Passionate Elopement* followed hotly by *Carnival*. The greatest success at about that time was his *Sinister Street*, a novel concerned with adolescence which was published in two volumes in 1913-1914.

In 1914 Mackenzie became a Roman Catholic and soon after was fighting in the Dardanelles and later worked for the Secret Service. He was awarded the OBE in 1919, he was not knighted until 1952.

One of his faculties was a quite phenomenal 'photographic' memory. He only *started* to write his biography when he was 80! A series of volumes entitles *My Life and Times Octave One*; *Octave Two* and so on right up until *Octave Seven* appeared.

MACKENZIE Scotland, April 12, 1858
(Sir) James London, January 26, 1925
Physician Golders Green

17, Bentinck Street, W1
133, Harley Street, W1, 1907-1924
53, Albert Hall Mansions, SW7, 1925

MacKenzie of highland Scottish stock became an authority on diseases of the heart. He invented the 'Polygraph' which graphically recorded the actions of the heart.

One of his patients was Lord NORTHCLIFFE, who, not long before he died in 1922 (in a demented state) threatened to shoot him!

MACKENZIE
(Sir) Morell
Physician

Leytonstone, July 7, 1837
London, February 2, 1892
St Mary's Church, Wargrave

64, George Street, W1, 1862
5, Kingly (formerly King) Street, W1, 1870
19, Harley Street, W1, from 1888 until he died here

MacKenzie was knighted in 1887 after he had been consulted on the health of the German Crown Prince (son-in-law of Queen Victoria and, for a few weeks before his death, Emperor Friedrich III). MacKenzie's presence in the Imperial sick-room, not unnaturally, was resented by the Emperor's usual medical advisers and to make matters worse, MacKenzie's diagnosis and treatment were wrong. The Emperor had advanced and malignant throat cancer. When the situation was clearer, MacKenzie was 'officially censured' by the Royal College of Surgeons in January 1889. (The Emperor having died on June 15, 1888.) In probable anticipation of some form of criticism, MacKenzie published a book in October 1888 which he called *Frederick the Noble*. The general tone is rather nauseating. For instance, MacKenzie ends his Chapter Nine – the Emperor having died – with the sentence: 'He had gone down to his grave leaving us the memory and example of a stainless life and a beautiful death'.

MACKLIN
Charles
Actor

Ireland, May 1, 1690 (?)
London, July 11, 1797

19-20, Bow Street, WC2

There are many missing chapters in Macklin's life story, beginning with the real date of his birth. Some sources say that he was two months old when the Battle of the Boyne was fought. The battle took place on July 1, 1690 and, as Macklin really *did* die on July 11, 1797 this 'Boyne-set-date' means that he would have been over 107 years old when 'he took the final curtain'.
By 1725 he was appearing at the Lincoln's Inn Theatre and eventually became a hit as *Shylock* in 1741. When he was nearly 90 (or a 100?) he created the part of 'Sir Pertinax MacSycophant' in his own play, *The Man of the World*.
He was constantly in trouble because of his irrationally bad temper – he actually killed a fellow actor called Thomas Hallam on May 10, 1735 but the charge was somehow reduced from murder to manslaughter. The death was accidental, Machlin's stick pierced Hallam's eye. The incident took place in the Green Room at the Theatre Royal, Drury Lane and *Macklin's* ghost has 'been seen many times' crossing the theatre in front of what used to be the pit.

MACLISE
Daniel
Artist

Cork, Eire, February 2, 1806
Cheyne Walk, April 25, 1870
Kensal Green; Grave No 3325, Plot No. 33

85, Charlotte Street, W1, 1835-1836 (in his day, 63)
4, Cheyne Walk, SW3, where he died.

Having been born in Ireland, with a Scottish highlander as a father, MacLise could be fairly described as a true *Celt*. He began studying at the Royal Academy Schools in 1828; rather older than most pupils, and won acclaim for his 'subject' pictures.
Frith in his autobiography wrote that MacLise was '...out and away the greatest artist that ever lived'(!) Certainly he was a facile and talented artist and, in his day, popular. Some of his work hangs on the walls in the Houses

of Parliament. Typical of his style and choice of subject, they include *The Death of Nelson* and *The Meeting of Wellington and Blücher*.

MACMILLAN February 10, 1894
Maurice Harold (1st Earl of
Stockton)
Prime Minister

14, Chester Square, SW1, 1922-1929

Daniel and Alexander MacMillan started their publishing company on November 10, 1843 and it prospered almost immediately. By 1880 they were sufficiently selective to have turned down G.B. SHAW's first novel, *Immaturity*. By 1900 they were *very* prosperous and Maurice Crawford MacMillan was sufficiently wealthy to send his son, Harold, to Eton. After Eton he was an *Exhibitioner* at Balliol College, Oxford, where he obtained First Class Honours in Moderations in 1919.

He was appointed ADC to the Governor General of Canada, but resigned his post so that he could enter British politics. In 1920 he married Dorothy Cavendish, daughter of the 9th Duke of Devonshire (who was born in 1900 and died in 1966) and this marriage set the seal on his political suitability. He was elected as the Conservative member for Stockton-on-Tees in 1924, defeated there in 1929, but re-elected two years later. In 1940 CHURCHILL made him Parliamentary Secretary to the Ministry of Supply and two years later sent him to Africa in a newly created *Cabinet* post of Minister Resident at Allied Headquarters. He lost his seat in the Socialist avalanche in 1945 but later in the year came back into the Commons as member for Bromley (in Kent) a seat he held until he retired in 1964.

As was widely forecast, he became Prime Minister in 1957 and remained so until October 1963. This six-year period coincided with a real upturn in Britain's prosperity: exports boomed, 'money was cheap' and MacMillan told the British 'they had never had it so good!' Another phrase attributed to him was, 'The Wind of Change'; this was coined in reference to the inevitability of the gaining of independence by the African nations.

On his 90th birthday (February 10, 1984) he was awarded a hereditary Earldom, the first since the elevation of Anthony ARMSTRONG-JONES in 1963. MacMillan chose to be called the Earl of Stockton. (Sadly, his son and so his heir, died only a few days after MacMillan's ennoblement. He, too, was a politician.)

MACNEICE Belfast, September 9, 1907
Louis September 3, 1963
Poet

2, Sussex Place, W2, 1955-1960
10, Regent's Park Terrace, NW1

Louis's father was the Protestant Bishop of Down and he sent the boy to England for his education (Marlborough, then Merton College, Oxford). MacNeice was a Classics lecturer at Birmingham and then, in 1936, he came to London as a lecturer at Bedford College. Not long after he went to Iceland with Wystan AUDEN and jointly they produced *Letters from Iceland* in 1937.

In addition to his own published poems he also translated Goethe's *Faust*. In 1958 he was awarded the CBE an unusual honour for a poet in the 1950s.

MACREADY	London, March 3, 1793
William Charles	Cheltenham, April 27, 1873
Actor	Kensal Green, Catacomb B. V.96

45, Stanhope Street, NW1, here born
61, Lincoln's Inn Fields, WC2, 1832-1837
1, York Gate, NW1, 1839-1843
64, Frith Street, W1, 1843-1851

William MacReady was the son of the actor, William McReady (sic) and was sent to Rugby School intending to enter the law. Father's finances failed and when he was 17 he went on to the stage, making his début in Birmingham, 1810. In 1816 he was appearing at Covent Garden but it was not really until 1837 that he became prominent in the theatre. He took over the management of the 'Garden' and presented two of Shakespeare's plays.
In 1841 he became manager of the Drury Lane Theatre and stayed there for two years. He toured Europe and appeared in America. In May 1849 his reputation was put at risk by the actions of a jealous American actor called Forrest, who fomented a riot in which 22 people were killed and 36 injured.

MAGNUS	London, October 7, 1842
(Sir) Philip	August 29, 1933
Mathematician	Jewish Cemetery, Golders Green

16, Gloucester Terrace, NW1, 1904
44, Lancaster Gate, W2, 1933

Generally the Jewish Community in London only became socially 'acceptable' when Edward, Prince of Wales (later King Edward VII) admitted Jewish friends into his so-called 'Marlborough House Set'. Edward was neither intellectual nor, in 1886, was allowed to have any influence on the Honours List. (His mother saw to *that*!) A knighthood for a Jew, 15 years before Edward came to the throne, was an achievement and was bestowed on Magnus in 1886 as a *real* honour.

MAIDA

The 'Maidas' take their name from the Battle of Maida, where, on July 4, 1804, the British Army defeated the French under Jean Louis Ebenezer Reynier (1771-1814) a Swiss-French general. Maida is in Calabria, Italy, about 13 miles west of Catanzaro.

MAIDA VALE, W9
Bakerloo line to Maida Vale

16, Sir William Dick REID, 1961.
108, Kinglsey AMIS, 1968.
136, William FRIESE-GREEN (LCP 1954) 1888-1891. He was living here with his wife and child when he first made a fifty-foot length of cine film (on celluloid) of Hyde Park on a Sunday morning.

MAIDEN LANE, WC2
*Piccadilly and Northern lines
to Leicester Square*

This refined *sounding* little (one way going east) street, parallel with the Strand, owes its name, not to any form of femininity, but a genteel version of 'midden' – a dung heap! It came into being in 1631.

9, Andrew MARVELL, 1677. In the last year of his life he was a victim of political threats.
9 (today's number) was a wigmaker's shop in January 1728 (P). In that month Francois AROUET ('Voltaire') began lodging here during his exile after his quarrel with the Chevalier de Rohan.

26, J.M.W. TURNER lived with his hairdresser father from his birth here on April 23, 1775 until 1800.

MALLORD STREET, SW3
District and Circle lines to Sloane Square

Named after Joseph Mallord William TURNER, the great artist who came to live in Cheyne Walk and died there in 1851.

11 (subsequently renumbered 13) A.A. MILNE (LCP 1979) 1920-1939. He wrote most of his *Winnie-the-Pooh* books here.

28, Augustus JOHN (LCP 1981) 1908-1929. The house was built for him and said to be a copy of Rembrandt's in Amsterdam. The architect was Robert Van T'Hoff. John owned the house until the 1930s when he sold it to the singer Gracie Fields (born in 1898 as Grace Stansfield). In 1929, John was one of three artists in the street. At number One was Graham Petrie and at 30, Arthur Croft Mitchell.

MALONE
Edmund
Literary figure

Dublin, October 4, 1741
London, April 25, 1812
In the family vault at Kilbixy

1, Foley Place, W1, pre-1777
40, Langham Street, W1, from 1779 until he died here

Son of a judge, Malone went up to Trinity to study law but, coming in to a considerable fortune, he was able to indulge himself in his first love of literature. He came to London in 1777 and his first edition of Shakespeare appeared in 1790. The work was acclaimed and in 1797 he published an edition of REYNOLD's works, followed by an edition of DRYDEN in 1800.

His literary knowledge was deep, well-respected and his reputation enhanced when he was the first person to doubt *publicly* the authenticity of CHATTERTON's 'Rowley' poems.

MANCHESTER SQUARE, W1
Central line to Bond Street

This is the second largest square on the PORTMAN estate. The first house to be built was on the north side in 1776 for the 4th Duke of Manchester, but it was not finished until 1788. The Wallace Collection is now housed in it (today called Hertford House). In 1840 the French Ambassador, François GUIZOT lived in it.

2, Sir Julius BENEDICT (LCP 1934) from 1845 until he died here in 1885.
3, J.H. JACKSON (LCP 1932) 1871-1911.
14, Lord MILNER (LCP 1967) 1920-1925. His widow lived on in the house until 1937.

MANSFIELD
Katherine Mansfield
Author

Wellington, N.Z., October 14, 1888
Fontainebleau, January 9, 1923

41, Harley Street, W1, 1901-1906
131, Cheyne Walk, SW3, 1910-1911
102, Edith Grove, SW10, 1914
47, Redcliffe Road, SW10, 114
3, Gower Street, WC1, 1917
141 A, Old Church Street, SW3, 1917

Katherine was the daughter of a new Zealand banker called Beauchamp (who was later knighted). Her first published work appeared when she was just nine years old. Later when she came to Queen's College, London, she edited the College magazine and was beginning to wonder whether or not she should make music her career.

In 1909 she married Charles Bowden, but left him in just over a week! Two years later she met John Middleton MURRY, became his mistress and finally married him in 1918.

She had always been troubled with a *chesty complaint* and was frequently searching the Continent for a more congenial climate. In 1920 her *Bliss and Other Stories* made her famous. Other short stories, a genre of which she was mistress – a 'female Chekhov' – followed, plus some poems. Posthumously, *Journal* and *Letters* appeared in 1927 and 1928 (edited by Murry) which kept her name before a growing, appreciative public.

MANSFIELD Scone, Scotland, March 2, 1705
William Murray (1st Lord) London, March 20, 1793
Jurist Westminster Abbey, in the North Cross

5, King's Bench Walk, EC4, pre-1756
28-29, Bloomsbury Square, WC1
(Kenwood House, Highgate, now a museum open year round, admission free.)

Murray was the fourth son of Viscount Stormont and, despite his predominately Scottish forbears, was educated in London at Westminster School and then Christ Church, Oxford, leaving there with a BA in 1727. He was soon called to the Bar and before long had a lucrative legal practice.

He was only 37 when he was made Solicitor-General, entered the House of Commons; became Attorney General in 1754 and Chief Justice of the King's Bench in 1756; together with a seat in the Cabinet.

As a judge he was renowned for his impartiality but he was *not* universally popular. His Bloomsbury Square house was burnt down in the Gordon Riots of 1780 and the mob destroyed his fine library.

Mansfield sat for Joshua REYNOLDS who asked him if the portrait was a good likeness. Mansfield replied that, '...it was totally out of his power to judge of its degree of resemblance, as he had not seen his face in a glass during the last thirty years'. His servant had always dressed him and put on his wig, '...which therefore rendered it quite unneccessary for him to look at himself in a mirror'(!) (Only a *really* conceited man could think like that!)

The Mansfield family motto is: *Uni Aequus Virtute*, Friendly to virtue alone. In 1795, FLAXMAN made a statue of Mansfield which now stands in Westminster Abbey.

MANSFIELD STREET, W1 *Bakerloo, Central and Victoria lines to Oxford Circus*

Once again a Harley estate related name, Henry Cavendish, Duke of Newcastle was also Viscount Mansfield. His granddaughter married Edward HARLEY, 2nd Earl of Oxford. Much of the street was built originally by the ADAM brothers around 1770.

2, Sir Robert MAYER, 1950-.
10, Dr. Malcolm MORRIS was born here on August 17, 1849, the 10th son and 15th child of John Carnac Morris.
13, John Loughborough PEARSON, 1880s.
13, Edwin LUTYENS (LCP 1962) from 1919 until he died here in 1944. He bought the house with a loan from Lady Sackville. She had also given him a Rolls-Royce. Dame Nellie Melba used to live next door. (The house is now divided up.)
20, Charles, 3rd Earl STANHOPE (LCP 1951) 1787-1795. In 1794 a mob attacked this house because 'Citizen Stanhope' openly supported the

French revolutionaries even when Britain was officially at war with Napoleon.

MARCONI
Guglielmo (Marchese)
Pioneer of Wireless

Bologna, April 25, 1874
Rome, July 20, 1937

71, Hereford Road, W2 (LCP 1954) 1896–1897
34, Charles Street, W1, 1906–1907

Marconi was the younger son of an Italian father and an Irish mother (which fact Ireland, for some reason, has never exploited) and was educated privately in Bologna, Florence and Leghorn. He had a scientific bent and in 1895 became convinced of the possibility of transmitting sound via electromagnetic waves.

Despite fairly convincing experimentation, Marconi could not interest the Italian Government in the potential of wireless and so he came to London in 1896 and on June 2 took out the first ever patent for wireless telegraphy – 'Improvements in Transmitting Electrical Impulses and Signals and...Apparatus therefor'. In 1897, Italy, having realized it had missed an opportunity, invited Marconi to demonstrate his new device and transmit messages from Spezia to some Italian warships, twelve miles offshore. These were followed by demonstrations in Rome when King Umberto and Queen Margherita were present. In 1897, a company was formed to acquire Marconi's patents *except* those valid in Italy.)

He succeeded in sending wireless messages across the Atlantic on December 12, 1901: from Poldhu in Cornwall to St John's, Newfoundland. In 1909 he was awarded the Nobel Prize and in 1910 messages were sent from Clifden, in Ireland, to Buenos Aires.

During the First World War, Marconi served in both the Italian Army and Navy. Soon the uses of *short waves* were being discovered and, in 1919, King Vittore Emmanuele III of Italy appointed Marconi to be delegate plenipotentiary at the Paris Peace Conference.

Marconi was also a pioneer of *broadcasting* and was sending out programmes from Writtle, near Chelmsford, for some time before the British Broadcasting Corporation was even formed.

MARGARET STREET, W1

*Central, Bakerloo and Victoria lines
to Oxford Circus*

This street is named after Lady Margaret Cavendish, heiress to the Harley estates, who married the 2nd Duke of Portland in 1734.

56, P.B. SHELLEY in 1814, whilst he was still arranging the legal separation from his first wife, Harriet.

70, Charles DICKENS, as a boy, when his father was (again) hiding from his creditors.

MARLBOROUGH
(Duchess) Gladys Marie
Mistress, then wife of the 9th Duke

Paris, February 7, 1881
Northampton, October 13, 1977

3, Hyde Park Place, W2, 1902
11, Savile Row, W1, 1911
15, Great College Street, SW1, 1922
7, Carlton House Terrace, SW1, 1928

Gladys Deacon was a Parisian born Bostonian American, who became a woman of great beauty. She also became mistress of Charles, 9th Duke of Marlborough, remained in that position for a number of years and married him when she was 40 years old.

The marriage broke up acrimoniously: the Duke practically tried to starve her out of the enormous house in Carlton House Terrace. She was reduced to cooking what food she could find in the house over an oil stove in the drawing room. The Duke had removed all the servants, had water, gas and light cut off and had barred all tradesmen's deliveries.

MARLBOROUGH

One can only suppose that these two St John's Wood 'Marlboroughs' *were* named after the only Duke (John Churchill, the 1st Duke) worth remembering, even though he died in 1722 and Marlborough Hill did not even begin to be built upon until 1830. Nearby is Blenheim Passage (and Hill and Road) so probably the developers used these *Marlburian* names to give their developments a 'touch of class'.

MARLBOROUGH HILL, NW8
Jubilee line to
St John's Wood

30A, Edmund BENTLEY, 1934-1938. His *Trent's Last Case* was a hit when it was published in 1913 and it was here he wrote *Trent Intervenes*; published (with less success) in 1938.

MARLBOROUGH PLACE, NW8
Bakerloo line to Maida Vale

10, Henry JAMES, as a boy in 1855. His father had rented the house for £250 a year. Ladies and gentlemen practised archery on a 'large green expanse' opposite the house.
38 (formerly 4) Thomas HUXLEY (LCP 1910) 1872-1890. Leonard Huxley later described the house as being '...not without character, and certainly was unlike most London houses. It was built for comfort, not beauty.'
58, Travers HUMPHREYS, for some years until he died here in 1983.

MARLOES ROAD, W8
District and Circle lines to
High Street Kensington

Originally Holland family property and one of many roads named after their Welsh connections. Marloes is a village in Dyfed, seven miles west of Milford Haven.

1, Andrew LANG (LCP 1959) 1876-1912. Whilst living here he wrote his most influential work, *Odyssey*, then three more books, ending with *The Making of Religion* in 1898.
3, Sir Edward ELGAR, 1889. He married Alice Roberts in this year.

MARRYAT	London, July 10, 1792
(Captain) Frederick	Langham, Norfolk, August 9, 1848
Author	St Andrews and St Mary's Church, Langham

8, Duke Street, St James's, SW1, 1830s
3, Spanish Place, W1 (LCP 1953) early 1840s

Marryat's grandfather, Thomas (1730-1792) was a doctor; his father, a wealthy man, an MP and once a Chairman of Lloyds. There was no lack of money but Frederick ran away when he was 14 and joined the Royal Navy as a midshipman under Lord COCHRANE's command. He served with distinction in many parts of the world, including Burma in 1824 and retired from the service when he was 38.
He became Equerry to the Duke of Sussex (Augustus Frederick, son of King George III: 1773-1843) and from 1832 edited the *Metropolitan Magazine* for

three years. He had already become a published author in 1829 with *Frank Mildmay, or the Naval Officer* but it was his *Midshipman Easy,* which appeared in 1836, on which his fame has rested.

MARSDEN   Sheffield, Yorks., September 16, 1796
William   Richmond, Surrey, January 26, 1867
Physician   Norwood Cemetery

23, High Holborn, WC1, 1816
65, Lincoln's Inn Fields, WC2, 1846

As an eighteen-year old Marsden came south to London *without* his parents' blessing and apprenticed himself to a Doctor Dale in High Holborn (having studied for a time under ABERNETHY).
Just before Christmas 1827, after Christmas shopping, he came across a pauper girl, nearly frozen, huddled in a doorway in Holborn. Marsden took the waif to a widow he knew at 2, Thavies Inn, who took the girl in and looked after her properly. It was this experience that determined him to found a hospital where treatment would be FREE and open to all, regardless of circumstances.
He had virtually no money of his own but by persistence he raised funds from older and wealthier friends and was able to take a house at 16, Greville Street, off Hatton Garden; the rent was £82.10s 0d. (£82.50) a year. In it he installed an apothecary called Watson who gave of his services in return for two living rooms on the top floor and a retainer of £30 per annum (plus another £30 for 'coal and candles'). A Charity was established called, 'The London General Institution for the Gratuitous Care of Malignant Diseases'. This was the beginning of two establishments (The Royal Free Hospital and the Royal Marsden Hospital) to be found in London today. Over the years tens of thousands of people, many, many of them suffering from cancer, owe Marsden an incalculable debt.

MARSH   London, November 18, 1872
(Sir) Edward   London, January 13, 1952
Artistic patron

38, Guildford Street, WC1, here born
30, Bruton Street, W1, 1877-1879
36, Bruton Street, W1, 1879-1899
3, Gray's Inn Place, WC1, 1899-1903
See under Grays Inn, 1903-1945
86, Walton Street, SW3, where he died

'Eddie' Marsh was a many faceted (but be-monocled) person. Some of the facets shone in his capacity as Personal Private Secretary to CHURCHILL, ASQUITH *and* BONAR LAW.
Marsh never married and was obviously attracted by handsome young men, some of whom *were* homosexual (Ivor NOVELLO for one). As a boy Marsh had had a bad attack of mumps and, as Christopher Hassall, Marsh's true friend and biographer wrote that the 'legacy' of mumps, '...enabled his affections to grow more intensely in the mind and, as a result, he cultivated a capacity for friendship which, untroubled by physical desire, could develop into devotion'.

MARTINEAU   Norwich, June 12, 1802
Harriet   Ambleside, June 27, 1876
Author and economist   Birmingham

6, Conduit Street, W1, 1832
17, Westbourne Street, W2, 1849

Harriet came from a very proper (and once prosperous) Huguenot family.

Her home life was 'industrious, intellectual and austere'. She was a sickly child and had been born without the senses of taste and smell. Worse, she grew to be completely deaf. In 1817 she was sent to live with her aunt, a Mrs. Kentish, who kept a school in Bristol. She was happier there and, by 1821, she had begun to have articles published (anonymously) in the *Monthly Repository* a Unitarian (ie 'Non-Conformist') periodical magazine.

Her father died in 1826 in dire financial straits; Harriet's brother died soon as did her lover and so, Harriet, suffering from these cruel blows, had to write for her (and her family's) living. In 1831 she was able to find a publisher for her *Illustrations of Political Economy* and in the following year she moved to London. Soon she made friends in pretty rarified circles; men like Henry HALLAM, Thomas Malthus, Richard MONCKTON-MILNES, Sydney SMITH, Sir Henry Buliver and Thomas CARLYLE.

In 1834 she paid an extended visit to the United States, where she was *not* popular at the time and less so, after 1837, when she had published *Society in America*. After a visit to the continent in 1839 she became unwell and remained an invalid until 1844. In that time she produced a novel, *The Hour and the Man* and some stories for children called *The Playfellow* in 1841.

MARVELL	Kingston-upon-Hull, Yorks., March
Andrew	31, 1621
Poet	London, August 16, 1678
	St Giles-in-the-Fields, Holborn

9, Maiden Lane, WC2, 1677

When Marvell was three years old his father left the Rectory in which Andrew was born, to become the master of the Hull Grammar School and master of the Charterhouse, also in Hull. Andrew was educated at the Hull school and afterwards went up to Trinity College, Cambridge. In 1639 Andrew got his BA and then travelled in Europe for nearly four years. He was a 'King's Man' in the Civil War and the subsequent Commonwealth, but he was also a law-abiding citizen and so lived happily, though warily, under Cromwell's regime.

Marvell was a great friend of John MILTON (and helped him get his secretaryship to the Council of State). He was elected in January 1659 as a member of Parliament for Hull, again in 1660 and again in 1661 (after the restoration of King Charles II) *and* he represented the borough until his death. Despite being a monarchist, Marvell thought the Court of Charles II immoral and corrupt. The King was supposed to have offered Marvell £1,000 (through his friend Danby) to take up some sort of place at Court. But nothing doing: 'I live here to serve my constitutents' [of Hull] 'the ministry may seek men for their purpose; I am not one', replied Marvell.

MARX	Dean Street, W1, January 16, 1855
Jenny Julia Eleanor	Sydenham, SE23, March 31, 1898
Socialist	Cremated at Woking (ashes in parents' grave)

55, Great Russell Street, WC1, 1884–1890
135, Gower Street, WC1 (in lodgings) 1898
(For earlier address look under Karl Marx.)

Only two of Marx's six children survived him; his second daughter, who had married a Cuban mulatto (who qualified as a doctor) committed suicide in 1911 and Eleanor, who committed suicide before her.

It happened through *theatrical* circles, that she met Dr. Edward Aveling. He was both a Socialist and a scientist. They were immediately attracted to each other and they were soon living as man and wife. Their mutual dedication to 'Socialism' enabled them to break the very rigid social *mores* of the late 19th century. In 1886 they travelled in America on a lecture tour and on their return to London, Aveling involved 'Tussy' in East End politics. Their relationship was not altogether happy but 'Tussy' was completely shattered to discover that Aveling was already married – and to an actress!

It was more than she could bear and she committed suicide by swallowing Prussic acid.

MARX	Trier, May 5, 1818
Karl Heinrich	London, March 14, 1883
Communist	Highgate Cemetery: Square 111, East IX

28, Dean Street (LCP 1967) W1, 1850-1856
46 (in Marx's day it was 9 and it changed to 38 at one time) Grafton Terrace, NW5, 1856-1864

Marx was the son of Herman Marx (1819-1842) a Jewish lawyer. He was also a descendent of Jehuda ben Elieser, a Paduan Rabbi who died in 1508. Karl began to study law first at Bonn, then Berlin, later turning aside to study history. In 1842 he was appointed editor of *Rheinische Zeitung* but his editorials were so critical of the government that the paper was banned. He married Jenny von Westphalen in 1843, moving to Paris, but was expelled in 1845 and the Marxes moved on to Brussels.

With ENGELS collaborating, Marx re-organised the Communist league when they met in London in 1847. Their manifesto ended with the immortal phrase; 'The Workers have nothing to lose but their chains. They have a world to win. Workers of all lands, unite!' Such sentiments were not acceptable to bourgeois Brussels and so, once again, the Marxes moved on: this time to London in 1849.

Here the family settled and experienced poverty and hardship. But London had wide arms and a compassionate nature and they stayed. Marx got a ticket for the British Museum Reading Room in June 1850 and here, after much research, he began to write *Das Kapital*. The first volume, which was to set the world agog, was published in 1867.

MARYLEBONE ROAD, NW1   *Bakerloo, Circle, Metropolitan and Jubilee lines to Baker Street (for low numbers on both sides of the road, Bakerloo line to Regents Park is perhaps better)*

The first land owners recorded in this area were both women: Aelgiva, Abbess of Barking and Eideva, probably another religious lady. In the Domesday Book, the area covered about 1,500 acres (647 hectares) but supported only about 150 people; compare this to the mid-19th century peak of 160,000! The Tyburn stream separated the property of these two ladies and the name Marylebone comes from either St Mary-by-Tyburn or St Mary-à-la-Bourne. Perhaps the manor would have been better called *Tyburnia* as THACKERAY once called Portman Square.

69,   William Hale WHITE, in the 1880s. In 1881 he had published *The Autobiography of Mark Rutherford*. He adopted 'Mark Rutherford' as a pen-name, but he also published, under his own name, a translation of Spinoza's *Ethic* in 1883.

190, Octavia HILL at the time of her death in 1912.

MASEFIELD Ledbury, Worcs., June 1, 1878
John Edward Burcote, May 12, 1967
Poet Laureate Ashes in Westminster Abbey ('Poet's
Corner')

8, Barton Street, SW1, 1901
18, Mecklenburgh Square, WC1, 1932-1935

Masefield's father was a country solicitor and his mother died when John
was only six years old. He was educated as a 'boy sailor' on *HMS Conway*
and was only 15 when he went to sea as an apprentice on a windjammer and
sailed around Cape Horn. (He did *not* sail 'before the mast': i.e. as a common
sailor whose quarters would have been in the *fo'c's'le* as was later alleged.) In
Chile, Masefield fell ill, he abandoned ship and, later, lived for three years in
New York. There he worked in a bakery, a stable, a saloon and eventually in
a carpet factory.

He was back in England by 1897 and began to sell some articles to various
magazines. He became editor of the *Speaker* and his first book of poems, *Salt
Sea Ballads*, appeared in 1902. Their success was followed by more poems
until *The Everlasting Mercy* was published in 1911. His public was *outraged* at
some of his more *earthy* references. (An example: 'And fifteen arms went
round her waist./ And then men ask, Are Barmaids chaste?')

Collected Poems, published in 1923 sold over 200,000 copies. Probably a
record for any poet, before or since.

MASON Dulwich, London, May 7, 1865
Alfred Edward Woodley London, November 22, 1948
Author

51, South Street, W1, 1948

Mason was educated at Dulwich College, 'just round the corner' from the
house where he was born and, after Oxford, joined the Benson company as
an actor.

His career took a sharp turn, when he was elected Liberal member of
Parliament for Coventry (in the industrial Midlands) in 1906. He was able to
combine his politics with his writing; though his first published novel had
been out in 1895, his most famous, *The Four Feathers* was published in 1902.
This be-monocled, laughing author, with his thick black hair, was regarded
(in some circles) as a potential Prime Minister.

In 1910 Mason published *At the Villa Rose* a detective story which featured
'Inspector Hanaud' of the Sûreté, who became one of the great figures in the
'school' of *detective fiction*.

MATTEI Campobasso, Naples, May 24, 1841
Tito London, March 30, 1914
'The King of Italy's' pianist

79, Baker Street, W1, 1914

He began his education in Naples but, at the age of 11, he was appointed
Professor of the Santa Cecilia Academy in Rome! For him actually, eleven
was quite an age, as he had given his first public concert in Turin, when he
was only *five* years old.

Basically, he was a pianist and had studied under Sigismond Thalberg – a
Swiss born, piano virtuoso. Mattei settled in London in 1863, gave many
concerts and conducted a season of Italian Opera at the Lyceum Theatre in
1870.

MAUGHAM Hackney, July 10, 1879
Syrie Gwendoline Maud London, July 25, 1955
Interior Decorator

9, Grosvenor Square, W1, 1924
43, Bryanston Square, W1, 1924-1927
213, Kings Road, SW3, 1927-1936
36, Chesham Place, SW1, 1936-1940
24, Park Lane, W1, 1944-1955

Syrie Maugham was the daughter of (the self-styled) Doctor Barnado, founder of the Barnado Homes for Waifs and Strays. Her mother, née Elmsie, was later nicknamed 'The Begum' which no doubt derived from her haughty manner.

On June 25, 1901, Syrie married Henry Solomon Wellcome at Surbiton. Wellcome, an American, put his age on the marriage certificate as 43 when he was nearer 50. They lived in some style style in Hayes, Kent, but the marriage did not work – Wellcome had some rather bizarre sexual tastes. However, they had a son, Mounteney, to whom Sir H.M. STANLEY stood as godfather. The Wellcomes remained together for eight years, but he was known in Syrie's family as 'Ghastly Old Wellcome'. They were divorced in 1915 and she was granted £2,400 pa alimony.

After the Wellcome divorce Syrie met Gordon Selfridge (c.1858-1947) and though they never actually lived together, they were lovers when Selfridge could take time off from the 'Dolly Sisters' and minding the store he had set up in Oxford Street in 1909. He established Syrie in a house in Regents Park and it was here she met Somerset MAUGHAM.

Despite Maugham being in love with Gerald Haxton, a bi-sexual, alcoholic, American opportunist (he died in New York in 1946) Syrie became pregnant by Maugham and married him in Jersey City on May 24, 1916. Predictably this marriage soon ran aground and they separated. Syrie started an interior decorating business and it was she who created the vogue for the 'all-white' room in the 1920s.

MAUGHAM Paris, January 25, 1874
William Somerset Nice, December 16, 1965
Author and playwright (his ashes were scattered near the
  'Maugham Library' at King's School,
  Canterbury)

27, Carlisle Mansions, SW3, 1904
23, Mount Street, W1, 1910
6, Chesterfield Street, W1, 1911-1918
2, Wyndham Place, W1, 1918-1924
43, Bryanston Square, W1, 1924-1927
213, Kings Road, SW3, 1927, shared with Syrie Maugham (qv)

Maugham was born in the British Embassy in Paris. His father, Robert Ormond Maugham, was a senior partner in an English law practice in Paris and took the precaution of having his son delivered on 'English territory', as there was a proposal that all people actually born on French soil would automatically become French citizens.

Willie was a small, sad, stuttering boy whose schooldays at the ancient King's School, Canterbury were a painful chapter in his life.

He qualified as a doctor of medecine but never practised. In 1897, his first novel, *Liza of Lambeth*, was published with such success that he turned his back on medecine. Soon after he became a playwright and was so popular that in 1908 there were four Maugham plays playing in the West End at the same time. A record; not even broken by Alan Ayckbourn in the 1970s.

In 1903 Maugham met Gerald KELLY in France and they became friends for life. Kelly painted 18 portraits of Maugham (15 of which are in the Humanities Research Centre of the University of Texas in Austin).

MAURICE   Lowestoft, August 29, 1805
John Frederick Denison   London, April 1, 1872
Theologian   Highgate Cemetery, West 11

21, Queen Square, WC1, 1846-1856
5, Russell Square, WC1, 1856-1860
2, Upper Harley Street, NW1 (LCP 1977) 1860-1866

Maurice, the son of a Lowestoft Unitarian minister, eventually went to Cambridge, then gravitated to London, where for a short time he edited the *Athenaeum* magazine.

He became Chaplain to Guy's Hospital, but in 1840 accepted the appointment as Professor of English Literature and History at King's College, London. He became a prominent figure in the Christian Socialist fringe of politics/religious thinkers and for a short time edited their magazine. He was dismissed from his chair at Kings as he said he could not believe in 'Hell and Eternal Damnation'.

In 1854 he was one of the founders of the Working Men's College of which he became Principal. His last official appointment was to be Professor of Moral Philosophy at Cambridge in 1866.

MAYER   Mannheim, June 5, 1879
(Sir) Robert   January 9, 1985
Musical philanthropist

2, Mansfield Street, W1, 1950-1984

Mayer who was the Chairman of the First British American Foundation, took over responsibility for the Robert Mayer Concerts for Children and was involved in many musical organizations on both sides of the Atlantic. He was originally a banker.

In 1919 he married Dorothy Piper, who was born in London in 1886. Lady Mayer (as she became in 1939, when her husband was knighted) was musical and had studied under Von zur Muehlen. Lady Mayer died in 1974 and Sir Robert remained a widower for six years, then quietly married Mrs. Jaqueline Noble on November 10, 1980. The bridegroom was a dashing one hundred and one years old. A record? Another record Sir Robert *may* have established was a letter he wrote to the editor of the *Times* on the subject of Jews in Russia, when he was over 100 years old. Had the *Times* ever published a letter from a centenarian reader before?

He was made a Companion of Honour in 1973 and six years later published a book, modestly (and truthfully) entitled, *My First Hundred Years*.

MAYHEW   London, November 25, 1812
Henry   London, July 25, 1887
Journalist   Kensal Green (catacomb A, Vault 52, now sealed off)

55, Albany Street, NW1 (LCP1953) 1840-1851

Mark Lemon and Mayhew were joint editors of the humorous weekly, *Punch* but Mayhew's real fame rested on greater reality in his book *London Labour and London Poor*, published progressively between 1851 and 1862.

He had run away from Westminster School and co-operated with his now unsung brother Augustus (1826-1875) in producing a number of light-hearted novels with appropriately light hearted titles like, *The Good Genius that Turns Everything to Gold* (1874). He also worked with yet another brother, Horace (1816-1872) who periodically contributed to *Punch*. The first issue of *Punch* appeared on July 17, 1841. Its originators were probably Henry Mayhew and Ebenezer Landells (1808-1860) a wood engraver. They gathered a team consisting of Douglas Jerrold (1803-1857) a savage, Radical wit, Mark Lemon and Stirling Coyne (1803-1868). The first issue sold 10,000 copies at threepence (1½p).

MAZZINI   Genoa, June 22, 1805
Giuseppe   Pisa, March 10, 1872
Italian Patriot   Genoa

5, Hatton Garden, EC1 (P)
183, Gower Street, WC1 (LCP 1950) 1837-1840
18, Fulham Road, SW6, late 1840s, early 1850s

As a 16-year old he had been moved by the plight of the refugees who were suffering as a result of the Piedmontese revolt. By the time he was only 19, he was a practising advocate and, in 1829, he joined the *Carbonari*. (A secret society formed in Naples during the reign of Murat, 1808-1815. Originally most of the members were refugees from the mountains of the Abruzzi provinces, many of them charcoal burners: so, *Carbonari*.) Mazzini was betrayed to the Sardinian Police and held in prison for a year. He then formed the 'Young Italy Association' in Marseilles, but was expelled from France two years later.

MECKLENBURGH SQUARE, WC1   *Piccadilly line to Russell Square*

Here stood the original buildings of Captain Coram's Foundation and the Square was so named as a compliment to Queen Charlotte (consort of King George III) who was a Princess of Mecklenburg. Poor Charlotte, who was *not* pretty; produced 15 children, none of whom seemed grateful and finally had the problem of dealing with a deranged husband. She died in 1818, aged 74.

18, John MASEFIELD, 1932-1935. When he moved here he had been Poet Laureate for two years.
37, Virginia WOOLF. She and Leonard took a ten-year lease in 1939 and this was their London address until her suicide in 1941. Leonard stayed on her for another year; the property being quite badly damaged in the *Blitz*.
44, D.H. LAWRENCE, 1917; not long after the publication of his novel, *The Rainbow* which was suppressed.
44, Dorothy L. SAYERS, 1920. Here she had had to cook for the first time in her life. She had little money and, 'Food', she wrote, 'is my most sinful extravagance'. It was here she first *produced* her aristocratic detective, 'Lord Peter Wimsey', whose exploits were so well recorded and received that she was able to afford the most luxuriant food for the following 30 years.
46, George Augustus SALA, c.1890. By now, 62 years old, he was at the pinnacle of his career.

MELBOURNE   London, March 15, 1779
William Lamb (2nd Viscount)   November, 24, 1848
Prime Minister

39, South Street, W1, 1835-1841

After school at Eton, University at Trinity College, Cambridge and Glasgow, Lamb became a Whig MP for Leominster, in Herefordshire, when he was 26. Surprisingly, under the Tory Government of Canning in 1827, he was appointed to the Chief Secretaryship for Ireland. He retained the post under the Earl of Ripon (1782-1859) the second son of Lord Grantham, who, as Lord Goderich was, for a short spell, PM. Actually, he was only created an Earl in 1833. Under WELLINGTON, too, Melbourne held the post. His father died in 1828 and so Melbourne had to leave the House of Commons and take his seat in the Lords. He was Prime Minister in 1834, again in 1835 and was still at Number 10 when Queen Victoria came to the throne in 1837. She was hardly 18 and Melbourne took great pains to introduce her gently to the burdens of a sovereign. At first she relied on him almost entirely and some catty wits in Court and Commons often referred to Victoria as 'Mrs. Melbourne'.

MELBURY ROAD, W14

Circle and District lines to High Street Kensington

Originally part of the Holland estate. The land here was part of the inheritance (in 1859) of Henry Fox-Strangways, 5th Earl of Ilchester. Melbury was the Ilchester's country home in Dorset.

2A, Sir Hamo THORNYCROFT (LCP 1957) 1878-1925. In Sir Hamo's day the house was called 'Moreton House'.

6, G.F. WATTS, 1876-1904. Ten years after moving here Watts had another go at marriage, his first having failed before it had begun. In 1886 he married Mary Fraser-Tytler.

18, William Holman HUNT (LCP 1965) lived and died in this house in 1910. Hunt, a stickler for authenticity, was not satisfied with the anatomical exactitude of the *donkey* he had painted in *The Triumph of the Innocents* (which he had worked on in Palestine). So he had a *horse* carcase delivered here, which was cut up into convenient sized joints, carried *through* the house and laid out on the grass in the back garden! (Despite this his widow stayed on in the house until 1929.)

MELVILLE	New York, August 1, 1819
Herman	New York, September 28, 1891
Author	

25, Craven Street, WC1, 1849

Melville's father was a merchant of Scottish descent whose business failed and was bankrupted in 1832. Soon after this the 15-year old Herman had to leave the Albany Academy, where he was a pupil and start to earn a living. In turn, he became a clerk, a farm hand, even a teacher, but eventually, in 1839, he signed on as a cabin boy on *SS Highlander* and sailed for Liverpool. This maiden voyage gave Melville sufficient background material for his novel, *Redburn*, which was published in 1849. Next he sailed the Pacific in the whaler, *Acushnet* and this inspired *Moby-Dick, or the Whale*, based on his whaling experience. When the boat reached the Marquesas Islands, Melville 'jumped ship' and was captured by cannibals. Somehow he managed to persuade them that a whale hunting son of a bankrupt Scottish merchant would probably give them indigestion and he lived with them amicably for some weeks. An adventure which appears in *Typee, a Peep at Polynesian Life*, which was his first published effort in 1846.

MEREDITH	Portsmouth, Hants; February 12, 1828
George	Box Hill, Surrey, May 18, 1909
Author and poet	His ashes are at Dorking (burial in Westminster Abbey was refused by the Dean.)

26, Great James's Street, WC1, 1840s
153, Ebury Street, SW1
193, Piccadilly, W1, June 1864

Meredith's father was a naval outfitter who had George educated in

Portsmouth and later in Germany. He had little money as one of his trustees made a considerable error in judgement and lost the young man a large proportion of what was not a very large income. He was articled to a London lawyer, but he had no stomach for the law and leaned toward literature. His first published effort appeared in *Chamber's Magazine* in 1849. In this year, too, he married Mary Ellen Nicholls, the widowed daughter of Thomas Love Peacock (novelist and poet, son of a London merchant: born in Weymouth, 1785, died 1866). The marriage was a failure from its early days and she eloped with Henry Wallis in 1858.

His first novel, *The Shaving of Shagpat*, appeared in 1855, followed by the very well known *The Ordeal of Richard Feverel*, four years later. His most famous, *Diana of the Crossways* finally appeared in 1885. In 1862 he published a sonnet sequence called *Modern Love* which was based on his own unhappy marriage. In its day the poem caused quite a stir.

However, he did find love eventually and married Marie Vulliamy when he was 36 years old.

MESSEL	London, January 13, 1905
Oliver Hilary Sambourne	July 13, 1978
Designer	

16, Yeoman's Row, SW3, 1929-1946
17 *and* 19, Pelham Place, SW3, 1953

Messel sprang to fame at 21, when he designed the décor and costumes for the *Cochran's Revue* of 1926. He did not have 'stageblood' in him and he had been conventionally educated at Eton. His artistic capabilities were no doubt inherited from his maternal grandfather Linley SAMBOURNE who was a frequent contributor to *Punch* and really a very talented artist.

Messel was always socially acceptable and never more so than when his sister's son, Anthony, married HRH Princess Margaret. At the time of Anthony's wedding his mother was the Countess of Rosse.

METTERNICH	Coblenz, May 15, 1773
(Prince) Clemens Lothar Wenzel	Vienna, June 11, 1859
Statesman	

44, Eaton Square, SW1 (LCP 1970) 1848

A diplomat to the toenails, Metternich studied at Strasbourg and Mainz and was then attached to the Austrian Embassy at The Hague. In 1807 he concluded the Treaty of Fontainebleau and, in 1809, negotiated the marriage of Napoleon to the Archduchess, Marie Louise of Austria.

It was Metternich who declared war on France in 1813 and, after the *Grand Alliance* was signed at Teplitz, Metternich was made a Prince of the Empire. After the French 'revolution' in 1848, half the crowned heads of Europe were toppled and Metternich fled to England, only returning to his Rhine castle of Johannesburg in 1851. His third wife, the Princesse Mélanie went into exile with him, thinking that everyone in England revelled in every European disaster. (She was probably right.)

MEW	London, November 15, 1869
Charlotte Mary	London, March 24, 1928
Poet	

10, Doughty Street, WC1, here born
9, Gordon Street, WC1, for most of her life
15, Delancey Street, NW1, not long before she died.

Charlotte's father was an architect and reasonably prosperous. Charlotte lived all her life in or near Bloomsbury. Despite her father's means she was to suffer both from poverty as well as ill health. She was awarded a small Civil List pension, which alleviated the former but did nothing for the latter which depressed her to such an extent that she committed suicide.

Her first published works were actually in prose and appeared in the *Yellow Book*. She did publish two volumes of poetry and Thomas HARDY said that she was the 'best woman poet of her time'.

MEYNELL	Barnes, Surrey, October 11, 1847
Alice Christina Gertrude	London, November 27, 1922
Poet	St Mary's Catholic Cemetery, Kensal Green

11, Inkerman Terrace, W8, 1877
21, Upper Phillimore Gardens, W8, 1881-1888
2A, Granville Place, W1, 1905-1922

Alice and her sister Elizabeth were daughters of T.J. Thompson and spent much of their childhood in Italy.

Five years before Alice married Wilfred Meynell in 1877, she had become a Catholic and, also before her marriage, she had published a book of verse called *Preludes*. She was well equipped to help Wilfred in his editorial work and they kept a sort of literary 'open house'. Of necessity their hospitality was frugal but they were often 'at home' to the great 19th *century literatii* such as, TENNYSON, BROWNING, John RUSKIN, Dante ROSSETTI, 'George ELIOT', PATMORE and George MEREDITH. The Meynell's 'rescued' the dissolute poet, Francis THOMPSON who dedicated his book of poems called *Love in Diana's Lap* to Alice Meynell and spent the rest of his short, tubercular life living, on and off, in the Meynell's house.

MEYNELL	London, May 12, 1891
(Sir) Francis	July 9, 1975
Typographer	

16, Great James Street, WC1, 1924-1936
39, Woburn Square, WC1, 1930s
50, Gordon Square, WC1, 1936

Francis, the son of Wilfred and ALICE Meynell, was educated at a boys' Roman Catholic School near Bath and afterwards went on to Trinity College, Dublin.

Politically he was a Socialist and for two years was a director of the *Daily Herald*, which was the mouthpiece of the British Labour Party and partly supported by subscriptions from most Trade Unions. The Stationery Office (HMSO, a government concern) asked his advice on typographical matters and he gave them assistance from time to time without remuneration.

MIKES	Siklos, Hungary, February 15, 1912
George	
Journalist	

1B, Dorncliffe Road, SW6, 1960s

Mikes was London correspondent for a few Budapest papers from 1931-1938. By 1946 he had lived in England long enough to be able to publish his marvellous little book *How To Be an Alien*. This should be required reading for any one who is *really* trying to find out what the British are like. The book was graced with elegant line drawings by Nicholas Bentley (son of 'Clerihew' BENTLEY; but alas, no longer with us).

In 1950 he published *Down with Everybody* and in it describes his adopted city: 'London', he wrote, 'is chaos incorporated'.

MILES   Uxbridge, September 27, 1907
Bernard James (1st Lord)
Actor and actor manager

43, Acacia Road, NW8, 1946

Miles began his working life as a school teacher but, by the time he was 25, he had become totally involved in the theatre.

He and his wife, Josephine (née Wilson) founded the 'Mermaid Theatre' at Puddle Dock and it became the first permanent, live theatre to be open in the City of London for over 300 years. The original 'Mermaid' has given way to a new theatre on the same site yet, somehow, it does not have the same *charm* of the first one.

Lord and Lady Miles put £10,000 each into the building but, by August 1983, it looked as if the theatre could not survive. The Corporation of the City of London had placed (on average) £5,000 annually at its disposal. An appeal for £1 million was started, but after a few months less that £400,000 had been raised. (The first show to open in the newly constructed 'Mermaid' was *Eastward Ho!* which alone lost £80,000.)

MILL   Pentonville, London, May 20, 1806
John Stuart   Avignon, May 8, 1873
Philosopher   Avignon

40, Queen Anne's Gate, SW1, 1814–1831
18, Kensington Square, W8 (LCP 1907) 1837–1851

Mill was one of James MILL's sons and James tried to mould him into a natural successor to BENTHAM and himself. John S. was highly intelligent and by the time he was 15 he had a thorough knowledge of classical literature, logic, political economy and mathematics (as a matter of fact, he was probably a priggish child).

Still only 15, he was sent to France where Sir Samuel Bentham (Jeremy's brother) kept an eye on him. Two years later he entered the Indian Office (as his father before him) and eventually became the Examiner of Indian Correspondence. The post was later abandoned and Mill was pensioned off on a liberal scale.

Mill stood as a 'working man's' candidate for Parliament in 1865. Early in his political career he made a speech in the House of Commons, which caused DISRAELI to raise his 'quizzing glass' and murmur to his neighbour, 'Ah, the Finishing Governess'.

In the Victoria Gardens, on the Embankment, near the Temple, is a bronze statue of Mill. It is by Thomas Woolner and was placed here in 1878.

MILLAIS   Southampton, June 8, 1829
(Sir) John Everett   London, August 13, 1896
Artist   St Paul's Cathedral

7, Gower Street, WC1
83, Gower Street, WC1, 1851–1854
7, Cromwell Place, SW7, 1862–1879
2, Palace Gate, W8 (LCP 1924) 1879 until he died here

The Millais family were originally from the Channel Islands but had been settled near Southampton for some years. Millais studied at the Royal Academy Schools and, when only 17, exhibited his painting, *Pizarro Seizing the Inca of Peru* (now in the Victoria and Albert Museum). Certainly he was precocious; he was, at 11 years old, the youngest Academy student ever.

Millais was angelically good looking and his mother had thought him too delicate to go to ordinary school. She used to read to him as he painted. He often used members of his family as models. His best known painting is almost certainly *Bubbles*, which was bought by the Pears Soap Company. Nearly as well known is *Boyhood of Raleigh*, which he painted in 1870 (now in the Tate Gallery).

In 1854 he was painting a portrait of John RUSKIN and, before the painting was finished, Mrs. Ruskin (Effie) told her husband she was in love with Millais; she went off with him and they were married that year.

Millais was dying from a painful and disfiguring cancer of the larynx in 1896, but in January of that year he had been elected President of the Royal Academy. (He had been made a Baronet in 1885.)

In the forecourt of the Tate Gallery there is a statue of Millais, brush in hand and palette ready. It is by Sir Thomas Brock and placed here in 1904.

MILNE	London, January 18, 1882
Alan Alexander	Sussex, January 31, 1956
Author	

11, Mallord Street, SW3 (LCP 1979) early 1920s
13, Mallord Street, SW3, 1925-1939

Milne, a schoolmaster's son, went to Westminster School and then to Cambridge (where he edited *Granta*). He began as a freelance journalist in London and, at the age of 24, was an assistant editor of *Punch*, a job which lasted until 1914. The war came and he served in the Royal Warwickshire Regiment. Just before the war broke out he had married Daphne de Selincourt and they had just one son, Christopher Robin.

After the War, Milne produced four books for his son: *When We Were Very Young* (1924) *Winnie the Pooh* (1926) *Now We Are Six* (1927) and *The House at Pooh Corner* in 1928. *Winnie the Pooh* (a bear of very little brain) has been enchanting children (and their parents) ever since Christopher Robin (who kept a book-shop in the waterside town of Dartmouth in Devon) himself grew up. He could be less than civil to people who hunt him out *just* because he was *the* Christopher Robin.

MILNER	Giessen, Germany, March 23, 1854
Alfred (1st Viscount)	Canterbury, May 13, 1925
Statesman	

8, York Street, W1, 1883-1885
47, Duke Street, SW1, 1885-1914
14, Manchester Square, W1 (LCP 1967) 1920-1925

Milner's father was a university lecturer at Tübingen (which is why he was born in Germany). Milner went up to Oxford in 1872 and had a brilliant record, winning a New College fellowship.

For a short while he was assistant editor of the *Pall Mall Gazette* and then became private secretary to Viscount Goschen (1831-1907) who recommended him for a financial post in Egypt in 1889. By 1892 he was Chairman of the Board of the Inland Revenue and five years later appointed as Governor of the Cape Colony. He was knighted in 1901 and given a Viscountcy the following year for his service to Britain during the Boer War.

In December 1916 he joined the War Cabinet and by 1918 was Secretary for War. In 1921 he was Colonial Secretary and, amongst other things, recommended that Egypt should be given its independence. By 1925 he was dead from *encephalitis lethargica*, a form of sleeping sickness.

There is a bronze medallion of Milner in the wall of the courtyard of Toynbee hall. It is a copy of the Milner Memorial in the Henry VII Chapel in Westminster Abbey. Both were executed by Gilbert Ledward in 1930.

MILNES
Richard Monckton
(1st Lord Houghton)
Wealthy, literary dilettante

London, June 19, 1809
Vichy, August 11, 1885
Fryston, Yorkshire

26, Pall Mall, SW1, 1837-1850
16, Upper Brook Street, W1, 1852-1870
27, Berkeley Square, W1, 1873

In his heyday Milnes either knew everybody who was anybody or else anybody who was nobody claimed to know him. He was in the literary swim from about 1830 and amongst his friends were: SWINBURNE, CARLYLE, TENNYSON and WORDSWORTH.

He also took the trouble to get himself elected as an MP (for Pontefract in Yorkshire: he had a country house called Fryston in that county) but he does not seem to have done much for his voters. His father had once rejected a peerage – much to his son's annoyance – but eventually Milnes was ennobled and styled himself as Lord Houghton.

MILTON
John
Poet

London, December 9, 1608
London, November 8, 1674
St Giles's Church, Fore Street, Barbican

19, Petty France, SW1 (at one time York Street) 1652-1660

Milton's father, who was a scrivener – a clerk, who copied important documents for eventual circulation – disowned his son when the young poet became a Protestant. A friend of his father, Thomas Young, a Puritan Scotsman, paid for John's early education, sent him to St Paul's School and on to Christ College, Cambridge. Here he spent seven years altogether. His first post-university poem *On the Morning of Christ's Nativity*, was published in 1629.

In 1632, *not* having taken holy orders (as was originally intended) Milton went to live near Windsor, where he wrote *L'Allegro* and *Il Penseroso* followed in 1633 by *Arcades*; *Comus* in 1634 and *Lycidas* in 1637. In 1638 he travelled in France, where he met Grotius and in Italy, where he met Galileo. He was back in England in 1639 and settled in London, earning a little 'pin-money' by tutoring his nephews, Edward and John Phillips. Four years later he married Mary Powell, the 17-year old daughter of an Oxfordshire cavalier. A month after the wedding, Mary went back to her father. John and she were reconciled in 1645 (and the three daughters they had were suitable evidence of that reconciliation). Mary died in 1652 and four years later Milton married Katherine Woodcock, who died in childbirth in 1653.

Ten years later, and totally blind, he married Mary Minshull, a 25-year old (he was 55) who had been 'recommended to him by a Doctor Paget'. In 1658 he began *Paradise Lost* but it was not published until 1667.

Paradise Regained, was printed, together with *Samson Agonistes*, in 1671. They were his last works and he died, '...of the gout...' three years later. Mary, his widow, lived on until 1727.

In the Church of St Giles, Cripplegate, in whose cemetery Milton was buried, is a bronze statue of the blind poet by Horace Mountford. There is also a bust of Milton in the church, dating from 1793, by BACON.

MITCHISON   Edinburgh, November 1, 1897
Naomi
Author

17, Cheyne Walk, SW3, 1919-1923

Born a Haldane (her brother was J.B.S. HALDANE) Naomi married G.R.
(later Lord) Mitchison in 1916. He died in 1970. Her first published work
was called *The Conquered* in 1923 and a number of books followed ranging
from autobiography through history, politics, philosophy to African affairs.
She was adviser in Botswana in 1963.

MITFORD   Alvesford, Hants., December 16, 1787
Mary Russell   Swallowfield, Berks., January 10, 1855
Author   Swallowfield

33, Hans Place, SW3, 1805-1820
49, Frith Street, W1, 1821-1829
56, Russell Square, WC1, 1835

Mary Mitford's father was a doctor of medecine who never practised as one.
He assiduously spent his wife's fortune, his own (such as it was) and the
£20,000 which his ten-year old daughter won in a lottery in 1797. Poor Mary
had to support her feckless father and she began trying to have her work
published.
Miscellaneous Poems appeared in 1810, which attracted little notice. *But* in
1819, the first volume of what was to become *Our Village* appeared in the
Lady's Magazine. Four more volumes were published, the last in 1832. She
also wrote three 'dramas' and her *Recollections of a Literary Life* only a year
before she died.

MITFORD   London, November 11, 1904
Nancy Freeman   Paris, June 30, 1973
Author   St Mary's Churchyard, Swinbrook,
                          Oxon (her ashes only, she was
                          cremated in France)

1, Graham Terrace, SW3, here born (used to be Graham Street)
49, Victoria Road, W8, 1923
26, Rutland Gate, SW7, 1926 (and later in the mews behind 26)
12, Blomfield Road, W9, 1939

Nancy Mitford was an aristocratic sprig from a rather dotty, aristocratic
family. Her father, the 2nd Baron Redesdale (a model for Uncle Matthew in
Nancy's 1945 novel, *The Pursuit of Love*).
She married the Hon. Peter Rodd in 1933, when she had already published
two novels which sold well: *Highland Fling* in 1931 and in 1932, *Christmas
Pudding*. Many of her relatives 'appear' in both *Pursuit of Love* and, in 1949,
Love in a Cold Climate. Her own pursuit of love was not so happy and her
marriage was dissolved in 1958 (she never remarried).
In 1956 Nancy edited a book called *Noblesse Oblige*. It was written by
Professor Alan (Strode Campbell) Ross. Ross was then a 49-year old
Professor of Linguistics at Birmingham University. The book was
composed of a number of satirical essays by various authors which dealt
with English snobbery and how it was evidenced in speech and
pronunciation. ('Fireplace' was 'Non-U'; i.e. not Upper Class. The 'U's'
warm themselves by the 'chimney piece', always go to the 'lavatory' and
never the 'toilet' and so on.) So a whole new linguistic field was opened up
and, because Miss Mitford was, almost by chance, involved in the book and
so *very* definitely 'U' herself, she was afterwards always associated with the
'U-non U' demarcations.

Like most 'U' English people she loved Paris and things Parisian. After *Pursuit of Love* she settled in Paris. *The Blessing* in 1951 was her last novel but she wrote three enchanting and authoritative biographies on, VOLTAIRE (*Voltaire in Love*) *Madame de Pompadour* and *The Sun King* (Louis XIV, 1638-1715, King of France from 1643) her last book in 1966.

MONTAGU
Elizabeth
'Blue Stocking'

West Layton, Yorks., October 2, 1720
London, August 25, 1800

22, Portman Square, W1, from 1781 until she died here (in her day it was Montagu House)

Née Robinson, Elizabeth married Edward Montagu, a grandson of the 5th Earl of Sandwich, a cousin, by marriage of Lady Mary MONTAGU on August 5, 1742. She soon established a *salon* to which the *ton* of the day flocked. Fanny BURNEY (Madame D'Arblay) wrote that Portman House, '...was magnificently fitted up and appeared to be rather appropriate for princes, nobles and courtiers rather than poets, philosophers and blue stocking votaries'.

MONTAGU
(Lady) Mary Wortley-Montagu
Literary lioness

(baptised) May 26, 1689
London, August 21, 1762
Grosvenor Chapel, Mount Street (the grave is not marked)

10, Soho Square, W1, 1734
19, Golden Square, W1, c.1737
44, St George Street, W1, where she died

Lady Mary was the eldest daughter of Evelyn Pierrepont, 5th Earl (and later, Duke) of Kingston and she acted as his hostess after the early death of her mother.
'Privately' in 1712, she married Edward Wortley-Montagu, a grandson of the first Earl of Sandwich. By him she had a son, Edwin, born in 1713 (probably less than nine months after their August wedding). She and her husband moved in literary circles and both ADDISON and POPE were among their intimate friends. They also had the entrée to Royal Circles. Caroline, Princess of Wales (who became Queen Caroline, as wife of King George II, in 1727) was probably her best female friend at one time.
Edward was appointed Ambassador at Constantinople and here she first encountered the small pox innoculation. She was responsible for bringing this remarkable medical prize to Britain in 1718. The marriage went astray and Lady Mary left England in 1738 and eventually settled in Venice. Horace WALPOLE wrote of her in 1740 as an '...old [she was just 51] foul, tawdry, painted, plastered personage'. She came back to London in February 1762.

MONTAGU SQUARE, W1
Central line to Marble Arch

The Square was begun c.1810 at the rear of Elizabeth MONTAGU's great house which she had built for herself c.1780. It was said that David Porter, who built the Square, once was a chimney sweep and so one of those who were given a feast on May Day every year by Mrs. Montagu. In 1937 the Square contained 63 houses: in twelve of them lived the Earls of Cromer, Lucan and Ancaster; the Countesses of Jersey, Mayo and Lichfield; Viscount Ashbrook and Lords Hutchinson of Montrose, Cantley, O'Neill and Mancroft. All *very* aristocratic.

15, Nancy CUNARD, after her unsatisfactory marriage to Sidney Fairbairn in November 1916.

39, Anthony TROLLOPE (LCP 1914). He moved in here in 1873 and was sufficiently well pleased with the house '...to hope to die in it'. He didn't actually die *in* it, but it *was* his last London address. (He died in 1880). He had a library of more than 5,000 books in the house.

63, Doctor Malcolm MORRIS, 1877-1887. His children's nurse was a girl called Amy Mustoe. She believed – and *drummed* into the heads of her small charges – that *the* Dreadful Day of Judgement, 'The Last Day', would take place, to the sounds of Heavenly Music, in Hyde Park, between the Marble Arch and the Serpentine! (Because *there* was the Centre of the World.) An election took place in 1880 and, with it, all the *hullaballoo*. The two younger children; Lilian, aged six, and Harold, only four (later to be Sir Harold Morris, QC) thought that the last Trumpet was about to be sounded and dashed out into the street, in their nightclothes, to join in the fun!

MONTPELIER SQUARE, SW7   *Piccadilly line to Knightsbridge*

Built around 1830: because the rarefied air of Brompton was considered healthy, it was likened to the salubrity of Montpelier, France, which, with its medical school founded in the 12th century, was still a fashionable resort in the 19th.

8, Arthur KOESTLER and his wife, Cynthia, committed suicide together here on Thursday, March 3, 1983. (Koestler had lived here off and on, since 1953.) The house was sold in April 1984 for nearly £350,000. It has only four bedrooms.

MOORE	Ballyglass, County Mayo, Eire,
George Augustus	February 24, 1852
Author	London, January 21, 1933

92, Victoria Street, SW1, early 1890s
8, King's Bench Walk, EC4, 1896
121, Ebury Street, SW1 (LCP 1936) from 1911 until he died here

When his father died in 1870 Moore went to Paris to study art, soon realized he had not sufficient talent to make a living and turned to poetry. In 1878 his first book of poems, *Flowers of Passion* was published, followed three years later by *Pagan Poems*.
He came back to London in 1883 and two years later his first novel, *A Mummer's Wife* appeared. However it was his semi-autobiographical novel, *Confessions of a Young Man*, which put him firmly on the literary map in 1888 *and* gave an insight into his life in Paris ten years earlier.

MOORE	12, Aungier Street, Dublin, May 25,
Tom	1779
Poet and Satirist	Devizes, February 25, 1852
	Bromham, Wiltshire

28, Bury Street, SW1, 1805-1811, moving to 19, in the same street, in 1826.
In between came:
81, Jermyn Street, SW1, in 1825
15, Duke Street, St James's, W1, 1833

Moore's father was a grocer in Kerry and his mother was a Codd (née Anastasia Codd)! After Tom finished his education at Trinity College, Dublin he came to London to study law in the Inner Temple. With him came his translation of *Anacreon*. (Anacreon was a Greek Lyric poet born in Teos about 563 BC and died about 478 BC. Moore's version was published in 1800 and sometimes he was called 'Anacreon Moore'.) He dedicated the work to the Prince Regent and it was well received.

In 1803 he was given the appointment of Admiralty Registrar in Bermuda (for no good reason!) He travelled home via America and his *Epistles, Odes and other Poems* appeared telling of his wanderings. In 1807 his *Irish Melodies* were set to music by Sir John Stevenson. The work was a triumph and Moore became a sort of 'Hibernian Poet Laureate'. The pieces continued to appear over the years and Moore was paid £105 for each 130 songs he composed and was now taken up by 'Society'. In 1811 he married Bessie Dyke and it was around then that his friendship with BYRON began. (Such was his fame that the publishers, Longmans, paid him £3,000 *sight unseen* for his *Lalla Rookh*.)

MOORE Hastings, Sussex, March 4, 1870
Thomas Sturge London, July 18, 1944
Poet and Engraver

31, Beaufort Street, SW3, 1895
20, St James's Square, Holland Park

The Moores in the middle of the 19th century were making a name for themselves in medecine and philosophy. Doctor Daniel Moore married, as his second wife, Henrietta Sturge, by whom he had four sons and three daughters. Thomas was the youngest and George, the eldest (1863-1958) became a leader in 'the philosophical revolution against idealism' and was prominent in those fields, while young Thomas became friendly with artistic and literary people, like Charles RICKETTS and his friend SHANNON (and lived off and on in their Beaufort Street house).

His mother, Henrietta, was a Quaker, but Thomas maintained friendly links with cousins of hers, the Appias, a French Roman Catholic family. His brother, Harry was at one time engaged to Marie Appia, but the engagement was broken off and Marie (1872-1957) became Thomas's wife.

In 1912, the Moores moved up to Hampstead to the house where John CONSTABLE had lived in Well Walk. Roger FRY called a house they had had in Highgate, the next 'village' to Hampstead, '...a house further from anywhere than anywhere else.' Early on in life, Thomas slightly altered his name to give the impression that he had a hyphen, Thomas Sturge-Moore, and many works list him as being 'double-barrelled'.

MORAN Yorkshire, November 10, 1882
Charles McMoran Wilson (1st April 12, 1977
Baron)
Physician

25, Bryanston Square, W1, 1964-1977

Moran was an eminent doctor, who received many honours and was involved in numerous medical and quasi-medical organizations. His father was a doctor and the family name was Wilson; Moran was the name chosen when Sir Charles Wilson was ennobled in 1943. He served as a doctor in the First World War and in time became the Chairman of the Army Medical Advisory Board.

However his place 'in history' is principally assured because in May 1940, only a few days after he became Prime Minister, Winston CHURCHILL appointed him as his personal doctor; a post Moran held until CHURCHILL's death nearly 25 years later.

In 1966 Moran published a book called *Struggle for Survival*, which dealt frankly with the life of his most illustrious patient. He wrote of matters which one would have thought (indeed *should*) have remained confidential between any patient and his doctor. Many eyebrows in Harley Street – and elsewhere – were raised, but Moran was unrepentant. The book is of consuming interest and, in places, well written.

MORGAN Kent, January 21, 1894
Charles Langbridge London, February 6, 1958
Author Gunnersbury Cemetery, W5

16, Campden Hill Square, W8, 1931-1958

Morgan's father was a railway engineer (though a knighted one) and Charles was educated at Osborne (Isle of Wight) and Dartmouth, both Naval Colleges. From 1911-1913 he served on the Atlantic and China stations, but in 1914 was taken prisoner by the Germans and spent the rest of the war in Holland on *parole*.

This enforced absence meant that he was 24 before he went up to Oxford where he became President of the Oxford University Dramatic Society (OUDS). Three years later he was dramatic critic on the *Times* and, in 1929 his novel, *Portrait in a Mirror* won the *Femina Vie Heureuse* Prize, which popularized his writing in France. In 1940 his book, *The Voyage*, won the Tait Black Prize.

He was a close friend of George (Edward) Moore, Professor of Philosophy at Cambridge. Moore, 21 years older than Morgan, made him his literary executor, but the older man outlived him, dying eight months after him, on October 24, 1958.

MORGAN Hartford, Conn., April 17, 1837
John Pierpont Rome, March 31, 1913
Millionaire

13, Prince's Gate, SW7 early 1900s-1913

John P. was a son of Junius Spencer Morgan (1813-1890) who, with George PEABODY, founded the firm of J.S. Morgan and Company in London and in time would control the banking firms of J.M. Morgan and Co. of New York, Drexel and Co. of Philadelphia (Anthony Joseph Drexel, 1826-1893) Morgan Grenfell of London and Morgan Harjes of Paris (John Harjes, 1828-1914).

However, all his money did not enable him to have a satisfactory love life. He had married Frances Tracey of New York in 1865 and by her had a son, John Pierpont (Junior) born in 1867 (and died in Boca Grande, Florida in March 1943) and three daughters. Despite a very large, triangular nose, brilliantly red and pitted by acne, many women claimed to find him 'fascinating' but, alas, they were probably more fascinated by the colour of his money than the colour of his nose.

MORNINGTON CRESCENT, NW1 *Northern line to Mornington Crescent*

This was part of the Fitzroy estate. Fitzroy was the family name of the illegitimate son of King Charles II and Barbara Castlemaine and his descendants. This son of the King was also made Duke of Grafton in 1675. *His* grandson was created Baron Southampton in 1780 and *his* son married into the Mornington family. The great Duke of Wellington was the son of the Earl of Mornington – an Irish peerage.

6, Walter SICKERT from 1907, about which time he established the 'Camden Town Group' of artists – really the first 'School of English Impressionism'.

25, Alfred TENNYSON lodged here in 1850. He left behind him the manuscript for his poem *In Memoriam*. Just by luck Coventry PATMORE was able to retrieve it for him.

MORNINGTON TERRACE, NW1 *(All details as for Mornington Crescent)*

12, H.G. WELLS lived here from 1894-1898 with his mistress, Catherine Robbins who had been a pupil of his. Here he wrote *The Time Traveller* (published in 1896 as *The Time Machine*) and the *Island of Doctor Moreau*.

20, Sir William CROOKES.

MORPETH TERRACE, SW1   *District, Circle, Victoria and BR lines to Victoria*

The Terrace, Carlisle Place and Howard Place were all developed in the middle of the 19th century and the man officially responsible for the changes was George, 8th Earl of Carlisle (1808-1889). Before he succeeded to the Earldom he was known as Viscount Morpeth. George died unmarried and was succeeded by a relative, George James Howard, as 9th Earl. The 9th Earl was a son of the fourth son of the 6th Earl! Morpeth Terrace and numbers one to three of Carlisle Place were designed by W. Jackson.

On the east side of the Terrace is a block of flats called MORPETH MANSIONS.

Flat 11, Winston CHURCHILL, 1938. On September 22, 1938, CHURCHILL asked Harold NICOLSON to meet him here at 4.30 pm to discuss the Czechoslovakian Crisis (when the country was being overrun by the Nazis). 'While I wait for the lift,' wrote Nicolson in his diary for that day, 'Winston appears from a taxi. We go up together. "This" [the Crisis] I say, "is hell". "It is the end of the British Empire", replied CHURCHILL.'

MORRELL   London, June 16, 1873
(Lady) Ottoline Violet Anne   Tunbridge Wells, April 21, 1938
Social and literary 'Queen Bee'   Holbeck Church, Welbeck

5, Portman Square, W1, here born
13, Grosvenor Place, SW1, 1878
22, Grosvenor Road, SW1, 1902
44, Bedford Square, WC1, 1904 and 1905
10, Gower Street, WC1, 1920s and 1930s

Ottoline's father was Lieutenant-General Arthur Bentinck of the Seventh Dragoon Guards and her cousin was the 5th Duke of Portland, 1800-1879, though it was a distant kinship. Her father died of a heart attack in 1877 and two years later the 5th Duke died. Ottoline's half-brother, Arthur, then 22, became the 6th Duke and in 1880, she was 'raised to the rank' of a Duke's daughter and received a lavish upbringing.

After a number of experiences (such as friendship with the then 40-year old Axel Munthe of *The Story of San Michele* fame) Ottoline went up to Somerville College when she was 25 and, during her time at Oxford, she met Philip Morrell, the elder son of a well-to-do Oxfordshire brewing family, who lived in a house called Black Hall. Philip and she were married at St Peter's, Eaton Square on February 8, 1902: they honeymooned in Italy and moved into 32, Grosvenor Road on their return to London.

One of Ottoline's lovers was Bertrand RUSSELL, an affaire which went on with very little attempt at concealment. Between 1911 and 1938, RUSSELL wrote her over 2,500 letters, all of which Ottoline kept. The Morrells had bought Garsington Manor, near Oxford and here, as well as at their London houses, they were hosts to the literary and artistic creatures, now loosely referred to as 'The Bloomsbury Set'. Vaslav Nijinsky (the Morrells were *balletophiles* as well) thought that, 'Lady Ottoline is *so* tall, *so* beautiful, *so* like a giraffe!' Tall, yes, but hardly *beautiful*.

MORRIS   London, August 17, 1849
Malcolm   Alexander February 18, 1924
Dermatologist

10, Mansfield Street, W1, here born
63, Montagu Square, W1, January 1877-1887
8, Harley Street, W1, September 1887

Morris was the tenth son and fifteenth child of John Carnac Morris, an employee of the East India Company and Malcolm was sent to school at Clifton, Bristol, not the public school Clifton College but a small private school for about 100 boys. He had an accident in Bristol docks and his subsequent treatment decided him to become a doctor. He persuaded his mother to let him leave school early and in September 1866 he began to study medecine at St Mary's Hospital, Paddington. He lived in rooms in St Mary's Terrace, just off Paddington Green and William Lewis, who became the much loved actor William Terriss, was a fellow lodger. (Born 1847 and tragically murdered in 1897 at the stage door of the Adelphi Theatre in the Strand, by a deranged bit-part actor.)

Morris graduated in 1870 and decided to specialize in diseases of the skin. In 1872 his brother Henry lent him £1,200 and he bought a general practice in Goole, Yorkshire. In the July of that year he married his Oxfordshire sweetheart, Fanny Cox. He moved south to London and, by 1886, was making £3,000 per annum. He moved to Harley Street as a skin specialist in 1887.

Two of his friends were doctors: one, Conan DOYLE, quit the profession for the more profitable pastures of detective fiction. Another was Frederick TREVES who had taken out the Royal appendix in 1902. In 1907 Treves asked Morris to treat the King for a spot under his left eye. Another specialist had tried but had nearly electrocuted His Majesty and so was *not* asked to continue. Morris, daringly bought £400 of radium and proceeded to eradicate the blemish with weekly exposures. It really was brave as Marie Curie, 1867-1934, only isolated radium and polonium in 1910. The treatment, part of which took place in Homburg, was successful and HM offered Morris 500 guineas (£525) or an 'honour'. Morris chose the honour and was made a Knight Commander of the Royal Victorian Order at Christmas 1907.

MORRIS   Walthamstow, March 24, 1834
William Samuel   Hammersmith, October 3, 1896
Artist, craftsman   Kelmscott, Oxfordshire

1, Gordon Street, WC1, 1856
17, Red Lion Square, WC1, 1857-1859
41, Great Ormond Street, WC1, 1861
8, Red Lion Square, WC1, 1861-1865
24, Queen Square, WC1, 1865

Morris was sent to Marlborough School in Wiltshire and then went up to Exeter College, Oxford, before being apprenticed to an architect. He took up painting and then, together with Edward BURNE-JONES and Dante Gabriel ROSSETTI, established a firm of furniture manufacturers. He was 'an all round man': he began the Oxford and Cambridge magazine – and included some of his own poetry in it. In 1868 he published *The Earthly Paradise* and *Love is Enough* in 1875. After he had made a tour of Iceland he produced *Sigard the Volsung* in 1876.

In 1890 he started the Kelmscott Press and designed type and some decorations for its printed output. He was a truly great craftsman (much better in that field than as an author or poet) but he really had rather too much of a 'folksy approach' to the work in hand.

MORSE　　　　　　　　　　　　Charlestown, Mass., April 27, 1791
Samuel Finley Breese　　　　　　New York, April 2, 1872
Artist and inventor

4, Buckingham Place, SW1, 1811
141, Cleveland Street, W1 (LCP 1962) 1812-1815

Morse's father was the Reverend Jedidiah Morse, a Massachusetts' geographer who was able to send Samuel to Yale in 1810. Not long after, he set off for England where he was going to study painting. He had already studied chemistry and electricity and, in 1832, he first thought of the idea of a *Magnetic Telegraph*. He showed his brain child to Congress and tried very hard to get full patent protection in Europe. Six years later Congress awarded Morse 30,000 dollars for a telegraph line between Washington and Baltimore. It was a success and the system soon widely adopted, together with the MORSE CODE.
Artistically Morse was highly regarded as well, once being referred to as the 'American Leonardo'. That may have been a little fulsome, but he was a competent artist though today only his *Code* is remembered.

MOSLEY　　　　　　　　　　　London, 1910
(Lady) Diana
Politician's wife

49, Victoria Road, W8, 1923
26, Rutland Gate, SW7, 1926-1928
10, Buckingham Street, SW1, 1928-1931
96, Cheyne Walk, SW3, 1931-1934
2, Eaton Square, SW1, 1934-1936

Diana, née Mitford, was the third daughter of the 2nd Lord Redesdale (1878-1958). Redesdale had six daughters – NANCY 1904, Pamela 1907, Diana 1910, Unity Valkyrie (sic) 1914, Jessica 1917 and Deborah Vivien 1920. His only son Tom, born in 1909, was killed in the Second World War so the title went to his younger brother, Bertram.
Diana was hardly ever called Diana – unless she was in trouble. Her mother called her 'Dana', her father 'Dina', Nancy 'Bodley', Pamela and Unity 'Nandy', Jessica 'Corduroy' and Deborah 'Honks'.
When she was only 18, Diana married Bryan Guinness, son of Colonel Guinness, a politician and part of the rambling, wealthy brewing family. Bryan was only 24 and, being well off, painted, as he did not have to earn a living. Two baby Guinesses appeared in due course, but so did Sir Oswald MOSLEY. Oswald and Diana met at a party given by the St John Hutchinsons for their daughter, Barbara in 1932. Bryan was divorced and Diana became Lady Mosley in Berlin in 1936.

MOSLEY　　　　　　　　　　　London, November 16, 1896
(Sir) Oswald Ernald (6th Bt.)　　France, December 3, 1980
British Fascist

5, Gordon Square, WC1
8 and 9, Smith Square, SW1, 1929
5, Lowndes Court, Lowndes Square, SW1, 1964

A product of Winchester and Sandhurst, Mosley became a Conservative MP for Harrow in 1918, a Labour member for Smethwick in 1922, was Chancellor of the Duchy of Lancaster in 1929 and, in 1932, founded the British Union of Fascists (the 'Blackshirts').
He married twice; firstly, in 1920, to Lady Cynthia Curzon (2nd daughter of Viscount CURZON) and they had two sons and one daughter. In 1936,

Lady Cynthia having died in 1932, he married Diana Mitford (sister of Nancy and also the Duchess of Devonshire). Diana had divorced Bryan Guinness to marry Mosley and this second wedding for both of them took place in Joseph Goebbel's drawing room in Berlin.
In the Second World War both Mosley and his wife were imprisoned under the Defence of the Realm Act, the Government of the day, not surprisingly, believing that Mosley, having begun the Blackshirt movement in Britain, would take sides with Britain's enemies, the Fascists.
Mosley had many qualities not the least of them being the ability to think that whatever *he* did was right. He once said, 'Before the organization of the Blackshirt Movement, free speech did not exist in this country'! Many Conservative thinkers in the 1920s saw in Mosley a new leader in the making, yet in a letter in the *Times* in 1968, he wrote, 'I am not, and never have been, a man of the right. My position was on the left and is now the centre of politics.'

MOTLEY   Boston (Mass.) April 15, 1814
John Lothrop   Dorset, May 29, 1877
Diplomat and historian   Kensal Green; Grave No. 24709, Plot
                              No. 104

31, Hertford Street, W1, 1859
17, Arlington Street, W1, 1869-1870

Motley, an ex-Harvard University man, travelled Europe in 1834 and afterwards was called to the Bar. Thirty five years later he was to be appointed as United States Minister to Great Britain for two years.
Of independent means, he could indulge himself in history and literature; his two great loves. He spent ten years working on his *Rise of the Dutch Republic*. It was published in three volumes simultaneously in London and New York in 1856. It covers Dutch history from the abdication of Charles V to the death of William the Silent in 1584. Later, he wrote *The History of the United Netherlands*. Both works were praised in America and Europe.

MOUNT STREET, W1   *Central line to Bond Street*

During the Civil War, London (rather surprisingly) was on the side of Cromwell and his Roundhead army. The Royalists fought hard to gain control of the capital and Cromwell, anticipating attack by the King's men from the west, had earthwork embankments put up in 1642-1643. These defences were nicknamed 'Oliver's Mounts' and the name stuck. In Whitechapel to the east of the City, Mount Terrace commemorates Cromwell's defence on that side.

4,   Washington IRVING lodged here in 1824.
22,   Fanny BURNEY (by now Mme. d'Arblay) was here in 1838, not long
       before her death.
23,   Somerset MAUGHAM, c.1910. In 1920, Hugh WALPOLE wrote in
       his *Vanity Fair*: 'The next time I saw Maugham was in that gay,
       discreet bandbox of a house in Mayfair' [ie this house] 'that became for
       many of us one of the happiest, most hospitable, most amusing houses
       in London. I was, I remember, struck by the strange contrast of the
       lower, social part of the house and the room on the top floor where he
       did his work. That top floor remains after all these years as the most
       ideal spot for a writing man that I have ever seen.' Despite Walpole's
       appreciation of his hospitality, Maugham portrayed Walpole as the
       rather unpleasant 'Kear' in his novel, *Cakes and Ale* in 1930. Walpole
       was very put out by this.

54, Prince Arthur of CONNAUGHT, immediately after his wedding to the Duchess of Fife on October 15, 1913. On August 9, 1914, the Princess gave birth to their only child, a son; Earl of MacDuff.

105, Winston CHURCHILL, 1904-1906. His uncle, the Duke of Marlborough gave him a two-year lease on a flat in this house. Winston wrote to his Aunt Leonie that the '...fine rooms here are much more comfortable than...at Cumberland Place' (his mother's house near Marble Arch).

MOUNTBATTEN
(Prince) Louis
Admiral

Graz, May 24, 1854
London, September 11, 1921
Whippinham, Isle of Wight

40, Grosvenor Gardens, SW1, 1900
4, Hans Crescent, SW3, 1901
87, Queen's Gate, SW7, 1911

Born a German prince, Mountbatten married Victoria of Hesse, granddaughter of Queen Victoria and joined the British Navy. He rose up through the service on merit and, in 1912, was made First Sea Lord. When the First World War broke out two years later, his German background was widely regarded with suspicion and he was forced to resign his post in October 1914. *Germanophobia* became so extreme King George V asked Mountbatten to renounce his German titles and, having toyed with calling himself Battenhill (his family name was Battenburg) he chose Mountbatten ...'we incline to' [Mountbatten] 'as a better sound', he wrote to his son Louis, then a fourteen-year old student.

MOUNTBATTEN OF BURMA
Louis Francis Albert Victor
Nicholas (1st Earl)
Admiral of the Fleet

Frogmore House, Windsor, June 24, 1900
Ireland, August 27, 1979 (murdered by 'Irish Patriots'
Romsey Abbey Church, Romsey, Hants (in the south transept)

Brook House, Park Lane, W1, 1929
2, Wilton Crescent, SW1, 1959

Lord Louis had the most distinguished career it is possible to imagine. His family connections were impeccable. His godmother was Queen Victoria. His nephew is HRH Prince Philip, Duke of Edinburgh, his aunt was the wife of Tsar Nicholas II of Russia and other blood ties connected him with practically every other European monarchy.

Had one ever have wanted to address an envelope *formally* to Lord Louis it should have looked something like this:

'Admiral of the Fleet, Viscount Mountbatten of Burma, KG, PC, GCB, CB, OM, GCSI, GCIE, GCVO, DSO, FRS, DCL, LLD.'

In addition to these British honours – and those are not all of them – he was entitled to show (when in full dress) the ribbons (and/or medals) of; the Legion of Merit, DSM of the U.S., the Greek Military Cross, Grand Cross of the Order of George I of Greece, the Special Grand Cordon of the Cloud and Banner of China, the Legion of Honour and Croix de Guerre, the Star of Nepal, the Order of the White Elephant of Siam, the Order of the Lion of the Netherlands, not to mention some ten other decorations not for war service!

MOZART Salzburg, January 27, 1756
John Chrysostom Wolfgang Vienna, December 5, 1791
Theophilus Vienna
Genius

20, Frith Street, W1, 1764
180, Ebury Street, SW1 (LCP 1939) 1764-1765

Although these were the four forenames given to Mozart at his baptism, when older, Mozart himself translated the 'Theophilus' from its Greek form to the German 'Amadeus' and dropped John Chrysostom altogether. Mozart and his sister, four years older than he, were the only two of Leopold Mozart's children to survive childhood. Leopold was a musician at the Chapel of the Prince Archbishop of Salzburg. The boy showed genius for both composing and performing music at an incredibly early age. When he was only six and a half years old, his father took him to Vienna where he played before the Emperor Francis I (1708-1765).

At 13 Mozart was appointed 'Director of Music' to the Archbishop of Saltzburg. In 1781 he married Constanze Weber, an actress. She was a loving wife but a bad manager. He was appointed Royal Organist to Joseph II (1741-1790) but with a salary of less than the equivalent of £80 a year, poor Mozart got deeper and deeper into debt. He was 'in-the-red' more or less permanently, yet he still managed to compose cheerful music.

Constanze was distraught with grief, when her beloved husband of only ten years died. Yet, neither she, nor any of his friends, followed his coffin to its unmarked grave. The circumstances of Mozart's burial still excite the curious. Why, for instance, should Vienna's most popular composer of the day, be given only a 'pauper's grave'? It now appears that a 'third class burial' had already been arranged *before* he was dead!

Admirers and students of Mozart's music owe much to Ludwig Ritter von Kochel. He was an Austrian musicologist, born in Stein in 1800. By the time he died in 1877 he had compiled the exhaustive and complete catalogue of all Mozart's compositions in the chronological order of their original composition. These are the 'K' numbers, universally in use today (and phonetically sound like 'Kirkel' number so-and-so).

MULBERRY WALK, SW3 *Piccadilly, District and Circle lines*
to South Kensington

The Walk lies on land that once formed Chelsea Park. In 1719 an ambitious scheme to create a domestic silk industry was launched. Over 2,000 mulberry trees were planted to provide the staple diet of the silkworm. The worms, however, turned (as some worms will) and, not liking the London climate, refused to co-operate and the whole scheme foundered.

1, Anthony EDEN, 1929. At this time he was merely a member of Parliament but held no governmental offices.

21, Evelyn WAUGH, 1937, not long after his second marriage, to Laura Herbert.

MURRY Peckham, August 6, 1889
John Middleton Norfolk, March 13, 1957
Author 47, Redcliffe Road, SW10

102, Edith Grove, SW10, 1914
18, York Buildings, WC2, 1925

Murry's father was a fairly lowly clerk in Somerset House, but somehow managed to pay the fees for the boy at Christ's Hospital and later the cost of Brazenose College, Oxford. Murry went into journalism not long after coming down from university, first working on the *Westminster Gazette* and later on the *Nation*.

Having lived with Katherine MANSFIELD for some time he eventually 'made an honest woman of her' in 1913. She exerted considerable influence on his literary style, as did their mutual friend, D.H. LAWRENCE.

He became editor of the *Athenaeum* and in 1923 founded the *Adelphi* magazine. He published a number of books of literary criticisms and some religious works. In 1933, ten years after Katherine's death at Fontainebleau, he published *The Life of Katherine Mansfield* and two years later an autobiography which he called *Between Two Worlds*.

NAPOLEON III
Charles, Louis-Napoleon Bonaparte
Emperor

Paris, April 20, 1808
Chiselhurst, January 9, 1873
Abbey Church of St Michael,
Farnborough, Hants.

1, Carlton Gardens, SW1, 1839-1840
1C, King Street, SW1, 1848

This Napoleon was the third son of the Bonaparte who was the third brother of Napoleon I. Most of Charles Louis' youth was spent at his mother's castle at Aveneuberg in Switzerland. He joined the rebels in Italy and it was in this abortive campaign his brother, Louis, died of a fever. In 1832 the Duke of Reichstadt and Charles Louis became head of the Dynasty. Europe was 'not yet ready for him' and he went off to America.
In 1840 he tried again to set himself up in France, but got little further than Boulogne and was imprisoned ('perpetually') in the fortress of Ham. From here he escaped in May 1846 and came to London. Two years later, after his plebiscite in his favour, he took control of the Republic. In 1853 he married the beautiful Eugénie de Montijo, a Spanish countess. (She did not die until 1920 at the age of 94.) Napoleon was not entirely satisfied with Eugénie – he was in any case, a compulsive womaniser – and one of his dalliances was with the Marquise Taisey-Chatenoy. She told of Napoleon coming to her room and becoming more than just romantic. During the subsequent gymnastics, the Marquise said that the Emperor's ardour melted the wax on his moustache and it (the moustache, anyway) drooped!
Rather surprisingly, Queen Victoria liked Napoleon, despite his well known reputation as a philanderer. She *quite* liked Eugénie. Victoria wrote in her journal that the French Empress's shoulders '...are very beautiful. The pictures of Winterhalter are very like her. The hair light brown, the face very pale, the mouth and teeth lovely. She does *not* bear standing well.' (How typical of HM! She could not allow *anybody* – except Albert – to be perfect. The last diary sentence is so like a school report!)

NELSON
Horatio (1st Viscount)
Admiral

Burnham Thorpe, Norfolk,
September 29, 1758
off Trafalgar, October 21, 1805
St Paul's Cathedral

5, Cavendish Square, W1, 1787
147, New Bond Street, W1 (P) 1797
103, New Bond Street, W1 (LCP 1958) 1798
19, Piccadilly, W1, 1803

Nelson, the son of the Vicar of Burnham Thorpe, went into the navy when he was only 12 years old. He was in the West Indies, followed by an Arctic expedition in 1773 then, three years later, in the East Indies, coming back to England in ill health. Whilst in the West Indies he married the widow of a Dr. Nesbit of Nevis.
In 1793, with Lord Hood in the Mediterranean, he was struck in the face by gravel shot and lost the sight of his *right* eye. In 1797 he was despatched to intercept treasure-laden Spanish ships at Santa Cruz. Nelson's attack was beaten off and his right elbow so shattered by grape shot that the arm had to be amputated just below the shoulder. It is said he even refused a deadening

draught of brandy and went through the operation silently. Early in 1798 this courageous little man was on *HMS Vanguard* in the 'Med.' to keep an eye (literally) on the French Fleet. He eventually attacked the French at Aboukir Bay and all but two French ships were sunk or captured. Nelson sailed back into Naples and was met there in triumph by Sir William Hamilton, the 63-year old British Ambassador and his 33-year old wife, EMMA. Nelson was given a barony (Lord Nelson of the Nile) £10,000 by the East India Company and the Dukedom of Brontë by the King of Naples. In March 1805 the French Fleet, under Villeneuve (1763-1806, who was destined to support Napoleon's projected invasion of England) set out from Toulon to the West Indies. Nelson followed and eventually, on the return journey the 33-strong French and Spanish Fleet were induced to stand and fight Nelson (with only 27 ships) off the Cape of Trafalgar at daybreak on October 21, 1805. At noon Admiral Cuthbert Collingwood (1750-1810) broke through the enemy's line and Nelson turned the rest of the fleet into the very centre of the engagement. As he passed astern of Villeneuve's ship, the French managed to fire a salvo at Nelson's ship, the *Victory*. The Admiral was on deck speaking to Captain Thomas Masterman Hardy (1769-1839) when a shot lodged in his left shoulder. (That actual piece of metal can be seen in a showcase in the hall of Windsor Castle.) He fell, was carried below and three hours later died from the wound, but knowing that the enemy fleet had been totally routed. His last words, some say were. 'Kiss me Hardy' – they were old friends – but others say he muttered 'Kismet, Hardy'.

The Nelson motto is *Aimam qui Meruit Ferat*, – Let him wear the palm who has deserved it.

Nelson's statue atop the Trafalgar Square column is by E.H. Bailey (1788-1867). The column is made from Devon granite and was designed by William Railton (d.1877) and based on a column in the Temple of Mars Ultor in the Forum, Rome. The whole monument is 185 feet (56 metres) high. It took three years to build, being finished in 1843. The bas-reliefs at the base of the column, cast in iron salvaged from French guns, were: (north face) Nelson's Nile victory by Woodington (east face) Copenhagen, by Ternouth (west face) St Vincent, by Watson and the scene of his death, by J.E. Carew, faces down Whitehall. The lions, by LANDSEER, were not finished until 1868.

NEW BOND STREET, W1   *Central line to Bond Street*

This busy street was built up around 1720 and named after Sir Thomas Bond, a wealthy financier who lent money to King Charles II and was Treasurer of the Household of Henrietta Maria, the widow of Charles I. It was Bond who developed 'Old' Bond Street about 1660.

146, General, Sir Thomas PICTON, 1797-1800, not long after he had been Commandant of Tobago in the West Indies.

147, Lord NELSON (P 1876). He lived here for only a few months in 1797, after he had lost his arm at Cape St Vincent. Lady Nelson attended to the daily dressing of the stump personally. In 1798 he moved back up the street to 103 (LCP 1958).

148, Lord CAMELFORD, 1803-1804; his last address before being killed in a duel over his mistress. He was 29.

150, Lady HAMILTON, 1813, not long before she was arrested for debt in the King's Bench. Alderman Joshua Smith bailed her out and helped her escape across the Channel to Calais.

154, Ugo FOSCOLO, 1819. His rooms were '…classic and pagan with an Apollo in the sitting room and a Jupiter in the entrance hall'.

160, H.M. STANLEY, 1886. His large and expensive flat was used to store the equipment for his final expedition to Africa.

NEWBOLT Bilston, Staffs., June 6, 1862
(Sir) Henry John London, April 19, 1938
Poet

177, Victoria Road, W8, 1889-1896
23, Earls Terrace, W8, 1900-1910
29, Campden Hill Road, W8, from 1918 until he died here.

Newbolt's father was a Vicar in the unlovely town of Bilston for some years, but, thanks to a private income, he was able to educate both his sons, Henry and Francis (as day boys) at Clifton College in Bristol. Henry went on to take First Class Moderations at Christ Church College, Oxford and Francis (who was just over a year younger) was up at Balliol.
His lasting fame is as a poet and of his poetry, the opening lines of *Vitai Lampada* are most certainly the best remembered. The 'Close' is the name of the cricket field infront of the main block of Clifton's buildings and the poem is describing the dying moments of a cricket match being played on it.
> 'There's a breathless hush on the Close tonight –
> Ten to make and the match to win'

NEWMAN STREET, W1 *Northern and Central lines*
to Tottenham Court Road

William Berners began to develop around here, building Berners Street in 1738 and Newman Street not long after. He (probably) named it after a house at Quendon, in Essex, which he owned called Newman Hall.

14, Benjamin WEST, lived here from 1777 until his death here in 1820. In 1790 his studio, which had two windows looking into a little garden had, '...an Italian look. The room was hung with engravings and coloured prints.'

28, Thomas STOTHARD when his family had outgrown his previous house. Stothard probably bought this house in 1790 – complete with all the furniture in it.

70, J. McNeil WHISTLER and also William DE MORGAN, pre-1860. WHISTLER passed the rooms on to DU MAURIER.

70, George DU MAURIER, in 1860 then in 1885; in Lionel Henley's rooms. From here du Maurier wrote, 'I don't think I could live without Henley – he's as good as a wife and makes 85, Newman Street feel like home'. In June 1861 he moved to 91 and, in the same year, to 90, where he stayed until 1862.

NEWTON Woolsthorpe, Lincs., December 25,
(Sir) Isaac 1642
Scientist London, March 20, 1727
Westminster Abbey Nave

88, Jermyn Street, W1 for three years, then;
87, Jermyn Street, W1 (LCP 1908) 1700-1709
35, St Martin's Street, WC2, 1720-1725

After the local Grammar School, Newton went up to Trinity College, Cambridge, taking his BA in 1665. It was in his last year at the university that his train of thought led him to consider the question of gravity. (Whether or not it was the falling apple, a fancy circulated by 'Voltaire', that triggered off the idea is speculative!) Some of his original calculations were wrong and he turned to the question of the nature of light. He worked on the construction of telescopes and was able to show how to produce instruments with far greater powers of definition than ever before. Without this fundamental thinking by Newton, neither HERSCHEL nor Rosse would have been able to produce the sophisticated telescopes with such perfection as they did.

Newton became a Fellow of Trinity and Lucasian Professor of Mathematics, two years later, in 1669. In 1671 he was elected to the Royal Society and again took up his study of gravity. This time there were no mistakes in his calculations and his findings were published under the title of *De Mora Corporum*.

When he was 50, he began to suffer from a form of madness that effectively ended his scientific career. It has been argued that his mental breakdown was caused by mercury and lead poisoning which entered into his system during his 'passionate researches' into Alchemy.

He had few pleasures outside science and he most certainly disliked music. In 1720 he told the Reverend William Stukeley that he had only once been to the opera: the first act he heard with pleasure, the second stretched his patience and in the third he ran away!

There is a rather penny-pinched head of Newton in Leicester Square, W1. The piece was by William Calder Marshall and erected here in 1874. There is also a statue of Newton on the first floor of the City of London School on the Embankment just before Blackfriars Bridge. The Abbey monument of Newton on the Choir Screen is by William Kent (1685-1748) and John Michael Rysbrack (1694-1770).

NICOLSON   Tehran, November 21, 1886
(Sir) Harold George   Sissinghurst, Kent, May 1, 1968
Diplomat and biographer

182, Ebury Street, SW1, 1916-1919
9, Bentinck Street, W1, 1916
5, Gordon Square, WC1, 1930s
C 1, Albany, W1, 1953

Nicolson's father, Arthur (later to be made Baron Carnock), who was born in 1849, was the British Chargé d'Affaires in the Embassy in Tehran. However, Harold was brought back to England for school at Wellington College and then Balliol College, Oxford.

He entered the Diplomatic Service in 1909 and held posts successively in Madrid, Istanbul (Constantinople) Tehran and Berlin. In 1929 he resigned from the Corps and went into journalism. Six years later he expanded into politics and was elected Liberal MP for West Leicester.

He wrote a number of biographies, the most brilliant one being that of King George V. He also published books on history, art and even good manners. In 1913 he married Victoria Sackville West, daughter of the 3rd Baron Sackville. (She was his only child, born in 1892.) The Nicolsons had two sons, Benedict, an artist who died, aged 68, in 1982 and Nigel, who went into publishing. Victoria, called by everybody 'Vita' and by her husband, 'Viti', died of cancer on June 2, 1962, aged 70. Her ashes were placed in the Sackville Crypt in Withyam, Sussex. Their marriage was an odd one. After the birth of Nigel (when Vita was 25) they hardly had any sexual relations. Anyone wondering at this should take into account that Nicolson was homosexual and Vita lesbian. In September 1941 Nicolson visited his doctor, Sir Kenneth Goadby. In his diary for September 23, Nicolson wrote, 'It seems that my skull is thicker than that of most people and that this has inhibited the full expansion of the pituitary gland. It may be owing to this excess of calcium in babyhood that I became homosexual.'

NIGHTINGALE	Florence, Italy, May 12, 1820
Florence	London, August 13, 1910
Nursing pioneer	East Wellow, Hants. (grave identified by initials)

10, South Street, W1 (LCP 1955) from 1856 until she died here

Florence persuaded her reluctant and hardly believing father to let her study nursing. In the middle of the 19th century, a girl of such a good family would be lowering the standards by earning a living. Certainly 'nursing', midwives apart, and there were many *Mrs. Gamps* among *them* was usually carried out by careless harridans who were hardly better than harlots. She began a training of sorts at Kaiserwerth in 1851 and later on in Paris.

After the Battle of Alma (when 3,000 British troops were killed and wounded) Florence offered to go out to the Crimea. She was allowed to do so with many provisos and so, with 38 nurses, none of her calibre but the best she could muster (and not inebriates) Florence set out from England in October 1854 and eventually set up hospital in Scutari.

On November 5, the Battle of Inkerman was fought with heavy losses and soon there were some 10,000 soldiers in dire need of treatment either from wounds or fever. Florence and her dedicated band had to cope with this *Augean* situation often with actual opposition from the existing British administration.

Florence came back to England in 1856 and some £50,000 was subscribed for her to form nurses' training schools at St Thomas's and King's College Hospitals in London. She extended her range of fire beyond mere nursing and continually attacked the sanitary standards in hospitals generally and many reforms were instigated as a result of her zeal.

A statue to Miss Nightingale forms part of the Guards' Crimean memorial at the bottom of Regent Street, facing Waterloo Place. Her statue was by Arthur Walker. Her cousin Sydney, who was given a peerage and became Lord Herbert of Lea, appears beside her. There is a less formal statue of her by Frederick Mancini on the terrace of St Thomas's Hospital, next to Edward VI. The bronze was *stolen* in 1970 and has been replaced by a figure made of composite material.

NORTH BANK, NW8   *Jubilee line to St John's Wood*

Once (before the railway line was driven through into Marylebone) an elegant row of houses stood here.

21,   George Henry LEWES and his mistress Marian Evans ('George Eliot') lived here from 1863 until LEWES died here in November 1878. Here she wrote *Middlemarch*, which was published in 1871. Mathilde Blind, an Anglo German poetess, wrote of Lewes and Marian that they were '...a strange looking couple – she, with a certain sibylline air, he not unlike some unkempt Polish refugee of vivacious manners – swinging their arms as they hurried along at a pace as rapid as their talk.'

36,   Mary SHELLEY in 1836, when she had been a widow for 14 years.

41,   Thomas HUXLEY; briefly, in 1851.

NORTHCLIFFE	Dublin, July 15, 1865
Alfred Charles William Harmsworth	London, August 14, 1922
(1st Viscount)	Marylebone Cemetery
Newspaper tycoon	

12, Clarges Street, W1, 1894
36, Berkeley Square, W1, 1897
2, Carlton Gardens, SW1, where he died

Though Irish born, Harmsworth was brought up in London where he exhibited early journalistic skill in editing his school magazine – complete with a 'gossip column'! Soon after leaving school he became editor of a magazine called *Youth* (appropriately enough). He then founded *Comic Cuts* ('amusing without being vulgar') and by 1894 had acquired enough financial muscle to absorb the *Evening News* and two years later he stood Fleet Street on its head by founding the *Daily Mail*. All the time this was going on in London, Harmsworth and his brothers Cecil, Harold, Hildebrand and Robert were buying up provincial papers and bringing them into the group. In 1903 the *Daily Mirror* appeared, the first paper intended to be especially for women and about this time he established the Amalgamated Press. After much secret negotiation in 1908, he bought *The Times* – the 'Old Thunderer' itself and then lowered its price to one penny (less than a half penny).

As his paper empire grew (and his wealth) his mental balance became more and more uncertain. He saw himself as a sort of Fleet Street Napoleon and when he was awarded a Viscountcy he chose the name of Northcliffe, which conveniently began with 'N'. By 1919 he was almost entirely unhinged.

There is a bronze bust of Northcliffe in the tiny forecourt of the Church of St Dunstan-in-the-West, at the Temple Bar end of Fleet Street. It is by Lady Scott, widow of Captain SCOTT. It dates from 1930. Northcliffe shares the site with Queen Elizabeth I.

NORTHCOTE London, October 27, 1818
Henry Staffor (1st Earl of Iddesleigh) London, January 12, 1887
Politician Upton Pyne, Derbyshire

23, Portland Place, W1, here born
86, Harley Street, W1, in the 1880s

Northcote became private secretary to GLADSTONE in 1842 and was called to the Bar five years later. He inherited his grandfather's baronetcy in 1851 – his father having died previously. He entered Parliament as an MP for Dudley and became Chancellor of the Exchequer in 1874. After DISRAELI's death in 1881, Northcote became joint leader of the Tory party, together with the Marquis of Salisbury. In 1885 he was elevated to the peerage, choosing the title of Viscount St Cyres (a hamlet in Devon) and Earl of Iddesleigh.

Many political observers saw in Northcote a future prime minister. (Not all, however, Lord Randolph CHURCHILL nicknamed him 'The Goat'.) In 1887 Lord Salisbury was made Prime Minister and it was thought, (understandably) that Northcote would be upset. Then he was deprived of his office of Foreign Secretary, a post he had held for a year. Salisbury asked him to come round to 10, Downing Street so that he could break the news to him as gently as possible. It was not gently enough and Northcote had a heart attack and died at Salisbury's feet!

The Iddesleigh motto was, *Christi Crux est Mea Lux* – the Cross of Christ is my Light.

NORTHCOTE Plymouth, Devon, October 22, 1746
James London, July 13, 1831
Painter the 'New' Church of St Marylebone

2, Old Bond Street, W1, 1780-1782
39, Argyll Street, W1, 1804-1806
8, Argyll Place, W1, where he died

Northcote was an historical and portrait painter who prospered and the richer he became, the stingier he got. In addition to being a successful artist he also wrote biographies of Sir Joshua REYNOLDS and Titian (c.1490-1576).

Northcote and his brother Samuel fled from Plymouth and their overbearing father and came to London in May 1771. They walked all the way which took five days. They had a letter to Sir Joshua REYNOLDS and James began to work in Reynold's studio. Samuel, however, preferred Plymouth and went back there to face his father's wrath.

James stayed with Reynolds until 1776 and then toured Europe, spending two years in Rome. On his return to London he set up as a portrait painter and began to command high fees. His *self*-portrait is in the National Gallery.

NOVELLO	Cardiff, January 15, 1893
David Ivor (Davies)	London, March 6, 1951
Composer and playwright	Golders Green

11, The Aldwych, WC2, in a top floor flat, 1914 until he died here

When he was 22, Novello wrote the music for a song called *Keep the Home Fires Burning*. The words were written by Lena Gilbert Ford whose son was killed during an air raid coming out of Warwick Avenue Underground station in 1918. Britain was in the second year of the First World War and this rather trite song met the needs of the day. It has joined *It's a Long Way to Tipperary* (written by a Birmingham man, Jack Judge, who died in 1938). The words were written by Harry Williams who lived at Temple Balsall, not far from Birmingham. It was published in 1912 and became a song to sing in 1914 when the troops were embarking for the front. The words of the refrain were inscribed on his tombstone. The last three lines of it were:

'Goodbye, Piccadilly; farewell to Leicester Square;
It's a long way to Tipperary,
But my heart's, [pause] right there.'

By the time Novello was in his twenties he was appearing regularly on the London stage (first appearance in 1921) and in 1928 he appeared in a comedy called *The Truth Game* which he wrote and produced himself. Others like it followed but the most popular ones were the brash, tinselly *Ruritanian* epics, such as *Glamorous Nights* in 1936 and *The Dancing Years* in 1937.

In the Second World War his reputation had been tarnished by a stupid mistake he had made concerning the private use of petrol and he was sent to prison on what was really a purely technical charge.

He recovered and so did his reputation. In 1945 came *Perchance to Dream* and, four years later, *King's Rhapsody*. He died suddenly and probably painlessly, as he would have liked – over a theatre – *and* still 'in harness'.

NOYES	Wolverhampton, September 16, 1880
Alfred	June 28, 1958
Poet	

85, Cadogan Gardens, SW1, c.1920s
13, Hanover Terrace, NW1, 1927-1936

Noyes had begun writing poetry while still an undergraduate at Exeter College, Oxford, though his university career was marked by his proficiency as an oarsman. However, encouraged by George MEREDITH, he stuck to poetry rather than the sliding seats of an Oxford '8' and, in 1902, his collection of poems called *The Loom of the Years* was printed. This had a satisfactory reception and his next piece – an epic sea poem, *Drake* – appeared in 1906.

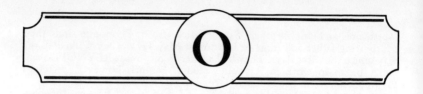

OAKLEY

Sir Hans SLOANE, Lord of the Manor of Chelsea died in 1753 leaving two daughters. The younger, Elizabeth, married Lord Cadogan of Oakley and this union introduced a number of Cadogan family names into Chelsea.

OAKLEY STREET, SW3

District and Circle lines to Sloane Square

56, Captain Richard Falcon SCOTT (LCP 1935) 1905-1908. He was hardly ever actually resident here as he was on active service with the Royal Navy during this time.

57, the Duke of St Albans, 1960s.

87, Lady WILDE ('Speranza') from 1886 until she died here in 1896. Her son, Oscar, spent a few days here in April 1895 just before his 'last' trial at the Old Bailey. His brother, Willie, also stayed here between marriages.

OLD BOND STREET, W1

Piccadilly, Jubilee and Victoria lines to Green Park

Built in 1686 and called after Sir Thomas Bond, controller to the Household of Queen Henrietta Maria, widow of Charles I. Bond was very much the confidant of her younger son James, Duke of York (later James II). In 1688, when James fled the country, Bond went into exile with him. In 1708, Hatton wrote that Bond Street was '...a fine new street, mostly inhabited by nobility and gentry'.

2, James NORTHCOTE, 1780-1782. He had recently returned from an extended tour of Europe and was now beginning to be a portrait painter in demand in London.

13, P.B. SHELLEY, 1914, just before he and Mary Wollestonecraft decamped to Europe.

14, Alexander POPE, c.1710.

24 (formerly 29) Sir Thomas LAWRENCE. HOPPNER having died in 1810, Lawrence was held to be the best portrait painter then working in London.

48, Laurence STERNE died here in lodgings (above Mrs. Mary Fourmantel's shop: she was 'Hair-bag maker to His Majesty') in 1768. The building was demolished in 1904.

OLD BROMPTON ROAD, SW5

Piccadilly, Circle or District lines to Gloucester Road or South Kensington

The old village of Brompton was apparently divided into new and Old Brompton and this road led through the 'Old' part. New Brompton really began to be established in the early 19th century. Holy Trinity Church (behind the Oratory) was dedicated in July 1829.

185 (Flat 3) Brigid BROPHY (alias Lady Levey) 1960s-1980s.

189 (which used to be in Moreton Gardens) Jenny LIND (LCP 1909) 1876-1886. After they were married, she and Otto Goldschmidt had a house, called Oakleigh, built for them in Wimbledon. It was too far out of London to keep in touch with the musical life of the city, so they moved in here. Otto had founded the Bach Choir which performed, for the first time in England, a mass in B minor in 1876.

OLD BURLINGTON STREET, W1

Piccadilly, Victoria or Jubilee lines
to Piccadilly Circus

The third (and last) Lord Burlington came into his title when he was nine years old in 1704. In 1717 he began to develop the land around here and this street was one of the projects most nearly finished when he died in 1735.

9, Mary Ann CLARKE, 1807. For the previous three years, she had been the mistress of King George III's favourite son, HRH the Duke of York.

10, James WOLFE, 1742-1752.

12, Mark AKENSIDE, from 1762 until he died here in 1770.

29, Samuel WYATT made alterations (including the porch) to this house in 1785.

OLD CAVENDISH STREET, W1

Central, Bakerloo and Victoria lines
to Oxford Circus

Edward Harley, who married Lady Henrietta Cavendish Holles in 1713, began to develop the property in the early years of the 18th century. Development was brought to a grinding halt by the 'bursting of the South Sea Bubble', a disastrous city swindle that ruined many people financially in 1720.

15, James BARRIE, 1892. He was still eking out a living, writing miscellaneous articles for various newspapers and magazines.

18, Thomas CAMPBELL, 1829. He lived here after his wife, Matilda, died and here their only surviving son went insane (hardly a happy house).

OLD CHURCH STREET, SW3

District and Circle lines
to Sloane Square

The street leads, appropriately enough, to Chelsea Old Church. The South Chapel, built by Thomas More in 1528, luckily was the least damaged part of the building when it was the subject of a direct hit by bombs in 1941. More's tomb is in the church and, on the Cheyne Walk Side is a statue of this 'Scholar, Saint and Statesman'. It is a bronze (coloured) by L. Cubitt Bevis, put here in 1969. Bevis 'signed' the work on the underside of the brim of Sir Thomas's hat.

56, Charles KINGSLEY (LCP 1979) 1836-c.1840. His father was the Rector of St Luke's Church in Sydney Street, SW3

68, Arthur Reed ROPES ('Adrian Ross'). He was living here in 1933, the year he died.

127, William and Evelyn DE MORGAN (LCP 1937) 1910-1917. He died in this house and Evelyn only lived for another two years.

141A, Katherine MANSFIELD, 1917. At this time she was the mistress of John MURRY. (She married him a year later.) This was her last address in London; she died in France in 1923.

147, Adrian JONES (P) 1892-1938. He moved here not long after he retired from the army having been a veterinary surgeon in it for 23 years and he spent the last 46 years of his life here, sculpting.

OLDFIELD	London, 1683
Anne ('Nance')	London, October 23, 1730
Actress	Westminster Abbey (South Aisle)

60 (today's numbering) Grosvenor Street, W1, where she died

Anne, a vintner's daughter, joined the theatrical company of Christopher Rich, manager of Drury Lane, who paid her 15 shillings (75p) a week when she first started, rising to one pound after a few months.

In 1704, Colley CIBBER gave Anne the part of Lady Betty Modish in his own play, *The Careless Husband,* and it made her reputation. Two years later she was held to be the equal of the 43-year old 'star' Anne Bracegirdle. For some years 'Nance' lived with the wealthy and handsome Arthur Maynwaring who was 15 years older than herself. She had his son but after his death in 1712 she 'came under the protection' of General Charles Churchill.

The Church must have turned a blind eye to 'Nance's' private life as they allowed her the final honour of burial in Westminster Abbey. Before the interment she lay 'in state' in the 'Jerusalem Chamber' on the south side of the building. King Henry IV actually died in this room on March 20, 1413. The room is so called because it used to be hung with tapestries depicting the history of Jerusalem. It dates from 1386.

OLIPHANT Musselburgh, Scotland, April 4, 1829
Margaret Wimbledon, June 25, 1897
Author

14, Victoria Square, SW1
44, Hans Place, SW3, 1880s
85, Cadogan Place, SW1, 1890-1897

She was the daughter of Francis Wilson and, in May 1857, she married her cousin who, rather confusingly, was another Francis Wilson!

Her early works (better now forgotten) were produced from the age of 20 onwards and she wrote prolifically until 1896. Her best novels were written between 1861 and 1865 – a series, *The Chronicles of Carlingford.* She produced biographies, historical works and novels like *The Beleaguered City,* in 1880, which is almost *Space fiction.*

O'NEILL Kensington, March 14, 1875
Norman Houston London, March 3, 1933
Composer Golders Green

16 (formerly 13), Young Street, W8, here born
18, Victoria Road, W8, 1897-1899
7, Edwardes Square, W8, 1899-1904

Norman was the youngest of six children, three girls and three boys (though Kathleen and Alice died young). Their father was a reasonably successful painter and 1875 was the most financially rewarding year he had had. Much of Norman's early youth was spent at the house in Kent his father had bought not long before his youngest child's birth.

This was sold in 1886 and then Norman spent all his time in Kensington.

In May 1891 Norman was travelling to Piccadilly on the top of a horse omnibus and happened to sit next to a *very* colourful Kensington inhabitant who styled himself *Count* Eric STENBOCK. This chance meeting led to an understanding friendship between the two men. Though STENBOCK was 15 years older, the two kept in touch when O'Neill went to Germany to study music. STENBOCK helped Norman financially (and left him £1,500 in his will when he died in 1895). This windfall allowed Norman to have a valuable final year of study at the Frankfort *Conservatoire.*

O'Neill was by now composing 'seriously' and his first important orchestral work, *In Autumn,* an overture dedicated to Sir Henry Wood, was played in the Queen's Hall (London) in October 1901.

On December 9, 1909 there was a first night at the *Haymarket Theatre* (which had been taken over by the poet, Herbert Trench) for a performance of Maeterlink's *Blue Bird.* The music for it had been written by O'Neill with some help from Gustav Holst.

ONSLOW

Many of the street names in this part of Kensington were a result of the development of land owned by the 'Smith's Charity'. In all, this organization owned something like 84 acres (34 hectares). Viscount CRANLEY was one of the Charity's Trustees and his father was the Earl of ONSLOW.

ONSLOW GARDENS, SW7   *Piccadilly, District and Circle lines to South Kensington*

5,   W.M. THACKERAY's daughters, Anny and Minny moved here after their father's death in 1863. They paid £1,800 for the house. After Minny's marriage to Leslie STEPHEN in 1867, all three lived here until March 1873, when they moved to Southwell Gardens, SW7.

5,   James Anthony FROUDE (LCP 1934) 1873-1892. By this time all ten volumes of his *History of England* had been published.

14,   James LEES-MILNE, 1927, where he had been 'placed' in lodgings by his father who paid his son's rent in advance. The rather dotty landlady was a Mrs. Roxburgh who claimed intimate relationship with (what seemed to the youthful James) half the aristocracy at least.

24,   Andrew BONAR LAW (LCP 1958) 1920-1923. He was living here when he made his political come-back, after retiring on the grounds of his ill-health. He became Prime Minister from October 1922 until May 1923, and died six months later.

38,   W.E.H. LECKY (LCP 1955) from 1874 until he died here in 1903.

ONSLOW SQUARE, SW7

The south side of the Square is a 'listed' terrace. It was built by FREAKE in 1849.

16,   Edwin LUTYENS at the time of his marriage to Emily Lytton in 1796.

36,   W.M. THACKERAY (LCP 1912) 1854-1862. Here he finished *The Virginians* (in 1859) and began as editor to the *Cornhill Magazine*. He paid £2,000 for the house and spent a lot of money improving it.

38,   Admiral Robert SINCLAIR (LCP 1981) from 1854 until, in the depths of a nervous breakdown, he committed suicide here in 1865.

OPIE
John
Artist

St Agnes, Nr. Truro, Cornwall, May 16, c.1761
London, April 9, 1807
St Paul's Cathedral

63, Great Queen Street, WC2, 1783-1791
8, Berners Street, W1, 1792-1807

Doctor WOLCOT ('Peter Pindar') found 19-year old Opie in Cornwall and admired his talent to such an extent that he brought him as his protege to London, where the prodigy was nicknamed 'The Cornish Wonder'.

About this time Opie was painting portraits to order and romantic, rustic, 'fancy' pictures. Sir Joshua REYNOLDS himself praised young Opie's work. Later, Opie moved to historical painting such as the *Death of Rizzio*, which was destroyed when the City of London Guildhall was bombed in 1941.

ORME SQUARE W2   *Central line to Queensway*

Named after Edward Orme, a Bond Street print seller who made some money 'on the side' by selling gravel to Czar Alexander I.

1, Sir Rowland HILL (LCP 1907) 1839-1844. It was whilst he lived here that his *Penny Post* came into being.

2, Jeremy THORPE and his second wife, Marion. She had lived here previously with her first husband, Lord Harewood. Thorpe moved in here after marrying Marion in 1973.

12, Richard WAGNER, 1877. He used to walk across Kensington Gardens to the Albert Hall (which, by then, had been open for six years) to conduct his concerts.

'ORWELL, George', see BLAIR, E.A.

OSBORNE London, December 19, 1929
John James
Playwright

11A, Curzon Street, W1, 1960s
15, Woodfall Street, SW3, 1970s

Osborne left Belmont College in Devon at the age of 15 and worked as a journalist for a year before becoming a repertory actor with various companies.

His first play was *Epitaph for George Dillon* (in conjunction with Anthony Creighton) but it was not staged until 1958. In the meantime, *Look Back in Anger* had appeared in 1956, establishing Osborne as King of the Kitchen Sink School of Drama and netting him substantial sums of money. The play attacked the 'Establishment' – if it ever existed – and the play's hero (or anti-hero) was the original 'angry young man'.

'OUIDA', see DE LA RAMEE

OUTER CIRCLE, Regent's Park, NW8 *Jubilee line to St John's Wood*
The 'Outer Circle' really *is* the circle which forms the outer periphery of Regent's Park.

Hanover Lodge This house was built by John Nash in 1820 and its first occupant was Sir Robert Arbuthnot (1773-1853). Thomas COCHRANE, the Earl of Dundonald came immediately or soon after Arbuthnot left. He was certainly living here by 1835 (LCP 1974) and had left by 1845.
Admiral BEATTY had the house from 1912 until 1924 and he sold it to Prince Obolensky, or rather, perhaps to the *Princess*. Alice Obolensky was the daughter of John Jacob Astor. Even his millions could not keep him afloat when the *Titanic* went down on April 15, 1912. J.J. went down with it, but left a million pounds to Alice, his daughter by Ava, Lady Ribblesdale.

OVINGTON SQUARE, SW3 *Circle and District lines to Sloane Square*
There are also Ovington Gardens and an Ovington Street but no apparent reason for so naming them. There is a place Ovington in Essex, which gets *its* name from being once the TUN, a homestead of UFA's people.

1, Lady WILDE; 'Speranza', mother of Oscar WILDE. She was living here in 1880 having come over to London after her dirty fingernailed husband had died in Dublin in April 1876.

OWEN
Wilfred
Poet

Oswestry, Salop., March 18, 1893
Killed in action in France, November
4, 1918

21, Devonshire Street, W1, 1915 and also at the Poetry Workshop at:
25, Devonshire Street, W1

Physically frail and precocious, Owen came up to London University from
school at Birkenhead. He had always been fond of poetry though he did not
begin to write until 1917. From the age of 20 until he was 23, he was tutor to
a French boy in a family who lived near Bordeaux.

In 1915 he enlisted with the Artists' Rifles but was invalided out in less than
two years. He spent some time in Craiglockhart Hospital and became
friendly with Siegfried SASSOON who was also a patient. It was he who
encouraged Owen to write poetry.

Tragically, in 1918, he was sent back to France as a Company Commander
and was rewarded with the Military Cross for bravery. Exactly a week
before the Armistice he was killed at the crossing of the Sambre Canal.

PAGE
Walter Hines
United States Ambassador

Cary, North Carolina, August 15, 1855
North Carolina, December 21, 1918

6, Grosvenor Square, W1 (P) 1913-1918

Page's father, Allison, was of Scottish descent and his mother, née Catherine Raboteau, of partly Huguenot stock. He was a rather weakly child but a diligent and endearing student. One of his teachers at the Randolph-Macon College, in Ashland, Virginia was Thomas Randolph Price, an enthusiastic Classicist. Price secured for Page one of the first 20 fellowships at the new John Hopkins University in Baltimore.

As a young man Page taught English in Louisville and then went into journalism, eventually joining the publishers Houghton, Mifflin and Co. in 1895. Four years later he helped Frank N. Doubleday establish the publishing house of Doubleday, Page and Co. They began the magazine *World's Work* and Page edited it from 1900 until 1913.

One of the first duties for President Woodrow Wilson was to appoint Page as United States Ambassador in London. It was Page who *really* understood the threats of Germany and strongly advocated America joining as a combatant with the British and their Allies. On April 2, 1917, with only 19 months of the war to go, Wilson asked Congress to declare war on Germany.

The plaque in Grosvenor Square was placed there in appreciation of Page's worth and friendship by the English Speaking Union. This organisation was founded in 1918 and its headquarters are just around the corner in 37, Charles Street, W1.

PAINE
Thomas
Deist and Radical

Thetford, Norfolk, January 29, 1737
New York, June 8, 1809
New Rochelle (plus a monument erected in 1839)

77, Fetter Lane, EC4, 1790-1793

Paine came from humble Quaker stock, his father being a stay-maker in Norfolk. Thomas tried his hand at school teaching ('Those that can, do, those that can't, teach', G.B. SHAW) and as a tobacconist. He was living in Lewes, Sussex, burdened with an unhappy marriage when he met Benjamin FRANKLIN. Franklin advised him to go to America.

This Paine did. Before long he was editing the *Pennsylvania Magazine* and was appointed to sit on a commission to treat with American Indians!

Paine more or less *had* to leave England because of his sympathies with the revolutionaries in France. In 1787 he came back to London and published *The Rights of Man* in 1791. Owing to the unpopularity it caused he crossed over to Paris where he so upset the Robespierre faction, that he was actually imprisoned in Paris in 1794! He had already published Part I of *The Age of Reason* Part II appeared in 1795 and the last volume not till 1807. Parts I and II were enough to alienate George Washington. The British Government (under PITT) tried, unsuccessfully, to stop their publication.

PALACE GARDENS TERRACE, W8

Central, District and Circle lines to Notting Hill Gate

52, Max BEERBOHM was born here in 1872.

61, Wyndham LEWIS in the 1920s. By this time in his mid-thirties, Lewis's behaviour was becoming more and more eccentric.

PALACE GATE, W8

2, Sir John MILLAIS (LCP 1926) from 1878 until he died here in 1896. His son, Everett, lived on here for a year before he died, only 41 years old. Millais had paid CUBITT £8,400 for the site in 1873. Philip Hardwicke designed the house which had Sicilian marble hall floors and a fountain designed by Edgar Boehm. Millais's studio was equally grandiose, being 40 feet (12 metres) long, 25 feet (7.6 metres) wide and 20 feet (6 metres) high.

PALACE GREEN, W8

2, W.M. THACKERAY (LCP 1863) from 1862 until he died here. He had bought the land and a dilapidated large house on it, which was unsafe and was pulled down. The new house, designed by Frederick Heming in red brick (partly in imitation of Wren's Marlborough House in the Mall, before the Prince of Wales 'improved' it) was to have cost £4,000, but ended up at over £6,000 – 'all made out of the inkstand' as Thackeray put it. It was nicknamed the 'Palazzo'.

8, Samuel COURTAULD, 1929. He was still, at this stage, involved in the running of the Courtauld rayon business.

PALACE STREET, SW1

District and Circle lines to St James's Park

From Buckingham Palace it leads from almost opposite the entrance to the Royal Mews (which, incidentally, are open to the public on most Wednesday and Thursday afternoons from 2-4 pm) and bends round into Victoria Street.

3, John GALSWORTHY, 1894. By this time he had been called to the Bar of Lincoln's Inn (but never practised law) and had gone on a tour of the Far East where he had met Joseph CONRAD.

Roebuck House (on the west side of the street, on the corner of Stag Place. A block of flats designed by CLRP Architects).

Flat 24, Sir Alec Douglas-Home, in the 1960s, but then known as the 14th Earl of HOME and Baron Dunglass.

PALGRAVE

PALGRAVE	Great Yarmouth, September 28, 1824
Francis Turner	London, October 24, 1897
Compiler of The Golden Treasury	Barnes Cemetery, London

5, York Gate, NW1 (LCP 1976) 1862-1875

Palgrave's father was Jewish, but became a Christian on his marriage, changing his name from Cohen to Palgrave – a subtle choice, as it was the surname of his mother-in-law! Cohen/Palgrave was Deputy Keeper of the Records from 1838 until his death in 1861.

For five years he was secretary to W.E. GLADSTONE and then Vice-Principal of the Teachers' Training College at Kneller Hall. Later he went into the Department of Education, ending up as an Assistant Secretary. In 1854 he published some of his own verse, called *Idylls and Songs*. Not long after he spent a holiday with TENNYSON who gave him considerable help in shaping the *Golden Treasury of Songs and Lyrics*, which was published eventually in 1861 and dedicated to Tennyson. In 1861 Palgrave was elected to the Oxford Chair of Poetry, in which he sat for ten years.

PALL MALL, SW1   *Piccadilly, Jubilee and Victoria lines*
                                                     to Green Park

King Charles I (and probably his father James) used to play a game not unlike croquet in which a ball (*palia*) was moved on the ground by striking it with a mallet (*maglia*) and the original pitch was somewhere along what today is Pall Mall. Sir Robert Dallington wrote in 1598 (five years before James came to the throne and 30 years before Charles's accession) about the game, which he described as *paille-maille*. After the Restoration of the Monarchy in 1660, Charles II ordered that a new pitch be made in St James's Park, parallel to today's Mall. A parcel of land by St James's Square was described as 'Pell Mell Close' in a Crown Land Survey of 1650, and the rate books for 1656 show that people were by then living 'In the Pall Mall'.

26, Richard MONCKTON MILNES (later Lord Houghton) 1837-1861. The house has been completely rebuilt since his day, but in 1840, there was a room in the house with a bow-windowed *alcove* where 'DISRAELI and Louis NAPOLEON could speak without being overlooked'.

49A, Ronald FIRBANK, 1922. This was his last (semi-permanent) address in London.

79, Nell GWYNN, 1671-1687, where she dallied with her lover, King Charles II. The property used to be the only freehold in Pall Mall.

82, Thomas GAINSBOROUGH. In the west part of Schomberg House, from 1774 until his death in 1788.
In 1784, Gainsborough had a row with the Royal Academy and so he organized a sort of 'mini-Academy' in Schomberg House. He took over part of the house from John Astley (who had been a fellow student with him under Joshua REYNOLDS) and paid £150 a year for it. Gainsborough was an ardent amateur musician. Once when he was playing a bassoon for Christian Bach (born Leipzig 1735, a son of the great J.S. Bach) Bach shouted at Gainsborough, '*Pote* it away man, *pote* it away. Do you want to burst yourself like der frog in der fable?' (Gainsborough died in Schomberg House and his last words were supposed to have been 'We are all going to Heaven and Van Dyke is of the company'.)

PALMER   Surrey Square, London, January 27,
Samuel   1805
Artist   Redhill, Surrey, May 24, 1881

1A, Victoria Road, W8, 1848-1851
6, Douro Place, W8 (LCP 1972) 1851-1861

Palmer's father was a bookseller who encouraged his son in his artistic bent. The boy was a precocious artist and actually had drawings (landscapes) in the Royal Academy when he was only 14.
At the age of 16 he met John Linnell (1792-1882) and he introduced the boy to William BLAKE. Blake's influence affected the younger artist's mystic approach to his art. When he was 21 he went to live for a while at Shoreham, in Kent, where he produced numerous sepia drawings and water colours.

PALMERSTON
Henry John Temple (3rd Viscount)
Prime Minister

London, October 20, 1784
Welwyn, October 18, 1865
Westminster Abbey (North Transept,
centre aisle)

20, Queen Anne's Gate, SW7 (LCP 1925) here born
4, Carlton Gardens, SW1 (LCP 1907) 1854
94, Piccadilly, W1 (LCP 1907) 1855 onwards

Palmerston was the Irish branch of the ancient English family of Temple. When he was just 16 he went to Edinburgh University, but his father died two years later and the new, young 3rd Viscount came south to Cambridge to complete his education, 1803–1806.

He stood as a Tory for the University seat, but failed, then in 1807 he was elected Member for Newport, Isle of Wight (being an Irish peer he could not sit in the Lords). He was to lose that seat when he supported the Reform Bill. He came back as member for Tiverton and became a junior Lord of the Admiralty. He moved up to be Secretary for War under PERCEVAL, then under LIVERPOOL, CANNING, Goderich *and* the Duke of WELLINGTON. (Luckily there was usually a war going on somewhere in which Britain was involved; Palmerston was very much a 'send-out-another-gunboat' type of politician.)

Always outspoken, his manner was brusque and he never attempted conciliation. His nickname was 'Firebrand Palmerston'.

When the Earl of ABERDEEN's Coalition Government fell in 1855, Palmerston stepped up from Home Secretary to Prime Minister. He stayed there until he failed over the Conspiracy Bill and went out of office. His time came again quite soon and in June 1859 he was back in 10, Downing Street and there he stayed until his death seven years later.

Thomas Woolner made the bronze statue of Palmerston (looking like a tailor's dummy) which has been in Parliament Square since 1876.

PANKHURST
Emmeline
Suffragette

Manchester, July 4, 1858
London, June 14, 1928
Brompton Cemetery

8, Russell Square, WC1, 1889–1893

Emmeline Pankhurst always seems to be referred to as *Mrs. Pankhurst* (rather like the *Doctor* in Doctor ARNE). Today, she would probably insist upon the unmusical 'Ms'. In fact her maiden name was Goulden and she married Richard Marsden Pankhurst, a lawyer, who, like Arne again, was usually referred to as the *Doctor* as he held a doctorate in law from the University of London. He was 20 years older than his wife and they were to have Christabel in 1880, Sylvia in 1882, Henry Francis in 1884 and, finally, Adela 15 months after, in May 1885. Henry Francis died of polio ('infantile paralysis') when he was 26. His sister, Sylvia, nursed him for four months. Mrs. Pankhurst was in America and came home in time only to see him 'breathe his last'. Sylvia chose the words which were inscribed over his grave: 'Blessed are the pure of heart'.

Mrs. Pankhurst, her family and her followers were prepared to go to considerable lengths to bring the cause of the 'Suffragettes' to both public and offical notice. Sometimes their actions, which were 'violence of a passive sort' (if that is not too great a contradiction) met *real* violence. The Suffragettes would chain themselves to the railings outside 10, Downing Street and elsewhere. The *Suffragettes* were frequently imprisoned, went on 'hunger strike' and had often to be forcibly fed, which frequently caused unnecessary injury. Luckily Mrs. Pankhurst lived long enough to see enfranchisement for some women, but it was not till 1929 that all women over 21 were allowed a vote.

There is a bronze statue of Emmeline Pankhurst in the gardens by the river near the Victoria Tower of the House of Lords. It was erected in 1930 and A.G. Walker was the sculptor.

PANKHURST   Manchester, May 5, 1882
Sylvia   Addis Ababa, September 27, 1960
Artist and feminist   Addis Ababa

165, Hampstead Road, NW1, 1886
8, Russell Square, WC1, 1888-1893
42, Linden Gardens, W2, 1910

Daughter of Emmeline and sister of the redoubtable, Christabel, Sylvia Pankhurst supported her relative's views on Women's Suffrage and worked for the 'Cause', but it was not really an integral part of her life. She was a talented artist (and often used her artistic abilities for political use).
When she became a suffragette she designed red Phrygian 'caps of Liberty', inspired by those worn by the insurgents in the French Revolution. She studied at the Manchester School of Art during the period of the Boer War (the family having moved north again after the five-year lease on the Russell Square house expired). She won a travelling scholarship and went to Venice to continue painting and study at the Accademia delle Belle Arti, coming home to England in the Spring of 1903. She next went to the Royal College of Art, living penuriously in a 'tall house off the Fulham Road'. At this time she met the family 'hero', Keir HARDIE and visited him at 14, Nevill's Court in Fetter Lane.

PANNIZI   Modena, Italy, September 16, 1797
(Sir) Anthony   London, April 18, 1879
Bibliophile   Kensal Green, St Mary's Cemetery

31, Bloomsbury Square, WC1, c.1856

Though Pannizi had a degree in law from Parma University (the Duchy of Parma, in Pannizi's lifetime, was annexed to France in 1802, then 'given' to Marie Louisa by the Congress of Vienna in 1847 and, after an 1849 revolution, incorporated into the Kingdom of Italy in 1860) Pannizi had dipped his toe into the warming waters of the Italian revolutionary movement and was obliged to flee the country. He ended up in Liverpool in 1823.
Five years later he was appointed Italian Professor at University College, London and then Assistant Librarian at the British Museum. In 1856 he was Chief Librarian. In the ten years he occupied the post he devised the British Museum Catalogue systems and arranged the layout of the great, circular Reading Room there.

PARK CRESCENT, W1   *Bakerloo line to Regent's Park*

For once, a logical name both for its configuration and its position. The statue facing down Portland Place is of the Duke of Kent (1767-1820) father of Queen Victoria. The sculptor was Sebastian Gahagan, a pupil of Nollekens. Gahagan was active between 1800 and 1835 and had a sort of office in King Street off the Edgware Road.

12, Lord LISTER (LCP 1915) from 1876 for some years.
19, Sir Charles WHEATSTONE, from 1866 until his death nine years later.
24, Dame Marie TEMPEST (LCP 1972) 1899-1902. She was then married to her second husband, C.C. Gordon-Lennox (1869-1921).

PARK LANE, W1   *Central line to Marble Arch*

Originally called Tyburn Lane, as it ran from the gallows at Tyburn Tree –
the site now covered by the Marble Arch – to Piccadilly.

21, Lady Palmerston, after PALMERSTON's death in 1865, bought this
house from Edward Bulwer in 1868 and lived in it for a year.

24 (where the 'Hilton' now stands) Syrie MAUGHAM lived, from 1944
until her death in 1955.

36 (on the corner of Brook Street) 'Brook House', Lord Louis
MOUNTBATTEN lived here 1936, when he was a mere Lieutenant
Commander, RN. He married Edwina Ashley in 1922, the
granddaughter of the *extremely* rich Sir Ernest Cassell. Brook House
was his and on the grand scale. The vast downstairs, marble hall was
called 'The Giants' Lavatory'! The Mountbattens' flat had 30 rooms. It
was on the top floor reached by an express lift from a private side
entrance in Brook Street. The lift achieved fame when HM Queen
Mary (widow of King George V) got stuck in it. Cassell was an
intimate friend of King Edward VII. An unkind wit had nicknamed
him 'Windsor Cassell'.

Between South Street and Deanery Street, and almost part of the
'Dorchester Hotel', are a number of very expensive flats; the postal
address being 55, Park Lane. When he died in 1972, this was Nubar
GULBENKIAN's address.

93 (formerly 1, Grosvenor Gate) Benjamin DISRAELI, 1839-1873. This
house belonged to his wife, the tactlessly lovable Mary Anne Lewis.
He moved in here after their marriage and lived here until her death in
1872.

PARK STREET, W1   *Central line to Marble Arch*

In this case the park is Hyde Park and it used to be called Hyde Park Street.

7, Angelica KAUFFMANN, 1780. Her first husband, 'Count de Horn'
had died and she was on the verge of marrying Antonio Zucchi, who
was 15 years older than she.

26, Sir Humphry DAVY, 1825-1829. This was his London house when he
died.

31, John RUSKIN, brought his bride, 'Effie', here in 1848 at the start of
their sexless marriage.

41D, Thomas HUGHES in the 1840s. Later he lived successively at numbers
113, 33 and 40.

111, Sir Patrick HASTINGS, 1929. At this time he was still MP for the
staunch Socialist constituency of Wallsend.

PARKER   Camden East, Canada, November 23,
(Sir) Gilbert Horatio George   1862
Author and politician   London, September 6, 1932

20, Carlton House Terrace, SW1, 1904-1920
24, Portman Square, W1, 1922-1928
2, Whitehall Court, SW1, 1929-1932

His father, Captain Joseph Parker, of the Artillery, sent Gilbert to the
Ottawa Normal School then on to Trinity College, Toronto, where he
became a lecturer in English in 1883.

Two years later, after a nervous breakdown, he took a convalescent world
cruise and ended up in Sydney, spending four years there, and became the
assistant editor of the *Morning Herald*. He settled down to a literary career,
coming to London for good in 1898. Three years before he married Amy
Van Tine of New York.

From 1900 until 1918 he sat as a Conservative MP for Gravesend. He had been made a Knight Bachelor in 1912 and upped to a Baronetcy in 1915 for his services to 'war propaganda in the United States'.

His most famous novel, *The Seats of the Mighty* – a story of the siege of Quebec – appeared in 1896. He produced a clutch of historical novels from 1895-1904. His last book, *Tarboc*, was an autobiographical piece, appearing in 1927.

PARRY	Bournemouth, February 27, 1848
(Sir) Charles Hubert Hastings	Rustington, October 7, 1918
Musician	St Paul's Cathedral crypt

17, Kensington Square, W8 (LCP 1949) 1887-1918

Parry came from a squirearchical Gloucestershire family and went up to Oxford from Eton in 1867. His muscial bent showed early. On October 19, 1864, the 16-year old Parry wrote in his diary, 'I have now finished reading through both the Preludes and the Fugues of the 48 of Bach. What a wonderful volume it is! It is to me a companion in travel, my comfort in trouble, my solace in sickness and my sharer of happiness.' In 1883 he became Professor of Music at the Royal College of Music; and Director of the school in 1895. He succeeded Sir George Grove (1820-1900, editor and genius behind *Dictionary of Music and Musicians*, first edition 1879, 6th edition 1981).

As a composer, Parry's music ranged wide. His piano concerto met with great approval in the Crystal Palace in 1880 with Edward Dannreuther (1844-1905) as soloist: he produced operas, choral works, symphonies and concerti. His best remembered piece is undoubtedly his setting of William BLAKE's poem, *Jerusalem*. It was written for the Suffragettes to use at their 'Fight for the Right' meeting in the Queens Hall. The words and music have become the song for the Womens' Institute throughout Great Britain. (Anybody who has been to, or listened to, the last night of the 'Proms' from the Albert Hall every summer, will know what happens to *Jerusalem then*.)

PATMORE	Woodford, Essex, July 23, 1823
Coventry Kersey Dighton	Lymington, Hants., November 26,
Poet	1896

12, Greek Street, W1, 1820s
12, Arundel Street, WC2, 1840s
14, Percy Street, W1, 1863-1864

For many years Patmore was a fairly humble assistant in the library at the British Museum. After-hours he mixed with brighter companions and became associated with the Pre-Raphaelite Brotherhood. Dante Gabriel ROSSETTI had been an admirer of Patmore's poetry since *Poems* were published in 1841. Many years later Patmore wrote, 'I was intimate with the Pre-Raphaelites when we were little more than boys together; they were all very simple, pure-minded, ignorant and confident.'

The Victorian public placed his poetic celebration of married love, *The Angel in the House* high on their list of permitted reading. The book would not stand a chance today and even then, Swinburne poked fun at it. His next major piece was the mystical *The Unknown Eros*. This was in 1864, after his first wife, Emily had died. Three years later he was received into the Church of Rome.

PAYNE   New York City, June 9, 1791
John Howard   Tunis, April 9, 1852
Actor, dramatist and Consul

29, Arundel Street, WC2, 1825-1827

Payne made his American stage début in February 1809 and in 1813 appeared on an English stage for the first time, playing at Drury Lane. For a while he lived in Paris making adaptations and arrangements from French drama.
For over 30 years he worked for the stage, 20 years being spent in London. One of his great friends was Washington IRVING who helped him with his very popular play, *Charles the Second*. In 1823 his opera *Clari, or the Maid of Milan* was performed at Covent Garden. This lightweight opera, the music of which was written by Sir Henry Bishop (1786-1855) contains the song *Home Sweet Home*, which must have been sung hundreds of thousands of times by singers who did not know who wrote the words, or the music, or where it was from.
Rather strangely Payne was appointed American Consul in Tunis in 1842. President John Tyler (1790-1862) who succeeded President Harrison in 1841, recalled Payne in 1845. Six years later, though, he was re-appointed to Tunis and it was there that he died.

PEABODY   South Danvers, Mass. February 18,
George   1795
Philanthropist   London, November 4, 1869
    Danvers, United States (now
    Peabody, Mass.)

11, Devonshire Street, W1, 1837
15, Cork Street, W1, 1861
80, Eaton Square, SW1 (LCP 1976) where he died. (The house was the home of Curtis Miranda LAMPSON.)

Peabody made a fortune from a 'dry goods' store in Baltimore, established in 1829. He came to London in 1837 and set up as a banker.
His prosperity continued and the sight of the poor quality of housing in which the poor of London lived touched him. With typical Peabody dynamism he set about improving the housing conditions. He paid for the erection of 29 blocks of flats from Shadwell to the east of the city to Hammersmith in the west. Many a poor family has grown up in a 'Peabody Trust'. The first of these blocks was opened in Spitalfields on February 29, 1864, Peabody had given £150,000 in March 1862; in January 1866 he gave another £100,000 and then, less than a year before his death, he gave a further £100,000 on December 5, 1868 – making £350,000 to just one charity in four years.
He was offered a baronetcy but he refused it, as he did the ultimate London honour – burial in Westminster Abbey. His body did 'lie-in-state' in the Abbey, though, before being taken back to his homeland on *HMS Monarch*. He had also given – amongst other donations – some £100,000 for education in the Southern States.

PEARSON   Durham, July 5, 1817
John Loughborough   December 11, 1897
Architect   Westminster Abbey, nave

13, Mansfield Street, W1 (LCP 1962) 1897

His father, a painter, apprenticed his son to Joseph BONOMI (the 'Younger') and in due course Joseph was to become an architect much in demand. He has often been referred to as the 'Founder of Modern Gothic Architecture in England'. In his early life he was most probably influenced by Durham Cathedral itself. This imposing building, set high upon a steep bank above the river Wear, was founded at the end of the 11th century and practically completed by 1150, though there are substantial Norman parts still in evidence.

In London, the Church of St. Augustine's in Kilburn, NW is his largest single ecclesiastical work. He also restored the west side (ie the side facing the Abbey) of Westminster Hall. The Astor family used him to build their Estate office on the Thames Embankment.

For a man who spent his life building, restoring or patching up churches, he chose a bride with the totally apt name of Jemima Christian! In 1880 he was elected a member of the Royal Academy.

PEEL	Bury, Lancs., February 5, 1783
(Sir) Robert	London, July 2, 1850
Prime Minister	

4, Whitehall Gardens, SW1, from 1825 until he died here

Peel's father was made a baronet in 1800, having made himself a fortune from the Lancashire cotton spinning industry. He died in 1830, leaving his 47-year old son very well-off indeed.

Robert was sent to Harrow and then went on to get a 'Double First' from Christ Church, Oxford in 1808. The following year he entered the House of Commons as the Tory Member for Cashel (a town in Tipperary, Eire – then part of Great Britain). In 1812 he was Secretary of State for Ireland, but was rabidly *anti*-Catholic. His nickname was 'Orange Peel'. The Orange Order was a society, founded in Ulster in 1795, to maintain the PROTESTANT Constitution in Ireland. The 'Order' still exists today and impresses its anti-ecumenical views severely and, not infrequently, violently. He was without a Parliamentary seat from 1818 until 1822, when he made his political comeback and was appointed Home Secretary with George CANNIN as Foreign Secretary in Lord Liverpool's Ministry.

It was Robert Peel who organized a proper London Police Force (hence *bobbies* or *peelers*). In 1834 he accepted the office of Prime Minister but stood aside for the 56-year old MELBOURNE the following year.

The 1841 election was fought principally over the Free Trade issue and the Tories, headed by Peel, came to power. His was a turbulent Ministry and, in 1846, he was defeated on the Irish Protection of Life Bill. He resigned his office and not long after left politics altogether.

He was a difficult man to get along with, Queen Victoria thought him, 'a cold, odd man'. Someone else (DISRAELI?) likened Peel's smile to '...a gleam of wintry sunshine on the brass handles of a coffin'. 'Socially sensitive society' thought him rather *common* as he never bothered to lose his Lancashire accent.

On June 29, 1850 he was thrown from his horse and, after four days in agonizing pain, he died at his London home.

The Peel family motto is *Industria* – With industry; which was the one chosen by the cotton spinning, 1st baronet in 1800.

A bronze statue of Peel by Matthew Noble (1818-1876) was placed in Parliament Square the year that Noble died, much nearer to Westminster Abbey than it is today. Marochetti was originally given the Peel commission, but his design was rejected in 1863. Marochetti even made another, at his own expense, but this was rejected too. William Behne also made a Peel statue which was erected in Cheapside, EC2, in 1855. Eighty years later it was moved to Postman's Park, off Aldersgate, EC1. It was finally given a permanent home in 1871, when the statue was placed in the Police College at Hendon, north-west London.

PEEL STREET, W8 *Central, District and Circle lines*
to Notting Hill Gate

This little street, begun in 1824, was intended to house workmen. It was named after Sir Robert PEEL who was the Home Secretary of the day. Most of the houses have been 'gentryfied' and change hands at shamefully high prices.

80, this cottage was built in 1872 by a gardener called Henry Evans. From 1877 to 1886 Matthew Ridley Corbett, an English artist lived in it. After Corbet, Sir Frank Dicksee, President of the Royal Academy lived here; then, in 1925, Sir William Russell FLINT arrived. When he came, the studio was in very bad repair, but Flint did it up and turned it into a warm, well-lit workroom. Flint lived here until his death in 1969. In 1983 Brian Clarke, an artist in stained glass, together with his wife Liz, his assistant Martin, and Pablo, a Colombian cook, moved in. Clarke was born in Oldham in 1943 and studied in Florence. His most exotic commission was when he designed the windows for the King Khaled International Airport at Riyadh, the capital of Saudi Arabia.

95, Sir Edward HULTON, 1983.

PELHAM

Another 'Smith's Charity', the details of which can be found in the introduction to Onslow Square. Henry Pelham, the 3rd Earl of Chichester (who died in 1867) was a Trustee of the Charity in 1835, about which time the 'Pelhams' were built.

PELHAM CRESCENT, SW7 *Piccadilly, District and Circle lines*
to South Kensington

Known in the early 1800s as Amelia Place.

15, Emlyn WILLIAMS, 1953-1960.
19, Dame Margot FONTEYN, 1946.
20, Francois GUIZOT, 1848-1849, having fled from France, when Louis, the 'Citizen King', to whom he was an adviser, was deposed in the *February Revolution.*
26, Sir Nigel PLAYFAIR (LCP 1965) 1910-1922. This house, like some others in the Crescent, was part of the original development by BASEVI.

PELHAM PLACE, SW7

8, Sir Cecil BEATON. He moved here in April 1940 and lived here, off and on, until his death in 1980.
17 and **19,** Oliver MESSELL, 1953. A brilliant designer, he and BEATON (at No. 8) really did have a lot in common.

PEMBERTON Birmingham, June 19, 1863
(Sir) Max February 22, 1950
Author

41, Hertford Street, W1, 1929
197, Queen's Gate, SW7, 1946

Pemberton always wanted to write and, soon after getting his Cambridge degree (Caius College) he began to make himself seen and heard in (and around) Fleet Street.

By 1892 he was editor of *Chums*, then editor of *Cassell's Magazine* until 1906. He produced a number of novels (today, largely forgotten, but they all had 'thrilling titles' like; *The Iron Pirate*, 1883, *The Impregnable City*, 1895, and so on.)

His lasting achievement, however, *is* the 'London School of Journalism', which he *created* and whose instructions have been absorbed by a number of 'ace' journalists.

PEMBROKE

The Edwardes family (of Edwardes Square) was descended from the Lords of Radnor – or so they said, and by the time Elizabeth, heiress to the Holland (of Holland Park etc.) fortune married into the Edwardes family, the Edwardes had settled themselves in and around the country of Pembrokeshire (now Dyfed) in Wales.

PEMBROKE GARDENS, W8

*Piccadilly and District lines
to Earl's Court*

6, Angela THIRKELL, 1898. 'A grandiose house, double fronted with high ceilinged, cold rooms; the narrow stairs were covered with dark green linoleum.'

8, Samuel SMILES, from 1874 until he died here in 1904.

PENNELL Philadelphia, United States, July 4,
Joseph 1860
Artist April 23, 1926

14, Buckingham Street, WC1, 1904
1 (formerly 3) Robert Street, WC2, 1909-1917

Pennell was an artist as well as an engraver and his wife, Elizabeth Robins, an author. They lived in Philadelphia and London for long periods, possibly spending more time out of America. They would take extended tours (which provided the raw material both for words and ·pictures) and they published books on Provence and Hungary.

He wrote a rather fulsome biography of WHISTLER which was published in 1908. His wife – who was five years older than he, though she did not die until ten years after him – wrote a passable biography of Mary Wollstonecraft.

PEPYS London, February 22, 1633
Samuel Clapham, May 26, 1703
Diarist and Civil Servant St Olave's Church, Hart Street, EC3

12, Buckingham Street, WC2 (LCP 1947) 1684-1688
14, Buckingham Street, WC2 (LCP 1908) 1688-1701

Today Pepys and diaries are thought of rather as pepper and salt. Certainly he kept a diary for a long time and a very interesting one too. But Pepys was much more than a philandering journalist.

His life was spent working in the Admiralty and it is arguable that had it not been for Pepys' foresight and good housekeeping, Britain may not have had the Navy which was able to beat all comers, not all that long after his death.

During the years of the Commonwealth (1649-1660) Pepys did not fare very well. He was very much a 'King's man'. He married Elizabeth Marchant de Sainte Michel who was only 15 when they became man and wife in 1656. Young, she may have been, but she could easily see the roving eye that her Samuel had – even in Church.

In 1660 Charles II swept back into London and Pepys, with the help of a distant cousin, the 1st Earl of Sandwich, prospered in the Civil Service and was Secretary to the Admiralty when he was only 39.

He was accused of involvement in the Popish Plot of 1679, but was completely cleared and re-appointed in 1684. He was as honest as a Civil Servant often can be and more diligent than most.

The famous diary ran from January 1, 1660 to May 31, 1669; fascinating years for England and taking in the two greatest disasters that had overtaken London – the Plague of 1665 and the Great Fire of the following year. It contains about one and a quarter million words and Pepys stopped writing it the year his wife died. In the closing pages he said that its furtherance would make the total blindness, he feared so dreadfully, inevitable. 'So I betake myself to that course which is almost as much to see myself go into my grave – for which and all the discomforts that will accompany me being blind, then God prepare me.' In fact not only did he not go blind, he lived on and kept his grave waiting for 34 years.

PERCEVAL	London, November 1, 1762
Spencer	London, May 11, 1812
Prime Minister	In the Egmont family vault at Charlton

59, Lincoln's Inn Fields, WC1 (LCP 1914) 1791-1808

Perceval was the younger son of the 2nd Earl of Egmont, a graduate of Trinity College, Cambridge and was called to the Bar in 1786. Ten years later he became a member of Parliament for Northampton, being a strong supporter of PITT. In 1802, under Henry Addington (1757-1844, Prime Minister from March 1801 to May 1804) he was appointed Attorney General and then, under the Duke of Portland (1738-1809, Prime Minister from March 1807) he was Chancellor until Portland died, when Perceval himself became Prime Minister in December 1809.

On May 11, 1812, Perceval walked in to the lobby of the House of Commons at 5.15 in the afternoon and received a shot from the firearm of a Liverpool broker called John Bellingham. By the time Perceval had been carried to a sofa in the Speaker's room, he was dead. His body was taken to Downing Street and Nollekens was called and 'took a death mask' of the late Prime Minister.

When Perceval was killed, Mrs. Perceval was pregnant with her *20th* child and Perceval had only £106.5s.1d (106.26) in his account. Parliament voted his widow a lump sum of £50,000 and an annuity for her lifetime. Eventually the fund (despite the multitude of little Percevals) had the resource to pay out small sums of money to *bona-fide* descendants of Perceval. One such, and the last beneficiary of the fund, was Sir Edward MARSH, who used to refer to his quarterly payment from the Perceval residue as his 'Murder Money'.

PERCY STREET, W1 *Northern line to Goodge Street*

Perhaps called after the Percy Coffee House which used to be round the corner in Rathbone Place.

4, Wyndham LEWIS. He lived here in the 1930s and also at number 31.
14, Coventry PATMORE (LCP 1960) 1863-1864. This was the last year he lived in London and just before his second marriage. 'You will be very glad to hear', wrote Patmore, 'that I am very comfortable in my new place' [except] 'I have had to call a policeman many times to the organ boys who prevent me from reading and writing and thinking. One was very rude and *would* not go away and I could not find a policeman: so I had to go out to him and pour some water over him and *that* made him go away.'
15, Constant LAMBERT, 1936.
23, On September 23, 1792, William COWPER visited a friend at this house on his last ever visit to London.

PETTY FRANCE, SW1 *District and Circle lines to St James's Park*

Not as many guides (and guide books) will tell you: a corruption of 'Petit France and only coming into being after the Edict of Nantes in 1685'. The street was existing and duly recorded in 1490 and was called Petefraunce. Later a number of French refugees *did* set up in the area and a nearby street was once called 'Petty Calais'. In 1792 Petty France was called York Street. The change of name was made, '...to perpetuate to posterity the detestation we, the said inhabitants, have to French principles, politics and all things that bear an affinity with the disordered system at present prevailing with that deluded people'. (So much for *entente cordiale!*) Tempers cooled and, in 1920, Petty France was back on the maps of London.

19, John MILTON. His first wife, Mary, died here in 1652, leaving him with three young daughters. Bad luck dogged him and his second wife died here only two years later. He began to work on *Paradise Lost* here and wrote his *Pro Populo Anglicano Defensio* in this house in 1651.

19, a few years later Jeremy BENTHAM bought the house and rented it to James MILL. William HAZLITT was another tenant from 1811 to 1819. Hazlitt's admiration for MILTON's genius led him to put a tablet in the garden, under an arch of trees inscribed to the 'Prince of Poets'. Hazlitt was later (perhaps justifiably) annoyed that Bentham cut down the trees and the tablet then became, '...subject to the continual inroad of the members of a *Chrestomathic* School'. (A school intended to be used in the acquirement of a language.)

'PHIZ' see BROWNE, H.K.

PICCADILLY, W1 *It is a long street and can be most easily reached by three Underground stations, depending on the street number Hyde Park is on the Piccadilly line and best for numbers 100-149 on the north side of Piccadilly. Green Park is on the Piccadilly, Victoria and Jubilee lines and best for 55-100 on the north side and 160-180 on the south side. Piccadilly Circus itself is on the Piccadilly and Bakerloo lines and best for 1-99 on the north and 181-228 on the south side.*

The origin (or origins) of probably the best known street in the world has been subject to discussion for years. Research shows that it *probably* all began with young Robert Baker from Somerset in the reign of Queen Elizabeth I. He was a tailor and would probably have made 'peccadilles' or 'piccadillies', which were a sort of ruff worn by men of fashion in the 16th century. Baker prospered and, about 1612, bought land in what is now Great Windmill Street. A number of houses were built and the one occupied by Baker himself was nick-named 'Pickadell Hall'. Baker spread his property wings and bought more land around Piccadilly Circus. He died in 1623 after which the family squabbled. (In the account books of the parish of St Martin's £3 is entered as a gift for the poor, 'Of Robte Baeker of Pickadilley Hall gewen by wille'.)

On the north side.

2, Thomas CAMPBELL, 1803. This was his first address in London just before he married.

16, Lord BYRON, 1805. It was this year he went up to Trinity College, Cambridge.

19, Lord NELSON lodged here immediately after his mistress's husband, Sir William Hamilton, had died at number 23, in 1803.

23 (now 99) in January 1805, Emma HAMILTON gave birth to

NELSON's daughter, Horatia here. (Her husband, William, having died here in April 1803.) The Hamiltons were resident here in April 1801 and the news of Nelson's great victory at Copenhagen was brought to them.

90, Hugh WALPOLE, 1920s and 1930s. The second and third books of his autobiographical novels of his *Jeremy* trilogy were published while he lived here.

94, Lord PALMERSTON (LCP 1961) from 1857, until his death in 1865. It was in this house that Lady Palmerston used to hold her 'Saturday evenings'.
It is now the Naval and Military Club, widely referred to as the 'In-and-Out' because these words, as instructions to drivers, are very prominently painted on the gateposts of the forecourt.

173, John HATCHARD, bookseller, from 1797 to 1801, when he moved to 190 and bought a 24-year lease on the property for £1,050.

193, George MEREDITH, 1864. At the time he was filling-in questionnaires (literally) concerning his fitness to marry Marie Vulliamy (who died in 1885).

210 (now part of Simpson's shop). On this site stood the London version of *Stage Door Canteen*, which opened its doors in 1944. In the next two years, until it closed in 1946, more than two million members of the Allied Services came to the 'Canteen'.

PICTON	Poyston, Dyfed, August 16 c.1758
(Sir) Thomas	Waterloo, Belgium, June 18, 1815
Soldier	

146, New Bond Street, W1, 1797-1800

Picton joined the Army when he was only 13. His rise in it must have been fairly speedy, as in 1794 he was in the West Indies and was involved in the capture of some of the islands from the French, the Spanish and sometimes the Dutch. He was appointed Governor of Trinidad and then commandant of Tobago. He was accused of having permitted (under old Spanish laws) a female prisoner to be tortured. Back in England he was found 'technically guilty' but, on appeal, acquitted altogether.
After the Walcheren expedition in 1809, he was made Governor of Flushing, a seaport in Zealand; then next year was off fighting again in Spain where he was in command of the 'Fighting Division' and distinguished himself at the capture of Badajoz in 1812.

PINERO	London, May 24, 1855
(Sir) Arthur Wing	London, November 23, 1934
Playwright	

62, Hamilton Terrace, NW8, 1896
14, Hanover Square, W1, 1904
115A, Harley Street, W1 (LCP 1970) 1909-1934

Pinero's father was a Portuguese Jew and young Arthur was all set to study law, but the lure of the greasepaint was too compelling and when he was 19 he made his debut in Edinburgh. The following year he joined the Lyceum Company.
In 1877 his first play *£200 a Year* was staged but his greatest play was *The Second Mrs. Tanqueray* in 1893 with Mrs. Patrick CAMPBELL in the lead.
Altogether, Pinero wrote over 50 plays and his glorious reward was a knighthood in 1909. This was only 14 years since the first 'theatrical knighthood' was given to Henry IRVING and shows the growing acceptance of 'theatrical people' by 'Society'.

His appearance was a little surprising and his eyebrows featured *prominently*. Max BEERBOHM once said they were actually 'the skins of some small mammal just not large enough to be used as mats'.

PINTER
Harold
Playwright

October 10, 1930

7, Hanover Terrace, NW1, 1960s
52, Campden Hill Square, W8, 1980

As well as being a dramatist, Pinter has also been an actor (stage name: 'David Baron') and a director. Probably such experiences were of very real help when it came to *writing* for the stage.

He was educated at Hackney Downs Grammar School and went straight into repertory from there. In 1956 he married the actress, Vivien Merchant and they had one son. By the 1970s the marriage had shaken apart and, after a divorce, he married Lady Antonia Fraser (daughter of Lord LONGFORD).

Pinter's best known plays are undoubtedly *The Caretaker* and *The Go-Between*, but he has written over 20 others. Perhaps Lady Antonia might re-read her second husband's play, *The Caretaker* (first staged in 1960 and filmed three years later). Pinter's character is made to say, 'Fortnight after I married her, no not so much as that, no more than a week, I took the lid off a saucepan, you know what was in it? A pile of her underclothing, unwashed. The pan for the vegetables it was. The vegetable pan. That's when I left her and I haven't seen her since.'

PITT
Thomas (2nd Lord Camelford)
Aristocratic loony

Cornwall, February 19, 1775
London, March 10, 1804
St Anne's, Soho Square, W1

47 (formerly 64) Baker Street, W1, 1779-1780
148, New Bond Street, W1, 1780-1783

During his short life Pitt managed to quarrel with just about everybody he came across, and one of his principal (and inexplicable) hatreds was the explorer George Vancouver, whose life he made miserable. Over his fireplace in his London lodgings, Pitt kept an assortment of bludgeons and horse whips on display and was not backward in applying them when he was aroused. He has sometimes been described as a 'duellist' (by the *Dictionary of National Biography* for one) and he certainly had many a fight, but he was hardly a 'professional duellist'. However it *was* a duel that was to be the end of him.

Both he and a Captain Thomas Best had shared the physical favours of a Mrs. Loveden (Pitt having begun his liaison with this '...very pretty little woman' in 1801, after Best had done with her). On March 3, at the Haymarket, Best spurned the lady's advance and she threatened to 'set Lord Camelford' (ie Pitt) upon Best's back. Pitt challenged Best and though more than one person tried to call off the fateful duel, the two men, with their seconds, met at dawn almost within sight of Holland House in Kensington. Pitt fired first, missing Best, who returned the fire wounding Pitt in the right chest; the bullet piercing his lung lodged in his spine. He lived for another three days and died peacefully holding the hand of his friend, Robert Barrie. An inquest, held on March 12 at the White Horse Inn, Kensington, returned a verdict of 'felonious homicide' but no steps were taken to arrest Best.

PITT
William (1st Earl of Chatham)
Prime Minister

Westminster, November 15, 1708
Hayes, Kent, May 11, 1778
Westminster Abbey (north transept)

10, St James's Square, SW1 (LCP 1910) 1760-1761
14, York Place, Portman Square, W1

Pitt's father, Robert, of Boconnoc in Cornwall, had sufficient means to send his son to Eton and then up to Trinity College, Oxford; after which he bought William a commission as a Cornet in the Blues Regiment. However, Pitt's only battles were on the hustings or in the House of Commons. He became a Member of Parliament for the borough of Old Sarum (now Salisbury) in Wiltshire.

In the clash between George II and his son, Frederick, Prince of Wales ('Poor Fred') Pitt took the Prince's side. All the Georges seemed to quarrel with their children but the dislike George II (1683-1760) and his consort, Queen Caroline of Ansbach, had for their first born was vicious. Pitt, therefore, did not enjoy the trust or confidence of the King. He was also opposed to WALPOLE and called himself a 'Patriotic Whig'. In 1746 there was a change in the Government and, under Pelham, Pitt was made Paymaster General, a post he retained under the Duke of Newcastle.

The Duchess of Marlborough, Sarah Churchill, died in 1744 (aged 84) and left Pitt £10,000. Sir William Pynsent left him £3,000 a year and an estate, Burton Pynsent, in Somerset, which became Pitt's country seat.

In 1757 Pitt resigned owing to continual differences with the King. This was in April but by June he was back 'by popular demand'. Pitt was determined to wage war unremittingly with France and everywhere, on land and sea, the British forces overwhelmed the French. In 1761 the Cabinet felt that Britain had had enough of War, albeit a successful one, and refused to extend the hostilities to take in Spain as well. Pitt was retired on a pension of £3,000 and his wife (a sister of George Granville) was created Baroness Chatham. He was against the official policy of harsh treatment of the 'American Colonies' and on April 2, 1778 he staggered into the House of Lords and by sheer will power made his feelings felt. He took his seat again but the effort of rising to answer a question put to him was too great. He fell back and was carried from the House. He died a month later.

PITT
William (the 'Younger')
Prime Minister

Hayes, Kent, May 28, 1759
Putney, January 23, 1806
Westminster Abbey (in his father's tomb)

4, Stone Buildings, Lincoln's Inn, WC2, 1779-1780
12, Park Place, W1, 1801
38, Hill Street, W1
120, Baker Street, W1 (LCP 1949) 1802-1806

Pitt was born in the house where his father was to die 21 years later. He was never given a formal education but entered Pembroke Hall, Cambridge, when he was only 14. From his earliest days he had been trained to become England's first *professional* politician. He became Member for Appleby in the Commons before he was 22, was Chancellor of the Exchequer the following year, once refused the Premiership, but, on being asked a second time, became the Prime Minister of Great Britain on December 7, 1783, when he was still only 24 years old.

His Government was repressive in its dealing with Home Affairs and Napoleon was giving Britain cause for alarm overseas. Pitt resigned his post in February 1801, but was back leading a new government on May 16, 1804.

The Treaty of Amiens was not held to be binding and war had broken out again in earnest. In 1805 Lord NELSON had routed the French Navy at Trafalgar and Pitt was the civilian hero of the day. By now his health had broken down completely and he was dead before he was 47.

So 'young' Pitt – 'Pitt the Schoolboy', as he was sometimes sneeringly referred to and the man COBBETT called a 'loud, snorting bawler', died too young, bitter and broken hearted.

A bronze statue of Pitt by Sir Francis CHANTREY was erected on the south side of Hanover Square in 1831. The statue ten feet (3.04 metres) high stands on a granite base 16 feet (4.8 metres) high.

PLACE	London, November 3, 1771
Francis	Hammersmith, London, January 1,
Political Reformer	1854

21, Brompton Square, SW3 (LCP 1961) 1833-1851

Place's father was a 'dissipated baker' who later went on to further 'dissipation' (one suspects) as a keeper of a Public house. Young Francis was apprenticed to a maker of leather breeches and, on the strength of having a trade, got married when he was only 19 and, as newly weds, lived in one room off the Strand. For a time he ran a tailor's shop at 29, Charing Cross, behind which he kept a small library, which was of sufficient quality to attract those great political reformers, James MILL, George BENTHAM and Robert Owen.

Leather breeches started to go out of fashion and an industrial dispute began in 1793. Place was chosen by 'the workers' to be their spokesman and leader. He was able to steer a bill through the Commons in 1824, to repeal the Combination Act, which effectively had made trade unions illegal.

PLAYFAIR	London, July 1, 1874
(Sir) Nigel Ross	August 19, 1934
Actor and Theatrical Manager	

26, Pelham Crescent, SW7 (LCP 1965) 1910-1922

Playfair began in law but by the time he was 28 he had gravitated to the stage and achieved success early on as a 'character actor'.

In 1918 Playfair 'discovered' the 'Lyric Opera House', King Street, Hammersmith. This theatre had opened originally in November 1888 as 'Lyric Hall'. Revamped, it opened again in 1890 as a regular theatre. 1895 saw its ownership change again and it was mostly rebuilt to the design of Frank Matcham. It opened in July and Lily LANGTRY spoke the *prologue* on the first night. The early 1890s saw it falter again, compulsory renovations were made to comply with safety regulations in 1909 and it reopened as 'The People's Popular Playhouse'. The cinema arrived and the P.P.P. became used for practically any function as the new medium replaced the stage in Hammersmith. Locally the Lyric was called the 'Blood and Flea Pit'. It was in this state that Playfair found it.

POE	Boston, Mass., January 19, 1809
Edgar Allan	Baltimore, October 2, 1849
Poet and author	

146, Sloane Street, SW3, 1816-1817

Poe was orphaned when he was three and then adopted by a childless, wealthy merchant called John Allan, who brought the boy to England in

1815. They stayed in England until 1820; Poe having been educated in, or near, London, they all went back to America. He went to the University of Virginia, where, initially he was thought to be a very bright student. But even then his gambling debts were too large and he had to be removed from the College.

West Point followed but here it was the *booze* that interfered with his curriculum and he was dismissed in 1831. John Allan died in 1834 and Poe was then able to take up literature as a career. Two years later he married Virginia Clemm, a cousin, he treated badly.

Two years before Virginia's death, Poe published his poem, *The Raven*. The death of his wife nearly unhinged him and he began to drink more heavily than ever, eventually dying after a prolonged alcoholic session.

POLAND STREET, W1 *Central, Bakerloo and Victoria lines to Oxford Circus*

Until destroyed by bombs in 1940, there used to be a public house called 'The King of Poland' on the Oxford Street (east) corner. There are other pubs called 'The King of Poland' in Britain, but the King remembered in Poland Street (for no apparently good reason) is King John Sobieski (1624-1696) and his victory over the Turkish armies outside Vienna on September 12, 1683.

15, Percy SHELLEY lodged here in 1811, he and Thomas Hogg having just been sent down from Oxford. It was while they were here that Shelley met Harriet Westbrook, whom he later married – with disastrous results. (Harriet was a friend of Shelley's sisters and they used to use her to take pocket money to Percy.) In the house was a '...quiet sitting-room, its walls papered with trellised vine-leaves and clustering grapes', and a bedroom leading out of it, similarly decorated. On first seeing these rooms, Shelley whispered 'We must stay here for ever'. 'For ever' lasted until August 1811, when Shelley and Harriet eloped to Edinburgh.

28, William BLAKE lived here from 1785-1791 and he wrote his *Songs of Innocence*.

50, Fanny BURNEY (Madame d'Arblay) lived here as a child in the 1750s.

PONT STREET, SW1 *Piccadilly line to Knightsbridge*

In 1830 the River Westbourne was still above ground in this part of what was Chelsea and over it was a bridge of which Pont Street formed part in 1830. It would appear that the property exploiters of the day felt that *Pont* Street was a more inviting name than plain Anglo Saxon *Bridge* Street.

18, Lily LANGTRY in the 1880s then...

21, in 1892, she moved in and lived here (LCP 1980) until 1897. Her house is now *totally* absorbed into the Cadogan Hotel.

22, Rafael SABATINI in the 1930s, by which time he enjoyed a good income from his 'swashbuckling' novels.

52, W.S. GILBERT, c.1901-1911.

57, Sir George ALEXANDER. He moved here in 1896 and remained, a resident of Chelsea, until he died in 1918.

64, Mrs. Patrick CAMPBELL, 1928-1940. Her last house in London before dying slightly deranged.

POPE Lombard Street, London, May 21,
Alexander 1688
Poet Twickenham, May 30, 1744

14, Old Bond Street, W1, c.1710

Pope was born in the year that King James II had to leave the throne of England because of his Catholicism and that of his wife, Mary of Modena, who he had married in 1673. So one could suppose that the deformed son of a linen-draper could hardly expect to be *persona grata* in English 'society' in the 1790s and onwards. Pope's father was a Roman Catholic who had a draper's shop in the Strand. What is more, such education as Alexander had was scant, but at Catholic shools.

When he was quite young, father Pope sold his shop and moved west to Binfield which then was *in* Windsor Forest. When he was 12, young Pope was severely ill (polio?) and he more or less stopped growing upwards: as a man he was only about four foot six inches (137 centimetres) tall and cruelly deformed.

He composed the *Pastorals* in 1704 (but they were not published until 1709) and *Windsor Forest* was published in 1713. In 1718 his father died and Alexander and his mother moved nearer town to Twickenham, where they lived in a villa not far from the banks of the Thames. The *Rape of the Lock* appeared in 1714 and Pope became *the* literary figure of the day. This put ADDISON's nose considerably out of joint and the two men were never friendly again.

In 1715 his translation of the *Iliad* came, which made him £5,000. His *Odyssey* came out in 1725 and took his poetic earnings up to £8,000.

POPE-HENNESSY November 20, 1916
James murdered in London, January 25, 1974
Author Kensal Green, Grave No. 59083: Plot
 No. 180

74, Avenue Road, NW8, from youth to 1942
9, Ladbroke Grove, W11, 1942-1974

Pope-Hennessy came from a fairly high powered family: his father was Major General L.H.R. Pope-Hennessy, his mother, Dame Una and his brother, three years senior and of whom he was very fond, became Sir John Pope-Hennessy in 1971. (Sir John was Director of the British Museum in 1974; he lived at 41, Bedford Gardens, W8.)

James went to Downside (a Catholic boys' Public School, near Bath) then to Balliol. He had just been appointed private secretary to the Governor of Trinidad and Tobago when the Second World War broke out; he went first into the Royal Artillery and later was commissioned in the Intelligence Corps.

James wrote a number of books, the first, *London Fabric,* won him the Hawthornden Prize in 1939; a two-volume biography of Monckton MILNES (Lord Houghton) travel books, a fine biography of Queen Mary (consort of King George V) and another on Queen Victoria.

In 1946 he said, 'I think I am only capable of companionship tempered by stray sexual obsessions'. It was a 'stray obsession' which was to kill him. He must have invited some more than usually 'rough trade' back to 9, Ladbroke Grove. He was found the following morning battered to death. No one was ever charged with his murder.

PORCHESTER

Much of the land in the Paddington area belonged to the Church of England and was leased out by the Church. One such tenant, in 1741, was Sir John Frederick, who was the wealthy grandson of the Lord Mayor of London, hence Frederick's Place in the City. Frederick came from Burwood in Surrey and his younger daughter, Selina, married Robert Thistlethwaite of Southwick Park. He owned extensive tracts of land in Hampshire, in and around, Portsea, Widley and Porchester. Building in this area began before 1800 but was continually being developed for the next 100 years or so.

PORCHESTER TERRACE, W2   *Central line to Queensway*

3/5, John and Jane LOUDON, in 1823 when Loudon signed a building contract for both houses. What he built was a house, '...furnished with verandahs extending nearly round the whole building for taking exercise in inclement weather...'

7,   Pearl CRAIGIE in the late 1860s, as a child and again, after 1895, with her only son, John, when she had divorced her husband.

10, E.C. BENTLEY, 1939-1956. This was his last house in London; he died in march 1956.

31, William WHITELEY, 1880-1907. The house was just around the corner from the Department Store he established and in which he was murdered in 1907.

PORTLAND PLACE, W1   *Central, Bakerloo and Victoria lines to Oxford Circus.*

Hans Bentinck (1649-1709) a favourite of King William III was given the title of *Earl* of Portland in 1689 (William seemed to be attracted by young men) and given considerable property by his Royal benefactor. His grandson the 2nd *Duke* of Portland (the Dukedom being bestowed on his father in 1716) married the heiress to the Harley estate, Margaret Cavendish and both the estates stayed in the family until 1879 when the 5th Duke, William, died unmarried and childless.

The width of Portland Place was dictated by Lord Foley (Thomas, the 3rd Baron, who died 1833). He owned a house at the south end of the Place (the present building was once the Langham Hotel) and stipulated that he must have an uninterrupted view from his house, to the north, in perpetuity. This did not worry John NASH, the architect, at all: he merely made Portland Place as wide as Lord Foley's house was long!

The Portland's motto was *Craignez Honte* – fear disgrace.

30, Lord CLARK, 1930-1938. During part of this period, Clark (then only *Mr.* Clark) was Director of the National Gallery.

31, Edgar WALLACE, 1928. He lived here for only one year. He was earning over £50,000 pa. He had a sound proof glass cabinet built in the house and from it he dictated his stories to a secretary in another room at the rate of 3,000 to 4,000 words an hour.

39, Edward FITZGERALD. This was his address until he graduated from Cambridge.

40, Ethel SANDS, 1888-1897.

47, Field Marshall, Lord ROBERTS (LCP 1922) 1902-1906. During this time he became Commander-in-Chief of the British Army.

49, SUN-YAT-SEN. He was 'held prisoner' here in 1896.

51, Prince TALLEYRAND, 1792. He was here in exile, having been elected President of the French Assembly only two years before.

54, James BRYCE, 1914. He had returned from Washington where he had been British Ambassador since 1907.

63, Frances Hodgson BURNETT (LCP 1979) 1893-1898. In the last year here she divorced her American doctor husband.

76, Lord TWEEDSMUIR, 1912-1919. Better known as John BUCHAN whose adventure novel *The Thirty-Nine Steps*, published in 1915 (and written here) was one of his best selling books.

80, Viscount JELLICOE, 1929. He was President of the British Legion at this time.

88, Sir George LEWIS at the time of his death in 1905. Lewis's first wife died in 1867 and after re-marriage his new wife was able to make use of his 'patronage of the arts'; 'The cellars were packed with rich gifts from his clients – gold and silver, oriental curios, weapons, vases, cigar-cases'.

98, Henry Brook ADAMS (LCP 1978). This house was the American Embassy and Adams was Ambassador in London from 1833-1836.

There are statues of Lord LISTER and Quintin Hogg in Portland Place. They are described under each of those people. In between them is a statue of Field Marshall Sir George White, on horseback. The piece is by John Tweed (1869-1933) and was erected here in 1922. White won the Victoria Cross for bravery in the Afghan campaign of 1879-1880 and was Governor of Gibraltar from 1900-1904. He was at the relief of the siege of Ladysmith on February 28, 1900 in the Boer War and became the Governor of Chelsea Hospital. By 1907 he had '...considerably fattened out...' since 1900 but he still had '...brilliant light blue eyes and that delightful gay Irish manner.'

PORTMAN SQUARE, W1 *Central line to Marble Arch*

The Portman estate was one of the richest north of Hyde Park. It dates back to 1553 when Sir William Portman bought the Marylebone estate. Two years later he was dead, but his grandchildren produced, from one branch; Henry SEYMOUR and from the other; Phillipa, who married Edward Berkeley. Many of the streets hereabouts have 'Portman' names, most of them being connected with the west of England, the best example was ORCHARD street; the family seat being Orchard Portman in Somerset. Other Portman properties in the adjoining county of Dorset are remembered in streets like BLANDFORD, NUTFORD, ENFORD, CLENSTON, BRIDPORT, MELBURY, SHERBORNE and so on.

5, Lieutenant General Arthur Bentinck. His daughter, Ottoline, who married Phillip MORRELL, was born here in June 1873.

18, Mary Ann CLARKE lived here, 'under the protection' of the Duke of York (favourite son of King George III, Commander in Chief of the British, *Grand Old Duke* in the nursery rhyme and whose statue is atop the 124 foot high Tuscan granite pillar in Waterloo Place.) Mary Ann kept more than 20 servants in the house and ten horses in the stables for her personal use. The Duke allowed her £1,000 a *month* in 1813.

20, Sam and Lilian COURTAULD. After he died in 1947, the house became the Courtauld Institute of Fine Art. The house was built by Robert himself between 1773 and 1777 for Elizabeth, Countess of Home, daughter of a West Indian Merchant and referred to by her neighbour, Mrs. Montagu, as 'the Queen of Hell'.

24, Sir Gilbert PARKER, 1922-1928. Here he wrote his autobiographical novel *Tarboc*, which was published in 1927.

PORTSEA PLACE, W2 *Central line to Marble Arch*

Much of the land near here was leased from the Church of England to Sir John Frederick of Burwood in Surrey about 1741. His younger daughter married a wealthy man called Thistlethwaite who owned land at Portsea in Hampshire.

16, Olive SCHREINER. She only lived here from August 1885 to January 1886.

Portsea Hall in Flat 45 – on the sixth floor lived Anthony (once *Sir* Anthony) BLUNT. He was here from the 1960s until he died here on Saturday, March 26, 1983. He lived here with his great friend, John Gaskin. Gaskin said that Blunt, '...got up from breakfast to look up a telephone number and then dropped dead'.

POTTER	London, July 28, 1866
Beatrix	Near Sawrey, December 22, 1943
Author and artist	

2, Bolton Gardens, SW5, 1866-1913

Beatrix was educated at home by a governess and later, by a tutor. She was always passionately fond of animals and there are letters of hers to an invalid friend filled with anecdotes and thumbnail sketches of her pets. Expanded, these letters were carefully edited and developed into a story called *Peter Rabbit*, which was published in 1900. This was followed by *Benjamin Bunny* in 1904. Probably *Peter Rabbit* and *Mickey Mouse* are the greatest of all animal creations of the 20th century.

In 1906 she bought a farm near Windemere (see *Jemima Puddleduck*, 1908). Her publisher, Norman Warne, had proposed marriage to her and been accepted. However, he died of leukemia only a month later. Seven years later, when she was 47, she married William Heelis, a country solicitor in the Lake District and their happy marriage lasted 30 years. Heelis was (or became) very secretive about his late wife and seemed to try to create a myth about her.

POTTER	London, February 1, 1900
Stephen	London, December 2, 1969
Author and 'gamesman'	

56, St George's Square, SW1, 1924
135, Harley Street, W1, 1945-1950
23, Hamilton Terrace, NW8, 1964

Potter was educated at Westminster School and then went on to join the British Broadcasting Corporation as a producer and scriptwriter after getting a second class degree in English Language from Merton College, Oxford. (One of his happiest radio programmes were the *How* series with Joyce GRENFELL.)

His first book to be published was *The Young Man* in 1929, which was followed by a number of books which did not attract too much attention. In 1947 all that changed. He published a book on *Gamesmanship* the sub-title for which was, *How to win games without actually cheating*. Basically his advice, if followed, would upset your opponent and the more conventional he was, so much the better. An example: to upset your opponent at tennis, turn up on the court wearing *violently coloured, unmatching* socks.

POULTRY, EC2   *Central and Northern lines to Bank*

Like so many other street names in the City (Bread Street, Ropemaker Street and so on) a very real reason existed for their names as the product, trade or craft was carried on in the thoroughfare. The good wives of London came here to buy their fowls at what was West Cheap Market (now Cheapside).

Cheap in Anglo Saxon was to sell or barter, not necessarily *cheap* as is understood by the word today.

22, James BOSWELL lodged here at his publishers, Edward and Charles Dilly.

31, Thomas HOOD was born here, 'at the sign of the "Peacock"', in 1779. His father kept a bookshop here.

POUND	Hailey, Idaho, October 30, 1855
Ezra Loomis	Venice, November 1, 1972
Poet	

48, Langham Street, W1, 1908

After a degree from Pennsylvania University, Pound taught at Wabash College. He came to England in 1906 and became friendly with T.S. ELIOT, James Joyce and Wyndham LEWIS, amongst other literary lights of the day. He became editor in London of the Chicago-based *Little Review*, in 1917 and then Paris correspondent of the *Dial* in 1920.

Two books of his poems had been published before 1912 and he was in the forefront of the 'Imagists' before joining the 'Vorticists'. Between 1924 and 1945 he lived in Italy, at Rapallo and there produced his series of *Cantos* – 70 of them being published in this 20-year period.

During the years of the Second World War, Pound, undoubtedly unhinged by now, broadcast from Italy about the evils of usury and the Americans, moving up through Italy in 1944, 'captured' Pound in Pisa and eventually took him back to the States where he was tried for treason, found of unbalanced mind and was placed in a Washington mental institution.

He was back in Italy in 1967 and appeared to have taken a vow of silence. 'Does he never speak?' asked Diana MOSLEY of Dominique de Roux; '*Non, non, ah, non. Jamais*', was the reply.

POYNTER	Paris, March 20, 1836
(Sir) Edward John	London, July 26, 1919
Artist	St Paul's Cathedral Crypt

106, Gower Street, WC1, 1866-1868
28, Albert Gate, SW7, 1870-1890s
70, Addison Road, W14, 1905-1919

Poynter's fobears were Huguenots; his father, Ambrose (1796-1886) was an architect. Young Poynter was sent to Westminster School and then went to study art, firstly in Rome from 1853 to 1854, then on to Paris, coming back to London about 1860.

He was a prolific water colourist and was elected to the Royal Academy in 1876, eventually succeeding MILLAIS as President in 1896. Additionally he was Slade Professor of Art at London University, Art Director at South Kensington for a while and a Director of the National Gallery for eleven years.

PRIESTLY	Birstall, Yorks., March 13, 1733
Joseph	Northumberland, February 6, 1804
Scientist	Quaker Burial Ground, Northumberland

54, Berkeley Square, W1, 1744

Priestley was the son of a cloth-dresser, who was a Presbyterian (by faith) and spent four years at the Dissenting Academy at Daventry. He was appointed Minister at Needham Market in 1755. On visits to London he met Benjamin FRANKLIN, who was able to provide material for his book, *The History of Electricity*. He began to study Chemistry seriously (still as a Minister of the Faith) at Mill Hill, Leeds, in 1767.

As a result of his published, scientific findings he was branded as an atheist in Britain, but in France he was elected to the French Academy of Sciences in 1772.

In 1791 a mob attacked his house in Birmingham and wrecked the contents because of his published reply to BURKE's *Reflection on the French Revolution*.

He settled in Hackney, in north-east London, after that upset and, in 1794, '...removed to America'. Priestly was a true pioneer of the chemistry of gasses and the *real* discoverer of oxygen.

His three sons were all in America and Priestley was warmly welcomed there. He founded the first Unitarian Church in Philadelphia.

A stone statue of Priestly by Gilbert Bayes was put up outside the Royal Institute of Chemistry at 30, Russell Square. He does not look very comfortable but, poor man, he has been here since 1914.

PRINCE's SW7 *Piccadilly line to Knightsbridge*

Named after Albert, the Prince Consort, as is practically everything else in this area, lying as it does practically in the shadow of *his* memorial (Queen Victoria, in her letters, was a great little *underliner*).

PRINCE'S GARDENS, SW7

36, W.S. GILBERT, 1894-1898. By this time the great partnership was over. The last *real* 'G. and S.' was *The Gondoliers* in 1893.

44, Aldous HUXLEY, in the 1920s, during the first months after his marriage to the Belgian, Maria Nys.

PRINCE'S GATE, SW7

7, Baroness SPENCER-CHURCHILL lived here after the death of her husband, Sir Winston CHURCHILL, in 1965, until her own death 13 years later.

13/14, J.P. MORGAN bought two houses here in the early 1900s (they had been originally built about 1850) and made them into one residence.

14, John F. KENNEDY (P) 1939-1940. J.F.K. probably *did* stay here sometimes as it was the London home of his disagreeable father Joseph (at that time the, deservedly unpopular, United States Ambassador to the Court of St James's). In June 1940 when Britain stood alone, without declared allies, against the Axis, Kennedy, senior publicly announced that Britain was as good as defeated.

15, Robert BADEN-POWELL, 1902. He was here during the period between the end of the Boer Wars and his establishing the Scout movement in 1908.

PROCTER	Leeds, Yorks., November 21, 1787
Bryan Waller ('Barry Cornwall')	London, October 5, 1874
Poet	

25, Bedford Square, WC1, 1825-1832
38, Harley Street, W1, c.1840-1861

Procter, an amiable man, was described by Thomas CARLYLE as a

'...decidedly pretty, little fellow, bodily and spiritually'. He most certainly did good by stealth and both BROWNING and SWINBURNE were in his debt.

In 1816, his father (a business man from farming stock) died. Procter took a house in Brunswick Square and was sufficiently affluent to keep a hunter there. He met Leigh HUNT and Charles LAMB, who both encouraged his poetic leanings and, in 1819, he published *Dramatic Scenes* (which was considerably influenced by LAMB).

He dabbled in play writing and it was for this literary output he employed the pseudonym of 'Barry Cornwall' (an imperfect, very imperfect, anagram of 'Bryan Waller'). His wife, by whom he had three daughters and three sons, was a daughter of Basil Montagu.

PUGIN	London, March 1, 1812
Augustus Welby Northmore	Ramsgate, September 14, 1852
Architect	(in his own church of St Augustine)

106 (today) Great Russell Street, WC1, 1822-1832

His father, Augustus Charles, also an architect, was born in France in 1762. Early in life he came to London and for a while worked for John NASH. Unlike Nash, Pugin senior did much for the Gothic architectural revival which was to reach its apotheosis in the House of Commons, partly designed by his son.

The young Pugin once wrote that, 'There is nothing worth living for but Christian architecture and a boat'. However, after serving a period of training with his father (who died in 1832) he worked on the Kensal Green Cemetery and also designed furniture for Windsor Castle. When he was only 19, he married, but his young wife died in childbirth only a year later. Pugin went bankrupt but, eventually, he was to pay off all his creditors in full.

In 1834 the Houses of Parliament burnt down and Charles BARRY was chosen as the architect for their rebuilding. In turn he chose the 24-year old Pugin as his principal assistant. For six years Pugin was fully employed making the detailed drawings for the House. In 1867 when both Barry and Pugin were dead, Edward Welby Pugin, the elder brother of Augustus, claimed that it was he, Augustus, who had actually produced the successful design, *not* Barry.

PYE	Faringdon, Berks., February 20, 1745
Henry James	Pinner, Middx., August 11, 1813
Poet Laureate	

2, James Street, Buckingham Gate, SW1, 1799-1800

Pye was a graduate of Magdalen College, Oxford but little seems to be known about him between the time he left Oxford in 1776, and 1784 when he turned up in the House of Commons as Member of Parliament for Berkshire. He supported PITT whole heartedly and this might have had some bearing on his being appointed Poet Laureate to succeed Thomas Warton in 1790.

As Laureate, Pye's poetic output was apt, punctual and incredibly boring. So much so that his poems became a byword for 'flatness and frigidity'. In a slightly more praiseworthy style he published *Comment on the Commentaries of Shakespeare* in 1807.

If today any children read (or have read to them) Nursery Rhymes as in days of yore, they will find an echo of Henry Pye. On one of King George III's birthdays, Pye produced a more than vapid poem to celebrate the anniversary. George Steevens (1736-1800) who was an English Shakespearian commentator heard Pye's tribute and (so said) 'off-the-cuff-, produced the following:

> 'And when the Pye was opened
> The birds began to sing
> And wasn't that a dainty dish
> To set before the King?'

Pye was the first Laureate to have a salary of £27 instead of a 'tierce' (42 gallons – like today's barrels of crude oil) of wine.

QUARTERMAINE
Leon
Actor

Richmond, Surrey, September 24, 1876
June 25, 1967

32, Cumberland Terrace, NW1, 1929
61, Clarence Gate Gardens, NW1, 1946

Quartermaine's mother was an Egg! (Alice Ann Egg; probably related to an English artist; Augustus Leopold Egg, RA, who died in 1863, aged 47.) Leon was at Whitgift School and made his stage début in Sheffield when he was only 18. Later on that year, he acted at the Pavillion Theatre, in the 'East End of the City'.

Over the years he played dozens of different parts, but he never got *Star Status*. Despite that, he was rarely out of work, though he managed to find the time to marry, first; Aimée de Burgh, second, Fay COMPTON and finally Barbara Wilcox.

QUEEN ANNE STREET, W1   *Central line to Oxford Circus*

Dating from 1714, the last year of the last of the Stuart monarchs, Queen Anne.

23,   J.M.W. TURNER from 1811 and where he painted much of his best work. He had a gallery built in the house in 1819/20. Later he moved to 22 and then to 45. The Gallery here was even longer than the one he had built at 64, Harley Street and it was top lighted.

23,   was rebuilt by Lord Howard de Walden in 1937. Over the garage is a bust of TURNER by W.C.H. King.

58,   Hector BERLIOZ (LCP 1969) 1851. He had been asked to be a member of a sort of International jury to judge the musical instruments which had been sent to the Great Exhibition, Prince Albert's brainchild, for which the Crystal Palace was originally built. His apartment was just above the main staircase of the house.

QUEEN ANNE'S GATE, SW1   *Circle and District lines to St James's Park*

The street was originally built for William Paterson (1658-1719) who founded the Bank of England in 1694. Not long after the buildings were completed (c.1705) a wall, projecting from the house today numbered 15, was erected, which divided the street in two. On 15 is a statue of Queen Anne, sculptor unknown, but he did not finish the job off as the robes on the Queen's back are still 'roughcast'. In March 1723, Sir Theodore Janssen (1658-1748; a half Dutch, half English director of the 'South Sea Bubble' scheme) was obliged to sell the house to pay some of his debts. The statue was listed on the 'sale specification'. The house has changed hands a number of times in the last 250 years but was bequeathed to the Gardener's Company by its ex-Master after the Second World War and bequeathed by them in 1974 to the Nation.

9,   Henry HYNDMAN, 1900 onwards.

16,   William WORDSWORTH stayed here as a guest of Joshua Watson (1776–1855) in 1853.

16, Admiral Lord FISHER (LCP 1975). When he lived here 'Jackie' Fisher was First Sea Lord, for the second time.

20, Lord PALMERSTON (LCP 1925). He was born in this house in 1784.

22, Henry Brook ADAMS, 1880s.

28, Lord HALDANE (LCP 1954) 1907-1928. Albert Einstein (1879-1955) used to stay here. 'Kaiser Bill', Kaiser Wilhelm II of Germany, Queen Victoria's oldest grandson, lunched here in 1911. He used to call it, 'Haldane's Doll's House'. The house bears the date 1704 and so is one of the originals.

40, John Stuart MILL, 1814-1831.

QUEEN SQUARE, WC1   *Central and Piccadilly lines to Holborn*

'Queen' (note, *not* Queen's) Square was built in the reign of 'Good Queen Anne' (1702-1714) but the statue in the Square gardens (of lead, by an unknown sculptor) is thought to be of Queen Charlotte, the plain, but fecund, consort of King George III. Originally the north side of the Square was not built upon and so views of Hampstead were to be had by fortunate residents.

20, Dr. John CAMPBELL, 1757-1775. Samuel JOHNSON often visited him here.

21, J.F.D. MAURICE, 1846-1856. Two years before he left this house he had founded the Working Mens' College of which he was appointed Principal.

26, William Samuel MORRIS moved his business here, together with his family in 1865.

29, Jerome K. JEROME, 1880s. Just about the time his best selling *Three Men in a Boat* was published (1889).

QUEEN'S GATE, SW7   *District, Circle and Piccadilly lines to Gloucester Road*

Named after Queen Victoria, in 1870, when Lord Mountstuart rented a house here for the season. It was in such 'rural' surroundings that he used to tell cab-drivers taking him home from Westminster, to 'Drive along the Cromwell Road until you come to a hedge, then turn right'. (Today's instructions, coming out of town along Cromwell Road would be, '…until you come past the Natural History Museum, *then* turn right'.)

48, Denis WHEATLEY, 1931-1938, after his second marriage. Here he wrote his first book, *Forbidden Fruit* which was reprinted seven times in less than two months in 1933.

87, Prince Louis MOUNTBATTEN, 1911. (Though at this time he was still Prince Louis Battenburg. He did not anglicize his name until his cousin, King George V, changed his 'dynastic' name to Windsor from Saxe Coburg Gotha in the Great War.) The Prince was on half pay and had just been given command of the 3rd and 4th Divisions of the Home Fleet.

102, Ronald FIRBANK 1912, in the early part of the year. In the autumn he was in Venice and by December was back to England, staying at Laura Place in Bath.

197, Sir Max PEMBERTON, 1946. He was 83 years old and this was his last address in London.

QUEEN'S GATE GARDENS, SW7

10, Sir James OUTRAM, 1862. Unwell, he had resigned from the Supreme Council of Calcutta. He went to 'winter' at Pau, in the south of France, where he died.

42, Harry QUILTER, who died here aged 56, in 1907.

Where Queen's Gate joins Kensington Gore, there is an equestrian statue of Field Marshall, Lord Napier of Magdala. This Bronze, begun by Sir Joseph Boehm and completed by Sir Alfred Gilbert, was originally erected in 1891 by Carlton House Gardens but was moved to its present site to 'make way' for King Edward VII in 1920. Anyone having been to Calcutta will probably have seen the replica of Napier's statue.

QUEEN'S GATE PLACE MEWS, SW7

5, Tom DRIBERG, 1935. He had a small flat here with two bedrooms, which was the scene of an incident which resulted in Driberg appearing in the Number One Court of the Old Bailey, charged with indecent assault. The Complainants were *two* Scotsmen who had shared Driberg's bed – with Driberg in it as well! Albert Westlake, Driberg's man servant, was asked by the judge if he (Westlake) had measured the bed in question. On oath, Westlake testified that the bed was 'three feet and six inches wide' and the mattress slightly smaller'. Despite this evidence of (at least) overcrowding, Driberg was acquitted.

QUILTER
Harry
Barrister, artist and author

Lower Norwood, January 24, 1851
London, July 10, 1907
Norwood

The White House, Tite Street, SW3, 1876
42, Queen's Gate Gardens, SW7, where he died

Quilter was that very British being – the 'gifted Amateur'. He studied law, he workèd on the *Times*, conducted the *Universal Review*, single handed, painted competently in oils and lectured on a wide variety of subjects.

In September 1900 he, '...originated a guide book to Modern Life entitled *What's What*. The title of the work was suggested by his wife, being a parody on *Who's Who*. It contained over 2,500 articles, more than 800 of them written by Quilter himself. He also published poems, which he said were '...fortunately anonymous and forgotten'. He was even the first President of the Society of Accountants.

He bought WHISTLER's house in Tite Street after the waspish American genius was bankrupted over the law suit he instigated against RUSKIN in 1876. Quilter paid £2,700 for the property. Whistler used to refer to him as 'the Philistine' and, when he was told Quilter was making alterations to the house, he wrote, 'Shall the birthplace of Art become the tomb of its parasite in Tite Street?'

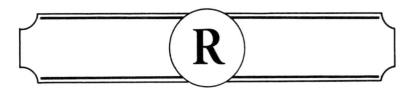

RACKHAM　　　　　　　London, September 19, 1867
Arthur　　　　　　　　　　September 6, 1939
Artist

6, Primrose Hill Studios, Fitzroy Road, NW1, 1929

Rackham studied Art at the Slade School in London and afterwards in Paris.
He became a member of the Royal Watercolour Society and this medium
was certainly his strength.
In Europe he enjoyed a reputation as a true artist, but in England he only
seems to have been thought of (and remembered for) his book illustrations.
Probably the finest of these was his series for the *Ingoldsby Legends* in 1907
and, for *Grimm's Fairy Tales* two years later.

RADCLIFFE　　　　　　Wakefield, Yorkshire, 1650
John　　　　　　　　　　　London, November 1, 1714
Physician　　　　　　　　St Mary's Church, Oxford

19-20, Bow Street, WC2 (LCP 1929) 1687-1714

Radcliffe studied at University College, Oxford (founded 1249). He took his
MB in 1675 and two years after getting his MD came to live in London in
1684.
He soon found fame, not only as a doctor, but as a rather capricious (and
often intemperate) *character*. Despite rather non-professional traits, he treated
both King William III and Queen Mary II. Such patients as this for Radcliffe
are even more surprising when it is remembered that he was a Jacobin and so
supported the very causes that King William had come from Holland in 1688
especially to repress!
Another Royal Patient was added to his list of *By Appointments*: in 1708 he
treated the boozy Prince George of Denmark, husband of Queen Anne. His
treatment was either wrong or ineffective, however, as HRH expired on
October 28 in the same year. As Queen Anne herself lay dying, she
summoned Radcliffe, who sent back his reply to say that he was too busy!

RADCLYFFE-HALL　　　Bournemouth, Hants., August 12,
Marguerite　　　　　　　　1880
Author　　　　　　　　　London, October 7, 1943
　　　　　　　　　　　　　Highgate Cemetery (west) N6

59, Cadogan Mansions, SW3, 1907-1916
1, Swan Walk, SW3, 1916
37, Holland Street, W8, 1929

Though christened Marguerite she became generally known to her friends as
'John'. In 1901 she left her parents' home and came to live with her
grandmother in South Kensington. She dressed very 'mannishly' and never
really let it be misunderstood that she preferred her own sex in and out of
bed. Her first, long standing *liaison* was Mabel Batten but she died in 1915. It
was Mabel who encouraged her to write, as did her second great love, Lady
Troubridge, who, funnily enough, was a cousin of Mabel Batten.
In 1928 Radclyffe-Hall became the talk of the literary one percent of Great
Britain. She had a book published by Jonathan Cape called *The Well of*

Loneliness, which dealt explicitly with female homosexuality. The Home Secretary ordered that it be withdrawn ('...it is an obscene book, a book which is prejudicial to the morals of the community'). It was printed in Paris and copies smuggled into Britain; any copies seized were destroyed. It was freely available in America, however.

Una Troubridge was the wife of Admiral, Sir Ernest Troubridge and had had a daughter by him. They were married in 1908 when he was 46: Una was his second wife.

RAGLAN (1st Baron)
Fitzroy James Henry Somerset
Soldier

Badminton, Glos., September 30, 1788
Crimea, June 28, 1855

85, Pall Mall, SW1
5, Stanhope Gate, W1 (LCP 1911) 1835-1854

Raglan was the youngest son of the 5th Duke of Beaufort, educated at Westminster School and joined the Army in 1804 with a Cornet's commission.

He served with WELLINGTON in the Peninsular War and had an arm shot off at Waterloo. It was not until he was 66 years old he saw action again. He had been made a Baron in 1852 and chose 'Raglan' for his title; he had a DCL from Oxford and was a member of the Privy Council. He was sent out to the Crimean battlefields; to a savage, senseless war and Raglan was just too old. He repeatedly referred to the enemy as 'the French', when that nation was one of our allies! *Russia* was the enemy. So was the Crimea. Raglan died while his Army was still besieging Sevastopol.

His legacy is the 'Raglan Sleeve', a tailoring trick where the sleeve is not 'set in' to the shoulder, and so a great help to a one-armed man.

The Raglan motto is; *Mutare Veltimere Spero* – I scorn to change or fear.

RAMBERT
(Dame) Marie
Dancer

Warsaw, February 2, 1888
June 12, 1982

19, Campden Hill Gardens, W8, 1946

Dame Marie was born Myriam Ramberg in Poland (her family name had been Ramban but Marie's father had had it changed to Ramberg). However, by 1910, she was calling herself Rambert and was in Paris (supposedly) studying medecine. There she met Isadora DUNCAN and mixed generally with a definitely *non*-medical set.

In 1914 she moved to London where she became a teacher and, by 1920, began her own dance studio in Kensington. She had married the playwright Ashley Dukes and, in 1931, they opened the Ballet Club at the Mercury Theatre. The School flourished until the Second World War began in 1939 and Marie Rambert then formed a touring company – even playing in *French* seaside resorts until just before the surrender of France. Back in England she toured the British cities despite falling German bombs.

RATHBONE PLACE, W1

*Central and Northern lines
to Tottenham Court Road*

In the 1720s this was the first development to be finished north of Oxford Street. Some claim that a carpenter called Rathbone was one of the workmen involved in the original building. Another surmise is that Thomas Rathbone, a naval captain, had had a house here since 1684. Both are theoretical explanations.

12, William HAZLITT, 1799-1803, when he occupied his brother John's 'back painting room'.

50, John CONSTABLE, 1801. 'I have just got three rooms in very comfortable house', he wrote, 'my large room has three windows in front. I shall make that my shop.'

RATTIGAN London, June 10, 1911
(Sir) Terence Mervyn Bermuda, November 30, 1977
Playwright

19, Stanhope Gardens, SW7, 1934-1936
K 5, Albany, W1, 1946
29, Eaton Square (penthouse flat) SW1, 1952

Rattigan's family was well-to-do middle class and could afford his education at Harrow (where he played cricket for the First XI in 1927, '28 and '29) from whence he went up to Trinity College, Oxford for a degree.
After Oxford he was very undecided what he really wanted to do in life and his father (on the 'give-him-enough-rope...' principle) let him live at home and '...he'll soon settle down'. He lived staidly in Stanhope Gardens for two years and in this time wrote a play which was to become a smash hit, called *French Without Tears*. It opened in London in November 1936 and ran for 1,030 performances. Rattigan never looked back.
During the Second World War he served in the Royal Air Force and during that time wrote *Flare Path, While the Sun Shines* and *Love in Idleness*. All were successful.
By 1945 he was earning £600 a *week*. He enjoyed his well-earned fame and the trappings of wealth. However, he found it increasingly difficult to come to terms with his homsexuality. (One of his 'romances' was with 'Chips' CHANNON.) Like many successful dramatists, before and since, he went to Hollywood but did not find the ambience congenial or fruitful.

READE Ipsden House, Oxon, June 8, 1814
Charles London, April 11, 1884
Author Willesden Churchyard

6, Bolton Row, W1, 1850
70, Knightsbridge, SW7, 1868-1882

Reade was the seventh son and the youngest of eleven children, whose father was 'a country gentleman' in Oxfordshire. Initially Charles was privately 'tutored' then after five years more ('all flogging') he won a demyship to Magdalen College, Oxford in 1831. Five years later he entered Lincoln's Inn and was called to the Bar in 1843. He never practised law but began writing dramas. He wrote some thirteen, 'which nobody would play'; even the remarkable *Masks and Faces*. Though this never saw a stage, Reade re-wrote it in 1852 and it was published in that year as the novel *Peg Woffington*. He was not a successful playwright, but his interest in the stage brought him into the world of the theatre and he formed a 'platonic' friendship with an actress, Mrs. Seymour (who had the proverbial 'heart of gold') and she kept house for him from 1854 until she died in 1879.
His novels *did* make money and the most lucrative of all was *The Cloister and the Hearth*, a long (*very* long) historical story set in the 15th century.
He died from 'complicated disorders of the lungs and liver'. In the winter of 1883/1884 he had been in Cannes and his doctor's orders were to drink two quarts (2.27 litres) of milk and eat 12 eggs a day.

REDCLIFFE ROAD, SW10 — *District line to West Brompton*

All the 'Redcliffes' were built by George GODWIN about 1860. One of his previous architectural successes had been in the Redcliffe district of the City of Bristol; the church of St Mary Redcliffe was considered to be the fairest parish in England by Queen Elizabeth I.

26, Christopher ISHERWOOD, 1926, in rooms 'bequeathed' to him by Roger Benford. His landlady, Mrs. Clarke, became 'Mrs. Partridge', the permanently debt-ridden landlady in *Lions and Shadows* (1935).

37, Wyndham LEWIS lodged here in 1920. His novel *Tarr* had been published with mixed success a few months previously.

47, John Middleton MURRY. In 1912, where he was joined by his mistress, Katherine MANSFIELD, whom he later married.

RED LION SQUARE, WC1 — *Piccadilly and Central line to Holborn*

The square was originally built up about 1698 and named after a long established tavern called the 'Red Lion' in Holborn. It was to this tavern the exhumed bodies of Ireton, Bradshaw and Cromwell were brought in 1660.

Summit House (on the corner of Dane Street, so called because the land belonged to the Church of St Clement Dane) by the Law Courts, on the south side. John HARRISON, 1752-1776, died in a house on this site.

8, William Samuel MORRIS and Edward BURNE-JONES, 1856. 'Although the front window had been cut to give a higher light, the rooms were shabby, dark and unfurnished and had apparently not been cleaned for the last five years, since ROSSETTI, supervising, was still able to recognize an address which poor Deverell' [a Pre-Raphaelite painter who had died in 1854, aged 28] 'had scribbled on the wall.'

Halsey House (on the other corner of Dane Street) Flat 7, Arnold BENNETT, 1908. He had just come back from eight years living in Paris.

REED — London, December 31, 1906
(Sir) Carol — April 25, 1976
Film Director

42, Charles Street, W1, 1946
213, Kings Road, SW3 (P?) 1948-1976

Reed had not long left King's School, Canterbury (founded AD 600) when he was appearing on the stage of the Empire Theatre, Leicester Square, in 1924. Later he joined Edgar WALLACE as stage director, but left the stage for the cinema in 1930.

Reed's wife, Penelope, whom he married in 1948, was one of the two daughters of Freda Dudley Ward (later the Marquesa CASA MAURY, who at one time in the 1930s was on the gossip writers' short lists as a wife for the 'King-who-gave-up-his-throne-for-love'; Edward VIII.) Reed had previously been married to the actress Diana Wynyard. They wed in 1943, but the marriage was dissolved four years later.

He was knighted for his contribution to the art of the cinema in 1952.

REGENT STREET, W1 — *Central and Bakerloo lines to Oxford Circus (or Piccadilly or Bakerloo lines to Picadilly Circus for the southern end).*

The street was designed by John Nash (under an Act of Parliament of 1815) as part of the Regent's Park Scheme to provide a princely carriage-way from Carlton House Terrace (where the Regent's town house was) to Regent's Park, a mile or so to the north.

14, John NASH built this house for his own•occupation. He had hanging here copies of some of Raphael's paintings. They were made by special permission of the Pope and Nash had copyists working on them in Rome for four years.

86, 'Buffalo Bill' CODY took rooms here, over Hope's (a gentlemen's outfitters) shop, in 1887. He found himself '...embarrassed by an overwhelming mass of flowers which come hourly from hosts of female admirers'.

REGENT'S PARK ROAD, NW1   *Northern line to Camden Town*

2, Cecil Sharp House. Sharp was born in London in 1859 and died in 1924. In 1902 he published a *Book of British Song* and *Folk Songs from Somerset* in 1905. He founded the English Folk Dance Society in 1911 which is now housed in the present building designed by H.M. Fletcher in 1930. In the main hall there is a 70 foot (21 metre) mural painted by Ivon Hitchens in 1954. Sharp noted over 5,000 folk tunes and their variants and left all his notebooks to Clare College, Cambridge.

121, Frederick ENGELS (LCP 1972) 1870-1894. For the last 11 years of his life Engels was able to give Karl MARX practical help with his literary and political work and financial help. Before moving here Engels was 'married' to *two* Irish sisters, Mary and Lydia Burns. Mary died in 1863 as his 'common law' wife and Lydia came with Engels to this house as his *second* 'common law' wife. When Lydia lay dying here Engels married her by special licence, on September 11, 1878.

RESCHID   Constantinople, 1802
Mustapha Pasha   Candia, January 7, 1858
Statesman and reformer

1, Bryanston Square, W1 (LCP 1972) 1839

Reschid was Minister of Foreign Affairs a number of times under Mahmud II and Abdul-Medjid who succeeded him in July 1839 when Reschid was, for the second time, Ambassador for Turkey in London. That year, too, he was made Hatti-Sherif of Gulhane.
Reschid's experiences of the Western way of life were valuable to him in his attempts to bring the Ottoman Empire up to date and he achieved some considerable success in the reformation of Turkey, both politically and socially.

REUTER   Kassel, Germany, July 21, 1816
(Baron) Paul Julius Freiherr von.   Nice, February 25, 1899
Founder of Reuters

18, Kensington Palace Gardens, W8, 1867-1899

Born Israel Beer, the to-be-Baron Reuter formed an organization in Aachen for transmitting commercial news by telegraph in 1846. A cable was laid on the Channel bed; Reuter moved his company to London in 1851 and began to supply the news to English papers.
In 1865 he turned *Reuters* into a limited liability company with himself as Managing Director. *Reuters* is still a potent force in the supply of news to the world.
A bust of Reuter by Michael Black was erected in the passage behind the Royal Exchange in the city in 1976. Black used a method sometimes called 'term' – a bust or head which 'grows' out of the column which supports it; the column and the sculpture all being of one piece.

REYNOLDS　　　　　　　　　Plymouth, July 16, 1723
(Sir Joshua)　　　　　　　　　London, February 23, 1792
Artist　　　　　　　　　　　　St Paul's Cathedral

5 (10 and 11 today) Great Newport Street, WC2 (P) c.1750-1760
47 (Fanum House) Leicester Square, WC2 (LCP 1960) 1760 until he died
Reynolds was the seventh son of a Plymouth Minister and, at the age of 17, he was sent to London to study art. In 1749 he set off for Rome where he studied the works of Raphael and Michelangelo assiduously. Whilst in the Vatican he caught a chill which left him slightly deaf for the rest of his life.

He was back in London by 1760 on the crest of his artistic wave. He founded a literary club in 1764 and Samuel JOHNSON, Edmund BURKE, Oliver GOLDSMITH and James BOSWELL were all members. In 1768 the Royal Academy of Art was founded and Reynolds was its first President. Eighteen years later he was appointed Court Painter to King George III, the same year, 1784, he finished one of his best known portraits; Sarah SIDDONS as *The Tragic Muse.*

By 1789 his sight had become so bad he was obliged to give up painting altogether. His last portrait was of Charles James FOX and he was able to finish it with a few, altering brush strokes in November, 1791.

At his death his body was opened by John HUNTER and his liver was found to weigh nearly 11 pounds (4.8 kilogrammes). A normal, human, adult, male liver would weigh about five pounds (just over two kilogrammes). Despite this (and whatever the cause) he was not an alcoholic and right up to his death he always looked years younger than his age.

There is a full length statue of Reynolds, palette in hand, in the courtyard of Burlington House, Piccadilly. Alfred Drury was the sculptor and it was placed here in 1931. In 1813 FLAXMAN sculpted Reynolds, the piece is now in St Paul's Cathedral.

RICHARDS　　　　　　　　　Glasgow, October 21, 1872
Grant Franklin Thomas　　　　February 24, 1848
Publisher

10, Barton Street, SW1, 1890
46, Buckingham Court, W11, 1848

Richards was the son of a man who described himself as, '...always a student and a scholar'. He apprenticed Grant to a firm of wholesale booksellers in Paternoster Row when the boy was not yet 16; but, he was paid eight shillings (40 pence) a week!

When young Grant was 17 he went to work with W.T. STEAD on the *Review of Reviews.* From here he went on to become a publisher on his own account in 1897 and made a varied collection of authors who were published under his imprint.

Richard's first publication of his own was *Caviare* in 1912, but the work of his which has really stood the test of time is his autobiography, published in 1932, entitled *Memories of a Misspent Youth.*

RICHARDSON　　　　　　　Cheltenham, December 19, 1902
(Sir) Ralph David　　　　　　　October 10, 1983
Actor

1, Chester Terrace, NW1, for many years

Richardson was the third son of the Art Master at Cheltenham Ladies' College and as a boy, thought of being a priest (being fascinated by ritual). He was sent to a Jesuit seminary (the Xavieran College, Brighton) but ran away and became a tea-boy in a Brighton insurance company. He got his first job on the stage – in a disused bacon factory – at the age of 18, by paying a premium for his own 'stage education' with a company run by R.H. Growcott.

He first appeared in London in a revival of *Outward Bound* at the Garrick when he was 21. A year later he married Muriel Hewitt, an actress with Charles Doran's Company. She died in 1942.

Richardson's range was remarkable: Shakespeare, of course, SHAW, Eden Philpotts, Ibsen, Pirandello, SHERIDAN and Graham Greene, all were accomodated in his very individual style.

Up until he was 80 he rode an extremely high powered motor cycle and he was (for some reason, unknown) keen on ferrets!

In 1950 he was awarded the Order of St Olaf of Norway – probably being the only English actor to have been so honoured. He was a widower for two years until 1944, when he married Merriel Forbes, who was 31 years old. She, too, was an actress but their son did not follow them onto the stage.

RICKETTS	Geneva, October 2, 1866
Charles de Souzy	London, October 7, 1931
Artist	

51, Beaufort Street, SW3, 1896-1902
Lansdowne House, Lansdowne Road, W11 (LCP 1979) 1904-1923
Townsend House, Albert Road, NW8, 1931

Partly French, Ricketts spent his early years roaming around Europe with his mother. After her death he came to London and apprenticed himself to a wood engraver when he was 16. It was here he met Charles SHANNON, with whom he was to spend the rest of his life.

In 1896 they founded the 'Vale Press' and produced a number of beautiful books, well illustrated and of very original design. Among the more notable of these was *The Sphinx* by Oscar WILDE. They also published his *House of Pomegranates*.

Ricketts also designed for the theatre and he had a collector's eye for works of art. Shannon and he built up a collection which eventually was valued at £40,000.

RIMBAUD	Charleville, France, October 20, 1854
Arthur Jean Nicholas	Marseilles, November 10, 1891
Poet	

35, Howland Street, W1, 1872

Son of a Belgian Army captain and his shrewish wife, young Rimbaud had a brilliant academic career and had actually had a book published when still only 16. His home life, however, was not happy and he soon 'fell into bad ways'; drinking heavily and keeping immoral company. The worst of the company was probably Paul VERLAINE. Their relationship was almost certainly homosexual, though Verlaine was married and both men denied more than once that their relationship was a physical one.

They came to London in 1872 and in the following year Rimbaud was wounded by Verlaine during a drunken squabble and Verlaine was (at first) imprisoned for attempted murder. In this same year Rimbaud published a prose work, *Une Saison en Enfer*, in which he described the 'Season in Hell' when he was struggling to rid himself of his dissolute ways and his corrupt friends.

RIPON	London, October 24, 1827
(Earl of) George Frederick Robinson	Ripon, July 9, 1909
Statesman	Studley Park, Ripon

9, Chelsea Embankment, SW3 (LCP 1959) 1890-1909

George Robinson succeeded his father as Earl of Ripon *and* his uncle as Earl de Grey. But before this he sat as a member for the Liberals and was appointed Secretary for War in 1863. He was made Secretary for India in 1866 and was Grandmaster of the Freemasons in 1870.

Then, rising to become Viceroy of India in 1880 (having been converted to Catholicism) he was the first Catholic Viceroy. Four years later he was First Lord of the Admiralty; in 1892 Colonial Secretary and Lord Privy Seal in 1905.

Ripon's motto was *Qualis ab inceptus* – the same as from the beginning.

RITCHIE London, June 9, 1837
(Lady) Anne Isabella Isle of Wight, February 26, 1919
Author Hampstead (beside her husband)

(see under THACKERAY for addresses until 1861)

8, Onslow Gardens, SW7, 1867–1873
153, Gloucester Road, SW7, 1877
27, Young Street, W8, 1878–1895
109, St George's Square, SW1, 1901–1912
9, St Leonard's Terrace, SW3, from 1912 until her death.

W.M. THACKERAY always wrote of his elder daughter as 'Anny' and Anny probably inherited his literary genius. Luckily she avoided the mental handicaps suffered by her mother Isabella Shawe. She wrote a number of novels, some of which were popular in her day; the best was probably *The Village on the Cliff*, which appeared in 1867.

In 1877, when she was 40, she married Richmond Ritchie, who was just 23. (It was said that he had proposed marriage to her when he was still at Eton!) Lionel Tennyson was Ritchie's best man and they had a week's honeymoon in Guildford before Ritchie returned to his desk at the India Office. Eventually he did well in the service and became Permanent Under-Secretary of State for India. He was given a knighthood for his work there. They had a daughter, Hester, in 1878 and a son, William Makepeace Denis, in March 1880 (always known as 'Billy').

The Ritchies' marriage was happy but after Lionel Tennyson died in April 1886, Richmond fell in love with his widow, Eleanor. Annie was most understanding but eventually Richmond made his decision to stay with his wife and children. His near-*affaire* was afterwards referred to as 'our perturbations'.

ROBERT STREET, WC2 *Northern, Jubilee, Bakerloo and BR lines to Charing Cross*

This was once part of the Adelphi development. The men responsible were the architectural brothers (*adelphos* Greek for 'brother') Adam. The oldest brother was ROBERT (1728–1792).

1-3, called Adelphi Terrace House, was occupied, at various times by: Thomas HOOD, Joseph PENNELL from 1909 to 1917, John GALSWORTHY from 1917 to 1918 and James BARRIE from 1909 to 1937. Barrie lived in a flat on the top floor, overlooking the river.

ROBERTS Cawnpore, India, September 30, 1832
Frederick Sleigh (1st Earl) France, November 14, 1914
Field Marshall Hornsey Churchyard

47, Portland Place, W1 (LCP 1922) 1902–1906

Roberts was sent back to England for his schooling, first at Clifton, then Eton from where he went on to Sandhurst. He joined the Bengal Artillery in 1851 and was at the siege of Lucknow; and, at the relief of that place, won the Victoria Cross for gallantry. He went from India to Abyssinia and the Afghan War of 1878, after which he was made a Major-General and given the KCB.

In 1880 the Kandahar Garrison was besieged by the forces of Amir Abdul Rahman. Roberts set off with 10,000 men and marched through Afghanistan, routing the enemy around Kandahar. He was made Commander-in-Chief in India in 1892 and given a peerage. Choosing the title of Lord Roberts of Kandahar and Waterford.

A few years later the Boer War was going badly for the British and Roberts was sent out to Africa to take command of a very nearly defeated British Army. He relieved Kimberly and made advances into Pretoria, coming back to England in 1901 to be appointed Commander-in-Chief and given an Earldom.

The motto Roberts chose on his elevation to the peerage was *Virtute et Valore* – By virtue and valour.

On the Downing Street side of Horse Guards Parade there is an equestrian, bronze statue of 'Bobs' by Harry Bates. It was placed there in 1924. There is also a stone bust of him on the pediment over the first floor windows of 69, Knightsbridge, placed there in 1902.

ROBERTSON	London, July 8, 1866
Walford Graham	September 4, 1948
Dramatist and artist	

21, Rutland Gate, SW7, 1889

This elegant, red-headed, Old Etonian, homosexual, young man can be seen in all his glory in the Tate Gallery. His portrait by John Singer SARGENT was painted when Robertson was in his twenties.

Robertson was a skilled artist and a not unsuccessful dramatist. One of his most popular pieces for the stage was called *Pinkie and the Fairies*. This was first performed in 1908 with Ellen TERRY and a *very* young Hermione Gingold in the cast. It was produced by Beerbohm TREE at His Majesty's Theatre, with music by Frederick Norton. It opened on December 19 and was revived on December 16, the following year.

In 1931, Sir Nigel PLAYFAIR produced Robertson's *Fountain of Youth* and in that year a new, struggling firm of publishers, Hamish Hamilton, brought out Robertson's autobiographical book, *Time Was*. It was a great success and went into many editions. Its popularity certainly gave Hamilton's the boost they needed.

Robertson bred grey, bob-tailed sheep dogs, then a very *non*-fashionable breed and in 1908 he kept two of them, 'Bob' and 'Portly'. He also collected (very expertly) works of William BLAKE.

At the very end of his long life, Robertson became almost totally paralysed. The last two sentences of his final instructions were '...no funeral, no mourning, no flowers. By request. If these arrangements are carried out one may perhaps manage to die without making a public nuisance of oneself.'

ROBEY	London, September 9, 1869
(Sir) George	November 29, 1954
Comedian	

334, Kennington Road, SE1, here born
83, Finchley Road, NW8, 1901-1907
70, Finchley Road, NW8, from 1907 for a year
59, Sloane Street, SW1
35, Circus Road, NW1, 1908
10, Victoria Road, W8, 1929

Robey (born George Edward Wade) first drew breath a stone's throw away from the house in which that other great comic, Charlie Chaplin, was born 20 years before. Robey, though, unlike Chaplin, came from a reasonably prosperous background. In fact he did nothing to dispel a rumour that he had had an 'Oxbridge' education.

He went on the stage in 1891, using the name Robey. His stocks-in-trade were: black, very bushy eyebrows, a sort of parsonical coat, a black, collarless shirt beneath it, all surmounted by a reddened bulbous nose. He played in practically every Music Hall in Britain and became a National Landmark.

Once in Mr. Justice Darling's Court, Darling asked from his bench, 'And who, pray, *is* George Robey?' To which F.E. SMITH (later Lord Birkenhead) the barrister, replied immediately, 'Mr. George Robey, M'lud, is The Darling of the Halls' – laughter in court.

ROBINSON
Henry Crabb
Diarist and Lawyer

Bury St Edmunds, May 13, 1775
London, February 5, 1867
Highgate Cemetery, Swain's Lane

30, Russell Square, WC1, 1839-1867

Robinson lived for a while in Germany where he met Goethe and Schiller. Later he became a correspondent for the London *Times* and covered the Peninsular War for that paper.

Two of the Institutions in which he was involved survive; the Athenaeum Club in Waterloo Place and University College in London. After his involvement with the *Times* he was called to the Bar in 1813 and became leader of the Eastern Circuit.

ROBINSON
Mary ('Perdita')
Actress and Royal Mistress

Bristol, November 27, 1758
Englefield, December 26, 1800
Old Windsor Churchyard

13, Hatton Garden, EC1, 1775

Mary was the daughter of an American sea captain called Darby, who had become a native of Bristol. She was only 15 when she married a Mr. Robinson who was 'in pecuniary difficulties' and to make ends meet she decided to go on the stage. She was lucky enough to attract the attention of GARRICK himself and he saw to it that she was given work at Drury Lane. In her third season she played 'Perdita' (the shepherdess daughter of 'Leontes' in Shakespeare's *Winter's Tale*) and this became both her nick-name and, eventually, her pen name.

Robinson seemed as careless with his wife as he was about money and made no objection when she began to have casual love affairs. In 1780 she met the 18-year old Prince of Wales ('Prinny') and they became lovers. Being the mistress of the Prince was a full time occupation and she gave up the stage, only to be thrown over two years later by her Royal friend. He pensioned her off on a £10,000 bond, which was never paid. Not untypically.

She was painted more than once by both REYNOLDS and GAINSBOROUGH. Charles James FOX took a passing interest in her and it was he who probably arranged a pension of £500 a year for her.

Unable to get work in the theatre she turned her attention to literature. She published a volume of poems in 1775, two years later a novel called *Lydia* and then *The Effusion of Love*, which purported to be her correspondence with the Prince.

She also composed a song, *Bounding billow, cease thy motion*, which became a drawing room favourite of the day. (Maybe the title reflected her memories of her corpulent Prince?) She had had a daughter by Robinson, also Mary, who published a three-volume collection of her mother's poetry in 1806.

ROCKINGHAM   1730
Charles Watson Wentworth (2nd   July 1, 1782
Marquis)
Prime Minister

10, Grosvenor Square, W1, where he died

Rockingham was the first politician to be called *Prime Minister,* he succeeded
to his father's Marquisate. He had been made the Earl of Malton, in his own
right, when he was only 20. The following year he was made a Knight of the
Garter but he was opposed to the policies of John, 3rd Earl of Bute, who was
one of the Principal Secretaries of State and, effectively 'Prime Minister'
from May 1762 to April 1763.

When Bute's power declined, Rockingham, as Leader of the Whig
Opposition, was called on to form a Government in 1765. He repealed the
Stamp Act and probably would have put through a number of overdue
reforms had there been less intrigue in Court circles.

ROGERS   Newington Green, London, July 30,
Samuel   1763
Banker   London, December 18, 1855
                                       Hornsey Churchyard

22, St James's Place, SW1, 1808-1855

At 17, Rogers started work in his father's bank and, just before he was 30,
became head of it. In that same year he inherited a small fortune giving him
£3,000 per annum. Ten years later he retired from the Bank on £5,000 a year
and settled into St James's Place to 'cultivate his mind'. He had begun
writing whilst in his 20s, having essays published in *The Gentelman's
Magazine* and he also published a book of poems, *The Pleasure of Memory*, in
1792.

He was quietly philanthropic and gave great help to Tom MOORE and
Thomas CAMPBELL. In 1830 he published (in a deluxe edition costing
£15,000) a magnificent book *Italy,* which contained 114 illustrations by
STOTHARD and J.M.W. TURNER.

Rogers became a small wizened man often wearing a blue coat and a nankeen
waistcoat. He was a natty dresser but sometimes cruelly referred to as 'The
dug-up Dandy', owing to his corpse-like face.

ROGET   London, January 1, 1779
(Doctor) Peter Mark   London, September 12, 1869
'Polymath'   St James's Churchyard, West Malvern,
                                       Worcs.

27, Gower Street, WC1, 1800
3, Great Titchfield Street, W1, 1800
46, Great Russell Street, WC1, 1800
39, Bernard Street, WC1, 1808-1843
18, Upper Bernard Street, WC1, 1843

Roget's most lasting achievement was his compilation of the *Thesaurus*
(from the Greek word for treasury or storehouse). It is probably the most
widely known – and used – reference book in the English language. It is all
the more amazing when one considers that Roget was over 70 when he
began to assemble it!

By training he was a doctor of medecine and was descended from a
Huguenot family. His interests outside medecine and philology were truly
catholic. He was a member of: the Geological Society in 1806, the Royal
Astronomical Society in 1822, a charter member of the Athenaeum Club in
1824, a founding member of the Society for the Diffusion of Useful

Knowledge in 1826, the Zoological Society in 1827, the Royal Geographical Society in 1830, the British Association for the Advancement of Science in 1831, The Royal Entomological Society in 1833 and, most prestigious of all, Secretary to the Royal Society from 1827.

ROLFE London, July 22, 1860
Frederick William ('Baron Corvo') Venice, October 26, 1913
Author Cemetery Island of San Michele

61, Cheapside, EC2, here born

In his 53 years Rolfe managed to be poet, poseur, playwright, possible priest and pederast. His father was a piano maker in London. Rolfe left school when he was fourteen yet became a school teacher and for a while taught at the Stationers' Company School in London.

He became a Roman Catholic when he was 26 and the following year entered Oscott College with a view to becoming a priest; he was expelled from there, as he was a year later from Scots College in Rome. Both expulsions were as a result of his 'unseemly behaviour'. From then on Rolfe seemed to think the world owed him a living. His first published work was *Stories Toto Told Me* in 1898. These were a number of tales retelling stories of Catholic saints ('Toto' of the tales in real life was Toto Maidalchini, the 'passionate, ripe and beautiful' boy who was the gang leader of a crowd of Italian youths whom Rolfe got to know in Italy in the Summer of 1890.) The first *Toto* tales appeared in the *Yellow Book*.

When he was about 30 years old he was described by 21-year old John Holden, the nephew of Rolfe's landlady at Holywell as, '...a little below the average height, with fairly broad shoulders and decidedly bandy legs...He had a smooth high forehead, a rather pointed nose and a somewhat aggressive chin; his hair was of a faded light brown, and he was bald over the temples and the crown...' Holden, according to Rolfe had 'a wondrous beauty', which 'gratified his sensuous palate'. (Rolfe was always in and out of love with practically every boy he met.)

ROLLS August 27, 1877
(Hon) Charles Steward Bournemouth, July 12, 1910
The Rolls of 'Rolls Royce'

14 and 15, Conduit Street, W1 (the house was actually next door to Kent House in Knightsbridge)

Rolls was the third son of the first Baron Llangattock and, after Eton, went up to Trinity College, Cambridge (founded 1546) where he got a 'half blue' for *cycling*. He graduated, with a degree in engineering in 1898. His family was wealthy and he drove in many of the very earliest motor car races, breaking the London to Monte Carlo speed record in 1900. He was a founder of the Royal Automobile Club, whose premises are on the south side of Pall Mall. For Rolls, the family motto, *Celeritas et Veritas* – quickness and truth, was indeed apt.

He met Henry (later Sir Henry) Royce in 1904. Royce had founded an electrical and motor engineering firm in Manchester in 1884 (he was 14 years older than Rolls. He died in 1933). The two men saw eye to eye about quality in engineering and, two years later, despite the very different social backgrounds, they founded the firm of Rolls Royce Ltd.

Two years later, when production of the first 'Silver Ghosts' had begun, they were on sale at £1,000. By 1928, 6,175 Rolls Royces had been sold, of which an incredible number survive. Today Rolls estimate, of all the cars they have built in the last 80 years or so, 60 percent are still *in running order*.

In July 1910 Rolls was flying his own aeroplane at an aviation meeting at Bournemouth when he landed at too high a speed. He tried to pull up, the aircraft overturned and he was killed instantly. So he became the first English man to die in an air crash.

There is a bronze bust of Rolls in the front hall of 65, Buckingham Palace Road, SW1, and also one of Royce. They are copies of the originals, which are at the company's factory in Crewe. They were the work of William MacMillan in 1934 and the copies were made in 1978. There is also a memorial window by Comper in the north nave of Westminster Abbey.

ROMILLY   London, March 1, 1757
(Sir) Samuel   London, November 2, 1818
Law Reformer   Knill, Herefordshire

18, Frith Street, W1, here born
6, Grays Inn Square, WC1 (P) 1778-1791
54, Gower Street, WC1, 1798-1802
21, Russell Square, WC1 (P) from 1804 until he committed suicide here in 1818.

Descended from Huguenot stock, Romilly was admitted as a member of Gray's Inn when he was only 21 and called to the Bar five years later. He was greatly influenced by the philosophical thinking of Jeremy BENTHAM in England and by Mirabeau and Diderot in France. He was actually in France during the closing stages of the French Revolution.

In 1806 he became Solicitor General and did much to lessen many of the savage penalties meted out by the courts at that time. He reduced the number of offences for which the sentence of death was demanded. He also actively supported William WILBERFORCE in his efforts to end the slave trade.

His beloved wife died on October 31, 1818 and he was so depressed he committed suicide three days later.

The Romilly motto was *Persevere*.

ROMNEY   Beckside, Lancs., December 15, 1734
George   Kendal, November 15, 1802
Artist   St Mary's Church, Dalton-in-Furness, Cumbria

32, Cavendish Square, W1, 1777-1799

As a young man Romney worked in his father's cabinet making business, but, by 1755, he began painting seriously. In 1762 he married and came to London to set up as a portrait painter, leaving his wife and two children back at home in the north of England. Sir Joshua REYNOLDS had told him that, 'art and marriage do not mix'.

He made two visits to France and lived in Italy for nearly two years, but details of his life in the period are very hazy. Back in London by 1786, he had a very successful year with portrait painting and earned over £3,500. He became infatuated with Emma HAMILTON, mistress of NELSON and painted her portrait more than 30 times!

ROPES   Lewisham, December 23, 1859
Arthur Reed ('Adrian Ross')   Kensington, September 10, 1933
Lyricist

13, Campden Grove, W8, c.1880s
31, Addison Road, W11, c.1910
68, Old Church Street, SW3, 1933

Ropes' father was a fairly prosperous merchant who traded principally with Russia. His son was able to go up to Cambridge, where he won the Chancellor's medal for English verse.

Ropes ('Ross') composed lyrics and wrote *libretti* for *dozens* of musicals and light operas. His first work, *performed* was in 1884. By January 1891 he was using his pen name for *Joan of Arc*. It ran for a year (in those days a considerable success.)

ROSS   Calcutta, May 6, 1922
Alan
Poet, novelist and editor

2, Walton Street, SW3, 1968
5, Pelham Crescent, SW3, c.1975
30, Thurloe Place, SW7, 1983

After Haileybury (also known as the Imperial Service College) and St John's College, Oxford (founded 1555) Ross went straight into the Navy for the duration of the War. Soon after demobilization he joined the *Observer* newspaper. He also kept writing on more literary planes and, in 1947, his *The Derelict Day* was published.

Today he is the editor of *London Magazine* and a director of the Company which publishes it. He is also a keen cricketer and has played for the Oxford XI and the Royal Navy side.

ROSS   Tours, France, May 25, 1869
Robert Baldwin   London, October 5, 1918
Literary friend of many

11, Upper Phillimore Gardens, W8, 1893-1900
40, Half Moon Street, W1, c.1910-1918

Ross's grandfather was Robert Baldwin (1804-1858) the first Prime Minister of Upper Canada and his father, Robert Ross, Attorney General. Robert died in 1871 and young Robert was brought to England to be educated.

No details remain of Robert between his arrival in England in 1871 and his appearance at King's College, Cambridge in 1888. Apparently he did exert himself enough to row in the College's Second '8', but he got into *hot* water for being openly critical of the method of electing Fellows of the College, then got thrown into *cold* water (River Cam) contracted pneumonia and 'came down' rather hurriedly in 1889.

Before all this had taken place, Robert, at the age of 17,had somehow met Oscar WILDE and some of the *coterie* around Wilde later used to say that Robbie Ross was the first boy that Wilde 'had had'.

Ross remained friends with Wilde and not only organized his funeral in Paris (paid for by 'Bosie' DOUGLAS) but he, with Reggie Turner, had had to clean up the poor hotel room in Paris, where Wilde eventually (and 'explosively') expired.

ROSSETTI   London, December 5, 1830
Christina Georgina   London, December 29, 1894
Poet   Highgate Cemetery, West XIV

110, Hallam Street, W1 (formerly 38, Charlotte Street) here born
12, Bloomsbury Square, WC1
30, Torrington Square, WC1 (LCP 1975) from 1876 until her death

When she was just 20, some of Christina's poems were published in *The Germ* a rather arty magazine founded by the Pre-Raphaelite Brotherhood. She lived very retiringly, looking after her mother who did not die until Christina was 56 in 1886. She had refused two proposals of marriage as she regarded it her duty to care for her mother (who was widowed in 1854).

ROSSETTI London, May 12, 1828
Dante Gabriel Birchington, Sussex, April 9, 1882
Artist and Poet All Saint's Church, Birchington

110, Hallam Street, W1 (formerly 38 Charlotte Street) (LCP 1906) here born
7, Cleveland Street, W1, 1848
72, Newman Street, W1, 1850-1851
38, Arlington Street, W1, 1851
17, Red Lion Square, WC1 (LCP 1911) 1851
16 (then Tudor House) Cheyne Walk, SW3 (LCP 1949) 1862-1882

In April 1824, 41-year old Gabriele Pasquale Giuseppe Rossetti arrived in London. Two and a half years previously he had been the Assistant Curator in the Naples Museum, at a salary of £32.2s 6d – £32.12½p per annum. He was a well known revolutionary figure and an inflammatory poet. He was smuggled aboard a British Naval vessel (part of the British Fleet was lying in the Bay of Naples) and set sail for Malta. Rossetti was on that island for nearly two and a half years, giving Italian lessons. Early in 1824 he travelled on *HMS Rochfort* to London and very soon was appointed Professor of Italian at King's College. On April 8, 1826, Rossetti married Frances Mary Lavinia Polidori. She was just 26 and her mother, who had been a governess was English. Any children of that marriage, therefore, would be three quarters Italian. The newly-weds moved into a decaying house at 38, Charlotte Street (later this address became 110, Hallam Street) and here Dante Gabriel was born.

Both he and his younger brother WILLIAM MICHAEL were sent to Kings College School by which time the family were living at 50, Charlotte Street. Dante began to study painting seriously in 1841 and for four years he went to a Bloomsbury drawing school run by a Mr. Cary (whose father, Henry, 1772-1844, was a well-known translator of Dante). Dante Gabriel was *not* a model student and he fretted under the academic yoke.

But in 1848 his life changed considerably. He, with Holman HUNT and MILLAIS, founded the 'Pre-Raphaelite Brotherhood' together with the painter, Collinson, the sculptor, Woolner and two critics, Stephens and young William Rossetti. It was Rossetti's painting called *The Girlhood of Mary Virgin* painted under Hunt's baleful supervision that was the first finished work to be exhibited publicly carrying the initials, *P.R.B.*

In 1860 Rossetti married his chestnut-haired model, Elizabeth Siddal. She had appeared in many of his paintings but tragically she died only two years later. Grief stricken, Rossetti insisted that some of his unpublished poems be buried in the coffin with her. Seven years later the coffin was exhumed and the poems recovered. Elizabeth's death was to set him on drug-taking which addiction eventually killed him.

ROSSETTI London, September 25, 1829
William Michael London, February 5, 1919
Literary Civil Servant Highgate Cemetery, West XIV

3, St Edmunds Terrace, NW8, 1904-1919

William came between Dante Gabriel and Christina, but did not seem as 'artistic' as either. At the age of 16 he began as a clerk in the Inland Revenue Department. 49 years later he was a Senior Assistant Secretary.

After working hard for a pension William Michael was not idle. In 1865 he translated and transcribed Dante's *Divine Comedy; Hell* into blank verse. In 1878 came his *Lives of Famous Poets* and then a number of works, some of them about his more glamorous siblings. In 1902, Sands published his *Versified Autobiography*.

ROSSI Nottingham, March 8, 1762
John Charles Felix London, February 21, 1839
Sculptor

116, Lisson Grove, NW8, 1808

His father was a native of Siena who practised as a doctor (but without proper qualifications) and sent his son to study in the studios of John Baptist Locatelli in London. When he finished his studies with Locatelli Rossi went to work for Mrs. Eleanor Coade at her 'artificial stone' factory in Lambeth. He entered the Royal Academy Schools in 1781 and in that year won the Silver Medal there. Three years later he won the Gold Medal for his group, entitled *Venus conducting Helen to Paris*. After travelling on the Continent for a year or so he came back to London in 1788 and took over the business of John BACON, being kept extremely busy as a result. Despite the success of earlier years, commissions became hard to come by and, in 1835, he was reduced to auctioning off the works which remained in his Lisson Grove studio.

His straitened means were not made any easier as he had had two wives and eight children by *each* of them.

ROTHENSTEIN Bradford, January 29, 1872
(Sir) William Far Oakridge, Glos., February 14,
Artist 1945

52, Glebe Place, SW3, 1890-1901
18, Sheffield Terrace, W8, 1920s
13, Airlie Gardens, W8, 1929-1935
10, Devonshire Place, W1, 1940s

Rothenstein was the second son of Moritz Rothenstein a Bradford (Yorkshire) wool merchant and began studying at the Slade School in London when he was only 16. The following year he was a student at the Academie Julian in Paris, under Doucet and Jules Lefebvre and in this period he met Jean Louis Forain and Puvis de Chavannes – though the latter was nearly 50 years older than Rothenstein.

He was not yet twenty when he had his first exhibition (at Galérie Thomas in Paris) which he shared with Charles CONDER: the arrangements were made by Henri Toulouse-Lautrec. In Paris he was friendly with Oscar WILDE, Camille and Lucien Pissaro, the de Goncourts and many other literary figures.

His first exhibition in London was at the Dutch Gallery, with SHANNON in 1894 and he contributed to the *Yellow Book*. In June 1899 he married Alice Mary Knewstub (whose father Walter John Knewstub had been a pupil of RUSKIN) and their son John, who was born in 1901, was to be Director and Keeper of the Tate Gallery. William was very much at the centre of things artistically and well liked (WHISTLER used to call him the 'Parson').

ROTHSCHILD Vienna, 1839
Ferdinand London, December 17, 1898
Banker Jewish Cemetery, Buckingham Road,
E15

143, Piccadilly, W1, for some years before his death

Ferdinand was one of the Rothschild's Austrian branch (son of Solomon, 1774-1855, who was made an Austrian baron in 1822). Ferdinand came to England, married his cousin Evalina and became a British citizen. (Evalina was Lionel Rothschild's daughter. Sadly she died in 1865 and Ferdinand never married again.) He endowed the Evalina Hospital in Southwark

Bridge Road in her memory. He also built her a domed tomb in the East End of London. Incorporated in the decoration hundreds of times was the word 'Eva' or just her initials, as a cypher, 'ER'. He was buried beside her 33 years later.

ROTHSCHILD London, November 22, 1808
Lionel de London, June 3, 1879
Banker Willesden Jewish Cemetery

148, Piccadilly, W1, from 1865, until his death

A very active member of the great banking family, Lionel was in charge of the funding operation to raise £20 million to pay the slave owners compensation when Britain finally abolished slavery in 1833. Success attended nearly all Lionel's efforts and in the 43 years he was head of the bank, over £1,000 million was raised by Rothschilds for foreign loans, including a massive one in 1839 for America (changed days!).
Lionel was the first *professing* Jew to become a Member of Parliament, in 1858. (Benjamin DISRAELI, later Lord Beaconsfield, is often referred to as being the first Jew to be in Parliament and the first Jew to be ennobled. True, he was born into the Jewish faith, but when he was 13, he was baptized into the Protestant faith.) He sat for ten years in the Commons but never got on his feet once. When GLADSTONE suggested that Rothschild be created a Lord, Queen Victoria thought differently. Imperiously (if a little ungrammatically) she wrote to GLADSTONE, '*To make a Jew* a peer is a step she *could not consent to*'. Lionel's son, Nathaniel Mayer Rothschild – already a Baron of the Austrian Empire and an English baronet (the latter inherited from his Uncle Anthony in 1876) was made a Baron (UK) in 1885. (Time must have softened the attitudes of HM.)

ROTHSCHILD Frankfurt-am-Main, September 16,
Nathan Mayer 1777
Banker Paris, July 28, 1836
  Brady Street Cemetery, Whitechapel

New Court, St Swithin's Lane, EC4, 1810
107, Piccadilly, W1, 1829-1836

Nathan was the first 'English' Rothschild even though he never bothered to learn the language properly. In appearance he was almost clown-like, having an enormous belly, bulging blue eyes, red hair and great blubbery lips. In contrast his wife, Hannah, was very good-looking. She bore him four sons and three daughters and was the only person in the world he trusted implicitly.
As there were so many Rothschilds, stories about them are often wrongly attributed, but let us say it was Nathan Mayer who was questioning a visitor about a recent visit to Tahiti. What had struck this chap was that in Tahiti there was '...a total absence of Jews and pigs'. So Rothschild said, 'My dear fellow, let us *both* go there at once. We'll make our fortunes!'

ROUSSEAU Geneva, June 28, 1712
Jean Jacques Ermonville, Paris, July 2, 1778
Philosopher

15, Buckingham Street, WC2, 1766

Rousseau's mother died not long after his birth and Papa seems to have spent most of *his* time either mending watches or 'dancing'. Jean Jacques was apprenticed to an engraver but, in his time, he was to become a 'lackey', a musician, a clerk, a seminary student, a private tutor and a music copyist. In addition he changed his religion a few times, sometimes just for money. Somehow, at the age of 38, he won a prize at Dijon for the best dissertation on, *Whether the progress of the Sciences and of Letters has tended to corrupt or elevate Morals.* (His *own* morals allowed him to father five illegitimate children by Thérèse Le Vasseur, all of whom were packed off to orphanages.)

The success that followed his Dijon prize was very real and literary triumph followed triumph until, eventually, his *Emile ou de L'éducation* led to exile from France and he wandered England or Switzerland until he was allowed back into France, *providing* he published nothing more. A Mme. D'Epinay wrote that 'It is said that he' [Rousseau] 'is in ill health, but that he carefully conceals his sufferings from some motive of vanity; it is apparently this which, from time to time, makes him shy.'

In his last two or three years he developed a persecution mania and finally died of 'apoplexy'. There was even talk of Rousseau being a suicide.

ROWLANDSON London, 1756
Thomas London, April 22, 1827
Artist

16, John Adam Street, WC2 (LCP 1950) in 1800
1, James Street, Adelphi, WC2, where he died

Rowlandson was lucky enough to be sent to Paris when he was not yet 16 to study drawing and painting. (He also studied other practices in Paris where his teachers were probably more expert than their London counterparts.) An aunt left him £7,000 and he spent practically all of it on the gaming tables. He came back to London and took up his studies at the Royal Academy Schools in 1775.

He roamed around England, enjoying the taverns en route, often in company with the likes of George Morland (1763-1804) James Gillray (1757-1815) or Henry Bunbury (1750-1811).

When Rowlandson exerted himself he was one of the most talented of English draughtsmen. When hurried his work often lacked finesse and was crude. His political lampoons were acid (Napoleon being a constant butt of his) and this biting aspect of his work was in great contrast with his sketches of country life. He travelled the rural areas of France, Germany and the Low Countries extensively.

For the last two years of his life he was a complete invalid in his James Street lodgings.

ROY Carluke, Scotland, May 4, 1726
William London, July 1, 1790
Surveyor

10, Argyll Street, W1 (LCP 1979) from 1779 until he died here

At 21, Roy was surveying his native Scotland and was commissioned into the Army in 1755. Twelve years later he was elected to the Royal Society and by the time he retired he was a Major-General. He laid the foundations for the Ordnance Survey which was established in 1791, a year after he died. This unique organization has mapped the whole of the British Isles with great accuracy and clarity. It fulfills a number of needs and is unparalleled in any other country in the world.

In 1764 Roy studied the Roman remains in Scotland and the Society of Antiquaries published his investigations in 1793 under the title of *Military Antiquities of the Romans in Britain.*

RUSH Philadelphia, August 29, 1780
Richard Philadelphia, July 30, 1859
Statesman

20, Baker Street, W1, 1817-1825

Richard, son of the noted physician, Benjamin Rush (one of the signatories to the Declaration of Independence: 1745-1813) was appointed Attorney General of the United States when he was only 34. In 1837 he came to London as American Minister to Britain. He negotiated the Fisheries Treaty of 1818 (much good *that* did) and went on to Paris, as American Minister there from 1847 to 1851.
In 1836-1838, Rush was Commissioner to receive the *Smithsonian Legacy*. James Lewis Macie Smithson, an English scientist, born in France about 1765, an illegitimate son of the First Duke of Northumberland who, as Sir Hugh Smithson, assumed the family name of Percy in 1750 and was created Duke of Northumberland in 1766 and died 20 years later. Smithson became a chemist and a mineralogist and a Member of the Royal Society. He died at Genoa on June 27, 1829. In his will, he left £105,000 to found, '...at Washington an establishment, under the name of the Smithsonian Institution for the increase and diffusion of knowledge among men'.

RUSKIN London, February 8, 1819
John Brantwood, Coniston, January 20,
Art Critic 1900
  Coniston Churchyard, Cumbria

31, Park Street, W1, 1848
6, Charles Street, W1, 1848

Ruskin was the son of a prosperous wine merchant and, until the age of 18, was educated 'privately'. He then went up to Christ Church College, Oxford. Here he discovered that he was most unsophisticated and found it hard to fraternize with his fellow undergraduates. This inability to get on easily with his fellow men (and women – one in particular) lasted the rest of his life.
Ruskin married Euphemia Gray in 1848 but the marriage was doomed (and unconsummated) from the very beginning. 'Effie' married, happily, John MILLAIS after her union with Ruskin was annulled.
It was in the year of the marriage that Mary Russell MITFORD, then 61, met the 29-year old Ruskin and she wrote of their meeting to her friend, Charles Boner that Ruskin, '...the Oxford Graduate, is a very elegant and distinguished looking young man, tall, fair and slender – *too* slender, for there is a consumptive look and, I fear, a consumptive tendency – the only cause of grief that he has ever been to his parents. He must be, I suppose, twenty-six or twenty-seven, but he looks much younger and has a gentle playfulness – a sort of pretty waywardness, that is quite charming.'
Ruskin's next brush with artists came when he took up with the Pre-Raphaelite Brotherhood (ROSSETTI, HOLMAN HUNT, MILLAIS et al) and at this time began on his greatest work, *the Seven Lamps of Architecture*. This and the later *Stones of Venice*, which began to be published in 1851, are certainly his finest memorials.
In 1858, when he was 39, Ruskin met nine-year old Rose La Touche who came to him for drawing lessons. The child stirred something in Ruskin and his adoration of the child changed with the years to love for the woman. When she was 18 he proposed marriage, she asked him to wait for three years, when she would be legally adult. Ruskin counted the days. In 1870 she rejected him, 'Effie' having written to Rose counselling her not to marry the ageing Ruskin. In 1875 Rose died; the grief-stricken Ruskin found a lost love letter from Rose and he carried the note – protected between gold leaves – until he died.

RUSSELL   Trelleck, Wales, May 18, 1872
Bertrand Arthur William (3rd Earl)   Merioneth, February 2, 1970
Philosopher   (his ashes scattered)

14, Cheyne Walk, SW3, early 1900s
34, Russell Chambers, Bury Street, SW1, 1911
57, Gordon Square, WC1, 1918-1919

Considered to be one of the greatest British philosophers and mathematicians ever, Russell was educated privately and then went up to Trinity College, Cambridge, from there graduating with First Class Honours in Mathematics. In the following year he graduated in the Moral Sciences. He spent a few months as an *attaché* at the British Embassy in Paris and then went on to Berlin. In 1896 he published his first book, entitled *German Social Democracy*. In the same year he married Alys Pearsall-Smtih, from an American family who, as well as being Quakers, had made a lot of money making glass bottles. In his autobiography, published *seventy-one years later* Russell wrote of Alys that, 'She had been brought up as American women always were in those days, to think that sex was beastly, that all women hated it and that men's brutal lusts were the chief obstacle to happiness in marriage.'

In 1902 his brilliant *Principles of Mathematics* was published and then, with Alfred WHITEHEAD, he published the even more brilliant *Principia mathematica* in 1910, which put Russell in the forefront of living philosophers.

He became a Professor in Peking, was divorced by Alys (who did not die until 1951) and married Dora Black in 1921. Dora was a Fellow of Girton College, Cambridge and she and Russell ran a 'progressive' school near Petersfield for a while. In 1935 they were divorced; perhaps all the more interesting because in 1932, he published a book called *Marriage and Morals*. (A cynic might be tempted to say that Russell had many of the former but practically none of the latter.)

Married or not, Russell usually had the inclination (and made the time) to dally with other – usually married – women. He and Ottoline MORRELL, for instance, had a long drawn out *affaire*. (She complained that he always had bad breath!)

Russell wife number three was Patricia Helen Spence. She had been in the Russell household anyway since 1930, as governess to the children. He married her in 1936. The marriage might have appeared a little confusing as Patricia was always called *Peter*. Despite that, Peter produced a son for Russell, but the marriage was dissolved in 1952.

Ever game, Russell married the American novelist, Edith Finch, daughter of Edward Bronson Finch of New York, in the same year.

In 1931 Russell succeeded to his elder brother (who died without sons) as Earl Russell. So he was one of that rare breed: an intellectual aristocrat. He had been elected to the Royal Society in 1908, was awarded the Order of Merit in 1949 and won the Nobel Prize for Literature in 1950. All his life he had been a 'Pacificist' – and suffered because of his beliefs; but, in 1945 he actually advocated the use of atomic weapons.

There is a bronze of Russell in Red Lion Square. It is by Marcelle Quinton and was placed here in 1980.

RUSSELL   London, August 18, 1792
John (1st Earl)   Richmond, May 28, 1878
Prime Minister

17, Hertford Street, W1, here born
66, South Audley Street, W1, 1823-1826
30, Wilton Crescent, SW1, 1835-1841
36, Chesham Place, SW1 (LCP 1911) 1851-1870

Russell was the third son of the 6th Duke of Bedford and so, unlikely to succeed to the Dukedom. He studied in Edinburgh and, after that, was returned as MP for Tavistock (in Devon). He was in favour of Reform and it was this policy that won the Liberals many votes (and seats) in 1830, when the Duke of WELLINGTON was defeated in the polls. In the 1841 election, Lord John became MP for the City of London.

When PEEL failed in 1845, Russell was asked to form a Government. This he could not do and PEEL was re-instated. However, in 1846, Russell did become Prime Minister and occupied the post until 1852. In the Coalition Government which followed, Russell was Foreign Secretary. He made a number of tactical mistakes over the prosecution of the Crimean War and he resigned in January 1855.

In the Government formed by Palmerston in 1859, he was made Foreign Secretary (again) and created Earl Russell in 1862. When Palmerston died in 1865, Russell became Prime Minister again, but only lasted two months, being defeated in June on his Reform Bill.

RUSSELL SQUARE, WC1   *Piccadilly line to Russell Square*

The Square is on land which belonged to the Russells (family name of the Dukes of Bedford). It began to be built in 1800 and is probably the largest *true* square in London. The gardens themselves were laid out by Humphrey Repton (1752-1818) the market gardener from Bury St Edmunds.

5,   Frederick MAURICE, 1856-1860. He was Principal of the Working Men's College, which he had helped found in 1854.

8,   the PANKHURST family from 1888 to 1893, when the lease expired. The house was decorated in 'brilliant' hues. The coach house which went with it was 'full of mystery'. Henry, Emmeline's fifth child, was born here in July 1889. He died of infantile paralysis (as polio was then called) in January 1910. He had been taken ill not long after his 21st birthday: Emmeline was in America and rushed home, but only to see him die.

13,   Sir George WILLIAMS at the time of his death in 1905.

21,   Sir Samuel ROMILLY (LCP 1919) from 1804 until he committed suicide here a few days after the death of his wife in 1818.

30,   Henry Crabb ROBINSON, from 1839 until the time of his death in 1867.

37,   Sir Edward CLARKE, 1894-1900. The house was originally built in 1801 for Sir James Park (a Scottish judge, 1763-1838). When Clarke took it over it had six reception rooms – the drawing room and the principal bedroom above it, being 30 feet (9.1 metres) long. Together with the stables, Clarke paid £1,700 for a 17-year lease and there was a ground rent on the lease of £50 per annum.

56,   Mary Russell MITFORD, 1835. By this time she had finished the fifth and last volume of *Our Village*. WORDSWORTH visited her here. In 1836 she gave a dinner party, after which she wrote: 'Mr. Wordsworth, Mr. LANDOR and Mr. White dined here. I like Mr. Wordsworth, of all things, Mr. Landor is very striking-looking and exceedingly clever. Also we had a Mr. BROWNING, a young poet...'

61,   Mrs. Humphrey WARD, 1881-1900. This was their first house in

London after Humphrey (having been a Fellow of Brasenose College, Oxford) came to work for the *Times*.

62, William COWPER, c.1750-1754. He lived here when he was a law student.

63, Ralph Waldo EMERSON lodged here in July 1833. His landlady Mrs. Fowler had been recommended to him by a friend of his in Paris.

65, Sir Thomas LAWRENCE, lived and died here in January 1830 of 'ossification of the heart'.

71, Richard D'Oyly CARTE (pre-1888). By this time his support of GILBERT and SULLIVAN had made him a wealthy man.

On the south side of the garden in the square is a statue of Francis, 5th Duke of Bedford – 1765-1802. The sculptor, Sir Richard Westmacott, has the Duke sharing the pedestal with a sheep as the Duke was a member of the first Agricultural Board. The statue was erected in 1809. In October 1941 someone painted the word 'TRAITOR!' on the statue. This was not only a waste of valuable paint but a pointless gesture. The 12th Duke had refused to allow iron railings outside his house in Lowndes Square to be cut down and make scrap metal to provide the raw material for weapons that Britain needed so desperately in those dark days.

RUSSELL STREET, WC1   *Piccadilly line to Covent Garden*

Once Bedford property and so their family name of Russell appears again. In the late 1790s, '...the ground behind the north west end of Russell Street was occupied by a farm...' [lived in] '...by two old maiden sisters of the name of Capper. One rode an old grey mare...the other sister's business was to seize the clothes of the lads who trespassed on their property to bathe.'

20, Charles LAMB lodged here with his sister Mary. In 1817, Lamb wrote to Dorothy Wordsworth that, 'Bow Street, where the thieves are examined' [is] 'within a few yards of us'. The Lambs lived here until 1823. Charles no longer invited visitors as regularly as he used to do, but when he did so, his invitations were very specific. One to Ayrton read, 'cards and cold Mutton in Russell Street on Friday at 8 and 9. Gin and jokes from past that time to 12. Pass this on to Mr. Payne, apprize Martin' [Burney] 'thereof'.

94, Mary SOMERVILLE (née Fairfax) came to live here in 1805 with her husband (and cousin) Samuel Greig. He died in 1807 leaving her alone with their infant son. She moved out in 1808 and did not come back to London until after her second marriage. The house she actually lived in, has been demolished.

RUTLAND GATE SW7   *Piccadilly line to Knightsbridge*

Here stood the 18th century red brick house of the Dukes of Rutland. Rutland was, for centuries, England's smallest county, now extinguished at the stroke of a bureaucratic pen. The family sold the property in 1833 and it was soon demolished, the site being redeveloped between 1838 and 1840 (the 3rd Duke of Rutland had died in the house in 1779, the last of the family to do so).

21, W. Graham ROBERTSON, after 1884. It was not long after his residence here that he got to know Oscar WILDE.

39, Sir Edward (later Lord CARSON, 1899. He was appointed Solicitor General not long after moving here.

42, Sir Francis GALTON (LCP 1972). He had lived here since 1861 and he died six months after leaving the house in 1911.

SABATINI
Rafael
Author

Jesi, Italy, April 29, 1875
February 13, 1950

22, Pont Street, SW3, 1920s-early 1930s

Sabatini was educated at Zoug in Switzerland and in Oporto. History was his best subject as a student and to this original interest Sabatini added a fluent and imaginative pen: his first historical novel, *The Tavern Knight*, was published in 1904.

He married Ruth Dixon in the following year and they settled in Herefordshire. In the 1914-1918 war, he worked for British Intelligence. (The Italians were Britain's Allies in that war.)

In the 1920s and 1930s came a succession of swashbuckling adventure stories, always with a well-researched historical background, the two best known being *Scaramouche* in 1921 and *Captain Blood* the following year. A previous novel *The Sea Hawk* (1915) was made into a very successful film a few years later.

SAINT ALBANS
Charles Frederick Aubrey de Vere
Beauclerk
13th Duke

August 16, 1915

57, Oakley Street, SW3
30, Cheyne Walk, SW3, 1975

Not content with being a 13th Duke (and having Royal blood, albeit diluted, in his veins) St Albans is also Earl of Burford and Baron of Heddington, Baron Vere, Hereditary Grand Falconer of England *and* Hereditary Registrar of the Court of Chancery.

The first Duke was the son of King Charles II and Nell GWYNN. Nell was probably one of the least demanding of all the King's mistresses (and possibly the nicest one as well). However, she did demand some sort of recognition of the King for their son. So, in 1686, he made the boy Baron of Heddington and he was then also the Captain of the Band of Gentlemen Pensioners! After Charles died the St Albans never got back into Royal Circles again. The nearest to it was probably when the 3rd Duke carried the Queen's crown at the Coronation of King George II in 1727.

The motto of St Albans is *Auspicium Melioris Aevi* – A pledge of better times.

ST GEORGE'S SQUARE, SW1
Victoria line to Pimlico

Laid out in 1839 as two parallel streets, it developed into a proper square by 1843. Until 1874 it had its own pier for steamers sited where Pimlico Gardens now lie. It was the only residential square open to the river in London. The parish in which this square lay began in Hanover Square and, like the Church of St George's there, this square was given its name as an oblique compliment to the four Hanoverian Georges, who had occupied the British throne for 126 years between them. The stone statue by John Gibson, 1790-1866, was finally placed here in 1915. It depicts William HUSKISSON, MP rather selfconsciously wearing a toga. Sir Osbert SITWELL described the piece as 'Boredom rising from a bath'.

26, 'Bram' STOKER died here of tertiary syphilis in April 1912.

56, Stephen POTTER, 1924. He lived here and taught at a 'crammer' housed in No. 68. Frank and Mary MacNalty owned both the houses and the school.

109, Lady Anne RITCHIE, 1901-1912.

ST GEORGE STREET, W1 *Central line to Bond Street*

Begun in 1713, but not finished until 1724, by which time the first of the four Georges had been on the throne for a decade. This street was named as a delicate compliment to a rather indelicate King.

7, David MALLET died here in 1765, having lived here for seven years.

9, Richard Brinsley SHERIDAN, with his son Thomas, lived here between 1803-1805.

12B, Arnold BENNETT, 1919-1921. Here he wrote part of *Riceyman Steps*.

12B, Sir Thomas BEECHAM, at the time of his death in 1961.

44, Lady Mary Wortley MONTAGU died here in 1726.

80, Cyril CONNOLLY, 1926-1927. Connolly was just down from Oxford and some of his more *precious* attitudes had been dropped.

ST JAMES'S, SW1

When Henry VIII set about developing this area to build his palace he had to move an ancient leper hospital which had been here for over 500 years. The hospital was endowed for, '...14 sisters, maidens that were leprous, living chastely and honestly in divine service'. Henry gave all the chaste maidens a pension (a sort of Tudor 'golden handshake') to go and live somewhere else. The only thing he retained was the name – Saint James, the patron saint of lepers.

ST JAMES'S PLACE, SW1 *Victoria line to Green Park*

Built up about 1694

4, Frederic CHOPIN (LCP 1981). In 1848 Chopin left this house to go to the Guildhall to give his last public performance.

21, 'Chips' CHANNON. On October 9, 1935, his wife, lady Honor, gave birth to their son Paul in this house.

28, William HUSKISSON, MP (LCP 1962) 1804-1806. In 1830 he became the first Englishman to die in a railway accident, referred to by the Duke of WELLINGTON, who loathed Huskisson, as a '...real Act of God'.

29, Lord Randolph CHURCHILL, 1878. His next door neighbour was Sir Stafford NORTHCOTE, who was Churchill's nominal leader in the House of Commons.

37/38, Sir Edward ELGAR, 1929, in the closing stages of his life.

ST JAMES'S SQUARE, SW1

The Square was laid out soon after 1660 by Henry Jermyn, 1st Earl of St Albans. The statue in the middle of the Square is of King William III. It was originally designed by John BACON but had to be finished by his son and was not finally put here until 1804, 102 years after the King's death. It's pedestal had stood waiting for its Royal burden since 1732. Bacon even included the molehill, which had caused the King's horse to stumble, throwing William off, causing physical complications which were to kill the King a few days later in 1702. The Catholic supporters of the Royal House of Stuart were delighted and used to offer a toast to 'the little gentleman in black velvet', who, unwittingly was the cause of the death of their despised

Protestant enemy. Apart from all that Bacon did not even give the King a pair of stirrups, so no wonder he was thrown off!

4, Lord ASTOR, 1912-1942, when he sold the house on condition that the building should become the headquarters of the Arts Council.

10, William PITT (the 'Elder') Lord Chatham (LCP 1910) 1759-1762. The Heathcote family owned the house from 1736 until 1890, but Pitt paid the local taxes (the 'rates') during his occupancy. Pitt's wife found the house cramped because her husband used to hold Cabinet meetings in it! 'There is to be a meeting of the Cabinet here this evening, which always engrosses *my* Apartment.' She wrote to one of her friends.

10, Earl of DERBY, 1837-1855. He only inherited his father's title in 1851 and so, for the first 14 years of his occupancy here, he was known as Lord Edward Stanley. He was to become Prime Minister three times.

10, W.E. GLADSTONE, 1890. He only occupied the house during the Parliamentary Session. That he occupied it at all, must make it the most 'Prime Ministered' house in London (10, Downing Street excepted). Gladstone was Prime Minister four times; DERBY three and PITT once: so this one building has housed eight Prime Ministers!

11, Lord Blessington bought this house in 1818 and moved into it with his new bride MARGUERITE. After Blessington's death she sold it to Windham's Club.

18, Lord CASTLEREAGH, 1815-1822. Not a popular man with the mobs, very often his windows were smashed by politically motivated 'yobboes'.

22, Flat 3, Sir Edward Hulton in 1975.

32, Sir Robert WALPOLE, 1732-1735. In January 1734, extremely high winds blew down the kitchen premises of WALPOLE's house.

ST JAMES'S STREET, SW1

8, Lord BYRON, was living here, when, on March 10, 1812, the first two cantos of *Childe Harold's Pilgrimage* were published and, as Byron later wrote, he, '...awoke one mornig and found myself famous.' (He was to awake many a morning later and find himself *infamous*.) The property is now called 'Byron House'.

76, Edward GIBBON, lived here over a bookshop in 1793 and died here in 1795.

88, W.M. THACKERAY, 1845-1846. Here he wrote *Barry Lyndon*.

ST LEONARD'S TERRACE, SW3 *District and Circle lines to Sloane Square*

This attractive row of houses was built in the 1820s by John Tombs, whose native village was Upton St Leonards, about nine miles from Cheltenham. He also gave Cheltenham Terrace, which is just around the corner, its name. Tombs, however, chose to live in Smith Square, Westminster.

9, Lady Ann RITCHIE. She moved here after her husband's death in 1912. Her son, Billy, lived nearby. Early in 1918 a German bomb fell on Chelsea College (killing a Major Ludlow and his family) and shattered the windows in number 9.

ST MARTIN'S LANE, WC2 *Piccadilly and Northern lines to Leicester Square*

The lane takes its name from the Church of St Martin-in-the-Fields at its southern end. The site of the Church is actually one of the oldest consecrated Church plots in London and dates back to the 13th century *at least*. It was first officially mentioned in 1222. It was rebuilt in 1544 and completely re-created by James Gibbs between 1722 and 1726. The steeple, however, was only finished in 1842.

100, Henry FUSELI, 1779-1785. He had not long been back in London, after studying art in Italy.

104, Sir James THORNHILL, 1710 and, after him, Francis Hayman (1708-1776) an artist who was principally a book illustrator. Some critics considered Hayman *on a par* with HOGARTH (Thornhill's son-in-law).

SALA	London, November 24, 1828
George Augustus Henry	Brighton, December 8, 1895
Journalist	

46, Mecklenburgh Square, WC1, c.1890

Born in London of Italian parents, Sala was, in part, educated in Paris, where one of his contemporaries was Alexander Dumas, the 'Younger' (1824-1895). He started to earn a living in London as a book illustrator but, by 1851, he was absorbed in journalism and literature. He was appointed by the *Daily Telegraph* to 'cover' the American Civil War and, eight years later, he was in Italy with Garibaldi, who was 21 years older than he.

He developed a particularly flamboyant manner and became 'one of the Sights of Fleet Street'. He habitually sported a frock coat and an immaculately starched, white waistcoat. The overall effect may have been marred by his *gargoylesque nose* which resulted, supposedly, from Sala having been 'coshed' in the Haymarket.

Charles DICKENS printed some of Sala's work in *Household Words* in 1851 and then sent him off to Russia. (To extend the 'Dickens Connection'; CRUIKSHANK illustrated a number of DICKENS' books and Sala was a pall bearer at Cruikshank's funeral in February 1878.)

By 1892 Sala was at the peak of his fame and he established a paper unwisely called *Sala's Journal*. It failed disastrously and only a few months before his death he was obliged to sell some 13,000 books from his own library. Lord Roseberry arranged a Civil List Pension of £100 per annum for him, but the now impoverished Sala did not live long enough to draw a penny of it.

SALISBURY	Hatfield House, Herts., February 3,
Robert Gascoyne-Cecil	1830
(3rd Marquess)	August 22, 1903
Prime Minister	

21, Fitzroy Square, W1 (LCP 1965) 1858-1862
20, Arlington Street, W1, 1878-1903

After Eton, Salisbury went on to Christ Church, Oxford. He was elected a Fellow of All Souls and then entered Parliament as member for Stamford as Viscount Cranbourne. He was the second son of James Brownlow, the 2nd Marquess, but his elder brother died and so Robert Arthur became the 3rd Marquess in 1868 and was obliged to move up into the House of Lords. By this time he had already been Secretary of State for India and, in the year of his succession, he was elected Chancellor of Oxford University.

DISRAELI and he went to the Berlin Congress of 1878 and, when Disraeli died three years later, Salisbury became leader of the Conservative Party. Four years later he was Prime Minister and also Secretary of State for Foreign Affairs. Backed by the Liberal Unionists he again became Prime Minister in 1886.

Outside politics, he was Chairman of the Great Eastern Railway; owned some 20,000 acres of good land and had four country houses.

The Salisbury motto is: *Sero sed Serio* – Late but with consideration.

There is a very poor little bust of Salisbury on a pediment over a first floor window at 87, Knightsbridge – put up there in 1902 to celebrate the Coronation of King Edward VII during Salisbury's Premiership.

SANDS   Newport, R.I., July 6, 1873
Ethel   London, March 3, 1962
Artistic patron

40, Portland Place, W1, 1888–1897
15, The Vale, SW3, 1913–1937
51, Chelsea Square, SW3, 1937
18, Chelsea Square, SW3, 1944

Ethel Sands was the daughter of wealthy American parents who first brought her to London when she was only three years old. She returned, 'under her own steam', liked what she saw and stayed. She came to know many artists and musicians working in England, who she encouraged, often giving hospitality to them.
She was in Paris in 1914 and met another American girl, Nan Hudson. They lived together, the very best of friends, from then until Miss Hudson's death in 1957.

SARGENT   Florence, Italy, January 12, 1856
John Singer   London, April 15, 1925
Artist   St Paul's Cathedral

31, Tite Street, SW3 (P) from 1901 until he died here

Sargent was a doctor's son who studied art in Italy, the country of his birth and later in Paris.
As an established artist, specialising in portraiture, he maintained studios in Boston, Mass. and Florence, but painted principally in London where he became the most fashionable portrait painter of the day. He was elected to the Royal Academy in 1897, then the highest honour England could bestow on an artist.
Sargent never married and is said to have refused a knighthood. In July 1925, three months after his death, the contents of his London studio were sold in a sale which lasted two days and fetched £175,260.

SAVILE ROW, W1   *Piccadilly and Bakerloo lines to Piccadilly Circus*

This property lay on land owned by the Earls of Burlington and the 3rd Earl married a Dorothy Savile. Burlington Arcade was built by a grandson of the 3rd Earl in 1819, to prevent people throwing rubbish into his garden (or so he said). The Row, originally Savile Street, began to be built up in about 1773.

11,   Richard BRIGHT (LCP 1979) 1830–1858. When Bright moved here, the house only had three storeys, as it was built in 1734. A top storey was built on during his occupation.
12,   George GROTE (LCP 1905) from 1848 until he died here in 1871.
14,   Richard Brinsley SHERIDAN. Sheridan was lent this house by the Duke of WELLINGTON and he lived in it for some years. In October 1815, Sheridan had been out to dinner and (as was, too often, his wont) had had too much to drink. Despite the poet's intake, BYRON took 'poor, dear Sherry home'. 'We deposited him safe…where his man, evidently used to the business waited to receive him in the hall'. Poor dear Sherry, wracked by financial worries (and varicose veins) died here in 1816.
17,   George BASEVI (LCP 1949) from 1829 until 1845, when he died as a result of a fall in Ely Cathedral.

SAYERS Oxford, June 13, 1893
Dorothy Leigh Witham, Essex, December 17, 1957
Author and Playwright Cremated, ashes below the tower of St
Anne's Church, Soho W1 (P)

44, Mecklenburgh Square, WC1, 1920
24, Great James Street, WC1, 1920-1957

She was the only child of the Reverend Henry Sayers, who was Headmaster of Christ Church College Choir School, Oxford when Dorothy was born. She was a solitary child in every sense, not going to school until much later than was usual for girls of her background.

In 1911 she had measles complicated by pneumonia and her hair dropped out. For a while she wore a wig but her hair was thin and was always a problem to her for the rest of her life. Five years later she went to work in Basil Blackwell's bookshop in Oxford, at a salary of £2 a week, but was discreetly given the sack and went to work in a boys' private school, 60 miles from Paris. By 1920 she was back in London and on the bread line. She invented the character of Lord Peter Wimsey and he first appeared as the aristocratic, amateur detective in *Whose Body?* in 1923. The book was a success and, between then and 1937, eleven more detective novels were to be published and the name of Dorothy Sayers has passed into the pantheon of 'who-dunnit' writers with the likes of Agatha Christie and Ngaio Marsh.

In no way a pretty woman – in fact in later life she became enormously fat – she was highly sexed and though some people thought she might have had Lesbian tendencies (sometimes she dressed very mannishly) she not only had affairs of the heart before her marriage to Oswald Fleming in 1926, but gave birth to an illegitimate son, Anthony, on January 3, 1924. The name of the father was never made public.

For a while Dorothy worked with S.H. Benson, advertising agents, the firm providing the background for her book *Murder Must Advertise* (1933) and she was involved in one of Guinesses most successful advertising campaigns in the 1930s. She helped devise the 'Zoo' series of advertisements and wrote the immortal quatrain:

> 'If he can say as you can
> Guiness is good for you
> How grand to be a Toucan
> Just think what Toucan do.'

(The Toucan theme was resurrected by Guiness in 1981.)

SCHREINER Basutoland, March 24, 1854
Olive Emilie Albertina South Africa, December 12, 1920
Novelist and feminist

116, Guildford Street, WC1, 1882
32, Fitzroy Street, W1, 1884
9, Blandford Square, W1, 1885-1886
16, Portsea Place, W2 (LCP 1959) 1886
9, Porchester Place, W2, 1917-1920

Olive's father was a missionary, of German descent, who had been in South Africa for many years. At the age of fifteen she became a governess to a Boer family who lived on the edge of the Karoo Desert. In 1883 her first book, *The Story of an African Farm*, was published under the pseudonym of 'Ralph Iron'. It was well received and, in 1882, she came to London, soon to be involved in the literary swim.

She held very advanced views on Women's Rights and most feminist issues of the day. Her libertarian principles allowed her to take lovers and one of her *affaires* a long and extraordinary one, was with Havelock Ellis. Her principles also allowed her to get married and this she did in 1894.

SCOTT
(Sir) George Gilbert
Architect

Gawcott, Bucks., July 13, 1811
London, March 27, 1878
Westminster Abbey (centre nave)

39, Courtfield Gardens, SW7, where he died

Scott was the architectural 'father' of the *Gothic Revival* in England. To such an extent that almost every public building, church or not, called for Scott as its architect. London can demonstrate two typical 'Scott's'; one is the Albert Memorial (facing the Albert Hall) the other, St Pancras Station (facing extinction). The story about St Pancras is that Scott was commissioned to produce a new Foreign Office (buildings still standing on Whitehall, one entrance is in Downing Street, facing the front door of Number 10). He submitted a St Pancras type layout and PALMERSTON vetoed it. He wanted the building to have an Italian 'palazzo' look. His wish was granted – well, an English 'translation'.

Scott was knighted in 1872, just when he was about to give up any hope of official recognition. His son, Giles (1880-1960) also an architect, left his mark on the land as he designed the Anglican Cathedral in Liverpool. More to the point, for a visitor to London; he also restored the House of Commons, which had been blown out of existence by German bombs. Like father, he too was knighted (in 1924) and in 1944 was elected to the Order of Merit.

SCOTT
Robert Falcon
Explorer

Devonport, Devon, June 6, 1868
Antarctica, c. March 29, 1912
79°,40 south, 11 miles from 'One Ton'
Depot

56, Oakley Street, SW3 (LCP 1935) 1905-1908
174, Buckingham Palace Road, SW1

Scott joined the *HMS Britannia* when he was twelve and two years later was a midshipman on the *Boadicea*. By 1897 he was first lieutenant and in two years was recommended to be the leader of the National Antarctic Expedition. He was posted as a Commander to the ship *Discovery*. Returning in 1904 he was promoted to Captain.

In 1910, backed by the British and Dominion Governments, Scott sailed in June in the *Terra Nova* and by November 1911 was sledging towards the South Pole. He and his four companions reached the Pole on January 18, 1912, only to find Roald Amundsen and his Norwegian party had beaten them by a month. To avoid frightening off possible backers for his exploit, Amundsen did not reveal his true intention of getting to the Pole until he was nearly there. He sent a cable to Scott which read, 'Am Going South Amundsen'. Scott's party felt this was *not* sporting, but worse was to come. Amundsen's team, desperately short of food, killed 24 of their dogs; not at *all* British.

Blizzards and savage weather made travelling conditions intolerable on the journey back to the ship. On February 17, 1912, Petty Officer Evans died. A month later 'Titus' Oates knew he could travel no further and walked out of the tent into the blizzard to die rather than hold the three remaining members up any further. (This brave man, Lawrence Edward Grace Oates, was born in Putney in 1880. He chose death heroically; he was only 32.) It is estimated that despite Oates' gallant sacrifice, the rest of the party (Scott, Wilson and Bowers) all died on or about March 29, 1912. Their bodies were found by a search party on November 12 that year.

SCOTT   Edinburgh, September 12, 1812
William Bell   Ayrshire, November 22, 1890
Artist and poet

92, Cheyne Walk, SW3, 1860

As well as being a painter (though his elder brother, David, 1806-1849, was probably the better artist of the two) Scott was a poet and an art critic. He was a devoted admirer of the Rossettis and his poem, a dreary one, *Rosabell*, caught Dante Gabriel ROSSETTI's eye. (The one that followed, *The Year of the Worth*, was even drearier). Scott entered into the Pre-Raphaelite Movement more fervidly than the founding members could have hoped.

Scott's parents were both plunged into melancholy after the early deaths of some six of their children and William was glad to escape from the morbid atmosphere at home. He came south as far as Newcastle, where he began to teach at a Government Art School. When Scott came to London in 1845, the Rossettis found him to be tall, rather bony but well developed, dark haired (thick and flowing) and had 'very pale clear blue eyes'. William ROSSETTI thought him, 'handsome and highly impressive'.

SEVERN   Hoxton, London, December 7, 1793
Joseph   Rome, August 3, 1879
Artist   Protestant Cemetery, Rome (beside
                                       KEATS)

21, Buckingham Gate, SW1, 1820s

Joseph was the son of a music teacher and early on in his life showed artistic skills. His father apprenticed him to an engraver and somehow managed to attend the Royal Academy School. In 1817 he won a gold medal from the Academy for his painting, *The Cave of Despair*. In 1820, KEATS' 'oak friend', William Haslam, suggested to Severn that he should go with Keats to Rome. This he did and nursed the young poet through the last pain wracked year of his life.

As a younger man Severn had been both a miniaturist and portrait painter – he painted Keats a number of times. He also knew COLERIDGE and painted a striking work called *Spectre Ship*, illustrating part of Coleridge's work, *The Ancient Mariner*.

SEYMOUR   *Central line to Marble Arch*

The Seymours, Dukes of Somerset, married into the PORTMAN family on whose land this road stands.

SEYMOUR STREET, W1

12   (originally 7, Upper Seymour Street) Michael BALFE (LCP 1912) 1861-1865, during which time he bought a small property in Hertfordshire where he played at being a gentleman farmer for the last six years of his life.

30   (originally 16, Upper Seymour Street) Edward LEAR (LCP 1960) 1857 and 1858. Lear merely rented rooms here.

33, Dr. Victor HORSLEY, 1892-1900. His first son, Siward, was born here.

45, Robert PEEL married the daughter of Lady Floyd in 1820 in this house.

SHADWELL Weeting, Norfolk, 1640 (or 1642?)
Thomas London, November 19, 1692
Poet Laureate Chelsea Old Church

60, Cheyne Walk, SW3, where he died

Shadwell was the son of a member of Parliament and was educated at Cambridge, where he studied law. He never practised but, as a young man, travelled extensively and wrote a number of plays (which did *not* travel so well). In their day they pleased the audiences. They all had provoking titles like, *The Sullen Lovers* (1668) or *The Miser* (1672).
Politically he was a Whig and when John DRYDEN attacked the Whig party in his *Absolom and Achitophel*, Shadwell was referred to contemptuously as 'Og'. Shadwell had called Dryden, '...an abandoned rascal, a half-wit and a fool'. Dryden replied in kind, calling Shadwell a '...drunken mass of foul corrupted matter...an opium taker, of mountain belly who never deviates into sense'.

SHAFTESBURY London, April 28, 1801
Anthony Ashley Cooper (7th Earl) October 1, 1885
Politician and philanthropist

24, Grosvenor Square, W1, here born
5, Belgrave Square, SW1, where he died

Shaftesbury was educated at Harrow, then Christ Church College, Oxford. He entered Parliament when he was only 25, as Lord Ashley, and led the way in the factory reform movement. He became a pioneer who brought about many Acts which were to alleviate the cruel working conditions suffered by the (often) grossly underpaid workers. His Coal Mines Act of 1842 prohibited the use of women and children under the age of 13 working below ground in the pits.
He was Chairman of the Ragged Schools Union for 40 years and he also supported Florence NIGHTINGALE in her efforts to ease the lot of the British soldier. He was a devoted Evangelist, yet despite the nature of the various Acts which were the results of his untiring efforts, he was strongly opposed to 'Radicalism'. He did, however, try to work with the up and coming Trade Union Movement.
His son was 54 years old when Shaftesbury died in 1885, but was only the 8th Earl for less than a year. Inexplicably he committed suicide by shooting himself in a four wheel carriage in Regent Street.
The Motto of the Shaftesburys was 'Love, Serve'.
Shaftesbury Avenue, leading off Piccadilly Circus is named after the 7th Earl. In the Circus itself is one of the best known statues in the world. It is always called *Eros* but its proper name is *The Angel of Christian Charity* and is a memorial to Shaftesbury's humanitarian work. *Eros* was the god of sexual love and Piccadilly Circus was one of the usual cruising places for harlots.

SHANNON Sleaford, Lincs., April 26, 1863
Charles Hazelwood Kew, March 18, 1937
Artist

51, Beaufort Street, SW3 (LCP 1979) 1896-1902
Lansdowne House, Lansdowne Road, W11 (LCP 1979) 1904-1923

Shannon, a vicar's son, first met Charles RICKETTS at the City and Guilds School of Art, where they were both pupils.
They lived (and loved) and worked together for the rest of Rickett's life.
Shannon had been trained as a wood engraver and they founded the 'Vale

Press', which produced some beautifully illustrated, superbly well designed books with handsome bindings.

He was made an ARA in 1911 and a full Academician in 1921. In 1929 he suffered a fall from a ladder, whilst hanging a picture.

From then on he was a permanent invalid. His brain was affected by the injuries and for quite long periods he was totally deranged; not even recognizing his beloved Rickets.

SHAW
George Bernard
Playwright

Dublin, July 26, 1856
Ayot St Lawrence, November 2, 1950
His ashes scattered in the garden at
Ayot (together with those of his wife)

13, Victoria Grove, W8 (now demolished)
36, Osnaburgh Street, NW1, 1882-1887 (demolished)
29, Fitzroy Square, W1 (LCP 1975) 1887-1898
10, Adelphi Terrace, WC2, 1899-1920s (demolished)
4, Whitehall Court, SW1, 1930s-1940s

Shaw's father was a drunkard and it is more than possible that the frequent sight of his inebriated father put G.B.S. off alcohol for life. Shaw's mother was a talented musician and she left her intemperate husband in Dublin while she came to London. Shaw stayed on in Ireland, working as a cashier in a land agency but in 1871 he followed his mother to London.

He started work with the Edison Telephone Company. In his spare time he began writing, completing four novels which, though serialized in magazines were not otherwise successful. The best of them is certainly *Cashel Byron's Profession*.

In 1885 he became the music critic on the *Star* and then the *World*. He wrote under the name, 'Corno di Bassetto'. Ten years later he became dramatic critic of the *Saturday Review*.

He was still writing (pieces like *The Quintessence of Ibsenism*) and in 1884 he joined the Fabian Society, having professed Socialism since 1882. Through overwork he had a mild form of a nervous breakdown in 1898. The same year he married Charlotte Payne-Townshend, also a Fabian (but a very rich one) who had 'green eyes'. The marriage was to be based on no sexual activity between them. Remarkably this held true and the marriage was never consumated. Blanche Patch (1879-1966) who was Shaw's secretary for 30 hectic years, once said to Charlotte Shaw: 'You *say* you are fond of kittens and small animals, yet you don't like babies'.

'Babies,' snorted Charlotte, 'who *could* like them? Disgusting little things!'

For the stage, his first play was *Widowers' Houses* in 1892, which he used as a vehicle to attack slum landlords. Play now followed play quite speedily and he soon became a well-known (if 'cranky') figure.

He was awarded the Nobel Prize for Literature in 1925 and in 1934 he was given the medal of the Irish Academy of Letters.

SHEFFIELD TERRACE, W8
*Circle and District lines to
High Street Kensington*

Built up around 1849 opposite a house which had been left to Robert Sheffield by Lady Jane Berkeley (of Berkeley Square). The house was demolished in 1960.

23, G.K. CHESTERTON (P) was born here in 1874 and lived here until 1881. This house, too, has been demolished. Perhaps the air of Sheffield Terrace is particularly inspiring for writers of detective fiction. Agatha Christie lived in the terrace for a time. (Could Hercules Poirot still be found 'talking shop' with Father Brown?)

31, Prebendary Wilson CARLILE (LCP 1972) 1881-1891. Wilson was living here when he left the Church to found his *Church Army*. The house is part of a long row of houses built by Jeremiah Little in 1850. The architect was probably Thomas Allason.

SHELLEY London, August 30, 1797
Mary Godwin London, February 21, 1851
Author St Peter's Churchyard, Bournemouth, Dorset

36, North Bank, NW8, 1836
24, Chester Square, SW1 (P) where she died

Mary was the only child of William GODWIN and Mary Wollstonecraft, his first wife. In 1814 Mary went to the Continent with Percy SHELLEY and married him in 1816 after his ill-used first wife had died.

She saw much of Lord BYRON and it was at his rented villa on Lake Geneva that she was inspired to write *Frankenstein, or the Modern Prometheus* which first appeared in 1818. Sir Walter Scott, in the *London Quarterly Review* of May 1818, commented: 'When we have thus admitted that Frankenstein has passages which appal the mind and make the flesh creep, we have given it all the praise (if praise it can be called) which we dare to bestow. Our taste and our judgement alike revolt at this kind of writing...' Nothing she wrote afterwards achieved either notoriety or fame. After Shelley's death in 1822 she edited all his poems.

SHELLEY Horsham, Sussex, August 4, 1792
Percy Bysshe Drowned in the Bay of Spezia, July 8, 1822
Poet His ashes buried (near Keats) in the Protestant Cemetery, Rome

15, Poland Street, W1 (LCP 1979) 1811
56, Margaret Street, W1, 1814
13, Bond Street, W1, 1814
41, Hans Place, SW1, 1815
101, Great Russell Street, WC1, 1816
13, Norfolk Street, EC4, 1816

Shelley's father, Sir Timothy Shelley, was a well-to-do country squire. He sent his son to Eton which perhaps was *not* a good idea. Percy Shelley was a beautiful boy, too sensitive to get along with his tougher school mates. He was known at Eton as 'Mad Shelley'. He may have been, he certainly had two 'lurid and romantic' novels published before he left the school.

He went up to University College, Oxford where he maintained his reputation for eccentricity. In 1811 he wrote a pamphlet called *The Necessity of Atheism*. The result was that he and Thomas Jefferson Hogg, a fellow 'revolutionary' were 'sent down'. The young men, Shelley was not yet 19, hid in London until Timothy Shelley cooled down sufficiently to make Percy an allowance. It was at this time that he met Harriet Westbrook, daughter of a coffee house keeper. She was only 16, but they eloped and were married in Edinburgh. (The Scottish marriage laws were kinder to runaway lovers than their English counterparts). Papa Shelley gave the young couple £400 and they roamed around England and Wales for a few months.

In 1813 a daughter was born, whom they called Ianthe. Shelley had his poem *Queen Mab* published about the same time. He also met William Godwin, whose radical philosophies appealed greatly to the 21-year old poet, as did Godwin's daughter, Mary. Another elopement took place, with Mary, to the Continent. Strangely Shelley asked poor Harriet to join them! Shelley's grandfather died easing Shelley's financial problems and he made Harriet quite a decent allowance. Mary gave birth to a son in 1816, who was christened William. The same year they met Lord BYRON, another unsteadying influence on the volatile Shelley. Harriet returned to London and, in despair, drowned herself in the Serpentine in Hyde Park, leaving Shelley free to marry Mary. The pair moved south to Pisa.

His *Laon and Cythna* (later re-titled *The Revolt of Islam*) was published in 1817. In 1819 his greatest work, *Prometheus Unbound*, was printed, followed by *Ode to a Skylark*.

In 1822 the Shelleys moved to a villa on the Gulf of Spezia. Shelley and his friend, Edward Elliker Williams, an Anglo Indian soldier, one year younger than Shelley, bought a boat which they christened *Ariel*. Sailing back from Leghorn, they were overtaken by a sudden, violent Mediterranean storm, the little *Ariel* sank and both the young men were drowned.

SHEPHERD	France, January 16, 1793
Thomas Hosmer	Islington, London, July 4, 1864
Artist	

2, Colebroke Row, N1 (the Bird's Buildings)

When the Shepherds lived at Batchelor Street they were on the edge of open countryside, but Thomas drew his inspiration from the city and became one of the best known topographical London painters of his day.

He made the aquatints for *A Picturesque Tour on the Regent's Canal* in 1825 and the following year was responsible for the 159 steel engravings which were the illustrations for a 'book' called *Metropolitan Improvements* which was published in 41 parts. His last commissioned work was for *Mighty London*, published after moving to Colebroke Row.

SHERIDAN	Dublin, September 30, 1751
Richard Brinsley	London, July 7, 1816
Dramatist	Westminster Abbey in 'Poets' Corner'

55/56, Great Queen Street, WC2, 1777-1790
10, Hertford Street, W1 (LCP 1955) 1795-1802
9, St George Street, W1, 1803-1805
14, Savile Row, W1 (P) where he died

Like a number of great 'English' literary figures, Sheridan was an Irishman, but brought up almost entirely in England. His father was an actor who could number Doctor JOHNSON amongst his friends. His mother wrote plays, so it was hardly surprising that Richard should gravitate toward the theatre.

Two of his plays, *School for Scandal* and *The Rivals*, have been, and will probably remain, in the repertoires of stage companies throughout the English-speaking world.

Away from the make-believe world of the theatre, Sheridan's own life was almost as comic. He and a Major Matthews both fell in love with an Elizabeth Linley and Sheridan fought a duel and won her hand, but perhaps only because he had packed her off to a French nunnery for safe keeping!

SICKERT	Munich, May 31, 1860
Walter Richard	Bath, January 22, 1942
Artist	

15, Cleveland Street, W1, 1884
6, Mornington Crescent, NW1 (LCP 1977) 1907
19, Fitzroy Street, W1, 1911-1913

Sickert had Danish and Irish blood in his veins. He set out for a career on the stage but soon changed to art and studied at the Slade School under Alphonse Legros (1837-1911) and also in Whistler's studio. In 1888 he was in Paris working with Dégas (1834-1917). It was about this time he began working from photographs (or memory) rather than 'on-the-spot'.

In 1895 he was working in Venice; in Dieppe from 1900-1905 and then came back to London. He taught at the Westminster School of Art until 1918, when he was succeeded by an ex-pupil, Walter Boyes (1869-1956). As a young girl, Clementine CHURCHILL (then Hozier) once asked Sickert who was the greatest living painter? 'My dear child', he replied, 'I am.' And he meant it.

Sickert married three times. His first wife was Alice Margaret Crook (1885-1950). Sickert claimed that she was the illegitimate daughter of the Duke of Clarence, the elder son of the Prince of Wales and heir presumptive to the throne. Some people believed that 'Eddie' Clarence was involved in the Cleveland Street scandal. Nothing is certain. He was also, at one time, seriously considered as a suspect in the JACK the RIPPER murders! Sickert claimed that he *knew* who the 'Ripper' was.

SIDDONS	Brecon, Wales, July 5, 1755
Sarah	London, June 8, 1831
Actress	St Mary's Church, Paddington Green

149, The Strand, WC1, 1782
226, Baker Street, W1
14, Gower Street, WC1, 1784-1789
54, Great Marlborough Street, W1, 1790-1802
27, Upper Baker Street (now Baker Street, see Clarence Gate) NW1, 1812-1831, where she died

Roger Kemble, an actor (1721-1802) married his manager's daughter, Sarah Ward and their first born was Sarah. Greasepaint coursed their veins: Sarah became an actress as did their other four daughters, Frances, 1760-1822; Jane, 1805-1875 (and her six children) Elizabeth, who married Charles Whitelock, who was both an actor *and* a dentist, and finally, Ann, who died in 1838. Ann married an actor too, called Curtis. As if that was not enough, Roger and Sarah Kemble had four sons as well and they *all* went on to the stage! – John Philip, Stephen, Charles and Henry. Sarah married the actor William Siddons in 1773. Their children rather let the side down; their elder boy, Henry (1774-1815) was on the stage and married Harriot Murray, an actress; the younger boy, George went into the Bengal service; their daughter, Cecilia, married a phrenologist.

Her white marble statue, by Leon-Joseph Chavalliand, was unveiled by Sir Henry IRVING on June 14, 1897. It now overlooks the never ending surges of traffic on the Western Avenue approach to London, but one can get to the statue through Paddington Green. In 'Poets' Corner', Westminster Abbey, there is a bust of Sarah by Thomas Campbell (1790-1858) a Scottish sculptor who studied in Rome.

SIMON	London, October 10, 1816
(Sir) John	London, July 23, 1904
Public Health pioneer	Lewisham Cemetery

40, Kensington Square, W8 (LCP 1959) from 1868 until he died here.

Simon was only 29 years old when he was elected to the Royal Society (he became President in 1879). His election resulted from the publication of his paper on the thyroid gland. A paper he had prepared whilst apprenticed to J.H. Green, Professor of Surgery at Kings College, London.

He became the first Medical Officer of Health in London in 1848. His reports on the general level of health amongst Londoners were published in 1858 and 1859. In 1890 he published *English Sanitary Institutions* which was – and is – a classic of its kind.

SIMPSON   Pennsylvania, June 19, 1896
Wallis Warfield
'Crown Toppler'

16, Cumberland Terrace, NW1, 1935

Originally she was known as Bessie Warfield around Blue Ridge Summit, where she was born. She soon insisted on being called Wallis and she set off on a career that would eventually rock the English 'establishment'.

In 1916 she married a pilot who drank more than he flew and the marriage broke up. Twelve years later in Chelsea Registry Office on July 21, 1928, she married Ernest Simpson. Their 'wedding breakfast' was taken in a sitting room of the Grosvenor Hotel at Victoria Station and they set off on a honeymoon to France in a chauffeur-driven, yellow Lagonda. On their return to London they moved in fairly elevated social circles and though Wallis's dress sense and general 'chic' was admired, no one could have called her a beauty.

History does not accurately date the time or place where Mrs. Simpson first met HRH Edward Albert Christian George Andrew Patrick David Windsor, Prince of Wales, who was two years older than she. Lady CUNARD claimed to have played 'Cupid'.

King George V died peacefully on January 20, 1936 and his eldest son became King Edward VIII at the age of 41. 'Society' had long known that their new King was more than a little friendly with 'that Mrs. Simpson'. Their association and its implications were headline material in America, but there was a conspiracy of silence in the British press. The country set about preparing for the Coronation of its King. Inevitably the 'secret' got out. Mrs. Simpson had obtained a *very* quiet divorce from Ernest Simpson on the basis of her husband having committed adultery with one 'Buttercup' Kennedy. At about the time of the divorce the Bishop of Bradford (from his pulpit) made a reference to the fact that the King was not the most regular churchgoer in the country. It was not intended as a comment on divorce but the 'crisis' did not take long to loom large. Stanley BALDWIN was Prime Minister and he and the Archbishop of Canterbury, Cosmo Land (1864–1945) tried to reason with the King. There could be no compromise, no morganatic marriage. Either give up this twice divorced American woman or leave the throne. He abdicated on December 11, 1936.

SITWELL   Scarborough, September 7, 1887
(Dame) Edith   December 9, 1964
Poet   St Mary's Churchyard, Weedon Lois,
                                             Northants

3, Arlington Street, W1, here born in 1887
'Sesame' Club, 49, Grosvenor Street, W1 (off and on for many years)

Edith was the eldest child of Sir George Sitwell, Bt (who was decidedly odd) and Ida. Her childhood was unhappy. She never married – though her life was not without love – and she grew to be nearly six feet tall. She affected 'medieval-like' garments and 'barbaric' jewelry.

In 1916, she and her two brothers, OSBERT and Sacheverell, founded the Magazine *Wheels* which set out to attack contemporary poetic practices. Her brothers and she also took the young William WALTON under their collective wing and, in 1922, there was a performance of *Façade* in Osbert's Chelsea house. It consisted of Walton's musical setting to a number of Edith's poems, the words of which she declaimed through a loud speaker device called a 'Sengerphone', from behind the backcloth. Her work was not confined to poetry entirely; she produced a number of Royal biographies, notable *Victoria of England* (1936).

SITWELL   London, December 6, 1892
(Sir) Osbert   Italy, April 5, 1969
Author

3, Arlington Street, W1, here born in 1892
25, Chesham Place, SW1, 1900
2, Carlyle Square, SW3, 1920-1960

Osbert, elder son of Sir George Sitwell (1860-1943) and brother to EDITH and Sacheverell, was sent to Eton (though his education was acquired during the holidays). In the First World War he went into the Brigade of Guards but was invalided out in 1919.
He was an erudite and often very humorous man as can be seen in his autobiography, the first volume of which, *Left Hand : Right Hand* was published in 1944. The fifth and final instalment, *Noble Essences*, appeared in 1950. He travelled extensively very much in the manner of an eighteenth century young English aristocrat on a 'Grand Tour'. One of his best books arising from his peregrinations was *Winters of Discontent* in 1932.
On the death of the dotty Sir George, Osbert became the 5th baronet in 1943 and became a Companion of Honour in 1958. He contracted PARKINSON's disease and, by 1959, was very disabled with the *agitans* and the last ten years of his life were miserable.

SLOANE

Sir Hans SLOANE was born in County Down in 1660 and he died in London in 1753. Sloane became the Lord of the Manor of Chelsea and so any streets in, or near, Chelsea Manor called 'Sloane' are due to him. His younger daughter married a Cadogan (pronounced KADDUGGAN) and this explains the Cadogan Street, Squares etc.

SLOANE   County Down, April 16, 1660
(Sir) Hans   London, January 11, 1753
Physician and botanist   Chelsea Old Church

4 (and later 5) Bloomsbury Place, WC1 (LCP 1965) 1695-1742.

Sloane, who had Scottish blood in him, came to Chelsea to study botany. He studied at Paris and Montpelier, to broaden his medical skills and was back in London in 1684. When he was only 27 years old he was made a Fellow of the Royal College of Physicians and in that same year, 1687, was appointed physician to the 34-year old (2nd) Duke of Albermarle who was going, as Governor, to Jamaica. They sailed on September 12, eventually landing in the West Indies on December 19, 1687. Within a year Albemarle was dead and Sloane came back to England with Albemarle's widow, arriving in May 1689. This curtailed stay enabled Sloane to publish his superb *Natural History of Jamaica* in 1707, with a second volume of it in 1720. As well as botanical specimens and the surviving flora, which he gave to the 'Physic' Garden (still there on Chelsea Embankment between Chelsea and Albert bridges) Sloane left Jamaica with an alligator, which died, an iguana, which jumped overboard, and a yellow snake, which escaped on the ship and was shot by the Duchesses' footman.
George I made him a baronet in 1716 and appointed him Physician General to the Armed Forces. He was the first doctor of medecine to be raised to the aristocracy. In 1695 he married the wealthy Elizabeth Langley, by whom he had four children, but only two daughters survived and so the baronetcy died with him.

At his death Sloane had directed that the Nation should be offered his collection and most of his library for £20,000. The Government paid and this purchase consisting of 200 volumes of dried plants, 30,600 objects of natural history, a library of 50,000 volumes and 3,566 manuscripts effectively formed the nucleus of what was to become the British Museum today.

SLOANE STREET, SW3
District and Circle lines to Sloane Square.

In 1850 this street was dismissed as 'a very long row of third-rate houses lying between Knightsbridge and the King's Road'. They should see it now.

42, J.McN. WHISTLER lodged here with his sister and her husband, Seymour Haden, in 1846.

44, Ronald FIRBANK, 1912.

59, George ROBEY rented this house, furnished, from the Lovat-Frasers in 1919.

76, Sir Charles Wentworth DILKE (LCP 1959). He lived here as a boy in the 1840s and 1850s. He returned to it as an adult and his wife, who was so involved in his political downfall, died here. It was also his address when he died in 1911.

77, Sir Herbert Beerbohm TREE and his half brother, Max BEERBOHM in the 1890s.

146, Edgar Allen POE went to a school run by the Misses Dubourg here when he was a seven-year old in 1816.

SMART
(Sir) George Thomas
Organist

London, May 10, 1776
London, February 23, 1867
Kensal Green; Catacomb B, Vault 175

91, Great Portland Street, W1, 1826
12, Bedford Square, WC1, from 1864 until he died here.

Smart was the son of a seller of sheet music and, as a boy, was a chorister at the Chapel Royal. He sang at the *first* HANDEL commemoration festival at Westminster Abbey and he conducted the *last* one in 1834. He was only *fifteen* when he was appointed organist at St George's Chapel in the Hampstead Road.

In 1811 he was knighted in Dublin by the Duke of Richmond, who was Lord Lieutenant of Ireland (the 4th Duke). In 1822 Smart was made Organist of the Chapel Royal at St James's Palace. Later he became Musical Director at Covent Garden and conducted the first Norwich Festival.

SMILES
Samuel
Doctor, railwayman, author

Haddington, New Brunswick,
December 23, 1812
London, April 16, 1904
Brompton Cemetery

8, Pembroke Gardens, W8, from 1874 until he died here.

Smiles trained as a surgeon but was 'too young for sucess', even after having practised for six years. He then became Secretary of the Leeds and Thirsk Railway and soon forgot all about medecine.

He wrote a number of pamphlets and tracts, but the one that hoisted him into the literary firmament was, *Self Help*, which really did help many a Victorian working man.

It was published in 1859 and over 20,000 copies were sold in that year. 55,000 copies had been sold by 1864 and Smiles gracefully retired from the railways. By the turn of the century over 120,000 copies, in English, had been sold and it had been translated into most foreign languages, including Turkish, Arabic and many of the tongues of India.

SMIRKE London, October 1, 1781
(Sir) Robert Cheltenham, April 18, 1867
Architect Kensal Green

A 14, Albany, W1, 1811–1832
81, Charlotte Street, W1 (LCP 1979) 1833–1842
28, Berkeley Square, W1, 1842

Sir Robert's father (also Robert) was a painter and book illustrator and young Robert inherited sufficient of his talent to become an architect. He moved ahead rapidly and was an RA by the time he was 30. He worked for the Board of Works and in recognition of his achievements there, was knighted in 1831.
Smirke's greatest single (and most evident) work is the British Museum. The Museum was originally housed in Montagu House in 1759. Soon, available space was not enough for the rapidly accumulating exhibits they owned and Smirke's 'Grecian' design for a new building was immediately accepted. The superb library belonging to George III was presented to the Museum by his eldest son, George IV, and the building to contain it was begun in 1823. Work on the magnificent porticoed façade of the Museum was still progressing in 1840.

SMITH Woodford, Essex, June 3, 1771
Sydney London, February 22, 1845
Clergyman Kensal Green; Grave No. 5680, Plot 131

14, Doughty Street, WC1 (LCP 1906) 1803–1806
77, Guildford Street, WC1, 1804
8, Cavendish Square, W1, 1804
47, Hertford Street, W1, 1824
58, Jermyn Street, W1, 1825
26, Hunter Street, WC1, 1835
25, Brook Street, W1, 1835
18, Stratford Place, W1, 1835
34, Hunter Street, WC1, 1836
33, Charles Street, W1, 1836–1839
42, Charles Street, W1, 1839

Smith, the son of a 'gentleman of independent means', was educated at Winchester and then New College, Oxford.
Sydney took Holy Orders and became a curate in Amesbury in Wiltshire. Soon after he travelled north and became tutor to a boy in Edinburgh. In this city (the 'Athens of the North') he met many young intellectuals, most of whom were politically, liberal; and so 'Whigs'. He was a co-founder of the *Edinburgh Review*, which was to become very well-regarded. He married – in Edinburgh – in 1802 and then came south to London to become a Preacher in the Foundling Hospital. His very real wit and an ability to please made him one of the 'favourites of society'. In those circles he also talked politics and did much to further the cause of Catholic Emancipation.

SMITH   London, September 22, 1756
William   London, May 31, 1835
Religious pioneer

16, Queen Anne's Gate, SW7 (LCP 1975) 1794–1819
5, Blandford Square, W1 (now demolished) his son's house where he died.

Smith was MP for Sudbury in Suffolk in 1784 and for Camelford between
1791 and 1796. He was an active and outspoken *anti-slaver*. Non-Anglicans
found in him a champion for their true worship and the basic rights of
citizenship. He became Chairman of the Committee of the Dissenting
Deputies; one of the fellow reformers being Charles James FOX.
Smith had sufficient inherited wealth to allow him to buy Joshua
REYNOLDS' portrait of Sarah SIDDONS at the *Tragic Muse*. He also
owned two Rembrandts and had enough money to bring up five sons and
five daughters, one of whom was to become the mother of Florence
NIGHTINGALE.

SMITH   London, June 24, 1825
William Henry   Walmer Castle, Kent, October 6, 1891
Bookseller

12, Hyde Park Street, W2 (LCP 1966) from 1858 for a number of years after.

Smith's father, also William Henry (1792-1865) entered his father's
newsagent's business in the Strand in 1812. Together with his brother,
Henry Edward Smith, they became the largest newsagents in Britain.
William Henry (junior) went into partnership with his father in 1846 and
very soon assumed total control of the business. In 1849 he obtained the
concession to sell his books and newspapers at *all* railway stations. The
business grew and grew until it was the largest seller of books in the UK; a
position it still holds.
He refused a Viscountcy but his widow was made a Viscountess in her own
right. She chose the title Viscountess Hambledon in 1891 and the title has
descended from her. She was born Emily Danvers in 1828. She married
Benjamin Leach in 1854, who died the following year and three years later
Emily married Smith. After Smith's death she moved to 23, Belgrave
Square. Her son, and heir to her own Viscountcy, was William Smith, who
was born in 1868. She had one daughter, Mary, by Leach and four daughters
by Smith. She was an aunt of Baroness Stocks, who wrote that her '…Aunt
Emily was extremely stupid'.
Smith was a man of the highest principles: so much so that *Punch* magazine
nicknamed him 'Old Morality'. The shades of 'Old Morality' still linger
within the giant firm of W.H. Smith and Sons. They still exercise a form of
censorship over the magazines they will allow to be sold from the chain of
shops.

SMITH SQUARE, SW1   *District and Circle lines to Westminster*

The Smith family owned two parcels of land in Westminster and Sir James
Smith built Great Smith Street in 1708. It was described as '…a new street of
good buildings' and Sir James himself lived in it with a Henry Smith –
probably his son, who was Treasurer to the Church Commissioners. Henry
sold the Square to them and they employed Thomas Archer to design the
Church of Saint John, which was built in the centre of the Square between
1713 and 1725. The Church (now used for concerts rather than religion) is
often jokingly referred to as 'Queen Anne's Footstool'. (Imagine it
upside-down and the four corners could well be turned wooden legs on a

rather plump footstool.) Sadly it has suffered from subsidence, caused by the infirm nature of the soil around its foundations.

8 and **9,** Sir Oswald MOSLEY in 1929. At this time he was still married to Viscount CURZON's daughter, Cynthia: she died in 1929.

SMOLLETT Dalquhurn, Scotland, March 19, 1721
Tobias George Pisa, Italy, September 9, 1771
Physician and author Leghorn, Italy

16, Lawrence Street, SW3 (LCP 1950) 1747-1762

Having been through Dumbarton Grammar School and Glasgow University, Smollett went on to become an apprentice with a 'Doctor-Apothecary' called Gordon in Glasgow. Smollett was supposed to have used Gordon as a model of his character 'Potion' in his *Roderick Random.*
In 1739 he came south to London, with hopes that his play *The Regicide* might be staged. This was not to be and in 1741 he sailed as a ship's surgeon's mate on the expedition to Carthagena. He was disgusted by the conditions of the service and quit the ship in the West Indies and lived in Jamaica. Here he met Anne Lascelles whom he later married. He was back in London by 1746, but did not find it easy to practice as a doctor and so decided to become a literary man. His *Roderick Random* was published in 1748 followed in 1751 by *Peregrine Pickle.* In 1776 he published *Travels in France and Italy*, which caused Lawrence STERNE to christen Smollet, 'Smelfungus'.

SNOW October 15, 1905
Charles Percy (1st Baron) July 1, 1980
Academic, author and socialist

199, Cromwell Road, SW7, 1964-1975
85, Eaton Terrace, SW1, 1975-1980

Snow was at Alderman Newton's School in Leicester, then College there, before going up to Christ's College at Cambridge.
He was Parliamentary Secretary at the Ministry of Technology from 1964 (when he was given a Life peerage) to 1966. He had published a large number of books, beginning with *Death Under Sail* in 1932, a sequence of novels – eleven books – under the general title of *Strangers and Brothers* right through to quasi-scientific, political and philosophic titles, not to mention a number of plays.
By some people Snow seemed to be regarded as a sort of *guru* but he was certainly not always as right as the impression he tried to give. He wrote, for instance, to his younger brother in October 1938, 'I don't think there is now any chance of a major war in Europe for years...'. One wonders what he was saying on September 3, 1939.

SOANE
(Sir) John
Architect

Goring-on-Thames, September 10,
1753
London, January 20, 1837
St Pancras Old Church

12, Lincoln's Inn Fields, WC2, from 1792, plus
13 and 14, which he bought about 1812

Soane's father was of very ordinary stock, a mason by trade and the Soane
family lived in a little village called Swan, near Reading, 40 miles or so west
of London in Berkshire. Soane's skills were appreciated and he was awarded
a travelling scholarship by the Royal Academy. On it he spent three years in
Italy and came back to settle in London in 1780.

Architecturally his greatest work was the Bank of England. Unfortunately
Soane's design was practically destroyed by the powers-that-were, who let
Sir Herbert Barker (1862-1946) loose on the building. Luckily, most of
Barker's bodging is at the top of the enormous building and he did leave
Soane's great classical columns.

At his death Soane gave his houses in Lincoln's Inn Fields to the nation. It is
called a museum (open Tuesdays – Saturdays, 10.00-15.00, all year round,
free) but it is really a personal collection, albeit an enormous one and nearly
all the exhibits and paintings in it are hung or stand on the sites of Soane's
choosing. Here the sarcophagus of Seti I of Egypt can be found rubbing
shoulders with the series of eight paintings by HOGARTH called *The Rake's
Progress*. Soane paid £598 for them in 1802. (In what was the dining room is a
portrait of Soane by LAWRENCE.)

On the north side of the Bank of England in the City there is a statue of
Soane set into a niche. It was put here in 1937 and is the work of Sir William
Reid Dick.

SOHO

'So-Ho!' it is said, was the medieval hunting cry used by hare coursers (just
as 'Tally Ho!' is the cry of the fox-hunter.) Certainly the area used to be
hunting country up until the early 17th century. 'Soho' was also the
pass-word that Monmouth's men used at the battle of Sedgemoor on July 6,
1685. The Duke of Monmouth (1649-1685) the bastard son of King Charles
II by his mistress, Lucy Walter, or Walters (1630-1658) headed a rebellion in
an attempt to overthrow his uncle, King James II (1633-1701) who reigned
from 1685 until he fled the country in 1688. At Sedgemoor – the last real
battle fought on English soil – Monmouth was completely defeated and he
was subsequently executed. 'So Ho' didn't do him much good, but he chose
it as he had a substantial house on the south side of what is today Soho
Square. (His neighbours were Colonel Rumsey, Mr. Pitcher, Sir Henry
Inglesby and Henry Grey, 1st Earl of Stamford.)

SOHO SQUARE, W1   *Central and Northern lines to Tottenham Court Road*

The Lord Mayor of the City of London and some of his aldermen once came
hunting foxes here in 1562. Richard Frith built the Square in about 1681,
where, in 1638, there had been brick kilns.

The rather time worn statue in the centre of Soho Square's garden is of King
Charles II by Caius Gabriel Cibber (1630-1700) and was here in 1681. For
some reason it was given to F.A. Goodall who took it out to W.S. Gilbert's
timbered house at Grimsdyke, Harrow Weald. Lady Gilbert handed it back
eventually and it was finally replaced here in 1938.

11,   Ugo FOSCOLO, 1816-1818. He stayed here rather longer than was
usual for him. One can only suppose his creditors were not too
pressing at this period.

26,   Rupert HART-DAVIS had his publishing house offices here, the outside was painted in the Old Etonian colours (he was an Old Etonian) of black and pale blue. Hart-Davis kept a flat 'over the shop'.

29,   Charles and Fanny KEMBLE, 1822-1825.

32,   (originally number 30, renumbered 32 in 1800) Sir Joseph BANKS, 1777-1820. Richard BRIGHT visited Banks here in 1818 and found Banks, '...an old man' [he was 75] 'in a wheel chair, knotted with gouty tumours'. This house, was built in 1680 and rebuilt in 1936.

SOMERVILLE	Jedburgh, Yorks., December 26, 1780
Mary Fairfax	Naples, November 29, 1872
Mathematician	English Cemetery, Naples

94, Russell Street, WC1, 1805-1808
12, Hanover Square, W1 (LCP 1908) 1818-1827

Fairfax was Mary's maiden name. When she was 24, she married her cousin Samuel Greig and soon after their marriage they came to London. Three years later she was a widow and she left Russell Street. In 1812 she married William Somerville (1770-1860). They moved into the Hanover Square house and only moved when it was necessary on his appointment connected with the Royal Hospital, Chelsea.

After the death of her first husband she began to study 'physical sciences' and encouraged by William (who, incidentally, like Greig before him, was Mary's cousin) she published a translation of La Place's *Mécanique Céleste* in English titled *The Mechanism of the Heavens*, in 1831. Four years later her *Connection of the Physical Sciences* appeared and she was to publish two more serious scientific works before she died. Her *Personal Recollections* appeared posthumously.

SOUTH AUDLEY STREET, W1   *Piccadilly line to Hyde Park corner*

Originally built in 1730 and named after the maiden name of the mother Sir Richard and Sir Thomas Grosvenor.

66,   Lord John RUSSELL, 1823-1826, when Member of Parliament for Tavistock, Devon.

SOUTH EATON PLACE, SW1   *Circle and District lines to Sloane Square*

Eaton Hall is the vast country house in Cheshire, built by the Duke of Westminster, whose family own most of the land in this part of 'Belgravia' and Pimlico.

16,   Viscount CECIL of Chelwood (LCP 1976) from 1922 until his death in 1958. (He also had a house at Haywards Heath, in Sussex.)

32,   Brian JOHNSTON, 1938-1939. The house was destroyed in the *Blitz* but Johnston had lodged here with William Douglas-Hume, playwriting brother of Alec DOUGLAS-HUME (ex 14th Earl of Hume) and quondam Prime Minister. Jo Grimond, one-time leader of the (by this time) pathetically small Liberal Party once lodged here, too.

37,   Christmas HUMPHREYS, 1933-1942. By this time he was a committed Buddhist.

SOUTH STREET, W1   *Piccadilly line to Hyde Park Corner*

So called as it was once the southern 'boundary' of land owned by the Grosvenors (the family name of the Dukes of Westminster) of their properties north of Piccadilly. The Street was originally built up in 1737 but has been largely rebuilt since then.

9, Charles FOX, 1792–1796. In 1795 he married a Mrs. Ormistead, who had been his mistress for a number of years. 'Fortunately she' [Mrs. Ormistead] 'was endowed with strong affection, good sense and unbounded devotion to Mr. Fox'.

10 (now sadly an office block) is the house where Florence NIGHTINGALE (LCP 1955) lived from 1856 until she died in it in 1910. She paid £3,000 for it. Her house was demolished in 1929.

15, Catherine WALTERS from 1872 to her death here in 1920. 'Skittles', as she was nicknamed, was the last of the great Victorian courtesans.

24, George, 'Beau' BRUMMELL after 1810. This began his period of his influence during the Regency. Six years later he fled the country.

39, Lord MELBOURNE, 1835–1841. During this period Melbourne was Prime Minister and, from 1837, a great help to the 18-year old Queen Victoria in the first four years of her reign. It was said that he never gave a dinner nor even had meat cooked for himself in this house:
> 'His cooks with long disuse their trade forgot;
> Cool was his kitchen.'

51, A.E. MASON, 1948, this was his last home in London.

SOUTHAMPTON

Thomas Wriothesley (1505–1550) was a lawyer, a social nobody who became the first Earl of Southampton. He was a 'King's Man', the King being Henry VIII, and rose to be Lord Chancellor, one of the most influential offices in Tudor England. He was given a mansion in High Holborn as well as the Manor of Bloomsbury. His property descended through his successors to the 4th (and last) Earl, who, in 1652, demolished Southampton House and built Southampton buildings. The Row and the Place followed not long after.

SOUTHAMPTON BUILDINGS, WC2   *Central line to Chancery Lane*

9, William HAZLITT, 1820–1824. In 1824 he married a Mrs. Bridgewater who had '£300 a year'. In 1807 he had lived at Number 34 for over three years.

34, Charles LAMB, 1809. By this time he and his sister Mary were well advanced with their *Tales from Shakespeare*.

SOUTHAMPTON ROW, WC1   *Central line to Holborn*

17, Edward FITZGERALD, 1830. He was in his last year at Cambridge University.

39, Edgar Allen POE was at school here in 1816. His adoptive parents were living at 146, Sloane Street.

SOUTHAMPTON STREET, WC2   *Piccadilly line to Covent Garden*

17, Colley CIBBER lodged here from 1714 to 1720. Cibber wrote in *Colley Cibber's Apology* that, 'I was born in London on the 6th of November, 1671 in Southampton Street, facing Southampton House'.

17, W.S. GILBERT was *probably* born here in 1836.

27, David GARRICK, from 1747 to 1772. This house and number 26, are the only two survivors of the original street and date from 1707–1708. Over the doorway of 27 is a bronze medallion of Garrick by H.C. Fehr, placed here in 1901. (In GARRICK's day the house was 'chocolate coloured'.)

SOUTHERNE   Oxmantown, Dublin, Autumn 1660
Thomas   London, May 26, 1746
Dramatist

4, Tothill Street, SW1, where he died.

After Trinity College, Dublin, Southerne came to London about 1681 to read law at the Middle Temple. Then his life seemed to take on a military flavour and he was to be found in the Army, under the Duke of Berwick (James Fitzjames, 1670-1734, a French General; illegitimate son of King James II of England, by the Duke of Marlborough's sister, Arabella Churchill). When this rather suprising military interlude was over, Southerne took up play writing. The first real success he had was with *The Fatal Marriage* in 1694, then the even more popular (but less pronounceable) *Oroonoko* or *The Royal Slave*. In it, Southerne made a passionate appeal to stop the slave trade. It was probably the first literary 'voice' to speak out publicly against that degrading commercial activity.

SOUTHWICK STREET, W2
Metropolitan, Bakerloo, Circle and District lines to Paddington

Much of the land here was leased out by the Church of England. One of their tenants married a Robert Thistlethwaite whose country house was called Southwick Park.

31, Max BEERBOHM in 1915. He and his wife, Florence, came back here from Italy for the duration of the First World War.

37, John LANE stayed here with Dr. Owen Pritchard in the 1880s when his 'Bodley Head' publishing house was being established.

SOYER
Alexis Benôit
Chef

Meaux-en-Brie, 1809
London, August 11, 1858
Kensal Green, Grave No. 3714, Plot No. 80

3, Kensington Square, W8, 1850s
15, Marlborough Hill, NW8, where he died

Soyer was originally intended for the church, but he preferred the cooking stove to the altar and the creed of culinary art attracted him both executively and intellectually. In 1830 he came to London and was appointed head chef at the Reform Club in Pall Mall in 1837, staying there for 13 years. Members of other clubs were understandably jealous of the pleasures afforded at the Reform's table.

In 1846, Ibrahim Pasha, Viceroy of Egypt, paid a visit to London and the Reform gave a dinner in his honour. Soyer created a suitable confection for the event; *Crème d'Egypte à l'Ibrahim Pasha*. It was a two foot (60 centimetres) high pyramid of meringue cake in imitation of 'solid stones', surrounded by grapes and other fruits, which supported an '...elegant crème à l'ananas on which rested a highly finished portrait of the illustrious stranger's father, Mehemet Ali, carefully drawn on a round shaped satin carton, the exact size of the top of the cream'. Below was a portrait of Ibrahim himself surrounded by an apparently *gilt* frame (in fact made of *eau de vie de Dantzic* and gold water mixed with jelly). Whew!

Though capable of producing such *exotica* Soyer was *totally* practical. He designed a stove for the Army field kitchens and actually went out to the battlefields of the Crimea to teach army cooks how best to use it.

SPANISH PLACE, W1
Central line to Bond Street

The Wallace Collection is housed in Hertford House in Manchester Square. Spanish Place runs into the North East corner of the Square and, at one time, Hertford House was the official residence of the Spanish Ambassador in London.

3, Captain Frederick MARRYAT (LCP 1953) 1841-1843. It was one of the '...tiniest of houses, furnished according to his' [Marryat's] 'taste, a very gem in its adornment...he received the visitors who made the little rooms brilliant with their conversation and their wit'. So, wrote Mrs. Ross Church, one of Marryat's daughters.

SPENCER	London, April 27, 1820
Herbert	Brighton, December 8, 1903
Philosopher	Cremated; but his ashes are in Highgate Cemetery, near 'George Eliot'

6, Hinde Street, W1, 1862-1863
29, Bloomsbury Square, WC1, 1864
64, Avenue Road, NW8, 1889-1890s

Spencer came to London as sub-editor of the *Economist* in 1848 and stayed with that publication until 1853. Through this period he came to know 'George Eliot' and T.H. HUXLEY. He was a strong supporter of DARWIN and defined his idea of evolution as a '...change from an indefinite, incoherent homogeneity to a definite heterogeneity'.

His American publisher once came to London specially to see him. Their meeting was opened by Spencer telling the American 'I beg of you to state your business as succinctly as possible as I cannot *endure* the human voice for more than six minutes'.

SPENCER-CHURCHILL	London, April 1, 1885
(Baroness) Clementine Ogilvy	London, December 12, 1977
Prime Minister's wife	Bladon Churchyard

75, Grosvenor Street, W1, here born
7, Prince's Gate, SW7, 1966-1977

Clementine Hozier, daughter of Sir Henry Hozier married Winston Churchill in 1908. He was already almost a public figure, but not yet the giant he was to become. They had one son and four daughters. She gave her husband – and he must have been difficult to live with – the support any really public figure *must* have.

Churchill always refused any honours above a baronetcy, because had be accepted, he would have had to leave his beloved House of Commons. (It was rumoured that Queen Elizabeth II offered him a Dukedom.) He became Sir Winston when he accepted the Garter, but after his death, the Queen created Lady Churchill a Baroness in her own right.

Winston CHURCHILL was at school at Harrow and now, nestling at the foot of the *Hill* is an American owned, expensive, 90 or so bed hospital. In 1981, Lady Soames officially opened it as it is, very happily, called the Clementine Churchill Hospital.

Oscar Nemon's double statue was erected in Kensington Gardens in 1981, not all that far from the Chruchill's Hyde Park Gate home, where Sir Winston died. The Churchill's are shown, seated and larger than life size.

SPOONER	July 22, 1844
William Archibald	August 29, 1930
Academic	

17, Chapel Street, W1, here born

Spooner was an albino and so suffered from bad eyesight, but despite this handicap became a clergyman and eventually a Dean. His name lives for ever in the English dictionary in 'Spoonerism. An, accidental or facetious transposition of the initial letters or syllables or words': e.g. 'a half warmed fish' instead of 'a half formed wish'. Research has found few people (indeed *any*) who actually heard a Spoonerism on the Dean's lips.

He was Warden of New College, Oxford for many years. His full brother, also in holy orders, was a true blonde and known as 'Golden Spoon', whilst William was known as 'Silver Spoon'.
Spooner was an archetypal 'absent-minded professor'. One day he met Stanley Casson, then a young archaelogist, in the quadrangle of New College and asked him to '...come to dinner tonight and meet our new Fellow, Casson'. Flushing, Casson replied, 'But, Warden, I *am* Casson.' 'Oh', said Spooner, 'never mind, come along all the same.'

STAEL-HOLSTEIN   Paris, April 22, 1766
Anne Louise Germaine Necker   Paris, July 14, 1817
(Baronne)
'Bluestocking' and novelist

3, George Street, W1, c. 1812
29 (formerly 30) Argyll Street, W1 (P) 1813-1814

She was the daughter of Jacques Necker (1732-1804) the French financier and Suzanne Curchod (1739-1796) who was the Swiss miss who captured Edward GIBBON's heart a few years before Germaine de Stael was born. Even as a child, Germaine was '...a romp, a coquette and passionately desirous of prominence and attention'. By 1786, '...her large eyes and buxom figure' had attracted Eric Magnus, Baron of Stael-Holstein, an attaché at the Swedish Legation and they were married on January 14, 1786; she was 20, he 37.
The marriage was not happy, he accused her (understandably) of extravagance and so, in 1797, they came to an amicable separation. She had already embarked on a number of *affaires*, the most notable being her friendship with Benjamin Constant, who was just that. They remained 'good friends' from 1794 until 1811 and it was she who probably inspired his most durable work – a short novel, called *Adolphe*.

STAFFORD TERRACE, W8   *District and Circle lines*
                                   to High Street Kensington

The Stafford here has no connection with the illustrious, if unlucky, aristocratic family of Staffords, but was named after the Reverend Charles Stafford of Oxford and/or Dr. Richard Stafford, a West End surgeon. Both these men had leased land here in the 1840s. The street was built up from 1870 onwards.

11, Charles CONDER, 1899. This was his second address in London having come from Paris (*en route* from Australia) not long before.

18, this house is now a Museum, kept up by the Victorian Society. It is open from March to October on Wednesdays (10-4) and Sundays (2-5). In it are a number of works of other Victorian artists, such as TENNIEL and CRANE.

STANFORD   Dublin, September 30, 1852
(Sir) Charles Villiers   London, March 29, 1924
Composer   Ashes in the North Aisle, Westminster
                         Abbey

56, Hornton Street, W8, 1894-1916
9, Lower Berkeley Street, 1923

Stanford studied music in London under Ernst Pauer and, in 1870, won a scholarship to Queen's College, Cambridge, later transferring to Trinity College, at the same university, three years later. Here he became organist (succeeding J.L. Hopkins) a position he held for 19 years. He was also conductor of the Cambridge University Musical Society and this afforded him many *entrées*. Previously he had also been to Germany to study under both Reinecke and Kiel.

He was knighted in 1902, having set very high standards in the composition of English Church Music. Also he actually composed an opera called *The Veiled Prophet of Khorassan* which had *one* performance in London and *one* in Hanover! He produced seven symphonies but his real *forte* was choral music. In 1878 he married Jennie, the daughter of a man who rejoiced in the name of Champion Wetton.

STANHOPE	Chevening, August 3, 1753
Charles (3rd Earl of)	London, December 16, 1816
Reformer and inventor	Westminster Abbey

20, Mansfield Street, W1

Charles, the Eton-educated father of Lady Hester Lucy STANHOPE, became a Member of Parliament and married PITT's sister. He had supported the aims of the French Revolution, despite the fact that, had he been a French aristocrat rather than English, he probably would have lost his head. Later he advocated making peace with Napoleon (in 1800) but the 'little Corporal' had 15 years to go, before his Empire fell about his ears.

However, politics were secondary to the lasting fame he achieved through his inventions. He gave scant attention to his wife and family when he was in an inventive mood. He devized a 'bio convex' lens to 'eliminate spherical aberrations' (ie to eliminate either fuzziness or distortion at the edges of the lens). He also took great interest in the development of mechanical calculators; he perfected a printing press and a method of stereotyping. (This last, was a way of copying the original set type by modelling it, first in a sort of *papier mâché* later called *flong* then casting it in metal.) A similar type setting could be printed in more than one place at once. Such a process was a great step forward in the burgeoning uses of printing presses at the end of the 18th century and the method was adopted by the Clarendon Press in Oxford.

STANHOPE	Chevening, March 12, 1776
(Lady) Hester Lucy	Mount Lebanon, June 23, 1839
Eccentric	In her garden at Mount Lenanon

120, Baker Street, W1, 1803–1804

Hester was a daughter of the 3rd Earl STANHOPE and kept house for her uncle, William PITT (the 'Younger') in Baker Street. When uncle William died in 1806, she was granted a pension of £1,200 by George III and, in 1810, grieving (it was said) for Sir John Moore, who fell at Coruna, and who she had loved, she left England for the Middle East.

When there she adopted the habit and habits of the Bedouin and settled on Mount Lebanon, in 1814. She was regarded by these nomads as a sort of prophetic fulfilment; certainly she was a bit 'off her head' as many 'prophets' are. She died in poverty, largely because she gave away such money as was hers to any person with a hard luck story. Her mental imbalance was certainly inherited from her father, who, though a brilliant man, was not '*quite* right in the head'.

STANHOPE GATE, W1   *Piccadilly line to Hyde Park Corner*

This little street led originally to the town mansion of Philip Stanhope, Earl of Chesterfield (Chesterfield Street and Gardens, just along the road, have acquired their names in a similar manner).

5,   Lord RAGLAN (LCP 1911) (he, of the sleeve) lived here from 1835 until his departure for the Crimean War, where he was the

Commander of the British Forces (and, at 66, past it). He died of illness at Sevastapol in June 1855.

19, Terence RATTIGAN, 1934-1936. Here, living in his parent's house, he wrote his first dramatic (and deserved) stage success, *French Without Tears*.

STANHOPE STREET, NW1   *Northern line to Mornington Crescent*

Henry, Duke of Grafton, bastard son of Barbara Viliers (later Duchess of Cleveland) and King Charles II, had a son called Charles who inherited some considerable property in this area. He built up what is now the Euston Road. He had two daughters, one of whom was Caroline Stanhope, Countess of Harrington, who married in 1746.

45, William MACREADY was born here on March 3, 1793
53, Matthew FLINDERS, c. 1790.
92, Ellen TERRY lived here with her parents, as a very young girl, c. 1850.

STANHOPE TERRACE, W2   *Central line to Lancaster Gate*

Once this was called Stanhope Street on land leased by the Church of England. Arthur Stanhope was a trustee of the Church Land, which was leased to his brother-in-law, Robert Thistlethwaite of Southwick.

3, George DU MAURIER, 1893, by which time he was failing fast and had only one more year to live.
3, Rupert HART-DAVIS, 1908. 'The house had four storeys and a basement. There was a large 'L-shaped' drawing room on the first floor and a similar bedroom for my mother above'. His sister, Deidre, was born in that bedroom in July 1909.
11, Lord BADEN-POWELL was born here in 1857.

STANLEY

STANLEY	Denbigh, June 10, 1841
(Sir) Henry Morton	London, May 10, 1904
Explorer	St Michael's Church, Pirbright, Surrey

34, De Vere Gardens, W8, 1872-1874
160, New Bond Street, W1, 1886
2, Richmond Terrace, SW1, where he died

Stanley was born in Wales the son of a man called Rowlands, who had him christened John. Young John Rowlands worked his passage across the Atlantic as a cabin boy. In New York he had a job with a merchant called Stanley, whose surname he adopted. He was in the Confederate Navy and later served in the U.S. Navy.

He drifted into journalism, but such was his talent, he was sent by the *New York Herald* to Africa to try and find the missing Doctor David Livingstone in 1869. In November 1871 he did find the tyranical doctor at Ujiji (where Stanley was supposed to have uttered those four famous words).

In 1890 he was back in London and he married (in Westminster Abbey) Dorothy Tennant, an artist. The marriage was more or less conditional on Dorothy, when married, promising to live at Richmond Terrace with her awesome mother. Mrs. Coombe-Tennant was bilingual in French and English and had been a friend of Gustave Flaubert. She held regular 'salons' on Sunday afternoons, to which affairs the eminents of the day (such as KITCHENER) would come to drink their intellectual fill. Her daughter, Dorothy (almost always called 'Dolly') was supposed to have been the result of an illicit liaison with John MILLAIS. (Perhaps she inherited her artistic talents from her mother's irregularity?)

The Stanleys duly stayed on with Mummy and they adopted a son. Stanley insisted that the boy be of Welsh origin.

STEAD	Alnwick, Northumberland, July 5,
William Thomas	1849
Journalist	Drowned on the *S.S. Titanic*, April
	15, 1912

5, Smith Square, SW1, 1880s

Leaving his school in Wakefield (Yorks.) when he was only 14, Stead had become editor of the *Northern Echo* newspaper by 1873. By 1880 he was working in London on the *Pall Mall* and was editor of it from 1883 to 1889. In 1885, however, he spent three months in Holloway Gaol (then a men's prison) where he was prisoner 245, for an article called *Maiden Tribute of Modern Babylon*, researched and written by Stead and printed in the *Pall Mall Gazette* (a London evening newspaper) on Monday, July 5, 1885. It was the story of a 13-year old girl called Eliza Armstrong, who lived with her family at 32, Charles Street (now demolished, but it used to be between the Edgware Road and Lisson Grove). Eliza had been 'bought' from her mother on June 2, 1885, through a third party. £3.00 was the 'down' payment and a further £2.00 was to be paid to Mrs. Armstrong after Eliza's virginity had been professionally certified. This being established by a midwife, Eliza was taken to a brothel and sedated with choloroform, to be woken by the attentions of one of the brothel's customers.
The trial opened at the Central Criminal Court ('Old Bailey') on October 3. The trial lasted twelve days and at the end of it Stead was found guilty of 'abduction'. A petition was got up for his release but, though signed by more than 200,000 people, to no avail. However, the original purpose of Stead's involvement, the exposure of the very real 'traffic' of young girls being sold into a life of prostitution in London was highlighted and also the law regarding the 'age of consent' (to be 16) was pushed through Parliament. On the river wall of the Embankment is a medallion to Stead by George Frampton, placed here in 1920 and paid for by fellow journalists.

STEER	Birkenhead, Lancs., December 28,
Philip Wilson	1860
Artist	London, March 21, 1942

109, Cheyne Walk, SW3 (LCP 1967) from 1898 until he died here

Steer was the painter son of a portrait painter. Philip studied at the Gloucester School of Art and later at the Academie Julien and L'Ecole des Beaux Arts in Paris. He was an admirer of J.M.W. TURNER and has sometimes been referred to as an English *Impressioniste* but none of his so called Impressionistic pictures were painted in London. He became a Founder Member of the New English Art Club and assistant teacher of Painting at the Slade.
He never married and was looked after by his Welsh nurse, Mrs. Raynes, who had looked after him from his birth, when his mother became a chronic invalid, until not long before he died in 1942. (He once complimented her – it was said – on a pudding she had made and she replied, 'There's art in everything, even in painting pictures'.)

STEIN	Alleghemy, U.S., February 3, 1874
Gertrude	Paris, July 27, 1946
Poet and Critic	

20, Bloomsbury Square, WC1, 1920

As a very small child Gertrude lived in Vienna and Paris and, as a girl, in Oakland and San Francisco. She went on to study psychology under

William James at Radcliffe College and, finally, medecine at John Hopkins. When she was 29, she returned to Paris to live. Here she met many of the *avante-garde* of the literary and artistic lions of the day, like Picasso and Matisse. On her part, she developed a literary style that was said by some to be incomprehensible and thought by many critics to be some form of intellectual joke.

Four years later she met Alice Toklas who became her secretary, lover and general 'bottle-washer'. In 1933 a book entitled *Autobiography of Alice B. Toklas* was published. In fact it was written by Stein. Stein called Toklas 'Pussy' and Toklas called Gertrude 'Lovely'.

In June 1946 she agreed to undergo a surgical operation which (probably even today) most doctors would have thought to be hopeless. As she was wheeled towards the operating theatre she questioned Alice Toklas, 'What is the answer?' Toklas did not reply. 'In that case,' pursued Gertrude, 'what is the question?' Those were her last words.

STENBOCK
Cheltenham, 1860
(Count) Eric Magnus Anders Harry Sussex, April 1895
'Aesthete'

21, Gloucester Walk, W8, 1890–1894

Arthur SYMONS wrote of Stenbock that he, '...was one of the most inhuman beings I have ever encountered: inhuman and abnormal; a degenerate who had I know not how many vices'.

The Count's rooms were usually kept dark during the daylight hours and often filled with the smoke of incense. He was a very *camp* homosexual, kept snakes in his sitting room and encouraged people to believe that he practised Black Magic.

He could not have been *all* bad. He did have a sense of humour and he helped Norman O'NEILL to be musically educated. He paid for O'Neill to learn in Germany and left him £1,500 in his will.

STEPHEN
James Kenneth
Northampton, February 3, 1892
Tutor to Royalty and...?

32, De Vere Gardens, W8, 1890–1892

Stephen, an old Etonian, was the son of Sir James Fitzjames Stephen, a judge. (He was the judge at the poisoning trial of Mr. Maybrick. It was during this trial that Sir James exhibited noticeable signs of mental derangement. He died, aged 65, in 1892. His younger brother, Leslie, was the father of Virginia WOOLF. It is possible, therefore, that mental troubles were not unusual in the Stephen blood.)

James Kenneth was appointed to the amiable, if not very bright, Duke of Clarence, elder son of the Prince of Wales – and so Stephen's pupil was second in succession to the throne. It has been suggested that Stephen had some sort of homosexual liaison with the young Duke, who then 'dropped' his tutor and Stephen, spurned, took his revenge on six (or more) East End prostitutes and was, in fact, 'JACK the RIPPER'. Other investigators of the 'Ripper' affair suggest that Stephen actually killed *ten* prostitutes.

Whatever the basis for such speculation it is known that Stephen died in 1892 of 'Mania; two and a half months. Persistent refusal of food, 20 days. Exhaustion'. These were the notes of the mental home where Stephen was locked up. His death occurred just 20 days after the untimely death of the Duke of Clarence.

STEPHEN　　　　　　　　　London, November 28, 1832
(Sir) Leslie　　　　　　　　　London, February 22, 1904
Biographer　　　　　　　　　Ashes buried in Highgate Cemetery

42 (today's numbering) Hyde Park Gate, SW7, here born
8, Onslow Gardens, SW7, 1867-1873
22, Hyde Park Gate, SW7 (LCP 1960) from 1876 until he died here

As a school boy at Eton, then an undergraduate at King's College, London and finally at Trinity Hall, Cambridge (where he was made a fellow) he distinguished himself both academically and athletically. He was a keen oarsman and a good long distance runner. He also once *walked* the fifty miles from Cambridge to London in 12 hours.

When he was 32 he settled in London and began to write for the *Saturday Review* and the *Cornhill* magazine – he was to be editor of the *Cornhill* for eleven years. In 1882 he was asked to become the first editor for the *Dictionary of National Biography*. He saw the first 26 volumes through the press and wrote many of the biographies himself thereby setting a very high standard, which, mercifully has been maintained by the many volumes which have followed, and will continue to be published every decade or so. This occupied him for nine years. His last published work was *English Literature and Society*, which was actually published on the day he died from cancer.

On June 19, 1867, he married Minny Thackeray, younger daughter of W.M. THACKERAY and for the first few years of his married life they shared the house with Minny's elder and beloved sister, Anny (who married Richmond RITCHIE in 1877).

On December 7, 1870, Laura Makepeace Stephen made her premature appearance. In 1875 Minny again became pregnant. On November 28, 1875 (Stephen's birthday) Minny gave birth to a premature and stillborn child and within hours Minny herself was dead.

Julia Duckworth, a niece of Mrs. Cameron (one of the first and greatest portrait photographers) recently widowed by Herbert Duckworth, who left her with three children, called on the Stephens on the night Minny died. After considerable 'cajoling' Stephen married Julia on March 26, 1878. They had four children: Virginia, who was to marry Leonard WOOLF, Vanessa, who married Clive BELL, Thoby, who died young in 1907 and, finally, Adrian.

Leslie Stephen was knighted in 1902 which really gave him little pleasure, the honour being so long delayed. Never really a very *easy* man to get to know at any time.

STEPHENSON　　　　　　　Newcastle, October 16, 1803
Robert　　　　　　　　　　　London, October 10, 1859
Railway pioneer　　　　　　　Westminster Abbey (beside
　　　　　　　　　　　　　　　TELFORD)

34, Gloucester Square, W2, where he died

Robert was the son of George Stephenson (1781-1848) who really invented a practical steam locomotive. Robert was put into the coal trade at Killingworth and then, when he was 19, father sent him to Edinburgh University for six months.

When he was 20 he helped his father to survey the lines for the Stockton and Darlington Railway. He then went to Colombia for three years, returning to England to become Manager of his father's locomotive engine works in Newcastle.

Independently of George, Robert is worthy of his own fame as a bridge builder. He constructed the Britannia Tubular Bridge (the bridge that links

Wales with the Island of Anglesey) in 1850, the Conway bridge (1848) and the bridge at Montreal, Canada.
In the forecourt of the reborn Euston Station is a bronze statue of Stephenson by Baron Marochetti. It was originally outside the old Euston from 1871 and came in out of the cold in 1968.

STERNE	Clonmel, Eire, November 24, 1713
Laurence	London, March 18, 1768
Novelist	St George's Burial Ground, Paddington

48, Old Bond Street, W1, where he died (the building was demolished in 1940 and rebuilt)

Sterne was the son of an Infantry Ensign and the grandson of the Archbishop of York (Richard Sterne, c.1596-1683). Laurence was early put in the care of a relation in Halifax, where his schooling really began and he went up to Jesus College, Cambridge in 1730. He left University as a parson (but unsuited to a strictly academic life) and, through family influence, was given a 'living' in Yorkshire. He married Elizabeth Lumley (a parson's daughter) but they were unsuited and he was more than glad to leave both his wife and the neighbourhood of his early years and come south to London by himself. It was not until 1760 that the first two volumes of *Tristram Shandy* were published and gained him very widespread popularity. Such was his fame that he was presented by a 'nobleman' with the perpetual curacy of Coxwold in Yorkshire. Volumes Three and Four of *Tristram Shandy* appeared in 1761. In 1768 Sterne followed up the success of *Shandy* with his *Sentimental Journey*.
By this time he was 'officially' separated from his wife and daughter and run down in health. John MacDonald, in his book. *Travels in Various Parts of Europe, Asia and Africa* (1790) wrote of a visit he had made to see Sterne on his death bed. Sterne had been taken violently ill in '...the silk-bag shop in Old Bond Street...I went to Mr. Sterne's lodgings: the mistress opened the door; I inquired how he did...I went into the room and he was just a-dying. I waited ten minutes, but in five he said; "Now, it is come!" He put up his hand as if to stop a blow and died in a minute' (and in debt).

STOKER	Dublin, November 8, 1847
Abraham ('Bram')	London, April 20, 1912
Author	Golders Green

27, Cheyne Walk, SW3, 1879
4, Durham Place, SW3
18, St Leonard's Terrace, SW3, 1904
26, St George's Square, SW1, where he died

Stoker, today, would appear to be remembered solely as the author of *Dracula* which appeared in 1897. In fact he was a barrister. He wrote another dozen or so books and was Sir Henry IRVING's acting manager at the Lyceum for 27 years. When Irving died in 1905 Stoker had a stroke which left him practically blind for some months.
The year he began at the Lyceum he married Florence Balcombe in Dublin. Florence had been a romantic childhood friend of Oscar WILDE's.

STOTHARD	Long Acre, London, August 17, 1755
Thomas	London, April 27, 1834
Illustrator	Bunhill Fields

28, Newman Street, W1 (LCP 1900) from 1794 until he died here in 1834
Stothard was apprenticed to a pattern drawer who taught his student well

and Stothard became a very capable and prolific engraver and designer. He painted as well; his first picture to be hung in the Academy, was an oil of *The Holy Family*. He was made an Academician in 1794 and in 1813 became librarian to the Academy.

Some 3,000 of his designs were engraved and his illustrations to Boydells *Shakespeare*, *The Pilgrim's Progress* and *Robinson Crusoe* were well thought of. In the autumn of 1833 he was knocked over by a carriage in the street and he never really recovered from the accident.

STRACHEY   London, March 1, 1880
Lytton Giles   Nr. Hungerford, January 21, 1932
Author

69, Lancaster Gate, W2.
51, Gordon Square, WC1 (LCP 1971) 1919
60, Frith Street, W1, 1917

Lytton was the fourth of five sons of Lieutenant-General, Sir Richard Strachey. At Cambridge this very un-military young man won the Chancellor's Medal, though he failed to get a First Class degree and Cambridge did not achieve the intellectual haven he had hoped to find. When, eventually, he came down he worked for the *Spectator*, at that time edited by his cousin, John St Loe Strachey. He had decided on 'literature' as a career and quite soon found himself a central figure in the so-called 'Bloomsbury Group' (see WOOLF, GRANT, KEYNES and MACCARTHY).

Despite Sir Leslie STEPHEN, Virginia WOOLF's father, being the first editor and founding father of the *Dictionary of National Biography*, Strachey held other views on the art of biography and proved them when he published *Eminent Victorians* in 1918 and, even more triumphantly, with *Queen Victoria* in 1921 (for which he was awarded the Tait Black Memorial Prize).

Strachey was homosexual and his love *affaires* both within and without the 'Group' have been told frequently and variously. He made little or no attempt to conceal his sexual preference and, indeed, it was perhaps part of the 'Group's' aims to be bolder about taboos, like homosexuality. His last companionship, however, was with Dora CARRINGTON who had no illusions about Strachey's tastes. In the First World War it was obvious that a 34-year-old man as physically badly shaped as he, would not be required in the firing line. 'God', he said, 'has put us on an island and Winston [CHURCHILL] has given us a Navy; it would be absurd to neglect those advantages.'

THE STRAND, WC1   *Northern, Bakerloo and Jubilee lines*
                                        to Charing Cross

So called because it once *was* a 'strand', the water's edge, or shore of the River Thames. It was a pre-Roman track and by 1185 it was called 'Stronde'.

33,   Frank HARRIS, when editor of *Vanity Fair* in 1911.
103 and **104** (today's numbering). Here used to be Fountain Court. William BLAKE lived from 1821 until his death here, in 1827.
149, Sarah SIDDONS, 1782. In October of that year, Sarah made her London début. At that time 149 was a lodging house, by the 1880s it had become the office of a publication called *Pictorial World*. After the first performance, Sarah, her husband and her father, Roger KEMBLE, ate a necessarily frugal supper here.
163, Mrs. Elizabeth INCHBALD, c.1780. By this time widowed, she began writing plays and became involved in theatrical management.
165, William GODWIN had a bookshop here in 1783/84. (He also stayed at number 195.)

342, Benjamin HAYDON lodged here when he first came to London in 1804. His very first morning in the city, he went to see the exhibition of pictures in Somerset House, but through ignorance went into the church of St Mary-le-Strand (in the middle of the road opposite the main gateway of Somerset House) and tried to pay the verger of the church his exhibition entrance fee of one shilling (5p).

STRANG	Dunbar, Scotland, February 13, 1859
William	Bournemouth, April 12, 1921
Artist	Kensal Green, Grave 47122, Plot 16

20, Hamilton Terrace, NW8 (LCP 1962) 1900-1921

Strang came south to study at the Slade under Legros and it was from Legros particularly he absorbed the finer points about etching. He produced over 700 plates, some of them being illustrations for *The Ancient Mariner*, which was published in 1896. Four years later an illustrated edition of Kipling's short stories with plates by Strang was published.

His paintings were vivid and imaginative, owing something perhaps to the Venetian colourists and also sharing a little of the influence of the Impressionists.

STRATFORD PLACE, W1   *Central line to Bond Street*

Here stood one of the original conduit heads supplying water to the city. By 1770 other supplies had been opened up and the area hereabouts became the province of speculative builders. The City Corporation leased this part to Stratford Edward who laid out the street in such a way as to thwart a competitive property gamble along the road which was backed by Sir Thomas Edwardes who, beaten, had to let off his leased tracts to the Parish scavengers.

7, Martin VAN BUREN (LCP 1977) 1831, when he became United States Ambassador in London, Washington IRVING often visited him here.

17, Edward LEAR, 1850-1852. He had returned after a holiday near Hastings with Holman HUNT in 1852 to find the ceiling in the front room had fallen in; he moved into the room behind and its ceiling followed suit. Lear went back to Hastings.

18, Sydney SMITH, 1835. In this same year he moved his address three times!

STRATTON STREET, W1   *Piccadilly, Jubilee and Victoria lines*
                                           to Green Park

Built up originally about 1693 on land owned by Baron Berkeley of Stratton. Stratton is a village in North Cornwall where John, the first Baron Berkely, won a battle, called Stratton Fight, for the Royalist cause in the Civil War.

1, Angela BURDETT-COUTTS for 50 years or more, until her death in 1906 and before her, her mother, the Duchess of St Albans. Baroness Burdett-Coutts was probably the richest woman in England, her millions coming from Thomas Coutts the banker (1735-1822).

14, William Stone from about 1887 to 1893, when he moved to (the) Albany.

17, Sir Henry IRVING at the time of his death in 1905. His corpse 'lay in state' in Baroness BURDETT-COUTTS' drawing room, just up the road.

STREET Woodford, Essex, June 20, 1824
George Edmund London, December 18, 1881
Architect Westminster Abbey

33, Montague Place, WC1, 1855-
14, Cavendish Square, W1 (LCP 1980) -1870
51, Russell Square, WC1, 1870

Street was one of the greatest architects of the Victorian era. He had worked for a time under Sir Gilbert SCOTT and, in turn, he was to have under him, Norman Shaw, Philip Webb and William MORRIS.

His greatest single work is the Law Courts Building on the north side of the Strand just before Fleet Street starts. It was finally completed in 1882 and had used some 35 million bricks, a million cubic feet of stone and eleven miles of heating pipes. It was not received enthusiastically in some quarters. *The Builder* magazine denounced it as a '...deformity and an eyesore'.

STUART Dysart, Scotland, September 7, 1815
John McDonall London, June 5, 1866
Explorer Kensal Green, Grave 19,834; Plot 9-15

9, Campden Hill Square, W8 (LCP 1962) from 1864 until he died here

Stuart emigrated (of his own free will, not at 'Government' expense) to Australia when he was 23 and first worked there as a surveyor. He joined Charles Stuart's expedition to the interior in 1845 after much effort had been expended on a workable route, north to south across the country. The telegraph had already reached India and if it could be linked with settlements in South Australia would be of great value in the extension of the British Empire.

He crossed overland in 1862 having been backed by the Government and, on his return, he was rewarded with £2,000 and the Gold Medal of the Royal Geographic Society.

Mount Stuart was named after him and in 1942, the 'Stuart Highway' was built, following the trail he had blazed 80 years before.

SULLIVAN London, May 13, 1842
(Sir) Arthur Seymour Tunbridge Wells, November 22, 1900
Composer St Paul's Cathedral

3, Ponsonby Street, SW1, 1861
139, Westbourne Terrace, W2, 1864
47, Claverton Terrace, SW1, 1864-1867
1, Queen Anne's Mansions, Queen Anne's Gate, SW1, 1881-1900

Sullivan's father was Bandmaster at Sandhurst Military College in Surrey and at the age of 14, Sullivan entered the Royal Academy of Music as their first Mendelssohn Scholar. He studied under William Sterndale Bennett. Sullivan followed Bennett's earlier example and went to Leipzig, where he became friendly with George (later Sir George) Grove, the editor of the musical dictionary which still bears his name. Together, Sullivan and Grove found the lost score of Schubert's music for *Rosamunde*.

Sullivan's first flirtation with the Theatre was his music for Morton's *Box and Cox*. Not long afterwards he met William Schwenk GILBERT and formed a partnership which was to last 25 uneasy years.

Apart from the operettas, Sullivan's best known single composition is probably *The Lost Chord* (1877) the setting of a poem by Adelaide Anne Procter, '...in sorrow at my brother Fred's death'. Another work to have lasted is the hymn tune *Onward Christian Soldiers*. Hymn tunes may not be commercially very successful, but his operetta music was and he left over £54,000 when he died, a batchelor. On his death, the obituary in the *Times*

read, in part, 'the death of Sir Arthur Sullivan...may be said without hyperbole, to have plunged the whole of the Empire in gloom...'.
There is a bronze bust of Sullivan in the Embankment Gardens immediately behind the Savoy Hotel. It was the work of Sir William John and placed here in 1903. A weeping girl with a sweeping skirt (but with bosoms bare) has attached herself to the plinth on which the bust is placed.

SUN YAT SEN
(or SUN WEN)
'Father of the Chinese Republic'

1866
Peking, March 12, 1925
Nanking

4, Gray's Inn Place, WC1 (P) 1895
49, Portland Place, W1, 1896

Though a qualified doctor, Sun Yat Sen founded a political organization in Honolulu in 1892 with the object of overthrowing the Canton Government, which was attempted unsuccessfully in 1895, after which he remained in exile from China until 1911.
In 1896 he was captured by Chinese factions and held prisoner in the basement of the Chinese Embassy on the corner of Weymouth Place and Portland Place. He managed to have a note smuggled to Sir James Cantlie, a surgeon, an expert in tropical diseases and his former tutor, who lived at 140, Harley Street, W1. Sir James was able to save him from almost certain death.

SUSSEX

The 'Sussexes' in W2 are all named after HRH Prince George Augustus, Duke of Sussex, 6th son of King George III and brother of 'Prinny', who became King George IV in 1820. Augustus was born in London on January 27, 1773 and died in London on April 21, 1843. By comparison to most of his many brothers, he was a *paragon* of virtue! He was Presdient of the Royal Society from 1830-1839. Despite a slight veneer of respectability, Prince George had, in his time, been arrested for debt and also had married illegally.

SUSSEX PLACE, W2

Central line to
Lancaster Gate

2, Louis McNEICE, 1955-1960. During this period he was honoured (unusually for a *poet* of that time) with a CBE

SUSSEX SQUARE, W2

2, Winston CHURCHILL (P) 1920-1925. The mews, which were available, then, behind the house were bought as well so that a studio could be built for 'Churchill – the artist'. From this house he moved to 11, Downing Street as Stanley BALDWIN's Chancellor of the Exchequer.

SWAN

There used to be an inn called the 'Swan' on the river bank before the Chelsea Embankment was built. It was locally famous as it was the 'finishing post' for the annual watermans' race for the Doggett's Coat and Badge. The 'pub' was demolished when the Chelsea Embankment was built. Samuel PEPYS recorded a visit to it (when his wife was in a bad temper).

SWAN WALK SW3

1, Marguerite RADCLYFFE-HALL, 1916. She stayed here (as a paying guest of her cousin, Dorothy Clarke) after her older lover, Mabel Batten had died. It has a fine 18th centry panelled room on the first floor.

SWINBURNE	London, April 5, 1837
Algernon Charles	London, April 10, 1909
Poet	St Boniface's Church, Bonchurch, Isle of Wight

7, Chester Street, SW1, here born
16, Grafton Street, W1, 1860
18, Grosvenor Place, SW1, 1862
77, Newman Street, W1, 1862
124, Mount Street, W1, 1862
22, Dover Street, W1, 1863
36, Wilton Crescent, SW1, 1865
22A, Dorset Street, W1, 1865-1870
12, Upper Woburn Place, WC1, 1872
16, Cheyne Walk, SW3, 1877
25, Guildford Street, WC1, 1878 until October 1879

Algernon was the elder son of Admiral Swinburne; educated at Eton (where it is most probable he acquired a taste for flagellation) before going up to Balliol College, Oxford; from whence he came down without a degree. He had written two plays that gained no popular success (or money) but in 1865, he published the poem *Atlanta in Calydon*, which brought him fame (and fortune) practically overnight.

His private tastes could hardly be considered 'healthy'. He drank too much and had a morbid interest in flagellation. In 1862 he proposed marriage to an American actress called Adah Isaacs Mencken, who was about the same age as himself. She rejected him and (was said to have) told Dante Gabriel ROSSETTI that it was difficult '...to get Algernon up to scratch'.

Despite his wayward life style, he was considered as a possible contender for *Poet Laureate*. In 1879 he was taken by Theodore WATTS-DUNTON, solicitor with literary rather than legal leanings to live at 'The Pines', a respectable semi-detached (ugly) villa at the foot of Putney Hill. He lived here for 30 years; his habits, especially alcoholic ones, were carefully regulated and for years his intake of drink was allowed to be only one bottle of light ale at lunchtime.

SYMONS	London, 1900
Alphonse James Albert	Colchester, August 26, 1941
Biographer	Finchingfield, Essex

17, Bedford Square, WC1, 1928

Symonds was a sort of 'intellectual con-man', and more than just something of a poseur. As a boy, the family were not well off and he was obliged to leave school early and work for a furrier; a job he detested. Somehow he broke free of his suburban background and the work he hated and founded the 'First Edition Club'. He started the 'Wine and Food Society', together with epicure, André Simon. He also wrote a biography of 'Baron' CORVO (Frederick Rolfe) in 1934, which is a model of the biographers' art and remains the standard work on the life of that strange man.

Symonds composed an epitaph for himself which surely wins a gold medal for brevity. It ran:

'A.J.A.S.
A L A S'

TALLEYRAND PERIGORD
Charles Maurice de (Prince of Benevento)
Statesman

Paris, February 13, 1754
Paris, May 17, 1838
Valençay

51, Portland Place, W1, 1792
36-37, Kensington Square, W8, 1793
21, Hanover Square, W1 (LCP 1978) 1830-1834

Originally intended for the Church, Talleyrand cultivated the pose of a rake and cynical wit. In 1790 he was elected President of the French Assembly but by 1792 he was in exile in London, only returning to France after the fall of Robespierre in 1796.

Talleyrand recognized the genius of Napoleon Bonaparte and had originally supported him but deserted the Emperor's cause in 1814. He became Minister for Foreign Affairs under King Louis XVIII, retiring when he was 80 years old.

He was lame (possibly from poliomyelitis) and wore a leg 'iron'. His *pantaloons* were cut so as to allow as much room as possible for the caliper. John Wilson Croker (an English political writer, 1780-1857) met Talleyrand in 1815 and described him as '...fattish, for a Frenchman, his ankles are weak and his feet deformed and he totters about in a strange way. His face is not at all expressive, except it be of a king of drunken stupor: in fact, he looks like an old, fuddled, lame, village schoolmaster and his voice is deep and hoarse'. In 1814 Lady Shelley, wife of Sir John Shelley, wrote in her journal for December 8, that Talleyrand, '...is a frightful object to look at and rolls his tongue about in a disgusting manner; in spite of all that the *French* ladies find him irresistible'.

TAVISTOCK

John Russell, the Patriarch of the Bedford tribe (1485-1555) was granted land in the County of Devon by King Henry VIII. Most of the properties lay in or near the towns (or villages) of Tavistock, Taviton, Crowndale and Morwell. Russell's West Country land holdings are reflected right across the once immense Bedford properties in London. The eldest sons of the Dukes of Bedford carry the courtesy title of the Marquess of Tavistock.

TAVISTOCK PLACE, WC1   *Piccadilly line to Russell Square*

26, Sydney SMITH, 1835
34, Mary Ann CLARKE, while still the mistress of the Duke of York, the Prince Regent's brother, in the 1820s.
34, Sydney SMITH, again, in 1836.

TAVISTOCK SQUARE, WC1

What is now BMA House on the east side of the Square was Tavistock House into which Charles DICKENS moved, from about 1851 until 1860. By this time Dickens was in love with Ellen Ternan.

In the centre of Tavistock Square is a statue of Mahatma Gandhi by Freddie Brilliant, which was unveiled by Harold (now Sir Harold) Wilson in 1966. The statue cost £10,000; a sum that would have appalled the Mahatma.

33,   Thomas BURKE, in the 1920s and 1930s. Out of this period came his book, *Living in Bloomsbury*, which was published in 1939. Of the area, he wrote that Bloomsbury, '…is indeed, as pleasant a quarter to live in as any of the quarters farther west. Its squares are quieter than many of those in other parts, and it is central for almost anywhere. Those who like London at all must, I think, find Bloomsbury agreeable. It is true London, and as one who is never really happy outside London, I have found it more than agreeable.'

52,   Virginia and Leonard WOOLF, for some years until 1941 when the house was badly damaged by a bomb. When they acquired it after the First World War, it had four storeys and a basement in which the Hogarth Press was first established. The Woolf's living quarters were on the second and third floors.

On the south east corner of the square is a remarkable sculpture of a remarkable woman. It is a double sided monument to Dame Louisa Aldridge-Blake (1865-1925). Dame Louisa was the Dean of the Royal Free Hospital.

TEARLE	New York, October 12, 1884
(Sir) Godfrey Seymour	London, June 8, 1953
Actor	

79, Knightsbridge, SW7, 1929

Though born in America, Tearle was educated at Carlisle Grammar School and made his stage début at the age of nine as the infant Duke of York (one of the 'Little Princes' in the Tower) in *Richard III*.

At 15 he had become a professional actor and toured with his father's company for two years. His father died in 1901, whereupon Tearle formed his own company and took the play *Soldier of Fortune* out into the provinces. It was five years before he made an entrance on a West End stage. His acting range became truly vast in the 'live' theatre, but he did not appear on film until after 1940.

He married three times (his second wife, Stella Freeman, died; numbers one and two were divorced). In 1949 he met 17-year old actress Jill Bennett at Stratford-on-Avon. She was taking the part of Banquo's son and, finding her behind the scenes; suitably grubby for her part, Tearle asked her to lunch. For the next four and a half years they had a friendship, affording them a period of 'curiously uncomplicated happiness', which ended with Tearle's death. He died with Jill Bennett at his side (literally: she was lying beside him on his bed in London Clinic) when he murmured, 'You are my sunshine' and, '…then he was gone'.

TEMPEST	London, July 15, 1864
(Dame) Maria	London, October 14, 1942
Actress	

24, Park Crescent, W1 (LCP 1972) 1899-1902

Dame Maria's real name was Mary Susan Etherington and her father (who was illegitimate) was a stationer.

She made her début as a singer in 1885 in Suppé's *Bocaccio* with considerable success. Her first acting role was as Becky Sharp in *Vanity Fair* a play by Robert HICHENS. This established her as a straight actress in comedy parts.

In 1885 she had married Alfred Izard, a professional pianist; the marriage failed and in 1895 she married Cosmo Gordon Lennox. This, too, failed and, third time lucky, she married William Graham Browne, an actor, in 1921. (She only had one child, a son by Izard.)

She had an immutable routine when she was actually in a part. She slept for two hours in the afternoon and *never* went to parties.

TENNYSON Somersby, Lincs., August 6, 1809
Alfred (1st Lord) Haslemere, Surrey, October 6, 1892
Poet Laureate Westminster Abbey in 'Poet's Corner'

60, Lincoln's Inn Fields, WC2, 1842, 1846
16, Egerton Terrace, SW3, 1846
225, Hampstead Road, NW1, 1849-1850

Tennyson must be one of the very few poets who was acclaimed by the ultra-literate, appreciated by the general public and afforded a place in 'society'. He was a 'household word' at one end of the scale and a favourite of Queen Victoria's at the other. The Queen elevated him to the peerage in 1854 and he chose the title of Baron Tennyson of Aldworth and Farringford; Aldworth being the name of the house he built and Farringford, a village in the Isle of Wight where he had settled in 1853.

Alfred became great friends at Cambridge with Monckton MILNES (afterwards Lord Houghton) and, very especially, with Arthur Hallam (1811-1833). Arthur's all too early death inspired the greatest of Tennyson's earlier poems, *In Memoriam*. In 1829 he won the Chancellor's medal with his poem *Timbuctoo*. In 1832 he travelled (with Hallam) in Europe and in that year published *Poems*, which included *The Lady of Shalott*. The year after Hallam died, he published *In Memoriam* and became engaged to be married to Emily Selwood. (They were not married, however, until 1850.)

The year he finally married Emily was the year he was elevated to the Laureateship on the death of WORDSWORTH. In 1854 he wrote *The Charge of the Light Brigade*. This epic work commemorated the action in the Crimean War at Balaclava when Lord RAGLAN (1788-1855) who lost an arm at the Battle of Waterloo in 1815, ordered Lord Lucan (1800-1888) to charge the Russian artillery at the northern end of the valley of Balaclava. The British cavalry routed the Russians but in the engagement only 168 of the original 670 British cavalrymen were to survive. His poem *Maud* was badly received on its publication in 1855. Tennyson suffered from piles and his doctor, on reading *Maud* for the first time, is reputed to have commented, 'Poor Alfred, he's got 'em again'. His *Idylls of the King* was spectacularly popular in 1859. Many poems followed, not all with success, but *Locksley Hall, Sixty Years After* (1886) and *Crossing the Bar* (1889) re-established him as probably the most successful of all English poets.

TERRY Coventry, February 27, 1847
(Dame) Ellen Tenterden, Kent, July 21, 1928
Actress St Paul's Church, Covent Garden

92, Stanhope Street, NW1, c.1850
33, Longridge Road, SW5, 1877-1888
215, King's Road, SW3, 1904-1920

Ellen was one of four daughters of the Irish actor Benjamin Terry, who went on stage. Benjamin (1818-1896) and his wife Sarah (née Ballard) also an actress, had 14 children in all. Ellen made her first stage appearance (as a boy) in *The Winter's Tale* in Charles KEAN's production at the Princess Theatre, London in 1856. She was to become Sir Henry IRVING's leading lady: forming a partnership with him which lasted from 1878 to 1902. She was triumphant in almost all the leading roles in Shakespeare.

Off the stage, life was not so good. At the age of 17 she married (or, more accurately, was married to) George WATTS, who was 47. She cried continuously throughout the wedding ceremony and this hapless, unconsummated marriage was over in less than a year. In 1868 she began to live with the architect, E.W. GODWIN, by whom she had a daughter Edith, who became an actress and a son, Edward Gordon Craig, who became a stage designer of international repute.

She tried marriage for the second time with an actor, Charles Kelly. This (probably unconsummated) union also broke up within a year. (Kelly died in 1885.) The third time was equally unlucky. At the age of 60 she married yet another actor, James Carew, who was a 30-year old American (d.1938). In about 1897 Ellen began a flirtatious correspondence with G.B. SHAW. (Shaw also carried on an even more flirtatious correspondence, beginning in 1899, with Mrs. 'Pat' CAMPBELL, whom he called 'Stella'. In a letter to 'Stella' on December 30, 1921, Shaw wrote, '...I wrote a wonderful string of love letters to Ellen Terry and got a wonderful string of replies from her. Ellen afterwards wrote her memoirs and wrote them very well indeed'. (How Shaw knew this in 1921, when Ellen's *Memoirs*, edited by her son Gordon Craig, were not published until 1932, is interesting.) 'Ellen must have bushels of love letters; and she has been adored by all the poets of her day.'

Towards the end of her life she became very absent minded and before she had left the King's Road she was blind. Her great-nephew, Sir John Gielgud said of his great aunt Ellen, '...with her lovely turned up nose and wide mouth, and that husky voice – a "veiled voice" – somebody called it once – and her enchanting smile, no wonder everyone adored her!'

Ellen was made a Dame of the British Empire in 1925. She was the second actress to be so honoured. The first was Dame Genevieve Ward, an American-born actress, who was 'be-Damed' in 1921.

THACKERAY	Calcutta, July 18, 1811
William Makepeace	Kensington, December 24, 1863
Author	Kensal Green, Square 36, Row 1

13, Coram Street, WC1, 1837-1843
27, Jermyn Street, SW1, 1843-1845
88, St James's Street, SW1, 1845-1846
16, Young Street, W8 (LCP 1965) 1846-1854
36, Onslow Square, SW7 (LCP 1912) 1854-1861
2, Palace Green, W8 (LCP 1887) from 1861 until he died here.

Thackeray was at Charterhouse School and in the last three years there, he was a day boy lodging at 9, Charterhouse Square. In his 18th year he was taken ill and three months later, rose from his sick bed, bald, but having increased his height by nine inches (23 centimetres) to six feet three inches (190 centimetres). His hair grew again, but for a while he wore a wig. In 1829 he went up to Trinity College, Cambridge, lost a poety prize (fittingly) to Alfred TENNYSON and came down without a degree. In 1830 his taste for gambling lost him £1,500 in *one* sitting. It took years to repay the debt. He went to Paris to study art – he was a more than competent artist and, in 1836, married Isabella Shaw, despite the antagonism of her dreadful, widowed mother. There were two surviving daughters of the marriage. Anny married Sir Richmond Ritchie and, as Lady RITCHIE, became a successful author herself. The other girl, Harriet, married Sir Leslie STEPHEN in 1867, but sadly died only nine years later. Their mother became totally unbalanced mentally and Thackeray 'became, as it were, a widower'. Isabella never recovered her sanity but did not die until 1892.

He went into Chambers at 5, Essex Court in 1831, but he forsook the law for literature and his first published effort was a short novel which appeared in installments in *Fraser's Magazine* in 1839-1840. He also contributed to *Punch* from its first issue. *Vanity Fair* in 1850, began Thackeray's reputation as a novelist; followed by *Pendennis Esmond* and *The Newcombes*. He lectured, with indifferent success, in America in 1852 and 1853 and later he even tried his hand at politics.

Thackeray had left explicit instructions that here was to be no 'Westminster

Abbey' for him and wished to be buried beside his first daughter, Jane, who died in 1839, only eight months old. Between 1,500 and 2,000 people attended Thackeray's funeral, amongst whom were DICKENS, BROWNING, TENNYSON, TROLLOPE, CARLYLE, MILLAIS, CRUIKSHANK and the *entire* staff of *Punch*.

THATCHER Grantham, Lincs., October 13, 1925
Margaret Hilda
Prime Minister

19, Flood Street, SW3, 1969-1984

Mrs. Thatcher's father was a shopkeeper in the small town of Grantham. (Despite being the home town of Sir Isaac NEWTON, Grantham was voted the 'Dullest Town in Britain' in 1981!) However, there has been nothing dull about Margaret Hilda Roberts. After local schooling she went up to Somerville College, Oxford where she graduated MA, BSc in chemistry and worked as a Research Chemist from 1947 to 1951. In 1951, she married Denis Thatcher, by whom she had twins in 1953; Mark and Carol.
Politics beckoned Margaret Thatcher more alluringly than chemistry and eventually she was elected as Conservative member for Finchley in North London. This constituency is a solid, true-blue Tory stronghold and, of the 54,000 electoral roll, it is estimated that over 9,000 voters are Jewish. She became joint Parliamentary Secretary to the Ministry of Pensions in 1961 and in 1964 Secretary of State in the Ministry of Education. (There her most memorable action was to cut back on the supply of free 'school milk')

THIRKELL Kensington, January 30, 1891
Angela Margaret Godalming, Surrey, January 29, 1961
Novelist

27, Young Street, W8, here born and lived with her family until 1900
108, Kensington Church Street, W8, 1911-1914
6, Pembroke Gardens, W8, 1935, her father's house
1, Shawfield Street, SW3, 1951-1961

Angela's father was J.W. Mackail and she was the granddaughter of Sir Edward BURNE-JONES (and a cousin of Rudyard KIPLING).
After her education at St Paul's School for Girls, she married J. Campbell McInnes when she was only 20 (in St Philip's Church, Kensington on May 5, 1911). By McInnes she had two sons. The younger, Colin, became a novelist and his first book, *City of Spades* in 1957 did *not* appeal to her. It was followed by *Absolute Beginners* in 1959 and *Mr Love and Mr Justice* in 1960.
In 1917, the McInnes were divorced and in the following year she married G.L. Thirkell, a Tasmanian. This marriage did not last either. She came back to London in 1931 and her first book, a form of autobiography, *Three Houses*, was published.
She then began to produce novels at the rate of about one every 18 months, the most popular titles being; *The Brandons* in 1939 and *Cheerfulness Breaks In*, 1940. Her last book, *Happy Returns*, was published in 1952.

THOMAS Swansea, October 27, 1914
Dylan Marlais New York, November 9, 1953
Poet

Flat 3, Wentworth Studios, Manresa Road, SW3, 1942-1944
54, Delancey Street, NW1, 1951

On leaving Swansea Grammar School, Dylan Thomas went to work as a junior reporter with the *South Wales Evening Post*. During this period the *Sunday Referee* accepted and printed some of his poems. Mark Goulden, editor of the *Sunday Referee*, began a feature called 'Poets' Corner' and Thomas was one of the first poets to be included. In 1934 Goulden published Dylan's *Eighteen Poems* – and paid for it himself. This little work was well thought of by Edith SITWELL and another book, *Twenty-five Poems*, was published in 1936.

During the Second World War, Thomas was found to be medically unfit for military service and he worked for the BBC. By this time he was drinking heavily and, when in his cups, could be decidedly *tiresome*. His widest known work is *Under Milk Wood*, which, written as a radio play – 'a play for voices' – had its first performance in Cambridge, Massachusetts, when Thomas himself read it in an unfinished edition. It was published as a radio play in 1954.

A plaque to Dylan Thomas was let into the floor by 'Poet's Corner' in Westminster Abbey in 1982.

THOMPSON	Framlingham, Suffolk, August 6, 1820
(Sir) Henry	London, August 18, 1904
Physician	

35, Wimpole Street, W1, 1904

Sir Henry was doctor to monarchs and noblemen. Using a plain-bladed *lithorite* he removed bladder stones from King Leopold of Belgium (and was paid £5,000 for doing so). He also operated on NAPOLEON III at Chiselhurst. The operation could hardly have been considered a success as the exiled emperor died soon after. (Thompson received a warm letter of thanks from a 'Red Republican' for 'his services to humanity in having so ably made away with a tyrant'!)

Thompson once asked THACKERAY how many bottles of wine he drank a year. Thackeray thought, then said; 'well – roughly – about 500'. Thompson looked grave, 'But', added Thackeray quickly '-it is almost all other people's wine you know'.

THOMSON	Belfast, June 26, 1824
William (1st Baron Kelvin)	Netherhall, Strathclyde, December 17,
Scientist	1907
	Westminster Abbey (central aisle of nave)

15, Eaton Place, SW1, for some years until his death

Baron Kelvin of Largs (which was the title he chose when he was created a Baron in 1892) was the son of James Thomson, Professor of Mathematics at Glasgow University. Kelvin, however, distinguished himself as an original thinker at Cambridge. He graduated as Second Wrangler, the first Smith's prizeman of 1845 and was made a Fellow of Peterhouse College.

In 1846 he was back in Glasgow as Professor of Natural Philosophy at the University. (His father, though now retired, lived to see his son appointed. He died in 1849, aged 63.) One of Kelvin's papers, earlier on, had dealt with electro-static problems and it was largely his work on research into the transmission of electric currents that made it possible for the submarine trans-Atlantic cable to be laid successfully and operating by 1865. He was knighted for this a year later.

Being a down-to-earth Scot, Kelvin chose a good plain English motto: 'Honesty with Fear'.

THORNHILL   Melcombe Regis, 1676
(Sir)   James Weymouth, May 13, 1734
Artist   St Nicholas's Church, Chiswick Mall

104, St Martin's Lane, WC2, 1710
12, Covent Garden, WC2, 1722-1724
75, Dean Street, W1, 1725-1733

Thornhill's father was a spendthrift and, when James was still a boy, the
family estate of Thornhill, near Weymouth in Dorset had to be sold.
Through the generosity of his uncle Thomas (Dr. Thomas Sydenham,
1624-1689) James was able to begin to study art in London. Thornhill's most
obvious works to a Londoner, or a visitor to the capital are the eight scenes
from the life of St Paul on the interior of the cupola of St Paul's Cathedral.
The work is in *chiar'oscuro* heightened in gold and Thornhill was paid at the
rate of forty shillings (£2) a square yard (0.836 of a square metre).
Thornhill's other works in conjunction with Christopher WREN's
architecture, can be seen at Hampton Court Palace to the west of the city and
at Greenwich in the east. (He was only paid the same rate for Greenwich as
he had been for St Paul's.)

THORNEYCROFT   London, March 9, 1850
(Sir) William Hamo   Oxford, December 18, 1925
Sculptor

2A, Melbury Road, W14, his studio in the 1920s, he lived at:
47, Marlborough Mansions, Hampstead, NW6

Sculpting seems to have been a speciality in the Thorneycroft family. His
mother, Mary (1814-1895) sculpted, as did his grandfather, John (1780-1861)
and his father, Thomas (1815-1885). His brother, Sir John Isaac
Thorneycroft, b.1843, was a Naval Architect, knighted in 1902.
William first exhibited at the Royal Academy in 1871, was elected a Member
of it in 1888 and was knighted in 1917. His work is well represented in
London: Queen Victoria in the Royal Exchange; General Gordon, now in
the Embankment Gardens (until 1953 it stood in Trafalgar Square) the
Gladstone Memorial in the Strand at the eastern end of the Aldwych and
Oliver Cromwell outside the Houses of Parliament. This was placed here in
1899, complete with his upside down spurs!

THORPE   April 29, 1929
Jeremy John
Politician

66, Marsham Court (corner of Page Street) Marsham Street, SW1
2, Orme Square, W2, 1973

Thorpe received some of his education at the Rectory School in Connecticut
(he was 'evacuated' from war-torn England in 1940) and the rest of it at Eton
after his return. He went up to Trinity College, Oxford in 1948, becoming
President of the Union there in 1951. Three years later he was a barrister in
the Inner Temple.
He was a political animal and, being possessed of some sort of 'private'
income, he chose to stand as the Liberal Candidate in the North Devon
constituency in October 1959. Jo Grimond was Party Leader – a party of
only a handful of seats in the House of Commons and, when Grimond
resigned at the age of 54, Thorpe stepped into his place.
His wife was tragically killed in a car crash in 1970; they had only been
married for two years and had one son, Rupert. Three years later he again
found happiness in a second marriage, to Marion, the divorced wife of Lord

Harewood (cousin of the Queen). She was strikingly good looking, intelligent and musical. The Thorpes moved into Orme Square, where Marion had held onto the house she had once shared with Harewood.

Then, strange stories began to circulate. The *Press* pricked up their collective ears and a series of bizarre incidents, seemingly unconnected began to fall into some sort of nightmare pattern. A large dog was shot dead on a Devon moor, a male model rented a flat in Draycott Avenue, SW3, paid for by a person 'in politics', the Parliamentary member for Bodmin, Cornwall, left Britain in a hurry. The link was Thorpe.

The whole matter erupted in 1971 with a long trial at the Old Bailey. Thorpe was accused of having a homosexual liaison with 'the male model', who turned out to be called Norman Scott. He had been to bed with Thorpe and had in his possession letters from Thorpe that left little room for doubt. Thorpe was also accused of plotting with others to have Scott 'eliminated'. The man for the job, the prosecution (the Crown) alleged, was to be an out-of-work air line pilot, who shot Scott's dog instead! The MP who had left both the Liberal Party and the country, in some haste, returned to London to give evidence on *oath* that he (Peter Bessell) and Thorpe had actually discussed the matter of Scott's *murder* on the terrace outside the House of Commons and the cost and the disposal of the body.

Many people gave evidence and many lies were told, but, after a long and *very* expensive case, Thorpe was cleared of all charges.

THURLOW	Norfolk, December 9, 1731
(Lord) Edward	Brighton, September 12, 1806
Lord Chancellor	The Temple Church, EC4

45, Great Ormond Street, WC1, 1771-1792

From Canterbury Grammar School, Thurlow went on to Caius College, Cambridge then into law, 'took silk' in 1761, was elected to a seat in the Commons for Tavistock (Devon) and was Solicitor General before he was 40.

He was violently *opposed* to the anti-slavery lobbies and a vigorous opponent of the American 'colonials' who wanted 'representation' if they were to be subject to British 'taxation'. In 1778, this bigoted man became Lord Chancellor and was elevated to the peerage.

His wit was caustic and he 'used profanity liberally both in his conversation and his speeches'. He had beetling black eyebrows over piercing black eyes and FOX said of him that he, '...*looked* wiser than any man ever *was*'.

TITE STREET, SW3	*Circle and Distric lines to*
	Sloane Square

Named in 1875 after Sir William Tite, MP (1798-1873) who was also a member of the Metropolitan Board of Works and much concerned with the building of the Thames Embankment, the 'upper reaches' of which, run across the southern end of the street.

8, Laurence BINYON, 1900, before he joined the staff of the British Museum.

13, J.McN. WHISTLER, 1881-1885. This was his first address after he had come back to London after the Ruskin court action had effectively bankrupted him.

31, John Singer SARGENT, from 1901 until he died here. The house, wrote Henry JAMES in 1913, has a '...beautiful, high, cool studio, opening upon a balcony that overhangs a charming Chelsea green garden, adding a charm to everything'.

33, Augustus JOHN, 1940. In that year he was *re*-elected to the Royal Academy.

34, Oscar WILDE, 1885-1895. He moved here with his beautiful, young wife, Constance. It was to be their only home together.

TORRINGTON SQUARE, WC1   *Northern line to Goodge Street*

This square, on Bedford owned land, was finished in about 1835. John, the 6th Duke, had married Georgina Byng whose father was Lord Torrington.

30, Christina ROSSETTI (LCP 1975) (P) from 1876 until she died here in 1894. During part of this period her brother. William, lived here as well. Their mother, a chronic invalid, held sway over the house.

TRAILL	Blackheath, London, August 14, 1842
Henry Duff	London, February 21, 1900
Author	

47, Gordon Square, WC1, 1880s

Traill's father was a magistrate and Henry was sent to the Merchant Taylors' School. He went up to St John's College, Oxford, read law and was called to the Inner Temple Bar in 1869. Two years later he joined the inspection department of the Government Educational branch and it was then he began to write commercially and thought about writing as a job rather than a hobby.

He joined the staff of the *Pall Mall Gazette* then moved to the *Saint James's Gazette*. From 1882 to 1897 he was a leader writer on the *Telegraph*. He wrote humorous verses, studies on STERNE (1882) COLERIDGE (1884) and the standard life of Sir John Franklin (1786-1847) the Arctic explorer who lost his life in King William's land.

TREE	London, December 17, 1852
(Sir) Herbert Beerbohm	London, July 2, 1917
Actor Manager	Hampstead Parish Church

76, Sloane Street, SW1 (P) 1898
A 1, Albany, Piccadilly, W1

In September 1887, Tree became the lessee of the Haymarket Theatre and moved into Her Majesty's ten years later. As an actor he had a curious, throaty delivery and his style generally was very much his own and (like Henry IRVING's) would not have had a chance today in the professional theatre. (W.S. GILBERT once said of Tree's playing of Hamlet, '...that it was funny without being vulgar'.) Tree's greatest financial success was in Du MAURIER's 'Trilby'.

Tree; like John Barrymore (but for different reasons) had great difficulty remembering his lines. One of Tree's contemporaries wrote that Tree, '...found it difficult to memorize the lines of his always leading parts and with the most fertile invention posted prompters under tables, behind rocks, jutting walls or ancient oaks as he moved in well-disguised anguish from cache to cache'.

TREVELYAN	Welcombe, Warks., February 16, 1876
George Macaulay	July 21, 1962
Historian	

8, Grosvenor Crescent, SW1, 1893
2, Cheyne Gardens, SW3, 1904-1918

Trevelyan, the son of Sir George Otto Trevelyan (1838-1928) was a grand nephew of MACAULAY and it is little wonder that he was a truly gifted historian himself. He first went to Harrow then up to Trinity College, Cambridge – of which he was to become Master in 1940. In 1904 he married Janet, a daughter of Mrs. Humphrey WARD.

In the First World War Trevelyan was commandant of a British Ambulance Unit in Italy. He was made a CBE in 1920 and, in 1930, King George V made him a Companion of the Order of Merit.

His *English Social History* was published in Britain in 1942, when the country was practically at its lowest ebb. By 1950 it had sold over half a million copies.

TREVES　　　　　　　　　　　Dorchester, Dorset, February 15, 1853
(Sir) Frederick　　　　　　　　　Verey, December 7, 1923
Physician　　　　　　　　　　　Ashes in Dorchester Cemetery

18, Gordon Square, WC1, 1879-1884
6, Wimpole Street, W1, 1884

Treves achieved fame and social standing when he removed the Royal appendix from the rotund King Edward VII in 1902. The operation necessitated the postponement of the King's Coronation but it also started a sort of 'appendectomy cult'. Of longer lasting fame was the work Treves did in the founding of the British Red Cross in the First World War.

At the age of 32 he had become Chief Surgeon at the London Hospital (where he had trained) and the hospital's House Governor recalled that Treves' operating coat was often so stiff with congealed blood that, '...it would stand upright when placed on the floor'!

In 1884 Treves 'exhibited' the now famous 'Elephant Man' to the Pathological Society. This poor man, John Merrick, had been exploited previously by travelling showmen. Merrick was terrifyingly hideous. He suffered from hypertrophy of the bones and pachydermatocele and papilloma of the skin. The circumference of his head was the same as that of his waist. The only outward part of him that did not shock or disgust was his left hand. Treves gave him sanctuary in rooms that he had had converted in the hospital, though there was nothing which the medical profession could do for him. Treves arranged it that willing people should 'drop in on' Merrick, without reacting to the near-monster he was. He even gave instructions that they offer to shake his right (and grossly deformed) hand.

TROLLOPE　　　　　　　　　London, April 24, 1815
Anthony　　　　　　　　　　　London, December 6, 1882
Novelist　　　　　　　　　　　Kensal Green: Square 138, Row 1

3, Holles Street, W1, 1872-1873
39, Montagu Square, W1 (LCP 1914) 1873-1880

Trollope worked for many years for the General Post Office, indeed it is said that it was he who *invented* the pillar box. He began writing to try and bolster his inadequate salary. He was 40 before he struck literary oil with *The Warden* in 1855, the first of the *Barchester* series, but did not resign from the Post Office for another 12 years.

He produced the staggering total of 50 novels and to achieve this he used to get up every morning (almost without exception) at 5 and write until 8 am. He could write at an average of 1,000 words per day. By the 1860s his literary output was earning him £4,500 per annum. The *Barsetshire* novels alone pulled in some £70,000 in his lifetime. This physical effort took its toll and he developed what can only be called writers' cramp. He had to have a secretary and he was lucky to have a niece, Florence Bland, who could do this work. Florence lived with the Trollopes almost as if she was their daughter. Her lot was *not* easy. She was not allowed to say *one* single word while Trollope was actually dictating, nor offer any suggestions.

Some one once said of Trollope that '...he came in at the door like a frantic windmill'. Locker-Lampson described him being, 'Hirsute and taurine of aspect, he would glare at you from behind two fierce spectacles. His ordinary tones had the penetrating capacity of two people quarreling.'

TRUMBULL Lebanon, Conn., June 6, 1756
John New York, November 10, 1843
Artist

72, Welbeck Street, W1, 1799
29, Leicester Square, WC1, 1808

Trumbull (son of Jonathan Trumbull, 1710-1785, one time Governor of Connecticut, who had taken a prominent part in the War of Independence) served as a deputy adjutant-general in the Revolutionary War. Afterwards he set himself up as a portrait painter in New York. He visited London in 1780 with a letter of introduction from Benjamin FRANKLIN to Benjamin WEST and was promptly arrested as a suspicious character. In 1784 he met Sir Joshua REYNOLDS and again in Paris in 1786. Trumbull married (unlike Reynolds) in London in 1800. One of his best known paintings is *The Surrender of Lord Cornwallis*.
The University of Yale collected more than 50 of Trumbull's paintings and, in 1831, granted him an annuity of 1,000 dollars.

TURNER Woodstock, Oxon., August 31, 1774
Charles London, August 1, 1857
Engraver Highgate

56, Warren Street, W1 (LCP 1924) 1799-1803
50, Warren Street, W1, where he died

As a result of Turner's father losing his job, Mrs. Turner started work in Blenheim Palace (the home of the Marlborough's, who also own the village of Woodstock) and was in charge of the china closet.
In 1795 Turner came to London and began to study at the Academy Schools. He became a highly skilled engraver and produced about 400 mezzotint or aquatint portraits.
He produced scenes from the Battle of Waterloo and one of Westminster Abbey during King George IV's Coronation in 1821. J.M.W. TURNER entrusted him to take the first plates of his *Liber Studiorum* to Charles. But the two Turners quarrelled (easy to do with J.M.W.) and the project failed.

TURNER London, April 23, 1775
Joseph Mallord William London, December 19, 1851
Artist St Paul's Cathedral

26, Maiden Lane, WC2, here born
51 (formerly 64) Harley Street, W1, 1800
23, then 22, and then 45, Queen Anne Street, W1
45, Harley Street, W1, 1803-1812
118, Cheyne Walk, SW3, from 1846 until his death here

The son of a barber and born over the barber's shop, Turner was to become England's greatest romantic artist. As a teenager he was employed as a copyist and colourist and later went to work with Thomas Girtin (1775-1802). He was admitted to the Royal Academy Schools and, in 1790 he had an exhibit in the Royal Academy Exhibition. In 1802 he went to Europe for the first of many a continental visit. Venice appealed to him particularly (as it *must* do for any 'romantic'). It was to be his painting, *Juliet and her Nurse*, an oil in a Venetian setting, which fetched a record of £2,689,076 at Sotheby's auction in New York on May 29, 1981; at that date the largest price paid for any painting by anybody.

He was not a sociable man and he never married, but there was speculation about his relationship with his 'housekeeper', Sophia Booth. Turner had met her whilst on holiday at Margate, where Sophia kept a lodging house. She was illiterate but she fully understood his genius.

TWAIN, M. see CLEMENS, S.L.

'UPPER' in every instance which follows, is merely a 'modification' of the street name it prefixes. The details of, say, Upper Berkeley Street' are the same as those given for Berkeley Street itself.

UPPER BERKELEY STREET, W1

20, Elizabeth Garrett ANDERSON (LCP 1962) 1860-1874. Five years after she moved here she became the first woman in Britain to qualify as a medical doctor.

48, Max BEERBOHM, 1898-1909. Two years previously (at the age of 24) he had published a book entitled, *The Complete Works of Max Beerbohm*.

UPPER BROOK STREET, W1 *Central line to Bond Street*

10, Stanley BALDWIN. The Baldwins moved here when the Conservative Party was beaten in the 1929 General Election and Baldwin had to leave 10, Downing Street. Mrs. Baldwin had yellow blinds fitted to all the rooms in the house, '...to create an atmosphere of permanent sunshine'.

16, Monckton MILNES (Lord Houghton) 1852-1870. His wife, Annabel, inherited this house from her aunt, Mrs. Cunliffe, together with its furnishing, pictures and a seven-year lease on it. Nathaniel HAWTHORNE had breakfast here on July 11, 1856.

39, Lord LEVERHULME, 1929.

50, Sir Edward HULTON, 1919, whilst still a schoolboy at Harrow.

UPPER CHEYNE ROW, SW3

10, Leigh HUNT (LCP 1905) 1818. On February 11, KEATS was HUNT's dinner guest. Another diner there was Thomas Love Peacock, an official in the East India Company, but today remembered as the author of *Headlong Hall* (1816) and *Nightmare Abbey* two years later.
Peacock was an intimate friend of P.B. SHELLEY.

22, Leigh HUNT, 1833-1840. In his day the house was number 4. (It had also once been number 10, just to confuse matters further.) He lived here with his wife and seven children, whose noise must have unsettled the dour Thomas CARLYLE, who lived at number 24.

UPPER HARLEY STREET, W1

2, Frederick MAURICE (LCP 1977) 1862-1866. He left here when he was elected to the Knightsbridge Chair of Moral Philosophy at Cambridge.

UPPER PHILLIMORE GARDENS, W8

11, Robert ROSS, 1893-1900.

21, Alice and Wilfred MEYNELL, 1881-1888. In 22 months the Meynells had had '...nine *different* cooks, five housemaids, one coming twice and making two changes, three nurses, one of them coming twice'.

UPPER WOBURN PLACE, WC1

12, Algernon SWINBURNE had lodgings here in 1872, but his 'well-bred' landlady had to ask him to leave 'because of his horrible drinking habits'.

24, Pearl CRAIGIE ('John Oliver Hobbes') in the 1870s. The whole family had come from Boston, Mass., to settle in London in 1868.

USTINOV   London, April 16, 1921
Peter Alexander
Actor and playwright

14, Chelsea Embankment, SW3, 1949-1953

Ustinov, the son of Iona Ustinov and the painter Nadia Benois, went to Westminster School and then straight into the Army, being demobilized in 1946. While still almost a school-boy he wrote his first play *House of Regrets* and it was produced at the Arts Theatre in 1942. Altogether he has some 15 plays to his credit, the most successful of them being *The Love of Four Colonels*, which was first played in 1951.

THE VALE, SW3 *District line to West Brompton*

Most of this street stands on the site of a paddock belonging to a house called Vale Grove, a villa in Old Church Street which was finally taken down in 1912. The 'paddock' was always referred to locally as 'The Vale'.

1, William DE MORGAN, 1887-1909, in a, '…quaint, rambling dwelling, shrouded in creepers with a verandah back and front…spruce with gay MORRIS papers and decorated with De Morgan pots and rich-hued paintings.'

2, J.McN. WHISTLER, 1886-1890 (both 1, 1B and 2 have all gone).

15, Ethel SANDS, 1913-1937. In 1934 Miss Sands rented this house to Alfred Lunt (a Milwaukee actor, then 41) and his lovely Lynn Fontanne, six years his senior (who was born in Essex). In January 1934 they both were playing in *Reunion in Vienna* at the Lyric, which had previously been a hit in New York.

VAN BUREN	Kinderhook, N.Y., December 5, 1782
Martin	Lindenwald, N.Y., July 24, 1862
8th President, United States	Kinderhook Cemetery

7, Stratford Place, W1 (LCP 1977) 1831-1832

Van Buren was the third of five children of a farmer and tavern keeper and, through his mother, Maria (the widow of Johanes Van Allen) was related twice over to Theodore Roosevelt, to be the 26th President of America. Van Buren, a lawyer, entered the New York State Senate in 1812 and was its Attorney General in 1815. In 1807 he married a cousin, Hannah Hoes (1783-1819) the daughter of a farmer and they had four sons.

Van Buren was the first President to be born a citizen of the United States. He was only five feet six inches tall and sometimes referred to as 'Little Matty'. (He also had other nicknames; 'The American Talleyrand', 'Little Magician' and the 'Red Fox'. He was even called 'Old Kinderhook' and sometimes just 'O.K.' Some people have advanced this last as being the true origin of the, now international, term 'O.K.'.)

VAUGHAN-WILLIAMS	Down Ampney, October 12, 1872
Ralph	London, August 26, 1958
Composer	Westminster Abbey, North Choir Aisle

13, Cheyne Walk, SW3, pre-1914
10, Hanover Terrace, NW1, 1953-1958

At Charterhouse, Vaughan-Williams was encouraged in his musical studies, at home too, his father being a vicar. He went on to the Royal College of Music and studied under Charles Villiers STANFORD, then under Max Bruch in Berlin and, finally, with Maurice Ravel in Paris. Despite his continental · musical education, Vaughan Williams' music was quintessentially English. He also had his MA (D Mus) from Cambridge. He was a collector and student of English folk song and Tudor Church music. His first real success was with his *Sea Symphony* in 1910. In 1909 he published his *Fantasia on a Theme of Tallis*, which still appears regularly in musical programmes around the world. (Thomas Tallis, who was born c.1505 and died in Greenwich in 1585, was a Gentleman of the Chapel Royal in the reigns of both Henry VIII and Queen Elizabeth I and joint organist with William Byrd, who was his pupil, some 38 years younger that Tallis and who died in Essex in 1623.)

VERLAINE
Paul
Poet

Metz, March 30, 1844
Paris, January 8, 1896

35, Howland Street, W1; 1872-1873

An 'Art-for-Art's-Sake' poet whose private life became involved with a wife, a child, alcohol and a depraved boy-friend ten years younger than he *and* a chronic shortage of money. In 1873 he shot at the boy-friend, Arthur RIMBAUD, only to wound him in a drunken brawl. He ended up in Mons gaol, where he wrote his *Romances Sans Paroles*.

He came to England to lecture on poetry, 'sponsored' by William ROTHENSTEIN in 1893 and behaved quite well, but drink and general debauchery had taken their toll.

Nina Hamnett once told Walter SICKERT (in the *Cafe Royal*) that she had lost her virginity in the same room once shared by Verlaine and his lover, Rimbaud. 'Should not,' she asked, '...the Council put up a plaque?' 'My dear', replied Sickert, 'they will put one up on the front for *you* and one on the *back* for *them*.'

VICTORIA ROAD, W8

*District, Circle and Piccadilly lines
to Gloucester Road*

Named after Queen Victoria, who had been on the throne some twelve years when this area began to be developed.

1A, Samuel PALMER, 1846-1851. Palmer and his wife, Hannah, moved in here not long after having returned from a two-year 'honeymoon' in Italy.

10, Sir George ROBEY. At this time Robey was still together with his first wife, Ethel. They left Victoria Road around 1929.

18, Norman O'NEILL, 1897-1899. He was not often here as he was in Germany for most of this period, studying at the Frankfurt Conservatoire.

26, Sir Patrick HASTINGS, 1908-1918. He moved from here immediately after he became a King's Council.

29, Nancy MITFORD was living here with her younger sister DIANA in 1923, just before Diana married her first husband, Bryan Guinness.

35, Sir Hugh CASSON, for many years until 1980, when they moved to W11.

79, Sir Rupert HART-DAVIS was born here in 1907.

177, Sir Henry NEWBOLT, 1889-1896, '...the one spot in London where we could live and flourish. It was small but not dark or cramped. It had a good outlook – a vista down a wide street leading out of our own and its front was pleasantly embowered behind two good trees, one an oak and the other an acacia...'

VILLIERS STREET, WC2

*Jubilee, Bakerloo and Northern lines
to Charing Cross*

George Villiers, Duke of Buckingham, acquired the former York House in 1617. The watergate for his house stands today, high and dry in Victoria Embankment Gardens. His son, the second and last Duke of Buckingham, sold the land for development in the 1670s on the understanding that five streets off the Strand were named after him. Accordingly, for some years there were to be found: George Court, Villiers Street, Duke Street (now gone) Of Alley (now York Place) and Buckingham Street.

24, Sir Charles MACFARREN was born here on the evening of March 2, 1813

43, Rudyard KIPLING, 1889-1891. He had lodgings in rooms 16, 17 and 18 on the second floor. In *Something of Myself* he wrote, 'Villiers Street was primitive and passionate in its habits. My rooms were small and not overclean or well kept but from my desk I could look out of my windows through the fan-light of Gatti's Music Hall entrance across the street.

'VOLTAIRE', see AROUET, F.M.

VON WEBER	Eutin, Germany, December 12, 1786
(Baron) Carl Maria Friedrich Ernst	London, June 4, 1826
Musician	St Mary's, Moorfields until 1844 when his remains were re-interred in Dresden

115, Great Portland Street, W1 (P) where he died

Von Weber has more than once been referred to as the 'Creator of the Romantic Opera'. He was of a noble, but impoverished Austrian family and, as a child, he and his parents, both musicians, travelled with a theatrical troupe. He was taught to play the piano before his feet could reach the pedals, but his musical education began in earnest when he was ten. His second opera, *Das Waldmadchen*, was written and performed at Freiburg before he was 14. He was welcomed as a pupil in Vienna by 'Abt' (George Joseph) Vogler (1749-1814) who got the boy the conductorship of the Opera in Breslau. At the age of 20, Weber became a sort of secretary to the King of Württemberg's brother, but soon was in trouble ('debt and dissipation') and, further, was charged with embezzlement. He and his father left the country, very hurriedly, in 1810.

His final masterpiece was *Oberon* and he conducted it often at Covent Garden. The piece had been composed originally for Charles Kemble. Weber overworked, for the few weeks in the late spring of 1826, whilst he was in London, and he died from exhaustion before he was 40. (The house in which he died belonged to Sir George SMART.)

W

WAGNER
Wilhelm Richard
Composer

Leipsic, May 22, 1813
Venice, February 13, 1883
In the garden of his house, *Wahnfried*, in Bayreuth

22, Portland Terrace (now Wellington Road) NW8, 1855
65, Balcombe Street, NW1, 1855
12, Orme Square, W2, 1877

Wagner received very little formal musical education until he was accepted by Weinlig of the Thomasschule when he was 17. His first opera, *Die Feen*, written when he was 20, was never performed in his lifetime; his second, *Liebesverbot* was given *one* performance at Magdeburg; it was a dismal failure. However, here he met Minna Planer and they were married here in 1836. She was a member of the company and he was, officially, the conductor of the Opera House. The Opera went bankrupt as did the next position he was to hold at Konigsberg.
Lohengrin was produced by Liszt at Weimar in 1850 and this encouraged Wagner to make a start on *Das Rheingold* in 1853, followed by *Die Walkure* and part one of *Siegfried*. Music did not take up *all* his time and, in 1859, he began a love affair with Mathilde, wife of his patron, Otto Wesendonck. The following year, Napoleon himself ordered a performance of *Tannhauser* in Paris (where it failed).
In 1861, Wagner was allowed to go back to Germany and it was about this time that the 16-year old King Ludwig II of Bavaria became attracted to Wagner's music. He summoned him to his Court where every facility was made available to the composer with no expense spared. *Tristan* was performed in Munich in 1865. Not long after politics reared its ugly head and Wagner hurriedly decamped for Switzerland again. He was joined by Cosima von Bulow (a daughter of Liszt and wife of the Music Director at Munich). Minna Wagner died in 1866, the von Bulow's were divorced and Wagner married Cosima in 1868. Cosima was *besotted* by Wagner. She ran the household with a military efficiency and ran Richard as well. When he died of a heart attack in her arms, she clung to his body for 24 hours. Later she cut off her long hair and placed it in his coffin to be buried with him.

WAKLEY
Thomas
Founder of the Lancet

Membury, Devon, July 11, 1795
Madeira, June 14, 1862
Kensal Green, Catacomb B, Vault 59
(visit by appointment)

35, Bedford Square, WC1 (LCP 1962) 1828-1848

Wakley came to London in 1815 and, not long after, prudently married into a well-to-do-family, before setting up as a medical practitioner in Argyll Street, W1. Later he moved a little south-east, to The Strand and, on October 5, 1823, launched a magazine which he called *The Lancet*. It was a *campaigning* publication, exposing medical malpractices and (inevitably) involved Wakley in a large number of libel suits. (Then, as now, there was a strong medical lobby in Parliament.)
Wakley joined Parliament as member for Finsbury in north London and represented this (even then) rather seedy suburb, taking his campaigns into

the House on a number of occasions. It was largely due to his pressures that, for instance, the 'Adulteration of Food and Drink Act' was brought into being in 1860.

WALEY   Tunbridge Wells, August 19, 1889
Arthur David   June 27, 1966
Orientalist   Highgate Cemetery

22, Great James Street, WC1, 1950s-1966

From 1912, Waley was Assistant Keeper of the Department of Prints and Drawings at the British Museum. During the Second World War he worked with the Ministry of Information. Waley translated (and had published in six volumes) the classic Japanese novel, *The Tale of the Genji*. The publication was spread over seven years, volume six appearing in 1932. It was his most important work. He also produced numerous translations from the Chinese and his life work was recognized when Queen Elizabeth bestowed the Companion of Honour in 1956.

Beryle de Zoete, a celebrated historian of the Dance, lived with Waley for years, unmarried, but they remained together until her death in 1962, when she was over 80. She affected the dress and mannerisms of someone much younger and Edith SITWELL – who was probably five years or so younger than she – always spoke of her as '*Baby* Beryl'.

WALLACE   Greenwich, April 1, 1875
Edgar Richard Horatio   Hollywood, February 10, 1932
Author

31, Portland Place, W1, c.1929

Wallace was the illegitimate son of an actor and was abandoned by his mother when he was only six days old. He was brought up by a Billingsgate fish-porter until he was 12 and went to an elementary school in Peckham. On leaving school he was in and out of a number of menial jobs and, generally disenchanted, joined the Army. He served in South Africa and, his army contract expired, became African correspondent for the *Daily Mail* in 1899.

From journalism to becoming an author was not a large step and, in 1905, his *Four Just Men* was published. From then on he never stopped. Eventually he published 170 books and a number of thrilling plays. The speed with which he worked was amazing. He used a 'Dictaphone' and employed a record breaking typist. The two together were sometimes referred to by *highbrow critics* as the 'Fiction Factory'.

On number 107, Fleet Street, on the north side at Ludgate Circus, at ground level of 'Ludgate House', is a bronze medallion of Wallace by F. Doyle-Jones.

WALLAS   Sunderland, May 31, 1858
(Professor) Graham   Cornwall, August 9, 1932
Economist

38, St Leonard's Terrace, SW3, 1894-1904

Wallas was sent to Shrewsbury School and then up to Corpus Christi College, Cambridge. Together with Beatrice POTTER (later Mrs. Webb then Lady Passfield) and others, Wallas helped found the London School of Economics, which first opened its doors in 1895. Wallas was Professor of Political Science there from 1912-1923.

He was a prominent Fabian and his philosophy and teachings were directed toward emphasizing the part that 'irrational forces' play in determining political attitudes and public opinion. The Fabian Society, founded in 1884, 'deprecates immediate attempts at revolutionary action'. (Named after the Roman, Fabius Maximus, Cunctator – 'The Delayer' who foiled Hannibal by employing dilatory tactics.)

WALPOLE   London, September 24, 1717
Horace (4th Earl of Orford)   London, March 2, 1797
Author

17, Arlington Street, W1 (LCP 1971) here born and lived until 1779
11 (in his day, number 40) Berkeley Square, W1, from 1779 until he died here

Walpole was at Eton then King's College, Cambridge, where, in both institutions, he had for a friend, the poet Thomas Gray. His father gave him one or more governmental sinecures, but Horace and Gray had set off on the 'Grand Tour' of Europe. At Reggio (Italy) they quarrelled and Walpole, feeling ill, returned to England in 1741. Not long after he took his seat in the House of Commons as member for Callington in Cornwall.
In 1745 Papa died and left 'ample means' for his younger son to live very agreeably. Two years later Horace bought a former coachman's cottage and a parcel of land at Twickenham, on the bank of the Thames, a few miles out of town. Gradually the 'cottage' was extended, finally battlemented (and 'gothicized') until 1756, when it was considered complete and called 'Strawberry Hill'.
His elder brother died in 1791 and Horace, unexpectedly, became the 4th Earl of Orford. However, the title made little difference to the way he lived and he was much more interested in capitalizing on his success as a novelist (his novel *Castle of Otranto* having been published with acclaim in 1764). He followed up with *The Mysterious Mother*, which added to his popularity some four years later.

WALPOLE   Aukland, N.Z. March 13, 1884
(Sir) Hugh Seymour   June 1, 1941
Author   St John's Churchyard, Keswick,
                                                      Cumbria

90, Piccadilly, W1, 1920, onwards

His father, a clergyman, eventually becoming Bishop of Edinburgh, sent young Hugh to school at King's School, Canterbury, Kent. Hugh went on to Cambridge, became a school master and then a book reviewer. His first novel, *The Wooden Horse*, was published in 1909 and two years later, *Mr. Perrin and Mr. Traill* appeared and was to become his best known novel.
During the First World War he worked with the Red Cross in Russia which became the background to his novels, *The Dark Forest* (1916) and *The Secret City* in 1919. This latter dealt with the Russian Revolution and he was awarded the Tait Black Memorial Prize for it. In the 1920s he produced a number of novels that sold well and he also wrote studies of CONRAD and TROLLOPE. A knighthood was his reward in 1930, he had already been given a CBE for his work in Russia.

WALPOLE　　　　　　　　　Houghton Hall, Norfolk, August 26,
Robert (1st Earl of Orford)　1676
Prime Minister　　　　　　　Houghton, March 18, 1745
　　　　　　　　　　　　　　St Martin's Church, Houghton Hall

17, Arlington Street, SW1, 1716
32, St James's Square, SW1, 1732-1735
5, Arlington Street, SW1 (LCP 1976) from 1742 until he died here

After Eton and Oxford, Walpole entered Parliament as Member for Castle
Rising in Norfolk in 1702. In 1708 he became Secretary for War (in those
days euphemisms were not used) in the Whig Government of the day. In
1712 Walpole supported Godolphin in the impeachment of Sacheverell and,
for his pains, was expelled from the House of Commons and sent as a
political prisoner to the Tower of London.
On the accession of the first Hanoverian monarch, King George I, in 1714,
Walpole was released, made a Privy Councillor; then, in 1715, Chancellor of
the Exchequer and First Lord of the Treasury.
After the 'South Sea Bubble' collapsed (as any reasonably honest and
intelligent person could have predicted) the investors and the public at large,
looked to Walpole to clean up the mess. By now, with all offices restored to
him, Walpole really controlled the Government single-handed and so,
perhaps, became the first Prime Minister. After a belligerent political career
he resigned his offices on February 2, 1742 and was created Earl of Orford.
The Walpole motto, *officially* was *Fari Quae Sentati* – To speak what he may
think. Unofficially, history tells us, it was 'Let sleeping dogs lie'.

WALTERS　　　　　　　　　Liverpool, June 13, 1839
Catherine ('Skittles')　　　London, August 5, 1920
Courtesan　　　　　　　　　Franciscan Monastery, Crawley,
　　　　　　　　　　　　　　Sussex

6, Chesterfield Street, W1, c.1860-1872
15, South Street, W1 (P) 1872-1920

Catherine was brought south by one of her first lovers, 'Black Jack' and was
not long in London before she found other well-to-do men who were more
than happy to pay well for her favours. By 1861, 'Skittles', by which
nickname she was universally known, had become a skilled horsewoman
and joined the upper classes who regularly rode in Rotten Row. There
remains a story of her disputing the 'right of way' with Lady Mary
Cambridge in the Park. Lady Mary was a member of the Royal Family, no
less. She is also supposed, at one hunt meeting, to have been complimented
by the Master on her rosy cheeks after a day in the field, 'That's nothing,'
said 'Skittles', 'you should see my arse'.

WALTON　　　　　　　　　　Oldham, Lancs., March 29, 1902
(Sir) William Turner　　　　Ischia, March 7, 1983
Composer

2, Carlyle Square, SW3, first in 1923 and a number of times afterwards

Walton received his general and basic musical education at Christ Church,
Oxford, as a chorister. He continued there as an undergraduate and, while
there in 1918, wrote his first substantial work – a piano quartet (which did
not get its first public airing until 1923, in Salzburg).
He became friendly with and was much helped by the SITWELL family.
One of his early pieces was *Facade* which was his musical setting to Edith
Sitwell's poems – and the first performance was in Osbert Sitwell's house in
Carlyle Square in 1923.

Walton produced some majestic film music, notably for Olivier's *Henry IV* and *Richard II*.

WALTON STREET, SW3
Piccadilly, District and Circle lines to South Kensington

George Walton was yet another trustee of Smith's Charity (see Onslow Square) and the Charity owned the land here. The street was developed in the 1840s.

2, Alan ROSS.

16, P.G. WODEHOUSE, in 1918, again in 1919 and yet *again* in 1920.

86, Sir Edward MARSH, from 1946 until he died here in 1952.

WARD
Mary Augusta
Author

Hobart, Tasmania, June 11, 1851
London, March 24, 1920
Alderley, Hertforshire

61, Russell Square, WC1, 1881-1900
25, Grosvenor Place, SW1, 1904-1911

She was born an Arnold, a granddaughter of Dr. Arnold of Rugby (and so a niece of Matthew ARNOLD). When she was 14 the family came back to England and settled in Oxford – an Oxford of Walter Pater, Benjamin Jowett (1817-1893) Master of Balliol and Thomas Hill Green (1836-1882) the 'neo-Hegelian'. Mary Arnold became Secretary to Somerville College (founded in 1879) having married T. Humphrey Ward, a Fellow of Brasenose College. When he was appointed to the staff of *The Times* in 1881, they came to live in London.

Three years later her first novel, *Miss Bretherton*, was published with little comment, but in 1888, *Robert Elsemere* appeared. It was the sensation of the day. It attacked Evangelical Christianity; yet GLADSTONE gave it a good review in *Nineteenth Century*.

WARDOUR STREET, W1
Piccadilly and Bakerloo lines to Piccadilly Circus

Until 1630 this, even then, ancient road had been known as Colman Hedge Lane. A nearby close was bought by Sir Edward Wardour, an Exchequer official who died in 1647. His grandson developed the land between 1695 and 1700.

27, John FLAXMAN, 1781-1787. He had married Ann Denman the previous year.

41, Willy CLARKSON (LCP 1966) from 1905 until he died here in 1934. He inherited his father's wig business and he began a theatrical costumier's business here.

WARREN STREET, W1
Northern and Victoria lines to Warren Street

Charles II's bastard son by Barbara Castlemaine (later the Duchess of Cleveland) was made Duke of Euston. His grandson inherited the land given to his family by the oversexed King and got himself declared Baron Southampton. He married Anne Warren and developed much of the area around Fitzroy Square in the 1790s.

56, Charles TURNER (LCP 1924) 1799-1803. Having lived here for four years, the Turners moved along the street to Number 50, so that they could more easily house their growing family.

WATTS London, February 23, 1817
George Frederick July 1, 1904
Artist

6, Melbury Road, W14, 1876

Watts first exhibited at the Royal Academy in the year Queen Victoria came to the throne but, of his many paintings, the ones of most interest to anyone who has read through *Capital Companion* this far are the numerous portraits of Victorian 'worthies' which can all be seen at the National Portrait Gallery (behind the National Gallery).

Another Watts' work is a copy of a really rather cumbersome statue of his, called *Physical Energy*, in Kensington Gardens. The original is part of a memorial to Cecil Rhodes which was erected at the foot of Table Mountain in 1902. Originally it was meant to be an equestrian statue for Hugh Grosvenor, the 1st *Duke* of Westminster. (Presumably the *Duke* would have been clothed, unlike the horseman of *Physical Energy* who is stark naked.)

WATTS-DUNTON St Ives, Hunts., October 13, 1832
Theodore Walter Putney, June 7, 1914
Solicitor and Swinburne 'Saviour' Norwood Cemetery

15, Great James Street, WC1, 1872-1873

Theodore's father was plain John King Watts, a country solicitor, but when Theodore was 64 years old, he *doublebarrelled* it by adding his mother's maiden name. He practised as a solicitor in London and wrote literary criticisms, from time to time, for the *Examiner* and the *Athenaeum* magazines. Moth-like, he fluttered around the literary and bohemian lights and cultivated the 'Pre-Raphaelite Brotherhood' in particular. He was a mousey, non-descript character – in fact, just like the son of a country solicitor.

By 1879, SWINBURNE was almost daily risking his life by his intake of alcohol and Watts-Dunton, seeing the problems, but also seeing potential advantages, wafted the little red-headed Algernon off to the (then) wilds of Putney Hill.

WAUGH London, October 28, 1903
Evelyn Arthur St John Somerset, April 10, 1966
Author St Peter and St Paul's Churchyard, Combe Florey

21, Mulberry Walk, SW3, 1937

Waugh went up to Hertford College, Oxford which he thought to be a little vulgar (apart from anything else, it was only founded in 1874) and just added to the sort of social 'chip-on-the-shoulder' which seemed to weigh him down so unnecessarily. Still, he joined in with the Oxford frolics and was arrested on April 7, 1925 for being drunk and disorderly and was fined 15 shillings (77½p). He gave the Court his occupation as 'Schoolmaster'.

His ability to write was never called into question and his first novel, *Decline and Fall*, in 1928, brought him immediately into the front rank of contemporary English novelists. In 1928 he married Evelyn Gardner, daughter of Lord Burghclere. The young couple were known (understandably) as 'The Evelyns'. The marriage was not happy and in 1930 they were divorced. The same year Waugh joined the Roman Catholic Church.

WEBB   London, May 22, 1849
(Sir) Aston   August 21, 1930
Architect   Gunnersbury Cemetery

1, Hanover Terrace, Ladbroke Square, W11, 1922-1930
19, Queen Anne's Gate, SW1, 1930

Webb's father was an engraver and his mother a water colour painter. Aston combined the talents of both. Not only was he a prominent architect, he was a Royal Academician (1903) and President of the Royal Academy in 1919, a post he held for five years and Honorary Fellow of the Royal Society of Pianter-Etchers.

His work is very much in evidence for a London visitor. He designed the present east front of Buckingham Palace and the Victoria Monument outside it at the head of the Mall. These projects were completed in 1912. By the time he was working on these he was already Sir Aston, having been knighted in 1904.

Another massive design of his is the Imperial Institute, behind the Albert Hall in Kensington, on Prince Consort Road, SW7.

WEBB   London, July 13, 1859
Sidney (1st Baron Pasfield) Liphook, Hants., October 13, 1947
Politician   Westminster Abbey

41, Grosvenor Road, SW1, 1904-1928

Webb, the son of an accountant, graduated with an LLB from London University in 1885 and married Beatrice POTTER when he was 33 years old. In the same year (1892) he met G.B. SHAW who introduced the Webbs to the Fabian Society The Society had been founded in January 1884 by a group of 'middle-class' intellectuals to promote social welfare generally by increasing 'state intervention' (nationalisation) in the economy. Two other prominent Fabians at that time were Graham WALLAS and Annie Besant (1847-1933). George D.H. Cole (1889-1959) later Chairman, and his wife, Isobel, wrote in their book, *The Common People*, that the Fabian Society, '...envisaged socialism as a heap of reforms to be built by the droppings of a host of successive swallows, who would in the end make a Socialist summer'. Webb was also to become an early 'Progressive' member of the London County Council.

WEIZMANN   Motol, Nr. Pinsk, November 27, 1874
Chaim   Rehovet, Israel, November 9, 1952
Scientist and Statesman

67, Addison Road, W14, 1917-1920

Weizmann became actively involved in Zionism when he was working as a bio-chemist at Manchester University at the outbreak of the First World War. He moved to London in 1915, becoming an adviser to the Admiralty. In that capacity he became caught up in political circles and began lobbying both BALFOUR and LLOYD-GEORGE about the possibility of establishing a totally Jewish state.

The house in Addison Road became a hub of the Zionist movement and, in 1900, Weizmann became President of the World Zionist Organization. When the State of Israel became a reality in 1948, he was made the first President of it.

WELBECK STREET, W1   *Central line to Bond Street*

When King Henry VIII 'did away' with the monasteries in the middle of the 16th century, Welbeck Abbey (somehow) fell into the hands of the

Cavendish family. Later their estates were added, through marriage, to the Harley land holdings and it was on these lands Welbeck Street was built.

29, Thomas WOOLNER (P) 1860-1892. By this time he was increasingly popular. His last work, sculpted here, was called *The Housemaid*.

48, Thomas YOUNG (LCP 1951) 1800-1825. This was his home as well as his surgery.

51, Maria De La RAMEE ('Ouida') with her mother, 1867-1883.

72, John TRUMBULL, 1799, when he was still a bachelor. He married a year later.

WELLINGTON	Dublin, April 30, 1769
Arthur Wellesly (1st Duke)	Walmer, Sussex, September 14, 1852
Soldier and Prime Minister	St Paul's Cathedral

11, Harley Street, W1, 1808-1814
Apsley House, 249, Piccadilly, W1, 1816-1852

Like that other English hero of his time, Horatio NELSON, Wellington did not live happily with his wife. (Wellington, however, did not have the solace of an Emma HAMILTON.) He had met Catherine, 'Kitty', Pakenham and proposed marriage to her in 1793 when Kitty was just 21. Her family felt that Captain Wesley (Wellington was born a Wesley but in 1898 took the surname of Wellesley) would not make a good husband but, as he rose in the Army, so did he in the Pakenhams' estimation. On the other hand Wellington had cooled, but, being an officer and a gentleman he felt bound, in honour, to marry Catherine and did so in 1806. They had two sons but she died in 1831 never really having played a supporting role as the wife of a great man. He was not a handsome man, but he was attractive to women. (Angela BURDETT-COUTTS, the wealthiest woman in England, proposed marriage to him more than once when she was 33 and he 78.)

Benjamin DISRAELI was always of the opinion that Wellington's true father was a son of Lord Blessington, General the Hon Charles Gardiner, and claimed that Wellington himself did not deny the charge.

Wellington was, and is all too often, referred to as the *Iron Duke*, but according to Sir John Pollock (b.1880) the nickname was never used in the Duke's lifetime. One of the first ironclad naval ships to be launched was named *The Iron Duke* and it was the ship, *not* the soldier, which carried the name. (Sir John's aunt had actually met Wellington and said of him '...he was a little man – a very little man, my dear'.)

In 1888, in front of Apsley house, Sir Joseph Boehm's bronze statue of Wellington, astride his old war horse, 'Copenhagen', was erected. Another equestrian statue of the Duke was unveiled outside the Royal Exchange on June 18, 1844 (the day on which Waterloo was fought) the Duke, himself, attending the ceremony. This was begun by CHANTREY, but he got no further than the *maquette* before he died in November 1842. It was finished off by Henry Weeks. This makes Wellington the only person to be honoured by having two *equestrian* statues in London. The Royal Exchange statue has Wellington seated on a saddle cloth only and having no stirrups. Another memorial to Wellington was erected, by command of King George IV on June 18, 1822, by the Hyde Park Corner end of Hyde Park. It is 18 feet (5.48 metres) and a modified copy of one of the 'Horse Tamers' on the Quirinal Hill in Rome. The metal for the casting came from cannons captured at Salamanca, Vittoria, Toulouse and Waterloo. It is the work of Sir Richard WESTMACOTT and cost £10,000.

WELLINGTON SQUARE, SW3   *Circle and District lines*
to Sloane Square

Named after the 'Iron Duke' whose brother was rector of Chelsea from 1805 to 1836.

11,   James LAVER, 1934-1950. The house had previously been occupied by Paul Villars, the London correspondent of *Le Journal des Débats* who, despite having lived in the house for 40 years, had had no bathroom. He did have a large wine cellar, however. George MOORE used to visit Villars here.

14,   Charles CONDER, 1902, after his marriage to Stella Maris.

32,   Thomas WOLFE stayed here in 1932 and worked on *A Portrait of Bascombe Hawke*, his short novel which was published before the end of the year.

WELLS   Bromley, Kent, September 21, 1866
Herbert George   London, August 13, 1946
Author

46, Fitzroy Road, NW1, 1889-1891
12, Mornington Crescent, NW1, 1894-1898
7, Mornington Place, NW1
4, (flat 20) Whitehall Court, SW1
Flat 47, Chiltern Court, 186, Baker Street, NW1, 1930
13, Hanover Terrace, NW1 (LCP 1966) from 1936, until he died here

Well's father had been a professional cricketer (who afterwards kept a china shop) and his mother, a lady's maid. He was sent to Midhurst Grammar School (where he was probably a little awkward 'socially') and leaving there, he was apprenticed to a draper, then a chemist and eventually won a scholarship to the Royal College of Science. Here he studied under HUXLEY and edited the College Magazine in his spare time.

When he was 25 he married his cousin Isabel Mary Wells. It was no-go right from the start; they separated in less than two years and were divorced in 1905. By this time Wells was a Science Instructor and he married Amy Catherine Robbins, one of his pupils. Neither 'believed' in marriage but they went through a ceremony to mollify their relatives. In some respects this marriage was successful. She was his secretary and literary critic, as well as housekeeper and wife. He called her 'Jane' and, despite her distaste for the sexual demands of wedlock, she bore him two sons. They discussed his sexual needs at length and with Jane's consent – almost her blessing – he was given the freedom of sexual involvement elsewhere. So they stayed 'happily' married; she typed his books and prepared his tax returns. Her understanding was wide: in 1908 Wells's current mistress, 22-year old Amber Reeves, became pregnant by Wells. Practically everybody was horrified. All except Jane who went out and bought a layette for the expected baby.

In 1912 Wells met Cicily Isabel Fairfield, then just 20. The world was to know this remarkable woman as Dame Rebecca West. She was made a DBE in 1959. They had a son, Anthony, who took her pen-name, West, as a surname and he too was to become a writer.

In 1893 Wells had some sort of nervous break-down and he left scientific, academic work on one side and began to write fiction. Two years later the first successful result, *The Time Machine*, appeared, followed by *The Invisible Man* in 1897. A year later came *The War of the Worlds*. Probably at that time no one (except, perhaps, Jules Verne) had produced fiction of this quality on 'sci-fi' topics.

WENTWORTH　　　　　　London, July 1, 1730
Charles Watson (2nd Marquis of　1782
Rockingham)
Prime Minister

10, Grosvenor Square, W1, where he died

Rockingham was certainly not the most brilliant of Prime Ministers – but nor was he the worst. He went into politics early and was created Earl of Malton in 1750. Shortly afterwards he inherited his father's marquisate and in 1751 he was made Knight of the Garter. However he crossed swords with the 3rd Earl of Bute (1713-1792) and he was dismissed from all his appointments.
He was leader of the Whig party in opposition and in 1765 was asked to form a government. He was a fairly forward thinking leader and undoubtedly had a number of reforms in mind (he repealed the Stamp Act, for example) but was thwarted by below-stairs intrigues. He resigned in 1766, opposing Lord North and his singularly stupid American policy.
In March 1782, a sick man, he again became Prime Minister, but within four months he was dead.

WESLEY　　　　　　Epworth, Lincs., June 28, 1703
John　　　　　　　　London, March 2, 1791
Methodist　　　　　　John Wesley Chapel, City Road, EC1

47, City Road, EC1 (LCP 1926) where he died

Though Wesley founded the Methodist Church, he had been ordained as a parson in the Church of England in 1725. His father was a vicar in Epworth, Lincs. John was invited to go to Georgia, United States as a missionary to the Indians and he worked in America in 1735, but left (rather hurriedly) in 1738, having been embroiled in some sort of 'romantic mis-understanding'. Back in London, Charles Wesley experienced his evangelical conversion on May 24, 1738, in a meeting room at 28, Aldersgate Street. (Brother Charles having entered into the Methodist faith three days earlier at John Bray's house at 12, Little Britain.) In the next 50 years Wesley travelled the whole of England, crossed the Irish Sea *42* times and, when he was 79, even set off on a mission to Holland. (It is estimated that in this time he preached over 40,000 sermons, a rate of two sermons a day with no days off.)
He was the first religious leader of consequence to speak out *publicly* against slavery.
The Wesley Museum in John Wesley's house at 47, City Road and is open all the year round except Sundays and Bank Holidays, from 10-4.
There is a bronze statue of Wesley by J. Adams Acton. It was erected in 1891 in the yard of the Wesley Chapel.

WEST　　　　　　Springfield, Pa., October 10, 1738
Benjamin　　　　　　London, March 10, 1820
Artist　　　　　　St Paul's Cathedral

14, Newman Street, W1, from 1777 until his death here

Having shown early artistic promise, West was sent to Italy to study and came to London in 1763. He was one of the first painters, producing pictures of historical events, to clothe the people depicted in their (more or less) correct contemporary clothing rather than bedecking them with togas or other bogus 'classical' garb.
West had the good fortune to enjoy the patronage of King George III for forty years (and the £1,000 annually that went with the honour). His rather grandiose oils can be seen in many public collections both in Britain and America.

He was elected President of the Royal Academy in 1792 and remained so until his death.

WESTBOURNE

The River Westbourne (which feeds the Serpentine in Hyde Park) runs underground into the Thames. It rises near 'Jack Straw's Castle' (a public house) in Hampstead and it can be briefly seen in Kensington, just by the Marlborough Gate before it plunges underground. When it was a 'surface river' it divided the villages of Paddington and 'Westeburne' (on the west bank). It can also be 'seen' in the underground station at Sloane Square. The river is contained by a huge iron conduit some 15 feet (4.5 metres) above the platform on its way to join the Thames near Chelsea Bridge.

WESTBOURNE STREET, W2   *Central line to Lancaster Gate*

10, Lady Randolph CHURCHILL died here in June 1921. When she moved here she created some small stir by having striped, waistcoated parlour maids instead of the usual footmen. (They were cheaper.)
17, Harriet MARTINEAU, 1849.

WESTBOURNE TERRACE, W2

139, Sir Arthur SULLIVAN, 1864. He was still ten years away from his very successful co-operation with W.S. GILBERT.
155, Aldous HUXLEY, 1921, not long after his marriage to Maria Nys and just before they removed to Italy.

WESTMACOTT	London, 1775
(Sir) Richard	London, September 1, 1856
Sculptor	Chastleton, Oxon

24, Mount Street, W1, 1800-1819
14, South Audley Street, W1 (LCP 1955) from 1819 till he died here 37 years later

Westmacott's father (also Richard: 1747-1808) was a sculptor and began his son in his own studio. When he was 18, young Richard went off to Italy to study under Antonio Canova (1757-1822) in Rome. He made such remarkable progress that he was elected a member of the Academy of Florence when he was 20 and also won a Papal medal for a bas-relief of *Joseph and his Brethren* in the same year.
He enjoyed Royal favour and made a chimney-piece for the Music Room in the Prince Regent's exotic Pavilion in Brighton for which he was paid (unlike many of the Regent's suppliers) £1,244. His last major work, easily to be seen today, is the group on the pediment of the British Museum.
In 1827 he succeeded FLAXMAN as Academy Professor of Sculpture and was knighted ten years later.

WETHERBY GARDENS, SW5   *Piccadilly, District and Circle lines to Gloucester Road*

Sir Robert Gunter, who had inherited land in this area, became a Member of Parliament for a Yorkshire constituency in the North of England and his home there was at Wetherby Grange.

24, Field Marshall, Lord ALLENBY (LCP 1960) 1928 until he died in 1936. He was a keen ornithologist and he built a small aviary in the back garden.

WHEATLEY
Dennis Yates
Author

Brixton, London, January 8, 1897
London, November 10, 1979
Cremated

48, Queen's Gate, SW7, 1931-1936
60, Cadogan Square, SW1, 1960-1979

Son of a Mayfair wine merchant, Wheatley went into business after he had finished his education on *HMS Worcester* in 1914. The business was lucrative but Wheatley had the urge to write. He sold the business in 1931 and one of his first books, *Old Rowley (a Private Life of Charles II)* appeared in 1933. However his reputation was successfully based on historic and/or novels dealing with both black and white magic, titles like *Black August* and *The Devil Rides Out* (published 1934).

Wheatley's thrillers achieved world wide popularity and have been reprinted regularly. Humbert Wolfe (1885-1940, an English poet whose *London Sonnets* were published in 1919) told Pamela Frankau that Wheatley had boasted to Wolfe that his works '...had been translated into every European language except one – I can't remember which...'. 'English,' said Miss Frankau.

WHEATSTONE
(Sir) Charles
Inventor

Gloucester, February 16(c), 1802
Paris, October 19, 1875
Kensal Green, Grave No.11,643: plot 41

19, Park Crescent, W1 (LCP 1981) 1866-1875

A country boy, Wheatstone came to London when he was 21 and established himself as a musical instrument maker. During this period he invented the concertina: a mixed blessing.

Later his interests and experiments led to the study of light and optics generally. He began to develop the electric telegraph and, in this field, he was appointed Professor of Experimental Physics at King's College, London in 1834. Four years later, in a paper to the Royal Society, he set out the principles of the stereoscope.

Working with Sir William Fothergill Cooke, Wheatstone perfected the electric telegraph between 1837 and 1847. He invented a form of meter for measuring and comparing electrical resistances, which ever after has been called *The Wheatstone Bridge*.

WHISTLER
James Abbott McNeill
Artist

Lowell, Mass., July 10, 1834
London, July 17, 1903
Chiswick Parish Churchyard (by the north wall of the new section, beside his wife)

62, Sloane Street, SW3, 1848
101, Cheyne Walk, SW3 (then 7, Lindsey Row) 1863-1866
96, Cheyne Walk, SW3 (then 2, Lindsey Row) (LCP 1925) 1866-1878
The White House, Tite Street, SW3, 1878-1879
13, Tite Street, SW3, 1881-1885
2, The Vale, SW3, 186
454, Fulham Road (the 'Pink Palace') SW10, 1887
21, Cheyne Row, SW3, 1890-1892
72, Cheyne Walk, SW3, where he died

Whistler's father was a railway engineer and had worked for some time in Russia. Whistler allowed this part of his life to be 'embellished' and let people think that he had been born in the fabulous St Petersburg (Leningrad since the Revolution). James *did* go to the Westpoint Military Academy (opened under an Act of Congress in 1794) but after one year there failed his examinations, left the Academy a few months later and left America altogether, never to return.

He studied art in Paris under Marc Gabriel Gleyre, was deeply impressed by the work of Gustave Courbet and 'discovered' the work of Hokusai, the Japanese wood engraver of the previous century. His mother came to England in 1863 and Whistler more or less settled in London from then on. He first gained recognition as a portrait painter, but in 1877 he exhibited some paintings he had entitled *Nocturnes* at the Grosvenor Gallery. These so infuriated the pompous John RUSKIN that he accused Whistler of '…flinging a pot of paint in the public's face'. Stung, Whistler sued Ruskin for damages. The court eventually found Ruskin guilty of libel but awarded the now *very* disgruntled Whistler 'one farthing's damages'. The costs of the whole, rather silly, case 'cleaned Whistler out' and he went to live abroad, but he was still declared bankrupt in 1879.

He was a very 'dandified' person and vain about the pure white lock of hair on his forehead. He was a considerable wit, sadly caustic and often hurtful. In 1890 he published a book called *The Gentle Art of Making Enemies* – a subject of which Whistler *was* a master.

WHITE	Bedford, December 22, 1831
William Hale ('Mark Rutherford')	March 14, 1913
Novelist	

69, Marylebone Road, NW1, 1880s

White's father was a bookseller and also doorkeeper to the House of Commons for 30 years. Originally intended for the Congregational Ministry, William was expelled from New College (having qualified there) for some of his views on 'inspiration'.

He put his inspiration into miscellaneous writing and, in 1883 published his translation of Spinoza's *Ethica* under his own name. But such fame as was eventually to be his were his books as *Mark Rutherford* beginning in 1881 with *The Autobiography of Mark Rutherford*. Under yet another nom-de-plume, that of 'Reuben Shapcott', he edited the *Revolution in Tanner's Lane* in 1887.

WHITEHALL, SW1

The road takes its name from Whitehall Palace which covered this area.

WHITEHALL COURT, SW1   *Northern, Bakerloo and Jubilee lines to Charing Cross*

A vast building by Archer and Green. Sir Nikolaus Pevsner says of it, 'Here after so much timid propriety is exuberance and no "ghastly good taste"'. Eight storeys, pyramid roofs, balconies, loggias – enough to make *Chambord* pale with envy'.

4,   George Bernard SHAW. This was his London home for many years and his wife, Charlotte, died here on September 13, 1943. (Previously Shaw had lived in 130, Whitehall Court, moving in October 1927.)

WHITEHALL GARDENS, SW1

2,   Benjamin DISRAELI, 1875-1880. This was after his wife (the ingenuous widow of Wyndham Lewis) had died in 1872.

4,   Sir Robert PEEL, from 1825 (16 years after he first entered Parliament) until he died here in July 1850.

WHITEHEAD   Ramsgate, Kent, February 15, 1861
Alfred North   1947
Mathematician

14, Carlyle Square, SW3, 1920s

With Whitehead, philosophy and mathematics went hand in hand.
'Philosophy', he wrote, in *Nature and Life*, 'is the product of wonder.' He
was educated at Sherborne School then Trinity College, Cambridge and was
Senior Lecturer in Mathematics there until 1911. In 1898 he had published
the highly original *Treatise on Universal Algebra*, in which he extended
Boolcian Symbolic Logic.
Whitehead, influenced by Giuseppe Peano (1858-1932, an Italian
mathematician who in addition to his work on mathematical logic, tried to
promote a universal language based on uninflected Latin) collaborated with
Bertrand RUSSELL on Russell's great *Principia Mathematica* between 1910
and 1913. This partnership and its product has been called 'the greatest single
contribution to logic since Aristotle' (c.384-322 BC).

WHITELEY   Wakefield, Yorks.,1831
William   London, 1907
'The Universal Provider'   Kensal Green

31, Porchester Terrace, W2, 1880-1907

A Northcountry man, Whiteley worked as a draper's assistant in a shop in
the City and somehow, on pitifully small wages, managed to save enough
money to open a fancy drapery shop at 31, Westbourne Grove in 1863. (At
that time Westbourne Grove had the cynical nick-name of 'Bankruptcy
Row'.) Thirteen years later, Whiteley owned 15 shops on both sides of
number 31 and was employing nearly 2,000 people.
In 1907 a young man, Horace George Rayner, shot Whiteley dead in his own
shop. Rayner was actually the illegitimate son of an old acquaintance of
Whiteley's but somehow he had got the idea that Whiteley was his father and
wanted to punish him for having begotten a bastard.

WIGMORE STREET, W1   *Central line to Bond Street*

The Harleys, on whose land this street stood, bought Wigmore Castle, one
time the fortress of the omnipotent Mortimer family. Roger Mortimer, Earl
of March became the lover of Isabella of France, wife of the homosexual
King Edward II of England. He virtually ruled Britain after Edward's
obscene murder in Berkley Castle in 1327.

7, (old numbering). Sir William HAMILTON and his wife, EMMA,
lived here for a short while after their marriage.
38, Sir Adrian BOULT.

WILBERFORCE   Hull, August 24, 1759
William   London, July 29, 1833
Statesman and Philanthropist   Westminster Abbey (north transept)

Gore House, Kensington Gore, SW7, 1808-1821
44, Cadogan Place, SW1 (LCP 1961) from 1831 until he died here

Wilberforce was brought up by an uncle, who left a considerable fortune to
young William (as did his grandfather). He went up to St John's College,
Cambridge (founded 1511). When he came down he entered into politics
and was a Member of the House of Commons – for Hull – when he was only
21. He was an intimate friend of William PITT (the 'Younger') who was
only three months older than he was.
In 1787 Wilberforce met Thomas Clarkson and, with him, took up the cause

of Anti-Slavery with enthusiasm. When he was 38 he married Barbara Spooner by whom he had four sons. They lived in Clapham until 1807. His evangelical fight against slavery found an outlet in his being a leading member of the 'Clapham Sect'.

Ill health forced Wilberforce's retirement from an active public and political life, but slavery *was* abolished 'within the British Dominions' in 1833 and some 800,000 slaves were set free.

WILDE
(Lady) Jane ('Speranza')
Poet

Ireland, c. 1826
London, February 3, 1896
Kensal Green, Grave No. 35,853, Plot No. 197

1, Ovington Square, SW3, c. 1880
116, Park Street, W1, 1883–1886
87, Oakley Street, SW3, 1886–until she died here

Lady Wilde was the wife of Sir William Wilde and mother of William Charles Kingsbury Wilde, Oscar WILDE and Isola Wilde (1859-1867). She was born Francesca Elgee and had played a leading role in the 'Young Ireland' movement in the 1840s. She wrote and published indifferent, (poetically) but inflammatory poems and articles under the *nom-de-guerre* of 'Speranza'.

She married Dr. Wilde in 1851 (he was not knighted until 1864) and in 1855 they moved to 1, Merrion Square, Dublin, where Isola was born. Wilde was an eminent oculist and ear surgeon. He was also an eminent lecher. He admitted to three illegitimate children (two of his bastards, young girls, perished when their floundering skirts caught on fire). Despite his medical genius, Wilde was personally very dirty, often unwashed. (A contemporary Dublin riddle indicates this:

'Q: Why are Sir William Wilde's nails so dirty?
A: Because he has just been scratching himself.')

WILDE
Oscar Fingal O'Flahertie (Wills)
Playwright

Dublin, October 16, 1854
Paris, November 30, 1900
Père Lachaise, Paris (finally)

1 ('Keat's House') Tite Street, SW3, 1880
34 (then 16) Tite Street, SW3 (LCP 1954) 1883–1895
10/11, St James's Street, SW1, 1893

Wilde, although he embroiled himself in one of the most scandalous law suits in 19th century history, is still justly famous: for the best of all his plays, *The Importance of Being Earnest*. It is frothy comedy at its wittiest and appears on practically every English speaking theatre company's repertoire. He had a brilliant academic career which began at Trinity College, Dublin and then Magdalen College, Oxford, where he got a First in *Greats* and won the Newdigate Prize for his poem *Ravenna* (actually not a very good poem). London first saw him in the autumn of 1879 and his first book of poems was published in June 1881. For the whole of 1882 he was on a lecture tour of America to boost the GILBERT and SULLIVAN opera, *Patience*. When he came back he was famous. In May 1884 he married the lovely Constance Lloyd, they moved into Tite Street; by November 1886 they had two attractive sons and he was the editor of the magazine *Women's World*.

Between then and February 1895, four of his brilliant plays had been staged and Wilde was fêted, lionized, adored and (comparatively) wealthy. By May 1895 he was in gaol and totally disgraced. He had been accused of homosexual behaviour for some years, with a number of young men. There was no doubt that he was guilty.

He spent *exactly* two years in gaol and on the day of his release crossed the Channel to spend the rest of his life – just over five years – drinking, lazing and pursuing boys in France, Italy and even Switzerland. He only produced one work, *The Ballad of Reading Gaol*; a long poem telling the story of a young soldier who was hung for killing his wife in a jealous frenzy.
Wilde died in a poor little hotel, the Hôtel d'Alsace, with his bill unpaid. He was first buried at Bagneux and then in 1909 he was re-interred in Père Lachaise. The grave was eventually covered by a memorial made by Jacob EPSTEIN.

WILKES　　　　　　　　　London, October 17, 1727
John　　　　　　　　　　　London, December 26, 1797
Politician　　　　　　　　　Grosvenor Chapel

30, Grosvenor Square, W1, where he died

Wilkes' father was a distiller who could afford to pay for his son's education in Leyden. The Wilkes lived in Clerkenwell (not, then, such a run-down district of London as it is today). To please his parents (it was said) he married the wealthy daughter of the eminent Doctor Mead. Wilkes was 22, Miss Mead was 33. Between them they produced a daughter but separated not long after.
As a supporter of PITT, Wilkes became a Member of Parliament for Aylesbury in 1757 and was also elected High Sherriff for the County of Buckinghamshire. He established a weekly journal, called the *North Briton* and in its pages Wilkes attacked Lord Bute's Government and, before the 27th edition of the *North Briton* was published, he was threatened with prosecution (and had to defend himself in a duel with Lord Talbot). On the publication of No. 45 of the paper, warrants for the arrest of *anybody* connected with it were issued and Wilkes was sent to the Tower. He was released and awarded quite substantial damages (by law) and became a 'hero' of the day.
Then the Earl of Sandwich read an extract of one of Wilkes's poems to the House of Lords, who found it to be obscene and Wilkes was summarily expelled from the House of Commons in January 1764. He was tried *in absentia* found guilty of 'obscenity' and remained out of England for four years. In 1769 he was back in the House, duly elected by the voters of Middlesex. Next: he was fined a thousand pounds, another 22 months in prison, then, though re-elected (again *in absentia*) four more times to the Commons, was excluded each time. Despite that he got back into Parliament (for Middlesex) and eventually retired from public life in 1790.

WILKIE　　　　　　　　　Cults, Fifeshire, November 18, 1785
(Sir) David　　　　　　　　　At sea, off Gibraltar, June 1, 1841
Artist　　　　　　　　　　　Buried at sea

8, Bolsover Street, W1, 1805-1812
144, Kensington High Street (formerly 24, Lower Phillimore Gardens) W8, 1805-1812

In his time, Wilkie was a fashionable painter, who, having studied in Edinburgh, came to London in 1805 and exhibited for the first time at the Academy in 1806.
When he was 40 he travelled in Spain which totally altered his painting style. He had established himself as a 'genre' artist but after Spain he worked almost exclusively on large scale historical subjects. He was appointed Painter-in-Ordinary to King George IV, who had a good eye for a good painter despite other blemishes.

WILLIAM II The Hague, December 6, 1792
Of Orange March 17, 1849
King of the Netherlands

8, Clifford Street, W1, 1813-1814

Son of William I (who abdicated in his favour in October 1840) William of
Orange was educated at Westminster School and then Oxford. He served
with distinction under WELLINGTON in the Peninsular War.

By most accounts he was hardly an attractive person physically; being,
'...ugly, sallow, slender and spindle legged'. Arrangements were well
advanced for him to be married to Princess Charlotte, only child of the
Prince Regent (later King George IV and so, potentially, a Queen *regnant* of
England). Luckily for England she rejected him and eventually he married
the Russian Grand Duchess Anne, sister of Alexander I.

WILLIAMS Mostyn, Wales, November 26, 1905
Emlyn
Actor and dramatist

15, Pelham Crescent, SW3, 1953-1960

Williams' father was an ironmonger in North Wales and so it was a very
great day when young Emlyn won a scholarship to Christ Church College
in Oxford. (Doubly so, perhaps, as Christ Church has always been thought
of as the 'gentleman's college'.)

He got his degree, but he had always been attracted by the stage and, in
1927, he joined Fagan's Repertory Company. Three years later he had his
first success as a playwright, with *A Murder has been Arranged* and then in
1935 with his highly successful *Night Must Fall*, a 'thinking man's thriller'.

WILLIAMS Dulverton, Glos., 1821
(Sir) George November 6, 1905
Benefactor Highgate Cemetery

13, Russell Square, WC1, 1897-1905

Williams came of humble stock and was educated at Gloyne's School in
Tiverton, Devon. He rose to be a partner in a prosperous draper's firm in the
City. In 1853 he married Helen (by whom he had five sons) daughter of
George Hitchcock. His father-in-law was also his boss; a good ploy.

He was an evangelical teetotaller and, at one time, a President of the Band of
Hope, a children's temperance association. It had been founded in 1847 and
in 1855 grew into the Band of Hope Union. He preached on the evils of
drink from friendly pulpits and also lectured to the hapless children in the
Ragged Schools.

WILSON Huddersfield, March 11, 1911
Harold James (1st Baron Rielvaulx)
Prime Minister

5, Lord North Street, SW1, 1960s and 1970s

In the history of 'Prime Ministers' since 1782, only two men have been
Premier four times: GLADSTONE and Harold Wilson.

Wilson was educated in Huddersfield and Cheshire before going up to Jesus
College, Cambridge (where, appropriately enough, he won the Gladstone
Memorial Prize). He graduated with a First Class Honours degree in
Philosophy, Politics and Economy and became a lecturer in Economics at
New College in 1937. He was appointed Director of Economics and
Statistics for the Ministry of Fuel and Power in 1943 and later moved to the

Board of Trade, from which he resigned in 1951. He became MP for Ormskirk in 1945 in the General Election when the Socialist Party were swept into power with a commanding majority. In 1950 he was returned to Parliament for Huyton (Liverpool) a seat he held until going into the Lords as Baron Rielvaulx. (In the 1981 election he had a *majority* of 16,233 and nearly 53,000 franchised voters actually voted.)

Wilson waited for Clement Attlee to resign after the Socialist defeat at the polls in 1951 and he waited again until the 'right-of-centre' Hugh Gaitskell died in 1963 (he was only 57). Wilson became the Leader of the Socialist Party in Opposition until October 1964, when Labour came to power and he became Prime Minister for the first time. His majority was disconcertingly small, but Wilson chanced his arm through a long winter and in April 1964 'went to the country' and came back to Westminster with a substantial working majority.

WILSON	Ireland, March 5, 1864
(Sir) Henry Hughes	London, June 22, 1922
Field Marshall	

36, Eaton Place, SW1 (on the front doorstep of which he was murdered)

Napoleon maintained that, '*Tout soldat Français porte dans sa giberne le baton de Maréchal de France*'. A comfort for Wilson as he failed to get into Sandhurst three times and had to get his baton by first joining the Irish Militia.

He rose upwards and his fluency in French enabled him to get along very well with Maréchal Foch (1851-1929). Wilson had been Director of Military Operations from 1910-1914 and he then became liaison officer with Joffre's HQ, where he constantly advised total co-operation between the British Expeditionary Force and the French Army. He was not universally popular: ASQUITH, still Prime Minister in 1914, referred to Wilson as 'That poisonous mischief maker'.

In 1922 Wilson became an MP for North Down in Ireland and became very much an 'Irishman's Irishman'. The last speech he made in the House of Commons included the words, 'I wonder when the moment will come when the Government will have the honesty and truthfulness to say: "We have miscalculated every single element in the Irish Problem"'. (Probably the same speech could be made of every British government since.)

Three weeks later, two 'heroic' Sinn Fein supporters called on the Field Marshall and shot him down in cold blood.

WILSON	Penegoes, Wales, August 1, 1714
Richard	Llanferras, Wales, May, 1782
Artist	

85, Great Titchfield Street, W1, 1776

Wilson came to London and studied painting under Thomas Wright for six years. He was still not yet 21 when he set himself up as a portrait painter. Not pleased with this he went to Italy in 1749 and stayed there for seven years, concentrating on landscape painting. He was before both CONSTABLE and GAINSBOROUGH in painting landscapes in a free, lyrical style (which these two masters were to perfect) rather than in the previous 'strait-laced classicism'.

WILTON CRESCENT, SW1   *Piccadilly line to Knightsbridge*

The first *Earl* Grosvenor successfully drained the marshy fields of 'Belgravia', so making it possible to develop the area. His wife was the daughter of the Earl of Wilton.

2, Lord Louis MOUNTBATTEN, 1960-1968. Lord Louis sold this seven-bedroomed house in May 1968 to the Republic of Singapore.

21, the 5th Lord Lonsdale was born here in 1857.

30, Lord John RUSSELL, 1835-1841.

36, Algernon SWINBURNE, 1856. He read his *Atlanta in Calydon* in proof here.

WILTON STREET, SW1

8, Rupert HART-DAVIS stayed here as a 17-year old schoolboy in 1924.

WIMPOLE STREET, W1   *Central line to Bond Street*

John Holles, Duke of Newcastle, bought both the Manor of Marylebone (this area) and Wimpole Hall in Cambridgeshire. His son-in-law, Edward Harley, having been financially debilitated by the 'South Sea Bubble' fiasco, had to sell off Wimpole Hall in 1740, but he had started to develop here by then.

32, Lord DAWSON of Penn, 1918.

35, Sir Henry THOMPSON. He used to give 'Octave' dinners here (eight eminent guests sat down to eight courses, beginning at eight o'clock). Such guests included the Prince of Wales (on more than one occasion) Conan DOYLE and 'Anthony HOPE'. The table was first rate, but Hope noticed that their host, '...ate next to nothing and drank water'.

50, where lived the Barretts of Wimpole Street. Robert BROWNING came here at three o'clock on the afternoon of Tuesday, May 20, 1845 and met the daughter of the house, Elizabeth, for the first time. He was 33, she 39. On the night of September 19, 1846, she wrote a letter to him ending with, 'Do you pray for me tonight, Robert? Pray for me and love me, that I may have courage'. The following day they eloped. Her bedroom was on the third floor, shielded from some of the noise by double green doors installed in 1844. Dark shades hung over the three windows and strips of paper were pasted around the frames to cut down draughts.

67, Henry HALLAM (LCP 1904) 1819-1841. In 1833 his son, Arthur, beloved by Lord TENNYSON, died at the age of 22 in Vienna.

82, Wilkie COLLINS died here in 1889.

WINANT
John Gilbert
Diplomat

1889
Concord, Mass., 1947

Flat 30, 3, Grosvenor Square, W1, 1941-1942
7, Aldford Street, W1 (LCP 1981) 1942-1946

Winant was to succeed the unlamented Joseph Kennedy as American Ambassador to London in March 1941. He was in the capital during the worst years of the bombing of Britain and for the period after the fall of France when Britain stood alone against the Axis.

John Winant arrived on March 2, 1941 and was met by King George VI and afterwards held a press conference. Fred Kuh, the United Press correspondent in London recalled that Winant, '...was embarrassed and fiddled with his glasses...like a school girl at commencement exercises'. One of the pressmen asked Winant what he thought of Joseph Kennedy. Finally Winant said, 'You better ask someone else that'.

F.D. Roosevelt was a great friend of Winant's and his death (on April 12, 1945 from a stroke) upset him profoundly. Three years later he committed suicide at his home in Concord.

WODEHOUSE Guildford, October 10, 1881
(Sir) Pelham Grenville Long Island, N.Y., February 14, 1975
Author

16, Walton Street, SW3, 1918, 1919 and 1920
23, Gilbert Street, W1, 1924

After Shakespeare, P.G. Wodehouse is probably the best known user of the English language. 'Jeeves', 'Bertie Wooster', 'Lord Emsworth' and many other Wodehousain immortals, have passed into English Literature's Hall of Fame.
Yet, in his day, Wodehouse was one of the greatest lyricists of the musical. His achievements here seem now forgotten. People have overlooked that Wodehouse and Gerome Kern practically *invented* the musical with the likes of *Oh Boy!* in 1917 and the Ziegfield productions that followed.
World War II caught Wodehouse in France after the French surrender and, in effect, he was taken prisoner by the Germans. He broadcast through their radio network, speaking half-humorously about his captivity and, as a result, found himself branded as a 'traitor' by a large number of people who, pre-war, had read and laughed over his books. An investigation showed him not to have been a *collaborateur* but he had to wait until 1975 to be given a knighthood as a sign of final 'official pardon'. By then he was 94 and only survived a few weeks knowing that the establishment had finally forgiven him.

WOFFINGTON Dublin, October 18, 1720
Margaret (or 'Peg') Teddington, March 28, 1760
Actress Teddington Parish Church

6, Bow Street, WC2, 1750

She was only a bricklayer's daughter but first appeared on stage at the age of 12 as Polly Peacham in the *Beggar's Opera*. She played regularly in Dublin, but came to London in 1740, when she appeared as Sylvia in *The Recruiting Officer*, becoming a 'star' overnight.
Once, when playing the stage part of an effeminate young man, she was supposed to have said: 'I think half London believes I *am* a man'. A rakish fellow, overhearing this small boast, replied, 'Yes, Madam, and the *other* half *knows* you are a woman'.

WOLCOT Dodbroke, Devon, May 9, 1738
John ('Peter Pindar') London, January 14, 1819
Physician and poet St Paul's Church, Covent Garden

1, Gildea Street, W1, 1800-1803

Wolcot practised medecine in the West Indies and was once the Physician-General in Jamaica. On his return to England he was ordained but remained a doctor, with a Cornish practice. John OPIE, the Cornish artist, came up to London and Wolcot came too, in 1780. He began to write satiric verse under the name 'Peter Pindar' (Pindar, c.522-443 BC, one of the great Theban Lyric poets) in which he attacked the 'establishment', George III, the Royal Academy and, on one occasion, James BOSWELL.

WOLFE Westerham, Kent, January 2, 1727
James Quebec, September 13, 1759
Soldier Greenwich Church

10, Old Burlington Street, W1, 1742-1751

Wolfe obtained his commission as a Second Lieutenant when he was only 14 and saw active service at the battle of Dettingen. (A village in Bavaria where, on June 27, 1743, the Anglo-German army under King George II defeated the French under General Vicomte Louis Marie de Noailles. It was the last battle where the British Army had a reigning King in command.) By the time Wolfe was 17 he was a Captain and took part in the battles of Falkirk and Culloden which put paid to the hopes of the Jacobites in 1745.

In 1759 Major-General Wolfe led an Army of 9,000 men to recapture Canada from the French. In June he attempted to take Quebec by an orthodox route but was repulsed by the French forces under Louis Joseph, Marquis de Montcalm Gozon de Saint-Veran (1712-1759). In September, Wolfe and his army, using the stupendously difficult route up the cliff face, known as the 'Heights of Abraham', surprised the French army, which tried to rally itself, but was soon beaten and the leaders of the two armies both died of their wounds, Wolfe on the day of battle and Montcalm 24 hours later. This decisive battle returned the whole of Canada into British hands.

WOLFE Asheville, N. Carolina, October 3,
Thomas Clayton 1900
Novelist Baltimore, September 15, 1938

32, Wellington Square, SW3, 1926
75, Ebury Street, SW1, 1930-1931
26, Hanover Square, W1, 1935

The youngest (and eighth) child of a stonecutter, Wolfe was supposed to have been able to talk fluently at the age of one and to read before he was two.

He grew to be six feet five inches (1.98 metres) and had a correspondingly large appetite for food, alcohol and sex. As a 25th birthday present he became the lover of Aline Bernstein, who was a theatrical designer, 20 years older than he. He had mistresses other than Aline (and an *affaire* with Jean Harlow) but he managed to avoid matrimony.

In 1929, his book *Look Homeward, Angel* appeared after having been rejected by a number of publishers. It met with both critical and popular success. He left England for the last time in 1935, settled in Brooklyn and produced four more novels before succumbing to pneumonia only a few days before his 38th birthday. As death grew near he became delirious and is said to have whispered, 'Where's Aline?...I want Aline...I want my Jew'.

WOOD Braintree, Essex, February 9, 1838
(Sir) Evelyn Henry London, December 2, 1919
Field Marshall

23, Devonshire Place, W1, 1896

Wood joined the Navy after schooling in England and fought in the Crimea with the Navy Brigade. He then deserted sea horses for the Cavalry and, as a Brigade-Major, won the Victoria Cross in action during the Indian Mutiny. The mutiny began on May 11, 1857 at Meerut, near Delhi. Improved Enfield rifles had been introduced into the Indian Army in 1856. Their cartridges had to be greased with animal fat and some sections of the Indian Army – depending on their religion – objected. Despite the discontinuance of the practice in January 1857, discontent grew and flared into open mutiny, which spread from the Delhi area to Lucknow on May 30 and to Bengal by June 1857.

In January 1879 he was commanding the Chatham District in the Zulu War and, with General Jacobus Joubert, the South African General (1834-1900), negotiated the Armistice in 1881. The following year he was a brigade commander in Egypt, where he stayed until 1888, during which time he practically created the Egyptian Army. During operations on the Nile, in 1884 and 1885, he was under the command of Lord Wolseley (1833-1913).

WOOLF   London, November 25, 1880
Leonard Sidney   London, August 14, 1969
Publisher

37, Mecklenburgh Square, WC1, 1939-1942
24, Victoria Square, SW1, 1944-1967

Leonard Woolf has too long (and too often) only been thought of as 'Virginia WOOLF's husband'. Apart from providing his wife with tender and loving support, it seems to be forgotten that he was 32 before he married and had very much a life of his own.
He went to St Paul's School (then in Hammersmith) and afterwards to Cambridge, then joined the Ceylon (now Sri Lanka) Civil Service in 1904. He spent seven years on that beautiful island which provided him with the material for his book, *The Village and the Jungle* published in 1913.
He married Virginia Stephen in 1912 and was a member of the Fabian Society, the 'done' thing to do for radical intellectuals of that era, and in 1916 the Woolfs established the Hogarth Press.

WOOLF   January 25, 1882
Virginia   Rodmell, Sussex, March 28, 1941
Author   (her ashes are buried in her garden at
          Rodmell)

29, Fitzroy Square, W1 (LCP 1974) 1907-1911
38, Brunswick Square, WC1, 1912
52, Tavistock Square, WC1, 1919-1941

Virginia was one of the daughters of Sir Leslie STEPHEN's second marriage, to Julia Jackson. She was never sent to school and was educated almost entirely at home.
In 1912 she married Leonard WOOLF and they both became part of the 'Bloomsbury Group' (or *Bloomsberries*) made up of artistic and 'intellectually skilled' people.
Her first novel, *The Voyage Out*, was published in 1915 and her reputation as a novelist, until, *The Waves* in 1931, six novels later, made her a 'Literary Priestess' and did much to perpetuate the idea that there *was* a 'Bloomsbury Group' in the first place.
Though married to Leonard and (probably) *really* in love with him, she had passionate friendships with women, interspersed with nervous and/or mental breakdowns. She must have been difficult to live with and additionally so because her actual writing caused her intense and worrying periods of doubt. Leonard and she had no children but her marriage *was* consummated. Her novel-writing technique has often been labelled as part of the 'stream of consciousness' school.
Her nervous breakdowns were 'signalled' in advance and Lionel *never* failed her before, during or after these mental storms. The Second World War and her terror of the bombing of totally innocent civilians, depressed her more and more and, finally in March 1944, she drowned herself in the River Ouse. She left a note for Leonard, 'I don't think two people could have been happier than we have been'.

WOOLNER　　　　　　　　Hadleigh, Suffolk, December 17, 1825
Thomas　　　　　　　　　　London, October 7, 1892
Sculptor　　　　　　　　　Hendon Churchyard

29, Welbeck Street, W1 (P) 1860-1892

Woolner exhibited early talent and his father, a Post Office employee, moved to London and put him to study under Henry Behnes. Not long after, Behnes died, but his brother William (1795-1864) kept young Woolner on in his studio for another four years. In 1842, on Behnes' advice, William enrolled at the Royal Academy Schools.

About five years later he met the ROSSETTI's and became a member of the 'Pre-Raphaelite Brotherhood'. Initially he was not very successful but in 1850 he made a medallion portrait of Mrs. Coventry PATMORE which was much admired. Despite this slight measure of success he decided to emigrate and, in 1852, set sail from Gravesend (Kent) to seek a fortune in the Australian goldfields. The painter Ford Madox Brown came to see him off and in 1855 used this experience in a painting he called *The Last of England*. The painting is now in the Art Gallery at Birmingham. But for Woolner it was *not* to be the 'last of England'. Australia did not agree with him and by 1854 he was back in London.

WORDSWORTH　　　　　　Cockermouth, April 7, 1770
William　　　　　　　　　　Rydal Mount, April 23, 1850
Poet Laureate　　　　　　　Grasmere Churchyard

16, Queen Anne's Gate, SW1, 1835 (as a guest of Joshua Watson)

He got his degree in 1791 and not long after paid his second visit to France. He prided himself on his Republican sympathies. The revolution in France, when it boiled over, gave Wordsworth cause to think again and, in 1793, his first work, *The Evening Wrath*, was published.

Two years later he met COLERIDGE and then firmly decided to become a poet. With his devoted sister, Dorothy, he settled first in Dorset, then at Alfoxden, not far from Coleridge's home at Nether Stowey in Somerset. The two poets planned to produce a combined publication, Coleridge's contribuition being, *The Ancient Mariner* and Wordsworth's *Tintern Abbey*. These, together with other pieces, appeared in 1978.

WREN　　　　　　　　　East Knoyle, Wilts., October 20, 1632
(Sir) Christopher　　　　　Hampton Court, February 23, 1723
Genius　　　　　　　　　St Paul's Cathedral Crypt

109, Great Russell Street, WC1

Sir Christopher's son, Christopher, had engraved on the stone above his father's simple tomb in the crypt of the great Cathedral, which owes its existence to Wren more than any one else, these simple words: *Lector, si monumentum requiris, circumspice*, which (freely) translated says 'Reader, if you seek my monument, look about you'. Wren could not have a happier or apter epitaph.

His father was the Dean of Windsor, who, during the early days of the Commonwealth after the execution of King Charles I, hid the great sword of King Edward III from Cromwell's destructive troops. The sword can still be seen in the St George's Chapel in the Castle. Wren was sent to school at Westminster (which lies almost in the arms of that other great church, Westminster Abbey) and then on to Wadham College, Oxford. He was appointed Professor of Astronomy in 1657 and Savilian Professor of Astronomy at Oxford in 1661. Together with the Hon. Robert Boyle (1627-1691) John Wilkins (1614-1672) and others, Wren laid the foundations of what was to become the prestigious Royal Society.

In 1663 he was commissioned to investigate the structure of St Paul's Cathedral which was destroyed just three years later in the Great Fire 1666. In 1669 he was appointed Surveyor General and chosen to rebuild the Church. The work only started, after much argument and interference from the King himself, in 1675 and went on building through the reign of King William III and Mary and into the last years of the reign of Queen Anne.

WYATT   1807
(Sir) Thomas Henry   London, 1880
Architect

77, Great Russell Street, WC1 (LCP 1980) from 1851 until he died here

Thomas Henry, Matthew Digby Wyatt's brother, was trained in the architectural office of Philip Hardwick (1792-1870) the designer of Limerick Cathedral.
Wyatt set up on his own and was responsible for a number of different buildings in England and Wales. In London examples of his work can be seen in the north gateway of Kensington Palace Gardens and in three nearby houses.

WYATVILLE   Burton-on-Trent, Staffs., August 3,
(Sir) Jeffry   1766
Architect   Windsor, February 18, 1840
                      St George's Chapel, Windsor Castle

39, Lower Brook Street, W1, 1820s

Born plain WYATT, a nephew of James, he was asked (so it was said) by King George IV to add the 'ville' to distinguish himself from all the other architectural WYATTS (who were, in quantity, greater than the Architectural ADAMS).
During the long reign (60 years) of George III and more especially in the last eleven years before his death in 1820, the king was virtually a prisoner in Windsor Castle, declared insane; but more probably suffering from *porphyria*. The Castle was literally crumbling and Wyatville was commissioned by King George IV to repair it entirely. Parliament was persuaded by the King to vote £300,000 for the refurbishment, a quarter of this sum to be spent on new furnishings. Eventually the bills added up to over a *million pounds*. Little or nothing has been added to the Castle proper since Wyatville's activities and so the shape seen today, is substantially the appearance he intended.

YEATS   Dublin, June 13, 1865
William Butler   Roquebrune, France, January 29, 1939
Poet   Sligo, Ireland

23, Fitzroy Road, NW1 (LCP 1957) 1867-1873
58, Eardley Crescent, SW5, 1887

Yeat's father was John Butler Yeats (1839-1922) an artist of some distinction and William was educated in both London and Dublin, eventually becoming an art student, though he never even tried to make a living as an artist.
He developed an interest in the occult and then took up writing poetry (and plays) seriously. His first publication, in fact, was a play – *Mosada*, in 1886. Poetry came later, in 1888, with *The Wanderings of Oisin* (an alternative spelling to *Ossian* a semi-historical Gaelic bard) then *Celtic Twilight* in 1893. The title of this book of peasant legends was used to 'label' a school for the renascence of Irish culture.
Yeats had a lively (and varied) sex life. At Woburn Walk he lived with Olivia Shakespear (sic) whom he christened 'Diana Vernon'. His real interest in Irish Nationalism was undoubtedly fuelled by his passion for the beautiful Maud Gonne. He actually served in the Irish Senate for six years after the separate state of Eire had been (so contentiously) created in 1921. Around this time Yeats apparently took a course of Voronoff Treatment. This had been developed by Serge Voronoff (1866-1951) and it was claimed that by grafting animal glands into the human body a greater sexual appetite could be created. Cruelly some wags then referred to Yeats as the 'Gland Old Man'.

YEOMAN'S ROW, SW3   *Piccadilly line to Knightsbridge*

This little *cul-de-sac* first appeared on the rate books in 1786 and was probably developed by a man called Yeoman.

16,   Dora CARRINGTON, 1916
16,   Oliver MESSEL, 1929-1946. James LAVER once found MESSEL's sister (Lord SNOWDON's mother and later Countess of Rosse) '...down on her hands and knees scrubbing her brother's studio floor because she could not find any one else to do it to her satisfaction'.

YORK BUILDINGS, WC2   *Jubilee, Northern, Bakerloo and BR lines*
                                           to Charing Cross

The buildings cover part of the site taken up by York House – the London residence of the Archbishops of York and taken over initially by King Henry VIII from Thomas Wolsey. Near here was the York 'waterworks' established by Charles II to supply the west side of London with fresh Thames water. Financially it was a failure.

18,   John Middleton MURRY, 1925. He had just founded the *Athenaeum Magazine*.
31,   Charles DICKENS (and his mother) in 1831.

YORK GATE, NW1 *Metropolitan, Circle and Jubilee lines to Baker Street*

Named after Frederick, Duke of York, George III's second (and favourite son) and brother of the Prince Regent.

1, William MACREADY, 1839-1843, during which time he was reputed to have lost £10,000 as manager of the Drury Lane Theatre.

5, Francis PALGRAVE (LCP 1976) 1862-1875. His first address after his marriage. He moved in here the year after his successful anthology of poems, *The Golden Treasury*, was published.

YORK PLACE, see BAKER STREET

YORK STREET, W1 *Bakerloo line to Marylebone*

Named after Frederick, Duke of York and Albany, the second and favourite son of King George III. This poor Fred died in 1827.

20, George Richmond (LCP 1961) 1843-1896. Richmond came here as a 34-year old and lived here till his death. He was a portrait painter and many distinguished people visited him here: the Duke of WELLINGTON was one.

47, Lord MILNER, 1885-1914. He lived here with his friend from Balliol College, Oxford, Henry Birchenough.

51, Sir 'Freddie' AYER, 1983.

YOUNG Milverton, Somerset, June 13, 1773
Thomas London, May 10, 1829
Scientist and linguist Farnborough, Kent

48, Welbeck Street, W1 (LCP 1951) 1800-1825

After studying at Edinburgh, Gottingen and Cambridge, Young set himself up as a doctor in 1800. The following year he became Professor of Natural Philosophy to the Royal Institution in order that he should have more free time to devote to various researches.

He was especially interested in Egyptology and his work in this field was invaluable in deciphering the inscriptions on the 'Rosetta Stone'. The stone was found by M. Boussard, a French engineering officer in 1799 at Fort St Julien, near Rosetta in the delta of the Nile. It bears inscriptions in hieroglyphic, the demotic and Greek. It was erected in 195 BC to honour Ptolemy Epiphanes. The stone is now in the British Museum. Young and Jean Francois Champollion actually 'cracked the code' in 1822.

YOUNG STREET, W8 *Circle and District lines to High Street Kensington*

Thomas Young built most of Kensington Square (into which Young Street leads) which he began in 1685.

9, Sir Patrick HASTINGS, 1902-1908.

16, W.M. THACKERAY (LCP 1905) 1846-1855. In his study, at the back of the house, '...where a vine shaded his two windows', THACKERAY wrote *Vanity Fair* (1848) *Pendennis* (1848-1850) and *Henry Esmond* (1852). Much of the action of this last novel takes place in Kensington Square. His rent here was £65 per annum. Thackeray wrote of the house: '...there's a good study for me downstairs and a dining-room and drawing room, and a little courtyard or garden and a little greenhouse: and Kensington Gardens at the gate, and omnibuses every two minutes. What can mortal want more?'

16, Norman O'NEILL was born here in 1875, two years after his father, an artist, had taken the house. He used THACKERAY's study as a studio.

27, Lady Anne RITCHIE, THACKERAY's daughter, also a novelist, from 1878-1883.

27, Angela THIRKELL was born here on January 30, 1890. The house itself was demolished many years ago.

YPRES	Ripple, Kent, September 25, 1852
John Denton Pinkston French (1st Earl)	Deal Castle, Kent, May 22, 1925
Field Marshall	

94, Lancaster Gate, W2, 1914-1923

His father was a naval officer and French (his surname until 1915 when he was raised to the peerage and adopted the title of Viscount French of Ypres and High Lake) followed him into the Navy, becoming a midshipman, but in 1874 he transferred into the Army and obtained a commission in the 19th Hussars. He served on the Nile Expedition in 1884 and commanded his regiment from 1889-1893. He saw much service in the Boer War and was made a Lieutenant General and Knight afterwards.

His Field Marshall's baton came to him when he was 61 and in 1914 he was in command of the British Expeditionary Force. He took charge of the Western Front in some of the bloodiest moments of that bloody campaign. The failure at Loos, for which he was in part responsible and his inability to get on with KITCHENER in London caused him to 'resign' and Douglas HAIG was put in his place. French became the Commander-in-Chief in the United Kingdom. He was made Lord Lieutenant of Ireland in May 1918, a post which was almost as bloody as Loos.

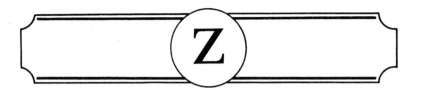

ZANGWILL
Israel
Novelist and playwright

London, February 14, 1864
August 1, 1926

3, Hare Court, Temple, EC4, 1904

Zangwill, the son of a Jewish refugee from Russia, was educated at the Jewish Free School and afterwards at London University. For two years after graduation, he taught at a school in Spitalfields in London's East End. Before the end of the 19th century, though, he had come to be recognized as a literary figure of great promise and, by 1900, he devoted himself entirely to writing. He began on a series of books dealing with Jewish history and Hebrew themes. Probably the first of these, *The Children of the Ghetto*, published in 1892, was the most successful.
Plays followed, *The Melting Pot* in 1908 and *Too Much Money* ten years later, were popular. He was an active Zionist, being the founder and first President of the International Jewish Territorial Organisation.

ZOFFANY
Johann
Painter

Frankfurt, 1735
Kew, 1810
St Anne's Church, Kew

9, Denmark Street, W1, 1768-1781

Zoffany's father was architect to the Prince of Thurn and Taxis, but young Johann was not happy and ran away from home when he was not yet 13 and somehow made his way to Rome where he stayed, studying painting, for nearly 12 years. He came to London in 1758 and legend has it that he was found, starving, in a garret in Drury Lane. Someone introduced him to Stephen Rimbault who gave him a job painting clock faces. Next he became a 'drapery painter' with Benjamin WILSON. (A drapery painter, as the description implies, used to paint in the draperies and other not so vital bits of portraits leaving the better known and better paid artist – in this case, Wilson – to work on the sitter's features and hands.) David GARRICK took up the young German, much to Wilson's annoyance, and not long after, Zoffany was a name by his own brush and was actually one of the founder members of the Royal Academy in 1786.
He painted King George III and all his children and engravings of this picture (or at least, details of it) were a great commercial success. His Royal sitter gave him an introduction to the Grand Duke of Tuscany and Zoffany went to Florence in 1772 and spent the next seven years there. After this, for no apparent reason, he went off to India, spending six years at the court of the Nabob of Oude and amassed a very tidy fortune. He left his wife and children in London.

ZOTOV
Anatoly Pavlovich
Spy?

Russia, c.1946

23, Campden Hill Gardens, W8 (ground floor flat) 1981-December 1982

In December 1982, Zotov and his good-looking wife, Nina, were given a week to pack up and get out of Britian by the British Foreign Office. Zotov enjoyed 'diplomatic privilege' and had he not been shielded by that widespread nonsense, he would have been arrested for spying.

He was what, in British Intelligence jargon, is called 'a big fish'. He was almost certainly in London to recruit and set up spy-rings for the Soviet Military Intelligence (the GRU). Some thought Zotov to be higher up the Kremlin ladder than Victor Popov himself (the Russian Ambassador then in London).

The Zotov's neighbours used to call them the 'Sputniks' and were amused to see Harrod's van deliver decadent, capitalistic goodies to Comrade Anatoly and Nina.

ZULUETA January 2, 1925
(Sir) Philip Francis de
Banker

11, Vicarage Gardens, W8, 1970s

From the Foreign Service (including two years in Moscow) after Oxford and the Welsh Guards, Zulueta became Private Secretary to three Prime Ministers in succession: Lord AVON (Anthony EDEN, as was) Sir Harold MACMILLAN (now 1st Earl of Stockton) and the then Sir Alec DOUGLAS-HOME. (Possibly a record; held with 'Eddie' MARSH?) In the early 1960s, Zulueta left the labyrinths of politics to grope through the mazes of merchant banking, not without success. In 1973 he was Chief Executive of Anthony Gibbs and Sons, Bankers.